T0338049

Globalization, Gating, and Risk Finance

Globalization, Gating, and Risk Finance

Unurjargal Nyambuu
New York City College of Technology
The City University of New York

and

Charles S. Tapiero
Tandon School of Engineering
New York University

Registered Offices
John Wiley & Sons, Inc., 111 River Street, Hoboken, NJ 07030, USA
John Wiley & Sons Ltd, The Atrium, Southern Gate, Chichester, West Sussex, PO19 8SQ, UK

Editorial Office
9600 Garsington Road, Oxford, OX4 2DQ, UK

For details of our global editorial offices, customer services, and more information about Wiley products visit us at www.wiley.com.

Wiley also publishes its books in a variety of electronic formats and by print-on-demand. Some content that appears in standard print versions of this book may not be available in other formats.

Library of Congress Cataloging-in-Publication Data

Names: Nyambuu, Unurjargal, 1980- author. | Tapiero, Charles S., author.
Title: Globalization, gating, and risk finance / Dr. Unurjargal Nyambuu,
    New York City College of Technology, The City University of New York,
    Dr. Charles S. Tapiero, Tandon School of Engineering, New York University.
Description: Hoboken, NJ : John Wiley & Sons, Inc., 2018. | Includes
    bibliographical references and index. |
Identifiers: LCCN 2017023321 (print) | LCCN 2017037256 (ebook) | ISBN
    9781119252689 (pdf) | ISBN 9781119252702 (epub) | ISBN 9781119252658
    (cloth : alk. paper)
Subjects: LCSH: International finance. | Financial risk management. |
    International trade.
Classification: LCC HG3881 (ebook) | LCC HG3881 .N885 2018 (print) | DDC
    332/.042–dc23
LC record available at https://lccn.loc.gov/2017023321

Cover Design: Wiley
Cover Image: © monsitj/Gettyimages

Set in 10/12pt Warnock by SPi Global, Pondicherry, India
Printed and bound in Malaysia by Vivar Printing Sdn Bhd

10 9 8 7 6 5 4 3 2 1

Dedicated to our parents: Nyambuu Khand, Selenge Tserenvanchig, and Violette Budestchu Tapiero

Chapters' Outline

The book is organized as follows.

Chapter 1, Globalization: Economies in Collision, provides a broad overview by introducing a selected number of problems motivating interest in global risk finance. This chapter provides a summary of foreign exchange (FX) markets, exchange rate regimes, and the evolution of reserve currencies from a macroeconomic perspective. We discuss the emergence of the Chinese yuan as a global exchange currency, its usage in global trade, and its inclusion in the International Monetary Fund's basket of foreign currencies. Further discussion of the yuan is relegated to subsequent chapters. Chapter 1 further outlines the history of globalization and presents a list of special issues for further discussion.

Chapter 2, **Data, Measurements, and Global Finance**, provides a review of standard statistical measurement approaches commonly used in economics and finance. We discuss national accounts, big data and model-less finance, technology and financial data, and data management. Particular attention is given to multivariate data and its treatment. For example, an introduction to data reduction and statistical measurement, principle component analysis, data modeling, copulas, implied volatility, autoregressive moving average, and related multivariate probability models are presented as an approach to the modeling and the study of global financial data. Autoregressive conditional heteroscedasticity (ARCH) and its extensions (generalized ARCH (GARCH), threshold GARCH, and GARCH-in-mean) are suggested for the measurement of FX volatility. This chapter assumes that the reader is already familiar with basic statistical techniques and seeks only to learn their relevance for practical problems. For the further study of data analytics and statistics, an extensive list of references is given.

Chapter 3, Global Finance: Utility, Financial Consumption, and Asset Pricing, outlines microeconomic and financial approaches to financial and asset pricing models and their extensions to a multi-country and multi-currency world. We develop the theoretical underpinnings underlying the Arrow–Debreu theory for complete market as well as the utility theory and its consumption capital asset pricing model (CCAPM). These theories are applied to valuation pricing in competing and a multi-agent framework. To do so, we introduce an approach based on the financial commitments to consumption. We then apply this framework to both standard and multi-country financial pricing and investment problems. This is shown to be far more representative of global finance based on competing agents. Examples for pricing foreign bonds, investments in securities, debt management, and currency wars are also outlined. CCAPM, in its multi-agent form, is shown to be particularly useful in pricing debt, financial leverage, inequality, swaps, and other aspects of global finance. Our tentative analyses are essentially essays which express the complexity of the pricing of financial products across national boundaries. Throughout the chapter, we introduce pricing and valuation models that are consistent with fundamental approaches, yet seek their marginal expansion to problems recurrent in global finance. The chapter's intent is to provide a relatively simple approach to some theoretical issues that occur in both conventional and multi-agent applications of global finance models.

Chapter 4, Macroeconomics, Foreign Exchange, and Global Finance. Global finance and international macroeconomics are intimately related to one another, yet they differ by the time scale of their statistics and by their concern with economic and financial global policies. This chapter presents several fundamental macroeconomic FX rate models required to provide a broader appreciation of global finance as well as to better predict sovereign state policies based mostly on macroeconomic statistics and political and geopolitical factors. We refer to the closed economy model introduced by Keynes and study its extension to an open economy by the Mundell–Fleming model. In this context, the implications of monetary and fiscal policies under the IS–LM–balance of payments model are discussed, describing the relationship between the goods and money markets and the balance of payments. Also, an equilibrium exchange rate determined by the demand and supply of currency is described, with further discussion on major factors affecting the exchange rate. Interactions between expenditures by the private sector, government, and transactions with foreign economies are highlighted. Their evolution underlies the relationships between cross-border trade, capital, and job flows. We discuss the importance of balance of payments in global finance and its implications. The sustainability of external debt, trends in foreign direct investment, and capital flows are highlighted. This chapter discusses recent trends in macroeconomic policies and exchange rate movements that shape global finance. At the same time, it highlights practical policy concerns and predictable scenarios concordant with macroeconomic finance. In addition, we analyze a correlation between globalization and income inequality and present the existing literature.

Chapter 5, Foreign Exchange Models and Prices, assesses FX rate pricing based on different models for FX. Purchasing power parity is explained using an application of the law of one price (concurrent to the no-arbitrage principle in finance) and empirical findings for its validity. Furthermore, FX rates and interest rates are studied based on covered interest arbitrage and uncovered interest parity (UIP). Monetary and asset-based approaches to FX rate determinations are presented along with the UIP model. We cover the Balassa–Samuelson model, the Dornbusch overshooting model, and the present-value models, all of which are outlined as extensions together with empirical evidence. A list of works for econometric and statistical analysis is suggested.

Chapter 6, Asia: Financial Environment and Risks, provides an overview of Asia's financial and economic development, emphasizing engines of growth and implications for the global economy and finance. Included is discussion of Asia's increasing international trade and its regional interdependence, FX rate issues, and foreign investment. We analyze the financial environment in Asia with an emphasis on the banking sector, bond market, and stock market development, and use different approaches to assess the financial and investment risks that Asia's financial industry is facing. Based on currency data, we discuss FX risks. We also consider regional systematic risk based on local stock exchange data. In addition to the study of Eastern and South-Eastern Asia, a detailed discussion on China and Japan is presented. In the case of China, while stressing the importance and achievements of the banking sector, we analyze the problem of shadow banking and look at challenges in equity markets, and corporate debt in particular. Econometric and statistical analyses for selected problems are provided.

Chapter 7, Financial Currency Pricing, Swaps, Derivatives, and Complete Markets, provides analysis of pricing the consumer price index and the FX-based securities in complete financial markets using modeling as well as empirical approaches. We present both relative and martingale-based FX models with an emphasis on risks and approaches found in US currency indices, global index reversion, the Ricatti FX model, and basket-based price reversion. We introduce a partial generalization by considering multivariate stochastic models and outline mean-reverting volatility-based models. Given the extensive use of options in finance, we assess their use only through some simple examples pertaining to FX options, cross-national boundary investments, and so on. The currency option pricing models and their applications are presented with further examples using spreads and other options (with references directing the reader to the extremely rich family of optional models). Furthermore, we look at option-based trading strategies, emphasizing protective puts, foreign trading, the covered call, and others. Finally, this chapter presents the, so-called, Greek analysis, which measures the sensitivity of option prices to parameters defining the price (e.g., interest rates, volatility). Although, in a global and heterogeneous economic world, "assumed complete markets" may in fact be incomplete, we note that the complete market framework may also be used to price specific and tailor-made financial products adapted to the needs of international financial transactions. To this purpose, we have also introduced swaps and some of their applications. More detailed developments and applications of swaps, accounting for a substantial part of foreign transactions, are introduced in Chapter 8, where loan-debt contracts are also defined as swaps.

Chapter 8, Credit Risk and International Debt, presents the growth of debt and debt dependency, highlighting both credit and global risks. This chapter analyzes country-specific risks, FX risks, credit trading, sovereign bond risks, as well as credit derivatives. In this context, different swaps (e.g., currency swaps, swaptions, credit default swaps, and securitized volatility) are defined and explained. This is important because, under assumptions of complete markets, option-based products (e.g., swaptions) are used extensively in global financial exchanges. We present credit and default risk pricing based on reduced-form models. Under this framework, bond prices are defined by the financial market in which they are traded. Then, we consider foreign bonds issued in a foreign currency as a pointer to the risk of bonds compounded by FX risk and extend this idea through the use of martingales. The utility approach is used to price and manage international credit risk and its option-based derivatives. Finally, this chapter describes the Merton debt model and its relationship to FX markets; it provides an example of the market pricing of both debt and credit risk and outlines Merton's continuous-time model for debt and options.

Chapter 9, Globalization and Trade: A Changing World, provides an overview of the evolution of trade based on conventional approaches, as well as its financial and gating aspects. We highlight the importance of trade in globalization and discuss its contributions to the changing world by analyzing its risks and other related issues; for example, inversion, outsourcing, risk externalities, strategic trade and gating, and trade barriers. This chapter reviews trade models based on Ricardo's theory and the implications of trade models for FX rates in a Cournot game. We introduce a strategic global and financial pricing approach to heterogeneous (and competing) agents (financial agents or countries) based on dependent utilities as well as competing suppliers. Therefore, our multi-country financial consumption approach is presented starting with a one-period utility consumption demand model integrated with a supply problem including imports and exports between two parties. Extensions to a Cournot multi-period financial consumption model accounting for both current and future consumption are, for brevity, considered in research papers we refer to. Owing to their complexity, the problems defined are relatively simple, providing a guideline for the development of a far more complex trade model that can be analyzed using simulation techniques. In this context, this chapter outlines our belief that essential issues underlying globalization (for the "rich" Western world, in particular) are their relationships between local consumption prices and strategic (game) problems fueled by cheap imports, the creation/loss of jobs, foreign dependence and the pursuit of short- and long-term political and geopolitical agendas.

Chapter 10, Compliance and Financial Regulation. Given the complex, growing, multi-headed, and multi-country financial and economic regulatory environment, this chapter is focused on compliance risks. A current trend, initiated by the USA, to regulate and tax globally will most likely lead to retaliatory actions by other countries. These retaliatory actions assume many forms; for example, creating competing markets where US laws cannot be enforced, a move away from the US dollar as the main exchange currency, stealthy finance seeking to elude controls, and so on. These and other new elements in global finance are having an impact which may be difficult to ascertain. Justice Stephen Breyer, in his book *The Court of the World: American Law and the New Global Realities,* raised some fundamental issues confronting the US legal framework and the future of democracy. One specific question he raised is, "Does foreign law have a place in interpreting the American Constitution?" Such a question is most relevant to almost all aspects of sovereign states' exchanges and relationships and, as a result, the world of global business and finance. On the one hand, legal isolationism would entail a USA divorced from the world; on the other hand, globalization renders foreign laws and international affairs simply unavoidable. From a practical viewpoint, regulated finance, both domestic and global, is confronted with an application of laws and asks "How do we comply?" and "Can we comply in a multi-polar world, with sovereign states and regulators pursuing multiple agendas?" These are complex questions that this chapter avoids. Instead, we introduce some of the issues and problems; we provide a partial view that emphasizes compliance in light of regulatory risks and their controls. We also point to the increased complexity of regulatory risks and compliance in a global, gated, and strategic finance. A number of quantitative and statistical compliance models are introduced based both on statistical and (random payoff) game constructs, raising a greater awareness of regulation and compliance risks and the consequences of these risks.

Although this book spans a wide breadth of problems, it is far from being exhaustive. The number of books and research papers that relate to the themes of study and featured in important international economics and financial journals, as well as those found in mathematical and quantitative finance and engineering books, is much larger. Our contribution seeks to create a greater awareness to the transformation of finance in an era confronting globalization and its gating and introduce their effects to financial pricing, trade, and compliance. In addition, we hope to provide the reader rational guidelines to economic and financial modeling in a global environment.

Acknowledgments

This book has profited from contributions from both authors' previous publications in academic journals and in books published by John Wiley & Sons, Springer, Elsevier, and others. In addition, we have referred, wherever we could, to our and others' many academic and professional publications that have addressed global finance from multiple perspectives. We apologize to those we missed and did not refer to. Throughout our research, we have benefitted from discussions with a number of students, academic researchers and practitioners. There may be too many to list, but among the many we thank Alain Bensoussan, Lucas Bernard, Dan Goroff, Ben Golub, Laurent Jacque, Konstantin Kogan, Peter Lewis, George Papanicolaou, Lorne Switzer, Pierre Vallois and three additional Tapieros: Daniel, Dafna and Oren, who are all immersed in real and global finance. Finally, Prof. Tapiero's involvement was supported by the endowment of the Topfer Chair and by the Sloan Foundation (for its support for the Regulation Chapter 10). To all we acknowledge our gratitude.

Contents

Motivation

Tom Friedman's (2005) book, *The World Is Flat*, has popularized the conventional wisdom that, in a global world, we are all codependent and that events occurring in one place may affect others. Globalization is a manifestation of this codependence. It underlies major economic, financial, and political trends with opportunities and risks. The purpose of this book is to outline perspectives on a gated global and risk finance, in a world where real finance is mutating into a far more complex finance, with political and social agendas, geopolitical realignments and the growth of A-national global enterprises, altering the conventional premises of economics and finance. Increasingly, sovereign states gate their economies explicitly and implicitly (through trade controls, taxation, and regulation, for example) to maintain economic advantages or pursue sovereign agendas. In this process, it is transforming underlying theoretical and rational financial foundations and free market principles, to be far more in "markets in collision" (and thus strategic). Currency, trade, and regulatory "wars," together with extreme economic inequality, underscore the concern that, despite its many benefits, globalization also embodies structural changes and comes with costs; further, global economic equalization is not always as "equal" as many would like. In such an environment, economic and financial exchanges are far more complex; for example, expanding from a mere exchange of goods to an exchange of "lower consumption prices" for a loss of "jobs"; from a gated environment to the free migration of people, technologies, industries, money, capital, and so on. Financial risks and pricing models, for example, are then far more subjugated to macroeconomic, political, geopolitical and social concerns, gating, regulation and its compliance, and to the many new and far more complex risks and opportunities that globalization entails. This book seeks to approach some of these issues using conventional economic and financial methods and to provide readers a broad outline of the challenges that global and risk finance raises. At the same time, we consider alternative and multivariate financial models that seek to appreciate the consequences of globalization and its strategic implications to fundamental issues in economics and finance.

The book is the product of our lectures and research projects, and is conducted with the intention of motivating students and professionals alike to be more aware of the complexity, the opportunities, and the consequences of a globalized and gated financial world. Therefore, we emphasize a global and strategic risk finance where economic powers, risks, and geopolitical issues are intermingled, creating a more real and complex finance. To do so, we emphasize both descriptive and qualitative aspects of current economic and policy issues as well as review a plethora of tools and statistical financial and economic models engineered to assess problems such as foreign exchange (FX) modeling, pricing and investing in a global and gated economy, compliance and risk pricing, related issues.

We review fundamental macroeconomic theories and their associated empirical evidence. We further point out that globalization contributes to a "global equalization of means and know-how" of developed and less developed economies which is intrinsic to their competition and gating for economic advantage. We emphasize that the growth of economic inequality within developed economies, where the rich get richer and the poor get poorer. Although such a process is ascribed at times to globalization, technology and the prominence of "capital over labor," in no small part, also contributes to such inequalities. Furthermore, issues that redefine the global economy relating to the migration of jobs, industrial capacities, and capital, are also assessed from the viewpoint of quantitative integrated models (e.g., Chapters 3, 7, 8, and 9). In Chapter 9, for example, trade is not presumed to be based entirely on comparative advantages and specialization, but also defined in terms of a far broader set of issues (e.g., socioeconomic and national agendas, supply risks, technology, loss of jobs, capital flows, and regulation). As a result, we conclude that the unhindered growth of globalization is also leading to a global competition and to a tendency to gate their national economies, yet confronted by consequences they failed to predict. Manifestations of globalization and gating risks abound, including a plethora of economic and finance "wars." For example, national and retaliatory explicit (or implicit) regulations, currency wars, financial and economic policies that seek to sustain their national and geopolitical agendas, and so on.

Globalization and gating are then parts of A-national enterprises (corporate entities increasingly independent of a national identification, regulation, or taxation) and global banking and finance and the many factors they set that underlie their governance, their financial and strategic policies, and their expansion of economic and financial outreach. Countries also implement gating policies and selective "openness" in order to achieve their economic, social, and political agendas.

However, in a "flat world," national powers are no longer as powerful as they once were. In such a world, financial agents are equally equipped with (or increasingly able to use) technologies that overcome distance, space, and time, and therefore are far less dependent on a home base. Further, globalization has led to a geographical diversification of consumption and supply markets as well as their many services. The business landscape has also been transformed from large corporate entities to global and extremely large networks of national and A-national entities. Global businesses, thus, are no longer a matter of orchestrated exchanges between national entities, a "few" importers or exporters, or international trading firms, but a far more diversified group of business entities that are self-serving and fuel the growth process of economic, industrial, and business entities that pursue the opportunities that an open world may provide. Examples of such processes are abundant, including competitive tax and supportive policies by sovereign states fueling inversions (firms moving their legal entities where their regulation and taxation advantages are greatest). For example, financial products, such as swaps, have been used increasingly in international exchanges to individualize economic and financial exchanges across national borders (Chapters 7 and 8). To meet new demands, traditional banking and finance and their associated regulatory sectors are changing. The former are expanding globally, while the latter leads to gating and attempts to manage the financial system.

Globally, we are witnessing the launch of financial exchange markets "everywhere," as well as the rise of electronic markets and IT systems supporting and managing an evolutionary development of finance. These include trading, information management and financial engineering, the stealthy movement of capital, and the core businesses of finance—banking, lending, liquidity supply, and trading, which are now embedded in a far more globally networked and complex finance. These transformations have important consequences for the quality of jobs in finance and its logistics. For example, increasingly, as savvy job seekers know, financial jobs require backgrounds in technology, risk finance, and regulation. These jobs are sought at the expense of traditional banking professional openings. Investment banking is shifting to standardized exchange traded funds, engineered to suit all potential investors' wants. In other words, in addition to a *boutique* finance, a *supermarket* finance with a global reach is altering the face of financial retail. Technologically, back-office automation, electronic markets, e-banking, e-currency, crypto-currency, artificial intelligence and robo-advisors are transforming the traditional financial environment. Such transformations combined with a banking system regulated by thousands of laws and costly sanctions have consequences, but it is not yet clear what these may be. For example, the global networking of financial institutions into a worldwide complex, together with unregulated networks, may emerge as A-national global financial systems, consisting of entities that need not function through conventional financial systems; they may appreciably affect their mechanisms.

Global equalization combined with the growth of inequality in rich Western economies, as pointed out earlier, have far-reaching consequences for their economic and political agendas, for industrial trade, and so on. A migration of industrial capacity in an increasingly sophisticated and technologically open world is also contributing to the growth of lagging economies equipped with newly found means and expectations that, in the near future, may lead the "haves" and "have-nots" to confront each other. When these trends are combined with job migration and losses accruing to the middle class, social and adverse economic effects arise, feeding a transformation of the job market, and challenging the globalization process and its underlying economic and financial processes. Global finance in such contexts is derived from "the global, political and social transition" to uncertain futures. For example, regulation and its compliance, currency wars, global warming, wars and peace, political and economic unions, and other issues are challenging globalization and, in their wake, financial futures. The challenges of globalization, raised daily by the media and in academic circles, define whether globalization is a win or lose proposition and for whom. Their outcome transcends their financial pricing and has consequences we can hardly assess. At the same time, it has radically changed the competitive economic platforms globally and challenged theoretical and conventional financial models.

Trade and investment policies have also become increasingly difficult to articulate when faced with unpredictable futures and conflicting sovereign policies. In such an environment, uncertainty prevails, financial theorists and practitioners emphasize risk management, the valuation of financial assets, and the legal and accounting aspects of compliance with regulations; all have a structural impact on the world of finance and its many institutions. Theoretically, complete market models are challenged by the increased complexity of trades and regulation, as well as by the many factors that contribute to financial markets' incompleteness. For example, international asset pricing, risk management, FX, external debt, trade financing, global investing, and assessing both currency and commodity price fluctuations are but samples of the many issues that global finance is confronting. They all involve a great number of risks (i.e., sources of randomness), often contagious and interdependent, and require more information to assess their consequences.

For example, the growth of and the complexity of compliance with the varying interpretations of the Dodd–Frank Act (2007–2009) have opened new vistas for financial regulators, causing financial institutions to scramble to comply with the thousands of ambiguous regulations. Financial reports are experiencing an increased demand by multiple regulators, domestically and across national borders; these are contributing to a gated and costly finance. These are due, in no small part, to the global reach of financial institutions and the sophistication of emerging financial products and the proliferation of financial markets and platforms globally. As a result, just as, at times, currency wars occur, regulatory wars occur as well. These elements underlie a regulatory eagerness, yet they are merely symptoms of the increased helplessness of sovereign states that seek to manage their economy as closed in an open and globalized economy.

Our Approach

The approach we chose to use in this book is based on broad and implied perspectives encompassing financial globalization, national (macro) economics, and the rational principles of fundamental finance. From a practical point of view, macroeconomic, sociopolitical and geopolitical factors are assuming greater importance. Although financial models are, by definition, restricted to specific problems, global finance may, in fact, be derived from macro-political and economic factors that alter and lead global finance. In this sense, our approach is based on the definition of "multiple factors," and thereby multivariate models as well as alternative models, some motivated by our observation of current financial practices. Figure 0.1 summarizes dependent factors omnipresent in the media and in the public discourse on globalization. Owing to their complex interactions, only some of their issues and mutual effects were selected for analysis.

Figure 0.1 Globalization and transformational finance.

At a mundane level, finance raises numerous questions and challenges. These include: How are currencies and FX priced? Why are efficient and stable currency prices important for trade? What are regulatory and compliance risks? How are gating policies applied through tariffs-taxation, controls, and incentives? Does globalization contribute to countries' economic welfare and to economic equality (or inequality)? What are the centrifugal and centripetal forces that fuel globalization, and why do they exist? How do contagious and extreme risks affect global sustainability? What are the policies and the repressive actions that sovereign states take (and why) to stifle their exposure to globalization?

These are a sample of many questions that global finance is concerned with. A seemingly endless number of newspapers and publications, statistics, and data sources provide a steady stream of information relating to political and geopolitical events, their analysis, their effects, theirs risks, and the opportunities they reveal. These data streams have redefined global finance into a new theoretically based profession that defines and evaluates the subcontexts of macroeconomics and geopolitics. The current economic and political discourse on jobs and their migration and on consumption prices (both as means to stimulate economic activity and prevent increasing inequalities) underlies political debates. For example, current US taxation on corporations' foreign income, not taxed unless repatriated, has created an incentive not to repatriate profits as well as to provide US corporate entities with a competitive advantage over foreign competitors (in their own land). Furthermore, untaxed profits accumulated over decades have been reinvested in foreign countries, thus contributing to the decline of job opportunities in the USA and the migration of US corporate and industrial might out of the country. These policy contradictions are contributing to self-defeating gating and a complex system of regulation based on political efforts to meet national agendas.

In its conventional and restricted sense, globalization is a term we use to describe the growing freedom of capital flows; to exchange and to trade economic resources among countries; to invest and to share opportunities and risks. In an ideal global finance there are no frontiers; in fact, media are increasingly pointing to sovereign gating policies, balking at impeded globalization, and raising trade restrictions, regulations, and providing incentives to their own while pursuing both geopolitical and economic agendas. At the same time, financial and statistical data are pointing to global finance pursuing a strong and unabated expansion fueled by the search for profits, tax and regulatory avoidance, and free financial flows seeking to capitalize on global financial opportunities. Global financial markets exchange trillions of dollars every day across a broad range of markets; this leads to a migration of capital, jobs, and people as never before, due to the continuously mutating economic and financial world. This mutation is assuming a life of its own, independent of sovereign rules, and is based on a global realignment based on the emerging perceptions of and the reality of globalization and its consequences. Some of these are based on previous economic misalignments; for example, the north–south euro economic imbalance (e.g., the Greek crisis and persistent weaknesses in the southern euro-based economies, compared with those economies to the north). We should also emphasize an increased vitality and development in emerging countries and in Asia that reflect new-found freedom, and the combating of economic inequalities everywhere.

Opportunities to borrow and lend money globally have increased, with well-informed and savvy traders speculating on global economic trends, currencies, and sovereign bonds. At the same time, global financial platforms may have created greater credit risk based on the stealth packaging of global assets (such as new families of exchange traded funds, structured financial portfolios, new families of collateralized debt obligations), as well as based on global trends and specific economic and geographical areas. These are contributing to an increasing risk dependence that may have caused the systemic financial failure of financial markets in 2007–2009. It also underlies the financial strategies of hedge funds speculating on global trends and constraints and investors seeking arbitrage opportunities across national boundaries. Such speculations and their inconsistent profit-making underscore that global finance is more complex than presumed and therefore more uncertain. In other words, both profits and risks have increased with globalization.

Globalization has also created more financial and speculative exchange venues due to asymmetries in regulation, culture, information, and opportunities. For example, prior to the launch of a program called "Shanghai–Hong Kong Stock Connect" in October of 2014, foreign investors had limited access to Chinese stock markets compared with that of Chinese traders (Shanghai Exchange with settlements in yuan). Another case concerns a foreign financial firm with assets in the USA that is subject to US regulation even though transactions occurred elsewhere; that may lead (and has led) to retaliation by sovereign states limiting the reach (although apparently unrelated) of global US corporations and financial interests. For example, the EU's decision (EC, 2016) to tax Apple's past income in Europe for €13 billion (or $14.5 billion) is a retaliation to the tax asymmetry between foreign and US corporations. The latter illustrates the case of avoiding taxation by not repatriating profits to the USA (as stated earlier).

These are not particular situations to the USA; most countries in their quest to sustain their own interest devise repressive and supportive actions to regulate their financial markets, subsidize economic trades, and support their economic growth and needs through their interventions in both FX and to their treasury interest rates. These are both current and pertinent issues that have expanded with changing financial world realities. For example, recent statistics indicate a growing trade in multiple currencies (rather than just in a dominant US dollar). Trade settlements in Chinese yuan were almost null in 2009, but they are now over 25% of global payments and growing in association with expanding currency blocs. By the same token, national financial markets are expanding in emerging economies, while Asia is seeking independence from Western financial institutions such as the International Monetary Fund and the World Bank. The growth of new economic power blocs based on common interests, embedding finance in a strategic framework with one bloc gaming the other, has led to a multipolar economic and financial environment with new powers seeking to assert themselves globally. Technology, social networking, big data, and the abundance of communications across cultural boundaries have amplified international transparency on the one hand and, on the other hand, muffled the understanding of their meanings. These are contributing to a greater "politicization" of finance and thereby to a "multi-agent" finance compared with a theoretical finance based on financial competing and complete markets—both vying for a theoretical predominance.

For some, global finance has increased their access to capital, contributed to economic development, increased their potential to diversify investments, and increased their wealth. For others, it has contributed to increased economic dependency and rendered sovereign states' abilities to manage their own economic affairs far more difficult. Firms have also grown from being national or international to being A-national (namely, "digital financial entities"), which are hidden from sovereign states' controls and respond to their self-interest by eluding all forms of national controls, regulation, and taxation. At the same time, these new corporate entities may also become political actors with well-defined agendas and powers that may exceed those of sovereign states. A stealthy economic environment is also growing through the reinvention of money using crypto-currencies, a new technology that evades any form of control. Thus, there are firms that are not subject to national jurisdiction. They may be stealthy or embedded in large and efficient supply chains tailored to meet demand, evade regulations, and shift profits and corporate seats from country to country to avoid taxation or seek local advantages. These firms are an outgrowth of multinational corporations which have assumed greater independence from their own and other sovereign states, thus rendering their control or their pursuit (by governments) ineffective. The impact of their actions, for better or for worse, pervades the new financial reality that is affecting all facets of our lives. For example, inversion, which we referred to previously, is used to avoid too harsh a regulatory environment, too high labor costs, and taxation. It also leads to a migration of national champions to the highest global bidders. Their development and growth, treating all markets as a single and global market, is leading sovereign states to protect their own advantages.

References

EC (2016) State aid: Ireland gave illegal tax benefits to Apple worth up to €13 billion. European Commission: Brussels. http://europa.eu/rapid/press-release_IP-16-2923_en. htm (accessed June 4, 2017).

Friedman, T.L. (2005) *The World Is Flat: A Brief History of the Twenty-first Century*. Farrar, Straus & Giroux: New York.

About the Authors

Dr. Unurjargal Nyambuu is an international economist with an extensive background in research, industry, and teaching. She specializes in macroeconomic policy and international finance, and is currently a professor of Economics in the Department of Social Science at the New York City College of Technology of The City University of New York. Previously, she was a research fellow in the Finance and Risk Engineering Department of New York University's Tandon School of Engineering. She has also served as an Economist for the Central Bank of Mongolia and has worked with the International Monetary Fund and the World Bank, where she was involved in analyzing exchange rates, commodity price dynamics, balance of payments, and developing global business and trade strategies. As a member of the South East Asian Central Banks' Expert Group, she specializes in capital flows and their impact on financial markets. Professor Nyambuu received her M.A. and doctorate degree (Ph.D.) in International Economics from The New School for Social Research in New York City. She completed an honors B.A. degree in Economics at Peking University in Beijing, China, with a specialization in Banking and Finance. She has worked as a consultant for the International Institute for Applied Systems Analysis, Vienna, Austria, and for the International Labor Organization, a United Nations affiliate based in Geneva, Switzerland. Professor Nyambuu is an active researcher with recent work published in the journal *Structural Change and Economic Dynamics*, in the journal *Economic Modelling*, and in John Wiley & Sons' well-known *International Journal of Finance and Economics*.

Dr. Charles S. Tapiero is the Topfer Chair Distinguished Professor of Financial Engineering and Technology Management at the Tandon School of Engineering, New York University. He is also founder of the Department of Finance and Risk Engineering, that he chaired until January 2016, as well as cofounder and co-editor in chief of *Risk and Decision Analysis*. An active researcher and consultant, Professor Tapiero has published over 400 papers and 15 books on a broad range of issues, spanning risk analysis, actuarial and financial risk engineering, and management. Some of the books include *Risk and Financial Management: Mathematical and Computational Methods* and *Risk Finance and Assets Pricing: Value Measurements, and Markets* published by Wiley; *Engineering Risk and Finance* (Springer), and others. Professor Tapiero has held numerous university positions in the USA and Europe (Columbia University, Case Western Reserve University, Hebrew University, ESSEC-France, and others), as well as held senior positions in quasi-governmental and government agencies. He received his Bachelor of Applied Science (Engineering) in Electrical Engineering, the MBA and doctorate degree (Ph.D.) in Operation Research and Management from New York University's Graduate School of Business Administration.

1

Globalization

Economies in Collision

Motivation

This chapter provides an overview of globalization. Our intent is to motivate and stimulate the reader to the compound challenges, opportunities, and risks that global finance provides. The economic and financial interdependence that geopolitics, macroeconomics, and finance entail has contributed to both global growth and concerns. Globalization has ushered in a transformation of economics and finance not only by encouraging the freedom to trade, but also through the movement of capital, resources, and money, as well as the migration of people and technology. It has led to major changes in financial institutions and in the practice of finance. This chapter seeks to highlight some of these issues as well as to present a number of trends that demonstrate the evolution of global finance and its current challenges. We provide a list of references for the motivated reader to better appreciate the impact of globalization on finance.

1.1 Introduction

Global finance is derived from and defined by countries' macroeconomic factors, trade, political, geopolitical and social agendas, and the global pursuit of national and individual financial interests. Sovereign states, corporate firms (both national and international), as well as a multitude of investors, traders, intermediaries, networked financial agencies, and globally distributed regulators are the elements that make up global finance; the extraordinary complexity that comprises it makes some of its elements more important than others, as they are able to sway trends, markets, prices, and, indeed, the evolution of global finance itself. Concurrently, global finance has, for better or for worse, introduced a global financial and economic interdependence through the growth of dominating institutions equipped with an extensive array of financial instruments allowing trade, investment, and the management of wealth globally. Currencies, and their derivatives, international investments, and exchange traded funds (ETFs) based on all aspects of the global economy have opened further opportunities for gain and loss. In fact, there are now more indexes than there are stocks (Bloomberg, 2017)! This has also allowed individuals to better define their preferences and identify global market trends.

Global finance is also evolving in a new era of multi-regulatory bodies; these seek to keep abreast of an evolving and complex finance, ensuring compliance with policy and laws, avoiding systemic risks, and maintaining market efficiency. The 2007–2008

Globalization, Gating, and Risk Finance, First Edition. Unurjargal Nyambuu and Charles S. Tapiero.
© 2018 John Wiley & Sons Ltd. Published 2018 by John Wiley & Sons Ltd.

financial crisis particularly contributed to the awareness that finance is truly global and interdependent, and therefore defined a new family of risks that sovereign regulation might not have been ready to deal with. These observations, as well as the economic consequences of globalization, have led to a reassessment of the global freedom that global finance was built on. Regulation and gating, both nationally and internationally, have altered the direction of their evolution, with the goal of better managing sovereign interests.

The global economy, fed by a global productivity growth, has grown unimpeded for decades, and is assuming an even greater importance due to political factors that have led to an economic and political realignment of emerging economies and global A-National corporate entities.[1] At the same time, networking and cyber-financial technologies have augmented the freedom of financial institutions, thus catalyzing a self-sustaining globalization trend into a complex economic development system that resists sovereign gating policies and seeks to protect its self-interest. This has led sovereign states to compete in global economic and financial markets and champion their own corporate entities; for example, the growth of increasing sovereign global corporations in China, Russia, and elsewhere. Global finance has thus contributed to the growth and the scale of financial institutions and to their economic and global outreach.

In 2011, state-owned enterprises (SOEs) accounted for more than 80% of the stock market capitalization in China, over 60% in Russia, and 35% in Brazil (*The Economist*, 2011). These statistics have systematically grown over time, indicating a new economic environment. More than 20 of these companies are listed among the world largest 100 multinational companies, and almost 30 of the top 100 companies are in the emerging markets. These firms are now found everywhere from China and Russia, to the Middle East. In some countries, where national champions are not politically common, the gradual loss of power has assumed other forms; for example, far greater regulatory intervention (as is the case in the USA, which uses the predominance of its currency as a tool to regulate what it can).

Trade is fueled by a global economic de-gating, economic growth, and increasingly competitive foreign firms. Technology, media, and social networking have rendered the world "a village" (Friedman, 2005). In the past, economic theories were based on Ricardo's theory of comparative advantage and specialization; in the present, trade is based on greater competition due to the global export of technologies and know-how, and will be more so in the future. Thus, changing patterns of consumption, geopolitical events, eco-political agreements, and corporate economic efficiencies are transforming trade. Industry has also changed based on globally networked supply, assembly, and retailing enterprises that contribute to the growth of trade. In Chapter 4, macroeconomic and financial issues of trade are addressed.

While trade is contributing to enrichment, it has also de-monopolized the power of some countries over their own economies. As a result, in times of crisis, it has led them to institute protectionist policies. This observation is consistent with sovereign states that have since expanded the breadth of the financial and economic policies they use. For example, in 2009 the G20 promised to refrain from protectionist action, yet then applied 122 new restrictions affecting 0.5% of the world imports between October 2010 and April 2011. In addition, the number of new trade restrictions was further

---

1 A number studies have examined globalization and economic growth. These include Sachs and Warner (1995), Rosenau (1996), Frankel (2000), Sachs (2000), Stiglitz (2006), Friedman (2005, 2012), and Spence (2011).

increased to 145 between October 2015 and May 2016 (see WTO (2016)). These restrictions were dominated by trade remedy measures and an increase in import tariffs (especially the initiation of anti-dumping investigations and duties in the metal industry). For example, the EU slapped anti-dumping duties on Russian and Chinese steel imports. New import tariffs on Chinese steelmakers were also imposed by the USA (266%)[2] and the EU (up to 13%) in 2016 and 2017. At the same time, a series of anti-dumping duties were imposed by China, especially between 2015 and 2016, on certain products imported from the EU, Japan, and the USA (see Chapter 9). There are many other examples. Egypt raised tariffs on over 300 goods (as much as 60% rate) in December 2016. Brazil increased tariffs on tools and toys, and imposed a 30% tax increase on cars with less than 65% local content in December 2011. Imported cars were taxed up to 55% on top of import tariffs (*The Economist*, 2012). Such taxes were imposed on the pretext of foreign imports fostering a deindustrialization of the Brazilian economy. In some cases, the EU was concerned with discriminatory taxes imposed by countries such as Brazil providing unfair advantages to its local manufacturers. At the same time, the USA has dampened the migration of professionals and others into the USA, imposing on foreign banks (with interests in the USA) to control bank accounts that belong to any US or foreign national who pays (also) taxes in the USA. Trade repression, seeking to gate and maintain corporate affiliations and safeguard jobs and capital, has also been revived and applied either directly or indirectly. Malaysia and Saudi Arabia, in the case of a firm's downsizing, have made it a priority to lay off foreign workers first. Such information, although reflected on the aggregate in globalization indexes and sovereign states' trade data, is explored on websites (either truthfully or partly truthfully) that report deviations in foreign trade practices.

Globalization and global finance are thus subject to push–pull forces. A "push" for open frontiers and a gating "pull." These have also unleashed two fundamental processes that have entered the political courses of sovereign states: *an equalization among countries, which we will allude to as a growth of entropy, combined with a growth of intranational economic inequalitiy*, as well as a loss of jobs in the rich Western countries subject to growing internal economic inequality. These two trends are creating a new environment that challenges national policies as well as basic academic macroeconomic theories that, in fact, are embedded in political dogma; thus, traditionally, this is called political economics. Equalization is further challenging Ricardo's principle of trade (comparative advantage); since in a maximum entropy-equalized world all have the same capacities and the same needs, whether financial or otherwise, "comparative advantage" might be irrelevant when there are no boundaries.

Globalization and global finance have thus articulated a complex system of worldwide networks of strategic partners. This has become a two-edged sword: on the one hand, it contributes to a global economic growth and creates greater mobility for ideas, technologies, labor, the transformation of social systems, and opportunities for a global economic equalization and growth; on the other hand, it changes traditional advantages for some and puts global competition on an equal footing for others.[3] Conventional finance, consisting of financial markets, credit risk and derivatives, corporate financial

---

2 See more in WSJ (2016a).
3 For further discussion on globalization, its management, and conflicting issues such as inequalities, poverty, resource curse, debt burden, and other problems, see Wood (1998), Sen (2001), The World Bank (2001), Stiglitz (2002, 2006), and Schneider *et al.* (2002).

Figure 1.1 Global finance: geopolitical, economic, and financial.

management, asset pricing, and other areas, has thus become far more complex in its global context, which is also defined by geopolitics, macroeconomics, and the complexity of an unruly world, as shown in Figure 1.1 and Figure 0.1, and outlined in this book's motivation.

Foreign exchange (FX) markets have evolved over many centuries to reflect the transformation of exchange rate regimes, the power of creditor states, and the international agreements which have sustained the stability of economic, business, and industrial exchanges, and so on. For example, prior to the Bretton Woods Agreement, currencies were fixed. On the one hand, it rendered speculative bets on exchange rates impossible; on the other hand, it contributed to economic dislocations due to mispricing and therefore to arbitrage opportunities that allowed currency traders to profit immensely. Financial arbitrage practiced by macro-hedge funds has allowed for windfall profits arising from economic imbalances, forcing sovereign states to revalue their currencies at great cost. Current financial currency markets have, to some extent, mitigated arbitrage opportunities, which resulted from economies in disequilibrium. In some cases, through strategic interventions by central banks, sovereign states may contribute to, and by their actions cause, FX markets to become more efficient. In the past decade, with the strong growth of globalization, FX markets have been freed in responding to macroeconomic policies and the market forces of supply and demand; these keep currencies in tune with global finance. For example, in 2016, China's economic and financial vows led it to accept a more flexible FX policy by letting the yuan fall freely and rendering it more sensitive to the market forces of supply and demand. As a result, we may surmise that in an era of economic openness, gating policies, in this case the control of FX currency, may be self-defeating.

In practice, however, we witness a broad number of cases where sovereign states intervene in FX markets explicitly and implicitly (with some costly interventions). Many emerging commodity exporting countries have aggressively intervened to support their weakened currencies following the contagious oil price decline between 2014 and 2016. These interventions were motivated by both economic and political agendas and by the need to stimulate employment through exports, to attract foreign funding (or investments) to domestic development programs, and so on. In particular, geopolitical agreements with Iran allowing it to free its oil exports as well as the political conflict underlying the supply of oil between Saudi Arabia and Iran and other countries led to a political (rather than just economic) price "war." The IMF (2016b), in its annual review of currency regimes, found that only one-third of member countries let their currencies float and that less than half of them rarely intervened—rarely enough to be classified as free floating. Both a country's economy and its multinational and A-National corporations' cash flows and returns are affected by fluctuations in FX prices and by the strategic interventions of sovereign states and their direct and indirect policies.

In recent years, the growth of back and front offices, along with financial technology, has contributed to the cross-border financial transactions underlying global financial markets. Such an evolution has grown and changed in tandem with A-National firms, international supply chains, and the evolution of political and economic agreements to regulate and streamline financial trades and international exchanges. At the same time, this has increasingly reduced the ability of sovereign states to gate and to regulate their financial markets and their associated complex financial transactions. Electronic markets (e.g., EURONEXT) and the proliferation of specialized financial markets have also bypassed and downgraded the capacities of sovereign states to regulate their own financial markets. In this environment, financial markets and FX have grown more independent, creating unique and global markets.

1.2 Trend and Challenges in Global Finance

1.2.1 Global Finance and the 2007–2008 Financial Crisis

The 2007–2008 financial crisis has awakened global finance to its global dependence and thus to its global risks. Nowadays, a trade on Wall Street can affect pensions in Norway, and where what was considered safe was in fact risky and therefore mispriced and without recourse. Global, systemic, and contagious events were proven, during the period from 2007 to 2008, to lead to disastrous financial phenomena (e.g., the loss of pensions, homes, jobs, and industries at national on an international scale).[4] Traditional finance, based on the assumptions of markets' rationality, independent of sovereign states, the predictability of future economic preferences, the uniqueness of prices, complete markets, and no arbitrage, may thus have been wrong or at least misleading. As a result, sovereign states reassess the globalization process, its costs and benefits, and their own position within such a world. Consequences of such assessment may have led some sovereign states to conclude that an unhindered global finance may lead to a financial jungle. To tame it, policies such as gating, multi-agent strategies, and the pursuit of complex agendas were enacted. However, this current state of affairs engenders its own risks.

Current questions frequently raised are: Is globalization sustainable? Is globalization contributing to growth and development? Is globalization increasing or decreasing national and global economic inequality? Is globalization irreversible? Does globalization cause a disappearance of middle-class jobs in the USA? Is globalization leading to the pursuit of greater profits or to the increased well-being of the planet? In a global setting, can we value and price international assets and their exchanges with simple financial models? Can there be a dominant US dollar (USD), or are there challenges to the dominance of the USD as an exchange and trade currency? Are multipolar financial markets and conflicts avoidable? Are digital (crypto) currencies an alternative to national currency markets? Can they be regulated, and by whom? What are the consequences of multipolar FX markets? Are

---

4 For causes and consequences of the global financial crisis and its global recovery, see Reinhart and Rogoff (2009), Stiglitz (2010), and Blanchard (2010) for example.

currency wars unavoidable?[5] These and many other questions are raised daily in the media, highlighting ongoing concerns and an awareness of the transformation of financial practice as taught and academically understood in classrooms. These are crucial and timely issues the world of business and finance are confronted by.

New facts are pointing to a greater role for emerging countries and to a global equalization; that is, to competition on an equal footing with developed countries. Equalization grows in many ways. On the one hand, historical trend of globalization shown by the KOF globalization index and illustrated in Figure 1.2[6] indicates that the USA had

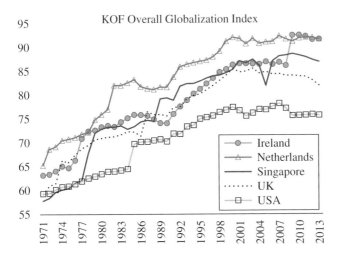

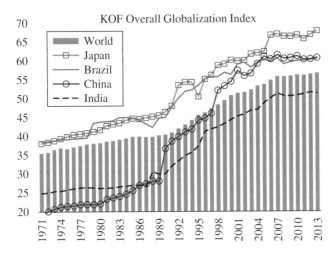

Figure 1.2 Globalization trend (KOF overall globalization index). *Source:* Data from KOF 2016.

5 For relevant discussions on some of these questions pertaining to globalization, financial markets, and instability, see papers by Lewis (1995, 1996), Krugman (2000), Stiglitz (2000), Rosenberg (2003), Blinder (2007), Boele (2002), Bruno and McLeavey (2003), Henry (2000, 2007), and Froot and Dabora (1999) for example.
6 For measurement of globalization, see papers by Lockwood (2001) and Kearney (2001) for example.

a gradual rise in globalization, but at a slower pace compared with other countries. Further, it has not shown much of an increase since 2000. On the other hand, countries that were less globalized in the 1970s and 1980s have increasingly become highly globalized. The migration of technologies, people, and industrial capacity, as well as the growth of financial markets and finance everywhere, is contributing to a global equalization process. Money, space, and time have become increasingly gateless, thereby maintaining an unhindered financial freedom and a preponderance and strengthening of A-National enterprises (whether large or small) trading across international and stealthy electronic networks. The pursuit of freedom and money thus leads to a transfer of know-how, jobs, and capital to access ever greater profits and, at the same time, to seek an independence of sovereign taxes, compliance, or collective responsibility.

These trends contribute to assertive corporate and national champions who expand their agendas and might globally. The Organization for Economic Co-operation and Development (OECD, 2014) provides a dataset on SOE sectors for 34 countries at the end of 2012. There are around 6 million employees working for the SOEs in these countries with a total enterprise value of over $2 trillion. The number of employees of the SOEs in most countries has increased from the previous survey period; in particular, French SOEs' employees doubled, increasing from 0.8 million in 2009 to 1.6 million in 2012, with almost half of the employees in transportation, followed by the electricity and gas industries. Major sectors of SOEs by company value in OECD countries are in electricity and gas, finance, transportation, manufacturing, and primary sectors. For example, SOEs in the financial sector dominate in Japan, the UK, and the USA, as shown in Figure 1.3. Note that the listed entities are majority-owned. The OECD database does not cover China. We emphasize the importance of China's SOEs and analyze this in Chapter 6.

1.2.2 Geopolitics and Finance or Geo-Finance

Geopolitics has several definitions, but all involve relating politics, power, and geography. Its aim is to provide tools for political action and define a strategic framework within which sovereign policies can be articulated. Thus, it is the art of political possibility. In a restricted and financial context, it defines the framework under which foreign (and global) financial policies are formulated. It determines the strategic alternatives that commit financial resources based on geographic access to economic and physical resources (such as oil), profit centers, and the geo-risks they entail. Geo-finance, a relatively unstructured financial discipline, is then important both due to its complexity and for the globalization processes it underlies. Among others, these include political, collaborative, and gating policies.[7]

The premise that financial markets define unique asset prices (in their theoretical sense and across national boundaries through the assumption of parity among equivalent or similar assets and products) is increasingly seen to be imprecise. A research report compiled by the Royal Bank of Canada points to the growing complexity and the multiplicity of financial markets, driven by computer-based trades, and each pursuing its own agenda to augment its profitability (NYT, 2016). Currently, there are 12 official exchanges making transactions through intermediaries; each one contributes to the layering of financial trades that lead to multiple prices and to a stealthy environment where prices need not be

---

7 For further discussions, refer to research by Walras (1954), Rabin (1993), Henderson (1999), Alberto *et al.* (1997), and Nunnenkamp (2002) for example.

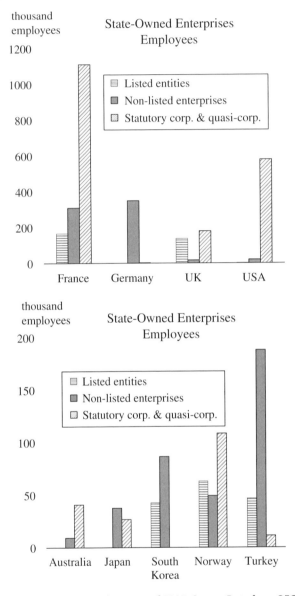

Figure 1.3 SOE employees as of 2012. *Source:* Data from OECD 2014.

the same for all traders. According to the Royal Bank of Canada, there are 800 pricing possibilities that generate profits mostly for a number of selected trading houses, determined by the volume of their trades and their exchange profits. The advantages of such trade houses are varied, and not limited to price only. Another advantage is the access to information and trading flexibility. On a global scale, these trading inefficiencies are augmented further by an increasing intractability of trades and the dominant role of large financial and global institutions. These elements raise risks that transcend the basic pricing of an asset in a specific financial market. In global finance, these inefficiencies are self-reinforcing and revealed only when financial crises erupt.

1.2.3 Population Growth

World population, currently over 7 billion, is predicted to reach 10 billion by 2050; this is also contributing to economic and socio-political transformations and migration. For example, countries endowed with large populations, such as China, have future prospects that will require large and long-term investments to meet local needs. At the same time, large populations provide economic opportunities for capital investors seeking returns. Symptoms of economic growth and economic equalization in emerging states are abundant, leading to a gradual departure of capital and well-paying jobs from the West to the East. At the same time, internal political challenges arise through the assumption of greater debt. Economic well-being is increasingly dependent on consumption at lower prices financed by increasing imports and maintaining lower domestic wages (and thus leading to a fall in domestic jobs with wages they cannot compete with). Economic and financial policies are, in their wake, becoming far more strategic and thus with colliding agendas. In this environment, financial reasoning based on ideals of rational expectations (i.e., based on an intertemporal financial equilibrium of demand and supply) is more difficult to justify. The axiomatic foundations of a complete market may not hold, and therefore economic markets may turn out to be less self-sustaining, more difficult to predict, and require financial and risk management to be far more in tune with real finance and its financial intents.

1.2.4 Geo-Finance and Gating

Geo-finance is defined by the growth of competing geopolitical groups that seek financial opportunities based on equal access to investors, traders, and financial markets. For example, the Eurogroup of countries was created for both political and economic reasons by first creating a common currency (to facilitate exchanges) to cement financial integration supplemented through political and fiscal integration (although a lack of fiscal integration has always been its Achilles' heel). On the one hand, its integration seeks to remove the risk of fratricidal wars with a political solution; on the other hand, it seeks to stimulate internal growth through an economic and political expansion of the euro. By the same token, trans-Atlantic market negotiations between Europe and the USA are not devoid of political concerns, encompassing the retreat of the USA as the sole dominant power (both politically and economically). The growth of Asian economies (e.g., China and India)[8] and their economic clout and expansion led to intensive discussion that finally led to a tentative trans-Pacific trade agreement between the USA and a number of productive and economically significant Asian countries (under President Trump, the USA withdrew from this partnership in January 2017). Questions regarding these agreements, political or economic or both, have been raised and point to the interdependence of finance and politics. In such contexts, trade agreements, financial regulation, and tariff/non-tariff barriers are part of the macroeconomic and financial policies applied within political agendas. These relationships and interconnected financial–economic–geopolitical events are shown in Figure 1.4. The rise of Donald Trump as president of the USA has introduced economic agendas which underlie his political policies.

---

8 For further information, see articles such as by Neftci and Xu (2007) and Keller and Rawski (2007).

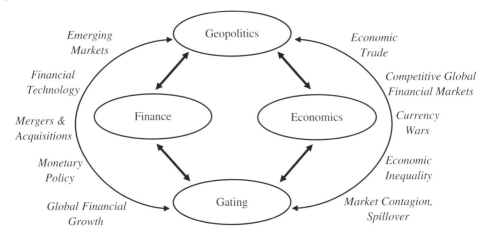

Figure 1.4 Interconnected financial–economic–geopolitical system under globalization and gating.

1.2.5 Culture and Social Norms

Culture and social norms are important elements that underlie globalization. For example, while the USA is sensitive to corruption and morality, as embedded in its constitution, it seeks to apply and export its moral arguments globally; that is, through US political means and global financial regulation. These cultural and social elements may alter markets with far-reaching economic and financial implications. At the same time, as discussed previously, sovereign states gradually lose the means to manage their own affairs by granting investors the freedom and the rights that would attract their interest to invest. Economic trends including the reduction of tariffs on trade (from a tax of 45% in 1947 to 3.7% in 1993) and the removal of non-tariff barriers are such examples. According to the World Trade Organization (WTO) Statistics Database on Tariffs (WTO, n.d.a), the current average tariff rate on imported agricultural products is 5% in the USA, but are 14% in Japan, with higher tariffs on sensitive products such as rice, dairy (32%), beef (38.5%), pork (8.5%), and wheat (25%) in 2015 (see Table 1.1). Other countries

Table 1.1 Import tariffs on agricultural products (%).

	Japan	USA	EU	China	India	Brazil
Meat of bovine animals	38.5	16.1	—	14.7	30	10.7
Frozen domestic ducks	9.6	—	—	20	30	10
Meat of swine	8.5	—	15.4	25	30	10
Milk and cream in solid forms	32.5	17.5	—	10	30	24
Wheat starch	25	—	—	20	30	10
Sweetcorn	10.6	14	—	10	30	10
Cocoa powder	22.4	7.5	8	10	30	18
Birds' eggs	10.5	—	7.7	12	30	4.8

Source: Data from WTO Statistics.

(e.g., India) have high tariffs, whereas the USA, the EU, China, and Brazil have much lower tariffs or no tariffs on many of these products. Japan has concluded several free trade agreements with countries, including Australia, India, and Mexico.

1.2.6 Emerging Economies, Equalization, and Risks

Emerging economies are striving toward equalization in their abilities to compete globally. Gating by sovereign states that seeks to counter global exchanges through regulatory and discriminatory policies and directional incentives have set the stage for strategic credit risks (see Chapter 4), thus pitting globalization and sovereign gating policy against those programs that seek to safeguard national advantages and pursue economic and political agendas. Such a process has underlain the evolution of globalization ever since the launch of the Industrial Revolution, fueled by the diffusion of sectorial technologies, with A-National firms and investors seeking greater economic freedom, greater access to global markets (through foreign intermediaries), higher yields, and less controls in expanding their might globally, regardless of their national origins. Equalization of means and capacities across nations and globalization is thus a self-reinforcing mechanism that reduces comparative advantages—both in technology and know-how. Financial technology is assuming a greater role in increasing the efficiency of global finance, but is also introducing new risks. For example, internet technology makes it possible to spread false information, contributing to contagion, and causing investor losses. Using the same technology, big data weakens those who do not wield it. Additionally, transparent and open information is easy prey to trolls who sell it to those who can use it. These provide, then, opportunities and information asymmetries that, in some contexts, may be equated with insider trading. In this environment, finance is inefficient.

These developments are reflected in the financial indexes of emerging economies. For equities' performances, we refer to the MSCI Emerging Markets (MSCI EM) index. This index covers 23 emerging markets with country weights of 28% China, 15% South Korea, 12% Taiwan, 9% India, 7% Brazil, and others, according to MSCI (2017). MSCI EM index's volatile movements correspond to both domestic and international macroeconomic factors. Sharp drops in these indexes occurred during the global financial crisis of 2007–2008 as well as the Asian financial crisis of 1997–1998, reflecting the increased global interdependence of economic activities around the world.[9] For example, weak currencies, slow economic growth, fiscal deterioration in some emerging countries (e.g., Russia and Brazil), and the plummeting of oil prices in 2014–2016 have contributed to the drop in the MSCI EM index with a sell-off of emerging market equities. These drops resulted from global economic, political, and financial patterns in commodity prices, and from political realignments in the Middle East rather than local economic issues.

Indexes' risks and returns can be calculated using MSCI data for overall emerging markets, as well as emerging regions of Asia, Europe, and Latin America. Latin American emerging markets are very volatile with very high risks and a standard deviation of returns in three digits since the early 2000s. During the financial crisis of 2007–2008, returns turned negative for all these regions with extremely high risks (even reaching

---

9 For analysis comparing the Asian financial crisis in 1990s and the global financial crisis in 2000s, see Andrew (2009) for example.

four-digit standard deviations of up to 1200% in Latin America). These statistics, of course, are not static, as they change over time following international and domestic trends and events. In this sense, global economic and financial states are in an off-equilibrium state, manifested by a continuous change.

1.2.7 Regulation and Politics

Financial institutions are currently affected by the complexity of US regulation and its outreach. For example, suppose that there were 7000 regulations that govern financial and bank compliance. In this case, the probability of being noncompliant would be extremely large, regardless of the efforts and the expenses that the firm undertook in order to be fully compliant (see Chapter 10 for a technical development). Such regulations imposed on banks often invite retaliation by sovereign states, discriminating between customers based both on wealth and deposits, and their origins. As an example, consider the preventive measures by retreating from businesses and markets—a preemptive strategy in the face of US regulation (*The Economist*, 2014). For example, the Red Cross transfers funds to help the displaced and alleviate tragedies in places such as Syria and other countries that are violating US financial regulation and thus became noncompliant, and running the risk of extremely large penalties. Further, the $110 billion collected as penalties pertaining to the mortgage bailout has, in fact, been used mostly for self-government and intractable expenses (WSJ, 2016b).

1.3 Global Finance and Trade in the Media and News

Media are filled with pronouncements and problems regarding global finance. A number of examples are presented in the following sections.

1.3.1 Taxing Foreign Returns When They Are Repatriated

US firms have acquired profits internationally; this has caused them to turn to foreign M&A (mergers and acquisition) to avoid tax liabilities in the USA. For example, the acquisition of Skype by Microsoft in 2011, for $8.5 billion, was paid from Microsoft's foreign cash reserves. Repatriating these profits to the USA would have entailed a tax rate of 35% they would have preferred to avoid. Many US firms with billions of dollars of earnings in foreign countries have contributed to global reinvestment and global growth of A-National firms. Are US firms at risk of foreign retaliation? Are such actions leading to the migration of American firms?

1.3.2 Sovereign Gating and Protective Tariffs, Trade Defense

In response to illegal subsidies provided by the Chinese government, the EU announced its decision to raise tariffs on Chinese high-end glossy paper exporters in May 2011 (see FT (2011)). Until then, the EU had imposed tariffs on countries that were dumping their exports (i.e., exporting at unjustifiable low prices). The EU's trade defense action's intent was to provide a signal that the EU would protect its high-end industries while essentially giving in to China's dominance of low-end and labor-intensive industries.

1.3.3 Global Insurance and Dependence

In 2012, Florida's residents were made to pay far greater premiums to be insured against hurricanes. This was not because of potential and costly hurricanes in 2011, but due to the extraordinary earthquake devastation in New Zealand and the deadly tsunami in Japan. In other words, in a global world with global insurance firms, events everywhere affect the overall risk premium we have to contend with. This is the case not only for insurance firms, but also for banks. Both Iceland's and Ireland's economies collapsed in 2009 not because of the domestic situations in these countries, but due to local banks that had become international and operated globally assuming risks in the mortgage-backed securities and engendering financial obligations that they were not able to meet.

1.3.4 Finance and Politics

At the G20 meeting in 2011, questions were raised about the US and Chinese modes of "participation in an international process that will review the risks that major economic powers pose to each other as well as to the global growth and its development" (NYT, 2011a). What are the intentions of such questions? As quoted in the same *New York Times* article, on the one hand, they hoped to "raise international pressure on China to stop increasing exports by keeping its currency artificially underpriced." On the other hand, the world might criticize the USA for its large current account deficits that fund its massive consumption and affect the price of its currency. As a result, each party necessarily has its own political agenda, sometimes resulting in gating, but at other times in collaboration. These events attest to the competitive nature of international and financial markets. They highlight the effects of taxation on capital flows: the strategic actions assumed by countries to maintain or gain competitive advantage. They also point to simple acts and events that can perturb the global business climate. Most governments' actions today, whether explicit or implicit, have global effects. Finance is thus derived from the information that emanates from the evolution of national interests and their consequences on global markets.

1.3.5 EU–US Regulation Risks in a Trans-Atlantic Market

Both the USA and the Eurogroup run risks in settling their differences while participating in a Trans-Atlantic market. For the eurozone, risks pertain to the protection of jobs (much weaker in the USA): a degradation of workers' collective rights and unions and weaker control of technological innovation (in agro-production, etc.). While in the euro world preventive measures are taken ex-ante, in the USA, most of the time, these measures are taken ex-post, after a disastrous event occurs. In the USA, it may result in restrictive immigration policy. A greater concern for sustainability in the eurozone (e.g., animal rights) compared with the USA (e.g., the reduction and protection of social services such as health care and transportation) is that they may become liberalized if the US approach to business is imposed. The trans-Atlantic market, with US firms demanding the opening of these markets, anticipates increased unemployment in Europe (as jobs will no longer be protected), the loss of confidentiality of data, submission to stringent rules and laws on intellectual property (which are weaker in Europe), and finally euro states will submit to a judicial system that may become far more tolerant of A-National enterprises.

For the USA, the challenges are important. For example, current financial and other regulations set by the USA and applied globally may face retaliation globally, and thus choke financial globalization. It may therefore be amended at some future time to account for resistance to being subjugated to the US regulatory rules. These may require a revision of the Volcker rule, of the Dodd–Frank regulations, a reintroduction of the Glass–Steagall Act of 1933 (ended by Congress under Bill Clinton's administration), other related regulation. Finally, even the USA will have to submit to the legal rules that the eurozone's A-National enterprises will bring to courts (not necessarily in New York or other US courts). As long as there will be broad differences, globalization will, necessarily, be in turmoil.

Evidently, these elements are to be accounted for by financial advisors and financial traders through their decisions to/not to invest, and in what and where investments are to be pursued.

1.3.6 Rare Earth and Strategic Trades

Supply constraints on strategic input factors have become one of the means to pursue both economic and political agendas. Rare earth minerals have attracted attention owing to their necessity for technological products; their mining in China accounts for over 95% of global production. Rare earth elements are needed, for example, for electronic items (such as tablet devices and wind power) and used in an extensive number of military items (NYT, 2010). However, production and exports of rare earth minerals have contributed to a number of pressing issues due to risk externalities. Explicitly, the extraction costs of rare earths are high and generate much pollution. Given their strategic importance, they can also be used as a political weapon, being supplied to some countries while being withheld from others, thus adopting discriminatory pricing and supply practices. Their extraction costs and related pollution have contributed to some rare-earth-rich countries (e.g., USA and Australia) foregoing their extraction, thus letting China gain a specialized monopoly. This situation has contributed to price discrimination in rare earths trade, with a price increase in dysprosium (a specific rare earth used in electronics) from $6.50/lb in 2003, to $132/lb in 2010. With such prices, a black market and illegal mining have set in, bypassing national and environmental controls. This has also led to a crackdown on illegal mining in order to institute both greater environmental controls and obtain a better political and economic control of rare earth exports. Keith Bradsher states (NYT, 2011b):

> China has long used access to its giant customer base and cheap labor as bargaining chips to persuade foreign companies to open factories within its borders. Now corporate executives say it is using its near monopoly on certain minerals—in particular, scarce metals vital to products like hybrid cars, cell phones and energy-efficient light bulbs—to make it difficult for foreign manufacturers of high tech materials to build or expand factories anywhere except China.

Companies can continue to expand their factories domestically, but may be subject to both price and supply discrimination that differentiates between domestic and foreign buyers and between foreign countries. Such practices are probably violating global trade rules. It is not clear, however, how they may be enforced due to China's current political and economic clout. On September 16, 2011, China clearly indicated that it was assuming full control of its rare earth mining and used its control for geopolitical ends. Since then, alternative sources of supply (e.g., Australia) have been developed to meet the demand for the mineral. At the same time, economies have reduced the demand for rare earth minerals, resulting in falling prices.

1.4 Global Risks

Financial risks are mutating, assuming many forms and becoming less amenable to the common methods we use to measure them. For example, while in a world lacking a basic (safe) and reference currency or a truly acceptable and agreed upon basket of currencies, the stability of currency markets is at risk. Instead of free and transparent markets, sovereign states may intervene through regulations and gating policies to maintain the stability of their currency. However, these actions have consequences. For example, in August 2011, Japanese intervention in its currency markets, in order to weaken their exchange rate against the dollar, eroded profits of its industrial champions (WSJ, 2011). This intervention followed a decision by the Swiss central bank to push down the value of its currency, slowing a spreading global response to a renewed economic weakness in the USA. Further, on October 11, 2011, the US Senate passed a bill that required the Treasury department to impose tariffs on certain Chinese goods if China continued to manipulate its currency—see NYT (2011c). However, as national economic environments have changed, these policies have also changed. Such actions are both political and economic, articulated with economic and financial tools which can be used strategically by trading nations. Similarly, an increase in complex and extensive sovereign regulation applied unilaterally and globally may contribute to greater confusion in the business of finance.

1.4.1 Factors Affecting Global Risks

Global risks are challenging finance theory and economic and financial management. They are compounded by countries' cultural, political, and eco-financial diversities and risks and result in a complex amalgamation of risks, which will be partly addressed in Chapter 10 (on financial compliance and regulation). A summary of factors follows:

1) *A multipolar world.* Competing financial markets combined with financial repression (taxation and local regulation, gating trades and other exchanges, applied locally and globally by some sovereign states). An increased transformation of national corporate entities into A-National firms evading national jurisdictions.
2) *Volatile and competing currencies areas.* Currencies' volatilities are amplified by USD fragility or resilience as well as national economies' performances, their interest rates, and their policies and politics. Ever since World War II, the USD has been a reference currency used to price assets and commodities globally. The USD dominance has led creditor nations (e.g., China, Japan, UK, and the rest of the world in smaller amounts) to indulge the US debt by holding extensive reserves in US dollars. When foreign nations hold US debt, they then have a strong incentive to see the USA succeed so that their dollar-denominated bonds become valuable. A retreat in the USD has, however, increased the credit risk of dollar creditors, augmenting the fragility of international exchanges. Thus, under an unviable and safe currency, the

global financial system and trade can falter. In this environment, competing currencies areas define FX prices, with potential currency wars (i.e., with a greater currency volatility) as well as augmenting the currencies' risks.

3) *Flight from risk.* This arises due to weak and uncertain yields in equity markets. It also contributes to a flight from globalization, a lack of financial liquidity, dampening economic growth and innovation. In such an economic environment, global risks might not be diversifiable. Global investments, usually where they are needed the most, are then reduced. In other words, a misunderstanding of global risks can contribute to their being overstated and may, in fact, increase global risk.

4) *Global environmental risk.* Creeping desertification, global warming and changing weather patterns, water shortages, population growth, and other environmental problems alter the economic, political, and social landscape for global finance. Contagious migrations, grass roots movements, and tyranny of minorities contribute to "re-evolutions" that pit political agendas internally and externally against each other, providing new sources of economic and financial instability.[10] In global finance, these assume a political risk premium.

5) *Statistical and contagious dependence.* Statistical dependence arises when the events in one country correlate with the events in another. A contagion arises, however, when one event not only correlates with, but triggers a statistical succession of other events. For example, consider the US economic well-being and its debt. A downgrade of the US economy can obviously have an impact on all of its trading partners (the world) and their dollar reserves. A contagious failure in one state is thus a threat inducing failure in another. States intervening to seek advantageous terms in trade through tariff and non-tariff barriers, quotas and taxes on imports, and incentives for exports can also cause contagious retaliations by other countries—with countries locked into costly retaliatory processes. By the same token, downgrading a whole banking sector subject to increased regulation may induce a tightening of its loan standards and anti-cyclical value-at-risk requirements that further dampens their ability to lend and make profit (and thus induce a greater probability of failure).

6) *A persistent transformation of information technology (IT) and cyber-financial risks.* Technology risks are based on the global leverage that information and misinformation technologies provide in addition to their social global outreach and cyberrisks. IT has contributed not only to instant global networking and distance-free communications and exchanges, but also to an increased complexity through networking; the liberalization of exchanges and stealthy exchanges that are difficult to regulate. In this environment, regulation of rogue financial transactions can be hard to control—increasing globalization, on the one hand, and contributing to sovereign state gating, on the other hand. By the same token, IT has been a social and networking two-edged sword: not only contributing to global social outreach, but also exposing both firms and societies to the scourge of cyber risks.

7) *Information and power asymmetry.* Moral hazard and adverse selection allow the few informed or powerful to profit at the expense of the many. Global finance requires global information and control on a global scale, and therefore financial agents and insider agents may have advantages that others do not have. For example, IT provides opportunities to powerful A-National firms as well as incentives to evade restraints in

---

10 For analysis on financial instability, see, for example, Minsky (1992, 2008).

their pursuit of growth and profitability. These contribute, potentially, to economic inequalities within countries arising from global and stealth profitability.

1.4.2 Global Finance and Risk Theories

Global risks are amplified by multi-agent, political, economic, external, and natural risks. Traditional financial analysis is based on theoretical assumptions that do not hold in a complex and interdependent environment. From a fundamental point of view, pricing is defined by value and opportunity to exchange with no arbitrage. These are translated into three essential assumptions:

- predictable asset's state preferences (future state prices are assumed known);
- a references measure is used to price assets (such as a risk-free rate or a basket of currencies with a known price with respect to which assets are priced);
- market rationality that defines a unique equilibrium.[11]

When any of these assumptions is lacking, markets are said to be incomplete and a unique market price for exchange cannot be set. In other words, complete markets' finance is not applicable and is essentially a model of economic–financial parametric equilibrium used by financial engineers to estimate parameters in an implied model based on available price information. Today, financial firms recognize that "no one can fully predict tomorrow's risks. But in today's fundamentally changed investment world, the risks are less foreseeable and more misunderstood than ever—and can cause lasting damage" (NYT, 2012a).

In the case when future events are unknown, and therefore unpredictable, probability distributions defining these events are incomplete. In physics, such situations are referred to as non-extensive systems. The calculus of probabilities requires that we define a mechanism to complete the probability distribution with all its probabilities summing to one. This terminology was coined by Knight (1921) as uncertainty, which he compares to risk when future events have known states and known probabilities associated with these states. In global finance, subject to many interacting economic models, these problems are more difficult to analyze.

Information regarding a reference asset (e.g., a risk free bond) or another related, but derived asset (e.g., various equity options with a common underlying stock and therefore a common source of risk) is needed to define a future price that is consistent with the financial model we use, as well as with all the information available regarding the asset.[12] Again, when such information is insufficient due to markets' complexity and future events and their consequences—ignored or presumed unpredictable—it is then much more difficult to price assets and pursue exchanges that presuppose an efficient global market. A greater understanding of these issues, as amplified in subsequent chapters, will provide a greater awareness and understanding of their consequences, albeit not necessarily providing resolution to that complexity. In Chapter 7, we shall suggest that, lacking a complete FX theory for pricing, we may consider the reciprocal tracking of FX and their baskets that best define and contribute to a sovereign agenda.

---

11 For a discussion on the rational market, see Fox (2009).

12 For research on risk theory, risk and uncertainty, international diversification, global stock returns, and other related issues see Knight (1921), Arrow (1965), Heston and Rouwenhorst (1994), Fontela (1998), Jermann (2002), Hoxha *et al.* (2009), and Hou *et al.* (2011).

1.5 Global Finance, Swaps and Financial Products

Swaps are, in principle, extremely simple. They entail an exchange between two parties or entities that have a common interest to engage in an exchange. Swaps are particularly important in global finance due to an increasing number of international and currency transactions, as well as with a large number of off-market transactions. For example, the barter agreement between two countries is, in fact, a swap contract. Another example can be a US firm seeking to sell an aircraft to a Romanian airline, thus engaging in an exchange where payments for the aircraft will assume many forms distributed over specific industrial activities; for example, the sales of agricultural products and/or payments distributed over time in multiple currencies. Similarly, if a party in France has euros but needs dollars to acquire a firm in the USA and it can find another party in the USA that has dollars but needs euros for another transaction in France, it may engage the two parties directly or indirectly. If the engagement entails a direct exchange it may be called an over-the-counter (OTC) exchange. If it is engaged through an intermediary (e.g., a broker that facilitates the exchange at a fee), it is an indirect contract. In such cases, brokers may act as market makers, profiting from both the spread and the trades they are able to engineer. By the same token, the French party buying dollars in the FX market is also involved in an indirect contract, but with a counterparty which is in fact, a financial market for currencies.

Financial swap products are engineered contracts that allow a personal exchange between parties. These products may involve guarantees that the counterparties to the contract will meet their obligations. To assure these obligations, a legal framework is defined that may be or may not be enforceable. Such exchanges may also be controlled by a third party, such as a government that would tax transactions or merely track transactions for other purposes (such as stealth money flow, and terrorism). In a global financial world, both the complexity and the number of purposes for which financial products may be engineered can be extremely large.

For convenience, we may categorize these products and their functions as follows:

- bilateral contracts or OTC;
- administered bilateral contracts (such as those handled by a broker, a dealer, or a regulator);
- freely market-traded products, albeit we may consider a regulator as an associate to the contract that makes no money but is assumed to maintain the legality of the contract.

For example, in real estate, when a transaction is assisted by a broker/agent, a fee is paid to the real estate agent—the intermediary. Homes may also be sold at an auction with buyers submitting bids to an auctioneer following specific rules or packaged as a portfolio which is then sold freely through a financial market and its property shared by the buyers of denominated shares in such a portfolio. Similarly, swaps underlie an extremely large variety of financial products exchanged between domestic and foreign partners or exchanged globally through financial markets. Such markets may further define derivatives such as options and swaptions (options on swap contracts). Credit products, including foreign debt, may be treated similarly, just as currency can be interpreted as a credit granted by the holder of the currency to the sovereign state issuing such a currency. Swaps, debt, credit, stocks, bonds, and so on thus underlie an extremely large number of tailored swaps. Swaps might therefore be exchanged for the following reasons:

- each party of the transaction has a perceived need or advantage;
- some of the parties may be better informed or able to assess value and therefore have an exchange advantage;
- markets are complete and therefore each exchange is fair to all, and reflects aggregate values.

Historically, a financial swap was created first in 1970 in the UK to circumvent FX controls and taxation that sought to prevent an outflow of capital. Previously, this was done by pairing two firms in different countries. One would agree to borrow locally and have the funds transferred to another, and vice versa. In this manner, none had any FX transactions. The evolution of such transactions to be administered by banks and other financial firms as intermediaries led to what we now call cross-currency swaps and interest rate swaps. These institutions, in fact, acted for a fee as brokers, while in other cases they became dealers— namely, market makers, helping to satisfy demand for such transactions.

The first currency swap was written in 1979 between the World Bank and IBM with Solomon Brothers as their intermediary. Their development led to commoditized (or standardized) transactions which, unlike OTC transactions, do not involve only a bilateral contract in which two parties (or their brokers or bankers as intermediaries) agree on how a particular trade or agreement is to be settled in the future. OTC markets are sometimes referred to as the "dark market" because OTC prices are neither published nor regulated. OTC derivatives, however, unlike traded swap contracts, may be used to construct a perfect hedge since traded standardized contracts are one-size-fits-all instruments that do not have as much flexibility as OTC contracts have. With OTC derivatives, though, a firm can tailor the contract specifications to best suit its risk exposure. OTC derivatives have counterparty risk; that is, the "other side" may default prior to expiration of the OTC trade. This is not the same as credit risk, where default is explicit in the contract. Thus, OTC products naturally incur liquidity risk not seen in standardized products. By definition, the OTC market does not have a formal "market maker."

In fact, swaps and OTC contracts can be structured and be extremely complex due to the multitude of wants and needs that parties have, as well as the logistical problems they encounter in engaging counterparties. As a result, a multitude of swaps and OTC contracts are tailored to meet markets, brokers, dealerships (intermediaries), and individual demand. The Bank for International Settlements (BIS, 2016a) provides detailed semi-annual data on outstanding global OTC derivatives for the 6 months ending each June 1 as the first half (H1) and at the end of December as the second half (H2) for each year. These contracts' gross market value surged from only a few trillion dollars in the early 2000s to a peak of $35 trillion (H2) and $20 trillion (H1) in 2008, but declined to $15 trillion (H2) and $21 trillion (H1) according to BIS (2016a, 2017). Popular derivatives include interest rate contracts, accounting for around 70% of total contracts, and FX contracts, which represent around 16% of such transactions (see Figure 1.5).

A brief list of variables defining such contracts may assume to include:

- currency, interest rates, commodities, financial commoditization, securitization;
- broker, dealer (market maker), and institutionalized and engineered financial markets portfolios, ETFs (firms such as BlackRock and many others have created these for a plethora of financial instruments and markets);

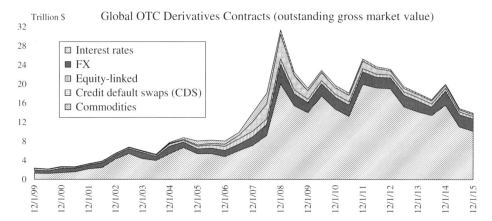

Figure 1.5 Global OTC derivatives contracts (semiannual outstanding gross market value). *Source:* Data from BIS 2016.

- time and money (debt, future returns);
- contracts, options (swaptions) as well as spreads and exotic options.

Subsequently, in Chapters 7 and 8 we will consider approaches to their valuation and pricing.

1.6 Currencies and Liquidity

An exchange rate is a relative price between two currencies that facilitates the exchange of one currency into the other. In antiquity, bronze coins were used as a medium of exchange, and therefore the legal tender of a currency was the metal minted. Subsequently, silver and gold were used and have since assumed a far greater importance. These coins provided the liquidity needed for economic exchange and development. Following the discovery and conquest of the Americas by Spain, silver and gold provided the liquidity to both its economic development and financing of their wars of conquests. Wars pursued by Spain strained its economy, leading to a growing indebtedness that contributed to the waning of its power. The silver and gold it held could no longer provide the liquidity needed to maintain its dominance (note the similarity with the financing of wars by the USA and its ability to sustain the price of the dollar and its global dominance). Today, money is liquidity, and therefore a sovereign state printing money increases its domestic liquidity. When its currency is recognized as a legitimate reference or safe exchange currency it may also contribute to a global liquidity. However, holding a denominated currency also entails FX risk, especially when such a currency is devalued due to political or inflationary forces. It can also be a speculative investment when the currency becomes stronger in value. Thus, currency is a *financial asset*.

The demand for liquidity has been an ever-present fact. Historically, it led to the rise of the Bankers Dynasty in Florence (the Medicis) and in Milan (the Sforza), both developing IOUs as legal tender, which were paper obligations. It has created paper money as an expanding medium of exchange. Paper money could then be redeemed by the Dukes of Venice, Sforza, and Venice. The paper created credit. Holding on to these paper obligations incurred necessarily credit risks, since dukes and their banks might not, in certain circumstances, meet the obligations paper money entitled its holders. Subsequently, Dutch and British banking dominance strengthened due to a financial innovation: reserves deposited in banks and financial markets to engineer and expand credit liquidity. This has led to the monetary system still currently in place and represented by the central banking system. Namely, a paper-based financial system arose based on the implicit fiduciary trust in the banking system. This trust has provided the required liquidity and the guarantees to holders of paper money. These guarantees assume many forms; for example, certificates of deposit that may or may not be safe, Federal Deposit Insurance Corporation insurance, which in some banks insures deposits up to $250 000, and so on. All of these are "money" and are priced to determine the currency of the country. The FX rate, therefore, expresses the relative trust one bestows on one country compared with another. As in past centuries, currencies used as paper money were priced by the relative trust in the value of the paper their creditors held. The FX price associating one currency with another therefore represents the relative and mutual trust of both the creditors and the debtors (countries) in a currency, reflecting the sustenance of its value and its risks.

Increasingly, attention is given to digital currencies providing an alternative denomination to the USD, thus evading its stringent regulation. Bitcoin and its technology have attracted some interest (mostly in the media). For example, British Barclays PLC together with Circle Internet Financial Ltd, is offering a free mobile app for receiving and sending British pounds. Through this digital currency exchange, US dollars and British pounds are exchanged to bitcoins and converted back to these currencies for the recipient. At the same time, big US banks are testing block chain, which is a bitcoin technology for swaps (e.g., credit default swap). It still has technical drawbacks that render it far from being accepted as a virtual currency or money that can be exchanged for currencies backed by sovereign states.

Paper money and FX prices are closely related to trade, terms of exchange, and their derived prices for credit and globalization. The FX rate is the price we ascribe to another country's paper money (as determined by financial markets). A stable FX rate is, thus, important as it allows lending and borrowing across nations with different currencies and trade. What happens when a country's debt increases beyond its ability to service debt? It increases its obligations and reduces its freedom to manage its own affairs and leads investors to invest in other countries. This contributes to a currency run and therefore to the currency's devaluation. In such cases, when a nation overprints paper money, it squanders its resources and becomes politically irresponsible; thus, its currency becomes risky. In other words, FX risk arises due to the lack of trust by global parties in the sovereign policies of the debtor currency, among other causes.

Currency and FX involve risks, including essentially:

- ***Market-related risks:*** When FX markets are unable to settle at a particular price for a currency, they become volatile and potentially extremely risky. For example, when Argentina could not reach a price for the FX rate, it simply resorted to pegging its currency to the dollar, with immense economic consequences. Similarly, Switzerland, faced with a flight from the dollar in September 2011, pegged its currency to the euro to stem the Swiss franc's appreciation and salvage its export industries.

- *Currencies and credit risks:* Under the Bretton Woods agreements (which we will summarize in the following), dollar holdings could be redeemed at the US Federal Reserve Bank in gold, with a price set to $35 for an ounce of gold. Since 1933, gold has been removed in the USA as legal tender. Instead, the currency debtor obligations are backed by the country's goods and services that can be met by buying or exchanging the currency held. When a country's price level changes (e.g., due to inflationary pressures), its exchanges are increasingly regulated, and/or the safety of its obligations is affected (e.g., the downgrading of sovereign bonds), and so there is FX risk due to holding of the weakening currency. Thus, for all countries, the strength of a currency or its weakness is relative to both global and alternative opportunities and to other countries' economic states. Economic growth, inflationary pressures, financial regulation and repression in FX, employment levels, balance of trade and payments, capital flows, import and export trends, interest rates, political stability, political clout, and other indicators are then part of a multitude of factors that intervene in determining a currency's exchange rate and its credit risk. Chapter 8 will provide a technical approach to pricing credit risk.
- *Counterparty-related risks:* These risks result, for example, from financial repression applied to trade, a power asymmetry that a sovereign state has over others, a concerted manipulation of FX prices, and so on. It may happen when a country is economically irresponsible or untrustworthy. In such cases, expropriation of assets, moral hazard, and adverse selection risks arise and trades make currencies to be inherently risky.
- *Latent and external risks:* Such risks may be rare events, such as the tsunami and nuclear meltdown that occurred in Japan in 2011, or latent and stagnating macroeconomic factors that take time to be detected; when they occur they have a particularly strong impact (such as the mortgage-backed securities crisis and the liquidity financial and contagious crisis that emanated from the USA).[13] These events have affected currency holders (such as China, Japan, and other countries with extremely large reserves of USD). These are particular risks, since when they occur they also affect a country's economic health and thereby the pricing of its assets. Such risks, however, are not easily defined or predictable, and are not therefore diversifiable.
- *Default model risks:* Such risks arise from misconstrued currency pricing models that are mostly based on few economic factors, giving only a partial assessment of the extent and the depth of dependency in a globalized financial and economic world. Furthermore, while the law of one price (LOOP) is a convenience we use to derive theoretical prediction of FX, in practice it might not reflect the real behavior of FX prices. In Chapter 7 we shall consider both application of the LOOP and departures from some of its assumptions.

Questions and Problems 1

Discuss the reasons that led to euro risks due to excessive indebtedness by some countries in the eurozone area (e.g., Greece). What are the repercussions for the euro FX rate and what are the consequences for other countries in the eurozone (e.g., France and Germany)? In particular, discuss what happens to capital flows and investment in

---

13 For analysis on financial contagion, see, for example, Allen and Gale (2000) and Soros (2008).

each country involved and why. What is the price of a loan one ought to assume to meet the obligations? What are the economic and political alternatives to the leading economies in the eurozone?

1.7   Foreign Exchange Regime and Markets, Global Payment, and Reserve Currency

FX markets are used as a platform to trade, invest, speculate, and exchange currencies and their derivatives. Thereby, they contribute to the determination of FX rates. As of 2016, these are huge financial markets with over $5 trillion being traded every day, providing both profit opportunities and risks for exporters and importers, international investors and speculators, and all economic agents affected directly or indirectly by globalization. FX rates have become a derived asset class which is difficult to manipulate by any specific agent, and is a function of different factors that contribute to the demand and supply of a currency. A country's macroeconomic fundamentals, such as GDP, debt and its fiscal policy, political environment, international and hazard risk events and attitudes toward globalization, are some of the factors that are used to explain and predict movements in these prices. FX rates, as a derived asset class, also allow investors and speculators to bet on the future states of world economies and, therefore, the economic parties to globalization. Financial bets can assume many forms; for example, buying long or short certain currencies, importing or exporting materials, commodities, or finished products, investing in foreign firms or international projects, as well as speculating on sovereign debt through buying and/or selling sovereign bonds. As we can see, these are an extremely diverse set of asset classes traded in continuously growing financial markets. Spot FX, treasury bonds, and their derivatives (such as forwards, futures, and options on bonds) are traded on exchanges in London, New York, Tokyo, Frankfurt, Zurich, Hong Kong, and all over the world. These financial markets, their trades, and prices reflect:

- the underlying geopolitical, real, and financial macroeconomic fundamentals of a country;
- the degree to which a currency is accepted and used as a reference asset in trades;
- belief and acceptance of a currency based on its issuing state's economic and political clout and reliability;
- the underlying financial credit and investment risks (and consequent ratings) associated with a country's currency.

Disparities between macroeconomic, microeconomic, and financial approaches can lead to different prices. Keynes (1972) pointed out that macroeconomic factors are based on demand for money and its supply in aggregate price determination, while in microeconomics it is based on marginal values (to buyers) and marginal costs (to sellers). Unlike these two approaches, in fundamental finance, prices are both relative and implied. They are relative to risk-free assets (or other assets), and implied in current trades about future state preferences (e.g., trading in forward and future options). These three approaches are used whenever they are needed. Chapters 4, 5, and 6 are focused on macroeconomic and financial approaches, and Chapters 7 and 8 consider the fundamental finance (complete markets) approach.

The exchange rate is based on the concept of purchasing power parity and determined by the prices in two countries. Furthermore, there are several exchange rates, including spot rate, real rate, effective rate, and forward exchange rates. The spot rate is quoted daily and continuously used in financial FX markets, while the real FX rate is defined in terms of the ratio of the consumer price index of countries. It may also be based on the ratio of domestic relative prices of tradable and nontradable goods between countries. Such a ratio, or its inverse, points to the balance of trade between countries. It is also used to indicate a country's competitiveness. Other real factors used to measure the real FX rate include unit (wages) labor costs within the domestic and foreign countries. Some of these elements will be treated subsequently in Chapters 3, 4, 5, and 9. An effective exchange rate is a measure relative to the rest of the world; namely, a weighted basket of exchange rates.

1.7.1 Foreign Exchange Markets and Global Trade Currency

In financial markets, the price of currencies is determined by the market forces of demand and supply of the currency, as well as the ability of sovereign and central banks' policies to sway, through their actions, the FX rates. The LOOP is then used to compound their mutual effects into an economic and traded FX price to convert one currency into another. Currencies are mostly priced relative to a reference currency, such as the USD, although, increasingly, several currencies can be used as a reference currency. For example, the IMF (2016a) has set up a basket of currencies consisting essentially of the USD, the euro (EUR), the pound sterling (GBP), the yen (JPY), and the yuan (CNY). Figure 1.6 summarizes the composition of the IMF basket of currencies during different periods. In the IMF basket (2011–2015), the USD is the dominant currency, albeit declining with an increase in EUR and GBP components. Starting in October of 2016, CNY was added to the SDR basket with a weight of 10.92%, resulting in smaller weights for other currencies (see Figure 1.6).

The IMF's inclusion of the CNY in its basket of foreign currencies recognized the growing role of China in global markets. For example, in August 2015, the CNY moved

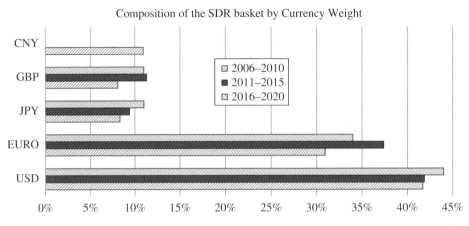

Figure 1.6 The IMF basket of currencies (composition of the special drawing right (SDR) basket by currency weight). *Source:* Data from IMF 2016.

to fourth place, accounting for 2.8% (from only 0.3% in 2012), in international payments. In order to promote and facilitate use of the CNY in trades and investments, the People's Bank of China signed currency swap agreements with over 30 central banks, including the European Central Bank, Brazil, Canada, Russia, South Africa, Switzerland, and the UK. It has also established official clearing banks in more than 15 cities, such as London, Frankfurt, Paris, Seoul, Singapore, and Zurich, since the end of 2008. Additionally, CNY is the third most widely used currency in trade financing (e.g., for letters of credit) after the USD and the EUR. The increased use of CNY and its role are being further enhanced by FX markets' platforms and a global network trading in CNY, pointing to the increased assertiveness of the Chinese currency and to the economic might of China.

These developments serve as signals pointing to changes in the roles of the USD and the EUR. In summary, we observe:

- a decline in the usage of major currencies such as the EUR and the USD;
- a rise in the use of Asian currencies;
- economic and political moves by China to make the CNY an exchange and global reserve currency.

Practically, currencies are bought and sold in FX markets with an average daily turnover of over 5 trillion USD. Market participants include individuals, firms, and private and public organizations. Their volumes not only indicate the relative dominance of their sovereign currencies, but also point to the global credit these currencies represent; that is, the safety, trustworthiness, and storage value of these currencies. The strength of these currencies allows for the issuance of treasury obligations and the printing of money. In other words, borrowing a strong currency globally is possible at prices that are less costly than would be the case for weaker currencies. For example, the dominant role of the USD as a prime currency is used by the USA to finance some of its activities by printing money without a consequential drop in the price of the dollar. The strength of the USD also contributes to the political clout and geopolitical primacy of the USA, allowing it to globally regulate firms trading in USD. Explicitly, it gives the legal right to US regulatory agencies to oversee USD trades and transactions. This regulatory power has both economic and political repercussions. For example, appreciably penalizing a European corporate entity due to a transaction done in USD in Argentina may be interpreted by the EU as anti-competitive. These transactions are particularly criticized when, in fact, both European and US firms may have been competing in Argentina. Whether justified or not, the legal status of the USD and its role, or any other reference currency, raise economic and political questions and motivate current efforts by other sovereign states to redefine or expand the definition of exchange currencies that would challenge the dominance of the USD.

The current trend to create alternative currencies to the USD as a means of exchange, such as the CNY, is partly due to the fact that major economies are, on the one hand, refusing to be regulated and penalized by US regulators and, on the other hand, it is an attempt to have their currency recognized as a reference trade currency. The growth of the CNY and the EUR, or a basket of currencies as reference currencies may provide an opportunity to print more money and issue more debt in these currencies. Currencies of choice and their many derivatives would then expand their economic opportunities and would also become global creditors, augmenting the liquidity of their currency. Figure 1.7 summarizes the development of FX markets that drive the extraordinary growth of both financial and global economic activities.

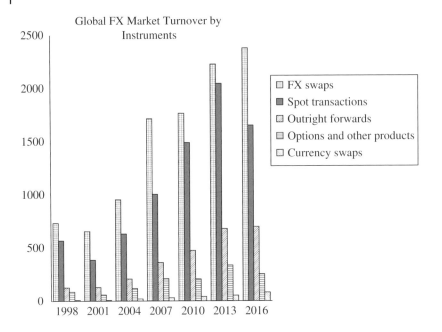

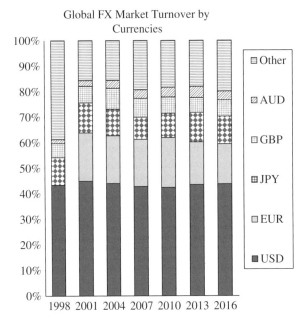

Figure 1.7 Global FX market turnover by instruments and by currencies (1998–2016). Note: top traded currencies include the USD, EUR, JPY, GBP, Australian dollar (AUD), and others including the Swiss franc (CHF), the Canadian dollar (CAD), the Mexican peso (MXN), and the CNY. Turnovers are expressed in billions of USD. *Source*: Data from BIS 2016.

According to the Bank for International Settlements (BIS, 2016b), the average daily turnover of FX trading that has fueled globalization is estimated to range from $1.5 trillion in 1998 and $4 trillion in 2010 to $5.4 trillion in 2013 and $5.1 trillion in 2016. Such growth has political and social implications for countries believing that globalization has short-changed their development. Financial engineering has, of course, contributed to these developments through numerous financial and option-based exchange products, thus facilitating these exchanges. However, most FX instruments were and remain FX swaps,[14] accounting for 47% of the total turnover in 2016, followed by spot transactions (33%), as Figure 1.7 indicates.

Furthermore, declining trends in the shares of the USD and the EUR in the global trade are also signaling greater assertiveness in other currencies; for example, the JPY and the CNY, as well as currencies of emerging economies. In particular, the share of CNY traded has increased fourfold from 2007, to 2% in 2016. This trend points to the weakening of the store-of-value function of the traditional leading currencies and, consequently, to a more complex environment for financial currencies, both competitive and strategic. As stated previously, these economic developments have occurred due to macroeconomic policies, the geopolitical posturing of emerging economies (Asia in particular), and regulatory sovereign assertiveness. Some examples include the surge of US public debt and the consequent credit rating downgrade a few years ago, presidential elections and the increased uncertainty regarding the future of US policy, the increasing assertiveness of regulatory agencies, and an increased number of technology-intensive global financial markets; all are contributing to a multipolar finance that besets the evolution of global finance with its gating by sovereign states.

The internationalization of the CNY, its introduction into a basket of currencies by the IMF (as stated earlier), the launch of an alternative (and Asia-based) World Bank (i.e., Asian Infrastructure Investment Bank (AIIB)), and The New Development Bank (established by the BRICS: Brazil, Russia, India, China, and South Africa) located in China and issuing large amounts of yuan-denominated bonds are elements used to position the CNY as an alternative currency for trade and financial exchanges. These are added to trends indicating an increase in the global demand for deposits denominated in CNY as well as in the rise of offshore investments in the yuan-denominated dim sum bond market (first opened in 2007 in Hong Kong). A number of international sources, such as the BIS and SWIFT,[15] highlight the importance of the CNY in international payment settlements and currency trading (increasing with the growing political and economic clout of China in international financial markets). At the same time, the economic growth of China and its political and economic policies concentrating these trends and contributing to its volatility have hindered the general acceptance of the CNY as a dominant reference currency.

---

14 According to the BIS (2016c: 17), FX swaps involve "the actual exchange of two currencies (principal amount only) on a specific date at a rate agreed at the time of the conclusion of the contract (the short leg), and a reverse exchange of the same two currencies at a date further in the future at a rate (generally different from the rate applied to the short leg) agreed at the time of the contract (the long leg)."

15 SWIFT stands for Society for Worldwide Interbank Financial Telecommunication (https://www.swift.com/).

1.7.2 Exchange Rate Regimes

The current global FX system is a mixture of different regimes ranging from hard and soft pegs to floating free markets. FX arrangements are classified in three broad categories: peg (fixed rate), mixed, and floating (market determined). Constant or fixed exchange rates require a central bank's intervention either through devaluation (reducing the value of the currency) or revaluation (raising the value of the currency) to maintain the exchange rate or bound it within given limits (the snake). Most sovereign states have been shifting toward more flexible FX rate regimes (FX rates determined by market demand and supply of currencies). An increased openness in the current account has also been upended due to improved economic growth, market conditions, and external balance. However, some nations, particularly in emerging and developing economies, have intervened frequently in FX markets to manage currency exposures associated with the volatility of capital flows and with domestic and social conditions. Thus, to gain a greater control of their currency, emerging economies have increasingly moved toward a more managed float regime.

There are geopolitical, economic, and financial reasons to seek a particular exchange rate regime. These include, for example, the size of the country, its geographical position, its openness to the world economy and trade, the diversity of its trading partners, and its macroeconomic indicators (e.g., GDP, inflation rate, money supply, capital flows). Table 1.2 provides a summary of different economies' exchange rate systems.[16] Some sovereign economies gave up the control of their currency due to internal economic reasons (e.g., such as uncontrollable inflationary pressures). One particular approach is adopting the USD as legal tender and using it for all transactions. Under this "dollarization," a sovereign economy foregoes its control, leaving its fiscal and monetary policies subject to volatility and trends in the USD. However, dollarization has led, at worst, to temporary capital flight and at best to a temporary stabilization. At worst, it challenges sovereign states to contend with both economic and social problems without the policy alternatives that a purely floating system would provide.

According to IMF (2016b), as of July 2015, there were 14 countries (e.g., Ecuador and Zimbabwe) which practice a formal dollarization, where the USD or other country's currency (e.g., EUR or AUD) circulates as a legal tender. These countries are classified as "no separate legal tender or currency boards" and do not report any official exchange rates; thus, they are not at risk of any speculative attacks on their currency. The number of sovereign economies turning to dollarization has, however, declined considerably over time. For example, in 2006 there were 41 countries in this classification group, including countries such as Congo, Mali, Niger, and Togo, whose arrangements are now reclassified as conventional peg. In the next arrangement, the currency board covers 11 economies, including Hong Kong. The Hong Kong dollar (HKD) has been exchanged with the USD at a fixed rate of 7.8 HKD/USD since 1983. This fixed exchange rate regime has contributed to the growth of investments in Hong Kong, principally by removing its exchange rate risk, as well as providing an investment channel to Chinese markets. In order to defend its currency peg, Hong Kong monetary authorities have frequently intervened in the FX market; for example, in 2014 and 2015 they sold billions of HKD to relieve a massive capital inflow. Previous pegged systems include, among others, the Mexican peso's (MXN) peg to the USD in 1994 and the CNY's peg to the USD between 1996 and 2005. A substantial reduction in FX market interventions over the years has, in

---

16 For the complete list of countries, refer to IMF (2016b) on current *de facto* exchange rate regimes.

Table 1.2 Classification of exchange rate regimes (as of July, 2016).

Arrangement	Description	Example countries
No separate legal tender	Another country's currency as the sole legal tender	Ecuador, Montenegro, Panama, Zimbabwe
Currency board	Monetary arrangement, fixed FX rate, legal obligation	Hong Kong, Brunei Darussalam, Bulgaria
Conventional peg	Formally pegs to another currency or basket of currencies at a fixed rate	Denmark, Morocco, Nepal, Qatar, Saudi Arabia, Turkmenistan, United Arab Emirates, Venezuela
Stabilized arrangement	Stability margin: within 2% for 6 months or more	Lebanon, Singapore, Vietnam
Crawling peg	Small adjustments at a fixed rate	Botswana, Honduras, Nicaragua
Crawl-like arrangement	Margin: within 2% relative to a statistical trend for 6 months or more	Jamaica, Sri Lanka, Tunisia
Pegged FX rate within horizontal bands	Within changes of at least ±1%	Tonga
Other managed arrangement		Algeria, China, Egypt, Malaysia, Pakistan
Floating	Market based; intervention to prevent undue fluctuations, pats are not preannounced	Brazil, Colombia, Hungary, Iceland, India, Indonesia, Israel, Korea, Mongolia, South Africa, Thailand, Turkey, Uganda
Free floating	Exceptional interventions for disorderly market conditions to moderate fluctuation	Australia, Austria, Canada, Chile, France, Germany, Italy, Japan, Luxembourg, Netherlands, Norway, Poland, Spain, Sweden, UK, USA

Source: Data from IMF 2016.

fact, been recorded. For example, China's regime was classified as a "crawl-like arrangement" in 2015 and then reclassified as "other managed arrangement" in 2016 (see Table 1.2). Following the IMF's decision to include the yuan in the SDR starting October 1, 2016, China's FX regime has become more flexible as its pricing is increasingly subject to market forces. Most countries are now either in soft peg or in a floating regime. Almost one-fourth of all IMF members have a "conventional peg," with a fixed peg of its local currency to a foreign currency or to a basket of currencies (e.g., Morocco and Venezuela). In addition, many countries have a market-based exchange rate: almost one-fifth of countries are practicing the floating regime (e.g., Brazil and Korea), and one-sixth have free floating arrangements (e.g., Japan, the USA, and the UK), with only exceptional interventions.

1.7.3 Foreign Exchange Reserve Currencies

A reserve currency plays an international money role as a store of value, providing a stable future value and purchasing power. The USD is still the dominant reserve currency for all countries for a number of reasons: it facilitates international trade transactions; the large US economy has deep financial markets; loans and deposits are often denominated in USD; it is the most liquid and traded currency in FX markets; many currencies are pegged to the

USD. Trades denominated in USD, however, are cleared through New York and are therefore subject to New York's financial regulators as well as numerous other US regulators. On the one hand, these provide appreciable economic and financial power to the USA. On the other hand, they contribute to the growth of US debt and its dependence on its currency creditors; for example, China, with trillions in USD and its geopolitical financial sway over the USA. Penalties imposed by US regulators on international banks (e.g., BNP, Deutsche Bank, Credit Suisse) for various violations of US laws or regulatory directives have provided US regulators the power to exercise their right globally, acting, in fact, as global regulators. These assumed powers are, as discussed earlier, due to the dominance of the USD and a lack of global and financial regulatory agencies and policies.

Trends and composition of reserve currencies for advanced, emerging, and developing countries were obtained from the Currency Composition of Official Foreign Exchange Reserves (COFER) Database (IMF, 2016c) and the International Financial Statistics (IMF, 2016d) and are shown in Figure 1.8. For example, as of the third quarter of 2016, the USD was the dominant reserve currency, accounting for 63% of total world allocated FX reserves, followed by other major currencies: the EUR (20%), the GBP (4%), and the JPY (4%) (see Figure 1.8a). However, the USD's share has declined from 70% (in 2000) while FX reserves have been growing rapidly in emerging and developing countries. For example, after the Asian financial crisis (1997–1998), Asian countries have accumulated large FX reserves (see Figure 1.8b). FX reserve assets held by the People's Bank of China reached almost $4 trillion at the end of 2014, reflecting a persistent positive trade balance and China's intervention in currency markets. China's foreign currency assets are mostly USD denominated, with its majority in US government bonds. Upon full liberalization of the capital account in China, FX reserves will account for a lesser part of the total assets held abroad by Chinese nationals. According to the IMF Spillover Report (IMF, 2013), this may lead to a substantial increase in foreign direct investment (FDI) as well as private portfolio investments by Chinese households and firms abroad. However, while FX reserves have grown globally in recent years, we note there is a recent decline in the trend for emerging and developing economies. This decline arose mainly due to important FX market interventions in emerging countries requiring their support to their weak currencies (2014–2015) as discussed earlier. For example, China's FX reserves declined to $3 trillion (as of December 2016) as a consequence of capital outflow pressures.

1.7.4 Exchange Rate in Emerging Markets

The Economist referred to certain emerging economies with large current account deficits in 2013–2014 as the "fragile five;" these include Brazil, India, Turkey, Indonesia, and South Africa. Ever since the fall of commodity prices in mid-2014, some of these emerging economies have been appreciably downgraded. A series of articles that appeared in *The Economist* (2014b–d) point to a Brazilian finance minister's statement regarding a currency war against the weak USD in 2010. This occurred when the USD depreciated against the currencies of several emerging markets, leading to an increase in demand for US goods and a decrease in goods from emerging economies. This movement was linked to the Fed's unconventional monetary policy, known as quantitative easing (QE),[17] wherein the Fed,

---

17 To maintain a low long-term interest rate aiming at higher spending, investment, and employment, QE3 was launched in 2012 with monthly bond purchases of $85 billion. The Fed ended this program in October 2014.

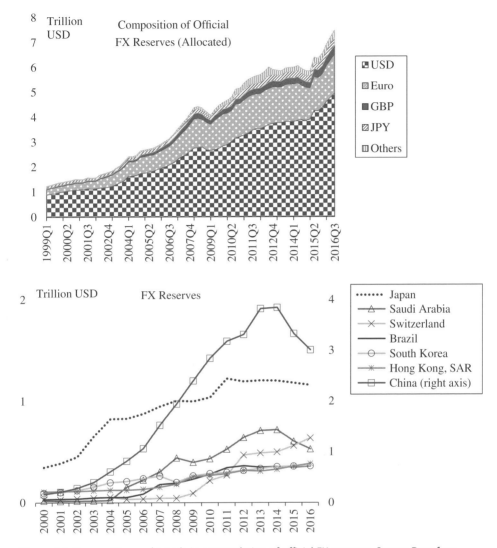

Figure 1.8 Composition and trends in accumulation of official FX reserves. *Source:* Data from IMF 2016.

basically, printed money in order to purchase bonds. Following the Fed's decision to slow down the pace of bond purchases, a reversal occurred in emerging economies' positions as their currencies declined in 2013 against the USD. For example, the value of the Indian rupee fell to a record low (68.8 per USD) in August 2013 following the record high current account deficit of 4.8% of GDP (Reuters, 2014). Similarly, the Turkish lira recorded a historic low (2.34 per USD) in January 2014. Figure 1.9 shows the evolution of exchange rate for Indian rupee, Turkish lira, South African rand, Indonesian rupiah, Brazilian real, and Argentine peso, with an increase indicating an appreciation of USD or depreciation of the domestic currency.

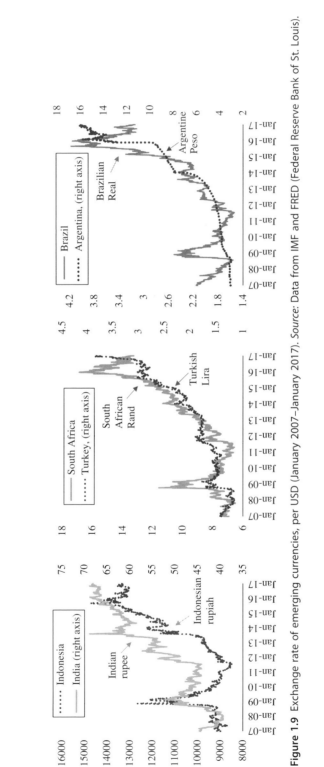

Figure 1.9 Exchange rate of emerging currencies, per USD (January 2007–January 2017). *Source:* Data from IMF and FRED (Federal Reserve Bank of St. Louis).

According to the Institute for International Finance (2016), flows of both bonds and equities into the emerging markets have declined sharply, indicating lower demand for emerging economies' assets. Some of the emerging markets included in these fragile five and Argentina used large sums of their international reserves to defend the currencies and prevent capital outflows. Other measures include a reduction in the current account deficits and restrictions on imports as in India (e.g., such as to curb gold imports in 2013).

1.8   Trade Incentives and Repression

Regional economic integration—such as the eurozone, North American Free Trade Agreement (NAFTA), and other agreements—is both economically and politically motivated. Lacking such agreements, some countries resort to export support and incentives combined with the gating of imports. These can include export insurance, export price support, tariffs, and levies, as well as controls and regulation.[18] For example, when Japan's electronic industries were emerging, it invaded an important part of French markets. To meet such challenges, the French government instituted a stringent quality control of all electronic items entering France. These were "attended to by *one* inspector in the city of Poitiers," resulting in a total stoppage of electronic imports from Japan. By the same token, some countries control export and import prices through interventions in the price of their currencies (in FX markets). The EU is taking measures to cope with tax evasion by multinational companies. In April 2015, the UK introduced profits tax, the so called "Google tax," at 25% especially targeting companies such as Apple, Google, and Amazon. These companies are currently being scrutinized carefully and globally. Similarly, the USA is struggling to define a tax policy that would create an incentive to repatriate foreign profits that are not currently taxed.

These controls have both short- and long-term trade effects. For example, trade incentives and repression through currency manipulations and sovereign states' interventions may have retaliatory consequences, inducing greater uncertainty in terms of trade. Globalization, whose intent is to remove barriers to the free movements of capital, goods, and labor between all countries in order to boost their economic growth, may then be hampered. Globalization leveling competitive advantage is also leading to fiercer competition. Traditional theories of trade support globalization based on the assumption that countries will move the bulk of their economic activity where they have an economic advantage and thereby contribute to global efficiency, and growth is thus dampened by the fact that such migration also leads to a loss of jobs and industrial infrastructure in some sovereign states.[19]

Globalization, when it is combined with a growth in income and consumption (thanks to increasing imports due to price reductions in imports), has also appreciably contributed to the growth of trading (export/imports) firms with extensive supply chains consisting of intermediaries directly and indirectly involved in trade. Table 1.3 indicates the ranking of a number of non-financial transnational corporations (TNCs) according to their foreign assets in 2015. Top TNCs from the UK, Japan, USA, France, and Germany

---

18 For further reading on strategic trade policy, trade theory, and other trade-related issues, see Krugman (1986, 1990), Frankel and Romer (1999), and Helpman and Krugman (1989).
19 For discussion on trade and jobs, refer to Krugman and Lawrence (1994).

Table 1.3 The world's top 10 non-financial TNCs, ranked by foreign assets, 2015.

	Corporation	Country	Foreign assets (billion USD)	Foreign/total assets (%)	Foreign employment (thousand)	Foreign/total employment (%)
1	Royal Dutch Shell plc	UK	288	85	68	73
2	Toyota Motor Corporation	Japan	273	65	149	43
3	General Electric Co.	USA	258	52	208	62
4	Total SA	France	237	97	66	68
5	BP plc	UK	217	83	47	59
6	Exxon Mobil Corporation	USA	193	57	44	60
7	Chevron Corporation	USA	192	72	32	52
8	Volkswagen Group	Germany	182	44	334	55
9	Vodafone Group Plc	UK	167	87	76	72
10	Apple Computer Inc.	USA	144	49	66	60

Source: Data from UNCTAD 2016.

are mostly involved in mining, petroleum, motor vehicles, and electronics. These companies also have a large share of foreign employees, as shown in Table 1.3. Furthermore, large financial TNCs are mostly from the EU and the USA, but there is a substantial increase in Asian firms as well as other sovereign state corporations. Table 1.3 also outlines the growth of new and international firms with a foreign base. For example, firms such as GE are essentially not paying taxes at all in the USA, with Apple producing the bulk of its products in China. The situation is more pronounced when one observes that, in addition to employers in the US industrial firms, including International Business Machines (378 000 employees, both local and foreign, in 2015), Hewlett-Packard Co. (240 000), General Electric (333 000), GM (215 000), the largest employers are in retail trade (e.g., Walmart with 2.3 million employees)—see UNCTAD (2016).

While these statistics may be explained by the changing economy, it is a fact that these jobs have moved elsewhere and, in the words of Steve Jobs, they are not returning to the USA. The implications of jobs migration and their replacement in a competing global economy are both a political and economic problem of gargantuan and dire consequences, as jobs in retail have a much smaller economic footprint than jobs derived from industrial activity. Explicitly, for every 1000 jobs created in retail, 240 additional jobs are created; for 1000 computer systems design services, 1190 additional jobs are created; for 1000 motor vehicles manufacturing, 4710 additional jobs are created; and

Table 1.4 The largest 10 banks in the world.

Rank	1995	2001	2013	2014	2015	2016
1	Japan	Germany	USA	China	China	China
2	Japan	France	USA	USA	China	China
3	Japan	Japan	China	USA	USA	USA
4	Germany	Switzerland	UK	UK	China	China
5	Japan	USA	USA	China	USA	China
6	France	Japan	China	USA	China	USA
7	Switzerland	Germany	Japan	Japan	USA	USA
8	UK	Japan	USA	USA	USA	USA
9	Netherlands	Japan	China	China	UK	UK
10	Germany	Japan	China	China	Japan	Japan

Source: Data from The Banker 2016.

finally, for 1000 jobs in steel product manufacturing, 11 890 additional jobs are created (NYT, 2012b).

Similarly, in the financial sector, there is a shift in the ranking of the largest banks, as shown in Table 1.4. Prior to 2012, the largest 10 banks were not US or Chinese banks. Rather, since 1995, the largest banks were Japanese (4/10) and German (2/10), with other European countries counting 1/10 or none at all. European international banks became leaders in bank size with a decline of Japanese banks. Then, starting in around 2010, due to the rise of China as an important global economic power combined with financial globalization by the US banking system, we note that banks of the largest domestic economies in the world, China and the USA, assume a global banking size, each with 4/10 largest, while Japan and the UK each has one bank (1/10) in the ranking of the top 10—see *The Banker* (2016). The Industrial Commercial Bank of China (ICBC) has claimed the first position in the world since 2014, with three other Chinese banks (China Construction Bank ranked second, Bank of China fourth, and Agricultural Bank of China fifth) ranked among the top 10 world banks in terms of tier 1 capital. The share of Chinese banks' profits in the world banking sector increased to almost 32% in 2016, up from 4.3% in 2006, whereas US banks' profits account for almost 22%, and for Japan 6%, and the UK at 2.6%. This implies that Asia, China in particular, has assumed an ever greater importance in global finance.

Finally, Figure 1.10 outlines the growth of GDP per capita in the USA, China, EU, Japan and other countries in USD. Note that the GDP per capita is much smaller for China because of its much greater population as well as its economic emergence since the early 2000s. Basic observed trends may be associated with the growth of the eurozone as well as increased economic activity. Japan, however, over a long period of time, has sustained a stagnant economy, as the graph indicates. A relationship between these trends and changes in FX rates suggests some linkage between FX rates and macroeconomic variables. Although per capita GDP is, on average, increasing in countries (e.g., China) with extremely large populations, they have experienced an appreciable GDP growth that is not accounted for by this graph.

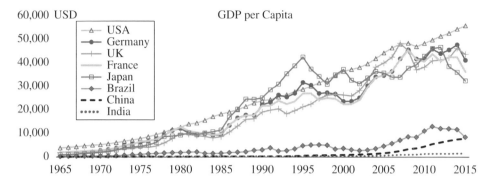

Figure 1.10 The growth of GDP per capita. *Source:* Data from The World Bank.

The potential of trade and its consequences have become particularly important to sovereign states, who meet regularly to confront their intended and nonintended consequences. The General Agreement on Tariffs and Trade (GATT), for example, was signed in 1947, after World War II, by 23 founding members to promote trade and reduce trade barriers. After the World War II, the average import tariff was very high (around 40%). Thus, to tackle trade restrictions and liberalize international trade, GATT included several rounds of trade negotiations. The "Kennedy" Round (1964–1967) cut the tariffs significantly and introduced an anti-dumping agreement. Then, the "Tokyo" Round (1973–1979) managed to reduce duties by one-third in the major industrial countries; it also focused on non-tariff measures. The last (the eighth round), the "Uruguay" Round (1986–1994), led to the creation of WTO in 1995; for details, see WTO (n.d.b).

Current negotiations at the WTO, IMF, and other organizations of sovereign states are particularly sensitive to the current growth of Asia, especially China and India, and its impact on the rest of the world (mainly the Western developed world). This has led, in some cases, to trade repression or support. These are strategic tools used by interested parties that may be either implicit or explicit. While some Western countries have resisted dumping (i.e., imports at prices that undercut fair competition) in their markets and imposed selective quotas and taxes on some imported items (from cheap labor exporters, in particular), other countries have retaliated against these same countries. A particularly blatant case was highlighted in NYT (2011d), where China conditioned its support for the euro in exchange for Europe's opening of its markets to Chinese products.

1.9 Historical Evolution

1.9.1 The Gold Standard System

In the gold standard monetary system, central banks maintained a fixed price of gold (thus, there was no exchange rate risk) in terms of their currencies by offering to buy or sell gold at fixed domestic currency prices. Exchange rates were set by relative national prices of gold, however. For example, in 1900, while a dollar was equal to 0.0484 ounces of gold, a pound sterling was equal to 0.2354 ounces; thus, the US dollar price of a pound was around 4.86 (McCallum, 1996). The UK adopted the gold standard in the early 18th century, and the system operated for a majority of the industrialized countries from 1879 to 1914. Only a few countries rigidly followed the rules of the specie flow system, David Hume's theory on balance of payments equilibrium. The system, however, operated in an approximate sense (Dunn and Mutti, 2004). In order to maintain the official parity between its currency and gold, the central bank needed an adequate stock of gold reserves.

The operative rule of the gold standard was defined as follows: whenever a balance of payment deficit occurred and gold was lost, interest rates were increased sufficiently to stop the gold outflow and attract foreign capital. Selling domestic assets in the face of a deficit and purchasing domestic assets in the face of a surplus. These rules increased the efficiency of the automatic adjustment process and were called the gold standard "rules of the game" (Krugman and Obstfeld, 2002). However, due to a strengthening of capital controls during World War I, the gold standard system could not operate well. Labor unions and oligopolistic industries made goods and labor markets less competitive. Owing to growing protectionist sentiments, free trade declined and tariff rates were increased. The gold standard collapsed in the early and mid-1930s, mainly because surplus countries such as the USA sterilized gold inflows, making the adjustment process too severe for deficit countries (Dunn and Mutti, 2004).

1.9.2 The Bretton Woods Agreement

In order to solve the gold standard's inadequacy problems and avoid competitive devaluation, the Bretton Woods system of fixed exchange rates based on the US dollar to gold was established in July 1944. Over time, fixed FX markets contributed to economic dislocations due to mispricing of currencies and stifling economic inefficiencies. This occurred due to a lack of auto-adjustments in FX rates when economic conditions called for such adjustments. It may have also stifled economic growth and encouraged arbitrage and speculative profits from trade mispricing. In some cases, it led to immense financial arbitrage profits with macro-hedge funds speculating on a country's ability to sustain their FX rates. The Bretton Woods agreement demise occurred when the USA announced a temporary suspension of a fixed conversion in the late 1960s.

Liberalizing FX markets to fluctuate in the early 1970s in order to respond to the market forces of demand and supply of currencies meant that sovereign states could no longer intervene in FX markets to seek an economic advantage for their exports. In practice, however, there were a large number of cases where sovereign states did intervene in FX markets, explicitly and implicitly, with some interventions ending very expensively due to a currency's misalignment. These interventions were motivated by political, domestic, and foreign agendas, and by the need to provide employment, attract foreign funding (or investments) to domestic development programs, and other purposes. These interventions were also intermingled with a decline in countries' economic growth that underlies trends of anti-globalization, seeking protection from risks and inequalities that are presumed to be due to globalization.

Whether FX rates should be fixed is not a simple question. Arguments in favor of free-floating flexible rates have essentially been based on a liberal policy expressing a lack of trust in governments' actions or their incompetence or incapacity to do so. This is particularly the case when several countries are considered at the same time. In practice, in an increasingly globalized and complex economic and financial world, there is ample evidence that fixed FX rates are not sustainable. On the other hand, fixed rates reduce FX rate volatility, and therefore FX risk can be managed by hedging; but this increases the costs of FX while at the same time it reduces the ability of other markets (e.g., the labor market) or economic growth to adjust to the evolution of the relative economic development of countries—see Jones and Kenen (1988). The imperfections of fixed and flexible FX rates lead some investors to seek stable exchange alternatives; for example, gold or money equivalents (such as barters). But these means can also be unstable with price fluctuations.[20]

1.9.3 The Yuan Exchange Rate: An Example

In a free market economy, the FX rate, with its strength and stability, plays an important role in the evaluation of a state's health. The basic trend in the FX expresses its long-run tendencies and random variations fueled by short-term speculations, news, expectations, and the many factors that motivate buyers and sellers in currency markets. The prediction of FX rates is therefore challenging and requires an appreciation of both the domestic and the global economy. The evolution of the Chinese yuan is shown in Figure 1.11. In January 1994, as an essential part of the socialist market economy reform, the yuan was devalued officially to 8.7 yuan against the US dollar and subsequently kept stable, as the economy was then managed by a central administration. China joined the WTO in 2001 with a commitment to make its currency more flexible. On July 21, 2005, The People's Bank of China announced a further reform to its exchange rate by adopting a managed floating exchange rate; this was done by determining its FX rate with reference to a basket of currencies. Since 2005, the yuan has gradually eased to adapt to the economic pressures of a mispriced exchange rate and to respond to international concerns that the yuan was undervalued. Such concerns regarding global trade imbalances due to China's massive trade surplus with the USA and other countries have persisted for the past few years. China's State Administration of Foreign Exchange has been reducing trade barriers and modifying its regulations to make the currency fully convertible through greater flexibility and an increased internationalization of the yuan. These measures include widening of the trading band against the US dollar (from 1% to 2% in 2014), trade payments in yuan, and currency swap deals with other countries (e.g., with the European Central Bank in 2013, Russia in 2014, and South Africa in 2015), with an increasing number of yuan clearing centers ranging from Asia to Europe. Direct conversion of euro and yuan is allowed in Frankfurt (November 2014). The yuan's usage in international payments has been accelerating, as discussed previously.

These observations clearly highlight China's economic growth, its gated and competitive FX and trade policy relative to the US dollar, and its export and import policies. China's yuan policy seemed to be, relative to the US dollar, far more volatile for a number of reasons (especially during the period 2015–2016). This can be seen, for example, in the

---

20 Textbooks, handbooks, research books, and papers provide foundations on international economic and financial market theories with practical issues and historical evolution. These include Jones and Kenen (1988a, b), Grabbe (1991), Grossman and Rogoff (1995), Obstfeld and Rogoff (1996, 2001), and Feenstra and Taylor (2008).

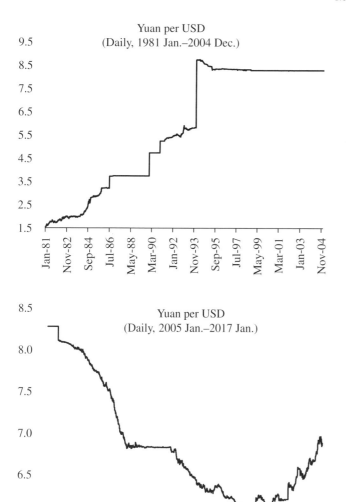

Figure 1.11 The evolution of the Chinese yuan spot exchange rate, per USD (1981–January 2017). *Source:* Data from The FRED (Federal Reserve Bank of St. Louis).

continuous depreciation of the yuan since August 2015 and in a drop in the yuan's usage in international payments during the first half of 2016, with a 1.72% share in SWIFT transactions. The US dollar is traded in free markets and is therefore open to the markets' vicissitudes. In addition, the dollar overtrends, compared with the yuan; this can be explained by a relative analysis of Chinese and the US macroeconomic factors. While the Chinese economy has pursued a high growth trajectory, the US economy has grown more slowly. The US dollar remains strong due to the US diversified economy as well as the usage of the dollar as a reference currency in global financial markets (with trade prices in dollars) and as a reserve currency in central banks.

1.10   Archaic and Modern Globalization: A Time Path

- **Archaic globalization**
  - *Roman times.* The foundation of modern global finance was established during Ancient Rome's global expansion. Various contracts were enforced in both domestic and foreign trade, and Roman citizenship was extended widely, which in turn promoted "the mercantile practices of the Greeks and Phoenicians to the entire Mediterranean world and into northwestern Europe" (Calomiris and Neal, 2013: 4).
  - *13th century.* Paper money was originally developed in Asia in the form of printed "bark of trees." This was introduced into Europe in the 13th century as a consequence of the Mongol invasion (for further information, see Polo (2015)). The Mongols established cultural and economic exchanges between the East and the West. Thus, globalization as we see it today has its roots in Genghis Khan. The "Silk Road," as it connected continents, linking East and West, was the first piece of infrastructure that directly contributed to globalization as we think of it today. It was the road for travelers and for traders, as well as for armies. Its current expansion by the Chinese revives its importance as both an economic and political tool.
- **Early modern globalization**
  - *15th century: discovery of the "New World."* A global exchange of new crops, plants, and livestock through Columbian Exchange[21] between Africa–Eurasia and America contributed significantly to the development of the agricultural sector.
  - *16th–17th century: a rise of European empires—Portuguese, Spanish, Dutch, and British.* The very first multinational corporations (MNCs), the British East India Company and the Dutch East India Company, were founded in 1600 and 1602 respectively.
- **Modern globalization**
  - *1848: the protectionist Corn Laws repealed in Britain, a landmark.* A victory for free trade and an important foundation for globalization. The rise of David Ricardo's theory of comparative advantage in trade.
  - *1870s: the beginning of the first Industrial Revolution.* Replacing artisanal-based manufacturing with systematic processes, expanding the role of specialization, technology and the need to exchange and trade materials and goods between industrialized countries and commodities' suppliers. The power of technological know-how was affirmed as essential to industrial and economic development.
  - *19th century.* Britain became the first global superpower and the pound sterling was the primary reserve currency.
  - *1914.* World War I forces countries to abandon the gold standard. Exchange rates fluctuated wildly as they lacked an acceptable basis for exchange, to the detriment of world trade.
  - *1930s: the Great Depression.* Mass unemployment, failure of thousands of banks, and dramatic slowdown in international trade and globalization cast doubt on free markets. The USA sought a greater and more strategic role for governments in stimulating economies using monetary and fiscal policy; that is, the manipulation of interest rates and money supply, and (deficit) spending and taxation; also, it implemented far greater control of global economic revenues and global firms (notice the

---

21 For details on consequences of the Columbian Exchange, see Crosby (2003).

similarity to 2011). In 1933, the Roosevelt government in the USA rendered the holding of gold illegal (there are similar suggestions to control US citizens' holdings of assets in general to allow the US government access to their capital holdings). Following the Great Depression, trends in deglobalization set in, a consequence of economic recovery.

– *1944: Bretton Woods.* The Allied powers met at Bretton Woods to devise a system to stabilize exchange rates based on freer exchanges to promote growth and trade. All currencies were tied to the US dollar, and the IMF and the World Bank were created. An immense boost to globalization, the US Marshall Plan for the reconstruction of Europe, and the dominance of the US dollar. Global political realignment following World War II based on economic and ideological paths.

– *1947: the GATT trade agreement.* Intended to reduce international trade barriers, this was signed by 23 nations. The initial construction of today's eurozone in the post-World War II agreement in Europe on coal and energy and Jean Monet's articulation of a United Europe based on its six leading economies.

– *1950s.* American MNCs expanded rapidly in developed and foreign markets, investments, innovation, and inventiveness in business and finance laying the infrastructure for its future global economic dominance.

– *1970s: stagflation (high inflation and unemployment) occurred.* European and Japanese firms grew to become MNCs. Keynesian economic policy (in support of a role for the government economic policies (Keynes, 1935, 1972)) was challenged by the University of Chicago Monetary School. The economy was managed financially, firms outsourced, and infrastructures for the rise of global supply chains were set in place supported by the increased use of computer logistics and accounting management and control software.

– *1971.* The USA abandoned the Bretton Woods system and the dollar became the reference dominant currency. Currencies were allowed to float against each another. It was the beginning of free FX markets and the rise of global financial entities. Large dollar funds accumulated outside the USA, creating a lack of confidence in the dollar/gold value. The US gold reserves were reduced by a third in the first 7 months, and President Nixon suspended official gold transactions. This was, in effect, a unilateral decision to abandon the Bretton Woods system and let the world's currencies "float" in relation to the dollar. By the end of the year, most of the major trading currencies had appreciated against the dollar. A second dollar devaluation occurred in 1973, when it fell to USD 42.22 per ounce, a drop of 10%. By June 1973, it had fallen by another 10%. In the floating exchange rate system, no currency is formally linked to any other, or to gold.

– *1973: the OPEC oil cartel hikes the price of crude oil.* The developed world is thrown into recession. During the oil crises of 1973 and 1979, when OPEC dramatically increased the price of oil, the floating system helped to minimize the chaos as the strain was taken by an adjustment in exchange rates (the OPEC countries' currencies suddenly became much stronger). Trade and exchanges were used as strategic economic and political tools. There was cleavage between commodity-rich and industrialized advanced nations. Politics and regional economics pointed to the limits of globalization.

– *FX policies.* Diverse ways of controlling exchange rates were applied. Some countries allowed their currencies to float freely with the market, while others "pegged" their currency to fluctuate within a fixed range against the dollar. Overall, the current system is best described as managed floating, with nations' central banks intervening in currency markets occasionally trying to influence their exchange rates.

- *1980s: the rise of developing countries.* A result of greater openness to the global economy through trade and FDI, particularly in Asia and in Latin America. Increased global capital and financial flows as well as seeding A-National corporations emanating from MNCs. These firms become truly global, with no national boundaries and no national controls to respond to.
- *1980s: debt crisis in Latin America.* Countries such as Mexico, Argentina, and Brazil borrowed extensively from international capital markets using their natural resources as collateral. Mexico defaulted on its debt in 1982.
- *Late 1980s–early 1990s.* The collapse of communist and socialist regimes and transition to a market-based economy (from a centrally planned economy). The Berlin Wall fell (1989), and USSR's dissolution (1991) formed 13 independent countries, promoting a market economy and greater openness to trade, investment, and travel.
- *1990s: IT—Internet boom.* It contributed to the expansion of globalization with development of global telecommunication and e-commerce, better and faster access to vast information networks, development of software, social networking, increased cultural exchange, trade, online shopping, and so on.
- *1993: conclusion of Uruguay Round of GATT.* It contributed to streamlining trade and the growth of globalization.
- *1993: the EU.* It was established with 12 countries under the Maastricht Treaty. Member states expanded to 28 countries as of 2015. First formal economic cooperation of European countries started after the foundation of the European Economic Community (EEC) in 1958.
- *1990s: globalization and free markets became a fact and unavoidable.* Barriers to free flows of capital and goods were partially removed (in some cases they were removed completely); globalization defines its own self-globalizing process.
- *1995: GATT succeeded by the WTO with an expanded list of partners.* Provision of a broader and more sustainable foundation for global trade and financial globalization was sought. Global outsourcing becomes a fact, providing the foundation for emerging industries in developing economies.
- *1997–1998: Asian financial crisis.* This showed how increased openness makes affected countries vulnerable to external shocks. Prior to the crisis, Asian countries encouraged trade and large capital inflows (including short-term foreign currency denominated bank loans) by offering higher yields to foreign investors. However, these countries lacked banking and financial regulations. Their capital markets were highly liberalized, and current accounts had large deficits. When the crisis hit, the valuations of the currency fell significantly, countries were exposed to FX risk and experienced a reversal of capital flows, deterioration of banks' balance sheets, a decline in foreign reserves, substantial fall in GDP growth, and flagging confidence of international investors in developing countries.
- *1999: the euro.* It was introduced and adopted by 11 EU member states (currently 19 members). By using a single currency, financial markets can be better coordinated and more efficient. Trade is expanded through reduced exchange costs.
- *2000: preliminary meeting of the WTO to discuss a new trade round.* In Seattle the meeting collapses amid recriminations between developing countries, the USA and the EU, while outside there were violent protests. An anti-globalization movement

gathered strength together with the awareness that globalization creates its own dislocating factors. Globalization is both benign and toxic.

- *2001: dot-com bubble.* Financial crisis with large stock market losses (speculative bubble) exposed the lack of financial regulations.
- *Securitization bubble begins to inflate.* A rapid rise in the use of structured financial products (e.g., mortgage-backed securities, collateralized default obligations) restructures the financial industry. Real estate, fueled by the removal of risk made possible with mortgage-backed securities, grows internationally.
- *2007: globalization has also led to global indebtedness.* A financial crisis emanates from unsustainable growth assumptions and a global financial contagion. The crisis is catalyzed by the rapid dissolution of the securitization bubble as firms divest themselves of structured financial products (e.g., the sub-prime crisis). Lehman Brothers fails. Global firms were both culprits and "too big to fail;" past assumptions were questioned, countries were financially destabilized and required economic recalibration. FX economic systems and FX markets were confronted with risky exchanges, a weaker dollar, the rise of FX alternatives (e.g., barter, gold), multipolar financial markets, a flight from risk, instabilities—greater volatility, greater uncertainty, and a strategic finance with economies in collision. The rise of developing countries to positions of financial and economic strength. Real estate values collapse worldwide.
- *2011: financial repression in FX markets, FX taxation (e.g., the new US regulation of 2010).* The growth of uncertainty in global finance and strategic finance. Globalization was challenged but was unavoidable. International finance in a critical post-crisis world was confronted by a global shift in the relative economic powers of Asian Basin countries assuming a far greater importance while traditional leading economies faced economic and safety challenges, unstable currencies, and the prospects of an Arab awakening potentially leading to a multipolar global and strategic world. At the same time, there are latent deglobalization forces to overcome the uncertainty that globalization and its complex processes induce. Unemployment explodes in Europe, with over 50% of young people without jobs in Spain, Greece, and Italy. Wage shares continue to fall globally.
- *2014: fluctuations in commodity prices.* Oil prices declined sharply from over $100/barrel in summer of 2014 to around $50, partly due to overproduction, especially in the USA where the new technology of fracking is used. This plunge in oil price, which at one point hit a low of $27 (January 2016), and slower demand from emerging economies (especially a slowdown in China's economy) had a negative impact on export revenues, which led to fiscal deficits in oil-exporting countries.
- *2014–2015: AIIB.* It is led by China with the support of many other founding member countries to finance the growing demand for infrastructure in Asia. Asian countries need investment in electricity, telecommunication, and a transportation system with high-speed rail, extension of railroads, new roads and ports to reduce transportation costs and increase trade. The AIIB was established to overcome challenges faced by the delay of US approval for IMF's governance reform to allow emerging markets more voting power. The AIIB is seen by the USA as a potential rival to the World Bank.
- *2014: Free Trade Area of Asia-Pacific (FTAAP).* Asia-Pacific Economic Cooperation leaders agreed to launch a regional free trade arrangement of FTAAP to increase trade and promote regional integration.

– *2015: the Trans-Pacific Partnership (TPP).* The TPP is a massive free trade agreement proposed by the US President Obama between the USA and 11 other countries (e.g., Australia, Canada, Japan, Mexico, and Singapore) to boost global economic growth through an increase in trade and investment, agricultural sector, creation of employment, innovation, and support of environmental protection. However, a number of US Democrats and Republicans, as well as environmental and labor groups, have opposed the TPP with concerns over issues such as labor standards, environmental regulation, and possible geostrategic implications of the free trade rationale. The USA withdrew from the TPP in January 2017.

– *2016*: Brexit. The UK voted to exit the EU because of concerns over sovereignty issues. Brexit (Britain's exit) affected the economic growth of not only the UK, but also the eurozone. Because of rising global uncertainty, global investors' demand for the government long-term bonds increased. Yield on 10-year government bonds plunged and even turned negative in some countries, especially in Germany. Globalization, gating, the growth of intra-nations' economic inequalities, and geopolitical challenges are causing some countries to assess the benefits of globalization and the openness of their borders to trade.

– *2016.* The expansion of the WTO's Information Technology Agreement was one of the most significant tariff liberalization deals, covering an enormous trade volume. An elimination of tariffs on 201 IT additional products, with an annual trade value of $1.3 trillion, acknowledges the massive technological change and a need to lower costs. This deal was described as a critical breakthrough that will lead to expanded technological development and increased trade of more IT products.

– *2017–2018.* Uncertainty and the retreat from globalization.

1.11 Discussions on Global Issues

The purpose of these discussions and themes is to stimulate the reader across various topics that are underlying the globalization of finance. Technology, financial regulation, and electronic markets, such as high-frequency trading, are both consequences and factors that contribute to growth and the gating of financial globalization. For brevity, we focus not on their importance, but on their potential manifestations.

1) Technology and globalization are changing finance, contributing to a realignment and to the profusion of financial markets, everywhere. How is this changing our conventional understanding of fundamental models of finance?

2) Virtu is the largest high-frequency trading firm as of April 2015. This firm is a market maker. It seeks to make arbitrage profits by offering (buy and sell) securities in the hope of capturing a tiny spread between those prices. It does so, however, by trading on an advanced and private technological infrastructure on global markets they have built allowing them to trade at high frequency. Technology and globalization have opened opportunities for them. Is such a firm a competitor or a monopolist in global finance?

3) US regulators have expanded their financial controls over global financial firms and banks, penalizing them, employing monitors at their expense, and setting rules in the USA and elsewhere such firms have to comply with. Explain why the US regulators can do this. What are the risks/benefits for the USA in imposing itself as the global finance regulator wherever they can? Discuss the role of the US dollar as the

major currency trades and transactions are made in and how the power of the US dollar as the dominant currency may also be threatened in the long run by unilateral actions.

4) Brexit refers to UK's vote to exit from the EU on June 23, 2016. Other countries may follow the UK in breaking away from Europe. What would be the financial consequences and their effects on globalization and gating? Discuss Brexit's potential impact on the UK and EU economies and on global trade and financial markets. Refer to the consequences (including British pound, British bond yields, stock market performance, foreign trade, and FDI) and reaction of the financial world. What are the implications of the downgrade of UK's credit rating? How are the British export/import companies affected in terms of tariff and other costs?

5) The state of Malta is currently offering the wealthiest persons in the world (the top 0.1%) the possibility of acquiring a Maltese passport and the freedom to travel freely through Europe and tax breaks they would not get elsewhere. The price tag is $1.3 million. How do globalization and the A-National growth of wealth contribute to the social make-up of the wealthy in the world? How does it contribute to the complexity of national taxation and regulatory controls? What are the potential future scenarios you believe can be entertained?

6) Globalization has ushered in a rush of free trade agreements. These include lower barriers to trade, and free movement of capital, technology, and labor. How has this profited financial banks and investors and how did it affect smaller enterprises (compared with big banks)? Who profits most from such globalization: smaller banks or bigger banks? Smaller countries or bigger countries? Job seekers or investors? Are such agreements reversible? What could be their financial consequences?

7) What is the future of financial markets such as Wall Street stock exchanges and electronic global markets? Which one is likely to be the dominant market? What are the regulation challenges for controlling electronic markets in particular high-frequency and ultra-high frequency trading?

8) Population growth, employment, and life expectancy have fueled demand all over the world—both in quantity and quality. How does this demand affect economic growth and business opportunities? How does the openness of demand changing the pattern of industries and trade contribute to greater globalization?

9) The apparent and systematic growth in trade as a percentage of GDP is pointing to its increased importance in economic development. How does the growth rate contribute to greater economic dependence between countries? How does such dependence affect capital flows? How do such trends affect regulation?

10) If we were to price currencies with respect to the dollar, what do such variations indicate relating to countries' macroeconomic indicators, trade, and internal pressures that these countries are confronted with? How can they be used to articulate a trading strategy?

11) What are the potential indicators of cross-country opportunities for arbitrage?

12) Crises have an impact on both the statistics and the memory of crises that linger on. How do investors use such an observation to profit and how do they use such information to hedge?

13) How do global macroeconomic factors affect trade, economic growth, and FX markets? In particular, discuss the effects of industrial specialization, technology, and

the essential macroeconomic factors (GDP, national income, interest rates, national debt, government fiscal policies, inflation, and balance of payments).

14) Does accumulation of wealth by poor countries contribute to a greater convergence between rich and poor countries (Landes, 1998; Spence, 2011); global dependence; access to capital markets and financial innovation augmenting liquidity and capital mobility?

References

Alberto, A., Spolaore, E., and Wacziarg, R. (1997) Economic integration and political disintegration. NBER Working Paper no. 6163.

Allen, F. and Gale, D. (2000) Financial contagion. *Journal of Political Economy*, **1**:08, 1–33.

Andrew, S. (2009) *From Asian to Global Financial Crisis: An Asian Regulator's View of Unfettered Finance in the 1990s and 2000s.* Cambridge University Press.

Arrow, K.J. (1965) *Aspects of the Theory of Risk Bearing.* Yrjö Jahnsson Lectures. Yrjö Jahnssonin Säätiö: Helsinki.

BIS (2016a) Semiannual OTC derivatives statistics. http://www.bis.org/statistics/derstats. htm (accessed July 11, 2017).

BIS (2016b) Triennial Central Bank Survey of foreign exchange and OTC derivatives markets in 2016. http://www.bis.org/publ/rpfx16.htm (accessed July 11, 2017).

BIS (2016c) Triennial Central Bank Survey: foreign exchange turnover in April 2016. http://www.bis.org/publ/rpfx16fx.pdf (accessed July 11, 2017).

BIS (2017) Semiannual OTC derivatives statistics. http://www.bis.org/statistics/derstats.htm.

Blanchard, O. (2010) Sustaining a global recovery. *Journal of Policy Modeling*, **32**(5): 604–609.

Blinder, A.S. (2007) *Offshoring: big deal, or business as usual? Working Paper no. 149, Center for Economic Policy Studies*, Princeton University.

Bloomberg (2017). There are now more indexes than stocks. https://www.bloomberg.com/news/articles/2017-05-12/there-are-now-more-indexes-than-stocks (accessed July 11, 2017).

Boele, G. (2002) *Strategic Market Analysis: EUR/USD Interbank Market as Diversified Organization.* Alan Guinn: Massapequa, NY.

Bruno, S. and McLeavey, D. (2003) *International Investments and Research Navigator Package*, 5th edition, Addison Wesley.

Calomiris, C.W. and Neal, L. (2013) History of financial globalization, overview. In *Handbook of Key Global Financial Markets, Institutions, and Infrastructure*, G. Caprio (ed.). Elsevier.

Crosby, A.W. (2003) The *Columbian Exchange: Biological and Cultural Consequences of 1492.* Praeger: Westport, CT.

Dunn M.R. and Mutti J.H. (2004) *International Economics*, 6th edn. Routledge: New York.

Feenstra, R.C. and Taylor A.M. (2008) *International Macroeconomics.* Worth Publishers.

Fontela, E. (1998) The era of finance: proposals for the future. *Futures*, **30**(8): 749–768.

Fox, J. (2009) *The Myth of the Rational Market.* HarperCollins: New York.

Frankel, J.A. (2000) Globalization of the economy. NBER Working Paper 7858, National Bureau of Economic Research.

Frankel J.A. and Romer, D. (1999) Does trade cause growth? *The American Economic Review*, **89**(3): 379–399.

FRED, Federal Reserve Bank of St. Louis. Board of Governors of the Federal Reserve System. https://fred.stlouisfed.org/series/DEXCHUS. (accessed March 5, 2017)

Friedman, T. (2005) *The World is Flat*, 1st edn. Farrar, Straus and Giroux.

Friedman, T. (2012) *The Lexus and the Olive Tree: Understanding Globalization*. Picador: New York.

Froot, K.A. and Dabora, E.M. (1999) How are stock prices affected by the location of trade? *Journal of Financial Economics*, **53**: 189–216.

FT (2011) EU acts over alleged Chinese subsidies: bloc to raise tariffs on high-end glossy paper. *Financial Times*, May 15. https://www.ft.com/content/b2919d04-7f04-11e0-b239-00144feabdc0.

Grabbe, J.O. (1991) *International Financial Markets*, 2nd edn. Elsevier.

Grossman G.M. and Rogoff, K. (eds) (1995) *Handbook of International Economics*, volume 3. Handbooks in Economics **3**. North Holland: Amsterdam.

Helpman, E. and Krugman P.R. (1989) *Trade Policy and Market Structure*. MIT Press, Cambridge, MA.

Henderson, D. (1999) *The Changing International Economic Order, Rival Visions for the Coming Millennium*. Melbourne Business School: Melbourne, Australia.

Henry, P.B. (2000) Stock market liberalization, economic reform, and emerging market equity prices. *Journal of Finance*, **55**: 529–564.

Henry, P.B. (2007) Capital account liberalization: theory, evidence, and speculation. *Journal of Economic Literature*, **45**: 887–935.

Heston, S. and Rouwenhorst, G. (1994) Does industrial structure explain the benefits of international diversification? *Journal of Financial Economics*, **36**: 3–27.

Hou, K., Karolyi, A.G., and Kho, B.C. (2011) What factors drive global stock returns? *Review of Financial Studies*, **24**(8): 2527–2574.

Hoxha, I., Kalemli-Ozcan, S., and Vollrath, D. (2009) How big are the gains from international financial integration? Working Paper 14636, National Bureau of Economic Research.

IMF (2013) Spillover Report. https://www.imf.org/external/np/pp/eng/2013/070213.pdf (accessed July 11, 2017).

IMF (2016a) SDRs Allocations and Holdings. http://www.imf.org/external/np/exr/facts/sdr.htm (accessed July 11, 2017).

IMF (2016b) Annual Report on Exchange Arrangements and Exchange Restrictions (AREAER). (Washington, October).

IMF (2016c) Currency Composition of Official Foreign Exchange Reserves (COFER) Database. http://www.imf.org/external/np/sta/cofer/eng/index.htm (accessed July 11, 2017).

IMF (2016d) International Financial Statistics (IFS). http://data.imf.org/?sk=5DABAFF2-C5AD-4D27-A175-1253419C02D1 (accessed July 11, 2017).

IMF (2016e). Exchange Rate Archives. http://www.imf.org/external/np/fin/ert/GUI/Pages/CountryDataBase.aspx (accessed July 11, 2017).

Institute for International Finance (2016) Capital Flows to Emerging Markets. April 7, 2016. https://www.iif.com/publication/capital-flows-emerging-markets-report/april-2016-capital-flows-emerging-markets.

Jermann, U.J. (2002) International portfolio diversification and endogenous labor supply choice. *European Economic Review*, **46**: 507–522.

Jones, R.W. and Kenen P.B. (eds) (1988a) *Handbook of International Economics, Volume 1: International Trade*. Handbooks in Economics 3. North Holland.

Jones, R.W. and Kenen P.B. (eds) (1988b) *Handbook of International Economics, Volume 2: International Monetary Economics and Finance*. Handbooks in Economics 3. North Holland.

Kearney, A. (2001) Measuring globalization. *Foreign Policy*, **122**: 56–65.

Keller, W.W. and Rawski, T.G. (2007) *China's Rise and the Balance of Influence in Asia*. University of Pittsburgh Press.

Keynes, J.M. (1935) *The General Theory of Employment, Interest and Money*. Harcourt, Brace and Company.

Keynes, J.M. (1972) *The General Theory and After. Part II: Defence and Development*. The Collected Writings of John Maynard Keynes, Volume 14. Royal Economic Society: London.

Knight, F.H. (1921) *Risk, Uncertainty, and Profit*. Hart, Schaffner & Marx; Houghton Mifflin Co.: Boston, MA:

Krugman, R.P. (1986) *Strategic Trade Policy and the New International Economics*. MIT Press: Cambridge, MA.

Krugman, P.R. (1990) *Rethinking International Trade*. MIT Press: Cambridge, MA.

Krugman, R.P. (2000) Technology, trade and factor prices. *Journal of International Economics*, **50**(1): 51–71.

Krugman P.R. and Lawrence, R. (1994) Trade, jobs and wages. *Scientific American*, **270**(4): 44–49.

Krugman R.P. and Obstfeld, M. (2002) *International Economics: Theory and Policy*., 6th edn. Addison Wesley: New York.

Landes, D. (1998) *The Wealth and Poverty of Nations: Why Some are So Rich and Some So Poor*. Norton: New York.

Lewis, K.K. (1995) Puzzles in international financial markets. In *Handbook of International Economics*, G. Grossman and K. Rogoff (eds). North Holland: Amsterdam.

Lewis, K.K. (1996) What can explain the apparent lack of international consumption risk-sharing? *Journal of Political Economy*, **104**: 267–297.

Lockwood, B. (2001) A note on the robustness of the Kearney/foreign policy globalization index. Working Paper No. 79.01, University of Warwick, Warwick, UK.

McCallum, T.B. (1996) *International Monetary Economics*. Oxford University Press: New York.

Minsky, H.P. (1992) The financial instability hypothesis. Working Paper No. 74, The Jerome Levy Economics Institute of Bard College.

Minsky, H.P. (2008) *Stabilizing an Unstable Economy*. McGraw-Hill: New York.

MSCI (2017) The MSCI Emerging Markets Index. https://www.msci.com/documents/10199/c0db0a48-01f2-4ba9-ad01-226fd5678111.

Neftci, S. and Xu, Y.M. (2007) *China's Financial Markets: An Insider's Guide to How the Markets Work*. Elsevier Academic Press.

Nunnenkamp, P. (2002) Why economic trends differ so much across developing countries: the globalization debate and its relevance to Pakistan. Kiel Working Paper No. 1091, Kiel Institute of World Economics.

NYT (2010) In China, Illegal rare earth mines face crackdown. *The New York Times*, December 29. http://www.nytimes.com/2010/12/30/business/global/30smuggle.html.

NYT (2011a) U.S. and China agree to a process to analyze risks in economies worldwide. *The New York Times*, April 15. http://www.nytimes.com/2011/04/16/business/global/16summit.html.

NYT (2011b) Chasing rare earths, foreign companies expand in China. *The New York Times*, August 24. http://www.nytimes.com/2011/08/25/business/global/chasing-rare-earths-foreign-companies-expand-in-china.html.

NYT (2011c) Senate jabs China over its currency. *The New York Times*, October 12. http://www.nytimes.com/2011/10/12/business/senate-approves-bill-aimed-at-chinas-currency-policy.html.

NYT (2011d) China trade numbers bear watching, up or down. *The New York Times*, September 16. http://www.nytimes.com/2011/09/17/business/up-or-down-china-trade-surpluses-bear-watching.html.

NYT (2012a) BNY advertising. *The New York Times*, January 22.

NYT (2012b) How the U.S. lost out on iPhone work. *The New York Times*, January 22, p. 22.

NYT (2016) Stock exchange prices grow so convoluted even traders are confused, study finds. *The New York Times*, March 2, p. B3. http://www.nytimes.com/2016/03/02/business/dealbook/stock-exchange-prices-grow-so-convoluted-even-traders-are-confused-study-finds.html (accessed May 5, 2017).

Obstfeld, M. and Rogoff, K. (1996) *Foundations of International Macroeconomics*. MIT Press: Cambridge, MA.

Obstfeld, M. and Rogoff, K. (2001) The six major puzzles in international macroeconomics: is there a common cause? In *NBER Macroeconomics Annual 2000*, Volume 15, B.S. Bernanke and K. Rogoff (eds). MIT Press: Cambridge, MA; pp. 339–412.

OECD (2014) *The Size and Sectoral Distribution of SOEs in OECD and Partner Countries*. OECD Publishing: Paris.

Polo, M. (2015) *The Book of Ser Marco Polo, the Venetian: Concerning the Kingdoms and Marvels of the East*, Volume 2. Arkose Press.

Rabin, M. (1993) Incorporating fairness into game theory and economics. *American Economic Review*, **83**(5): 1281–1302.

Reinhart, C.M. and Rogoff, K. 2009. *This Time Is Different: Eight Centuries of Financial Folly*. Princeton University Press: Princeton, NJ.

Reuters (2014) Government officials ready plan to ease gold import curbs – sources. *Money News*, May 21. http://in.reuters.com/article/uk-india-gold-imports-idINKBN0E110520140521.

Rosenau, J.N. (1996) The dynamics of globalization: toward an operational formulation. *Security Dialogue*, **27**(3): 247–262.

Rosenberg, M. (2003) *Exchange Rate Determination: Models and Strategies for Exchange Rate Forecasting*. McGraw-Hill.

Sachs, J. (2000) Globalization and patterns of economic development. *Review of World Economics*, **136**(4): 579–600.

Sachs, J. and Warner, A. (1995) Economic reform and the process of global integration. *Brookings Papers on Economic Activity*, **1**: 1–95.

Schneider, G., Barbieri, K., and Gleditsch, N.P. (2002) *Globalization and Conflict*. Rowman & Littlefield: Boulder, CO.

Sen, A. (2001) If it's fair, it's good: 10 truths about globalization. *International Herald Tribune*, July 14.

Soros, G. (2008) *The New Paradigm for Financial Markets: The Credit Crisis of 2008 and What It Means*. PublicAffairs: New York.

Spence, M. (2011) *The Next Convergence: The Future of Economic Growth in a Multispeed World*. Farrar, Straus and Giroux: New York.

Stiglitz, J.E. (2000) Capital market liberalization, economic growth, and instability. *World Development*, **28**(6): 1075–1086.

Stiglitz, J.E. (2002) *Globalization and Its Discontents*. W.W. Norton & Company.

Stiglitz, J.E. (2006) *Making Globalization Work*. W.W. Norton & Company.

Stiglitz, J.E. (2010) *Freefall: America, Free Markets, and the Sinking of the World Economy*. W. W. Norton.

The Banker (2016) The Banker Top 1000 World Banks 2016 rankings - WORLD Press release: For immediate release. http://www.thebanker.com/Top-1000-World-Banks/The-Banker-Top-1000-World-Banks-2016-ranking-WORLD-Press-IMMEDIATE-RELEASE/ (language)/eng-GB.

The Economist (2011) The company that ruled the waves. December 17. http://www.economist.com/node/21541753.

The Economist (2012) Brazil's trade policy: seeking protection. January 14. http://www.economist.com/node/21542780.

The Economist (2014a) International banking: poor correspondents. June 14. http://www.economist.com/news/finance-and-economics/21604183-big-banks-are-cutting-customers-and-retreating-markets-fear.

The Economist (2014b) Currencies: all go for the greenback? January 21. http://www.economist.com/blogs/buttonwood/2014/01/currencies.

The Economist (2014c) Locus of extremity. February 1. http://www.economist.com/news/finance-and-economics/21595485-developing-economies-struggle-cope-new-world-locus-extremity.

The Economist (2014d) Yuawn. June 21. http://www.economist.com/news/finance-and-economics/21604579-buzz-about-rise-chinas-currency-has-run-far-ahead-sedate-reality-yuawn.

The World Bank (2001) *Globalization, growth and poverty: building an inclusive world economy. Report No. 23591.* World Bank: Washington, DC.

The World Bank (2016) World Development Indicators. http://databank.worldbank.org/data/reports.aspx?source=world-development-indicators (accessed July 11, 2017).

UNCTAD. 2016. World Investment Report 2016. http://unctad.org/en/PublicationsLibrary/wir2016_en.pdf.

Walras, L. (1954) *Elements of Pure Economics, or the Theory of Social Wealth*, W. Jaffé (transl.). Allen and Unwin: London.

Wood, A. (1998) Globalisation and the rise in labour market inequalities. *The Economic Journal*, **108**(450): 1463–1482.

WSJ (2011) Japanese, Swiss move to push currencies lower. *The Wall Street Journal*, August 4. https://www.wsj.com/articles/SB10001424053111903366504576485781605927972.

WSJ (2016a) U.S. imposes 266% duty on some Chinese steel imports. *The Wall Street Journal*, March 1. http://www.wsj.com/articles/u-s-imposes-266-duty-on-some-chinese-steel-imports-1456878180.

WSJ (2016b) Big banks paid $110 billion in mortgage-related fines. Where did the money go? *The Wall Street Journal*, March 9. http://www.wsj.com/articles/big-banks-paid-110-billionin-mortgage-related-fines-where-did-the-money-go-1457557442.

WTO (2016) Report on G20 Trade Measures. https://www.wto.org/english/news_e/news16_e/g20_wto_report_june16_e.pdf.

WTO (n.d.a) Statistics Database on Tariffs. http://stat.wto.org/Home/WSDBHome.aspx?Language=E. https://www.wto.org/english/thewto_e/whatis_e/tif_e/fact4_e.htm.

WTO (n.d.b) Understanding the WTO: Basics. The GATT years: from Havana to Marrakesh. https://www.wto.org/english/thewto_e/whatis_e/tif_e/fact1_e.htm.

2

Data, Measurements, and Global Finance

Motivation

Global finance compounds the complexity of traditional finance by taking into account additional economic and financial factors together with political and geopolitical aspects. Financial models are then mostly multivariate, data based, networked, and generally interdependent. Further, data granularity is a constant problem. For example, macroeconomic data may be reported monthly, quarterly, or annually, while financial data are frequently reported daily (or even minute to minute or tic to tic). Therefore, data and measurements used to estimate trends and their properties may require analytic approaches that differ from traditional analysis. The purpose of this chapter is to summarize basic statistical tools, motivate the development of modeling techniques, and explore the empirical tools to better understand global and risk finance. In all subsequent chapters, examples and applications are further developed.

2.1 Data and Models

The choice and the measurement of data in a global and complex space are perhaps the most important aspects of statistical risk pricing and economic analysis. Data may be varied, consisting of qualitative events (such as political outcomes and decisions, time series of national macroeconomic statistics, and social and financial metrics). Data, whether big or small, are used to estimate multiple factors and their relationships. Practically, measurements are based on their availability and on the data needed and implied by the models we construct. Data are therefore partial, providing assessments that are embedded in their origins and in the manners they are used. Data measurements, their interdependence, and their statistical properties nonetheless provide only a partial assessment of global economic and financial predictions. Practically, models based on a fundamental understanding of geopolitical relationships, political events, macroeconomic and financial principles are so complex that, perhaps, only simulation models might assess the implied trends, risks, and their evolution. Guetzkow (1959, 1962), for example, introduced Monte Carlo simulation models to the study of political processes,

Globalization, Gating, and Risk Finance, First Edition. Unurjargal Nyambuu and Charles S. Tapiero.
© 2018 John Wiley & Sons Ltd. Published 2018 by John Wiley & Sons Ltd.

providing quantitative anchors to the study of political processes. For simplicity, we may consider three types of data:

- geopolitical, geo-risk, geo-finance, geo-social (such as economic inequalities);
- national macroeconomic statistical accounts;
- financial time series, quantitative and qualitative data.

We distinguish between four types of data sets:

1) Qualitative data, such as regulations and policies set by sovereign states, providing a reference frame within which financial models may be constructed or justified. For example, Chapter 10 provides an approach to compliance to regulation based on games and such data.
2) Granular time series measurements (generally recorded electronically or systematically assembled), events, or spurious changes occurring over time or subject to policy predictions. In this context, a model is nonstationary, changing over time either due to major model-external events or other causes.
3) Implied measurements embedded in the definition of predictive models (and therefore model specific). For example, models based on prices of options or their future volatility.
4) Big data consisting of databases treated algorithmically to search for patterned relationships between multiple factors, as well as states and events previously neglected or those whose importance has not been appreciated at their appropriate value.

Data sources have expanded at an exponential rate along all conceivable dimensions of globalization, creating an awareness of both its benefits and its risks. A cursory list of data sources includes the UN, the IMF, the OECD, EU KLEMS, and national statistics regarding everything from quality of life, population, employment, wages, military expenditures, and health care, to capital flows, export–import flows, FX, and macroeconomic accounts. Furthermore, commercial firms (e.g., Bloomberg (USA), Thomson Reuters (USA), Datastream (USA), FACTSET (USA), Wind (China), and others) assemble and sell data on stock prices and assets markets. Financial markets include categorized asset prices; for example, stocks, bonds, options, and exchange traded funds (ETFs). They may be specialized in certain commodities such as oil, metals, and "softs" (sugar, soybeans, coffee, etc.), or in certain technology-intensive markets (e.g., electronics/semiconductors). Additional data are found in corporate financial reports and guidance; that is, earnings predictions set by corporate entities.

2.1.1 National Accounts and Country-Specific Data

National accounts are macroeconomic reports of countries' economic activities. They are used to document and to help predict economic performance when used in macroeconomic models. Global financial information suppliers are increasingly expanding their databases to service sovereign states and cater to global financial investors and managers (see Chapter 4). Macroeconomic statistics are used to define economic and financial policies, while financial analysts use these data to improve their forecasts.

National accounts[1] also provide historical data, including the gross domestic product (GDP), consumer price index (CPI), jobs, industrial migration, inequality, trade balance, financial accounts (such as a net acquisition and disposal of financial assets and liabilities.

Table 2.1 summarizes some of these macroeconomic indicators. Real GDP percentage changes from 2014 to 2015 show growth in China, the USA, the UK, the euro area, and Japan, compared with contraction in Brazil and Russia, which were negatively affected by low oil prices. These two countries also have high inflation, as shown by the CPI growth. Furthermore, countries, including China and the euro area, recorded a significant increase in their trade surplus. Financial accounts indicate a significant change in all countries' growth in financial investments and capital flows with net lenders (e.g., China, euro area, and Japan) and net borrowers (e.g., USA, UK, and Brazil). Presuming that the USA maintains its economic, industrial, and technological leadership, its increased borrowing (as well as the extraordinary growth in its global debt) ought to be explained. One interpretation is that due to the strength of the US dollar and its global demand, it seems that printing dollars for the USA is necessarily an inexpensive way to finance itself. That, too, has risks, as we shall see in Chapter 8. In this sense, data are revealing what might not be self-evident.

2.1.2 Financial Data

Financial data are in the midst of a global transformation due to electronic markets, pricing financial assets in numerous and multipolar markets located in all time zones. Trades and exchanges are therefore technology based and assisted with a data lifetime that may in some cases be irrelevant, as is the case of "doctored data" sets by some stealth trading firms launching buy transactions for some assets to affect their price and canceling their orders at microseconds prior to their execution. In addition, the multiplicity of financial products—such as options of all sorts, ETFs, credit default swaps, and VIX (the fear volatility index)—provides new challenges to global investors.

2.1.3 Corporate and Statistical Measurements

Corporate objectives and statistical measurements feed one another. Their analysis is measured and assessed relative to their expectations and market trends. Their financial performance, however, provides the bulk of their statistics pertaining to their stock prices, their derivatives, and to many factors that contribute to an assessment of their risks. In global finance, data originating in some countries may be of poor quality, and therefore risky. For example, data may be generated by a corporate policy rather than a performance record. These include among many others:

- corporate stock prices, their bond prices and their associated future and option prices;
- credit and counterparty risks (both local and international);

---

1 Main aggregates and classifications of national accounts statistics are recommended in the United Nations System of National Accounts 1993 (SNA, 1993).

Table 2.1 National accounts and international macroeconomic indicators.

Country	GDP (constant 2010$, trillion $)			CPI (2010 = 100)			Trade balance in goods (net, billion $)			Financial account (net, billion $)		
	2014	2015	Growth (%)	2014	2015	Growth (%)	2014	2015	Growth (%)	2014	2015	Growth (%)
USA	16.2	16.5	2.4	109	109	0.1	-741	-759	2.4	-240	-209	-12.7
China	8.2	8.8	6.9	113	115	1.4	435	567	30.3	169	143	-15.6
Japan	5.6	5.7	0.5	103	104	0.8	-100	-5	-94.8	58	175	199.6
Euro area	12.8	13.0	1.7	—	—	—	223	327	46.6	335	490	46.1
UK	2.6	2.7	2.3	112	112	0.1	-202	-191	-5.4	-166	-143	-13.7
Brazil	2.4	2.3	-3.8	127	138	9.0	-7	18	-366.5	-101	-55	-45.6
Russia	1.7	1.6	-3.7	131	152	15.5	190	149	-21.7	24	74	205.9

Source: Data from The World Bank.

- corporate debt and risks, liquidity risks or a lack of funding for strategic investments;
- oprisks (such as lack of internal controls, data-measurements management, omissions, and, today, far more cyber risks);
- legal risks (including fraud risks, noncompliance risks, regulatory risks);
- reputation risks;
- propensity to contagious risks.

In global finance, corporate risks are amplified and mitigated at the same time by a global networking with interdependent global entities. For example, global connectivity has augmented cyber risks appreciably. Techniques to address these problems and their risks are emerging based mostly on networks modeling science, mathematical graphs defining the structure of their relationships, random graphs where their connections may be defined by probabilities, queue networks (Tapiero, 2004, 2013), statistical graph approaches consisting of statistical sampling over graphs and inferring their connectivity (Tapiero, 1975; Tapiero *et al.*, 1975; Tapiero and Hsu, 1988), learning networks such as Bayesian networks (Pearl, 1985), and network science in general (Kennet and Havlin, 2015) based on heterogeneous structures that exhibit power laws (defined by the number of links per node) distributions, and so on. These systems are called scale-free networks and include, for example, the internet, social networks, and airlines; for example, see Caldarelli (2007). They are equally useful in global finance to better understand contagion processes, experienced in financial bank runs. The difference between these scale-free networks and random graphs defined by Erdos and Renyi (1959) is the robustness of these networks—the former are far more robust than the latter. For further details on these networks, see, for example, Kennet and Havlin (2015), Havlin *et al.* (2012), Barabási and Albert, (1999), and Albert and Barabási (2002).

There are large number of sources for country and global risk analysis. For example, Duke University[2] provides on country risk analysis emphasizing global industries' risk exposure, financial, and political events, as well as behavior and challenges of markets; the *International Country Risk Guide* by the PRS Group[3] covers political, economic, and financial risks using over 30 metrics since 1980; *The Economist* Intelligence Unit[4] provides country analysis, risk analysis (with details on global risk scenarios, security risk, credit risk and operational risk), and industry analysis; the Global Risk Assessment Module (GLORAM) by Zurich[5] assesses 24 global risks and their impact with a scenario analysis; the World Economic Forum's global risk reports (e.g., World Economic Forum, 2016) analyze 29 global risks under five broad categories (economic, environmental, geopolitical, societal, and technological).

---

2 http://people.duke.edu/~charvey/Country_risk/couindex.htm.
3 http://www.prsgroup.com/about-us/our-two-methodologies/icrg.
4 http://www.eiu.com/Default.aspx.
5 https://www.zurich.com.

2.1.4 Big Data and Model-Less Finance

Big data is hammered by the media as a model-less alternative to complex modeling and statistical analysis. It is appealing because it presumes that "models are not needed" since data express "what really is, rather than what we believe it is or search for." It defines relationships that do exist based on what has happened or happening anywhere or everywhere (e.g., see Andersen *et al.* (2009), Callebaut (2012), *The Economist* (2010), Goodman and Wong (2009), Hey *et al.* (2009), Krohs and Callebaut (2007), Manyika *et al.* (2011)). Big data in practice is mostly used as a search engine applied to the discovery of any matter that would seem, once discovered, to be important. It may be applied to search for deviant traders, collusive trades across national boundaries, to detect credit default risks, trade opportunities in far out markets with built-in mispricing of assets, and so on. It may also be used to identify future scenarios previously unknown as well as to augment the relevance of financial models and thereby to reduce the uncertainty that financial models have by their own definition. For regulators, it may be used to better define the factors contributing to systemic risks and detect suspected noncompliance (at least based on the detection of noncompliance signals).

An increasing number of software programs and start-ups are proposing "big-data-black-boxes" that seek financial trends and consumers' moods, preferences, and intents using internet comments assembled globally on financial assets and economic variables. Algorithms and automatic learning machines are then created to seek and interpret images, to detect departures from expected trends, and to trace sentiments integrated into predictive mechanisms for stock markets performance. A rising tide of data-driven algorithms based on behavioral rationalities is thus emerging and engulfing large firms and business interests with an avid and information-dependent finance. Big data thus competes and at the same time complements the traditional statistical approach to data measurement and interpretation, providing a renewed interest to data analytic techniques (such as clustering techniques, data reduction approaches, decentralized data systems, networked data systems, and random matrices used to detect relevant factors). However, it may also increase the use of data to artificial and intelligent decision-making at the expense of the need to understand the decisions supported by big data. Big data may in this sense imply risks as well, since it imbues decisions with a certainty that by definition exists nowhere.

The traditional statistical approach, unlike information technology (IT)-intensive big data, is based on fundamental and structured hypotheses emanating from scientific statements or theories to be refuted or not, based on statistical (data) evidence (see Allen (2001), Weinberg (2010), and Callebaut (2012)). As a result, the statistical/scientific approach reveals uncertainty from a given and tested knowledge database. On the other hand, data-driven algorithms are based on a robotized artificial intelligence that has the capacity to treat large data sets to reveal covariations, associations, and patterns based on their search (in some cases improved by built-in learning algorithms) rather than theory. Thus, while the statistical/scientific approach is an evolutionary and evolving process, based on a cycle to hypothesize, measure, test, and confirm or not, the data-driven approach is a shortcut, seeking to know even though it may not know why. It is an interpretation of data at any one time with a predictive artificial intelligence that decision-makers might not understand as data revelations can be as complex and as stealthy as artificial intelligence may be to its users. It is, therefore, a statement of a current fact—a presumed certainty, rather than a recognition that all knowledge is partial—embedded in a greater uncertainty.

The British astrophysicist Arthur S. Eddington once wrote, "No experiment should be believed until it has been confirmed by theory" (NYT, 2012). In this sense, data-driven measurements can be misleading and reveal about anything one may choose to discover. To disprove its validity, a digitalization of Tolstoy's *War and Peace* and a search engine revealed secret intents. Similarly, other books have even predicted political stalemates in the Middle East and their resolution. In this sense, data-driven measurement models can make sense out of nonsense even though it is in fact nonsense. Similarly, in biology, where big data has already found its footing, Callebaut (2012: 69) raises important and philosophical issues, such as "Can data 'speak for themselves'?" And he discusses Carl Woese's concern about whether "a society that permits biology to become an engineering discipline, that allows that science to slip into the role of changing the living world without trying to understand it, is a danger to itself."

Big data, therefore, has its perils, with type II statistical errors (i.e., making a false discovery), enslaving decision-makers to rationalities they might not be aware of, and providing a new twist to the misuse of data measurement by seeking and finding the confirmation of one's certainty. The statistical approach is presented in comparison with the data analytic approach in Figure 2.1.

Finally, big data can turn out to be an unwieldy process victimized by the belief that a larger haystack may help to find a needle in that haystack. Yet, big data banks, if tamed, can complement the statistical/scientific approach to measurements by providing an opportunity to reveal new hypotheses and new directions that can set such approaches on a more certain footing. For example, scale analysis techniques, developed by Louis Guttman, have provided approaches to the measurement and the reduction of data dimensions into a scale (used profusely in the social sciences and psychology). The Guttman approach is described in Figure 2.2. It consists of a repeated and structural reduction of multivariate data resulting in an ordered scale, profusely used in psychology.

For banks, financial traders and suppliers of financial information, data and information are their primary assets. *The Economist* (2010) reports that the middle class grew by more than 1 billion people between 1990 and 2005, and the amount of data transferred over the internet has been rising exponentially. Companies like Amazon's Web Services, AT&T's Synaptic Hosting, AppNexus, GoGrid, Rackspace Cloud Hosting, the HP/Yahoo/Intel Cloud Computing Test bed, the IBM/Google and Micro Strategy BI Cloud are providing various types of cloud services to ease data storage problems.

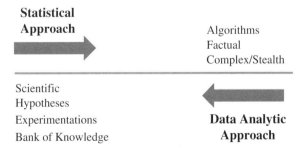

Statistical Approach

Algorithms
Factual
Complex/Stealth

Scientific
Hypotheses
Experimentations
Bank of Knowledge

Data Analytic Approach

Figure 2.1 Statistical versus data analytic approaches.

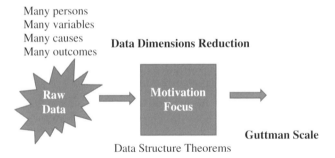

Many persons
Many variables
Many causes
Many outcomes

Data Dimensions Reduction

Raw Data

Motivation Focus

Guttman Scale

Data Structure Theorems

Figure 2.2 The Guttman approach.

Big data and global finance may fit to one another as both imply and are based on large volumes of data, a wide variety and types of data, and a high velocity of data streams, with data of various granularities and scale and their aggregates, both internally produced and externally supplied. While technologies from social media companies have shown a way to handle vast amounts of unstructured data, our abilities to translate these complex, diverse, and dynamic data sources into workable global and financial information remain challenging. From a technical and statistical viewpoint, they require quantitative and data modeling expertise regarding (i) algorithmic search or data mining, (ii) data detection, selection, and coding, (iii) data assembly, filtering, and reporting to construct a prior time path, (iv) data security and quality, and (v) data modeling and data dimensional scale reduction $\mathfrak{R}^n \Rightarrow \mathfrak{R}^P$. The latter include the application of statistical tools in global finance such as data parametric reduction, data models reduction, learning and inferences, and data visualization and data management.

Global financial systems that are becoming more digitized allow automatic context-specific interpretations, aggregation, and analysis of data (e.g., what information is relevant or not to a particular country, market, or stock). For example, information and/or knowledge extracted from digital records can render financial bank jobs easier in accurately diagnosing and detecting risky clients, in selected global areas. Similarly, digitized data may prevent cybercrimes more effectively and thus contribute to the management of increasingly complex systems of financial networks, e-financial markets, and financial retailing. Despite the potential for big data and data analytics for financial information, it is still immature, misunderstood, and misused. Michael de Crespigny, CEO at Information Security Information (ISF), points out regarding forensic finance that (Ashford, 2012):

> Only half of organisations surveyed by the ISF are using some form of analytics for fraud prevention, forensics and network traffic analysis, while less than 20% are using it to identify information related to subject matter requests, predict hardware failures, ensure data integrity or check data classification. "Few organisations currently recognize the benefits for information security, yet many are already using data analytics to support their core business."

The business of financial big data is bright and challenging. The following questions highlight some of the issues of global finance–big data:

- Is big data looking for a pin in a haystack by adding hay?
- Is big data in the future of global finance (and vice versa)?

- Can big data, based on past facts, be reconciled with implied volatility estimates?
- Is big data merely another IT data-driven tool to justify what we are doing or rather define what we ought to do?
- Is big data the end of privacy?
- Are big data algorithmic search models transparent to those who may want to use it? Is it a means to reveal outcomes a-priori sought or reveal the unknown and the unexpected?
- Is big data something new? Or the marketing of well-known data analytics tools up-ended with more information, expanded by new computational hardware?
- Is big data a means to increase or reduce complexity?
- Is the growth of data and our ability to deal with this data unsustainable?

2.1.5 Technology and Financial Data[6]

The evolution of IT combined with globalization has led to a transformation and management of data. Distributed databases and IT networking under a global and data-open environment are gradually changing finance. This does so from technological, data management, and not least from data intelligence viewpoints. The latter underlies algorithmic finance, feeding financial industries (banks, investment funds, hedge funds, high-frequency traders, financial advisory firms, etc.). Financial technologies and intelligence are not expectedly and uniformly distributed. Therefore, on the one hand, they have introduced risks for ill-equipped agents, and on the other hand, there is a fierce competition between financial firms able to acquire the technology but struggling to make it pay (since its financial intelligence is not distributed equally). For these reasons, the future of global finance is both complex and in a continuous search of itself and transformation.

Prior to 1995 (before distributed computing was introduced), data management was relatively simple. Generally, data were centrally maintained in mainframe computers, financial products were less complex, the velocity of systems change was much slower, and centralized system processing meant data standards were easier to manage and maintain. Since 1995, data management has become increasingly complex due to the financial freedom to trade in far greater types of assets, and incentives that have extended the outreach of banking and their competitive postures. Specific reasons include the following: Glass–Steagall Act gets repealed, and therefore banks were able to trade rather than just lend and manage clients' moneys; product innovation, such as future contracts, and a broad variety of optional products explodes; distributed computing and databases took hold and transformed data management, accessible from many locations; data processing standards are diluted and business silos are empowered.

The year 2000 (the Y2K syndrome) further challenged computer-aided data management and ushered changes both in markets and in financial products that began to change. Derivatives market began to explode, creating a notional size of over $400 trillion. Global capital markets became more interdependent as products were sold globally across jurisdictions. Further, following the repeal of the Glass–Steagall Act, separation between investment banks and depository banks was removed, enabling risk to flow freely between the bank and its entities, augmenting the financial outreach of banking institutions to areas where they were previously unable to function in.

---

6 Based on joint research with Michael Hayes from Goldman Sachs.

These also resulted in an unprecedented number of mergers and acquisitions; the line between risk and data control became blurred; comfort, instead of objective analysis, became acceptable; engineering standards were compromised. A "new complexity" invaded finance, augmenting the profits of those who could function in such complexity and increasing the risks for those who could not. From a data management viewpoint, distributed computing set in with new opportunities and risks. Some of its consequences included: data management going from being centralized to decentralized—hundreds if not thousands of database servers were created; businesses rapidly transformed themselves, creating distinct processing silos; federated ownership of data ruled the day, meaning that everyone owned the data, so no one effectively owned the data. In other words, owning data was not an advantage; businesses argued "data freedom" was better than "data anarchy"; product creation/experimentation increased at an exponential rate, and governance and data processing became compromised.

These consequences, faced with an ever-expanding financial system, created a sense of sovereign uncontrollability and sovereign risks that have prepared the groundwork to institute legally a far greater and far more powerful financial regulation. The 2007–2008 financial crisis increased the political commitment to reign in the financial system. If not completely, at least wherever it could.

According to the National Research Council (2010: 1), the post Lehman crisis in 2008 and its contagion evolving into the turmoil of the financial crisis has also pointed out that "rapid change in the financial system driven by innovation and deregulation … has altered the mechanisms and pace of financial intermediation to such an extent that regulatory tools, processes and data have fallen behind." These have provided a regulatory revolution that is in continuous transformation. Its challenges are expanding multifold in global finance, where all countries are confronted with their own problems, their regulation, and other countries' regulations. These elements introduce far greater risks and costs to financial institutions to comply with financial (and often contradictory) regulations. This environment calls then for a far greater Big Data Intelligence.

2.1.6 Transforming Data Management in Global Finance

The complexity of standardizing data and its quality in a global environment has led to a four-letter objective: "A-C-T-S" or accuracy, completeness, timeliness, and adherence to standards.

In managing big data, there are basically two general approaches:

- The first is enterprise information integration, which is a process of information integration that uses data abstraction to provide a unified interface (known as uniform data access) for viewing all the data within an organization and a single set of structures and naming conventions (known as uniform information representation) to represent data.
- The second is data virtualization, which uses technologies that offer data users a unified, abstracted, and encapsulated view for querying and manipulating data stored in a heterogeneous set of data stores.

The main benefits of these approaches are that users get a unified view of the data; data integration happens at middleware level (data quality improves because standards are promoted back into the database; engineering principles and practices are uniformly applied across the enterprise; encapsulation hides the technical details of the data so users can interact with data in a more natural manner; business intelligence tools can readily be put to use against the data; users can once again trust the data to conform to operating standard; and governance of information becomes effective.

2.2 Global Finance, Data Reduction, and Statistical Measurements

Global finance is both extensive and multivariate. To render data underlying global finance problems tractable, data are reduced to their meaningful interpretation. These include probability distributions, their probability moments, their granularity, and models of various sorts. In the following, we shall consider a number of specific approaches and models and provide examples to highlight their function.

2.2.1 Moments

Consider a data set of stock prices returns in N financial markets these stocks are traded in. Let their record in a specific kth market be

$$\{S_{1,k}, S_{2,k}, S_{3,k}, ..., S_{t,k}\}, \quad k = 1, 2, ..., N$$

A data matrix of $[t \times N]$ defines then a data set records of prices in all N markets over t time periods. These data may be fit to a model or transformed to another financial meaning. For example, letting

$$\frac{\Delta S_{t,k}}{S_{t,k}} = R_{t,k}, \quad \Delta S_{t,k} = S_{t+1,k} - S_{t,k}$$

where $R_{t,k}$ is a rate of return (ROR) obtained from the data set. Data matrices such as $[\mathbf{S}(t, k), \mathbf{R}(t, k)]$ may be both analyzed and reduced to specific moments and to model estimates providing a trend both in time and across national boundaries. The data granularity of such observed variables may be varied, being regional, state–country level, city wide, or time-granular defined in terms of daily, monthly, or yearly data as well as intraday and high-frequency data. For example, let $R_{1,1}, R_{1,2}, ..., R_{1,N}$ be the RORs over N countries at a specific time 1, say 1 day. The average return is then

$$\hat{R}_1 = \frac{1}{N} \sum_{k=1}^{N} R_{1,k}$$

and the variance is

$$\sigma_1^2 = \frac{1}{N-1} \sum_{k=1}^{N} \left(R_{1,k} - \hat{R}_1 \right)^2$$

The covariance and the correlation matrix of such observations may also be defined (as we shall see subsequently). By the same token, country data matrices may be used to summarize the data assembled for a country $j, j = 1, 2, ..., M$, over a number of factors (both macroeconomic and financial).

$$[\mathbf{S}^{(1)}(t,k)] = \begin{bmatrix} 1 \\ 2 \\ \vdots \\ t \end{bmatrix} \begin{bmatrix} S_{1,1}^{(1)}, S_{1,2}^{(1)}, S_{1,3}^{(1)}, \dots, S_{1,m}^{(1)} \\ S_{2,1}^{(1)}, S_{2,2}^{(1)}, S_{2,3}^{(1)}, \dots, S_{2,m}^{(1)} \\ \dots \\ S_{t,1}^{(1)}, S_{t,2}^{(1)}, S_{t,3}^{(1)}, \dots, S_{t,m}^{(1)} \\ \dots \end{bmatrix} \Leftrightarrow \begin{bmatrix} 1 \\ 2 \\ \vdots \\ t \end{bmatrix} \begin{bmatrix} R_{1,1}^{(1)}, R_{1,2}^{(1)}, R_{1,3}^{(1)}, \dots, R_{1,m}^{(1)} \\ R_{2,1}^{(1)}, R_{2,2}^{(1)}, R_{2,3}^{(1)}, \dots, R_{2,m}^{(1)} \\ \dots \\ R_{t,1}^{(1)}, R_{t,2}^{(1)}, R_{t,3}^{(1)}, \dots, R_{t,m}^{(1)} \\ \dots \end{bmatrix} = [\mathbf{R}^{(1)}(t,k)]$$

$$[\mathbf{S}^{(M)}(t,k)] = \begin{bmatrix} 1 \\ 2 \\ \vdots \\ t \end{bmatrix} \begin{bmatrix} S_{1,1}^{(M)}, S_{1,2}^{(M)}, S_{1,3}^{(M)}, \dots, S_{1,m}^{(M)} \\ S_{2,1}^{(M)}, S_{2,2}^{(M)}, S_{2,3}^{(M)}, \dots, S_{2,m}^{(M)} \\ \dots \\ S_{t,1}^{(M)}, S_{t,2}^{(M)}, S_{t,3}^{(M)}, \dots, S_{t,m}^{(M)} \end{bmatrix} \Leftrightarrow \begin{bmatrix} R_{1,1}^{(M)}, R_{1,2}^{(M)}, R_{1,3}^{(M)}, \dots, R_{1,m}^{(M)} \\ R_{2,1}^{(M)}, R_{2,2}^{(M)}, R_{2,3}^{(M)}, \dots, R_{2,m}^{(M)} \\ \dots \\ R_{t,1}^{(M)}, R_{t,2}^{(M)}, R_{t,3}^{(M)}, \dots, R_{t,m}^{(M)} \end{bmatrix} = [\mathbf{R}^{(M)}(t,k)]$$

In this case, the matrices are defined by entries $\left[S_{i,k}^{(j)}\right]$, $i = 1, 2, \dots, t$; $k = 1, 2, \dots, m$; $j = 1, 2, \dots, M$, where, for example, index i denotes time and index k denotes economic and other factors, such as trades, currency prices, wages, and employment rate. The analysis of such data may follow a number of alternative approaches, such as regression analysis, panel data analyses, and volatility estimates—see Rogers and Satchell (1991) and Yang and Zhang (2000). These estimates are based on financial models we construct for the purposes of understanding and predicting financial prices and the markets that produce such prices. For example, let the data history in a given country, up to and including time t, be defined by a filtration, which we note as $\{\mathfrak{I}_t^k\}$, where $\mathfrak{I}_t^k$ implies a data set over t past periods in market k. We now consider a number of statistics.

Reduction of specific RORs defined over all markets to a probability distribution

$$\{R_{i,1}, R_{i,2}, R_{i,3}, \dots, R_{i,N}\} \Rightarrow \text{Statistics} \Rightarrow f_{i,N}(R_i) \underset{N \to \infty}{=} f_i(R_i)$$

where $f_i(R_i)$ denotes a limit (assuming convergence) price across all countries. The expected RORs are then $E(R_{i,k}|\{\mathfrak{I}_{i,k}\})$, denoting a filtered conditional estimate of the current ROR and a filtered prediction of the next period's ROR. Additional moments may be defined as well. These include volatility, skewness, kurtosis, range, correlation, and autocorrelation, as will be indicated later. Each of these moments has a meaningful property we use to characterize the data set. Similarly, consider the RORs time series in a specific market k:

$$\{R_{1,k}, R_{2,k}, R_{3,k}, \dots, R_{t,k}\} \Rightarrow \Phi_{t,k}(R_{t,k}) \underset{t \to \infty}{=} \Phi_k(R_k)$$

where $\Phi_k(R_k)$ is a limit price in market k with a filtered conditional mean and predictive estimate with means at two subsequent periods: $E(R_{t,k}|\mathfrak{I}_{t,k})$ and $E(R_{t+1,k}|\mathfrak{I}_{t,k})$. In other words, the data matrix of, say, RORs provides both longitudinal (across financial markets) and latitudinal (over time) estimates. By the same token, other moments' estimates can be calculated. Risk theories and risk metrics are covered in studies such as by Gerber (1979) and Morgan (1995).

For simplicity, consider RORs time series and their moments.

- Averages (sample mean):

$$\bar{R}_{t,k} = \frac{1}{t}\sum_{i=1}^{t} R_{i,k}$$

- Volatility (standard deviation):

$$\bar{\sigma}_{t,k} = \sqrt{\frac{1}{t-1}\sum_{i=1}^{n}\left(R_{i,k}-\bar{R}_{t,k}\right)^2}$$

- Index of skewness: $\xi_{t,k}/\sigma_{t,k}^3$, for the third moment defining the distribution asymmetry.
- Index of kurtosis: $\psi_{t,k}/\sigma_{t,k}^4$, the fourth moment to the squared distribution variance, defining the existence of the distribution fat tails.
- Range: $\mathfrak{R}_{t,k} = \mathrm{Max}\{R_{1,k}, R_{2,k}, R_{3,k}, ..., R_{t,k}\} - \mathrm{Min}\{R_{1,k}, R_{2,k}, R_{3,k}, ..., R_{t,k}\}$, used to assess jumps and outliers in the sample statistics.
- Dependence statistics, an autocorrelation

$$\rho_{R_{i,k}, R_{t,k}} = \frac{E\left((R_{i,k}-E(R_{i,k}))(R_{t,k}-E(R_{t,k}))\right)}{\sigma_{R_{i,k}}\sigma_{R_{t,k}}}$$

expressing the co-movements of random returns at two instants of time.

- Dependence statistic, a correlation (expressing the correlation of two markets) at a given time:

$$\rho_{i,kj}(\tau) = \frac{E\left((R_{i,k}-E(R_{i,k}))\left(R_{i,j}-E\left(R_{i,j}\right)\right)\right)}{\sigma_{i,k}\sigma_{i,j}}$$

Example 2.1 Consider the data set in Figure 2.3 consisting of the monthly prices of 10 stock exchanges, each in different countries denoted by A, B, C, ... and recorded monthly over a period of 10 months. We let the entries of this matrix for a country J be $\left[SP_{i,\mathrm{Price}}^{(j)}\right]$, $i = 1, 2, ..., 10$; $j = 1, 2, ..., 10$. Their basic moments calculated across time (horizontally) and vertically (across stocks exchanges in different countries) provide their mean, volatility (or standard deviation), skewness, kurtosis, and the range. Given that their skewness is not null, their distributions both across time and across international markets are not normally distributed.

2.2.2 Skew and Kurtosis (Tails)

Skew and kurtosis are based on statistical third and fourth moments measurements deviating from their mean. Skewness indicates a measure of asymmetry, while kurtosis indicates a measure of tail thickness (fat tails) based on its fourth probability moment. The greater the kurtosis index, the greater the distribution tail and therefore the greater the probability of events deviating from their mean. For example, say that FX RORs time series are shown empirically to have a normal probability distribution of mean and variance (μ, σ^2). Since the normal distribution is symmetric, its third moment

	7/31/2015	8/31/2015	9/30/2015	10/30/2015	11/30/2015	12/31/2015	1/29/2016	2/29/2016	3/31/2016	4/29/2016	5/31/2016	6/30/2016	7/29/2016	8/31/2016	Average	Volatility	Skewness	Kurtosis	Range
SPX Index	−0.24%	−2.59%	−4.68%	4.14%	2.76%	−1.28%	−6.60%	−0.74%	6.17%	2.65%	−0.48%	0.89%	3.12%	1.33%	0.32%	0.034560744	−0.389119523	0.020952104	12.77%
CCMP Index	0.19%	−2.92%	−3.78%	2.76%	4.17%	−0.83%	−8.53%	−3.20%	6.53%	2.90%	−2.12%	1.42%	3.45%	3.84%	0.28%	0.040630168	−0.567736657	0.05298983	15.05%
SHCOMP Index	−19.89%	−6.61%	−12.97%	6.86%	6.54%	−0.43%	−15.87%	−6.04%	3.76%	3.32%	−4.83%	1.38%	4.06%	1.10%	−2.82%	0.084961301	−0.80893925	−0.424947271	26.65%
HSI Index	−7.32%	−7.23%	−8.00%	6.01%	−0.62%	−2.66%	−9.93%	−3.04%	6.09%	3.38%	−3.87%	2.34%	4.12%	5.42%	−1.09%	0.056842582	−0.121140854	−1.533955439	16.02%
TPX Index	−0.93%	−1.45%	−9.81%	3.49%	5.07%	−1.97%	−8.97%	−6.21%	2.54%	−1.67%	−0.09%	−3.42%	0.19%	0.98%	−1.59%	0.043544028	−0.586656232	−0.103715591	14.88%
CAC Index	0.57%	−1.39%	−7.38%	4.18%	4.13%	−4.98%	−6.98%	−3.58%	5.80%	0.40%	−1.61%	−1.82%	0.55%	2.49%	−0.69%	0.040865141	−0.154539099	−0.78840852	13.18%
DAX Index	0.46%	−4.16%	−7.99%	2.70%	7.47%	−2.85%	−7.93%	−5.45%	6.12%	1.66%	−0.13%	−1.51%	1.03%	5.72%	−0.35%	0.049601739	−0.056157442	−0.889370971	15.47%
IBOV Index	−3.60%	−7.51%	−2.88%	2.09%	−0.41%	−5.11%	−11.84%	4.15%	19.86%	5.45%	−1.61%	−1.68%	9.69%	5.39%	0.86%	0.078841115	0.872150619	1.557116728	31.71%
NYA Index	−1.43%	−3.00%	−5.45%	3.69%	0.98%	−2.17%	−6.82%	−0.77%	6.62%	2.82%	−0.06%	0.77%	2.61%	0.97%	−0.09%	0.035871594	−0.179902227	0.105694903	13.45%
UKX Index	−2.01%	−2.87%	−5.71%	4.16%	−0.53%	−2.29%	−3.89%	−0.69%	4.69%	1.86%	−1.71%	0.17%	7.78%	2.49%	0.10%	0.037040278	0.563144063	−0.089048753	13.49%
JALSH Index	−0.20%	−2.51%	−1.41%	6.21%	−0.83%	−4.96%	−3.86%	2.05%	6.67%	0.52%	0.18%	0.40%	−0.35%	0.42%	0.17%	0.032251426	0.735210998	0.784894431	11.63%
EGX30 Index	−7.94%	−4.93%	−4.18%	4.36%	−9.62%	−1.71%	−6.32%	−3.92%	15.95%	9.06%	−1.25%	−1.64%	2.25%	8.73%	−0.08%	0.073199312	0.875123975	0.172273697	25.57%
Average	−3.52%	−3.93%	−6.19%	4.22%	1.59%	−2.60%	−8.13%	−2.29%	7.57%	2.69%	−1.47%	−0.22%	3.21%	3.24%					
Volatility	0.058806727	0.021599559	0.032149983	0.014748465	0.04582722	0.016157531	0.033399826	0.032010985	0.050591291	0.026936591	0.015680212	0.017349647	0.030057894	0.025861193					
Skewness	−2.235578102	−0.670277378	−0.661274272	0.511965385	−1.191565307	−0.594854983	−1.038081448	0.688294662	1.87444372	0.962237746	−1.107668484	−0.343976911	1.069993294	0.868291833					
Kurtosis	5.424162346	−0.962367106	0.400454183	−0.535449445	2.375485076	−0.821530969	1.622088588	−0.080766657	2.878157967	2.293367812	0.687851266	−0.878262151	0.822983009	−0.020819577					
Range	20.37%	6.11%	11.56%	4.77%	17.10%	4.69%	12.01%	10.36%	17.32%	10.73%	5.02%	5.76%	10.04%	8.30%					

Average	Volatility	Skewness	Kurtosis	Range
Index Compare				
Time Compare				

Figure 2.3 Data set of stock exchanges. *Source:* Data from Bloomberg.

(and thereby its index of skewness) is necessarily null. For this reason, such an index expresses a departure from the normal assumption, which has important implications to financial theory and practice. By the same token, the thickness of a tail—the index of kurtosis—is an indicator of a distribution's predictability. Thick tails mean that there are many more states that have an appreciable probability mass; therefore, predicting the distribution's states is increasingly difficult. In other words, a data set exhibiting a very high kurtosis implies that prices are commensurably unpredictable. For a standard normal probability distribution with zero mean and constant variance, we have the following moments: $E(\varepsilon) = \mu = 0$, $E(\varepsilon^2) = \sigma^2 = 1$, $E(\varepsilon^3) = 0$, $E(\varepsilon^4) = 3$, where its index of skewness is null, while its index of kurtosis is

$$\frac{\psi}{\sigma^4} = \frac{4}{\sqrt{\pi}}\Gamma\left(\frac{5}{2}\right) = 3$$

In other words, if we estimate the probability moments of a security's RORs and observe that their third moment (skewness) is not null, this ought to point out that RORs do not have a normal probability distribution. Similarly, if the fourth moment reveals a kurtosis that differs from that of the normal distribution, then again, the RORs and their associated risks cannot be presumed to be normal. Such a distribution may have fatter tails than those of the normal probability distribution if its kurtosis is larger; therefore, the presumption of price predictability which is essential in fundamental finance falters. From a financial viewpoint, such differences across countries provide an opportunity to extract algorithms that may yield arbitrage trading strategies. For example, for the skewness and kurtosis in stock index returns which is implied by the prices of options, see Corrado and Su (1996).

2.2.3 Outliers, Extreme Statistics, and Fat Tails

Outliers are events in a data set that do not conform to their predicted occurrences. They may be extreme cases often modeled by extreme and exceedance distributions using extreme data (highs and lows) as well as range to standard deviation (R/S analysis) to estimate outliers (e.g., see Irwin (1925), Barnett and Lewis (1994), Tapiero and Vallois (2015, 2016), Mandelbrot and Van Ness (1968), and Mandelbrot and Taqqu (1979)). For time series, R/S sample statistics are used to construct models of greater (or smaller, depending on the R/S relationship to time) variability—examples are considered in further sections; see also Tapiero *et al.* (2016) and Tapiero and Vallois (2015). Additionally, for the analysis of heavy or fat tails, see Basi *et al.* (1998) and Lo (1997).

2.2.4 Extreme Risks

Extreme risks are characterized by rare events or by extreme consequences. Their rarity, however, can be measured by the hazard rate we associate with the probability of their occurrence; namely, the conditional probability that consequential events occur at time t defined by $h(t) = f(t)/(1 - F(t))$. In global finance, these events are rare and occur due to the conjuncture of many factors (see Tapiero (2013) and Tapiero and Vallois (2015)). For example, the 1987 stock crash, Cyclone Hugo, Barings losses, the hi-tech bubble, and Asian financial markets meltdown in 1997 were the events with extreme consequences, some of which have occurred for reasons that were not accounted for. These events may be difficult to characterize by probabilities as they seem to be nonrecurrent, although they do occur and recur surprisingly. Assuming N factors associated with such events, a conjuncture of such events may be assessed statistically if data and appropriate models are constructed. Their origins are as varied as unexpected and with consequences counted in many ways—by their number of deaths, by the financial losses sustained, by their causal and subsequent effects, and so on. They can be manmade (either on purpose, such as wars and terror, or inadvertently, such as malfunctions in nuclear plants) or arise from natural causes. Although some are observable when they occur, they may also be latent, contagious, and expanding over time. They may occur due to latent climatic changes or events (such as extreme drought, rain and floods, heat and cold), as well as due to external events (e.g., an asteroid entering our vital space). These events, in addition to their human and financial costs, may also have political and geopolitical repercussions. For example, it is estimated that, for each death in a natural disaster, there are an additional 3000 and more who will be affected; and for any disaster (such as an extreme terror case), there can be enduring costs, and in some cases transformational financial and social consequences. Accounting for extreme risks is therefore extremely challenging. Insurance firms in particular are assembling large databases to assess their differences and consequences and predict their costs. These are focused on their immediate and insurable costs and are therefore incomplete. For the study of insurance and claims processes and their modeling, see Embrechts *et al.* (1997) and Vallois and Tapiero (2009) for example.

2.2.5 Time Series and Filtration

In a time series, we use the expected notation as a conditional statement on the data sample that has previously occurred. Explicitly, given a data set $\mathfrak{I}_t = \{S_1, S_2, S_2, ..., S_t\}$, defining past and all relevant data used to construct financial and statistical estimates (or a filtration):

$$E(S_{t+1}|\mathfrak{I}_t) = E(S_{t+1}|S_1, S_2, S_2, ..., S_t)$$

$\mathfrak{I}_t$ is called a filtration based on past data. A financial model relating two periods is then an expression of a conditional filtration based on data up to time t relative to prior estimates and real observed data based on past filtrations.

Historical data are broadly available and in many frequencies, spanning the milliseconds of some electronic markets, daily data, monthly, as well as tick data tabulating transactions. Studies involving theory and estimations based on intraday data for volatility in a financial market include Admati and Pfleiderer (1988), Fung *et al.* (1994), and Andersen and Bollerslev (1997). For this reason, the models we construct ought to be concurrent to the data we use (see also Tapiero and Vallois (2016)). Historical data are used mostly for predictive purposes, while models-based implied estimates are using models to extrapolate theoretically potential (and statistical) future outcomes and seek their evidence at a current time. For example, statistical estimates of volatility are by definition conditional to a mean estimate, both of which are past data-based measurements (and therefore they are necessarily dependent if not treated appropriately to remove their dependence). These are implied by an autocorrelation, removed by using autoregressive conditional heteroscedasticity (ARCH) and generalized ARCH (GARCH) models profusely used in financial econometrics, as we shall see later.

2.2.6   Dependence

Practically, dependence arises because events may move statistically in a systematic manner. They may have latent and common causes or underlying factors (as they may depend on common information or common policies). In some cases, events may also feed each other, leading to complex feedback relationships and to a contagion. Generally, dependence can be spurious, measured by a correlation moment which would imply that prices tend to move in directions that are more or less concurrent. Dependence may also be causal. For example, a rise in a central bank's interest rate (in probability) affects the price of sovereign bonds, increases capital flows, and affects FX rates. When the probability of such events can be assessed statistically, estimates of the conditional events can be assessed by Bayes' theorem and over time by applying Bayesian (learning) recursive methods. Dependence may also be a signal and a symptom of common risk sources (e.g., macroeconomic factors affecting assets in a given portfolio) or result from real or statistical covariation. Although dependence is fundamental for economics and finance, it is loosely used, implying far more than is implied by a simple (non-causal) statistical covariation of prices and economic factors. In a global economy, dependence is prevalent at all levels and manifestations of the world economy. The definition of models that seek to structure causally the dependence of currencies and prices are therefore multivariate and complex.

Dependent processes are notoriously difficult to model and explain causally. For expository purposes, five types of dependence have been defined in the following, which summarizes their financial implications:

- Independence, with spurious prices' variations that are statistically independent of one another.
- Statistical dependence, with specific prices exhibiting a statistical covariation. Such situations testify to the effect that two securities' price movements seem to be statistically correlated without an explicit causal explanation of these movements. We differentiate between the correlation of two random variables and the autocorrelations in the same random variable at two different times. An autocorrelation, say at two instants of time, would mean that future states are in fact correlated to present states.
- Latent (or underlying) dependence occurs when two or more prices or events in two countries are subject to a common source of risk—whether arising due to rare events or not. In this case, the latent factor causes all prices to be affected at the same time, albeit in similar or other manners.
- Short-term memory dependence or persistence occurs when a price time path history determines subsequent unfolding probabilities of future prices. For example, if in the US presidential election a Libertarian is elected, we can expect that future financial policies will be altered accordingly and reflected in stochastic models that define stock prices.
- Long-run memory dependence (or autocorrelation) occurs when the long-past memory—or future expectations, singly or in concert—affects the evolution of prices, producing a nonlinear time growth in asset price variance and an autocorrelation of financial prices (i.e., stock prices at two different times are correlated). In such cases, in the long run, the variance of prices can be infinite, and therefore prices are presumed to be unpredictable (or to have an extremely large variance). Technically, long-run dependence or long-run memory is embedded in the autocorrelation of temporal events defined by a statistical regular property.

Each of these contributes to our approach to modeling and to the rich literature of quantitative modeling of financial models. From a global financial perspective, combining multiple factors, some of which are causal or conditionally causal, may be useful. For details on range process, long-range dependence, and long memory, see Barlow and Proschan, (1965, 1975), Taqqu (1986), Lo (1991, 1997), Beran (1994), Vallois and Tapiero (2007, 2009), and Tapiero and Vallois (2000, 2016).

The modeling of such dependence differs. The following are specific approaches which we will introduce by examples.

- Statistical functional dependence is model specific. For example, stochastic processes[7] are used to model and define stochastic relationships between current and future events.
- Spurious dependence or correlation is defined by a statistical property manifested in the measurements of two or more data sets.
- Copulas are algebraic models defining a multivariate density function by the distribution marginal density functions. As a result, dependence is probability-statistical parameterized by the algebraic model.
- Bayesian models are defined by the randomized probability that an event dependent on other occurs.

Example 2.2   Dependence and Correlation

The most common statistical approach to measurement of dependence is based on the correlation of two (or more) random variables. Let (x, y) be two random variables denoting the number of firms that defaulted in two countries. Their correlation ρ_{XY} is then defined, as stated earlier, by

$$\rho_{XY}\sigma_X\sigma_Y = E((x-E(x))(y-E(y))) \quad \text{or} \quad \text{cov}(x,y) = E(xy) - E(x)E(y)$$

where $\text{cov}(x, y)$ is the covariance of x and y and $\rho_{XY} \in [-1, +1]$. If $\rho = (0 >, < 0)$ is a correlation index indicating a dependence, with a volatility respectively growing and decreasing due to variables' codependence in defaults. In global finance, with increasingly dependent markets, their correlation may be far more complex due to a number of factors (whether economic, financial or otherwise) that ought to be accounted for. For example, let x_k be a CPI in a country k. Then, if $\text{cov}(x_k, x_j) = 0$, the CPIs of the two countries are independent. In global finance, these prices may be dependent, in which case $\text{cov}(x_k, x_j) \neq 0$. A global dependence assumes a greater number of factors, however. Say that a common global index CPI_G is defined by a continuous function $\text{CPI}_G = f(\text{CPI}_1, \text{CPI}_2, ..., \text{CPI}_n)$ and, therefore, the covariance with a CPI in country k with that index is $\text{cov}(\text{CPI}_k, \text{CPI}_G) \neq 0$. However, when we seek a more detailed relationship of codependence across countries, then, for a continuous function $f(\cdots)$ (Rubinstein, 1973; Stein, 1973; Wei and Lee, 1988), where CPI_j have a normal probability distribution, we have the following derived identity:

$$\text{cov}(\text{CPI}_k, f(\text{CPI}_1, \text{CPI}_2, ..., \text{CPI}_n)) = \sum_{j=1}^{n} E\left(\frac{\partial f(\text{CPI}_j)}{\partial \text{CPI}_j}\right) \text{cov}(\text{CPI}_k, \text{CPI}_j)$$

---

7 For details on stochastic processes, see for example Duncan *et al.* (2002) and Duncan (2006).

And for a single country, with a continuous functional random variable $f(y)$, we have

$$\text{cov}(\text{CPI}_k, f(y)) = E\left(\frac{\partial f(y)}{\partial y}\right)\text{cov}(\text{CPI}_k, y)$$

In this case, a covariance between a given country and an aggregate group of financial factors can be calculated.[8] The proof of the Stein–Rubinstein result is straightforward. Consider two normally distributed random variables x and y, where y is a standard variable, and set $x = \beta y + \varepsilon$, where $\text{cov}(y, \varepsilon) = 0$. Thus, $xy = \beta y_2 + \varepsilon y$ or $Exy = \beta E y_2 + E(\varepsilon y)$ and $\beta = \text{cov}(x, y)/\sigma_y^2$. Consider, the probability density function $g(x, y)$ and its covariance:

$$\text{cov}(y, f(x)) = \int_x \left[\int_y (y - \hat{y}) f(x) g(x, y)\, dy\, dx\right] \text{ or}$$

$$\text{cov}(y, f(x)) = \int_Y \left[\int_X (y - \hat{y}) f(ay + \varepsilon) g(y, by + \varepsilon)\, dy\, d\varepsilon\right]$$

Set $h(y, \varepsilon) = f(ay + \varepsilon)$ such that

$$\frac{\partial h}{\partial y} = \frac{\partial f}{\partial x}\frac{\partial x}{\partial y} = \frac{\partial f(ay + \varepsilon)}{\partial x}a$$

In this case, equating these results and assuming that $E\{\partial f(x)/\partial x\} < \infty$ and $E\{\partial h(y, \varepsilon)/\partial y\} < \infty$, we have the Stein–Rubinstein equation:

$$\text{cov}(y, f(x)) = E\left\{\frac{\partial h(y, \varepsilon)}{\partial y}\sigma_y^2\right\} = E\left\{\frac{\partial f(x)}{\partial x}\right\}\text{cov}(y, x)$$

For example, if $f(w, z) = aw^\alpha z^\beta$ is a cost estimate of production, a function of wages and capital, their covariance of the CPI and the cost of production estimate is

$$\text{cov}(\text{CPI}_k, aw^\alpha z^\beta) = E(a\alpha w^{\alpha-1} z^\beta)\text{cov}(\text{CPI}_k, w) + E(a\beta w^\alpha z^{\beta-1})\text{cov}(\text{CPI}_k, z)$$

These covariations are thus an indicator of dependence among both random variables and functional random variables. This assumes, however, that both wages and capital are normally distributed. Their applications to pricing and trade models within the capital asset pricing model (CAPM) and other models are considered in Chapter 9.

Example 2.3   Covariations Matrix
Using FX data from 2000 to 2016, Table 2.2 shows the covariations matrix for USD exchange rates to China's yuan (CNY), the Japanese yen (JPY), the Swiss franc (CHF), the euro (EUR), and British pound (GBP). We note that all currencies except for the British pound are positively correlated; namely, when one currency increases the other increases as well. In a mathematical model accounting for the correlation of currencies "noise," these correlations are to be considered.

---

8 A generalized formula replacing x by a polynomial function in x was suggested as well by Wei and Lee (1988). For an additional reference, see Losq and Chateau (1982).

Table 2.2 Correlations between exchange rates.

	USDCNY	USDJPY	USDCHF	USDEUR	USDGBP
USDCNY	1				
USDJPY	0.580	1			
USDCHF	0.860	0.614	1		
USDEUR	0.542	0.579	0.829	1	
USDGBP	−0.689	−0.713	−0.815	−0.868	1

Source: Data from IMF.

For a multivariate linear combination of random variables defining, say, baskets of FX currencies, we have then

$$\text{cov}\left(\sum_{i=1}^{m} a_i x_i, \sum_{j=1}^{n} b_j y_j \right) = \sum_{i=1}^{m} \sum_{j=1}^{n} a_i b_j \text{cov}(x_i, y_j)$$

Example 2.4   Covariations with Wages and Capital

Let y_1^1 and y_2 be two random variables denoting wages and capital in a country 1 and let $f_1(y_1^1, y_2)$ be a continuous function of these random variables, while y_1^2, y_2, and $f_2(y_1^2, y_2)$ are similar random variables in country 2. Then, assume a preference function (say a utility, as will be considered in Chapter 3), given by $u_1(c_1)$ and $u_2(c_2)$, their covariations are

$$\text{cov}(u_1, f_1(y_1^1, y_2)) = E\left(\frac{\partial f_1(y_1^1, y_2)}{\partial y_1^1} \right) \text{cov}(u_1, y_1^1) + E\left(\frac{\partial f_1(y_1^1, y_2)}{\partial y_2} \right) \text{cov}(u_1, y_2)$$

$$\text{cov}(u_2, f_2(y_1^2, y_2)) = E\left(\frac{\partial f_2(y_1^2, y_2)}{\partial y_1^2} \right) \text{cov}(u_2, y_1^2) + E\left(\frac{\partial f_2(y_1^2, y_2)}{\partial y_2} \right) \text{cov}(u_2, y_2)$$

As a result, we note that both countries have a common covariation with respect to y_2, resulting from their dependence on a common resource.

Examples 2.5   FX Data

Table 2.3 summarizes the statistics based on different time periods (not to be confused with time scales) of the FX including the euro, the British pound, Japanese yen, and Chinese yuan. We note that periods of upheaval are noted with greater range and greater volatility, while the skewness provides a preliminary indication that the underlying data depart from the normal probability distribution. These statistics vary by their FX since the economic relationships between countries and their FX differ both in kind and quantity. For example, Table 2.3 shows that while the EUR and GBP exchange rates were considerably stable during these periods, JPY and CNY became more volatile.

Example 2.6   Currency Baskets

Currency baskets can be used as a reference "currency" or as a "currency index" with respect to which a given currency can be compared or priced. Currently, the dominance of the US dollar has justified a currency price relative to that of the dollar. Such an approach underlies CAPMs and baskets consisting of international currencies with an

Table 2.3 Statistical summary of FX (1995–2016).

	January 1, 1995–December 31, 2005				January 1, 2006–December 31, 2008				January 1, 2009–June 30, 2016			
	EUR/$	GBP/$	$/JPY	$/CNY	EUR/$	GBP/$	$/JPY	$/CNY	EUR/$	GBP/$	$/JPY	$/CNY
Mean	1.1	1.6	114.2	8.3	1.4	1.9	112.5	7.5	1.3	1.6	96.2	6.4
St. Dev.	0.1	0.1	11.0	0.05	0.1	0.1	7.6	0.4	0.1	0.1	14.4	0.3
Kurtosis	−1.1	−0.2	0.6	10.1	−0.9	1.3	0.4	−1.4	−0.5	−0.1	−0.9	−1.2
Skewness	−0.2	0.5	−0.1	−1.5	0.5	−1.0	−1.0	−0.4	−0.6	−0.4	0.4	0.4
Range	0.5	0.6	66.6	0.4	0.4	0.7	36.7	1.3	0.5	0.4	49.8	0.8
Minimum	0.8	1.4	80.6	8.1	1.2	1.4	87.2	6.8	1	1.3	75.8	6
Maximum	1.4	1.9	147.3	8.4	1.6	2.1	123.9	8.1	1.5	1.7	125.6	6.8

Source: Data from IMF.
EUR/$ indicates USD per euro, GBP/$ is USD per pound, and $/JPY is Japanese yen per USD, $/CNY is Chinese yuan per USD. St. Dev.: standard deviation.

important part in dollars (see Chapter 3). Alternatively, consumption-based CAPMs (Chapters 3 and 8) or kernel pricing models are based on a consumer's rationality translated into an inter-temporal optimization of their utility of consumption (whether wealth or consumption). Although both these approaches are based on utility models, the treatment of these models in pricing financial assets and FX rates differs, as will be indicated in Chapter 3.

Table 2.4 presents daily RORs (excluding non-trading days: weekends and certain holidays) for selected currencies over different periods of time: period 1 for January 1995–December 2005, and period 2 for January 2006–June 2016. Emerging market currencies, such as for China and Singapore, show higher average returns as well as lower volatility than in other economies. Results for period 2 reflect the global financial crisis of 2007–2008, with lower or negative mean returns as well as increased volatility for certain developed and developing economies' currencies (such as GBP, EUR, Brazil, and South Africa) compared with the results for period 1. The reason for their fluctuations is that the global economic environment changes permanently, and in some cases certain periods might not be statistically comparable (as these periods would have underlying statistical population parameters that are appreciably different). A calculation of RORs' expectations, volatility, skewness, and kurtosis then indicates departure from normality, the prevalence of rare events, and other important aspects based on our interpretation of these statistical parameters.

Example 2.7   Market Indexes (Domestic and Global)
Consider a market index defined as a weighted sum of stock prices in a domestic market (and therefore in the same currency):

$$\tilde{S}_{\text{Index}}(t) = \sum_{i=1}^{n} w_i \tilde{S}_i(t)$$

where w_i is a weight associated with an asset i whose price at time t is a random variable $\tilde{S}_i(t)$. In this case, the index variance can be calculated easily if the assets have a known correlation. In this case:

$$E\left(\tilde{S}_{\text{Index}}(t)\right) = \sum_{i=1}^{n} w_i E\left(\tilde{S}_i(t)\right)$$

and

$$\text{var}\left(\tilde{S}_{\text{Index}}(t)\right) = \text{var}\left(\sum_{i=1}^{n} w_i \tilde{S}_i(t)\right)$$

$$= \sum_{i=1}^{n} w_i^2 \text{var}\left(\tilde{S}_i(t)\right) + 2\sum_{i=1}^{n}\sum_{k\neq i}^{n} w_i w_k \rho_{ik} \sqrt{\text{var}\left(\tilde{S}_i(t)\right)\text{var}\left(\tilde{S}_k(t)\right)}$$

Assuming that RORs have a normal probability distribution, the index of ROR can be written as

$$\frac{\tilde{S}_{\text{Index}}(t+\Delta t) - \tilde{S}_{\text{Index}}(t)}{\tilde{S}_{\text{Index}}(t)} = \sum_{i=1}^{n} w_i \frac{\tilde{S}_i(t+\Delta t) - \tilde{S}_i(t)}{\tilde{S}_i(t)} \quad \text{or} \quad \tilde{R}_{\text{Index}}(t) = \sum_{i=1}^{n} w_i \tilde{R}_i(t)$$

Table 2.4 Statistical summary of daily return for FX rates (1995–2016).

	January 1, 1995–December 31, 2005				January 1, 2006–June 30, 2016			
	Mean (%)	St. Dev.	Kurtosis	Skewness	Mean (%)	St. Dev.	Kurtosis	Skewness
R(CNY)	0.002	0.0004	2171.07	43.81	0.007	0.001	22.47	−0.95
R(JPY)	−0.0005	0.007	7.06	0.76	0.007	0.007	4.67	0.10
R(EUR)	0.0001	0.006	0.97	0.08	−0.0004	0.006	2.05	0.13
R(GBP)	0.005	0.005	1.23	0.03	−0.008	0.006	13.69	−1.15
R(CAD)	0.007	0.004	1.57	0.07	−0.002	0.006	2.66	−0.08
R(MXN)	−0.022	0.009	91.12	2.58	−0.017	0.008	9.74	−0.47
R(BRA)	−0.031	0.009	25.25	0.02	−0.006	0.011	5.11	−0.11
R(ZAR)	−0.016	0.010	15.73	0.15	−0.025	0.011	13.23	−0.96
R(INR)	−0.012	0.003	22.59	−0.68	−0.015	0.005	4.64	−0.09
R(KRW)	−0.005	0.011	117.62	1.38	−0.002	0.008	21.34	0.36
R(SGD)	−0.004	0.004	13.83	0.50	0.008	0.004	4.11	0.03

Source: Data from IMF.
GBP is British pound, JPY is Japanese yen, EUR is euro, CNY is Chinese yuan, CAD is Canadian dollar, ZAR is African rand, INR is Indian rupee, MXN is Mexican peso, BRA is Brazilian real, KRW is Korean won, and SGD is Singapore dollar.

Therefore, as indicated earlier:

$$E\left(\tilde{R}_{\text{Index}}(t)\right) = \sum_{i=1}^{n} w_i E\left(\tilde{R}_i(t)\right) \quad \text{and} \quad \text{var}\left(\tilde{R}_{\text{Index}}(t)\right) = \text{var}\left(\sum_{i=1}^{n} w_i \tilde{R}_i(t)\right)$$

Given the correlation matrix ρ_{ij}, we have

$$\text{var}\left(\tilde{R}_{\text{Index}}(t)\right) = \sum_{i=1}^{n} w_i^2 \text{var}\left(\tilde{R}_i(t)\right) + 2\sum_{i=1}^{n}\sum_{j\neq i}^{n} w_i w_j \rho_{ij} \sqrt{\text{var}\tilde{R}_i(t)} \sqrt{\text{var}\tilde{R}_j(t)}$$

If all these returns are positively correlated (if they are all subject to a common risk factor), holding on to an index would seem to be more risky than constructing one's own index, better suited to one's needs and exhibiting potentially a smaller variance. Further, if the index is subject to a specific source of risk, say a latent factor, that other securities are not affected by, a drop in the index price will necessarily affect the price of each of these factors. However, if an index falls suddenly due to a specific factor, the holder of the index may be partially protected by their holdings due to the index's compensation effect (i.e., its safety in an aggregate holding of factors' risks). In practice, statistical dependence is not easily expressed in terms of factors' price correlations and, therefore, requires other approaches—both empirical and modeling based. Assuming that globalization contributes to an increased dependence, domestic markets and foreign ones may be positively correlated and may lead in fact to greater risks (if indeed these are measured by the indexes' variance). If this is the case, financial globalization ought to be interpreted in its traditional sense, namely, greater risks demand greater returns.

A global financial index, however, combines securities' prices with two sources of risk: the security priced in local currency and its FX risk. For simplicity, say that a global index is defined by the local ROR of the country's treasury bills and their own market index. In this case, the global price in US dollars is not normally distributed, as assumed previously, since

$$\tilde{S}_{Gi}(t) = \sum_{k\neq i}^{n} w_k \tilde{\xi}_{ik}\tilde{S}_k(t) + \left(1 - \sum_{k\neq i}^{n} w_k\right)B_{f,i}(t), \quad \sum_{i=1}^{n} w_i = 1$$

Therefore:

$$E\left(\tilde{S}_{Gi}(t)\right) = \sum_{k\neq i}^{n} w_k E\left(\tilde{\xi}_{ik}\tilde{S}_k(t)\right) + \left(1 - \sum_{k\neq i}^{n} w_k\right)B_{f,i}(t)$$

$$E\left(\tilde{S}_{Gi}(t)\right) = \text{var}\left(\sum_{k\neq i}^{n} w_k\left(\tilde{\xi}_{ik}\tilde{S}_k(t)\right)\right) = \sum_{k\neq i}^{n} w_k^2 \text{var}\left(\tilde{\xi}_{ik}\tilde{S}_k(t)\right)$$

$$+ 2\sum_{k\neq i1}^{n}\sum_{j\neq k}^{n} w_k w_j \rho_{kj} \sqrt{\text{var}\tilde{S}_k(t)} \sqrt{\text{var}\tilde{S}_j(t)}$$

where

$$E\left(\tilde{\xi}_{ik}\tilde{S}_k(t)\right) = E\left(\tilde{\xi}_{ik}\right)E\left(\tilde{S}_k(t)\right) + \rho_{\tilde{\xi}\tilde{R}}\sqrt{\text{var}\left(\tilde{\xi}_{ik}\right)\text{var}\left(\tilde{S}_k(t)\right)}$$

$$\mathrm{var}\left(\tilde{\xi}_{ik}\tilde{S}_k(t)\right) = E\left(\tilde{\xi}_{ik}\tilde{S}_k(t)\right)^2 - \left[E\left(\tilde{\xi}_{ik}\tilde{S}_k(t)\right)\right]^2$$

and

$$E\left(\tilde{\xi}_{ik}\tilde{S}_k(t)\right)^2 = E\left(\tilde{\xi}_{ik}^2\tilde{S}_k^2(t)\right) = E\left(\tilde{\xi}_{ik}^2\right)E\left(\tilde{S}_k^2(t)\right) + \rho_{\tilde{\xi}_{ik}^2\tilde{R}_k^2(t)}\sqrt{\mathrm{var}\left(\tilde{\xi}_{ik}^2\right)\mathrm{var}\left(\tilde{S}_k^2(t)\right)}$$

The statistical moments of portfolios are therefore more complex to calculate and require greater numerical attention. In global financial models, such problems commonly recur and express the complexity of integrating FX rates and multiple countries' variables in the calculations of cross-national boundary portfolios. However, such simple observations imply that if one invests in a global portfolio with market prices measured in one's own currency, one would expect greater returns for the risk-variance that such a portfolio assumes.

2.2.7 Risk Exposure

Risk exposure is an ex-ante measure providing a probability estimate of loss over a specified period of time and over a specified potential loss. The common approach to risk exposure is based on a set of axioms suggested by Artzner *et al.* (1997, 1999). They define a rational measurement of actuarial risk[9] that consists of the following conditions:

- monotonicity, meaning that the riskier the assets held, the larger the required reserve;
- invariance by drift; that is, if the prices of a portfolio increase by a fixed quantity then their required reserve remains the same;
- homogeneity, requiring that reserve be proportional to a portfolio price;
- sub-additivity.

These conditions are an outgrowth of regulators' requirements for banks to set aside as part of their capital (VaR or value at risk) to meet future loss contingencies—for VaR, see Jorion (1997), Gourieroux *et al.* (2000), and Tapiero (2005a,b, 2013). These conditions imply convexity of the reserve; that is, the greater the risk, the greater the reserve; but greater risk acceleration reduces the required and proportional reserves. It also provides an economic advantage for merging portfolio holdings (i.e., diversification). These conditions have been broadly applied through Basel (II and III) regulation as well as by US regulators in the application of various forms of VaR (as we shall see subsequently in Chapter 10). For example, having no liquidity to meet a claim when it occurs due to a lack of capital set aside for such purposes. Various countries regulate their banks to hold liquid assets to reduce their risk of default. Each country, however, has different rules, controls, and penalties in case of banks' noncompliance (see Chapter 10). Financial compliance in a global environment is a multi-country compliance requirement, which is far more complex. First, most countries have their own regulation and differ in their legal procedures and intent when they regulate and apply penalties on corporate firms. A global compliance implies the compliance to an extremely large number of regulations, some ambiguous and difficult to comply with. Business in a global financial world also involves taxation issues, FX, political cultures, nationalization, and, not least, legal

---

9 For studies on actuarial risk see Bowers *et al.* (1997), Tapiero (2004), and Denuit *et al.* (2005).

and ownership rights and structures limiting foreign agents. These many factors compound the definition of the risks we may have to consider when assessing and pricing foreign ventures (see Chapter 10).

2.3 Volatility and Implied Models Estimates

Volatility is a fundamental statistic for financial pricing and risk measurements. Black (1976) and Christie (1982) show that volatility is a function of debt; Merton (1973) and French *et al.* (1987) point to a function of change in expected RORs and in interest rates. Similarly, excess volatility may be a signal revealing the economic instability in foreign lands, and so on. There are numerous approaches to measure volatility—whether based on historical data or implied volatility (based on future prices, currently traded options). Further, volatility estimates may depend on factors such as the date at which the volatility is estimated, and the measurements' granularity (the time span over which volatility is measured), the sample information used, and the prediction horizon. Predictive variables, such as market prices, interest rates, and external information, contributing to estimating stabilized or destabilized markets, render the estimate of volatility difficult. It is therefore a conditional expectation which is estimated based on the information, its granularity, and the models we use (the best prediction based on the sample information used). Volatility models are also varied, including assumptions of constant volatility, random walk volatility models, perturbed (stochastic) random walks, and continuous and discrete time stochastic volatility models—for references, see Stein and Stein (1991), Weiss (1994), Vallois (1996), and Vallois and Tapiero (1996, 1997a,b, 2007). Examples we consider subsequently highlight some of these approaches and their differences. Further, these problems will be considered in greater detail in Chapter 7.

2.3.1 Simple Volatility Estimates

Let FX RORs be defined by $R_{t+1} = \mu_t + \varepsilon_{t+1}$, where ε_{t+1} is a standard normal random variable. Then, $\mu_t = E_t(R_{t+1})$ while the variance is $\sigma_t^2 = E_t(\varepsilon_{t+1}^2) = E_t(R_{t+1}^2) - \mu_t^2$. A naive estimate of the variance is then

$$\hat{\sigma}_t^2 = E_t(R_{t+1}^2) = \frac{1}{T}\sum_{i=1}^{T} R_{t+i-1}^2$$

with $w_i(t) = 1/T$ the weight given to an observation at time $0 < i \leq T$. A generalization, still naive, consists of associating weights with these observations, in which case:

$$\hat{\sigma}_t^2 = E_t(R_{t+1}^2) = w_0 + \sum_{i=1}^{k} w_i(t)R_{t+i-1}^2$$

Further, to reduce the number of weight parameters, we can model weights by $w_i(t) = \theta^{i-1}(1-\theta)$, $0 \leq \theta^{i-1} \leq 1$, and obtain the risk-metric estimation:

$$\hat{\sigma}_t^2 = E_t(R_{t+1}^2) = (1-\theta)\sum_{i=1}^{\infty} \theta^{i-1} R_{t+i-1}^2$$

Estimates based on daily data also vary. Using end-of-day data, the mean-variance estimate based on the normal model treated above may be written as

$$\hat{\mu} = \frac{1}{n} \sum_{t=1}^{n} R_t, \quad \hat{\sigma}_2 = \frac{1}{n-1} \sum_{t=1}^{n} (R_t - \hat{\mu})^2$$

However, estimates of moments-skewness and kurtosis, may point out that the underlying assumption of "model normality" is not appropriate. For this reason, other estimates were suggested, such as the Parkinson (1980) estimator—which was also used in security price volatility (Kunitomo, 1995)—based on high (H_t) and low (L_t) day data statistics commonly available:

$$\hat{\sigma}_{\text{Park},t}^2 = \frac{[\ln H_t - \ln L_t]^2}{4 \ln(2)}$$

These estimates are based on a relationship between the range of an underlying normal probability distribution and its volatility. In this sense, it subsumes that data to be normally distributed. These estimates were adjusted further to better fit data, such as the weighted high/low statistic:

$$\hat{\sigma} = 0.627 \frac{\sum_{t=1}^{n} W_t \ln(H_t / L_t)}{\sum_{t=1}^{n} W_t}$$

Or, using the Garman–Klass statistics-based process (Garman and Klass, 1980) rather than RORs, or

$$\hat{\sigma}_{\text{GK},t}^2 = 0.5 [\ln(H_t / L_t)]^2 - 0.39 [\ln(\xi_t / \xi_{t-1})]^2$$

Finally, Mandelbrot and Van Ness (1968) pointed out that FX data are time auto-correlated and, therefore, long-run dependent. As a result, naive estimates that do not account for this autocorrelation are necessarily inappropriate. To overcome such problems, as well as to construct volatility models rather than naive models, ARCH and GARCH techniques have been suggested by Engle (1982) and Bollerslev (1986), leading to a broad variety of such models. These are considered later in this chapter.

2.3.2 Implied Volatility

Option prices are current prices of a future and random state (i.e., a random price). When a pricing of a future model price is given, and its future price is defined by its currently traded price, one price defines the other, and vice versa. In this sense, an implied price is a future price implied in a current price. Option prices (as we shall see in Chapter 7) may be defined in terms of a number of parameters we know for sure, except for the volatility. Thus, given a current observable price, its future volatility is uniquely defined, and vice versa. For these reasons, implied volatility models are essentially defined by inverse models. Calculating the volatility using options data, however, differs fundamentally from ARCH–GARCH estimates. The latter are based on past data, the former is based on a pricing model and current data (the past is in this case irrelevant). Thus, an implied volatility is defined by an inverse model price:

$$\text{Volatility} = \text{Model}^{-1}(\text{Data, Option price})$$

A volatility thus calculated provides an assessment of current beliefs regarding the future (or forward-looking) which is embedded in the model we use to predict the future price. Bankers use this information to assess the current market belief regarding future prices as well as hedge their future risks. It is also a tool for traders, investors, and speculators who assume financial positions based on their beliefs and the information they have (which might differ from the current market beliefs). In global finance, options are used to hedge future foreign risks and currency prices. Such an approach differs substantially from the statistical approach based on past prices; therefore, they need not be the same.

A simple example outlines this procedure. Let the evolution of an FX price be defined by a binomial model; in other words, the future FX can assume one of two prices:

$$FX_{t+1} = \begin{cases} FX_{t+1}^{+} & \text{If the price has increased in } (t,t+1) \\ FX_{t+1}^{-} & \text{If the price has decreased in } (t,t+1) \end{cases}$$

Say that an exchange (e.g., an insurance FX contract) is reached at time t, with the seller (insurer) collecting $\$C_t$ from the buyer (say on a foreign transaction) assuring the buyer of a price FX_{t+1}^{+} at time $t+1$, regardless of variations in the asset price. The payment set initially is thus an insurance risk premium guaranteeing the payment of (at an FX rate) FX_{t+1}^{+}.

By the same token, assume that the buyer (in the same country) pays C_t at time t for the guarantee that their price is at least K with $FX_{t+1}^{-}(\sigma_{t+1}) < K < FX_{t+1}^{+}(\sigma_{t+1})$, where σ_{t+1} is the unknown future volatility. The risk premium is then the price of the implied future volatility, which, although unknown at time t, is in fact surmised by traders that through their current transactions defines a relationship between the current and the future prices through an economic model we owe to Arrow and Debreu. In other words, setting

$$\text{Max}\{FX_{t+1}(\sigma_{t+1}) - K, 0\} = \begin{cases} FX_{t+1}^{+}(\sigma_{t+1}) - K > 0 \\ FX_{t+1}^{-}(\sigma_{t+1}) - K < 0 \end{cases}$$

Since its current price is C_t, the risk premium currently traded is defined by an appropriate financial model expressed by a probability (model) measure denoted by Q with the expectation establishing a unique relationship:

$$C_t \Leftrightarrow E^Q\{\text{Max}\{FX_{t+1}(\sigma_{t+1}) - K, 0\}\}$$

Such an approach defines the fundamental finance approach.

Example 2.8 The VIX—A Traded Volatility Index

The VIX is a weighted basket of implied volatilities with a maturity of a month ahead on the S&P financial index. Explicitly, these are volatilities implied by the prices of options currently traded on financial markets. The VIX was introduced by the Chicago Board of Exchange and its price reflects the predisposition of investors regarding the future volatility. It is also called a "fear index" as it is believed that it indicates the fear of investors regarding the financial market index as a whole. Trades on the VIX provide then investors the buying and the selling of future volatilities and thereby to manage future risks. The popularity of this index has been expanded to a number of financial indexes in different countries, providing thereby the means to compare the expectation of index price volatility in the future. The technique is simple and will be considered in Chapter 7.

2.3.3 Moving Average and Autoregressive Moving Average Models

Moving average (MA) and autoregressive moving average (ARMA) models are linear models based on past data. Consider n normally distributed random variables, each identically and independently distributed (iid) with zero mean and unit variance, $w_i \sim N(0,1)$, and let there be n constants c_n. Let z_t be a random variable given at time t by the MA weighted average model:

$$z_t = w_t + c_1 w_{t-1} + c_2 w_{t-2} + c_3 w_{t-3} + \cdots + c_n w_{t-n}$$

We can rewrite this process as a linear system as follows and set the vector:

$$x_t = [w_{t-n}, w_{t-n+1}, \ldots, w_{t-1}]$$

By definition, and in vector notation, we thus have

$$x_{t+1} = A x_t + B w_t$$

where

$$
A = \begin{bmatrix}
0 & 1 & 0 & 0 & \cdots & \cdots & \cdots & \cdots & 0 & 0 \\
0 & 0 & 1 & 0 & \cdots & \cdots & \cdots & \cdots & 0 & 0 \\
\cdots & \cdots & \cdots & & & & & & & \\
0 & 0 & 0 & 0 & & & & & 0 & 1 \\
0 & 0 & 0 & 0 & & & & & 0 & 0
\end{bmatrix}
; \quad B = \begin{bmatrix}
0 \\
0 \\
\cdots \\
\cdots \\
1
\end{bmatrix}
$$

Of course, we can construct processes which are combinations of AR (autoregressive) and MA models. These are called ARMA models and have been the topic of intensive study (e.g., see Barnard (1959) and Box and Jenkins (1976)). An ARMA process is defined by a vector difference equation of the form:

$$z_t + A_{1t} z_{t-1} + \cdots + A_{nt} z_{t-n} = B_{0t} v_t + B_{1t} v_{t-1} + \cdots + B_{mt} v_{t-m}$$

The variables $v_t, v_{t-1}, \ldots, v_{t-m}$ are zero mean and normally distributed random variables, while $z_t, z_{t-1}, \ldots, z_{t-n}$ are the process dependent variables. It is also possible to express the set of equations above into a multivariate linear system of difference equations taking the form

$$\mathbf{x}_{t+1} = \mathbf{A}_t \mathbf{x}_t + \mathbf{B}_t \mathbf{v}_t$$

where $\mathbf{x}_{t+1}$, $\mathbf{x}_t$, and $\mathbf{v}_t$ are vectors of appropriate dimensions and $\mathbf{A}_t$ and $\mathbf{B}_t$ are matrices which are defined according to the ARMA process used. Such a multivariate linear representation simplifies the analysis of such models.

2.3.4 ARCH–GARCH Volatility Models

For normal returns with known mean and known volatility, an observation can be written in terms of standard normal variations such as z-scores: $z_t = \left(\tilde{R}_t - \mu_t\right)/\sigma_t \sim N(0,1)$. Thus, for mean returns' estimates based on a data set consisting of returns (normally distributed), we can write $\tilde{R}_t = \mu_t + \sigma_t z_t$, with the mean estimated either by linear regression or by maximizing the likelihood of the data set. However, this procedure presumes that the standard deviation is known (as both depend on the other in a data sample). If the standard deviation (volatility) has to be estimated as well using the same data set, there are statistical problems due to the dependence of both parameters on the same data set. These situations have motivated estimation techniques coined ARCH and GARCH. Engle (1982) in particular has suggested that we remove this codependence between the means and the variance estimators and thereby deal with the heteroscedasticity of data. Note that a data set is homoscedastic if its residuals (once estimators are determined) are uniformly randomly distributed. When a data set exhibits non-uniformly distributed random residuals, and in particular a dependence, we call it heteroscedastic. Removing the dependence from the residual once a mean has been estimated and using the adjusted residuals to estimate the standard deviation defines the ARCH and GARCH approaches.

The assumption of constant volatility (homoscedasticity) has repeatedly been contradicted in financial time series. Fluctuations in returns of actual assets tend to cluster. A turbulent trading day tends to be followed by another turbulent day, while a tranquil period tends to be followed by another tranquil period. This means that there are memory effects where past fluctuations in returns influence current and future fluctuations. The normal model assumes, however, that all information is contained within the current asset price and hence it is reasonable to assume no memory (which is a contradiction).

There is an extensive literature on financial econometrics and its applications to the estimation of volatility (e.g., Brockwell and Davis, 1986; Bollerslev *et al.*, 1994; Beckers, 1996; Engle, 2002; Alizadeh *et al.*, 2002; Bouchaud and Potters, 2003; Ang *et al.*, 2006; Embrechts *et al.*, 2007; Andersen *et al.*, 2009) to the estimation of volatility. Consider, for example, the ROR on a financial index in any given country, and for simplicity say that it is modeled by the linear models $R_t = \mu + \varepsilon_t$, where ε_t is a normally distributed random variable with zero mean and variance σ^2. Such a model is extended in several ways including the linear models:

$$\text{Linear}: R_t = \mu + \sum_{i=0} \lambda_i \varepsilon_{t-i}$$

$$\text{MA}(q): R_t = \mu + \varepsilon_t - \sum_{i=1}^{q} \lambda_i \varepsilon_{t-i}$$

$$\text{ARMA}(p,q): R_t = \mu + \sum_{i=0} \lambda_i R_{t-i} + \varepsilon_t + \sum_{i=0} \lambda_i \varepsilon_{t-i}$$

These models, however, are heteroscedastic. Namely, the expected value of $E\left((\varepsilon_t)^2 | \sigma^2\right)$ is defined as a function of σ^2. Such a property occurs commonly in the statistical analysis of financial data. In this case, in a regression of $R_t = \mu + \varepsilon_t$, the estimate of μ is necessarily also a function of the variance and therefore of $\hat{\mu}(\sigma^2)$. Assuming a conditional hetero-scedasticity, we have then a condition we call homoscedastic:

$$E\left(\varepsilon_t|R_j, j=1,\ldots,t-1\right) = 0 \quad \text{and} \quad E\left(\varepsilon_t^2|R_j, j=1,2,\ldots,t-1\right) = \sigma^2$$

where $\varepsilon \sim N(0,\sigma^2)$. With these assumptions the following models may result:

$$R_t = \sigma_{t-1}\varepsilon_t \quad \text{and} \quad \sigma_t^2 = w + \beta_1\sigma_{t-1}^2 + \alpha_1 R_t^2$$

and more generally the GARCH model:

$$R_t = \sigma_{t-1}\varepsilon_t \quad \text{and} \quad \sigma_t^2 = w + \sum_{k=1}^{p}\beta_k\sigma_{t-k}^2 + \sum_{i=1}^{q}\alpha_i R_{t-i-1}^2$$

2.3.4.1 The AR(1)–GARCH(1) Model

The simplest model suggested by Engle (1982) is the AR(1)–GARCH(1) model, explicitly stated as follows. First, assume an autoregressive returns process AR(1) model as defined earlier:

$$\tilde{R}_t = \alpha R_{t-1} + \varepsilon_t, \quad |\alpha| < 1$$

where ε_t are assumed iid as defined earlier with zero mean and variance σ^2. Now let $\mathfrak{R}^{t-1}$ be a security returns time series observed and therefore available at time $t-1$, with $\mathfrak{R}^{t-1} = \{R_0, R_1, \ldots, R_{t-1}\}$. Assuming the AR(1) model, the returns expectation conditionally on the data set is

$$E(\varepsilon_t) = 0, \quad E\left(\tilde{R}_t|\mathfrak{R}^{t-1}\right) = \alpha R_{t-1}$$

while the variance estimator is also an unbiased estimator of the variance since

$$\text{var}\left(\tilde{R}_t\right) = \alpha^2\text{var}(R_{t-1}) + \text{var}(\varepsilon_t) \quad \text{or} \quad \text{var}\left(\tilde{R}_t\right) = \frac{\text{var}(\varepsilon_t)}{1-\alpha^2} = \frac{\sigma^2}{1-\alpha^2} \quad \text{or}$$

$$\text{var}\left(\tilde{R}_t\right) = \frac{\sigma^2}{1-\alpha^2} \quad \text{while} \quad \text{var}\left(\tilde{R}_t|\mathfrak{R}^{t-1}\right) = E\left\{\left[\tilde{R}_t - E\left(\tilde{R}_t|\mathfrak{R}^{t-1}\right)\right]^2|\mathfrak{R}^{t-1}\right\} = \sigma^2$$

Note that the variance estimators are constant over time. Further, these variances are independent of the information available up to time t, or $\{\mathfrak{R}^t, t \geq 0\}$. The need for conditioning the variance estimator on the available information (the time series) underlies ARCH and GARCH models. For the AR(1) model, Engle (1982) proposed that the error variance be set as a linear function of the past error, in which case

$$E\left(\varepsilon_t|\mathfrak{R}^{t-1}\right) = 0, \quad \text{var}\left(\varepsilon_t|\mathfrak{R}^{t-1}\right) = \alpha_0 + \alpha_1\varepsilon_{t-1}^2, \quad \alpha_0 > 0, \quad \alpha_1 \geq 0$$

where the information available on hand is now $\mathfrak{R}^{t-1} = \{R_{t-1}, R_{t-2}, \ldots\} = \{\varepsilon_{t-1}, \varepsilon_{t-2}, \ldots\}$ since by definition of the AR(1) process we have $\varepsilon_{t-i} = \tilde{R}_{t-i} - \alpha R_{t-1-i}$. The parameter $|\alpha| < 1$ assumes that the R process is stationary at the second order while the positive values for α_0 and α_1 guarantee that the conditional variance is positive. The AR(1) model with errors specified above is known as the ARCH(1) model. The error estimate term in this case is $\nu_t = \varepsilon_t^2 - \text{var}(\varepsilon_t|Y^{t-1})$, written by the AR(1) model: $\varepsilon_t^2 = \alpha_0 + \alpha_1\varepsilon_{t-1}^2 + \nu_t$. Further, if $\alpha_1 < 1$, it is easy to show that $\text{var}(\varepsilon_t) = \alpha_0/(1-\alpha_1)$ and, as a result, that

$\mathrm{var}\left(\varepsilon_t|\mathfrak{R}^{t-1}\right) - \mathrm{var}(\varepsilon_t) = \alpha_1\left(\varepsilon_{t-1}^2 - \sigma^2\right)$. Thus, the error variance is only a function of the information available up to this time. This approach can be generalized further by considering a general linear regression where the error term is also estimated. This brief introduction to ARCH and GARCH models highlights some of the considerations we must keep in mind when dealing with the estimation of an underlying process variance (its volatility).

An alternative model for the volatility is provided by the GARCH model (Bollerslev, 1986). It is specified by assuming that the conditional error term has a zero mean normal probability distribution with a model variance h_t, or $\left(\varepsilon_t|\mathfrak{R}^{t-1}\right) \sim N(0,h_t)$, where

$$h_t = \alpha_0 + \alpha_1\varepsilon_{t-1}^2 + \alpha_2\varepsilon_{t-2}^2 + \alpha_3\varepsilon_{t-3}^2 + \ldots + \alpha_q\varepsilon_{t-q}^2 + \gamma_1 h_{t-1} + \gamma_2 h_{t-2} + \ldots + \gamma_p h_{t-p}$$
$$\alpha_0 > 0, \alpha_i \geq 0, i = 1,2,\ldots,q \text{ and } \gamma_j, j = 1,2,\ldots,p$$

which defines a GARCH (p,q) model. In this case, the model is estimated by

$$z_t = x_t'\beta + \varepsilon_t, \quad t = 1,2,\ldots,T$$

with a conditional error $\left(\varepsilon_t|\mathfrak{R}^{t-1}\right) \sim N(0,h_t)$.

2.3.5   ARCH–GARCH Model: Empirical Evidence

We consider, for example, a data set consisting of the FX rates of the US dollar, the yen (JPY) and the British pound (GBP). The data are detrended from their mean evolution over time and therefore we have the data set residuals. Then, we also construct simple ARCH and GARCH models.

Based on historical data, a time-varying volatility is estimated for different FX rates through an ARCH(1) model first. Figure 2.4 shows the daily returns on \$/JPY and on GBP/\$ from January 1, 1990, through August 31, 2015. There are periods of increased volatility or turbulence and considerably sedate periods or tranquility indicating volatility clustering. Thus, these swings seem to exhibit a time-varying variance of the return for FX with autocorrelated swings. For the daily exchange rate returns for JPY, its variance is about 0.4618. The volatility in Figure 2.4 for return for JPY is obviously not captured by this variance. This is also seen from the GBP. An underlying volatility of the JPY as well as GBP returns is measured by the ARCH model and its extensions such as GARCH.

At first, we test for the conditional heteroscedasticity by plotting the autocorrelogram (autocorrelation function) for the squared returns (with 100 lags). The results in Figure 2.5 show a long memory with significant autocorrelation or ARCH effects (which will be analyzed in Section 2.4).

The "mean equation" for an estimation of the daily return for JPY is

$$\mathrm{JPY}_t = \mu + e_t, \quad e_t \sim \mathrm{iid}N\left(0,\sigma_t^2\right)$$

where μ is a constant that represents the mean and e is an error term that is assumed to be normally distributed with zero mean and variance of $v_t = \sigma_t^2$.

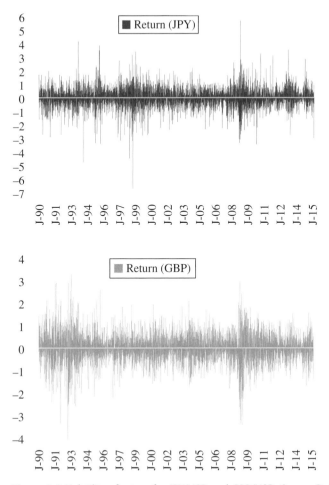

Figure 2.4 Volatility of return for JPY/USD and GBP/USD. *Source:* Data from Bloomberg.

Next, we introduce an ARCH effect. The "variance equation" for the error v_t for an ARCH(1) model is as follows, with a positive coefficient to ensure that variance is positive:[10]

$$v_t = \beta + \beta_1 e_{t-1}^2, \quad 0 < \beta_1 < 1$$

Since there is an ARCH effect, as shown in Table 2.5, further estimation of the ARCH (1) model and its results are presented in Table 2.6. The mean and the variance equations are shown separately. An estimated coefficient on the ARCH term in the variance equation, $\beta_1 = 0.1981$, is positive and statistically significant. Thus, we find that variance is autoregressive and conditionally heteroscedastic.

For additional lags of the variance in the ARCH model and to ensure that coefficients in the variance equation are positive, we estimate the GARCH model. In the following

---

10 Other independent variables, such as macroeconomic statistics and news, can be added to the regression model.

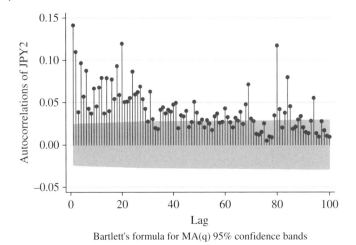

Bartlett's formula for MA(q) 95% confidence bands

Figure 2.5 Autocorrelation of squared returns, $/JPY.

Table 2.5 The LM test used for testing the ARCH effects.

	JPY			GBP		
Lags(p)	χ^2	Df	Prob $> \chi^2$	χ^2	Df	Prob $> \chi^2$
1	133.483	1	0.0000	123.213	1	0.0000

H_0: no ARCH effects versus H_1: ARCH(p) disturbance H_0: no ARCH versus H_1: ARCH(p) disturbance

Table 2.6 ARCH(1) estimation.

	JPY				GBP			
	Coeff.	SE	z	P	Coeff.	SE	z	P
Constant	0.0072	0.0078	0.93	0.354	0.0069	0.0069	1	0.316
ARCH Lag1	0.1981	0.0103	19.21	0.000	0.1523	0.0111	13.66	0.000
ARCH constant	0.3729	0.0053	70.02	0.000	0.2887	0.0042	68.69	0.000

Table 2.7 GARCH(1,1) estimation.

	JPY				GBP			
	Coeff.	SE	z	P	Coeff.	SE	z	P
Constant	0.0071	0.0071	1.00	0.318	0.0085	0.006	1.41	0.159
ARCH Lag1	0.4611	0.0028	16.64	0.000	0.0353	0.0026	13.81	0.000
GARCH Lag1	0.9411	0.0037	254.40	0.000	0.9587	0.0029	328.57	0.000
ARCH constant	0.0062	0.0007	8.56	0.000	0.0019	0.0003	5.96	0.000

GARCH(1, 1) model, it has 1 lag of squared residuals (ARCH term) and 1 lag of the variance:

$$v_t = \gamma + \beta_1 e_{t-1}^2 + \mu_1 v_{t-1}$$

The estimation for a GARCH(1, 1) model for the JPY return is shown in Table 2.7. For JPY return, coefficients on the ARCH and GARCH terms are both positive and statistically significant. Thus, we find evidence of an ARCH effect, as current conditional variance is affected by the lagged one.

A further extension of the GARCH model is threshold GARCH (T-GARCH) with asymmetric news (positive and negative news):

$$v_t = \gamma + \beta_1 e_{t-1}^2 + \mu_1 v_{t-1} + \beta_2 k_{t-1} e_{t-1}^2$$

where $k_t = 1$ with bad news ($e_t < 0$) and $k_t = 0$ with good news ($e_t \geq 0$). An estimation of this T-GARCH model for the return for JPY is shown in Table 2.8.

Another extension of the model is GARCH-in-mean (M-GARCH), where the mean regression function incorporates a risk factor, measured by the conditional variance v_t (for details, see Gujarati (2014)). A positive estimated coefficient on this variance will make the average return higher. This extension of the GARCH model estimates the following regression:

$$JPY_t = \mu + \vartheta v_t + e_t$$

Table 2.8 T-GARCH(1,1) estimation.

	JPY				GBP			
	Coeff.	SE	z	P	Coeff.	SE	z	P
constant	0.003	0.007	0.44	0.66	0.006	0.006	0.94	0.35
ARCH (1)	0.062	0.004	16.11	0.000	0.041	0.003	12.09	0.000
T-GARCH(1)	−0.028	0.004	−6.4	0.000	−0.014	0.004	−3.37	0.001
GARCH(1)	0.936	0.004	236.5	0.000	0.959	0.003	331.4	0.000
ARCH constant	0.007	0.001	9.25	0.000	0.002	0.000	6.35	0.000

Table 2.9 M-GARCH(1,1) estimation.

	JPY				GBP			
	Coeff.	SE	z	P	Coeff.	SE	z	P
Constant	0.0075	0.0160	0.47	0.639	0.0212	0.012	1.7	0.088
M-GARCH	−0.0010	0.0383	−0.03	0.978	−0.059	0.0417	−1.42	0.155
ARCH(1)	0.0461	0.0028	16.63	0.000	0.0417	0.0035	12.06	0.000
GARCH(1)	0.9411	0.0037	254.28	0.000	0.959	0.0029	330.18	0.000
ARCH constant	0.0062	0.0007	8.55	0.000	0.0021	0.0003	6.27	0.000

M-GARCH estimation results for return on JPY are shown in Table 2.9.

We can forecast the future conditional volatility using the estimated coefficients. For example, the next period volatility can be estimated based on the current variables as in the following GARCH(1, 1) model (we use the estimates of the coefficients in Table 2.7):

$$v_{t+1} = \gamma + \beta_1 e_t^2 + \mu_1 v_t$$

Conditional variances estimated from ARCH(1) and GARCH(1, 1) models are shown in Figure 2.6. There is a lot of volatility, especially during the late 1990s and the late 2000s for JPY, and early 1990s and late 2000s for GBP.

Questions and Problems 2

Analyze the volatility of daily returns for other currencies, such as AUD. Conduct the test for the ARCH effect and test if the variance is autoregressive conditionally heteroscedastic. Estimate the ARCH model first. For the number of lagged terms, use the Akaike or Schwarz information criterion. Estimate the GARCH, T-GARCH, and M-GARCH models.

2.4 Stochastic Models

Stochastic models, as stated earlier, establish a temporal relationship between random events. Models are varied and defined by theories, generally tested empirically. They consist of functional models, based on the hypotheses we make regarding the relationships that underlie data. For example, linear models, exponential models, or systems of simultaneous equations may define a prior set of relationships between, say, asset prices in several countries. In this case, data are applied to these models and their parameters are estimated and validated statistically. Alternatively, we define data sets and seek models, algorithms, and an "intelligence" that will construct the model that best accounts for the data. When the data set is extremely large (say big data), we first seek to downsize the number of factors or variables that characterize the data set so that it may become treatable. In the following, we consider a number of RORs models that may integrate well FX time-series prices. Spot FX rates will be transformed for convenience to RORs and

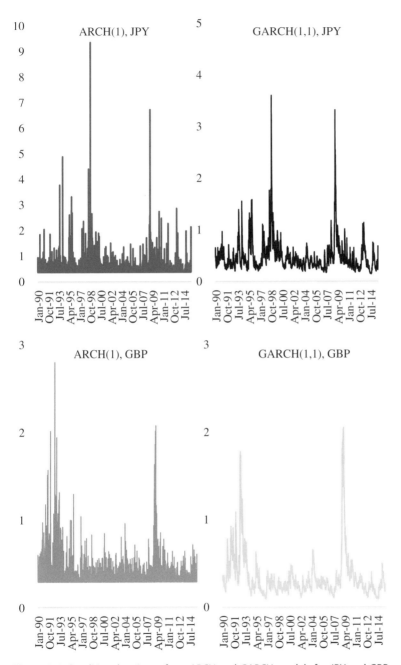

Figure 2.6 Conditional variance from ARCH and GARCH models for JPY and GBP.

modeled accordingly. ROR financial models abound and are based on extremely simple rationales tested by financial econometric statistics. Essential models include:

- the constant ROR model hypothesis;
- mean reversion models;
- implied (or inverse) financial models;
- ARCH–GARCH models.

2.4.1 The Constant Rate of Return Hypothesis

Let $\tilde{\xi}_t$ be an FX price at day t (say the price of 1 EUR for 1 USD). Today's ROR at t and future time $t + 1$ are by definition

$$\tilde{R}_t = \frac{\tilde{\xi}_t - \tilde{\xi}_{t-1}}{\tilde{\xi}_{t-1}} = \frac{S_t}{\tilde{\xi}_{t-1}} - 1, t = 1,2,3,\dots, \text{ and } \tilde{R}_{t+1} = \frac{\tilde{\xi}_{t+1} - \tilde{\xi}_t}{\tilde{\xi}_t} = \frac{\tilde{\xi}_{t+1}}{\tilde{\xi}_t} - 1$$

Note that $\tilde{R}_{t+1}$ is a random variable at time t while $\tilde{R}_t$ is a random variable at time $t-1$. Assume that $R_j = 1,2,\dots t$ are observed. The constant ROR hypothesis states that the expected ROR of a security or an FX is some (statistical population) constant μ defined by the following stochastic (random walk) model:

$$\tilde{R}_{t+1} = \mu + \sigma\tilde{\varepsilon}_{t+1}, \quad E\left(\tilde{R}_{t+1}\right) = \mu, \quad E\left(\tilde{\varepsilon}_{t+1}\right) = 0, \quad \mathrm{var}\left(\tilde{\varepsilon}_{t+1}\right) = 1$$

where $\tilde{\varepsilon}_{t+1}$ denotes a random error assumed to be iid as a normal probability distribution with zero mean and variance of 1. This model assumes that, at all time periods, returns have statistically identical and independent returns (of previous periods), with mean μ and variance σ^2. Combining these equations, the following linear RORs pricing model results (also called the lognormal model for asset prices):

$$\frac{\tilde{\xi}_{t+1} - \tilde{\xi}_t}{\tilde{\xi}_t} = \frac{\Delta\tilde{\xi}_{t+1}}{\tilde{\xi}_t} = \tilde{R}_{t+1} = \mu + \sigma\varepsilon_{t+1}, \quad S_0 > 0, \quad t = 1,2,3,\dots$$

When the time interval is defined by Δt, we have, instead, the lognormal models in discrete and in continuous time:

$$\frac{\Delta\tilde{\xi}_{t+1}}{\tilde{\xi}_t} = \mu\Delta t + \sigma\Delta W_t, \xi_0 > 0, t = 1,2,3,\dots, \text{ and } \frac{\mathrm{d}\tilde{\xi}(t)}{\xi(t)} = \mu\,\mathrm{d}t + \sigma\,\mathrm{d}W(t), \xi_0 > 0$$

where ΔW_t is used to denote standard normally distributed and independent random variables with zero mean and a linear time variance. Thus, for a small interval of time, the variance is linear in the time interval Δt. This can be verified by $E(\varepsilon_{t+\Delta t}) = E(\Delta W_t) = 0$ and $\mathrm{var}(\varepsilon_{t+\Delta t}) = \mathrm{var}(\sigma\Delta W_t) = \sigma^2\Delta t$. Although these two models are similar, they are also different due to their granularity.

Consider the transformation $h(\xi_t) = \ln(\xi_t)$ and a Taylor series expansion with respect to its previous price (say the previous day at the known price ξ_{t-1}). The first three terms of a Taylor series expansion yields

$$\Delta h(\xi_t) = \frac{\partial h(\xi_{t-1})}{\partial\xi_t}(\Delta\xi_t) + \frac{1}{2}\frac{\partial^2 h(\xi_{t-1})}{\partial\xi_t^{2}}(\Delta\xi_t)^2 + \frac{1}{2\times 3}\frac{\partial^3 h(\xi_{t-1})}{\partial\xi_t^{3}}(\Delta\xi_t)^3 + \cdots$$

where $\Delta \xi_t = \xi_t - \xi_{t-1}$. Applying the transformation $h(\xi_t) = \ln(\xi_t)$ for a previous instant of time Δt, we have

$$\Delta \ln(\xi_t) = \frac{(\Delta \xi_t)}{\xi_{t-1}} - \frac{1}{2}\left(\frac{(\Delta \xi_t)}{\xi_{t-1}}\right)^2 + \frac{1}{2 \times 3}\left(\frac{(\Delta \xi_t)}{\xi_{t-1}}\right)^3 + \cdots$$

where $\Delta \ln(\xi_t)$ is the day rate of change in the FX which at time t yields in expectation an expression which is a function of the first three moments of the FX ROR for that day, or the mean, the variance, and the skewness:

$$E(\Delta \ln(\xi_t)) = E\left(\frac{(\Delta \xi_t)}{\xi_{t-1}}\right) - \frac{1}{2}E\left[\left(\frac{(\Delta \xi_t)}{\xi_{t-1}}\right)^2\right] + \frac{1}{2 \times 3}E\left[\left(\frac{(\Delta \xi_t)}{\xi_{t-1}}\right)^3\right] + \cdots$$

If a priori we assume that $\Delta \xi_t$ is normally distributed, its third moment is null. Further, setting the first two moments to be $E(\tilde{R}_t) = \mu$ and $\mathrm{var}(\tilde{R}_t) = \sigma^2$, then

$$E(\Delta \ln(\xi_t)) = E\frac{(\Delta \xi_t)}{\xi_{t-1}} - \frac{1}{2}E\left(\frac{(\Delta \xi_t)}{\xi_{t-1}}\right)^2 = \left(\mu - \frac{1}{2}\sigma^2\right)dt$$

By the same token, using the fact that a normal probability distribution has no skewness and that $\mathrm{var}(\sigma \Delta W_t) = \sigma^2 \Delta t$, we have the linear RORs stochastic process:

$$\Delta(\ln(\xi_t)) = \left(\mu - \frac{1}{2}\sigma^2\right)\Delta t + \sigma \Delta W_t, \quad \xi_0 > 0, \text{ and } d(\ln(\xi_t)) = \left(\mu - \frac{1}{2}\sigma^2\right)dt + \sigma dW_t, \quad \xi_0 > 0$$

This model is widely used in financial modeling and underlies the Black–Scholes model. As noted earlier, it depends basically on a data normality assumption which is not always verified. A further estimation of the mean ROR is statistically problematic since

$$E[\Delta(\ln(\xi_t))] = \left(\mu - \frac{1}{2}\sigma^2\right)\Delta t$$

and is therefore a function of two parameters: the mean and the variance. Econometric techniques of ARCH–GARCH to be considered subsequently in this chapter provide a data treatment which will allow the resolution of this problem. Of course, in the case of an FX between two countries, the FX of the one is the inverse of the other; thus, if we consider the inverse relationship, for example the price of 1 USD in euros defined by the random variable $\tilde{\eta}_t = 1/\tilde{\xi}_t$ (if there is no "friction" between these exchange rates):

$$\Delta(\ln(\tilde{\eta}_t)) = \left(\mu_\eta - \frac{1}{2}\sigma_\eta^2\right)\Delta t + \sigma_\eta \Delta W_{\eta_t}$$

which empirically might not be the same model. Theoretically, the transformation $\Delta \ln \tilde{\eta}_t = -\Delta \ln \tilde{\xi}_t$ treating the ROR data from a domestic or from a foreign perspective will be identical. If this were not the case, it would imply that the mutual FX rates of two countries are not equivalent.

2.4.2 Autoregressive and Mean Reverting Models

Some financial models are defined as AR processes; namely, defined as a function of a previous outcome (as discussed earlier). Consider a simple AR(1) model defined by the following model:

$$R_t = \alpha R_{t-1} + \sigma \varepsilon_t, \quad |\alpha| < 1, \quad E(\varepsilon_t) = 0, \quad var(\varepsilon_t) = 1$$

where ε_t are assumed to be standard normal iid random variables. A general AR(n) model, accounting for past returns as well, is written similarly by

$$R_t = \sum_{i=1}^{n} \alpha_i R_{t-i} + \sigma \varepsilon_t, \quad |\alpha_i| < 1$$

Other models, based on a smaller number of parameters, can also be developed to estimate assumptions other than the constant ROR. For example, a simple extension of the constant mean ROR model $\tilde{R}_{t+1} = \mu + \sigma \tilde{\varepsilon}_{t+1}$ noted by regression estimates would be

$$R_t = \mu + \alpha R_{t-1} + \sigma \varepsilon_t, \quad |\alpha| < 1, \quad E(\varepsilon_t) = 0, \quad var(\varepsilon_t) = 1$$

Over a time interval Δt, we have

$$\Delta R_t = [\mu - (1 - \alpha)R_t]\Delta t + \sigma \Delta W_t, \quad |\alpha| < 1$$

This can be rearranged to

$$\Delta R_t = -\lambda \left(\frac{1-\alpha}{\lambda} R_t - \frac{\mu}{\lambda} \right) \Delta t + \sigma \Delta W_t$$

and $\Delta R_t = -\lambda(aR_t - \bar{\mu})\Delta t + \sigma \Delta W_t$. At the limit, when $\Delta R_t = 0$, we have $a\bar{R}_t - \bar{\mu} = 0$ or $a = \bar{\mu}/\bar{R}_t$, and thus $\Delta R_t = \lambda \bar{\mu}[1 - (R_t/\bar{R})]\Delta t + \sigma \Delta W_t$. Finally, letting $x_t = R_t/\bar{R}$, we obtain a unit reversion model (i.e. an ROR model in a continuous-time stochastic process—with time intervals infinitely small):

$$dx_t = \theta(1 - x)\,dt + \sigma\,dW_t, \quad \theta = \frac{\lambda \bar{\mu}}{\bar{R}}$$

An estimation of such models of different data granularity (i.e., daily or monthly data based on financial and macroeconomic data) would point to results that differ due to the time scale used (Tapiero and Vallois, 2016).

The mean reversion model is applied to interest rate models (and therefore potentially useful to model ROR FX, which is a function of sovereign interest rates) that were initially applied by Vasicek (1977) based on the hypothesis that FX rates have a stable trend and therefore their variations fluctuate along the long-run trend. Say that the current FX ξ_t is a weighted function of past FX variations $\Delta \xi_{t-i}$ which we denote by $\Delta \eta_{t-i}$ assumed to be normally distributed:

$$\xi_t = \sum_{i=1}^{n} \mu_i \Delta \eta_{t-i}$$

where $\Delta \eta_{t-i} = \Delta \xi_{t-i}$ and $\Delta \xi_{t-i} = \alpha \Delta t + \sigma \Delta W(t-i)$ with μ_i, α, and σ that are a set of parameters. For convenience, say that the FX is a continuous time function exponentially decreasing as a function of all past FX variations (in discrete time, it corresponds to a geometric probability distribution):

$$\xi(t) = \int_{-\infty}^{t} e^{-\mu(t-\tau)} \, d\eta(\tau)$$

Equivalently, its derivative with respect to time yields

$$\Delta\xi(t) = -\mu\Delta t \int_{-\infty}^{t} e^{-\mu(t-\tau)} \, d\eta(\tau) + \Delta\eta(\tau) = \Delta\eta(t) - \mu\xi(t)\Delta t$$

Since perturbations in RORs are random, and given by the random model $\Delta\eta(t) = \alpha\Delta t + \sigma\Delta W(t)$, we obtain the RORs process $\Delta\xi(t) = \alpha\Delta t + \sigma\Delta W(t) - \mu\xi(t)\Delta t$, which we rewrite as the mean reversion model:

$$\Delta\xi(t) = \mu\left(\frac{\alpha}{\mu} - \xi(t)\right)\Delta t + \sigma\Delta W(t) \quad \text{and} \quad d\xi(t) = \mu(\nu - \xi(t)) \, dt + \sigma \, dW(t)$$

In expectation $E(d\xi(t)) = 0$, and $E(\xi(t)) = \nu$. Such models will be developed further and applied to global finance problems in Chapters 7 and 8.

2.5 Multivariate Probability Models

Multivariate probability models are used naturally in global finance. The most common multivariate and continuous probability distribution is normal. For example, let the CPI in n countries be defined by vector random variables $[\mathbf{CPI}(t)] = [\text{CPI}_1(t), \text{CPI}_2(t), \ldots, \text{CPI}_n(t)]$. Let $\mathbf{CPI}(t)$ be normally distributed with vector mean $\mathbf{M}(t)$ and variance–covariance matrix $\mathbf{\Sigma}(t)$. Thus:

$$f(\mathbf{CPI}(t)) = \frac{1}{(2\pi)^{n/2}|\Sigma|^{1/2}} \exp\left[-\frac{1}{2}(\mathbf{CPI}(t) - \mathbf{M}(t))^{\mathrm{T}} \Sigma^{-1}(\mathbf{CPI}(t) - \mathbf{M}(t))\right]$$

For example, for a two-CPI model, we have

$$\mathbf{M}(t) = \begin{pmatrix} M_1(t) \\ M_2(t) \end{pmatrix} \quad \text{and} \quad \mathbf{\Sigma}(t) = \begin{pmatrix} \sigma_1^2 & \sigma_{12} \\ \sigma_{12} & \sigma_2^2 \end{pmatrix} \quad \text{and} \quad \sigma_{12} = \rho\sigma_1\sigma_2$$

where ρ is the correlation between these two prices. A linear transformation of the CPI vector to a linear model with a standard (zero mean, unit variance) normal vector is then defined by

$$\mathbf{CPI}(t) = \mathbf{M}(t) + \mathbf{A}(t)\mathbf{Z}(t), \quad \mathbf{\Sigma}(t) = \mathbf{A}^{\mathrm{T}}(t)\mathbf{A}(t), \quad \text{and} \quad \mathbf{Z} \sim \mathbf{N}(\mathbf{0}, \mathbf{I})$$

Let $f(x, y)$ be a bivariate normal probability distribution. If its random variables are independent, $f(x,y) = f(x)g(y)$, while when they are dependent

$f(x|y) = f(x|y)g(y) = f(x)g(y|x)$. As a result, the conditional distribution of $g(y|x)$ is also normal with mean and variance

$$g(y|x) \sim N\left(\mu_y + \frac{\sigma_{xy}}{\sigma_x^2}(x-\mu_x); \sigma_x^2 - \frac{\sigma_y\sigma_{xy}}{\sigma_x^2}\right)$$

Next, assume that consumption in these two countries is constant; then, financial expenditures are $C_1\text{CPI}_1(t) + C_2\text{CPI}_2(t)$ and, therefore, the mean and variance are

$$C_1M_1(t) + C_2M_2(t) \quad \text{and} \quad \text{var}(C_1\text{CPI}_1(t) + C_2\text{CPI}_2(t)) = (C_1)^2\sigma_1^2 + (C_2)^2\sigma_2^2 + \rho_{12}C_1C_2\sigma_1\sigma_2$$

Assume further that CPI is a function of another random variable, say $\tilde{U}(t)$, denoting the GNP. An explicit aggregate distribution has a joint probability distribution:

$$f_{U,V_i}\left(\text{CPI}_1(t),\ldots,\text{CPI}_n(t),\tilde{U}(t)\right) = \int_{-\infty}^{+\infty} f_{\text{CPI}_i|U}\left(\text{CPI}_1(t),\ldots,\text{CPI}_n(t)|\tilde{U}(t)\right)f_U\left(\tilde{U}(t)\right)\,d\tilde{U}(t)$$

The study of such distributions can then be used for a number of purposes:

- to study the factors dependence and their effect on the aggregate index and vice versa;
- to determine a subset of factors that have the greatest influence on the aggregate;
- to manage the aggregate index through its components.

The construction of multivariate models in global finance requires other tools, such as a copula, providing dependent multivariate probability distributions defined by an algebraic function of the marginal cumulative density functions. For references in different multivariate distributions, see, for example, Johnson and Kotz (1972), Stein (1973), Fang *et al.* (1987), Marshall and Olkin (1988), Oakes (1994), and Joe (1997).

2.5.1 Bernoulli and Codependence: Qualitative Data

A fundamental question in finance depending on a central bank decision or on some sovereign policy is essentially a binary decision. Namely, it "does or it does not." For example, a regulator auditing a firm; a supply contract with the national authority in Nigeria will be signed or not. In its simplest form, it may be defined by a Bernoulli probability $P(\tilde{x}) = p, \tilde{x} \in [1,0]$. This probability may, however, be conditional on a variety of factors, such as $P(\tilde{x}|y_1,y_2,\ldots,y_n) = p, \tilde{x} \in [1,0]$. Estimates of the probability of an event are then random and can be estimated as a function of observed factors and measured by $\{y_1, y_2, \ldots, y_n\}$. For example, a logistic (logit) distribution is often used to estimate this probability. It is given by a linear regression of the odds of a Bernoulli event occurring:

$$\ln\left(\frac{p}{1-p}\right) = \sum_{j=1}^{n} a_j y_j + \tilde{\varepsilon} \quad \text{or} \quad p = \frac{1}{1 + \exp\left(\sum_{j=1}^{n} a_j y_j + \tilde{\varepsilon}\right)}$$

where $\tilde{\varepsilon}$ is a random noise. Ordered logit proportional models have the following form, however:

$$\text{logit}(p_1) = \ln\left(\frac{p_1}{1-p_1}\right) = \alpha_1 + \sum_{j=1}^{n} a_j y_j + \tilde{\varepsilon}$$

$$\text{logit}(p_1 + p_2) = \ln\left(\frac{p_1 + p_2}{1 - p_1 - p_2}\right) = \alpha_2 + \sum_{j=1}^{n} a_j y_j + \tilde{\varepsilon}$$

$$\vdots$$

$$\text{logit}(p_1 + p_2 + \cdots + p_k) = \ln\left(\frac{p_1 + p_2 + \cdots + p_k}{1 - p_1 - p_2 - \cdots - p_k}\right) = \alpha_k + \sum_{j=1}^{n} a_j y_j + \tilde{\varepsilon}$$

Example 2.9   Hazard Rate and Survivability

Assume that $\tilde{p}$ is a random variable with a known Beta probability distribution and therefore its odds $\tilde{p}/(1-\tilde{p})$ have a Beta prime probability distribution, which we can estimate by standard estimation techniques. For example, let an estimate of the odds of (more or less similar) financial firms to be compliant with regulation be given with an average and a variance. Assuming that a Beta prime distribution is used, its corresponding probability of being compliant can be calculated and therefore used to decide whether to audit the financial firm or not. Similarly, let the conditional hazard rate be $h(t|\theta)$, defined by a conditional probability that an event occurs at a specific time t given that it had not occurred before, or:

$$h(t|\theta) = \frac{f(t|\theta)}{1 - F(t|\theta)}$$

Say that $h(t|\theta) = \theta A(t)$ where $A(t)$ is a known function for the hazard rate and uncertainty—see Klugman *et al.* (2008: 68). In this case, the survival distribution is

$$1 - F(t|\theta) = e^{-\theta \int_0^t A(\tau) d\tau}$$

The function $A(t)$ defines as well the survivability and the hazard rate. If $\partial A(t)/\partial t > 0$, the more that time passes, the greater is the probability of an event occurring, and vice versa when its derivative is negative.

Alternatively, the odds of such an event at a specific instant of time are thus $h(t|\theta)/(1 - h(t|\theta))$, which may be treated either as Bernoulli event or as a Bernoulli-derived distribution (whether random or not as indicated earlier).

2.5.2   Multivariate Qualitative Data

Global finance is often defined by multivariate quantitative and qualitative data. For example, countries may be classified as safe (1) or not safe (0). In this case, $n = 10$ countries would be labeled, for example, as (1, 1, 1, 0, 0, 1, 0, 0, 0, 1). Labeling may also be probabilistic values we may assume for simplicity and defined by a multivariate and dependent Bernoulli process (where each country probability is random or not). In particular, in

Chapter 10 we will define the following qualitative random variables $(\tilde{x}_i, \tilde{y}_j)$ $(i = 0,1; j = 0,1)$ denoting compliance to a specific regulation and the audit probability by a regulator.

A univariate Bernoulli process assumes two values, say 1 or 0, which we denote by a random variable $\tilde{x}_i \in \{1,0\}$ with probability $p(\tilde{x}_i = 1) = p_i$ (based on multiple estimations and defined as statistical estimates). Consider two dependent Bernoulli processes, defined by the random variables $(\tilde{x}_i, \tilde{y}_j)$, $i = 0,1; j = 0,1$. Four states are possible, $\langle\{1,1\}, \{1,0\}, \{0,1\}, \{0,0\}\rangle$, while their probability distribution is $\{p_{ij} = p(\tilde{x}, \tilde{y})\}$. A general expression for dependent bivariate Bernoulli random variables $(\tilde{x}, \tilde{y})$ is

$$p(x,y) = \{p_{11}\}^{xy}\{p_{10}\}^{x(1-y)}\{p_{01}\}^{(1-x)y}\{p_{00}\}^{(1-x)(1-y)},$$
$$(x,y) \in [1,0], \text{ with } p_{11} + p_{10} + p_{01} + p_{00} = 1$$

And generally for a K vector of multivariate Bernoulli probability distribution (note the change in notation):

$$p(x_1, x_2, \ldots, x_K) = \{p_{11\ldots1}\}^{\prod_{j=1}^{K} x_j}\{p_{011\ldots1}\}^{(1-x_1)\prod_{j=1}^{K} x_j}\ldots\{p_{00\ldots0}\}^{\prod_{j=1}^{K}(1-x_j)}$$

which for the bivariate case leads to the following moments (mean, variance, and covariation):

$$E(x_1) = p_{10} + p_{11}, \quad \text{var}(x_1) = (p_{10} + p_{11})(1 - (p_{10} + p_{11}))$$
$$E(x_2) = p_{01} + p_{11}, \quad \text{var}(x_2) = (p_{01} + p_{11})(1 - (p_{01} + p_{11}))$$
$$E(x_1 x_2) = p_{11}$$

Since the sum of probabilities for all events is equal to one, we can write $p_{11} = 1 - p_{00} - p_{10} - p_{01}$. Further, setting $1 - p_{00} - p_{01} = p_1$ and $1 - p_{00} - p_{10} = p_2$, we obtain

$$E(x_1) = p_1 = 1 - p_{00} - p_{01}, \quad \text{var}(x_1) = p_1(1 - p_1)$$
$$E(x_2) = p_2 = 1 - p_{00} - p_{10}, \quad \text{var}(x_2) = p_2(1 - p_2)$$

as well as

$$E(x_1 x_2) = p_{11} = E(x_1)E(x_2) + \rho\sqrt{\text{var}(x_1)\text{var}(x_2)}$$

where ρ is the correlation of the bivariate Bernoulli distribution with

$$E(x_1 x_2) = p_{11} = p_1 - p_{10} = p_2 - p_{01}$$
$$= p_1 p_2 + \rho\sqrt{p_1 p_2(1 - p_1)(1 - p_2)} \text{ and } \text{cov}(x_1, x_2) = \rho - p_1 p_2$$

Say that the probability of noncompliance in two regulation systems is $p_1 = 0.2$, $p_2 = 0.1$ with correlation $\rho = 0.3$. Then, $p_{11} = 0.038$, $p_{10} = 0.162$, $p_{01} = 0.062$, $p_{00} = 0.738$. For an independent process, we have $E(x_1 x_2) = p_{11} = p_1 p_2$ and $E(x_1 x_2) = p_1 - p_{10} = p_2 - p_{01} = p_1 p_2$, with $p_{10} = p_1(1 - p_2)$ and $p_{01} = p_2(1 - p_1)$. If an audit by a regulator is set to one or the other regulations, there is then a probability that even if audited there is a probability to be found compliant (due to regulators not detecting noncompliance).

Table 2.10 Bivariate Bernoulli in terms of controls and compliance.

x_1/x_2	Compliant	Not compliant
No inspection	p_{00}	p_{01}
Inspection	p_{10}	p_{11}

Example 2.10 Let $x_1 = 1$ be a Bernoulli regulation event, and let the event of noncompliance of the bank controlled be $x_2 = 1$. Assume that both events, noncompliance and a regulatory intervention, are statistically dependent as indicated by the probabilities in Table 2.10 (since noncompliance and the prospect of being inspected are assumed to be correlated).

The probability of being noncompliant in this case is $p_{01} + p_{11}$, while the probability of a regulatory intervention is $p_{10} + p_{11}$. Say that a sample of n factors is selected and tested for compliance. Given that there may be n countries where the bank is located, the probability distribution of a control of all n countries' banks has a bivariate binomial distribution whose probability generating function is

$$G^*(z_1, z_2) = (p_{11} + p_{01}z_1 + p_{10}z_2 + p_{00}z_1z_2)^n$$

with moments $E(x_1) = n(p_{01} + p_{00})$ and $E(x_2) = n(p_{00} + p_{10})$ and

$$E(x_1x_2) = n(n-1)[p_{00} + (p_{01} + p_{00})(p_{10} + p_{00})]$$

where $E(x_1x_2) = E(x_1)E(x_2) + \rho\sigma_1\sigma_2$. And

$$\rho = \frac{E(x_1x_2) - E(x_1)E(x_2)}{\sigma_1\sigma_2}$$

where $\sigma_1\sigma_2$ can be calculated by using the second derivatives of the probability generating function.

Example 2.11   Strategic Audit and Compliance
The example in Table 2.11 defines a simple audit-compliance model as a game where a firm is penalized for $\$P$ if the regulator audits and the first is not compliant. In this case, the expected probability of such a penalty is $p_{11}p_{01}P$. The penalties and the audits as well as the compliance probability of the financial firm are far more complex, however, as will be outlined in Chapter 10.

Table 2.11 Bivariate Bernoulli audit and compliance.

x_1/x_2	Compliant p_{00}	Not compliant p_{01}
No inspection p_{10}	0	0
Inspection p_{11}	0	P

Example 2.12   Bivariate Case

Similar distributions can be formulated in different ways. For example, let $(\tilde{x}_1, \tilde{x}_2, ..., \tilde{x}_n)$ be n bivariate random variables, defined as follows:

$$f(\tilde{x}_i = 1 | p_{1,i}) = p_{1,i}$$
$$f(\tilde{x}_i = 1, \tilde{x}_j = 1 | p_{2,ij}) = p_{2,ij}, \quad i,j = 1,...,n; \ i \neq j$$

$$\vdots$$

$$f(\tilde{x}_i = 1, \tilde{x}_j = 1, ..., \tilde{x}_n = 1 | p_{k,i,j,...,n}) = p_{k,i,j,...,n}$$

where $\{p_k\}$ is a parameter set (similar to that defined earlier). Since this is a binary variable, we have

$$E(\tilde{x}_i | p_{1i}) = p_{1i}, \quad E(\tilde{x}_i \tilde{x}_j | p_{2,ij}) = p_{2,ij}, \quad \text{cov}(\tilde{x}_i, \tilde{x}_j | p_{1i}, p_{1j} p_{2,ij}) = p_{2,ij} - p_{1i} p_{1j} \ (i \neq j), \text{ and}$$

$$\rho_{ij}(\tilde{x}_i, \tilde{x}_j) = \frac{p_{2,ij} - p_{1i} p_{1j}}{\sqrt{p_{1i}(1 - p_{1i}) p_{1j}(1 - p_{1j})}}$$

The number of parameters required to represent the dependence of such systems rises as the number of factors increases. For two, three, four, and more random factors, it will require an increasing number of parameters, which renders such an approach unrealistic. For this reason, other approaches can be devised to represent and capture the dependence essential characteristics, and at the same time maintain the model tractable.

2.5.3   Copulas and Multivariate Models

Copulas are algebraic structures (functional models) that represent technically the statistical dependence of joint distribution functions by their marginal probability distributions. Namely, a joint distribution function in two random variables, defined by

$$F(x,y) = \Phi(F_X(x), F_Y(y)) \quad \text{or} \quad \Phi(u,v) = P(U_X \leq F_X(x), U_Y \leq F_Y(y)), \quad u = F_X(x), \ v = F_Y(y)$$

with u and v denoting the marginal cumulative distributions. Copulas $\Phi(u, v)$ have the same properties as those of joint cumulative probability distributions, or $0 \leq \Phi(u,v) \leq 1$ ($0 \leq u \leq 1$, $0 \leq v \leq 1$), $\Phi(0,u) = \Phi(u,0) = 0$, $\Phi(1,u) = \Phi(u,1) = u$. Owing to their practical importance, copulas have been the subject of considerable research and application. Definitions of the copula are based on basic theorems and relationships, including the Sklar theorem (Sklar, 1959) as outlined later. Copulas are a convenient means to model the dependence of global and statistical relationships. While multivariate normal probability distributions are commonly used, based on empirical covariations, copulas allow the construction of more complex relationships that may be tested empirically.

Sklar theorem (1959): Let H be an n-dimensional distribution function with margins $F_1, ..., F_n$, then there exists an n-copula function C such that for all x in R^n

$$H(x_1,...,x_n) = C(F_1(x_1),...,F_n(x_n))$$

Conversely, if C is an n-copula and $F_1, ..., F_n$ are distribution functions, then the function H defined above is an n-dimensional distribution function with margins $F_1, ..., F_n$.

Remarks:

1) C need not be unique, but is unique if the margins are continuous.
2) For continuous margins, the unique copula function is

$$C(u_1,...,u_n) = H\left(F^{-1}(u_1),...,F^{-1}(u_n)\right)$$

where $F^{-1}(t) = \inf\{x \in \mathfrak{R} | F(x) \geq t\}$ for all t in $[0, 1]$.
3) A copula is a function which joins or couples a multivariate distribution function to its one-dimensional margins.
4) For independence, the copula function is $C(u_1,...,u_n) = u_1 \cdots u_n$.
5) For other copula functions, they generally contain parameter(s) that describe the dependence.

Example 2.13   Two-Dimensional Copulas

- A two-dimensional (2-dim) copula density function $C(u, v)$ (C-2-dim df) defined on $[0, 1]^2$ with uniform marginal has the following properties:

$$C(1, u) = C(u, 1) = u, \text{ for any } 0 \leq u \leq 1, \text{ and it is independent if } C_I(u, v) = uv.$$

- A co-monotonic copula is defined by $C_U(u, v) = \min\{u, v\}$ while a counter-monotonic copula is defined by $C_L(u, v) = (u + v - 1)^+$.
- The Frechet bivariate family of copulas is defined by $C(u, v) = uv[1 + \alpha(1 - u)(1 - v)]$.
- A mixture copula is defined by $C(u, v) = (1 - \rho)uv + \rho \min(u, v), \rho > 0$.

A mixture copula is defined by the mixture of two probability distributions, while co-monotonic copulas point to probability distributions that move in tandem (or vice versa for counter-monotonic copulas). Other copulas can be defined ex post to better fit observed empirical records, or any joint distributions. Their applications are indeed very large, and numerous publications document their characteristics (e.g., Frees and Valdez, 1998; Li, 1999; Nelsen, 1999; Embrechts *et al.*, 2002, 2003, 2007; Cherubini *et al.*, 2004; McNeil *et al.*, 2005; Patton, 2009; Kurowicka and Joe, 2011).

Frequently used copulas include the Gumbel copula, and for global finance conditional copulas may be applied carefully where financial random events are defined conditionally on macroeconomic events. We summarize their definitions in the following examples.

Example 2.14   The Gumbel Copula, the Highs and the Lows

Say that the joint cumulative probability distribution of the highs and the lows of two prices (say in a day trade) is defined by marginal Gumbel probability distributions with their copula given by

$$C(u, v | x, y) = uv \exp\left[-\theta\left(\frac{1}{\ln u} + \frac{1}{\ln v}\right)^{-1}\right]$$

where their marginal distributions are $[u(x), v(y)]$ and thus the Gumbel Copula (joint distribution) is

$$F(x,y) = u(x)v(y)\exp\left[-\theta\left(\frac{1}{\ln u(x)} + \frac{1}{\ln v(y)}\right)^{-1}\right]$$

Note that for such a distribution $u(x) = [x]^n$, $v(y) = 1 - [1 - y]^n$, and since the high and the low prices are drawn from the same probability distribution, we have $y = x = F(S)$. Thus, the bivariate (high and low prices for a day) copula $u = u(x)$, $v = v(y)$ is as defined earlier: $C(u,v|x,y)$. As a result:

$$C(x,y|S) = [x]^n(1 - [1 - y]^n) \exp\left\{-\theta\left[\frac{1}{n\ln[x]} + \frac{1}{\ln(1 - [1 - y]^n)}\right]^{-1}\right\}, x = y = F(S)$$

which provides a joint cumulative distribution for the high and the low which can be tested against empirical data. Alternatively, a type B Gumbel is defined by

$$C(u,v|x,y) = uv\exp\left\{\left[\left(\ln\frac{1}{u}\right)^m + \left(\ln\frac{1}{v}\right)^m\right]^{1/m}\right\}$$

And therefore its joint distribution is

$$F(x,y) = u(x)v(y)\exp\left\{\left[\left(\ln\frac{1}{u(x)}\right)^m + \left(\ln\frac{1}{v(y)}\right)^m\right]^{1/m}\right\}$$

where $m > 1$, $m = 1/(1 - \rho)^{1/2}$, with ρ being a coefficient of correlation between the high and the low. We can calculate the explicit joint probability distribution using the fact that

$$f(x,y) = \frac{\partial^2 F(x,y)}{\partial x \partial y}$$

and simulate such a joint distribution using Monte Carlo techniques to calculate its moments (mean, variance, covariance, skewness, kurtosis, etc.).

Example 2.15 Copulas and Conditional Dependence (Based on Embrechts et al. (2003))

Financial statistics are dependent both horizontally (across many securities and other economic variables) and conditionally on specific events that may occur randomly. For example, let a return in a foreign country be conditional on the country policy to increase or reduce the interest rate, or on an election result. Consider two financial prices, and postulate a joint cumulative distribution (S and C) defined by a bivariate copula, where $F_S(S_1)$, $F_C(c_1)$ are their marginal CDF and

$$C(F_S(S_1), F_C(c_1)) = \int_{-\infty}^{S_1} \int_{-\infty}^{c_1} f(x,y)\, dx\, dy$$

It might be more intuitive to express C conditional to S. To do so, we proceed as follows. We define the bivariate copula $C(u, v)$ and its first (risk factor) derivative with respect to u:

$$C_1(u,v) = \frac{\partial C(u,v)}{\partial u} \quad \text{or} \quad \frac{\partial C(u,v)}{\partial u} = C_{2|1}(v|u) = C_{2|1}(F_C(c_1)|F_S(S_1))$$

This conditional copula defines the conditional cumulative probability distribution of $(c_1|S_1)$, or

$$F_{c_1|S_1}(c_1) = C(F_C(c_1)|F_S(S_1))$$

The conditional probability distribution of the security C and that of S is thus

$$\frac{\partial F_{c_1|S_1}(c_1)}{\partial c_1} = f(c_1|S_1)$$

In practice, additional knowledge, both qualitative and quantitative, is needed to define a copula. To this end, families of copulas have been studied, providing a library of relationships one may select from. Next, an example developed by Embrechts *et al.* (2002, 2003, 2007) is used to derive copulas from their conditional (model) copulas.

For example, say that $C(u, v) = [u^{-\alpha} + v^{-\alpha} - 1]^{-1/\alpha}$, $\alpha > 0$, and calculate the conditional copula:

$$C_{2|1}(v|u) = \frac{\partial C(u, v)}{\partial u} = u^{-\alpha-1}[u^{-\alpha} + v^{-\alpha} - 1]^{-(1/\alpha)-1}, \quad \alpha > 0$$

Now set the conditional copula $q = C_{2|1}(v|u)$ and solve for v. Or, conditional density function given u:

$$v = \left\{ 1 + \left(q u^{1+\alpha} \right)^{-\alpha/(1+\alpha)} - u^{-\alpha} \right\}^{-1/\alpha}$$

In other words, for the two random variables x_1 and x_2, we have their CDF given by

$$v = F_2(x_2) = \left\{ 1 + \left(q u^{1+\alpha} \right)^{-\alpha/(1+\alpha)} - u^{-\alpha} \right\}^{-1/\alpha}, \quad u = F_1(x_1), \text{ and}$$

$$v = F_2(x_2) = \left\{ 1 + \left(\left[[F_1(x_1)]^{-\alpha-1}[[F_1(x_1)]^{-\alpha} + v^{-\alpha} - 1]^{-(1/\alpha)-1} \right] [F_1(x_1)]^{1+\alpha} \right)^{-\alpha/(1+\alpha)} \right.$$
$$\left. - [F_1(x_1)]^{-\alpha} \right\}^{-1/\alpha}$$

Set $z_1 = 1 - [F_1(x_1)]^{-\alpha}$ and $(v)^{-\alpha} = \left\{ z_1 + \left([v^{-\alpha} - v]^{-(1/\alpha)-1} \right)^{-\alpha/(1+\alpha)} \right\}$ or $v = \Phi_\alpha\{z_1\}$

An explicit conditional copula can be equally written as follows:

$$q = F_{2|1}(x_2|x_1) = \left\{ -1 + (F_1(x_1))^\alpha [(F_2(x_2))^{-\alpha} - 1] \right\}^{-(1+\alpha)/\alpha}$$

while the conditional probability distribution is given by its derivative:

$$f_{2|1}(x_2 x_1) = \frac{\partial F_{2|1}(x_2|x_1)}{\partial x_2} = (1 + \alpha) \frac{f_2(x_2)}{F_2(x_2)} \left(\frac{F_1(x_1)}{F_2(x_2)} \right)^\alpha \left\{ -1 + (F_1(x_1))^\alpha [(F_2(x_2))^{-\alpha} - 1] \right\}^{-(1+2\alpha)/\alpha}$$

In other words, given x_1, the probability distribution function of x_2 is given above. Generally, if we define the k-dimensional copula, with $C_1(u_1) = u_1$, $C_2(u_1, u_2)$, ..., $C_n(u_1, u_2, u_3, ..., u_n)$, with $C(u_1, u_2, u_3, ..., u_n) = C_n(u_1, u_2, u_3, ..., u_n)$, the conditional copula is then

$$C_k(u_k|u_2, u_3, ..., u_{k-1}) = P\{U_k \le u_k | U_2 = u_2, U_3 = u_3, ..., U_{k-1} = u_{k-1}\} \text{ and}$$

$$C_k(u_k|u_2,u_3,...,u_{k-1}) = \frac{\dfrac{\partial^{k-1}C_k(u_1,u_2,...,u_k)}{\partial u_1,...,\partial u_{k-1}}}{\dfrac{\partial^{k-1}C_{k-1}(u_1,u_2,...,u_{k-1})}{\partial u_1,...,\partial u_{k-1}}}$$

Thus, for $k = 2$ we have, as seen earlier:

$$C_2(u_2|u_1) = \frac{\dfrac{\partial C_2(u_1,u_2)}{\partial u_1}}{\dfrac{\partial C_1(u_1)}{\partial u_1}} = \frac{\dfrac{\partial C_2(u_1,u_2)}{\partial u_1}}{\dfrac{\partial}{\partial u_1}u_1} = \frac{\partial C_2(u_1,u_2)}{\partial u_1}$$

Such models are, of course, only modeling tools that allow us to construct broader and more comprehensive models of dependence even though their joint distribution is unknown. For extensions of such an approach, we refer the reader to Embrechts *et al.* (2003) and Nelsen (1999).

2.6 Statistical Data Reduction

When the number of variables is very large, a subset of factors might be dominant. The statistical approach consists instead of reducing data matrices to a series of dominant components, called principal components. For example, can a financial index (whether market based or based on multiple countries' statistical data) represent effectively the evolution of economic aggregates? Does an index based on a portfolio constructed from 25 firms selected in the stock market replicate the evolution of prices in such a market? In other words, from a matrix of thousands of firms' prices traded, what are the first 25 components and do they account for the thousands of firms' price variations? If this were the case, can we use the first 25 components as a market variability index? These questions can be applied to numerous problems, such as the price of water, which is not traded but is found to covary with hundreds of firms' and other economic, geographic, and political variables. A reduction is naturally not only in dimensions. It also includes replacing a data set by its statistical parameters. A number of approaches are possible, including:

- $\mathfrak{R}^n \Rightarrow \mathfrak{R}^P$ or dimensional reduction;
- statistical moments representative of data sets;
- parametric models estimated based on data sets;
- reducing data matrices or data "equivalents" by the eigenvalues.

Example 2.16   Data Reduction
Financial and corporate firms are defined in terms of extremely large numbers of variables and over many periods. Say we have 500 such firms. What can we get from this data? That is, what kind of questions can we ask? How can we proceed? What is the relationship between these variables? Are these variables dependent? How does the change in a data point affect other data points? Can we reduce the data sets to smaller and manageable dimensions? Projecting in some sense (quantitative) the data sets on a number of categories (factors), say $F_1, F_2, ..., F_P$, let each data point X_i be expressed as a function of these P factors:

$$X_i = \Phi_i\left(F_1, F_2, \ldots, F_p\right)$$

To do so, we define the kth factor by a weighted sum of a subset n_k points

$$\left\{ F_k = \sum_{i=1}^{n_k} a_i^k X_i, \quad k = 1, 2, \ldots, p \right\} \quad \text{and} \quad \left\{ X_i \Leftarrow \Phi_i\left(F_1, F_2, \ldots, F_p\right) \right\}$$

One approach is based on factor analysis and another is principle component analysis (PCA). Factor analysis is a quadratic metric reducing a number of factors to a smaller one (for a study of such an approach, see Tapiero (2010)). PCA considers instead a data matrix which is reduced based on its eigenvalues (and their eigenvectors). For example, given global financial portfolios expressed by stochastic models with many risk sources $\sum_{i=1}^{n} \sigma_i \Delta W_i$, such as

$$\frac{\Delta S_P(t)}{S_P(t)} = \chi_P(t)\Delta t + \sum_{i=1}^{n} \sigma_i \Delta W_i, \quad S_P(0) > 0$$

where ΔW_i are n dependent and normally distributed random variables. For example, assume a database consisting of time series of n variables, such as the RORs of currencies, and the matrix of their correlations. Let the resulting data matrix be D. The purpose of PCA is to use fewer variables to replicate the variability of the data matrix. For example, if the price of a given currency is a function of an extremely large number of other currencies, seeking the three or four principal components that reasonably approximate global currency variation would result in a simplified model (with fewer currencies to reckon with). The same idea applies to constructing market indexes or summarizing the variability of a term structure of interest rates (i.e., the variations in all interest rates) into a single factor. For references to such an approach, see Tapiero (2010). In the following we consider a very simple and analytical problem for a 2×2 matrix.

Example 2.17   Reducing the Number of Risk Sources
Define two random vectors $\mathbf{w}$ and $\mathbf{v}$ and let $\mathbf{Q}$ be the correlation matrix and set $\mathbf{w} = \mathbf{Qv}$. If the correlation matrix is square and invertible, one random vector can be defined in terms of the other (and vice versa) by solving $\mathbf{Q}^{-1}\mathbf{w} = \mathbf{v}$. For example, for two sources of risks and a matrix

$$\mathbf{Q} = \begin{pmatrix} q_{11} & q_{12} \\ q_{21} & q_{22} \end{pmatrix}$$

we have

$$\begin{pmatrix} w_1 \\ w_2 \end{pmatrix} = \begin{pmatrix} q_{11} & q_{12} \\ q_{21} & q_{22} \end{pmatrix}\begin{pmatrix} v_1 \\ v_2 \end{pmatrix} \quad \text{and} \quad \begin{pmatrix} v_1 \\ v_2 \end{pmatrix} = \begin{pmatrix} q_{11} & q_{12} \\ q_{21} & q_{22} \end{pmatrix}^{-1}\begin{pmatrix} w_1 \\ w_2 \end{pmatrix}$$

For a correlation matrix, we have $q_{ii} = 1$, $q_{12} = q_{21}$, $i = 1, 2$, and therefore

$$w_1 = v_1 + q_{12}v_2 \quad \text{and} \quad w_2 = q_{12}v_1 + v_2 \quad \text{or} \quad v_1 = \left(\frac{w_1 - w_2 q_{12}}{1 - q_{12}^2}\right), \; v_2 = \left(\frac{w_2 - w_1 q_{12}}{1 - q_{12}^2}\right)$$

To reduce the number of risk sources, we first determine the matrix $\mathbf{Q}$ eigenvalues λ_j ($j = 1, 2$) by solving the determinant equation $|\mathbf{Q} - \lambda I| = 0$, with

$$\mathbf{Q} - \lambda I = \begin{pmatrix} q_{11} - \lambda & q_{12} \\ q_{21} & q_{22} - \lambda \end{pmatrix} \quad \text{and} \quad \begin{vmatrix} q_{11} - \lambda & q_{12} \\ q_{21} & q_{22} - \lambda \end{vmatrix} = (q_{11} - \lambda)(q_{22} - \lambda) - q_{12} q_{21} = 0$$

Solution for the eigenvalues λ_i, $i = 1, 2$, is then

$$\lambda_1 = \frac{q_{22} + q_{11}}{2} + \sqrt{\left(\frac{q_{22} + q_{11}}{2}\right)^2 - q_{11} q_{22} + q_{12} q_{21}}$$

$$\lambda_2 = \frac{q_{22} + q_{11}}{2} - \sqrt{\left(\frac{q_{22} + q_{11}}{2}\right)^2 - q_{11} q_{22} + q_{12} q_{21}}$$

And for a correlation matrix, this is reduced to $\lambda_1 = 1 + q_{12}$, $\lambda_2 = 1 - q_{12}$. To determine the eigenvectors associated with each eigenvalue of this matrix, we solve the matrix equation $\mathbf{Q}\boldsymbol{\beta}_j = \lambda_j \boldsymbol{\beta}_j$, $j = 1, 2, \ldots, n$, or

$$\begin{pmatrix} q_{11} & q_{12} \\ q_{21} & q_{22} \end{pmatrix} \begin{pmatrix} \beta_1 \\ \beta_2 \end{pmatrix} = \begin{pmatrix} \lambda_1 & 0 \\ 0 & \lambda_1 \end{pmatrix} \begin{pmatrix} \beta_1 \\ \beta_2 \end{pmatrix}, \qquad \text{eigenvector for } \lambda_1$$

$$\begin{pmatrix} q_{11} & q_{12} \\ q_{21} & q_{22} \end{pmatrix} \begin{pmatrix} \beta_1' \\ \beta_2' \end{pmatrix} = \begin{pmatrix} \lambda_2 & 0 \\ 0 & \lambda_2 \end{pmatrix} \begin{pmatrix} \beta_1' \\ \beta_2' \end{pmatrix}, \qquad \text{eigenvector for } \lambda_2$$

Generally, since the matrix $\mathbf{Q}$ is symmetric non-negative definite, the eigenvalues are all non-negative and the eigenvectors are all orthogonal to each other. Normalization of the eigenvectors yields $\mathbf{Q}|\boldsymbol{\beta}_j| = \sum \beta_{ij}^2 = \lambda_j$, $j = 1, 2, \ldots, n$. If we order the eigenvalues in an increasing order such that $\lambda_1 \geq \lambda_2 \geq \lambda_3 \geq \cdots \lambda_n$, then $\boldsymbol{\beta}_1$ is called the first principal component and $\boldsymbol{\beta}_j$ is called the jth principal component. In our simple example, say that the first eigenvalue is larger than the second one, or $\lambda_1 \gg \lambda_2$, and say that we drop the second eigenvalue. Thus, the new data matrix (or correlation matrix $\mathbf{Q}$ if we decide to collapse such a matrix) can be defined in terms of the first principal component, or

$$\mathbf{Q_r} = \begin{pmatrix} \beta_1 \\ \beta_2 \end{pmatrix}^{\mathrm{T}} \begin{pmatrix} q_{11} & q_{12} \\ q_{21} & q_{22} \end{pmatrix}^{\mathrm{T}}$$

Practically, we may use only the first few principal components to capture the variations of the multiple risks, thereby significantly reducing the dimensionality of the risk sources to consider.

2.7 Complexity: The Global Risk Finance Scourge

Complexity is often used, but generally misused. It implies that a process has a large number of seemingly independent and dependent agents and processes that can spontaneously organize themselves into a coherent system (and bifurcate unpredictably). Events are then attributed often to uncertainty! Namely, it may be due to "structural geometry" of events that underlie extremely complex systems that we do not understand or ignore their existence. For example, when a market collapses with no specific reason, we simply may claim that this is due to the system complexity.

Thus, in complex systems the objects involved and the rules of operations are not identified. They appear in biological systems, computer systems, social structures, and increasingly in financial markets and global financial institutions. As a result, it alters the basic assumptions that we have been able to use to manage finance and risks in the real world (rather than virtual and theoretical risks). Examples to model such systems include neural networks, the World Wide Web, and complex interactions of globally distributed financial institutions. It may refer to biological dynamical systems (neural computation), social dynamical systems (transportation flows), and financial markets. It includes dynamic populations that appear in medicine (epidemiology), social sciences (migrations and public health systems), global trading, and in other fields.

These systems, usually combine different scales, address different levels of hierarchy, and involve deterministic as well as stochastic aspects. So what we can say about complexity is that nobody really knows. However, there are many theories that seek to explain why they are bifurcating, adaptive, self-organizing, apparently disordered (i.e., with a high entropy), and permanently in search of an equilibrium that they never reach. The question is then, why are systems in disequilibrium? There are many explanations, which we briefly summarize. First, systems left to themselves are subjected to external events that alter them and lead them to bifurcate in another or several trajectories. Second, they may be inherently (and structurally) unstable. Third, real dynamic systems are mostly nonlinear and interactive, creating responses that are not just the sum of their parts' responses. Prigogine (1976), for example, points out that an economic system is self-organizing with markets adapting to external changes. As evidence, we are currently confronted with a transformation of financial markets through globalization and technology, but also of political and geopolitical powers. Ashby (1956), in his seminal book on cybernetics, pointed to the positive feedback effects of both complexity and controls based on a law of requisite variety. These approaches lead to the application of techniques and approaches inspired by life sciences, with terms such as bio and neuro applied to economics and financial models and computational techniques.

The complexity of financial as well as life sciences and other systems is challenging mathematical and data analytic techniques that attempt to provide methodologies and coherent frameworks to better understand, appreciate, and manage complexity (or at least some of its manifestations). Core research areas include dynamical systems, stochastic systems, information and statistical entropic systems, graph and network theory, random graphs and the statistical analysis of random networks, various areas of geometry and topology, and others. By the same token, data analytic approaches based on large-scale data accumulation are integrating and departing at the same time from fundamental statistical approaches. Algorithmic techniques, such as genetic algorithms and Bayesian networks, are profusely applied to search for other complex models.

2.8 Discussion

Traditionally, measurements are sought to meet a specific purpose, such as tracking and control; for predictive purposes such as future prices, future decisions by governments on their interest rates directives; defaulting lenders; market sustainability; competitiveness, investments, and trade policies. Global financial measurements are far more comparative, explorative, and strategic, with consequences measured by the relative standing of countries' economic states. They have numerous derived measurements (e.g., sovereign states' treasury rates, balance of payments) used by both investors and sovereign states with respect to which their own policies and measurements are reached. A country's measurements are equally broad, with important implications for its macroeconomic indicators. For the various reasons we have discussed, risk measurements of global finance are far more strategic, complex, and ill-defined.

References

Admati, A.R.P. and Pfleiderer, P. (1988) A theory of intraday patterns: volumes and price volatility. *Review of Financial Studies*, **1**(1): 3–40.

Albert R. and Barabási, A.-L. (2002) Statistical mechanics of complex networks. *Reviews of Modern Physics*, **74**(1): 47.

Alizadeh, S., Brandt, M.W., and Diebold, F.X. (2002) Range based estimation of stochastic volatility models. *Journal of Finance*, **47**: 1047–1092.

Allen, J F. (2001) Hypothesis, induction and background knowledge. Data do not speak for themselves. *BioEssays*, **23**: 861–862.

Andersen, T. and Bollerslev, T. (1997) Intraday periodicity and volatility persistence in financial markets. *Journal of Empirical Finance*, **4**: 115–158.

Andersen, T.G., Davis, R.A., Kreiss, J.P., and Mikosch, T. (eds) (2009) *Handbook of Financial Time Series*. Springer Verlag: Berlin.

Ang, A., Chen, J., and Xing, Y. (2006) Downside risk. *Review of Financial Studies*, **19**(4): 1191–1239.

Artzner, P., Delbaen, F., Eber, J.M., and Heath, D. (1997) Thinking coherently. *Risk*, **10**: 68–71.

Artzner P., Delbaen, F., Eber, J., and Heath, D. (1999) Coherent measures of risk. *Mathematical Finance*, **9**(3): 203–228.

Ashby, W.R. (1956) *Introduction to Cybernetics*. Chapman & Hall: London.

Ashford, W. (2012) Big data analytics has the potential to reduce the growing number of cyber security risks and increase business agility, says the ISF. *ComputerWeekly.com*, August 1. http://www.computerweekly.com/news/2240160679/Big-data-analytics-can-reduce-cyber-risks-says-ISF (accessed May 14, 2017).

Barabási, A.-L. and Albert, R. (1999) Emergence of scaling in random networks. *Science*, **286** (5439): 509–512.

Barlow, R. and Proschan, F. (1965) *Mathematical Theory of Reliability*. John Wiley & Sons, Inc.: New York.

Barlow, R. and Proschan, F. (1975) *Statistical Theory of Reliability and Life Testing*. Holt, Rinehart & Winston: New York.

Barnard, G.A. (1959) Control charts and stochastic processes. *Journal of the Royal Statistical Society, Series B*, **21**: 239–271.

Barnett, V. and Lewis, T. (1994) *Outliers in Statistical Data*, 3rd edn. John Wiley & Sons, Inc.: New York.

Basi, F., Embrechts, P., and Kafetzaki, M. (1998) Risk management and quantile estimation. In *Practical Guide to Heavy Tails*, R. Adler, R. Feldman, and M. Taqqu (eds). Birkhauser: Boston; pp. 111–130.

Beckers, S. (1996) A survey of risk measurement theory and practice. In *The Handbook of Risk Management and Analysis*, C. Alexander (ed.). John Wiley & Sons, Inc.: Hoboken, NJ; pp. 191–192.

Beran, J. (1994) *Statistics for Long-Memory Processes*. Chapman and Hall: London.

Black, F. (1976) The pricing of commodity contracts. *Journal of Financial Economics*, **3**: 167–179.

Bollerslev, T. (1986) Generalized autoregressive conditional heteroskedasticity. *Journal of Econometrics*, **31**: 307–327.

Bollerslev, T., Engle, R.F., and Nelson, D.B. (1994) ARCH models. In *Handbook of Econometrics*, vol. 4, R.F. Engle and D.L. McFadden (eds). Handbooks in Economics 2. Elsevier: Amsterdam; pp. 2961–3038.

Bouchaud, J.P. and Potters, M. (2003) *Theory of Financial Risks and Derivatives Pricing from Statistical Physics to Risk Management*, 2nd edn. Cambridge University Press: London.

Bowers, N., Gerber, H., Hickman, J., et al. (1997) *Actuarial Mathematics*, 2nd edn. Society of Actuaries: Schaumburg, IL.

Box, G.E.P. and Jenkins, G.M. (1976) *Time Series Analysis: Forecasting and Control*, revised edn. Holden Day: San Francisco.

Brockwell P.J. and Davis, R.A. (1986) *Time Series: Theory and Methods*. Springer: New York.

Caldarelli, G. (2007) *Scale-Free Networks: Complex Webs in Nature and Technology*. Oxford University Press: Oxford.

Callebaut, W. (2012) Scientific perspectivism: a philosopher of science's response to the challenge of big data biology. *Studies in History and Philosophy of Science Part C*, **43**(1): 69–80.

Cherubini, U., Luciano, E., and Vecchiato, W. (2004) *Copula Methods in Finance*. John Wiley & Sons, Inc.: Hoboken, NJ.

Christie, A.A. (1982) The stochastic behavior of common stock variances: value, leverage and interest rate effects. *Journal of Financial Economics*, **10**: 407–432.

Corrado, C. and Su, T. (1996) Skewness and kurtosis in S&P 500 index returns implied by S&P 500 index option prices. *Journal of Derivatives*, **4**: 8–19.

Denuit, M., Dhaene, J., Goovaerts, M., and Kaas, R. (2005) *Actuarial Theory for Dependent Risks*. Measures, Orders and Models. John Wiley & Sons.

Duncan, T.E. (2006) Some bilinear stochastic equations with a fractional Brownian motion. In *Stochastic Processes, Optimization, and Control Theory: Applications in Financial Engineering, Queueing Networks and Manufacturing*, H. Yan, G. Yin, and Q. Zhang (eds). Springer Science + Business Media: Berlin; pp. 97–108.

Duncan, T.E., Hu, Y.Z., and Pasik-Duncan, B. (2002) Stochastic calculus for fractional Brownian motion I: theory. *SIAM Journal on Control and Optimization*, **36**: 582–612.

Embrechts, P., Klupperberg, C., and Mikosch, T. (1997) *Modelling Extremal Events in Insurance and Finance*. Springer: Berlin.

Embrechts, P., McNeil, A., and Straumann, D. (2002) Correlation and dependence properties in risk management: properties and pitfalls. In *Risk Management: Value at Risk and Beyond*, M. Dempster (ed.). Cambridge University Press: Cambridge.

Embrechts, P., Höing, A., and Juri, A. (2003) Using copulae to bound the value-at-risk for functions of dependent risks. *Finance & Stochastics*, 7: 145–167.

Embrechts, P., Furrer, H., and Kaufmann, R. (2007) Different kinds of risk. In *Handbook of Financial Time Series*, T.G. Andersen, R.A. Davis, J.-P. Kreiss, and T. Mikosch (eds). Springer Verlag: Berlin.

Engle, R.F. (1982) Autoregressive conditional heteroskedasticity with estimates of the variance of United Kingdom inflation. *Econometrica*, **50**: 987–1007.

Engle, R.F. (2002) Dynamic conditional correlation: a simple class of multivariate GARCH models. *Journal of Business Economics and Statistics*, **20**: 339–350.

Erdos, P. and Renyi, A. (1959) On random graphs I. *Publicationes Mathematicae*, **6**: 290–297.

Fang, K.T., Kotz S., and Ng, K.W. (1987) *Symmetric Multivariate and Related Distributions*. Chapman & Hall: London.

Frees, E. and Valdez, E. (1998) Understanding relationships using copulas. *North American Actuarial Journal*, **2**: 1–25.

French, K., Schwert, G., and Stambaugh, R. (1987) Expected stock returns and volatility. *Journal of Financial Economics*, **19**(1): 3–29.

Fung, H.-G., Lo, W.-C., and Peterson, J.E. (1994) Examining the dependency in intra-day stock index futures. *Journal of Futures Markets*, **14**: 405–419.

Garman, M.B. and Klass, M. (1980) On the estimation of security price volatilities from historical data. *Journal of Business*, **53**(1): 67–78.

Gerber, H.U. (1979) *An Introduction to Mathematical Risk Theory*. Monograph 8. Huebner Foundation, University of Pennsylvania, PA.

Goodman, A.A. and Wong, C. (2009) Bringing the night sky closer: discoveries in the data deluge. In *The Fourth Paradigm: Data-Intensive Scientific Discovery*, T. Hey, S. Tansley, and K. Tolle (eds). Microsoft Research: Redmond, WA.

Gourieroux C., Laurent, J.P., and Scaillet, O. (2000) Sensitivity analysis of values at risk. *Journal of Empirical Finance*, **7**: 225–245.

Guetzkow, H. (1959) A use of simulation in the study of inter-nation relations. *Behavioral Science*, **4**(3): 183–191.

Guetzkow, H. (1962) *Simulation in Social Science: Readings*. Prentice-Hall: Englewood Cliffs, NJ.

Gujarati, D. (2014) *Econometrics by Example*, 2nd edn. Palgrave.

Havlin, S., Kenett, D.Y., Ben-Jacob, E., et al. (2012) Challenges in network science: applications to infrastructures, climate, social systems and economics. *The European Physical Journal Special Topics*, **214**(1): 273–293.

Hey, T., Tansley, S., and Tolle, K. (2009) *The Fourth Paradigm: Data Intensive Scientific Discovery*. Microsoft Research: Redmond, WA.

IMF (2016a) Exchange Rate Archives. http://www.imf.org/external/np/fin/ert/GUI/Pages/CountryDataBase.aspx.

IMF (2016b) International Financial Statistics (IFS). http://data.imf.org/?sk=5DABAFF2-C5AD-4D27-A175-1253419C02D1.

Irwin, J.O. (1925) On a criterion for the rejection of outlying observations. *Biometrika*, **17**: 237–250.

Joe, H. (1997) *Multivariate Models and Dependence Concepts*. Chapman & Hall: London.

Johnson, N. and Kotz, S. (1972) *Distributions in Statistics: Continuous Multivariate Distributions*. John Wiley & Sons, Inc.: New York.

Jorion, P. (1997) *Value at Risk: The New Benchmark for Controlling Market Risk*. McGraw-Hill: Chicago, IL.

Kennet, Y.D., and Havlin, S. (2015) *Network Science: A Useful Tool in Economics and Finance*. Springer: Berlin.

Klugman, S.A., Panier, H.H., and Willmot, G.E. (2008) *Loss Models: From Data to Decisions*. John Wiley & Sons, Inc.: Hoboken, NJ.

Krohs, U. and Callebaut, W. (2007) Data without models merging with models without data. In *Systems Biology: Philosophical Foundations*, F.C. Boogerd, F.J. Bruggeman, J.H.S. Hofmeyr, and H.V. Westerhoff (eds). Elsevier; pp. 181–213.

Kunitom, N. (1995) Improving the Parkinson method of estimating security price volatilities. *Journal of Business*, **65**(2): 295–302.

Kurowicka, D. and Joe, H. (eds) (2011) *Dependence Modeling: Vine Copula Handbook*. World Scientific: Singapore.

Li, D.X. (1999) On default correlation: a copula function approach. Working paper 99-07, RiskMetric Group.

Lo, A.W. (1991) Long term memory in stock market prices. *Econometrica*, **59**(5): 1279–1313.

Lo, A.W. (1997) Fat tails, long memory and the stock market since 1960s. *Economic Notes*, **26**: 213–245.

Losq, E. and Chateau, J.P.D. (1982) A generalization of the CAPM based on a property of the covariance operator. *Journal of Financial and Quantitative Analysis*, **17**: 783–797.

Merton, R. (1973) An intertemporal capital asset pricing model. *Econometrica*, **41**: 867–887.

Morgan, J.P. (1995) *Introduction to RiskMetrics*™, 4th edn, J.P. Morgan: New York.

Mandelbrot, B. and Taqqu, M. (1979) Robust R/S analysis of long run serial correlation. *Bulletin of the International Statistical Institute*, **48**(Book 2): 59–104.

Mandelbrot, B.B. and Van Ness, J.W. (1968) Fractional Brownian motions, fractional noises and applications. *SIAM Review*, **10**: 422–437.

Manyika, J., Chui, M., Brown, B., *et al.* (2011) *Big Data: The Next Frontier for Innovation, Competition, and Productivity*. McKinsey Global Institute. http://www.mckinsey.com/business-functions/digital-mckinsey/our-insights/big-data-the-next-frontier-for-innovation (accessed May 14, 2017).

Marshall, A. and Olkin, I. (1988) Families of multivariate distributions. *Journal of the American Statistical Association*, **83**: 834–841.

McNeil, R., Frey, A.J., and Embrechts, P. (2005) *Quantitative Risk Management*. Princeton University Press: Princeton, NJ.

National Research Council (2010) *Technical Capabilities Necessary for Regulation of Systemic Financial Risk: Summary of a Workshop*. The National Academies Press: Washington, DC.

Nelsen, R.B. (1999) *An Introduction to Copulas*. Lecture Notes in Statistics, vol. **139**. Springer Verlag: New York.

NYT (2012) The trouble with data that outpaces a theory. *The New York Times*, March 26. http://www.nytimes.com/2012/03/27/science/the-trouble-with-neutrinos-that-outpaced-einsteins-theory.html (accessed May 14, 2017).

Oakes, D. (1994) Multivariate survival distributions. *Journal of Nonparametric Statistics*, **3**: 343–354.

Parkinson, M. (1980) The extreme value method for estimating the variance of the ROR. *Journal of Business*, **53**(1): 61–65.

Patton, A.J. (2009) Copula-based models for financial time series. In *Handbook of Financial Time Series*, T.G. Andersen, R.A. Davis, J.-P. Kreiss, and T. Mikosch (eds). Springer Verlag: Berlin.

Pearl, J. (1985) Bayesian networks: a model of self-activated memory for evidential reasoning (UCLA Technical Report CSD-850017). In *Proceedings of the 7th Conference of the Cognitive Science Society*, University of California, Irvine, CA; pp. 329–334.

Prigogine, I. (1976) Order through fluctuation: self-organization and social system. In *Evolution and Consciousness*, E. Jantsch and C.H. Waddington (eds). Addison-Wesley: London; pp. 93–133.

Rogers, C. and Satchell, S. (1991) Estimating variance from high, low and closing prices. *Annals of Applied Probability*, **1**: 504–512.

Rubinstein, M. (1973) The fundamental theorem of parameter-preference security valuation. *Journal of Financial and Quantitative Analysis*, **8**: 61–70.

Stein, C. (1973) Estimation of the mean of a multivariate normal distribution. In *Proceedings of Prague Symposium on Asymptotic Statistics*, September 3–6, vol. II, Charles University, Prague, J. Hájek (ed.).

Stein, E., and Stein, J. (1991) Stock price distributions with stochastic volatility: an analytic approach. *Review of Financial Studies*, **4**: 727–752.

Sklar, A. (1959) Fonctions de répartition á *n* dimensions et leurs marges. Publications de l'Institut de Statistique de l'Université de Paris, vol. 8; pp. 229–231.

SNA (1993) *The United Nations System of National Accounts*. http://unstats.un.org/unsd/nationalaccount/docs/1993sna.pdf (accessed May 14, 2017).

Tapiero, C.S. (1975) Random walk models of advertising, their diffusion approximations and hypothesis testing. *Annals of Economics and Social Measurement*, **4**: 293–309.

Tapiero, C.S. (2004) Risk management. In *Encyclopedia on Actuarial and Risk Management*, J. Teugels and B. Sundt (eds). John Wiley & Sons.

Tapiero, C.S. (2005a) Reliability design and RVaR. *International Journal of Reliability, Quality and Safety Engineering*, **12**(4): 347–353.

Tapiero, C.S. (2005b) Value at risk and inventory control. *European Journal of Operations Research*, **163**(3): 769–775.

Tapiero, C.S. (2010) *Risk Finance and Asset Pricing: Value, Measurements, and Markets*. John Wiley & Sons, Inc.: Hoboken, NJ.

Tapiero, C.S. (2013) *Engineering Risk and Finance*. Springer.

Tapiero, C.S. and Hsu, L.F. (1988) Quality control of an unreliable random FMS Bernoulli and CSP sampling. *International Journal of Production Research*, **26**(6): 1125–1135.

Tapiero, C.S. and Vallois, P. (2000) The inter-event range process and testing for chaos in time series. *Neural Network World*, **10**(1–2): 89–99.

Tapiero, C.S. and Vallois, P. (2015) Financial modelling and memory: mathematical system. In *Future Perspectives in Risk Models and Finance*, A. Bensoussan, D. Guegan, and C.S. Tapiero (eds). International Series in Operations Research and Management Science, vol. 211. Springer: New York; pp. 149–246.

Tapiero, C.S. and Vallois, P. (2016) Fractional randomness. *Physica A: Statistical Mechanics and its Applications*, **462**: 1161–1177.

Tapiero, C.S., Capobianco, M.F., and Lewin, A.Y. (1975) Structural inference in organizations. *Journal of Mathematical Sociology*, **4**: 121–130.

Tapiero, C.S., Tapiero, O.J., and Jumarie, G. (2016) The price of granularity and fractional finance. *Risk and Decision Analysis*, **6**(1): 7–21.

Taqqu, M.S. (1986) A bibliographical guide to self similar processes and long range dependence. In *Dependence in Probability and Statistics*, E. Eberlein and M. S. Taqqu (eds). Birkhauser: Boston; pp. 137–165.

The Economist (2010) Data, data everywhere. *The Economist*, February 25. http://www.economist.com/node/15557443 (accessed May 14, 2017).

The PRS Group (n.d.) *International Country Risk Guide*: http://www.prsgroup.com/about-us/our-two-methodologies/icrg (accessed May 14, 2017).

The World Bank. World DataBank. World Development Indicators. http://databank.worldbank.org/data/home.aspx. Accessed on Jan. 3, 2017.

Vallois, P. (1996) The range of a simple random walk on Z. *Advanced Applied Probability*, **28**: 1014–1033.

Vallois, P. and Tapiero, C.S. (1996) Run length statistics and the Hurst exponent in random and birth–death random walks. *Chaos, Solitons and Fractals*, 7(9): 1333–1341.

Vallois, P. and Tapiero, C.S. (1997a) The range process in random walks: theoretical results and applications. In *Computational Approaches to Economic Problems*, H. Ammans, B. Rustem, and A. Whinston (eds). Advances in Computational Economics, vol. 6. Kluwer: Dordrecht; pp. 291–307.

Vallois, P. and Tapiero, C.S. (1997b) Range reliability in random walks. *Mathematical Methods of Operations Research*, 45(3): 325–345.

Vallois, P. and Tapiero, C.S. (2007) Memory-based persistence in a counting random walk process. *Physica A*, **386**(1): 303–317.

Vallois, P. and Tapiero, C.S. (2009) A claims persistence process and insurance. *Insurance Economics and Mathematics*, **44**(3): 367–373.

Vasicek, O. (1977) An equilibrium characterization of the term structure. *Journal of Financial Economics*, **5**, 177–188.

Wei, J.K.C and Lee, C.F. (1988) The generalized Stein/Rubinstein covariance formula and its application to estimate real systematic risk. *Journal of Management Science*, **34**(10): 1266–1270.

Weinberg, R.A. (2010) Point: hypotheses first. *Nature*, **464**: 678.

Weiss, G.H. (1994) *Aspects and Applications of the Random Walk*. North-Holland: Amsterdam.

World Economic Forum (2016) *The Global Risks Report 2016*, 11th edn. World Economic Forum: Geneva. https://www.weforum.org/reports/the-global-risks-report-2016 (accessed May 14, 2017)

Yang, D. and Zhang, Q. (2000) Drift independent volatility estimation based on high, low, open, and close prices. *Journal of Business*, **73**: 477–492.

3

Global Finance

Utility, Financial Consumption, and Asset Pricing

Motivation

This chapter outlines the utility-based and Arrow–Debreu approaches to financial risk and asset pricing as used in global financial models. While the utility-based approach to pricing is founded on agents' preferences, the Arrow–Debreu approach is preference free. To put it another way, it is based on a number of specific conditions; for example, no arbitrage, unique equilibrium prices, and the predictability of all future state preferences. In this chapter, we extend conventional single-agent utility pricing to a multi-agent model and construct an approach to the "financialization" of utility decisions. In this context, prices are unique and defined by aggregate (global) demand for consumption, rather than by what each agent is willing to pay for consumption, as well as by the aggregate supply and its price. The multi-agent framework is applied to the study of several problems; for example, the multi-agent consumption-based capital asset pricing model (CCAPM), as well as to a variety of challenging problems in global finance, including investment in competing markets, credit pricing, and foreign exchange (FX) pricing. The Arrow–Debreu framework and its rationale, which underlies complete markets finance, is developed and applied to investment pricing using simple models. These are extended to continuous-time models in Chapters 7 and 8.

3.1 Introduction: Financial Models and Pricing

Adam Smith's (1994[1776]) theory of competitive economic markets distinguishes between value and price. Fundamental elements are defined in terms of:

- scarcity or excess (supply);
- need or consumption (demand);
- exchange (markets).

Value defines worth to an agent, while price is defined by an exchange, either between financial agents, each seeking to better their wealth, or by a financial market. When an exchange is made in a financial market, it sets a market price. The market price results from the exchanges of an extremely large number of financial agents, none of which has any advantages over the other with regard to the control of prices or information access. Market pricing theory is usually attributed to an extension of Walras' general equilibrium model as interpreted by Arrow and Debreu, who extended it to future risk markets.

Globalization, Gating, and Risk Finance, First Edition. Unurjargal Nyambuu and Charles S. Tapiero.
© 2018 John Wiley & Sons Ltd. Published 2018 by John Wiley & Sons Ltd.

Its theoretical foundations are based on simple elements. For example, no arbitrage; which implies that no profit can be made without assuming risks. In this framework, pricing is defined relative to known asset prices that define a probability measure. In other words, there is an implied risk-free distribution that allows current prices to be defined by the expected value of future prices. The utility approach is based instead on financial agents and consumers, each of which has their preference and risk attitude embedded in a utility function. Prices are then determined by marginal utility principles, defining the price the agent is willing to pay and not the price they will actually end up paying. The price is set by what all buying agents are willing to pay and at what prices all selling agents are willing to receive.

Both frameworks are useful, each with its advantages and limitations. In truly competitive markets, prices are set uniquely when an equilibrium is reached (i.e., when there is no scarcity and no excess). In other words, this occurs when the market clearing price results in an equilibrium of demand and supply. When markets are not truly competitive, one or the other (scarcity or need) may determine a price. For example, in the hand of a monopolist, the price is defined by what they may extract from buyers. In such cases, prices can differ across buyers, and thus do not need to be unique; that is, a price tailored to a buyer's need and ability to pay, rather than to a market-defined price. These situations occur in many instances. In the financial industry there is no scarcity of services, yet collusion and, in some cases, bank rights and rules allow the extraction of non-competitive profits because of their access to a controlling position. This is legal and referred to as proprietary (prop) trading, and it is a significant source of income for investment banks. Some banks may also implement policies that favor their interests by simply using the power they have over their clients. Further, not all risks are priced equally. Certain risks are exchanged (or traded) in a market, while others are not, both potentially resulting in different prices. When we refer to the price of risk, we do not consider the price of non-diversifiable, uninsurable, or incomplete risks—which are various names that refer to risks that are not traded (although they may be priced by specific agents entering into appropriate exchanges). For this reason, only diversifiable risks can be used in market pricing, albeit based on "a bounded rationality" embedded in the risk model. Risk models, however, may falter when they cannot account for complex transactions or unfair and discriminatory exchanges due to asymmetric information and other issues. Approaches to financial risk and asset pricing when markets are out of equilibrium (incomplete) are complex, and therefore challenging.

3.1.1 The Walras–Arrow–Debreu Preference-Free Q Framework

The fundamental approach to financial pricing originates in the economic law of supply and demand (J.-B. Says). Thus, a product which is in great demand and in short supply is scarce; consequently, its price will be greater than a product that is abundant or in excess supply. Such a premise underlies Walras' general economic equilibrium (Walras, 1874–1877). This theory essentially states that, in an exchange economy, a market price tends to increase as long as there is a positive excess demand; it tends to decrease when there is a positive excess supply. An equilibrium is reached when "negative feedback forces" lead to a unique price, or when demand and supply clear at a unique point. An adjustment process that moves such situations to be in equilibrium is termed a "tâtonnement process" (i.e., trial-and-error process) by Walras. Prices are then defined relative to the price of an asset or a basket of assets (the latter is termed a "numeraire").

For example, returns determined by using a risk-neutral measure are priced relative to a risk-free rate, while a consumer price index (CPI) may be priced relative to a basket of CPIs in multiple countries.

Walras' theoretical economic and competitive framework was applied to risk-free products, where all assets are countable and priced based on their relative need and scarcity. Arrow's (1951) and Debreu's (1953, 1960) important contributions to risk economics and financial pricing extended Walras' general competitive equilibrium to risk and future markets, providing thereby the means to price risk. They did so by framing future and predictable states into denumerable and price-accountable states, each state with a price defined by the law of demand and supply. An equilibrium model is then reached based on consumers' and investors' rationality, resulting in a state where there are no longer profit opportunities defined by a state we call no arbitrage. This framework leads to the convention to accept risk pricing models when markets are complete. Such an approach does not prescribe, however, how such prices are reached and often neglects the factors that in practice affect exchanges, and therefore their unique price. These models are then based on assumptions, including no-arbitrage opportunities, predictable future states, current and shared information, and an infinite number of consumers or financial agents (none of which matters as far as prices are concerned and none have an advantage over the other). In such models, the market price is unique and implies the expectation of completely and uniquely priced future states. In this sense, current prices derived from the expectation of a given set of underlying state preferences imply one another. Technically, this means that under an appropriate probability measure, future prices are implied in current ones. Inversely, a current price does not imply future ones since one price cannot imply uniquely many others. This asymmetry, of course, has implications that we often prefer to neglect as they undermine the statistical and predictive efforts we make to predict future prices from past or known financial data. This statement does not depreciate the essential and important need of applied financial econometrics, but rather seeks to build a greater awareness, that all models and their interpretations are bounded by their assumptions which might be needed but need not be necessarily true. The transformation of finance and its adaptation to a global framework through IT and networking technologies, the growth of A-National and globally networked financial citadels, globalization, have already eroded the reliability of the standard economic models accepted generally in the last century. These and other factors may thus alter the models of both domestic and foreign assets where we use their relative prices (or, say, FX). Lacking a general framework that could integrate environmental, geopolitical, macroeconomic statistics and factors, and markets' gating by sovereign states and regulation systems, we necessarily bound our models; therefore, in reality, and in the short term, prices are mostly incomplete and impossible (if not very difficult) to predict.

Rational expectations result in future prices to be implied in a current trade's price. In this sense, financial futures are priced in a present. Such an observation provides the mechanism to price future prices, including financial derivatives (options) and generally future and forward asset prices. In this approach, the past is no guide to the future, although a past informational base defines the quality of future models and their estimate (technically formulated as conditional estimates on a filtration as seen in Chapter 2). All prices result from conditional expectation (a filtration), changing over time as additional information accumulates, the environment changes, political events occur, news changes, and volatility occurs. These complex events alter future expectations, and therefore current prices! Their prices are thus measured relative to "a probability measure" defining uniquely the equilibrium no-arbitrage exchange price. The rationality underlying complete financial markets is then based on a number of assumptions, including:

1) The future is completely defined in terms of what we know about a complete set of future states, or state preferences.
2) Each future state is priced uniquely.
3) There is no arbitrage; namely, no profit can be made without assuming risk.
4) A current price is defined relative to a probability measure and its expectation of future states and define the unique price.

In this sense, probabilities of future states and future prices are mathematical constructs implied in current prices.

For these reasons, an attempt to price assets and their risks is always based on a prior definition of what financial models seek and can do. In this chapter, we consider both the utility approach based on preferences of financial agents and the Arrow–Debreu approach that defines prices based on financial agents' exchanges in complete (efficient) markets. Both approaches will be used in their univariate and multivariate (countries and multi-agent) frameworks. These two fundamental approaches to financial modeling, (1) rational expectations and (2) consumption utility-based models, will be extended and applied further in subsequent chapters.

3.1.2 Utility Finance

The fundamental utility approach is defined in terms of functions that express individual and subjective preferences for risk assets by specific individual (or representative) agents. Pricing is then a personal valuation that can generate demand and supply and in economic markets can result in exchanges between financial agents justified by their utility. An exchange occurs when there is an agreement between the buyer and the seller. In global finance, increased complexity and risks render such exchanges more complex, and therefore more "subjective." In the following, we shall consider first an individual *agent*, whose utility of consumption defines a price—a price that an agent is willing to pay for consumption. Subsequently, we consider several agents, each maximizing its own utility of consumption and paying a price—a unique price, defined by an equilibrium of the aggregate demand for consumption and aggregate supply. Such problems are in fact more complex, resulting in games between agents, each of which is equipped with its own information, the power to sway the market price or demand, and so on. In this chapter, elements of such an approach are presented; some of its elements are developed further in Chapters 7–10.

Both the Walras–Arrow–Debreu (WAD) and the kernel-utility pricing models are, as we shall see, practically inverse problems. Namely, future pricing models' expectations imply current prices. The WAD approach is based on a concept of financial equilibrium, while the utility approach is based on a rational model that values the preferences, attitudes, and behaviors of consumers or financial agents. Both approaches seek at the same time for models that are coherent with observed prices. However, theoretically, utility models define prices that consumers–investors are willing to pay for, rather than prices set in a fair, competitive, and efficient financial market. The utility multi-agent pricing models we shall consider extend the utility framework by pricing investors relative to a price resulting from all other agents. As a result, pricing is a strategic problem when financial agents are powerful, informed, and rich enough to sway the market price. Such a framework is relevant to global finance when countries, as well as large A-National and sovereign states with different agendas, affect the prices of financial markets. Thus, unlike the WAD financial markets, where all financial agents' decisions are independent, in a multi-agent framework there are sovereign and other agents competing for global resources or seeking to sway financial markets or FX currencies to their advantage. Their power, information, and decisions lead to strategic and dependent decisions, and therefore to markets that might not be efficient. For example, say that countries are consumers of a given good (e.g., oil) and say that we seek the price of this good. The kernel pricing framework would (for a country's utility) indicate a price that country would be willing (or prefer) to pay and not the price, which depends on aggregate demand and supply, it will in fact pay. For these reasons, in a global framework, "equivalence" or "parity" between countries' prices is in fact more complex than presumed by financial markets that in a global context are treated as complete. In summary, the WAD and the utility theoretical frameworks differ. One is based on a market equilibrium, and the other is based on the power, the information, and the agendas of financial agents that can sway prices to their advantage.

3.1.3 Utility Preferences and Pricing

Utility models are based on investors' preferences defining their rational decisions. For example, consumption utility models define mostly the utility of consumers by the maximization of consumers' utility. Such a maximization results in a unique marginal utility that defines both the price and the volume of consumption. When the utility of consumption is "financialized," the price the agent pays is random, and thus its consumption is also random. For example, if w_k is a financial expenditure for consumption at a given time, and if $\tilde{\pi}$ is an uncertain price to be paid for consumption (a function of aggregate demand and supply and suppliers' competition), then current consumption is necessarily random since $\tilde{c}_k = w_k / \tilde{\pi}$. By the same token, a consumer planning a level of consumption has a financial expenditure that is random, or $\tilde{w}_k = c_k / \tilde{\pi}$. At an aggregate level, we may therefore see that economic consumption markets and financial (money or stocks) markets are dependent. In such cases, consumption, wealth expenditures in consumption of financial markets, and prices are in fact all random, albeit intimately dependent on one another.

In a global and transformed economic environment, these issues are upended by sovereign states' political and geopolitical policies that move markets and their expectations. Economic and financial models as well as political simulation models (e.g., see Guetzkow (1959, 1962)) are combined to simplify the "global complexity" and reduce agents' future uncertainties to well-defined risks they may be able to value and price. For a typical consumer–investor, independent of other investors, consuming now and investing for future consumption is based on an inter-temporal substitution between "needs now" and "needs later." To simplify their predictions, future models are used that account for habits, reflecting the fact that a consumer may be resilient to a change in consumption habits or other economic patterns based on confirmed statistical analysis. Similarly, an appreciation of national governments' future decisions may define future stock prices. For example, when sovereign financial policies are expected to alter future political agreements that alter future consumption or define future financial opportunities, these may contribute to drastic internal market changes that can, in some cases, lead to new economic and financial trends.

Numerous issues result from our consideration of multiple and simultaneous financial and economic variables, as well as agendas. Sovereign agendas, of course, may differ, and thus their financial terms of exchange and risks are necessarily also different. Pricing models ought to recognize their differences, including the following:

- In a global setting, investors differ in their value, preferences, environment, technology, and so on, and are therefore heterogeneous rather than homogeneous or defined by a single representative agent.
- Central banks have different agendas; some are governed by macroeconomic, political, geo-finance, geo-regulations, or geo-risks concerns. Further, in some cases, they define policies that are based on national priorities.
- Sovereign states may not be equally and financially resilient. For example, different capacities to meet sovereign debt payments and failure to do so may have systemic repercussions that differ from country to country or between groups of countries (e.g., the European Central Bank and IMF relating to the 2014–2016 Greek financial crisis).
- Sovereign states differ in their ability to impose gating policies (such as financial regulation and taxation, trade restrictions, and control of various sorts) applied locally (in their domestic country) or globally (imposed across national boundaries). These abilities differ from country to country; therefore, the real price of assets and consumption may differ appreciably. For example, the strength of the US dollar and its use as a global currency for trade and exchanges provide a legal right used by the USA both to control transactions conducted in US dollars and to set global US regulatory rules.
- In global financial markets, investors and intermediaries tend to invest and trade in large sums (such as financial institutions and funds), some with agendas and the power to affect financial markets (as is the case of sovereign funds, as well as large banks such as Goldman Sachs and JP Morgan). Thus, rather than atomic investors unable to affect market prices individually, national enterprises and large financial institutions have the ability to coerce market prices, to better compete or seek arbitrage profits (e.g., as some banks collude in setting the Libor rate and FX rates). Elements vital to the efficiency of global exchanges, when not maintained, alter the assumptions we make regarding fundamental pricing and utility pricing models (such as the capital asset pricing model (CAPM) or kernel (CCAPM) pricing models).
- FX prices, although subject to global economic forces of demand and supply, may also be manipulated explicitly or implicitly by a sovereign state's macroeconomic and trade policies. These interventions render trade and FX financial markets far more strategic, as they depend more on the power of sovereign states to affect the terms of trade and determine their terms of exchange. In such an environment, currency wars, whether fought explicitly or implicitly, are common.
- Safety and security are of greater concern due to the free movement that globalization requires and the diffusion of technologies empowering agents to trade from anywhere in the globe. It contributes also to a "tyranny of a financial minority" that imposes its will through leverage, stealth transactions, and terrorism. These elements alter the calculus of global financial risks. At a more mundane level, these risks include nationalization of foreign assets, retaliatory actions set on foreign investors by national entities, cyber risks, and so on.

In these situations, geo-politics, macroeconomic principles, and sovereign states' agendas, combined with a far more aggressive and strategic financial regulation and gated finance and financial markets, alter the volume and the ability of financial enterprises, traders, and investors to function in concordance with the underlying assumptions of financial models. Anchor theories, such as fundamental finance (based on the WAD framework) and utility theory that are the mainstay of financial analysis and pricing models, are challenged by global finance. Subjective finance (i.e., individual rationalities aggregated over many financial agents), such as behavioral finance and microstructure finance, is contributing to complementary developments to rational financial models, although their (mostly) microeconomic concerns do not define the increasingly important impact of macroeconomic and geopolitical factors. Although it is presumptuous that we may provide answers and solutions to these problems, we will consider in this chapter a number of problems based on the application of these approaches. In Chapters 4 and 5 we consider the macroeconomic approach, underlying macro-finance. Chapters 7 and 8 will address these problems from a Quant-Finance approach (i.e., based on stochastic financial models and complete markets pricing), while Chapter 9 provides an introduction to elementary models for financial consumption and economic trade.

3.2   Review: Elements of Utility and Risk

Say that $\{\tilde{R}, P(.)\}$ is a set of rewards $\tilde{R}$ defined by a continuous probability distribution $P(.)$ and define a utility function $u(.)$ for such rewards. The expected utility provides a scale for the pricing of random rewards $\tilde{R}$ relative to certain (risk-free) return R_{CE}. This price is defined by their parity; namely, that the utility valuation of a risk-free return and that of risk-prone return have the same utility:

$$E\big(u(\tilde{R})\big) = \int_{r \in \mathfrak{R}} u(\tilde{R})f(\tilde{R}) \, d\tilde{R} \text{ and } u(R_{CE}) = E\big(u(\tilde{R})\big) \text{ or } R_{CE} = u^{-1}\big(E\big(u(\tilde{R})\big)\big)$$

Let the mean return be $\hat{R} = E(\tilde{R})$, then the risk premium is defined by $P = \hat{R} - R_{CE}$; that is, the financial rate of return (ROR) that a utility holder will be willing to pay to remove risk. It can be interpreted as an "insurance" premium paid by the utility holder whose expectation of future returns equals a risk-free rate. Thus, $\hat{R} = P + R_{CE} > P + R_f$. In other words, $R_{CE} > R_f$, and the utility holder will demand a risk-free interest greater than the market risk-free rate. If there is no arbitrage, the certain equivalent is necessarily the treasury's risk-free return R_f, and therefore $R_f = R_{CE}$, $\hat{R} = R_f + P$, while $\hat{R} - R_f = P$ is the risk premium. If, as indicated earlier, $R_f \neq R_{CE}$, there may be something else that we are missing when calculating the risk premium. This was observed in fact by Mehra and Prescott (1985), who pointed to a substantial difference between the equity premium using financial time series of stocks and using a utility model based on investors' preferences for future returns. This difference (although there are many papers and studies that seek to reconcile these differences) is called the *equity premium puzzle*. It highlights the necessity to reconcile the validity of financial models we use with the financial data at hand. When these cannot be reconciled, it implies that the model fails to explain what it purports to explain in the first place.

Such a *puzzle*, in its global setting, is complicated further. For example, let $u_D\left(\widetilde{R}_D,\widetilde{R}_{DF}\right)$ and $u_F\left(\widetilde{R}_{FD},\widetilde{R}_F\right)$ be the utility of two agents, one domestic and the other foreign respectively. We assume that $\widetilde{R}_D$ and $\widetilde{R}_{DF}$ are the RORs the domestic agent obtains from investments in domestic and foreign markets respectively, and similarly for the foreign agent. Let

$$E_D u_D\left(\widetilde{R}_D,\widetilde{R}_{DF}\right) = u_D\left(R_{CE}^D, R_{CE}^{DF}\right) \quad \text{and} \quad E_F u_F\left(\widetilde{R}_F,\widetilde{R}_{FD}\right) = u_F\left(R_{CE}^F, R_{CE}^{FD}\right)$$

Since $R_{CE}^F = R_f^F$ and $R_{CE}^D = R_f^D$ are the risk-free rates of the foreign and the domestic countries, we have a system of two equations and two unknowns, R_{CE}^{DF} and R_{CE}^{FD}, denoting the RORs each agent expects from another country to invest in. In other words, their solution is given by

$$E_D u_D\left(\widetilde{R}_D,\widetilde{R}_{DF}\right) = u_D\left(R_f^D, R_{CE}^{DF}\right)$$

$$E_F u_F\left(\widetilde{R}_F,\widetilde{R}_{FD}\right) = u_F\left(R_f^F, R_{CE}^{FD}\right)$$

Further, developments, extensions, and applications of dependent and multivariate utilities will be considered subsequently. These multivariate utilities, valued or priced depending on global agents, highlight the theoretical and practical challenges of confronting economic and financial models in an era of globalization and its gating.

3.2.1 Utility and Risk Preferences

Utility valuation is based on "risk-predictables" prospects given by a return: $\widetilde{R} = \hat{R} + \tilde{\varepsilon}$, where $\tilde{\varepsilon}$ is a random error, with $E(\tilde{\varepsilon}) = 0$ and $\mathrm{var}(\tilde{\varepsilon}) = \sigma^2$, where σ^2 is the payoff variance. An expected utility is then $E\left(u(\hat{R} + \tilde{\varepsilon})\right)$, which equals, as indicated earlier, the utility of the certain equivalent, or $u(R_{CE}) = u(\hat{R} - P)$. A marginal analysis based on a Taylor series valuation relative to the expected return then yields

$$E\left(u(\widetilde{R})\right) = E\left(u(\hat{R} + \tilde{\varepsilon})\right) = E\left(u(\hat{R}) + \tilde{\varepsilon}u'(\hat{R}) + \frac{\tilde{\varepsilon}^2}{2}u''(\hat{R}) \right) = u(\hat{R}) + \sigma^2\frac{u''(\hat{R})}{2}$$

However, an equivalent valuation yields $u(R_{CE}) = E\left(u(\widetilde{R})\right)$ or $E\left(u(\widetilde{R})\right) = E\left(u(\hat{R} + \tilde{\varepsilon})\right)$. Applying a two-term Taylor series expansion, $E\left(u(\hat{R} + \tilde{\varepsilon})\right) = u(\hat{R}) - Pu'(\hat{R})$ and $E\left(u(\widetilde{R} + \tilde{\varepsilon})\right) = u(\hat{R}) + \sigma^2\left(u''(\hat{R})/2\right)$. Equating these two terms, the risk premium is given (instead of our previous use of the certain equivalent) by:

$$P = -\frac{1}{2}\sigma^2\frac{u''(\hat{R})}{u'(\hat{R})}$$

Note that $u'(\hat{R}) > 0$; therefore, for a risk-averse investor the premium is positive if $u''(\hat{R}) < 0$ and for a risk-loving investor the premium is negative. In this spirit, a risk attitude is embedded in the utility function's derivatives, leading to the definition of an index of risk aversion, called the Arrow–Pratt index of risk aversion:

$$A_P(\hat{R}) = -\frac{u''(\hat{R})}{u'(\hat{R})} \quad \text{or} \quad P = \frac{1}{2}\sigma^2 A_P(\hat{R})$$

This index expresses the quantity by which a fair bet must be altered by a risk-averse decision-maker in order to be indifferent between accepting and rejecting the bet. These definitions provide a number of indicators where risk attitudes and their prices can be formalized and assessed quantitatively.

Analysis of risk aversion or risk loving has indicated that there may be other indexes indicative of such attitudes. For example, an index of prudence and temperance was suggested by Kimball (1990) and Eeckhoudt *et al.* (1996) based on the third derivative of the utility function (see Eichner and Wagener (2005) and Munier and Tapiero (2008) for their relationship and the returns' variance).

For example, measurements of various absolute risk attitudes characterized by a utility function $u(.)$ are defined (with respect to wealth) as follows:

$$A_k \equiv -\frac{u^{k+1}(W)}{u^k(W)}, \quad W \in \mathfrak{R}, \ k \in \mathbb{N}$$

where W is an investor's wealth and $u^k(W)$ denotes its kth derivative. Particular measurements of risk attitudes consist thus of A_1 —the Arrow–Pratt measure of absolute risk aversion defined earlier. Similarly, A_2 and A_3 are used to denote a quantitative estimate of absolute prudence and absolute temperance. When $k \geq 3$, a number of studies have suggested an interpretation embedded in a mixed risk aversion (Eichner and Wagener, 2005) and given by

$$B_k \equiv -z\frac{u^{k+1}(W+z)}{u^k(W+z)}$$

For $k = 1$, this yields a partial relative risk aversion, while $k = 2$ and $k = 3$ can be used as measurements of partial prudence and partial temperance. These indexes, although not commonly applied (relative to the index of risk aversion based on the second derivative of the utility function), may be useful when seeking to compare the "risk attitudes" across national boundaries. For example, investors in different countries may have different "attitudes" due to their social conditions, their wealth, their culture, and the private sense of safety they may have.

When an expected utility is subject to another source of risk, it is said to be risk robust if it is appreciably insensitive to it. A prudent investor, for example, will reach an investment decision based on a utility that reflects this prudence-robust attitude. For example, an investor with a precautionary motive will tend to save more to hedge against the uncertainty (i.e., future events that were not accounted for), which is common for an investor investing in a foreign market. This notion of prudence was defined first by Kimball (1990) and subsequently by Eeckhoudt *et al.* (1996), associating it with the optimal utility (measured by relative marginal utilities invariance), which is or could be perturbed by other sources of risk. A prudence risk premium ψ may then be defined as an additional insurance premium to be paid to maintain one's own marginal utility at its known level.

3.2.2 Selected Utility Functions

A utility function is defined by its behavioral and mathematical properties that are ascribed to the utility holder. In the following, we list a number of utility functions commonly used.

1) The exponential utility:

$$u(W) = 1 - e^{-aW}, \quad \frac{\partial u(W)}{\partial W} = ae^{-aW} > 0, \quad \frac{\partial^2 u(W)}{\partial W^2} = -a^2 e^{-aW} < 0$$

and therefore its Arrow–Pratt index of risk aversion is $A_P = a$, while its risk premium is $\pi = \sigma^2 a$.

2) The logarithmic utility:

$$u(W) = \ln(a + bW), \quad \frac{\partial u(W)}{\partial W} = \frac{b}{a + bW}, \quad \frac{\partial^2 u(W)}{\partial W^2} = -\frac{b^2}{(a + bW)^2} < 0$$

and therefore its Arrow–Pratt index of risk aversion is $A_P = b/(a + bW)$.

3) The hyperbolic absolute risk aversion utility:

$$u(W) = \frac{1-b}{b}\left(\frac{aW}{1-b} + c\right)^b, \quad \frac{\partial u(W)}{\partial W} = a\left(\frac{aW}{1-b} + c\right)^{b-1}, \quad \frac{\partial^2 u(W)}{\partial W^2} = -a^2\left(\frac{aW}{1-b} + c\right)^{b-2}$$

and therefore its Arrow–Pratt index of risk aversion is

$$A_P = a\left(\frac{aW}{1-b} + c\right)^{-1}$$

These, as well as other utility functions, will be used in various problems and applications.

3.3 The Utility of Consumption and its Price

Let c_0^k be the kth individual consumption choice at time $t = 0$. Its utility $u_k(c_0^k)$ defines a subjective measure for the value of consumption from an agent's vantage point. The rational price π_0^k that a kth agent would be willing to pay for is defined by the optimization of its net utility. The net utility is $U_k(c_0^k) = u_k(c_0^k) - \pi_0^k c_0^k$, and therefore

$$\underset{c_0^k}{\operatorname{Max}} U(c_0^k) = u_k(c_0^k) - \pi_0^k c_0^k, \quad \text{and} \quad \pi_0^k(c_0^k) = \frac{\partial u_k(c_0^k)}{\partial c_0^k}$$

Prices are not defined by what one is willing to pay, but by what the market bears. For example, consider two individuals, each willing to pay for consumption $\pi_0^1(c_0^1) = \partial u_1(c_0^1)/\partial c_0^1$ and $\pi_0^2(c_0^2) = \partial u_2(c_0^2)/\partial c_0^2$. The price they would pay will depend on numerous factors, potentially including aggregate consumption, aggregate supply, market structure, imports and exports tariffs, and so on. If the price depends only on aggregate consumption $C_0 = c_0^1 + c_0^2$, or $\pi(C_0)$, then for a rational utility optimizing consumer we have

$$\underset{c_0^1}{\text{Max}}\, U\left(c_0^1\right) = u_1\left(c_0^1\right) - \pi_0(C_0)c_0^1 \quad \text{and} \quad \frac{\partial u_1\left(c_0^1\right)}{\partial c_0^1} = \pi_0(C_0) + c_0^1 \frac{\partial \pi}{\partial C_0}, \quad \pi(0) = 0$$

$$\underset{c_0^2}{\text{Max}}\, U\left(c_0^2\right) = u_2\left(c_0^2\right) - \pi_0(C_0)c_0^2 \quad \text{and} \quad \frac{\partial u_2\left(c_0^2\right)}{\partial c_0^2} = \pi_0(C_0) + c_0^2 \frac{\partial \pi}{\partial C_0}, \quad \pi(0) = 0$$

Unlike the single-agent utility problem, where the agent is also a "price maker" (embedded in its utility), the two-agent problem defines a price where both agents contribute to the definition of the price and the aggregate market supply (assuming it equals the aggregate demand). In this sense, agents are "price takers," but each able to sway the price that depends on its utility of consumption. Their actions render their consumption and the price they will pay random. Such a formulation has implications for global finance and for its pricing commodities traded, consumed, and supplied globally.

3.3.1 Example: The Financial Utility of Consumption

Consider $u(\tilde{c})$, $\tilde{c} = W/\tilde{\pi}$, and a consumer buying insurance to maintain the same marginal utilities of money (or the price to π^*). Thus:

$$\frac{\partial u\left(\frac{W-\psi}{\pi^*}\right)}{\partial W} = E\left\{\frac{\partial u(W/\tilde{\pi}(W))}{\partial W}\right\} \quad \text{or} \quad \frac{1}{\pi^*}\frac{\partial u(c^*)}{\partial c^*} = E\left\{\left(1 - W\frac{\partial \ln \tilde{\pi}(W)}{\partial W}\right)\frac{1}{\tilde{\pi}(W)}\frac{\partial u(\tilde{c})}{\partial \tilde{c}}\right\}$$

Using a logarithmic utility:

$$\frac{1}{\pi^* c^*} = E\left\{\left(1 - W\frac{\partial \ln \tilde{\pi}(W)}{\partial W}\right)\frac{1}{\tilde{\pi}(W)\tilde{c}}\right\}$$

Thus, the risk premium ψ is

$$\frac{W}{W-\psi} = E\left(1 - W\frac{\partial \ln \tilde{\pi}(W)}{\partial W}\right) \quad \text{or} \quad \psi = W\left\{1 - \frac{1}{E\left(1 - W\frac{\partial \ln \tilde{\pi}(W)}{\partial W}\right)}\right\}$$

Alternatively, set $u(W-\psi) = Eu\left(W + \tilde{R}\right)$, where $\tilde{R}$ is a random (gain or loss) return; then:

$$\frac{\partial}{\partial(.)}u(W-\psi) = E\left(\frac{\partial}{\partial(.)}u\left(W + \tilde{R}\right)\right) \quad \text{or} \quad u'(W-\psi) = E\left(u'\left(W + \tilde{R}\right)\right)$$

And by the inverse utility:

$$\psi = W - {u'}^{-1}\left\{E\left(u'\left(W + \tilde{R}\right)\right)\right\}$$

By using a Taylor series approximation on the marginal utility, we have

$$u'(W-\psi) = u'(W) - \psi u''(W) \quad \text{and} \quad E\left(u'\left(W + \tilde{R}\right)\right) = u'(W) + u''(W)E(\tilde{R}) + \frac{1}{2}u'''(W)E\left(\tilde{R}^2\right)$$

And again:

$$\psi = -E(\tilde{R}) - \frac{1}{2}\frac{u'''(W)}{u''(W)}E(\tilde{R}^2)$$

Letting $E(\tilde{R}) = 0$, $E(\tilde{R}^2) = \sigma^2$ for convenience, we obtain a prudence premium:

$$\psi = -\frac{1}{2}\frac{u'''(W)}{u''(W)}\sigma^2, \quad \frac{u'''(W)}{u''(W)} < 0$$

For a risk-averse decision-maker, the utility second-order derivative is negative ($u'' \leq 0$), and therefore prudence will be positive (negative) if the third derivative u''' is positive (negative). Further, Kimball (1990) also shows that if the risk premium is positive and decreases with wealth W, then $\psi > \pi$. As a result, $\psi - \pi$ is a premium one would pay to render the expected utility of an investment invariant under other sources of risk (meaning a robustness of the utility with respect to other sources of risk it may depend on). These terms—*expected utility, certainty equivalent, risk premium, Arrow–Pratt index of risk aversion*, and *prudence*—are used profusely in insurance, economics, and financial applications.

In a global finance environment, the utility approach may be expanded (as we shall see subsequently and in Chapter 9) to utility of financial agents to be far more dependent among themselves as each agent may affect the utility of the other. Further, given the growth of risk due to the complexity and risk compounding in a global environment, attention is to be given to prudence and its risk premium.

3.3.2 The Utility of Financial Consumption

We assume that agents' consumptions are financial—that is, defined by the money they commit to consumption. Let W_0^k be the kth agent financial commitment, and let $\tilde{\pi}(C_0)$ be the price of consumption, a function of aggregate demand for consumption, $\tilde{C}_0 = \sum_{k=1}^{N}\tilde{c}_0^k$. Then, $\tilde{c}_0^k = W_0^k/\tilde{\pi}(C_0)$, which reduces the utility optimization problem to that of an expected financial utility:

$$\underset{W_0^k}{\text{Max}}\,U(c_0^k) = Eu_k\left(\frac{W_0^k}{\tilde{\pi}(C_0)}\right) - W_0^k$$

Note that $\tilde{c}_0^k = W_0^k/\tilde{\pi}(C_0)$ and therefore aggregate demand and aggregate supply are random, defined by agents' aggregate financial expenditures and suppliers, and economic costs and profits. For an agent, maximization of the net financial utility of consumption leads to the first-order condition

$$1 = E\left(\frac{\partial u_k}{\partial \tilde{c}_0^k}\frac{\partial \tilde{c}_0^k}{\partial W_0^k}\right)$$

where

$$\frac{\partial \tilde{c}_0^k}{\partial W_0^k} = \frac{1}{\pi(C_0)}\left(1 - \frac{W_0^k}{\tilde{\pi}(C_0)}\frac{\partial \tilde{\pi}(C_0)}{\partial W_0^k}\right), \quad \frac{\partial \tilde{\pi}(C_0)}{\partial W_0^k} = \frac{\partial \tilde{\pi}(C_0)}{\partial C_0}\frac{\partial \tilde{c}_0^k}{\partial W_0^k}$$

Therefore:

$$\frac{\partial \tilde{\pi}_0^k}{\partial W_0^k} = \left(\tilde{\pi}(C_0) W_0^k \frac{\partial \ln \tilde{\pi}(C_0)}{\partial C_0} \right)^{-1}$$

Elementary manipulations yield

$$1 = E\left(\frac{\tilde{\pi}_0^k}{\prod(W_0^k, C_0)} \right), \quad \frac{\partial u_k}{\partial \tilde{c}_0^k} = \tilde{\pi}_0^k$$

where $\prod(W_0^k, C_0) = \pi(C_0) + W_0^k (\partial \ln \tilde{\pi}(C_0)/\partial C_0)$. Note that $1 = E\left(\pi_0^k/\tilde{\pi}(C_0)\right)$ if $\partial \pi(C_0)/\partial C_0 = 0$. Further, π_0^k is the marginal utility price that agent k is willing to pay for consumption, while $\tilde{\pi}(C_0)$ is the price the agent will pay (which assumes that aggregate demand is met by aggregate supply). In other words, actual consumption is defined by the price the agent has to pay. However, when $\partial \tilde{\pi}(C_0)/\partial C_0 \neq 0$, we have instead

$$1 = E\left(\frac{\pi_0^k \left(p_0^k C_0 \right)}{\prod(W_0^k, C_0)} \right), \quad \Phi(.,.) = \frac{\pi_0^k \left(p_0^k C_0 \right)}{\prod(W_0^k, C_0)}, \quad c_0^k = p_0^k C_0 \text{ and } \sum_{k=1}^{n} p_0^k = 1$$

A first-order Taylor series approximation of $\prod(W_0^k, C_0)$ about $\tilde{\pi}_0^k$ yields

$$\frac{\tilde{\pi}_0^k}{\prod(W_0^k, C_0)} \approx \Phi(\tilde{\pi}_0^k, \tilde{\pi}_0^k) + \frac{\partial \Phi}{\partial \widetilde{\prod}} \left(\widetilde{\prod} - \tilde{\pi}_0^k \right) + \frac{1}{2} \frac{\partial^2 \Phi}{\partial \widetilde{\prod}^2} \left(\widetilde{\prod} - \tilde{\pi}_0^k \right)^2 + \text{residual}$$

where

$$\frac{\partial \Phi}{\partial \widetilde{\prod}} \left(\widetilde{\prod} - \tilde{\pi}_0^k \right) = -\frac{1}{\widetilde{\prod}^2} \left(\widetilde{\prod} - \tilde{\pi}_0^k \right) \text{ and } \frac{1}{2} \frac{\partial^2 \Phi}{\partial \widetilde{\prod}^2} \left(\widetilde{\prod} - \tilde{\pi}_0^k \right)^2 = \frac{\tilde{\pi}_0^k}{\widetilde{\prod}^3} \left(\widetilde{\prod} - \tilde{\pi}_0^k \right)^2$$

and therefore

$$\frac{\tilde{\pi}_0^k}{\prod(W_0^k, C_0)} \approx 1 - \frac{\tilde{\pi}_0^k}{\widetilde{\prod}^2} \left(\widetilde{\prod} - \tilde{\pi}_0^k \right) + \frac{\tilde{\pi}_0^k}{\widetilde{\prod}^3} \left(\widetilde{\prod} - \tilde{\pi}_0^k \right)^2 + \text{residual}$$

And in expectation:

$$1 = E\left(\frac{\tilde{\pi}_0^k}{\widetilde{\prod}(W_0^k, C_0)} \right) \approx 1 - E\left(\frac{\tilde{\pi}_0^k}{\widetilde{\prod}} \left(1 - \frac{\tilde{\pi}_0^k}{\widetilde{\prod}} \right) \right) + E\left(\frac{\tilde{\pi}_0^k}{\widetilde{\prod}} \left(1 - \frac{\tilde{\pi}_0^k}{\widetilde{\prod}} \right)^2 \right)$$

Or

$$E\left(\frac{\tilde{\pi}_0^k}{\widetilde{\prod}} \left\{ \left(1 - \frac{\tilde{\pi}_0^k}{\widetilde{\prod}} \right) - \left(1 - \frac{\tilde{\pi}_0^k}{\widetilde{\prod}} \right)^2 \right\} \right) = 0 \text{ and } E\left(\frac{\tilde{\pi}_0^k}{\widetilde{\prod}} - \left(\frac{\tilde{\pi}_0^k}{\widetilde{\prod}} \right)^2 \right) = 0$$

As a result, the mean and the variance correspond to a Bernoulli process whose probability is the expected ratio $E\left(\tilde{\pi}_0^k / \widetilde{\prod}\right)$, or

$$q = E\left(\frac{\tilde{\pi}_0^k}{\widetilde{\prod}}\right) \text{ and } \text{var}\left(\frac{\tilde{\pi}_0^k}{\widetilde{\prod}}\right) = E\left(\frac{\tilde{\pi}_0^k}{\widetilde{\prod}}\right)\left(1 - E\left(\frac{\tilde{\pi}_0^k}{\widetilde{\prod}}\right)\right) = q(1-q), \quad 0 < E\left(\frac{\tilde{\pi}_0^k}{\widetilde{\prod}}\right) \leq 1$$

Which implies that

$$\tilde{\pi}_0^k\left(p_0^k C_0\right) < \tilde{\pi}(C_0) + W_0^k \frac{\partial \ln \tilde{\pi}(C_0)}{\partial C_0} \quad \text{or} \quad \tilde{\pi}_0^k\left(p_0^k C_0\right) - \tilde{\pi}(C_0) < W_0^k \frac{\partial \ln \tilde{\pi}(C_0)}{\partial C_0}$$

As a result:

$$\tilde{\pi}_0^k\left(p_0^k C_0\right) < \tilde{\pi}(C_0) \quad \text{if} \quad \frac{\partial \ln \tilde{\pi}(C_0)}{\partial C_0} > 0$$

$$\tilde{\pi}_0^k\left(p_0^k C_0\right) > \tilde{\pi}(C_0) \quad \text{if} \quad \pi(C_0) - \tilde{\pi}_0^k\left(p_0^k C_0\right) > W_0^k\left|\frac{\partial \ln \tilde{\pi}(C_0)}{\partial C_0}\right|$$

Note that if p_0^k is very small, then $\tilde{\pi}(C_0) = \tilde{\pi}_0^k$.

The utility approach, therefore, provides a number of ways we can use to construct strategic pricing models for global and risk finance, providing a relationship between individual agents' financial decisions and prices when they are set as a function of aggregate macroeconomic and geopolitical factors. In such cases, the price of consumption may be far more complex, but it would account for the relative prices across national boundaries, the multiple interactive and complex relationships between suppliers, retailers, and demand, and political factors that can curtail or sponsor consumption and financial liquidity. Subsequently, these issues will be considered in the context of simple models to highlight the complexity of utility micro-/macro-financial models. It will be expanded further to define a price as an expectation over a probability measure, underlying the utility function. In Chapter 9, in particular we shall extend the implication of this approach to trade across national boundaries by introducing exports and imports as well as competitive supply factors. In Chapter 8, we shall also consider such models to define credit and lenders' borrowing contracts across national boundaries.

3.4 The Capital Asset Pricing Model

CAPM is a pricing model whose origin is with the Markowitz (1959) portfolio design problem, later expanded by Sharpe (1964) and Lintner (1965); all received Nobel Prizes in recognition of their contribution. This model, although criticized based on the observability of the market portfolio return (e.g., Fama and French, 1992; Constantinides and Duffie, 1996), it is still practiced today. The CAPM has assumed many extensions and developments, including the arbitrage pricing theory (APT) put forth by Ross (1976, 1977, 1978), the intertemporal CAPM (multi-factor) of Merton (1990), the Ingersoll (1984) alpha model, and others. For further study, see also Huberman (1982), Chamberlain (1983), and Connor (1984), for example. The purpose of CAPM and its various derived models is to obtain returns greater than the market index rate (called active trading) or obtain returns tracking the index rate. Active rates are analyzed based on multiple factors of a particular stock relative to an index (or a basket of assets) that is fully diversified (as implied by the Markowitz portfolio models).

The pre-CAPM may be interpreted in terms of the mean-variance return of a portfolio where we add a bond to the portfolio. Let $\tilde{R}_P$ be the ROR of a portfolio investment, part of which, say x, is invested in a risk-free bond whose ROR is R_f and its complement, $1-x$, invested in an all-equity portfolio index $\tilde{R}_E$. In this case, the portfolio ROR is $\tilde{R}_P = xR_f + (1-x)\tilde{R}_E$. Its mean and variance are then

$$\hat{R}_P = xR_f + (1-x)\hat{R}_E \quad \text{and} \quad \text{var}(\tilde{R}_P) = (1-x)^2\text{var}(\tilde{R}_E)$$

or

$$0 < \frac{\hat{R}_P - R_f}{\hat{R}_E - R_f} = 1-x < 1 \quad \text{and} \quad \sigma(\tilde{R}_P) = (1-x)\sigma(\tilde{R}_E)$$

In other words, the portfolio risk premium relative to the equity risk premium is smaller than unity, defined by the portfolio relative allocation to the risk-free asset. For example, for a mean-variance objective, consisting of optimizing

$$\underset{0<1-x\leq 1}{\text{Max}} \ \hat{R}_P - \frac{\rho}{2}\text{var}(\tilde{R}_P)$$

we have

$$1-x = \frac{\hat{R}_E - R_f}{\rho\text{var}(\tilde{R}_E)}$$

Therefore, the proportional wealth invested in equity is proportional to the ratio of the risk premium received due to an investment in equity relative to the variance of this portfolio and its risk aversion parameter ρ. Replacing the optimal allocation of equity by the portfolio mean and variance, we have

$$1 = \frac{\hat{R}_P - R_f}{\rho\text{var}(\tilde{R}_P)}$$

and therefore

$$\frac{\hat{R}_P - R_f}{\hat{R}_E - R_f} = \frac{\sigma(\tilde{R}_P)}{\sigma(\tilde{R}_E)} \quad \text{or} \quad \hat{R}_P - R_f = \frac{\sigma(\tilde{R}_P)}{\sigma(\tilde{R}_E)}(\hat{R}_E - R_f)$$

The relative risk premium of the portfolio to that of the equity is proportional to its volatility. However, the CAPM is an empirical extension of such an approach. Instead of a portfolio, consider a financial asset ROR, defined by:

$$\frac{\hat{R}_P - R_f}{\hat{R}_E - R_f} = \frac{\sigma(\tilde{R}_P)}{\sigma(\tilde{R}_E)} \quad \text{and} \quad \text{cov}(\tilde{R}_M, \tilde{\varepsilon}) = 0, \ \text{cov}(\tilde{R}_M, \tilde{\alpha}) = 0, \ \text{cov}(\tilde{\alpha}, \tilde{\varepsilon})$$

where M indicates market. In terms of risk premiums, setting $\tilde{\eta} = \tilde{\alpha} - R_f$:

$$\tilde{R}_k - R_f = \tilde{\eta} + \beta_k(\tilde{R}_M - R_f) + \tilde{\varepsilon} \quad \text{or} \quad \tilde{\pi}_k = \tilde{\eta} + \beta_k\tilde{\pi}_M + \tilde{\varepsilon}$$

where $\tilde{\alpha} - R_f$ is the Jensen alpha, which indicates a potential for arbitrage with $\tilde{\alpha} - R_f > 0$. If there is no arbitrage, then of course, $\tilde{\alpha} - R_f = 0$ and therefore $\alpha = R_f$ and the CAPM is reduced to $\tilde{\pi}_k = \beta_k\tilde{\pi}_M + \tilde{\varepsilon}$ and $\hat{\pi}_k = \beta_k\hat{\pi}_M$. To define β_k, we proceed as follows:

$$\tilde{\pi}_k = \beta_k\tilde{\pi}_M + \tilde{\varepsilon} \rightarrow \text{var}(\tilde{\varepsilon}) = \text{var}(\beta_k\tilde{\pi}_M - \tilde{\pi}_k) = \beta_k{}^2\text{var}(\tilde{\pi}_M) + \text{var}(\tilde{\pi}_k) - 2\beta_k\text{cov}(\tilde{\pi}_M, \tilde{\pi}_k)$$

However:

$$\text{var}(\tilde{\pi}_k) = \beta_k^2 \text{var}(\tilde{\pi}_M) + \text{var}(\tilde{\varepsilon}) + 2\beta_k \text{cov}(\tilde{\varepsilon}, \tilde{\pi}_M), \quad \text{cov}(\tilde{\varepsilon}, \tilde{\pi}_M) = 0$$

Setting $\text{var}(\tilde{\varepsilon}) = \text{var}(\tilde{\pi}_k) - \beta_k^2 \text{var}(\tilde{\pi}_M)$, we have

$$\beta_k = \frac{\text{cov}(\tilde{\pi}_M, \tilde{\pi}_k)}{\text{var}(\tilde{\pi}_M)} = \frac{\rho_{kM}\sigma(\tilde{\pi}_k)\sigma(\tilde{\pi}_M)}{\sigma^2(\tilde{\pi}_M)} = \rho_{kM}\frac{\sigma(\tilde{\pi}_k)}{\sigma(\tilde{\pi}_M)}$$

3.4.1 Discussion

The CAPM is based on a number of assumptions similar to those of the Markowitz model. These include risk-averse and rational investors; one asset is assumed to be riskless; and investors borrowing and lending at the market rate are unconstrained; and finally, the financial market is efficient in the sense that taxes and transaction costs are not accounted for. The CAPM as assumed earlier, $\tilde{\pi}_k = \beta_k \tilde{\pi}_M + \tilde{\varepsilon}$, was found to be restrictive, and therefore the assumption that $\tilde{\eta} = 0$ was removed, leading to the Jensen alpha model (standing for seeing arbitrage investments) as well as extending the CAPM to a multi-factor model (Roll and Ross, 1980). A passive investment strategy, unlike the CAPM seeking a stock to invest in, seeks to track (or replicate) a given financial index. The current usefulness of such an approach is that it reduces the trading transaction costs and augments the investment transparency. In a global and financial environment, the application of the CAPM as a tool for active trading or application of passive trading is, of course, more complex, as FX rate and other factors (e.g., safety of investments) are to be accounted for as well.

These approaches can then be compared relative to financial performance indices. Namely in terms of the Sharpe, Treynor, and Jensen ratios, expressed in the following at their risk premium, we have respectively

$$\frac{E(\tilde{\pi}_P)}{\sigma(\tilde{\pi}_P)}, \quad \frac{E(\tilde{\pi}_P)}{\beta_P}, \quad \text{and} \quad \alpha_P = E(\tilde{\pi}_P) - \beta_P E(\tilde{\pi}_M)$$

3.4.2 The Jensen Alpha Case: $\tilde{\eta} = \tilde{\alpha} - R_f \neq 0$

The Jensen alpha case corresponds to the existence of a potential alpha arbitrage investment (in which case, we arbitrarily set $\beta_\eta = 1$) as well as a two-factor CAPM (i.e., a return defined by two financial markets' indexes—say domestic and a foreign one). Let $\tilde{\pi}_k = \beta_\eta \tilde{\eta} + \beta_k \tilde{\pi}_M + \tilde{\varepsilon}$ and $\hat{\pi}_k = \beta_\eta \hat{\eta} + \beta_k \tilde{\pi}_M$. The variance of the error term is $\text{var}(\tilde{\varepsilon}) = \text{var}(\beta_\eta \tilde{\eta} + \beta_k \tilde{\pi}_M - \tilde{\pi}_k)$, and therefore

$$\text{var}(\tilde{\varepsilon}) = \beta_\eta^2 \text{var}(\tilde{\eta}) + \beta_k^2 \text{var}(\tilde{\pi}_M) + \text{var}(\tilde{\pi}_k) + 2\beta_\eta \beta_k \text{cov}(\tilde{\eta}, \tilde{\pi}_M) - 2\beta_\eta \text{cov}(\tilde{\eta}, \tilde{\pi}_k) - 2\beta_k \text{cov}(\tilde{\pi}_M, \tilde{\pi}_k)$$

Further:

$$\text{var}(\tilde{\pi}_k) = \beta_\eta^2 \text{var}(\tilde{\eta}) + \beta_k^2 \text{var}(\tilde{\pi}_M) + \text{var}(\tilde{\varepsilon}) + 2\beta_\eta \beta_k \text{cov}(\tilde{\eta}, \tilde{\pi}_M)$$

Replacing $\mathrm{var}(\tilde{\varepsilon})$, we obtain

$$0 = \beta_\eta{}^2 \mathrm{var}(\tilde{\eta}) + \beta_k{}^2 \mathrm{var}(\tilde{\pi}_\mathrm{M}) + 2\beta_\eta \beta_k \mathrm{cov}(\tilde{\eta}, \tilde{\pi}_\mathrm{M}) - \beta_\eta \mathrm{cov}(\tilde{\eta}, \tilde{\pi}_k) - \beta_k \mathrm{cov}(\tilde{\pi}_\mathrm{M}, \tilde{\pi}_k)$$

or the bi-quadratic equation in two parameters β_η and β_k:

$$\beta_\eta \mathrm{cov}(\tilde{\eta}, \tilde{\pi}_k) + \beta_k \mathrm{cov}(\tilde{\pi}_\mathrm{M}, \tilde{\pi}_k) = \beta_\eta{}^2 \mathrm{var}(\tilde{\eta}) + \beta_k{}^2 \mathrm{var}(\tilde{\pi}_\mathrm{M}) + 2\beta_\eta \beta_k \mathrm{cov}(\tilde{\eta}, \tilde{\pi}_\mathrm{M})$$

Using $\hat{\pi}_k = \beta_\eta \hat{\eta} + \beta_k \hat{\pi}_\mathrm{M}$, the beta parameters can be solved for. Explicitly, letting $(\hat{\pi}_k - \beta_k \hat{\pi}_\mathrm{M})/\hat{\eta} = \beta_\eta$, we can obtain β_k from

$$(\hat{\pi}_k - \beta_k \hat{\pi}_\mathrm{M})(\mathrm{cov}(\tilde{\eta}, \tilde{\pi}_k) - 2\beta_k \mathrm{cov}(\tilde{\eta}, \tilde{\pi}_\mathrm{M})) + \hat{\eta}\beta_k \mathrm{cov}(\tilde{\pi}_\mathrm{M}, \tilde{\pi}_k) = \hat{\eta}\left(\frac{\hat{\pi}_k - \beta_k \hat{\pi}_\mathrm{M}}{\hat{\eta}}\right)^2 \mathrm{var}(\tilde{\eta})$$

$$+ \beta_k{}^2 \hat{\eta} \mathrm{var}(\tilde{\pi}_\mathrm{M})$$

If $\tilde{\eta}$ is constant, we obtain again

$$\beta_k = \frac{\mathrm{cov}(\tilde{\pi}_\mathrm{M}, \tilde{\pi}_k)}{\mathrm{var}(\tilde{\pi}_\mathrm{M})}$$

3.4.3 The Arbitrage Pricing Theory

The APT is defined by multiple factors. Assuming two risk premium factors for simplicity:

$$\tilde{\pi}_k = \tilde{\eta} + \beta_k \tilde{\pi}_\mathrm{M} + \tilde{\varepsilon}$$

and

$$\mathrm{var}(\tilde{\pi}_k) = \mathrm{var}(\tilde{\eta}) + (\beta_k)^2 \mathrm{var}(\tilde{\pi}_\mathrm{M}) + \mathrm{var}(\tilde{\varepsilon}) + 2\beta_k \mathrm{cov}(\tilde{\eta}, \tilde{\pi}_\mathrm{M})$$

Similarly, letting $\tilde{\varepsilon} = \tilde{\eta} + \beta_k \tilde{\pi}_\mathrm{M} - \tilde{\pi}_k$, we have

$$\mathrm{var}(\tilde{\varepsilon}) = \mathrm{var}(\tilde{\eta}) + (\beta_k)^2 \mathrm{var}(\tilde{\pi}_\mathrm{M}) + \mathrm{var}(\tilde{\pi}_k) + 2\beta_k \mathrm{cov}(\tilde{\eta}, \tilde{\pi}_\mathrm{M}) - 2\mathrm{cov}(\tilde{\eta}, \tilde{\pi}_k) - 2\beta_k \mathrm{cov}(\tilde{\pi}_\mathrm{M}, \tilde{\pi}_k)$$

Replacing $\mathrm{var}(\tilde{\varepsilon})$ in this equation, we obtain the quadratic equation

$$0 = (\beta_k)^2 \mathrm{var}(\tilde{\pi}_\mathrm{M}) - \beta_k(\mathrm{cov}(\tilde{\pi}_\mathrm{M}, \tilde{\pi}_k) - 2\beta_k \mathrm{cov}(\tilde{\eta}, \tilde{\pi}_\mathrm{M})) + \mathrm{var}(\tilde{\eta}) - \mathrm{cov}(\tilde{\eta}, \tilde{\pi}_k)$$

When $\mathrm{var}(\tilde{\eta})$, this is reduced to $\beta_k = \mathrm{cov}(\tilde{\pi}_\mathrm{M}, \tilde{\pi}_k)/\mathrm{var}(\tilde{\pi}_\mathrm{M})$. However if $\mathrm{var}(\tilde{\eta}) \neq 0$, then

$$(\beta_k)^2 - \beta_k\left(\frac{\mathrm{cov}(\tilde{\pi}_\mathrm{M}, \tilde{\pi}_k) - 2\beta_k \mathrm{cov}(\tilde{\eta}, \tilde{\pi}_\mathrm{M})}{\mathrm{var}(\tilde{\pi}_\mathrm{M})}\right) + \frac{\mathrm{var}(\tilde{\eta}) - \mathrm{cov}(\tilde{\eta}, \tilde{\pi}_k)}{\mathrm{var}(\tilde{\pi}_\mathrm{M})} = 0$$

And therefore a solution of the quadratic equation is

$$(\beta_k)^2\left(1 + \frac{2\mathrm{cov}(\tilde{\eta}, \tilde{\pi}_\mathrm{M})}{\mathrm{var}(\tilde{\pi}_\mathrm{M})}\right) - (\beta_k)\left(\frac{\mathrm{cov}(\tilde{\pi}_\mathrm{M}, \tilde{\pi}_k)}{\mathrm{var}(\tilde{\pi}_\mathrm{M})}\right) + \frac{\mathrm{var}(\tilde{\eta}) - \mathrm{cov}(\tilde{\eta}, \tilde{\pi}_k)}{\mathrm{var}(\tilde{\pi}_\mathrm{M})} = 0$$

For example, for $\tilde{\eta} = 0$ we have

$$\beta_k = \frac{\text{cov}(\tilde{\pi}_M, \tilde{\pi}_k)}{\text{var}(\tilde{\pi}_M)}$$

For generality, the multi-factor model is

$$\tilde{\pi}_k = \lambda + \beta_\eta \tilde{\eta} + \beta_k \tilde{\pi}_M + \tilde{\varepsilon}$$

with λ a constant, which is null when the model is efficient and otherwise positive if it provides an "alpha return." These models are typically estimated statistically by regressions, and therefore the statistical quality of their estimates points to the validity of the model when it is applied.[1]

3.4.4 The Capital Asset Pricing Model and Foreign Exchange

Let R_i and R_m be the RORs of a given currency and the ROR of a currency basket. Both are assumed jointly and normally distributed with known means and known variances and covariances. Next, assume that $R_i \xi$ is a foreign ROR priced at a domestic rate. The expected ROR using the CAPM model is then

$$E\left\{\tilde{\xi}\left(\tilde{R}_i - R_f\right)\right\} = \beta_i E\left(\tilde{\xi}\left[\tilde{R}_m - R_f\right]\right) + \tilde{\varepsilon} \ \text{ or } \ \left(\tilde{\xi}\tilde{\pi}_i\right) = \beta_i\left(\tilde{\xi}\tilde{\pi}_m\right) + \tilde{\varepsilon} \ \text{ and } \ E\left(\tilde{\xi}\tilde{\pi}_i\right) = \beta_i E\left(\tilde{\xi}\tilde{\pi}_m\right)$$

$$\text{var}(\tilde{\varepsilon}) = \text{var}\left(\tilde{\xi}\tilde{\pi}_i\right) + \beta_i^2 \text{var}\left(\tilde{\xi}\tilde{\pi}_m\right) - 2\beta_i \text{cov}\left(\tilde{\xi}\tilde{\pi}_m, \tilde{\xi}\tilde{\pi}_i\right)$$

Therefore:

$$\beta_i = \frac{\text{cov}\left(\tilde{\xi}\tilde{\pi}_m, \tilde{\xi}\tilde{\pi}_i\right)}{\text{var}\left(\tilde{\xi}\tilde{\pi}_m\right)}$$

where

$$\text{var}\left(\tilde{\xi}\tilde{\pi}_m\right) = \text{var}\{R_m, \xi\}$$

$$= E^2\{\tilde{\pi}_m\}\text{var}\{\xi\} + 2E(\xi)E\{\tilde{\pi}_m\}\text{cov}\{\xi, \tilde{\pi}_m\} + E^2\{\xi\}\text{var}\{\tilde{\pi}_m\} + \text{cov}^2\{\xi, \tilde{\pi}_m\}$$

$$+ \text{var}\{\tilde{\pi}_m\}\text{var}\{\xi\}$$

while the covariation of $\tilde{\xi}\tilde{\pi}_i$ and $\tilde{\xi}\tilde{\pi}_m$ is

$$\text{cov}\left(\tilde{\xi}\tilde{\pi}_i, \tilde{\xi}\tilde{\pi}_m\right) = E\{\tilde{\pi}_i\}E\{\tilde{\pi}_m\}\text{var}\{\xi\} + E\{\tilde{\pi}_i\}E\{\xi\}\text{cov}\{\xi, \tilde{\pi}_m\} + E\{\tilde{\pi}_m\}E\{\xi\}\text{cov}\{\xi, \tilde{\pi}_i\}$$

$$+ E^2\{\xi\}\text{cov}\{\tilde{\pi}_i, \tilde{\pi}_m\} + \text{cov}\{\tilde{\pi}_i, \xi\}\text{cov}\{\tilde{\pi}_m, \xi\} + \text{cov}\{\tilde{\pi}_i, \tilde{\pi}_m\}\text{var}\{\xi\}$$

---

1 The APT model estimates are based on multivariate linear regressions providing estimates for the beta parameters. As a result, the regression goodness of fit (the R^2 for a fit between the dependent and independent variables) as well as the statistical quality of the beta parameters' estimates (their t-values) and, not least, missing financial factors, and covariations of the regression factors' variables render the evaluation of beta estimates far more carefully.

3.4.5 Pricing Foreign Exchange Rates and a Basket of Foreign Exchange Rates

Let $\tilde{R}(\xi_i)$ be the ROR, and consider $\tilde{R}_C$ a diversified portfolio of currencies—say a basket of currencies accepted by sovereign states as the portfolio to be used as a currency index $\tilde{R}_C = \sum_{i=1}^{n} w_i \tilde{R}(\xi_i),$ where w_i denotes a weight given to currency i in the reference basket. Given the importance of stability in a basket of reference currencies, these weights would be selected to account for smaller volatility in currency exchanges. Namely, the larger the currency FX rate volatility, the smaller its weight. Assuming that there are such weights, the CAPM is formulated as follows (with ε_i iid zero-mean, normally distributed random variables):

$$\tilde{R}(\xi_i) = a_i + \beta_{iG}\tilde{R}_G + \varepsilon_i, \quad E\varepsilon_i = 0, \quad \mathrm{var}(\varepsilon_i) = \sigma^2$$

Alternatively, in terms of risk premiums, each ROR would be priced relative to its national risk-free rate $\tilde{\pi}_i = \alpha_i + \beta_{iG}\tilde{\pi}_G + \varepsilon_i,$ where $\tilde{\pi}_i = \tilde{R}(\xi_i) - R_f^i,$ $\alpha_i = a_i - R_f^i,$ and

$$\tilde{\pi}_G = \sum_{k=1}^{n} w_k \left(\tilde{R}(\xi_k) - R_f^k \right) = \sum_{k=1}^{n} w_k \tilde{\pi}_k$$

Further, $E\varepsilon_i = 0,$ $\mathrm{var}(\varepsilon_i) = \sigma^2,$ and R_f^k is a risk-free rate associated with country k. We consider again the case $\varepsilon_i = \alpha_i + \beta_{iG}\tilde{\pi}_G - \tilde{\pi}_i$ and its variance

$$\mathrm{var}(\varepsilon_i) = \mathrm{var}(\alpha_i) + (\beta_{iG})^2\mathrm{var}(\tilde{\pi}_G) + \mathrm{var}(\tilde{\pi}_i) + 2\beta_{iG}\mathrm{cov}(\alpha_i, \tilde{\pi}_G) - 2\beta_{iG}\mathrm{cov}(\alpha_i, \tilde{\pi}_i)$$
$$- 2\beta_{iG}\mathrm{cov}(\tilde{\pi}_i, \tilde{\pi}_G)$$

By the same token:

$$\mathrm{var}(\tilde{\pi}_i) = \mathrm{var}(\alpha_i) + (\beta_{iG})^2\mathrm{var}(\tilde{\pi}_G) + \mathrm{var}(\varepsilon_i) + 2\beta_{iG}\mathrm{cov}(\alpha_i, \tilde{\pi}_G)$$

Replacing again $\mathrm{var}(\varepsilon_i)$ we obtain a quadratic equation in the beta factor of currency i. Or:

$$(\beta_{iG})^2\mathrm{var}(\tilde{\pi}_G) - \beta_{iG}(\mathrm{cov}(\alpha_i, \tilde{\pi}_i) + \mathrm{cov}(\tilde{\pi}_i, \tilde{\pi}_G) - \mathrm{cov}(\alpha_i, \tilde{\pi}_G)) + \mathrm{var}(\alpha_i) = 0$$

If $\mathrm{var}(\alpha_i) = 0,$ then $\mathrm{cov}(\alpha_i, \tilde{\pi}_i) = 0$ and $\mathrm{cov}(\alpha_i, \tilde{\pi}_G) = 0,$ and therefore:

$$\beta_{iG} = \frac{\mathrm{cov}(\tilde{\pi}_i, \tilde{\pi}_G)}{\mathrm{var}(\tilde{\pi}_G)} = \frac{\mathrm{cov}\left(\tilde{\pi}_i, \sum_{k=1}^{n} w_k \tilde{\pi}_k \right)}{\mathrm{var}\left(\sum_{k=1}^{n} w_k \tilde{\pi}_k \right)}$$

However, as indicated in Chapter 2 (see also Stein (1973) and Rubinstein (1974)), we also have

$$\mathrm{cov}\left(\tilde{\pi}_i, \sum_{k=1}^{n} w_k \tilde{\pi}_k \right) = \sum_{k \neq i}^{n} w_i \mathrm{cov}(\tilde{\pi}_i, \tilde{\pi}_k)$$

and therefore

$$\beta_{iG} = \frac{\displaystyle\sum_{k \neq i}^{n} w_i \text{cov}(\tilde{\pi}_i, \tilde{\pi}_k)}{\text{var}\left(\displaystyle\sum_{k=1}^{n} w_k \tilde{\pi}_k\right)}$$

However if $\text{var}(\alpha_i) \neq 0$ (i.e., there is an investment arbitrage in country i), then

$$(\beta_{iG})^2 - \beta_{iG} \frac{(\text{cov}(\alpha_i, \tilde{\pi}_i) + \text{cov}(\tilde{\pi}_i, \tilde{\pi}_G) - \text{cov}(\alpha_i, \tilde{\pi}_G))}{\text{var}(\tilde{\pi}_G)} + \frac{\text{var}(\alpha_i)}{\text{var}(\tilde{\pi}_G)} = 0$$

$$\beta_{iG} = \frac{1}{2} \frac{\Phi(.)}{\text{var}(\tilde{\pi}_G)} + \sqrt{\frac{1}{2}\Phi(.) - \frac{\text{var}(\alpha_i)}{\text{var}(\tilde{\pi}_G)}}, \quad \Phi(.) = (\text{cov}(\alpha_i, \tilde{\pi}_i) + \text{cov}(\tilde{\pi}_i, \tilde{\pi}_G) - \text{cov}(\alpha_i, \tilde{\pi}_G))$$

Note that in this case

$$\text{cov}(\tilde{\pi}_i, \tilde{\pi}_G) = \text{cov}\left(\tilde{\pi}_i, \sum_{k \neq i}^{n} w_k \tilde{\pi}_k\right) \quad \text{and} \quad \text{cov}(\alpha_i, \tilde{\pi}_G) = \text{cov}\left(\alpha_i, \sum_{k=1}^{n} w_k \tilde{\pi}_k\right)$$

In a global financial environment, markets might not justify the assumptions of a normal probability distribution, and therefore skewness may be used to obtain a better estimate of the beta associated with a financial asset or index. In this case, assuming for convenience that $\tilde{\pi}_i = \alpha_i + \beta_{iG}\tilde{\pi}_G + \varepsilon_i$, $\alpha_i = 0$, the index of skewness is

$$\text{SKEW}_i = \frac{E(\tilde{\pi}_i - \hat{\pi}_i)^3}{\text{var}(\tilde{\pi}_i)^{3/2}} = \frac{E(\alpha_i + \beta_{iG}\tilde{\pi}_G + \varepsilon_i - \hat{\alpha}_i - \beta_{iG}\hat{\pi}_G)^3}{[\text{var}(\tilde{\pi}_i)]^{3/2}} = \frac{(\beta_{iG})^3 (\tilde{\pi}_G - \hat{\pi}_G)^3 + E[\varepsilon_i]^3}{[\text{var}(\tilde{\pi}_i)]^{3/2}}$$

$$= \frac{(\beta_{iG})^3 \text{SKEW}_G [\text{var}(\tilde{\pi}_G)]^{3/2} + \text{SKEW}_\varepsilon [\text{var}(\varepsilon)]^{3/2}}{[\text{var}(\tilde{\pi}_i)]^{3/2}}$$

And therefore the beta is

$$\beta_{iG} = \left\{\frac{\text{SKEW}_i}{\text{SKEW}_G}\left(\frac{\text{var}(\tilde{\pi}_i)}{\text{var}(\tilde{\pi}_G)}\right)^{3/2} - \frac{\text{SKEW}_\varepsilon}{\text{SKEW}_G}\left(\frac{\text{var}(\varepsilon)}{\text{var}(\tilde{\pi}_G)}\right)^{3/2}\right\}^{1/3}$$

If the error ε_i is normally and identically distributed (iid), we have $\text{SKEW}_\varepsilon = 0$ and therefore

$$\beta_{iG} = \left(\frac{\text{SKEW}_i}{\text{SKEW}_G}\right)^{1/3} \left(\frac{\text{var}(\tilde{\pi}_i)}{\text{var}(\tilde{\pi}_G)}\right)^{1/2}$$

Example 3.1 Consider two currencies FD and DF. In this case

$$\tilde{\pi}_{DF} = \alpha_{DF} + \beta_{DF,G}\tilde{\pi}_G + \varepsilon_D, \quad E\varepsilon_D = 0, \quad \text{var}(\varepsilon_D) = \sigma_D^2$$

$$\tilde{\pi}_{FD} = \alpha_{FD} + \beta_{FD,G}\tilde{\pi}_G + \varepsilon_F, \quad E\varepsilon_F = 0, \quad \text{var}(\varepsilon_F) = \sigma_F^2$$

Applying the previous SKEW estimate, we have

$$\beta_{DF,G} = \left(\frac{\text{SKEW}_{DF}}{\text{SKEW}_G}\right)^{1/3} \left(\frac{\text{var}(\tilde{\pi}_{DF})}{\text{var}(\tilde{\pi}_G)}\right)^{1/2} \quad \text{and} \quad \beta_{FD,G} = \left(\frac{\text{SKEW}_{FD}}{\text{SKEW}_G}\right)^{1/3} \left(\frac{\text{var}(\tilde{\pi}_{FD})}{\text{var}(\tilde{\pi}_G)}\right)^{1/2}$$

3.4.6 Thought Experiment

In a financial world, the price of a currency is measured relative to the dominating currency (e.g., US dollar). In a CAPM, we then have a currency price (ROR) measured by

$$\beta_{iG} = \frac{\text{cov}(\tilde{\pi}_i, \tilde{\pi}_G)}{\text{var}(\tilde{\pi}_i)}$$

In other words, say that the dollar price is stable, in which case its variance is small and the foreign currency ROR premium $\tilde{\pi}_i$ is then larger. This means that compensation for holding the foreign currency is large since $\hat{\pi}_i = \beta_{iG}\tilde{\pi}_i$ (which implies greater risks in holding the foreign currency and thus holding of the dollar becomes "safe"). Next, assume that the dollar became more volatile. In other words, the foreign currency beta will be smaller and the reverse tendency occurs. Namely, a flight from the dollar to the foreign currency whose beta is smaller. This thought experiment points to the importance of a reference and stable currency. Lacking such a currency, we seek a basket of currencies, commodities, or global assets that can provide an alternative to the dollar. For example, consider a basket of currencies of leading economies such as the US dollar, the euro, the British pound and the yen. Is such a basket (based on proportional strength of their economy) an appropriate and stable basket? Further, will traders, exporters, and importers be willing to peg their transactions to such a basket? Also, should commodities such as oil, a basket of grains, or gold be part of such a basket? These are the types of questions that may be raised if in the future US dollar weakness is pervasive. Such concerns are already expressed in the price of gold, which is used by some as a "shadow currency" or as a "last resort" hedge against a contagious failure of major currencies.

3.4.7 Linear Regressions, Capital Asset Pricing Model, and Global Finance

The practical and empirical applications of pricing using the CAPM are simple since it is a linear equation we can estimate by standard linear regression. In this case:

$$\tilde{\pi}_i = \alpha_i + \beta_{iG}\tilde{\pi}_G + \varepsilon_i \quad \text{and pointwise} \quad \Pi_k^i = \alpha^i + \beta_k^{iG}\Pi_k^G + \varepsilon_k$$

Therefore, assuming a data set $\left(\Pi_k^i, \Pi_k^G\right)$, $k = 1, 2, 3, \ldots, n$, the following beta estimate is obtained:

$$\hat{\beta}_k^{iG} = \frac{\displaystyle\sum_{k=1}^{n}\left(\Pi_k^G - \bar{\Pi}^G\right)\left(\Pi_k^i - \bar{\Pi}^i\right)}{\displaystyle\sum_{k=1}^{n}\left(\Pi_k^G - \bar{\Pi}^G\right)^2} = \frac{\displaystyle\sum_{k=1}^{n}\left(\Pi_k^G - \bar{\Pi}^G\right)\Pi_k^i}{\displaystyle\sum_{k=1}^{n}\left(\Pi_k^G - \bar{\Pi}^G\right)^2}$$

Such a regression assumes that the risk premium variability is fully explained by the model variability. In a global and complex financial situation, the number of intervening variables is very large; therefore, some important factors explaining the risk premium $\tilde{\pi}_i$ may be lacking. Two possibilities arise then. First, we need to consider a multivariate regression model to estimate the premium risk model. Second, we need to estimate a bias due to missing factors (i.e., not accounted for). We consider the second case first, and assume that there is a true model defined by $\tilde{\pi}_i = \alpha_i + \beta_{iG}\tilde{\pi}_G + \gamma_i\tilde{x} + \varepsilon_i$ and pointwise $\Pi_k^i = \alpha^i + \beta_k^{iG}\Pi_k^G + \gamma_k^i X_k + \varepsilon_k$. In this case, the beta estimate is

$$\hat{\beta}_k^{iG} = \frac{\sum_{k=1}^{n}\left(\Pi_k^G - \bar{\Pi}^G\right)^2\left(\alpha^i + \beta_k^{iG}\Pi_k^G + \gamma_k^i X_k + \varepsilon_k\right)}{\sum_{k=1}^{n}\left(\Pi_k^G - \bar{\Pi}^G\right)^2}$$

Therefore:

$$\hat{\beta}^{iG} = \beta^{iG} + \gamma_k^i\frac{\sum_{k=1}^{n}\left(\Pi_k^G - \bar{\Pi}^G\right)^2(X_k - \bar{X})}{\sum_{k=1}^{n}\left(\Pi_k^i - \bar{\Pi}^i\right)^2} + \frac{\sum_{k=1}^{n}\left(\Pi_k^G - \bar{\Pi}^G\right)^2\varepsilon_k}{\sum_{k=1}^{n}\left(\Pi_k^i - \bar{\Pi}^i\right)^2}$$

As a result, $\hat{\beta}^{iG} \neq \beta^{iG}$, and therefore the beta estimate is biased. This observation may account for some of the difficulties one encounters in estimating the beta of a financial asset when based on a simplistic model.

We consider next a multivariate linear model defined by

$$\mathbf{\Pi} = [\mathbf{X}][\mathbf{\beta}] + [\mathbf{\varepsilon}], \quad [\mathbf{\varepsilon}]^T = (\varepsilon_1,\ldots,\varepsilon_n), \quad [\mathbf{X}] = [\mathbf{X}_1,\mathbf{X}_2,\ldots,\mathbf{X}_{p-1}]$$

An estimation of the beta vector in this linear regression is then (see Rencher and Christensen (2012) for the development of multivariate linear regression)

$$\left[\hat{\mathbf{\beta}}\right] = \left[\mathbf{X}^T\mathbf{X}\right]^{-1}[\mathbf{X}]^T\mathbf{\Pi}$$

A number of problems arise, such as a beta estimate may be constrained and, more importantly, the regression's factors may be multi-collinear (since economic and financial variables may be codependent). In this case, the data set $[\mathbf{X}^T\mathbf{X}]$ is nonsingular and therefore its inverse is extremely large. However, if the smallest eigenvalue of such a data set is very small, the data set is multi-collinear and the test t-statistic values are extremely small. In this case, it may be necessary to reduce the number of explanatory factors by adding restrictions on the parameters to estimate. Alternatively, one may orthogonalize the vector data space to remove the multi-collinearity (also called the Gramm–Schmidt approach). Other approaches may be used, such as vector autoregressive, moving-average, autoregressive, and autoregressive–moving-average model, and of course an extensive list of financial econometric models based on autoregressive conditional heteroscedastic (ARCH) and generalized ARCH estimation techniques, which were discussed in Chapter 2. For brevity, these important aspects of financial empirical applications to a global and interdependent finance are not considered here.

3.5 Review of Elements of Arrow–Debreu and Q Pricing

Rational expectations models are based on a general equilibrium theory that defines a unique price. This is a pricing model where all financial exchanges occur at the same price. An asset price is then based on engineering a probability measure which presumes that markets are complete. In this approach, prices are relative to the current information (what we know) and relative to specific known prices (e.g., the price of a risk-free bond or a basket of currencies). Explicitly, say that the future, a period hence, of a financial asset is defined by n presumably known future states $S_i(1)$, $i = 1, 2, ..., n$. Let the price of each of these states be $\pi_i(1)$, $i = 1, 2, ..., n$; in other words, each price is the outcome of a theoretical exchange of traders that defines the price uniquely. *In a complete market, future and current equilibrium prices are unique, while the current price is a linear weighted function of future state prices.* Since a current price $S(0)$ is unique, its price is

$$S(0) = \sum_{i=1}^{N} \pi_i(1)S_i(1)$$

In other words, the current price implies future state preferences and their prices. Inversely, future state preferences can be predicted based on current and observable prices of the assets and their derivatives—since derivatives are a function of the same state preferences. For example, say that future state preferences consist of two known values $S_i(1)$, $i = 1, 2$. The current price is thus $S(0) = \pi_1(1)S_1(1) + \pi_2(1)S_2(1)$ with prices $(\pi_1(1), \pi_2(1))$ unknown. If future states $S_1(1)$ and $S_2(1)$ have the same consequences (i.e., payouts are riskless since in all states investors collect the same payout, or $S_1(1) = S_2(1) = B(1)$), the current price is then $S(0) = B(0)$, with $B(0) = B(1) \sum_{i=1}^{N} \pi_i(1)$. Such risk-free payouts are necessarily equal to the payout for a risk-free bond (since the price of assets with identical risk-returns characteristics has necessarily the same price). Let the risk-free ROR in such a bond be R_f, with $B(1) = B(0)(1 + R_f)$; thus:

$$B(0) = B(0)(1 + R_f)\sum_{i=1}^{N}\pi_i(1) \text{ and } \sum_{i=1}^{N}\pi_i(1) = (1 + R_f)^{-1}$$

Define for convenience the proportions $p_i(1) = \pi_i(1) / \sum_{i=1}^{N}\pi_i(1)$, where $p_i(1)$, $0 \le p_i(1) \le 1$, and $\sum_{i=1}^{N} p_i(1) = 1$, have the property of a probability distribution, which we call for convenience a "risk-neutral probability" as it will allow us an estimate of price by a simple expectation. Since in a complete market $S(0) = \sum_{i=1}^{N}\pi_i(1)S_i(1)$, we replace $\pi_i(1)$ by $p_i(1)\sum_{i=1}^{N}\pi_i(1) = \pi_i(1)$ and $\sum_{i=1}^{N}\pi_i(1) = (1 + R_f)^{-1}$. As a result:

$$S(0) = \sum_{i=1}^{N}\left(p_i(1)\sum_{i=1}^{N}\pi_i(1)\right)S_i(1) = \sum_{i=1}^{N}\pi_i(1)\sum_{i=1}^{N}(p_i(1))S_i(1) = \frac{1}{1 + R_f}\sum_{i=1}^{N}p_i(1)S_i(1)$$

Or

$$S(0) = \frac{1}{1 + R_f}E^Q(S_i(1))$$

Thus, the current price is an expected future price based on a probability measure Q defined by the probability distribution $\{p_i(1)\}$, $i = 1, 2, ..., n$, and discounted by the price of a future risk-free bond price. Alternatively, we can write

$$\frac{S(0)}{B(0)} = E^Q\left(\frac{S_i(1)}{B(1)}\right) \text{ or } S(0) = \frac{B(0)}{B(1)}E^Q(S_i(1))$$

where $E^Q(.)$ is an expectation about the probability distribution we call a Q-probability measure, transforming the price process to "an equilibrium state" relative to the current information state (defined as conditional on the current filtration $|\Im_0$) with prices equal to the current price, since

$$\frac{S(0)}{B(0)} = E^Q\left(\frac{S(1)}{B(1)}\Big|\Im_0\right) = E^Q\left(\frac{S(2)}{B(2)}\Big|\Im_0\right) = \cdots = E^Q\left(\frac{S(t)}{B(t)}\Big|\Im_0\right) = \cdots$$

The Q-probability measure thus defines a martingale (since all future prices are equal under the chosen probability measure). In this context, all assets derivatives with an underlying stock price martingale are also a martingale and their current price is also equal to an expectation of the future prices (under the Q-probability measure). For example, current call and put option prices are defined by their expected future price. Inversely, current prices imply their future prices (or, equivalently, their risk-neutral probabilities); and vice versa, the Q-measure probabilities imply current prices:

$$\{S(0), C(0), P(0)\} \Leftrightarrow \{\{S(1), C(1), P(1)\} \text{ or } p_i(1), \ i = 1, 2, ..., n\}$$

If a future price is only a function of its volatility, the current price is necessarily a unique function of the future volatility. When multiple sources of risks and financial assets are considered, prices and future volatility estimates are necessarily more complex (as we shall see subsequently).

For example, let the price of a foreign asset bought in a domestic currency, and therefore priced relative to a domestic bond, be

$$S_D^F(0) = \frac{B_D(0)}{B_D(t)} E^Q\left(S_D^F(t)|\Im_0\right)$$

For a foreign asset, its price in a foreign currency (priced relative to the foreign bond) is

$$S_F(0) = \frac{B_F(0)}{B_F(t)} E^Q\left(S_F(t)|\Im_0\right)$$

In this case, when considering an asset pricing model across national boundaries, the FX risk compounds the foreign asset risk. Of course, when both the FX and the asset price risks are statistically dependent, these problems have to be treated by accounting for both the asset price in its currency and their correlation with its FX price, as will be considered in applications in the following.

These models are fundamental and provide a rationality which is based on a set of assumptions that might not hold when markets are not in equilibrium (or incomplete markets). For example, prices can be influenced by trends, information, news, risks and behavioral attitudes of investors. In a global environment, where sovereign states politics and geopolitical events have an important impact through financial exchanges, prices, financial agreements, and so on, the application of such a framework is of course more complex. Nonetheless, it provides a quantitative reference structure to better assess foreign financial prices as well as to manage international stocks and exchange traded funds. Furthermore, global finance's complexity may imply a prevalent Knight uncertainty, presuming *that not all future state preferences are known* and leading to assets' mispricing. This is the case when events are rare and therefore not accounted for, when future states are not known, when sovereign states' actions and major natural events that can affect financial states are unpredictable. In such cases, a number of approximations based on behavioral studies or numerical techniques are used to maintain the convenience of rational expectation and complete markets in asset pricing. The presumption of such an approach is that, although markets are mostly incomplete, the arbitrage opportunities they provide to investors and speculators are necessarily temporary. In this context, finance, although always incomplete, is moved by trends that seek to make it complete. The examples we consider in the following provide simple models treated with and without FX risks. We emphasize first the Arrow–Debreu framework and subsequently the utility approaches.

3.5.1 Applications of the Arrow–Debreu Framework

The applications we shall consider span a number of basic pricing models based on the Arrow–Debreu economic framework as well as the utility pricing framework. Throughout this chapter we emphasize discrete time problems (Chapters 7 and 8 consider continuous time problems). The problems we consider are initially defined as standard pricing problems, such as the price of domestic and foreign bonds, simple financial pricing of FX, valuation of a portfolio invested globally, as well as the discrete Merton model for pricing credit. Subsequently, we extend some of these problems to their multi-country and global framework. The intent of these applications is to formulate and contrast these problems in their domestic as well as global (multi-country) framework.

3.5.2 Pricing a Foreign Bond and Foreign Exchange Rates

This example uses a bond investment to price FX rates. This approach establishes a linkage between treasury rates of two countries to the FX rates that defines the countries' currencies. Assume a domestic investment of B_0^D in a foreign bond in domestic currency. The risk-free treasury rates in the respective domestic and foreign countries are (r_d, r_f), while ξ_{DF}^0 is the current FX rate for buying the foreign currency, allowing acquisition of the foreign bond. A period later, the foreign investment is priced relative to the foreign currency treasury rates and repatriated to the domestic country (and thus measured relative to a domestic bond). Its price $\tilde{P}_1^D$ is then random (due to the FX rate). These portfolio prices are defined by

$$P_0^D = B_0^D, \quad \tilde{P}_1^D = \left(B_0^D \xi_{DF}^0 \right)(1 + r_f)\tilde{\xi}_{FD}^1$$

Under an appropriate risk-neutral pricing (of the foreign bond relative to its investment in the domestic bond), it yields

$$\frac{P_0^D}{B_0^D} = E^Q \left(\frac{\tilde{P}_1^D}{B_1^D} \right)$$

and therefore

$$1 = E^Q \left(\frac{B_0^D(1 + r_f)}{B_0^D(1 + r_d)} \xi_{DF}^0 \tilde{\xi}_{FD}^1 \right) = \frac{1 + r_f}{1 + r_d} E^Q \left(\xi_{DF}^0 \tilde{\xi}_{FD}^1 \right)$$

Since $\xi_{DF}^0 \tilde{\xi}_{FD}^1 = \tilde{\xi}_{FD}^1 / \xi_{FD}^0$, we obtain the currency price discounted at a differential risk-free rate of the domestic and the currency treasury (bond) prices:

$$\xi_{FD}^0 = \frac{1 + r_f}{1 + r_d} E^Q (\tilde{\xi}_{FD}^1)$$

Since $\tilde{\xi}_{FD}^1 / \xi_{FD}^0 = 1 + R_1^{\tilde{\xi}_{FD}^1}$, with $R_1^{\tilde{\xi}_{FD}^1}$ an ROR of the FX $\tilde{\xi}_{FD}^1$, we have

$$1 = \frac{1 + r_f}{1 + r_d} E^Q \left(1 + R_1^{\tilde{\xi}_{FD}^1}\right)$$

In this case, holding a currency may be interpreted as a financial asset with returns and their associated risks. By the same token, currency options can be priced accordingly. For example, expressed for call and put options with (k_C, k_P) as their strike:

$$C_{FD}^0 = \frac{1 + r_f}{1 + r_d} E^Q \text{Max}(\tilde{\xi}_{FD}^1 - k_C, 0), \quad P_{FD}^0 = \frac{1 + r_f}{1 + r_d} E^Q \text{Max}(k_P - \tilde{\xi}_{FD}^1, 0)$$

If we consider instead a domestic agent acquiring a foreign currency, they would then become a foreign currency holder, priced relative to the foreign risk-free rate. In this case, currency pricing is reached relative to a foreign probability measure, and

$$\xi_{DF}^0 = \frac{1 + r_d}{1 + r_f} E^U (\tilde{\xi}_{DF}^1)$$

where we note that the probability measures Q and U are specific to the domestic and foreign agents. If the price of a currency in a domestic country is the inverse of the foreign currency price, then

$$\xi_{DF}^0 \xi_{FD}^0 = 1$$

and therefore each expectation is defined relative to a filter, a stand-in for all the information and other elements defining the pricing process in one country relative to another, or

$$1 = E^Q (\tilde{\xi}_{FD}^1 | \mathfrak{I}_D) \left(E^U (\tilde{\xi}_{DF}^1 | \mathfrak{I}_F)\right)$$

This implies that probability measures need not be the same even though prices maintain their equivalence by $\xi_{DF}^0 \xi_{FD}^0 = 1$. However, assuming that in the future a price reaches an equilibrium, then $1 = \tilde{\xi}_{FD}^1 \tilde{\xi}_{DF}^1$, and a process will lead to a price equivalence, reaching a unique currency price. In a multi-country environment, such an approach to pricing is more complex as its price is derived from numerous economic and other factors. Practically, valuation in one country does not need to be the same as the other, thereby providing arbitrage opportunities pertaining to future currency contracts. For these reasons, we may consider also a utility-based multiagent approach to FX and foreign asset pricing (as we shall subsequently see).

The aforementioned pricing model can be extended in several directions. Consider the case of transaction costs δ_{DF} for the domestic investor buying the foreign currency as well as another transaction cost when repatriating foreign investments δ_{FD}. In this case, for a domestic bond, $P_0^D = B_0^D$ and $P_1^D = B_0^D(1 + r_d)$, investing the same amount in a foreign country (i.e., converting to the foreign currency, paying transaction costs, and then repatriating the funds) yields

$$P_0^D = B_0^D, \quad P_1^D = B_0^D\left(1 + R_f^D\right), \quad \tilde{P}_1^F = B_0^F(1 - \delta_{DF})(1 - \delta_{FD})B_0^F\left(1 + R_f^F\right)\frac{\tilde{\xi}_{FD}^1}{\xi_{FD}^0}$$

If the FX market is complete, then prices are (for no arbitrage) given by $B_0^D = 1$, $B_1^D = 1 + R_f^D$, and

$$1 + R_f^D = E^Q\left(\tilde{P}_1^{FD}\right) = (1 - \delta_{DF})(1 - \delta_{FD})\left(1 + R_f^F\right)E^Q\left(\frac{\tilde{\xi}_{FD}^1}{\xi_{FD}^0}\right)$$

As a result:

$$\frac{1 + R_f^D}{1 + R_f^F} = (1 - \delta_{DF})(1 - \delta_{FD})E^Q\left(\frac{\tilde{\xi}_{FD}^1}{\xi_{FD}^0}\right)$$

For example, let the price of an ROR on the FX be 10% with no transactions costs:

$$\frac{1 + R_f^D}{1 + R_f^F} = E^Q\left(\frac{\tilde{\xi}_{FD}^1}{\xi_{FD}^0}\right) = 1.10 \quad \text{and} \quad R_f^D = 0.10 + 1.10R_f^F, \quad R_f^D > R_f^F$$

Say that a sovereign state seeks to provide an incentive not to invest in a foreign country that provides a greater ROR. Then, applying a 10% tax rate δ_{DF}, $1 - \delta_{DF} = 0.90$, yields

$$\frac{1 + R_f^D}{1 + R_f^F} = 1.10 \times 0.90 = 0.99$$

In this case, the rates are $R_f^D = -0.01 + 0.99R_f^F$. Say that $R_f^F = 0.07$, then $R_f^D = 0.0593$. Imposing a heavy tax on returning profits (say of 35%), from a domestic viewpoint, would reduce the profitability of foreign profits. Since foreign profits are not taxed if not repatriated, there are few prospects that these profits will return home. The EU requirement to tax Apple for $14.5 billion (September 2016) has motivated the US Treasury to review its taxation policy to both assure a tax payment in the USA and at the same time reduce the tax weight of US corporate firms paying taxes in Europe. These situations are underlying potential taxation wars.

Transaction costs incurred when converting a currency back and forth from a foreign country will also require that the foreign risk-free rate be greater to compensate for these costs. If δ_{FD} is very large (as would be implied by the aforementioned tax levy and against returning home foreign profits—as is the case with a 35% tax rate to repatriate foreign profits to the USA), it is quite possible that firms will prefer not to repatriate funds and instead reinvest their external funds. Such a process has certainly contributed to the growth of global financial expansion and to the creation of large and global firms increasingly less dependent on sovereign states' regulatory, political, and economic policies. By the same token, high transaction (and taxation) costs when repatriating foreign profits provide an incentive to invest their gains in the foreign country (or at least globally). In this sense, reducing currency barriers by removing hidden and intermediaries' currencies costs contributes to a growth of globalization that would lead to a global "common market." For example, the EU adopting one currency has rendered exchanges across national boundaries to be currency neutral. Removal of internal trade and gating barriers across euro boundaries has contributed to the integration of the EU. It has created other problems, however, due to the fiscal independence of EU sovereign states and the free flows of capital, the price of debt, and so on, across economies that were not equipped equivalently with the "shocks" that a common currency created.

Excessive taxation on repatriation of foreign returns, as well as inversion (where firms relocate to another country to avoid excessive domestic taxation), can lead to problems currently faced by the USA. Let the profit repatriation tax rate be τ, then expected profits are $\tilde{P}_1^{FD} - \pi_1^{FD}\tau$, where $\pi_1^{FD} = \tilde{P}_1^F - B_0^D$, and as a result expected foreign profits equal

$$E^Q \tilde{P}_1^{FD}(1-\tau) + B_0^D\tau \quad \text{or} \quad B_0^D\left[(1-\delta_{DF})(1-\delta_{FD})(1+r_d)(1-\tau) + \tau\right]$$

Thus, a foreign investment pays if

$$B_0^D\left[(1-\delta_{DF})(1-\delta_{FD})(1+r_d)(1-\tau) + \tau\right] \geq B_0^D(1+r_d)$$

In a complete market:

$$\tau < (1+r_d)\frac{(1-\delta_{DF})(1-\delta_{FD})-1}{1-(1-\delta_{DF})(1-\delta_{FD})(1+r_d)}$$

This implies that the assumptions of complete currency markets are not reasonable. Instead, global markets are currency incomplete (or at least in transition, till globalization reaches a point of global homogeneity) and provide profits due to the arbitrage they allow based on different terms and conditions that exist naturally in markets that differ substantially.

In a currency incomplete market, we will then have (without taxes)

$$E\left(\tilde{P}_1^F\right) = B_0^D(1-\delta_{DF})(1-\delta_{FD})(1+r_f)E\left(1+\tilde{R}_{FD}^\xi\right) > B_0^D(1+r_d)$$

The (speculative) required foreign bond ROR is greater than the domestic ROR, since

$$E\left(1+\tilde{R}_{FD}^\xi\right) > \frac{1}{(1-\delta_{DF})(1-\delta_{FD})}\frac{1+r_d}{1+r_f}$$

and if $\delta_{DF} = \delta_{FD} = 0$ then

$$E\left(1+\tilde{R}_{FD}^\xi\right) > \frac{1+r_d}{1+r_f}$$

3.5.3 Global Investment Pricing: A Binomial Model

International portfolio investments involve opportunities and potential risks, including political, FX, and other risks that define investment yields in various countries. These investments require a number of considerations, including:

- pricing and risk assessment of foreign investments;
- expected regime change inducing uncertainty regarding future investments;
- market frictions;
- anticipating natural future global change (desertification, global weather patterns change);
- sovereign debt and credit risk of sovereign states and rating of countries;
- price stickiness and overshooting.

Global portfolios may consist of specific investments, such as in mining firms in Australia in Australian dollars or in Chinese firms listed on the Hong Kong or Shanghai stock markets denoted therefore in Hong Kong dollars or in yuan. Such investments, while they may provide greater yields than those accessible in domestic markets, they may also have greater risks.

Combining a foreign investment with currencies transactions creates an asset with two risk sources, each potentially dependent on the other. The treatment of such assets is therefore more complex. For example, consider a binomial price model defined by

$$S_0^D \Leftrightarrow \left(S_1^{+D}, S_1^{-D}\right) \quad \text{as well as} \quad \xi_{FD}^0 \Leftrightarrow \left(\tilde{\xi}_{FD}^{+1}, \tilde{\xi}_{FD}^{-1}\right)$$

As a result, an initial investment S_0^D by a domestic investor in a foreign country ex-post currency conversion is $S_0^D \xi_{DF}^0 = S_0^D / \xi_{FD}^0$ whose future price in foreign currency is $\left(S_0^D / \xi_{FD}^0\right)\left(1 + \tilde{R}_1^{SF}\right)$, or

$$S_0^D \Leftrightarrow \left\{\left(S_0^D / \xi_{FD}^0\right)\left(1 + R_1^{+SF}\right), \left(S_0^D / \xi_{FD}^0\right)\left(1 + R_1^{-SF}\right)\right\}$$

Repatriating these assets to the domestic country (and therefore an initial investment in local currency S_0^D), the asset price at the currency price $\tilde{\xi}_{FD}^1 \equiv \left(\tilde{\xi}_{FD}^{+,1}, \tilde{\xi}_{FD}^{-,1}\right)$ is then

$$S_0^D \Leftrightarrow \left\{\left(S_0^D / \xi_{FD}^0\right)\left(1 + R_1^{+SF}\right), \left(S_0^D / \xi_{FD}^0\right)\left(1 + R_1^{-SF}\right)\right\}\left(\xi_{FD}^{+,1}, \xi_{FD}^{-,1}\right)$$

Explicitly, there are then four potential outcomes:

$$S_0^D \Leftrightarrow S_0^D \left\{\left(\left(1 + R_1^{+SF}\right)\frac{\xi_{FD}^{+,1}}{\xi_{FD}^0}; \left(1 + R_1^{-SF}\right)\frac{\xi_{FD}^{+,1}}{\xi_{FD}^0}\right); \left(1 + R_1^{+SF}\right)\frac{\xi_{FD}^{-,1}}{\xi_{FD}^0}; \left(1 + R_1^{-SF}\right)\frac{\xi_{FD}^{-,1}}{\xi_{FD}^0}\right\}$$

or

$$\frac{S_0^D}{B_0^D} = E^{Q_S, Q_\xi}\left(\frac{S_0^D}{B_1^D}\left(1 + \tilde{R}_1^{SF}\right)\frac{\tilde{\xi}_{FD}^1}{\xi_{FD}^0}\right) = \frac{S_0^D}{B_1^D}E^{Q_S, Q_\xi}\left(\left(1 + \tilde{R}_1^{SF}\right)\left(1 + \tilde{R}_{1FD}^{\tilde{\xi}1}\right)\right)$$

where $E^{Q_S, Q_\xi}(.,.)$ is an expectation taken with respect to two risks: a stock and a currency risk. If the FX and the foreign investment's returns are statistically independent, and since at its maturity the price of the domestic bond is $B_1^D = 1 + r_d$, we have

$$1 = \frac{1}{1 + r_d}E^{Q_S, Q_\xi}\left\{\left(1 + \tilde{R}_1^{SF}\right)\left(1 + R_{1FD}^{\tilde{\xi}1}\right)\right\}$$

As a result:

$$1 = \frac{1}{1 + r_d}\left\{E^{Q_S}\left(1 + \tilde{R}_1^{SF}\right)E^{Q_\xi}\left(1 + R_1^{\tilde{\xi}_{FD}^1}\right) + \rho\sigma_1^{Q, SF}\sigma_1^{Q, \tilde{\xi}_{FD}^1}\right\}$$

However, under the probability measure Q_ξ, $1 = [1/(1 + r_f)]E^{Q_\xi}\left(1 + R_1^{\tilde{\xi}_{FD}^1}\right)$ replacing $E^{Q_\xi}\left(1 + R_1^{\tilde{\xi}_{FD}^1}\right)$, we have

$$1 = \frac{1 + r_f}{1 + r_d}\left\{E^{Q_S}\left(1 + \tilde{R}_1^{SF}\right) + \rho\sigma_1^{Q, SF}\sigma_1^{Q, \tilde{\xi}_{FD}^1}\right\}$$

and, therefore, if $\widetilde{R}_1^{SF}$ and $R_{1FD}^{\tilde{\xi}1}$ are independent, $\rho = 0$, and as indicated earlier we obtain

$$1 = \frac{1 + r_f}{1 + r_d} E^{Q_s} \left(1 + \widetilde{R}_1^{SF}\right)$$

Global financial problems involve in general multiple risks, leading therefore to more complex models.

3.5.4 Global Investment Pricing: A Portfolio Problem

Let a consumer-investor's wealth be \$1, part of which, say I_0, is invested for its consumption in the next period, with $\tilde{I}_1 = I_0(1 + \tilde{R}_1)$, where $\tilde{R}_1$ is the investor's portfolio ROR. If the portfolio is invested solely in a risk-free bond, then $I_1 = I_0(1 + R_f)$. For a portfolio invested in both an equity k and in a risk-free asset, each of which has an ROR $\tilde{R}_k$ and R_f, we then have

$$\tilde{I}_1 = I_0\left(1 + \tilde{R}_1\right) = \alpha I_0(1 + R_f) + (1-\alpha)I_0\left(1 + \tilde{R}_k\right) \quad \text{or} \quad \tilde{R}_1 = R_f + (1-\alpha)\left(\tilde{R}_k - R_f\right)$$

where α is the proportion of one's initial portfolio invested in the risk-free asset. As already noted, under an appropriate probability measure for the equity investment risk, we have

$$\frac{I_0}{B_0^D} = E^Q\left(\frac{\tilde{I}_1}{B_1^D}\right)$$

$$\frac{I_0}{B_0^D} = \frac{1}{B_1^D}E^Q\left(\alpha I_0(1 + R_f) + (1-\alpha)I_0\left(1 + \tilde{R}_k\right)\right) = \frac{\alpha I_0(1 + R_f)}{B_1^D} + \frac{(1-\alpha)I_0}{B_1^D}E^Q\left(1 + \tilde{R}_k\right)$$

and

$$1 = \alpha + \left(\frac{1 - \alpha}{1 + R_f}\right)E^Q\left(1 + \tilde{R}_k\right)$$

By the same token, consider a domestic investor investing locally and in a foreign country in both risk-free and risky assets. The portfolio price involves then two risks: the equity price risk and the FX rate risk. A period hence, the following results:

$$\tilde{I}_1 = I_0\left(1 + \tilde{R}_1\right)$$

$$= \alpha_D I_0\left(1 + R_f^D\right) + \alpha_F I_0\xi_{DF}^0\,\tilde{\xi}_{FD}^1\left(1 + R_f^F\right) + \beta_D I_0\left(1 + \tilde{R}_k^D\right) + \beta_F I_0\xi_{DF}^0\tilde{\xi}_{FD}^1\left(1 + \tilde{R}_k^F\right)$$

where ξ_{DF}^0 and $\tilde{\xi}_{FD}^1$ are exchange rates at time $t = 0$ and at time $t = 1$ respectively. The former is a domestic expenditure rate to buy the foreign asset in a foreign currency price, and the latter is the FX to acquire back the domestic currency. Therefore, $\xi_{DF}^0 = 1/\xi_{FD}^0$.

$$\xi_{DF}^0\tilde{\xi}_{FD}^1 = \xi_{DF}^0\left(\xi_{FD}^0 + \Delta\tilde{\xi}_{FD}^1\right) = \frac{\xi_{FD}^0 + \Delta\tilde{\xi}_{FD}^1}{\xi_{DF}^0} = 1 + \tilde{R}_{FD}^\xi$$

where $\tilde{R}_{FD}^{\xi}$ is the ROR (or a loss) resulting from the foreign currency FX. Further, $\alpha_D + \alpha_F + \beta_D + \beta_F = 1$ denotes the proportions of one investment in both domestic and foreign markets. In this case, the portfolio ROR priced in the domestic currency is

$$\tilde{R}_1 = \alpha_D R_f^D + \beta_D \tilde{R}_k^D + \alpha_F \left(R_f^F \left(1 + \tilde{R}_{FD}^{\xi} \right) + \tilde{R}_{FD}^{\xi} \right) + \beta_F \left(\tilde{R}_k^F + \tilde{R}_{FD}^{\xi} + \tilde{R}_k^F \tilde{R}_{FD}^{\xi} \right)$$

Assuming we have the data providing an empirical estimate of the moments of $\tilde{R}_1$ (under a numerical and statistical estimate of the RORs of the first two moments), we then have

$$E\left(\tilde{R}_1 \right) = \alpha_D R_f^D + \beta_D E\left(\tilde{R}_k^D \right) + \alpha_F \left(R_f^F \left(1 + E\left(\tilde{R}_{FD}^{\xi} \right) \right) + E\left(\tilde{R}_{FD}^{\xi} \right) \right)$$
$$+ \beta_F \left(E\left(\tilde{R}_k^F \right) + E\left(\tilde{R}_{FD}^{\xi} \right) + E\left(\tilde{R}_k^F \tilde{R}_{FD}^{\xi} \right) \right)$$

where

$$E\left(\tilde{R}_k^F \tilde{R}_{FD}^{\xi} \right) = E\left(\tilde{R}_k^F \right) E\left(\tilde{R}_{FD}^{\xi} \right) + \rho \sqrt{\operatorname{var}\left(\tilde{R}_k^F \right) \operatorname{var}\left(\tilde{R}_{FD}^{\xi} \right)}$$

We can also calculate its variance:

$$\operatorname{var}\left(\tilde{R}_1 \right) = \operatorname{var}\left\{ \beta_D \tilde{R}_k^D + \alpha_F \left(1 + R_f^F \right) \tilde{R}_{FD}^{\xi} + \beta_F \left(\tilde{R}_k^F + \tilde{R}_{FD}^{\xi} + \tilde{R}_k^F \tilde{R}_{FD}^{\xi} \right) \right\} = E\left(\tilde{R}_1 \right)^2 - \left[E\left(\tilde{R}_1 \right) \right]^2$$

$$= \left\{ \left(\beta_D \right)^2 E\left(\tilde{R}_k^D \right)^2 + \left(\alpha_F \left(1 + R_f^F \right) \right)^2 E\left(\tilde{R}_{FD}^{\xi} \right)^2 + \left(\beta_F \right)^2 E\left(\tilde{R}_k^F + \tilde{R}_{FD}^{\xi} + \tilde{R}_k^F \tilde{R}_{FD}^{\xi} \right)^2 \right\}$$

$$+ 2\beta_D \alpha_F \left(1 + R_f^F \right) E\left(\tilde{R}_k^D \tilde{R}_{FD}^{\xi} \right) + 2\beta_D \beta_F \left(E\left(\tilde{R}_k^F \tilde{R}_k^D \right) + E\left(\tilde{R}_{FD}^{\xi} \tilde{R}_k^D \right) + E\left(\tilde{R}_k^F \tilde{R}_{FD}^{\xi} \tilde{R}_k^D \right) \right)$$

$$+ 2\alpha_F \beta_F \left(1 + R_f^F \right) \left(E\left(\tilde{R}_k^F \tilde{R}_{FD}^{\xi} \right) + E\left(\tilde{R}_{FD}^{\xi} \right)^2 + E\left(\tilde{R}_k^F \left(\tilde{R}_{FD}^{\xi} \right) \right)^2 \right)$$

$$- \left\{ \beta_D E\left(\tilde{R}_k^D \right) + \alpha_F \left(1 + R_f^F \right) E\left(\tilde{R}_{FD}^{\xi} \right) + \beta_F \left(E\left(\tilde{R}_k^F \right) + E\left(\tilde{R}_{FD}^{\xi} \right) + E\left(\tilde{R}_k^F \tilde{R}_{FD}^{\xi} \right) \right) \right\}^2$$

For these reasons, a "summary" ROR for a "global" investor ought to account as well for currencies' covariations. Under risk-neutral pricing, both risk sources are to be accounted for as noted previously.

If, instead, we were to consider a foreign investor investing locally (in their country) and domestically (for them, in a foreign country), the risks and the returns of such an investor would be assumed not to be the same (unless a stringent set of parity conditions were to be applied). If these were not the same, opportunities for arbitrage occur. Such an approach is statistical in the sense that it may be calculated by using observed financial time series. It is not, however, a pricing model.

The effects of the FX ROR on an ROR of a portfolio RORs are also important. For example, say that a bet on a foreign security disappoints, however. It may be compensated by an appreciable ROR on the currency, and vice versa. A portfolio's expected return and its standard deviation might also (most likely) not be normal. Its ROR might also be a function of the covariations of the foreign equity asset price and the country FX rate. Thus, the combination of multiple risk sources embedded in valuations and pricing across national borders will require a more complex approach to fundamental pricing. To do so, we shall consider a linear ROR model (the Black–Scholes model) in Chapter 7 and provide an approach to account for the statistical dependence of currency and asset prices.

3.5.5 Foreign Exchange, Consumer Price Index, and Purchasing Power Parity

The CPI is defined by a basket of goods and services and their prices. It is often used to compare prevalent prices in two different countries. Their equivalence, also coined purchasing power parity (PPP), defines the FX rate of two countries. Assume that PPP holds between two countries' CPIs; then, by definition:

$$\xi_{FD}^t = \frac{CPI_F^t}{CPI_D^t} \quad \text{and} \quad \tilde{\xi}_{FD}^T = \frac{(CPI)_F^T}{(CPI)_D^T} \quad \text{and} \quad \tilde{\xi}_{FD}^T = \frac{(CPI)_F^T}{(CPI)_D^T}$$

Note, however, that if expected inflation rates in CPIs over a period of time $T-t$ and in both countries are $\nu_D^{T,t}$ and $\nu_F^{T,t}$, then at time t we have

$$\frac{CPI_F^t + \Delta CPI_F^{T,t}}{CPI_F^T} = 1 + \frac{\Delta CPI_F^{T,t}}{CPI_F^T} = 1 + \nu_F^{T,t} \quad \text{and} \quad \frac{CPI_D^t + \Delta CPI_D^{T,t}}{CPI_D^T} = 1 + \frac{\Delta CPI_D^{T,t}}{CPI_D^T} = 1 + \nu_D^{T,t}$$

Since current expectation of the future inflation is embedded in the current inflation rates ν_F^t and ν_D^t and the probability measure Q, we have

$$\frac{1 + \nu_F^t}{1 + \nu_D^t} = e^{-(r_d - r_f)(T-t)} E_t^Q \left(\frac{1 + \nu_F^{T,t}}{1 + \nu_D^{T,t}} \right)$$

3.5.6 Relative Purchasing Power Parity

Define a relative rate of change in an FX rate as a function of relative CPI in both the domestic and the foreign country:

$$\frac{\Delta \xi_{FD}^t}{\xi_{FD}^t} = \frac{\Delta CPI_F^t}{CPI_F^t} - \frac{\Delta CPI_D^t}{CPI_D^t} \quad \text{or} \quad \frac{\Delta \ln \xi_{FD}^t}{\Delta t} = \frac{\Delta \ln CPI_F^t}{\Delta t} - \frac{\Delta \ln CPI_D^t}{\Delta t}$$

Therefore, it expresses an ROR in FX rates which is defined by a relative change in the inflation rates of both countries:

$$\frac{\Delta \ln \xi_{FD}^t}{\Delta t} = \frac{\Delta \ln \left(CPI_F^t \right)}{\Delta t} - \frac{\Delta \ln \left(CPI_D^t \right)}{\Delta t} = \nu_F^t - \nu_D^t$$

The actual FX rate, however, is changing due to market forces reflecting the preferences of the parties (sovereign states), their economic states, inflation, financial and trade repression, and incentives and risk attitudes. In other words, FX rates are defined globally and simultaneously by all countries' economic financial and risk characteristics. These are further fueled by investors and speculators in currencies markets who view FX rates as an asset that compounds the uncertainty of their real or financial international transactions. While we have considered here the domestic side of the FX rate, similar results are obtained from the foreign side. Their differences and manipulations by sovereign states contribute to a strategic evolution of currency markets.

We summarize these results in the following, where for notational simplicity we use

$$\frac{1}{1+\mathbf{R}^D} = \frac{(1-\nu_f)(1-\delta_{FD})(1+r_f)}{(1-\nu_d)(1+r_d)} \quad \text{and} \quad \frac{1}{1+\mathbf{R}^F} = \frac{(1-\nu_d)(1-\delta_{DD})(1+r_d)}{(1-\nu_f)(1+r_f)}$$

And therefore for the two countries D and F:

$$\left\{ \begin{array}{ll} 1 = \left(\dfrac{1}{1+\mathbf{R}^D}\right)^T E^Q\left(1+\tilde{R}^\xi_{FD}(T)\right), & 1 = \left(\dfrac{1}{1+\mathbf{R}^F}\right)^T E^V\left(1+\tilde{R}^\xi_{DF}(T)\right) \\[3mm] \dfrac{1+\nu_F^t}{1+\nu_D^t} = \left(\dfrac{1}{1+\mathbf{R}^D}\right)^{T-t} E^Q_t\left(\dfrac{1+\nu_F^T}{1+\nu_D^T}\right), & \dfrac{1+\nu_D^t}{1+\nu_F^t} = \left(\dfrac{1}{1+\mathbf{R}^F}\right)^{T-t} E^V_t\left(\dfrac{1+\nu_D^T}{1+\nu_F^T}\right) \end{array} \right\}$$

3.6 The Multi-Period Consumption-Based Capital Asset Pricing Model

The CCAPM is a kernel pricing problem. For a single agent, a "typical and rational consumer," assume its initial wealth is W at time t. Let $\pi_t c_t$ be a current consumption expenditure and its residual wealth invested for future consumption $I_t = W_t - \pi_t c_t$ with an ROR $\tilde{R}_{t+1}$. We assume that the price at time t is known to the consumer but its future price is not known for sure. Therefore, consumption at time $t+1$ is

$$c_{t+1} = \left(\frac{W_t - \pi_t c_t}{\tilde{\pi}_{t+1}}\right)(1+\tilde{R}_{t+1}) \quad \text{and} \quad \frac{\partial \tilde{c}_{t+1}}{\partial c_t} = -\left(\frac{\pi_t}{\tilde{\pi}_{t+1}}\right)(1+\tilde{R}_{t+1})$$

Since $\tilde{\pi}_{t+1} = \pi_t(1+\tilde{r}_{t+1})$, where $\tilde{r}_{t+1}$ is an inflation (or deflation) random rate, over two periods only, the consumer utility they seek to maximize is (Tapiero, 2015)

$$\operatorname*{Max}_{c_t} U^i_t(c_t) = u_t(c_t) + \beta E u_{t+1}(\tilde{c}_{t+1})$$

A necessary condition for optimality is thus

$$\partial \frac{U^i_t(c_t)}{\partial c_t} = \frac{\partial u_t(c_t)}{\partial c_t} + \beta E\left(\frac{\partial u_{t+1}(\tilde{c}_{t+1})}{\partial \tilde{c}_{t+1}}\frac{\partial \tilde{c}_{t+1}}{\partial c_t}\right) = 0$$

where

$$\frac{\partial \tilde{c}_{t+1}}{\partial c_t} = -\left(\frac{1+\tilde{R}_{t+1}}{1+\tilde{r}_{t+1}}\right)$$

As a result:

$$\frac{\partial u_t(c_t)}{\partial c_t} = \beta E\left(\frac{\partial u_{t+1}(\tilde{c}_{t+1})}{\partial \tilde{c}_{t+1}}\left(\frac{1+\tilde{R}_{t+1}}{1+\tilde{r}_{t+1}}\right)\right) \quad \text{or} \quad 1 = \beta E\left(\frac{\partial u_{t+1}(\tilde{c}_{t+1})/\partial \tilde{c}_{t+1}}{\partial u_t(c_t)/\partial c_t}\left(\frac{1+\tilde{R}_{t+1}}{1+\tilde{r}_{t+1}}\right)\right)$$

In this expression, the marginal utility of a consumer k defines the price the consumer is willing to pay rather than the price they will be paying; therefore, we set $\pi_t^k = \partial u_t(c_t)/\partial c_t$ and, as a result, we set

$$\frac{\partial u_{t+1}(\tilde{c}_{t+1})/\partial \tilde{c}_{t+1}}{\partial u_t(c_t)/\partial c_t} = \frac{\tilde{\pi}_{t+1}^k}{\pi_t^k} = 1 + \tilde{r}_{t+1}^k \quad \text{and} \quad 1 = \beta E\left(\frac{1+\tilde{r}_{t+1}^k}{1+\tilde{r}_{t+1}}(1+\tilde{R}_{t+1})\right)$$

To define a pricing model, we seek to define a probability measure for the rate of investments return $1 + \tilde{R}_{t+1}$. Since this expression is for all RORs, we assume that we invest in risk-free bonds with a constant ROR given by $1 + R_f$. As a result, $1 = \beta(1 + R_f)E(M_t)$, $M_t = \left(1 + \tilde{r}_{t+1}^k\right)/(1 + \tilde{r}_{t+1})$, with $M_t/E(M_t)$ defining a probability measure relative to its mean. In other words, since the propensity of the consumers to pay more (or less) for consumption at a rate $\tilde{r}_{t+1}^k$ relative to the increase (or decrease) of the price they will pay for consumption, the measure is a "relative risk measure" that is proportional to the bond risk-free rate, or $E(M_t) = 1/\beta(1 + R_f)$. In this case, the pricing model is

$$1 = \frac{1}{1+R_f}E\left(\frac{M_t}{E(M_t)}(1+\tilde{R}_{t+1})\right) = \frac{1}{1+R_f}E^M\left(1+\tilde{R}_{t+1}\right)$$

Assume instead that the pricing model does not account for the market price of consumption (which we assume set by external factors such as suppliers, imports, and exports). In this case, letting the probability measure be the inflation price that a consumer is willing to pay for consumption, we have $P_t^k = \tilde{\pi}_{t+1}^k/\pi_t^k = 1 + \tilde{r}_{t+1}^k$; therefore:

$$1 = \beta E\left(P_t^k\left(\frac{1+\tilde{R}_{t+1}}{1+\tilde{r}_{t+1}}\right)\right)$$

Since $(1 + \tilde{R}_{t+1})/(1 + \tilde{r}_{t+1})$ is an inflation-adjusted ROR, we consider the risk-free rate of treasury inflation-protected security (TIPS) bonds that are indexed to consumption inflation prices with an ROR $1 + R_f^T$, $R_f^T < R_f$. In this case:

$$1 = \beta\left(1 + R_f^T\right)E\left(P_t^k\right)$$

and therefore under a probability measure accounting for temporal substitution of the consumer marginal utilities we have

$$1 = \frac{1}{1+R_f^T}E\left(\frac{P_t^k}{E(P_t^k)}\left(\frac{1+\tilde{R}_{t+1}}{1+\tilde{r}_{t+1}}\right)\right) = \frac{1}{1+R_f^T}E^{P^k}\left(\frac{1+\tilde{R}_{t+1}}{1+\tilde{r}_{t+1}}\right)$$

In other words, the probability measure defines a kernel price which is a relative (to a risk-free rate) deflator of future return risks. The rationale of this approach is that investing in a risky asset implies that, once a risk premium is accounted for, its ROR is a risk-free rate and therefore its ROR is equal to the risk-free ROR. This is the case for a common bond as well as for TIPS bonds. The risk premium is then embedded in the probability measure that defines the pricing kernel. In our case, it is an expression of the relative prices and their expectation associated with the particular agent k. For example, let the TIPS trade at a rate of 2% per year and let the inflation rate be 5% while the market rate is $1 + \tilde{R}_{t+1}$. Then, under the consumer k probability measure, the expected inflation indexed ROR under the probability measure P_t^k is 7.1%, where

$$1 = \frac{1}{1.02 \times 1.05} E^{P_t^k} \left(1 + \tilde{R}_{t+1}\right) \quad \text{and} \quad 1.071 = E^{P_t^k} \left(1 + \tilde{R}_{t+1}\right)$$

Such an approach may be extended to the pricing of foreign transactions. The following example considers the transaction in a foreign country by a domestic financial agent. Such a transaction is set in both domestic and foreign currencies.

3.6.1 Example: Pricing Exports

Let W_t^D be the domestic agent's initial wealth and let c_t^{FD} be the export consumption of the agent with π_t^{FD} the foreign export price. Thus, its residual wealth for future consumption (in one period) is

$$I_t^D = W_t^D - \left(\pi_t^{FD} \xi_t^{DF}\right) c_t^{FD} \quad \text{and} \quad \tilde{W}_{t+1}^D = \left(W_t^D - \left(\pi_t^{FD} \xi_t^{DF}\right) c_t^{FD}\right) \left(1 + \tilde{R}_{t+1}^D\right)$$

where $\pi_t^{FD} \xi_t^{DF}$ is the domestic consumption price of exports at time t and $\tilde{W}_{t+1}^D$ is the residual wealth expended completely on foreign exports at time $t + 1$. As a result:

$$\tilde{c}_{t+1}^{FD} = \frac{\tilde{W}_{t+1}^D}{\tilde{\pi}_{t+1}^{FD} \tilde{\xi}_{t+1}^{DF}} = \frac{\left(W_t^D - \left(\pi_t^{FD} \xi_t^{DF}\right) c_t^{FD}\right) \left(1 + \tilde{R}_{t+1}^D\right)}{\tilde{\pi}_{t+1}^{FD} \tilde{\xi}_{t+1}^{DF}}$$

and therefore

$$\frac{\partial \tilde{c}_{t+1}^{FD}}{\partial c_t^{FD}} = -\frac{1 + \tilde{R}_{t+1}^D}{\tilde{\pi}_{t+1}^{FD} \tilde{\xi}_{t+1}^{DF} / \left(\pi_t^{FD} \xi_t^{DF}\right)} = \frac{1 + \tilde{R}_{t+1}^D}{\left(1 + \tilde{r}_{t+1}^{FD}\right)\left(1 + r_{t+1\xi}\right)}, \quad r_{t+1\xi} = \frac{\tilde{\xi}_{t+1}^{DF}}{\xi_t^{DF}}$$

Since $\tilde{\pi}_{t+1}^{FD} \tilde{\xi}_{t+1}^{DF}$ is the domestic price we may write the price of exports as $\tilde{\pi}_{t+1}^{FD} \tilde{\xi}_{t+1}^{DF} = \tilde{\pi}_{t+1}^{DE}$ and $\tilde{\pi}_{t+1}^{DE} = \pi_t^{DE} \left(1 + \tilde{r}_{t+1}^{DE}\right)$, which leads to

$$\frac{\partial \tilde{c}_{t+1}^{FD}}{\partial c_t^{FD}} = -\frac{1 + \tilde{R}_{t+1}^D}{\left(1 + \tilde{r}_{t+1}^{FD}\right)\left(1 + r_{t+1}^{\tilde{\xi}}\right)}$$

The price of exports in terms of domestic prices would then account for foreign prices risks, FX risks, and, of course, the ROR on domestic investments:

$$1 = \frac{1}{1 + R_f^D} E^{P^D} \left(\frac{1 + \tilde{R}_{t+1}^D}{\left(1 + \tilde{r}_{t+1}^{FD}\right)\left(1 + r_{t+1}^{\tilde{\xi}}\right)}\right)$$

Subsequently, problems relating to trading across national boundaries will be considered.

In the following, we extend this approach to a strategic framework by noting that the prices consumers pay are a function of both theirs and others' consumption. In this case, a consumer's decision to consume, provided their consumption is large enough, may affect the market price they will pay. For example, the USA drastically reducing its consumption of OPEC oil may have an important effect on its price.

3.6.2 Example: The Multi-Agent Consumption-Based Capital Asset Pricing Model

Let $W_k(t)$ be the initial wealth at time t of a consumer in country k, part of which is consumed at t and its remnant is invested for the next period $t + 1$ consumption. Let $s_k(t)$ be the consumer k saving rate. Since the current price is known, the current financial expenditure is $(1 - s_k(t))W_k(t) = \pi(C(t), t)c_k(t)$, where $C(t)$ is the aggregate demand for consumption and $c_k(t)$ is the kth agent's (country's) demand. A period later, the residual wealth invested $s_k(t)W_k(t)$ at an ROR $\tilde{R}_k(t + 1)$ yields a consumption $\tilde{c}_k(t + 1)$ (assuming that at the second period all wealth in consumed), when the future random price is $\tilde{\pi}(\tilde{C}(t + 1), t + 1)$:

$$\tilde{c}_k(t + 1) = \frac{s_k(t)W_k(t)\left(1 + \tilde{R}_k(t + 1)\right)}{\tilde{\pi}(\tilde{C}(t + 1), t + 1)}, \quad \tilde{C}((t + 1), t + 1) = \sum_{i=1}^{n} \tilde{c}_i(t + 1), \quad k = 1, 2, 3, \dots, n$$

The two-period utility multi-agent (multi-country) problem is then defined by the saving policy $s_k(t)$:

$$\underset{s_k(t)}{\text{Max}} U_k\left(\frac{(1 - s_k(t))W_k(t)}{\pi(C(t), t)}\right) + \beta E\left\{U_k\left(\frac{s_k(t)W_k(t)\left(1 + \tilde{R}_k(t + 1)\right)}{\tilde{\pi}(\tilde{C}(t + 1), t + 1)}\right)\right\}, \quad k = 1, 2, 3, \dots, n$$

The optimization of this problem is straightforward and yields

$$1 = \beta E\left\{\frac{\pi_k(t + 1)/\pi_k(t)}{\pi(\tilde{C}((t + 1), t + 1))/\pi(C((t), t))}\left\{(1 + \tilde{R}_k(t + 1))\left(\frac{1 - s_k(t)\dfrac{\partial \ln \pi(\tilde{C}((t + 1), t + 1))}{\partial \tilde{C}((t + 1), t + 1)}}{1 + (1 - s_k(t))\dfrac{\partial \ln \pi(C((t), t))}{\partial C(t)}}\right)\right\}\right\}$$

where $\pi(\tilde{C}((t + 1), t + 1))/\pi(C((t), t)) = 1 + \tilde{\eta}(t + 1)$ is the inflation rate of the price to be paid, while the price inflation rate that agents are willing to pay is $\pi_k(t + 1)/\pi_k(t) = 1 + \tilde{\mu}_k(t + 1)$, which allows us to rewrite the pricing model as follows:

$$1 = \beta E\left\{\frac{1 + \tilde{\mu}_k(t + 1)}{1 + \tilde{\eta}(t + 1)}\left\{(1 + \tilde{R}_k(t + 1))\left(\frac{1 - s_k(t)\dfrac{\partial \ln \pi(\tilde{C}((t + 1), t + 1))}{\partial \tilde{C}((t + 1), t + 1)}}{1 + (1 - s_k(t))\dfrac{\partial \ln \pi(C(t), t)}{\partial C(t)}}\right)\right\}\right\}$$

Note that if $\partial \pi / \partial C = 0$, then

$$1 = \beta E\left\{\frac{1 + \tilde{\mu}_k(t + 1)}{1 + \tilde{\eta}(t + 1)}\left\{(1 + \tilde{R}_k(t + 1))\right\}\right\}$$

In this case, a kernel pricing formula can be defined by noting that an investment in a risk-free rate yields

$$1 = \beta E \left\{ \frac{1 + \tilde{\mu}_k(t+1)}{1 + \tilde{\eta}(t+1)} \left\{ \left(1 + R^{\mathrm{TIPS}}(t+1)\right)\right\} \right\} \quad \text{and}$$

$$1 = \frac{1}{1 + R^{\mathrm{TIPS}}} E^{M_k^t} \left(\frac{1 + \tilde{R}_k(t+1)}{1 + \tilde{\eta}(t+1)} \right), \quad k = 1, 2, 3, \ldots, n$$

In this sense, consumer consumption prices are both financial and strategic, depending on other consumers' wealth capacities, their propensity to save, and their willingness to pay for consumption. This formulation is concurrent with global and dependent consumption problems.

3.6.3 Example: Portfolio Investment

Consider a two-period optimization problem for a domestic investor saving in the first period to consume their residual wealth in the second period:

$$U^{\mathrm{D}}(.) = \underset{B_{\mathrm{D}}^{\mathrm{D}}, B_{\mathrm{F}}^{\mathrm{D}}}{\mathrm{Max}}\, u_0^{\mathrm{D}}\left(c_0^{\mathrm{D}}\right) + \mu E^P u_1^{\mathrm{D}}\left(\tilde{c}_1^{\mathrm{D}}\right), \quad \left(c_0^{\mathrm{D}} = W_0^{\mathrm{D}} - P_0^{\mathrm{D}}; \tilde{c}_1^{\mathrm{D}} = \tilde{P}_1^{\mathrm{D}}\right)$$

For simplicity, let the domestic consumer invest in both domestic and foreign bonds $B_{\mathrm{D}}^{\mathrm{D}} + B_{\mathrm{F}}^{\mathrm{D}}(1 - \delta_{\mathrm{DF}})$, where δ_{DF} is the transaction cost D pays to invest in the foreign country. Finally, we let r_{d} and r_{F} be bonds returns with ν_{d} and ν_{F} transaction costs when exercising the right to cash in the bond. Finally, we let a currency ROR on the foreign bond be the random variable $\tilde{R}_{\mathrm{FD}}^{\xi}$. The following domestic consumer utility results:

$$U^{\mathrm{D}}(.) = \left\{ \begin{array}{l} \underset{B_{\mathrm{D}}^{\mathrm{D}}, B_{\mathrm{F}}^{\mathrm{D}}}{\mathrm{Max}}\, u_0^{\mathrm{D}}\left(W_0 - \left(B_{\mathrm{D}}^{\mathrm{D}} + B_{\mathrm{F}}^{\mathrm{D}}(1 - \delta_{\mathrm{DF}})\right)\right) \\ + \mu E u_1^{\mathrm{D}}\left((1 - \nu_{\mathrm{d}})B_{\mathrm{D}}^{\mathrm{D}}(1 + r_{\mathrm{d}}) + (1 - \nu_{\mathrm{d}})(1 - \nu_{\mathrm{f}})B_{\mathrm{F}}^{\mathrm{D}}(1 + r_{\mathrm{f}})(1 - \delta_{\mathrm{FD}})(1 - \delta_{\mathrm{DF}})\left(1 + \tilde{R}_{\mathrm{FD}}^{\xi}\right)\right) \end{array} \right\}$$

The currency (returns) pricing model for a domestic probability measure $M^{\mathrm{D}}/E(M^{\mathrm{D}})$ is then

$$E^{M^{\mathrm{D}}}\left(1 + \tilde{R}_{\mathrm{FD}}^{\xi}\right) = \frac{(1 - \nu_{\mathrm{d}})(1 + r_{\mathrm{d}})}{(1 - \nu_{\mathrm{f}})(1 - \delta_{\mathrm{FD}})(1 + r_{\mathrm{f}})} \quad \text{or} \quad \xi_{\mathrm{FD}}^0 = \frac{(1 - \nu_{\mathrm{f}})(1 - \delta_{\mathrm{FD}})(1 + r_{\mathrm{f}})}{(1 - \nu_{\mathrm{d}})(1 + r_{\mathrm{d}})} E^{M^{\mathrm{D}}}\left(\tilde{\xi}_{\mathrm{FD}}^1\right)$$

Proof
The necessary conditions for the portfolio optimality (with the utility of consumption defined equally for both periods) are

$$E^{M^{\mathrm{D}}}\left(1 + \tilde{R}_{\mathrm{FD}}^{\xi}\right) = \frac{(1 - \nu_{\mathrm{d}})(1 + r_{\mathrm{d}})}{(1 - \nu_{\mathrm{f}})(1 - \delta_{\mathrm{FD}})(1 + r_{\mathrm{f}})} \quad \text{or} \quad \frac{1}{(1 - \nu_{\mathrm{d}})(1 + r_{\mathrm{d}})} = E\left(\mu \frac{\partial u_1^{\mathrm{D}}(.)/\partial \tilde{c}_1^{\mathrm{D}}}{\partial u_0^{\mathrm{D}}(.)/\partial c_0^{\mathrm{D}}}\right)$$

and

$$\frac{\partial U^{\mathrm{D}}(.)}{\partial B_{\mathrm{F}}^{\mathrm{D}}} = -\frac{\partial u_0^{\mathrm{D}}(.)}{\partial c_0^{\mathrm{D}}}(1 - \delta_{\mathrm{DF}}) + \mu(1 - \nu_{\mathrm{f}})(1 - \delta_{\mathrm{DF}})(1 - \delta_{\mathrm{FD}})(1 + r_{\mathrm{f}})E\left(\mu \frac{\partial u_1^{\mathrm{D}}(.)/\partial \tilde{c}_1^{\mathrm{D}}}{\partial u_0^{\mathrm{D}}(.)/\partial c_0^{\mathrm{D}}}\left(1 + \tilde{R}_{\mathrm{FD}}^{\xi}\right)\right) = 0$$

Setting as indicated by the CCAPM probability measure

$$\tilde{M}^{D} = \mu \frac{\partial u_1^{D}(.)/\partial \tilde{c}_1^{D}}{\partial u_0^{D}(.)/\partial c_0^{D}}$$

we obtain

$$\frac{1}{(1-\nu_d)(1+r_d)} = E(\tilde{M}_0^{D}) \quad \text{and} \quad \frac{(1-\nu_d)(1+r_d)}{(1-\nu_f)(1-\delta_{FD})(1+r_f)} = E\left(\left(\frac{\tilde{M}_0^{D}}{E(\tilde{M}_0^{D})}\right)(1+\tilde{R}_{FD}^{\xi})\right)$$

And therefore, under the M^{D} probability measure, we have

$$\frac{(1-\nu_d)(1+r_d)}{(1-\nu_f)(1-\delta_{FD})(1+r_f)} = E^{M^{D}}\left(1+\tilde{R}_{FD}^{\xi}\right) \quad \text{or} \quad \xi_{FD}^{0} = \frac{(1-\nu_f)(1-\delta_{FD})(1+r_f)}{(1-\nu_d)(1+r_d)} E^{M^{D}}\left(\tilde{\xi}_{FD}^{1}\right)$$

where $E^{M^{D}}\left(1+\tilde{R}_{FD}^{\xi}\right)$ expresses the domestic investor expectation with respect to the probability measure. Q.E.D.

Note that in this case, the current FX rate is discounted by a number of economic variables, including the countries' risk-free rates, the transaction costs in FX, and the countries' inflation rates. Thus, under this measure, the ROR in the FX currency (an asset class in this case) is equal to the relative risk-free RORs between the domestic and the foreign countries. This expresses the domestic valuation of the FX rate. For the foreign country (investor), we have instead

$$\xi_{DF}^{0} = \frac{(1-\nu_d)(1-\delta_{DF})(1+r_d)}{(1-\nu_f)(1+r_f)} E^{M^{F}}\left(\tilde{\xi}_{DF}^{1}\right), \quad \xi_{DF}^{0} = \frac{1}{\xi_{FD}^{0}}$$

Again, ξ_{DF}^{0} expresses the valuation of the FX rate by the foreign party, which at time $t = 0$ must necessarily maintain the equality $\xi_{DF}^{0} = 1/\xi_{FD}^{0}$ (assuming no transaction cost). In this case:

$$\xi_{DF}^{0} = \frac{(1-\nu_d)(1-\delta_{DF})(1+r_d)E^{M^{F}}\left(\tilde{\xi}_{DF}^{1}\right)}{(1-\nu_f)(1+r_f)} = \frac{(1-\nu_d)(1+r_d)}{(1-\nu_f)(1-\delta_{FD})(1+r_f)E^{M^{D}}\left(\tilde{\xi}_{FD}^{1}\right)}$$

And therefore

$$E^{M^{D}}\left(\tilde{\xi}_{FD}^{1}\right)E^{M^{F}}\left(\tilde{\xi}_{DF}^{1}\right) = \frac{1}{(1-\delta_{DF})(1-\delta_{FD})}$$

If in our calculations $\xi_{FD}^{0} \neq 1/\xi_{DF}^{0}$, this means that FX prices are not priced equally across countries, providing opportunities for arbitrage as this will allow one party to transfer funds from one place to another and make a riskless and instantaneous profit (presuming that there are no transactions and other costs to include). If there is no inflation and no transaction costs, these equations are reduced to our previous results:

$$1 = \frac{1+r_f}{1+r_d} E^{M^{D}}\left(1+\tilde{R}_{FD}^{\xi}\right) \quad \text{or} \quad \frac{r_d - r_f}{1+r_f} = E^{M^{D}}\left(\tilde{R}_{FD}^{\xi}\right), \quad \frac{r_f - r_d}{1+r_d} = E^{M^{F}}\left(\tilde{R}_{DF}^{\xi}\right)$$

If $(1-\nu_d)(1+r_d) = (1-\nu_f)(1-\delta_{FD})(1+r_f)$, then $E^{M^{D}}\left(\tilde{R}_{FD}^{\xi}\right) = 0$ and $E^{M^{F}}\left(\tilde{R}_{DF}^{\xi}\right) = 0$, which points to an FX stability, as FX rates will be maintained at a given level over time. If FX rates are maintained at a fixed level arbitrarily, while countries' risk-free rates, transaction costs, and inflation rates differ, we will also have an expected zero ROR in the currencies market $E\left(\tilde{R}_{FD}^{\xi}\right) = E\left(\tilde{R}_{DF}^{\xi}\right) = 0$ which will contradict the "market price" for FX rates. Again, such a disparity opens up opportunities for betting for or against the currency in the expectation that, eventually, the true FX rate market price will prevail.

Note that the countries' risk-free deflator implied by kernel pricing is a function of both countries' discount rates as well as inflationary forces in both countries and currency transactions costs. For example, if foreign currencies' FX RORs are null for the domestic investor, then $E^Q\left(\tilde{R}_{FD}^{\xi}\right) = 0$ and thereby the interest rate on the foreign bond investment is a function of countries' relative inflation rates and currencies' transaction costs:

$$r_{\mathrm{f}} = \frac{(1-\nu_{\mathrm{d}})(1+r_{\mathrm{d}})}{(1-\nu_{\mathrm{f}})(1-\delta_{FD})} - 1 \quad \text{and} \quad r_{\mathrm{d}} = \frac{(1-\nu_{\mathrm{f}})(1+r_{\mathrm{f}})}{(1-\nu_{\mathrm{d}})(1-\delta_{DF})} - 1$$

These interest rates are not equal and provide, therefore, an incentive to investors to move their income from one country to another. For example, if a domestic investor repatriates their investment, the transaction cost is 10% while that of the foreign investor is 0%; then, *ceteris paribus* (zero RORs in currency speculation), we have

$$r_{\mathrm{f}} = \frac{(1-\nu_{\mathrm{d}})(1+r_{\mathrm{d}})}{0.90(1-\nu_{\mathrm{f}})} - 1 \quad \text{and} \quad r_{\mathrm{d}} = \frac{(1-\nu_{\mathrm{f}})(1+r_{\mathrm{f}})}{(1-\nu_{\mathrm{d}})} - 1$$

And interest rates differentials are necessarily not equal to zero, but a function of the countries' inflation rates. Or:

$$r_{\mathrm{f}} - r_{\mathrm{d}} = \frac{(1-\nu_{\mathrm{d}})^2(1+r_{\mathrm{d}}) - 0.90(1-\nu_{\mathrm{f}})^2(1+r_{\mathrm{f}})}{0.90(1-\nu_{\mathrm{f}})(1-\nu_{\mathrm{d}})} \neq 0$$

If countries have equal inflation rates, we have $r_{\mathrm{f}} = 0.0555 + 1.0555 r_{\mathrm{d}}$, which requires that the domestic sovereign treasury rate be much higher. If this is not the case, then capital investments will flow to the foreign country.

This result is generalized next by recursion over n periods. Assuming no transaction costs and no inflation, we have

$$1 = \left(\frac{1+r_{\mathrm{f}}}{1+r_{\mathrm{d}}}\right)^n E^{M_{\mathrm{D}}}\left(\frac{\tilde{\xi}_{FD}^n}{\xi_{FD}^0}\right) \quad \text{and} \quad \xi_{FD}^0 = \left(\frac{1+r_{\mathrm{f}}}{1+r_{\mathrm{d}}}\right)^n E^{M_{\mathrm{D}}}\left(\tilde{\xi}_{FD}^n\right)$$

Thus, at the limit, when n is large:

$$\lim_{n \to \infty}\left(\frac{1+r_{\mathrm{f}}}{1+r_{\mathrm{d}}}\right)^n = e^{-(r_{\mathrm{d}}-r_{\mathrm{f}})n}$$

therefore, over a period of continuous time t, we have the well-known pricing functions

$$\xi_{FD}^0 = e^{-(r_{\mathrm{d}}-r_{\mathrm{f}})t} E_0^{M_{\mathrm{D}}}\left(\tilde{\xi}_{FD}^t\right) \quad \text{and also} \quad \xi_{FD}^t = e^{-(r_{\mathrm{d}}-r_{\mathrm{f}})(T-t)} E_t^{M_{\mathrm{D}}}\left(\tilde{\xi}_{FD}^T\right)$$

where $E_t^{M_{\mathrm{D}}}$ indicates an expectation under the probability measure M_{D} at time t and based on all the information commonly available and shared by all investors. For call and put options on a foreign currency, the following holds:

$$C_{FD}^0\left(\xi_{FD}^0\right) = e^{-(r_{\mathrm{d}}-r_{\mathrm{f}})T} E_0^{M_{\mathrm{D}}}\left(C_{FD}^0\left(\tilde{\xi}_{FD}^T\right)\right) = e^{-(r_{\mathrm{d}}-r_{\mathrm{f}})T} E_0^{M_{\mathrm{D}}}\left(\mathrm{Max}\left(\tilde{\xi}_{FD}^T - \bar{\xi}_{FD}^C, 0\right)\right)$$
$$P_{FD}^0\left(\xi_{FD}^0\right) = e^{-(r_{\mathrm{d}}-r_{\mathrm{f}})T} E_0^{M_{\mathrm{D}}}\left(P_{FD}^0\left(\tilde{\xi}_{FD}^T\right)\right) = e^{-(r_{\mathrm{d}}-r_{\mathrm{f}})T} E_0^{M_{\mathrm{D}}}\left(\mathrm{Max}\left(\bar{\xi}_{FD}^P - \tilde{\xi}_{FD}^T, 0\right)\right)$$

where $\bar{\xi}_{FD}^{C}$ is the strike of the call option and $\bar{\xi}_{FD}^{P}$ the strike of the put option with T, the options exercise time.

3.6.4 The Capital Asset Pricing Model as a Special Case of the Consumption-Based Capital Asset Pricing Model

The CCAPM linear kernel model $M_{t+1} = a_t + b_t \tilde{R}_{M,t+1}$ defines also the CAPM model, where $\tilde{R}_{M,t+1}$ is a diversified financial index. For a given stock, whose ROR is $1 + \tilde{R}_{t+1} = \tilde{p}_{t+1}/p_t$, we have

$$1 = E\{M_{t+1}(1+\tilde{R}_{t+1})\} \rightarrow E(1+\tilde{R}_{t+1}) = \frac{1}{E(M_{t+1})} - \frac{\operatorname{cov}(M_{t+1}, 1+\tilde{R}_{t+1})}{E(M_{t+1})}$$

Inserting the linear kernel, we have $E(1+R_{t+1}) = (1+\tilde{R}_{f,t})(1-\operatorname{cov}(M_{t+1}, 1+\tilde{R}_{t+1}))$ and $E(1+\tilde{R}_{t+1}) = (1+R_{f,t+1})(1-\operatorname{cov}(a+b\tilde{R}_{M,t+1}, 1+\tilde{R}_{t+1}))$, which is reduced to

$$E(\tilde{R}_{t+1} - R_{f,t+1}) = \frac{\operatorname{cov}(\tilde{R}_{M,t+1} - R_{f,t+1}, \tilde{R}_{t+1} - R_{f,t+1})}{\operatorname{var}(\tilde{R}_{M,t+1} - R_{f,t+1})} E_t(\tilde{R}_{M,t+1} - R_{f,t+1})$$

Or in terms of a risk premium, it is reduced to

$$E(\tilde{\pi}_{t+1}) = \frac{\operatorname{cov}(\tilde{\pi}_{M,t+1}, \tilde{\pi}_{t+1})}{\operatorname{var}(\tilde{\pi}_{M,t+1})} E_t(\tilde{\pi}_{M,t+1})$$

while its beta is

$$\beta = \frac{\operatorname{cov}(\tilde{R}_{M,t+1} - R_{f,t+1}, \tilde{R}_{t+1} - R_{f,t+1})}{\operatorname{var}(\tilde{R}_{M,t+1} - R_{f,t+1})} = \frac{\operatorname{cov}(\tilde{\pi}_{M,t+1}, \tilde{\pi}_{t+1})}{\operatorname{var}(\tilde{\pi}_{M,t+1})}$$

The hypothesis that the kernel is linear may be limiting, however. Some studies have suggested that we use a quadratic measurement of risk with a kernel given by

$$M_{t+1} = a_t + b_t R_{M,t+1} + c_t R_{M,t+1}^2$$

In this case, the skewness of the distribution has to be accounted as well when valuing the stock.

Kernel pricing models are therefore both rational and empirical, since under an appropriate measure an investment and its outcome ought, in expectation and with respect to a probability measure, be the same. If this is not the case, it provides an opportunity of arbitrage. In such a case, prices are incomplete and investors can make money without any financial commitment or risk—an impossibility in the long run.

3.6.5 Foreign Exchange Rates, Bonds, and Equity

Assume an investment portfolio consisting of a domestic and foreign portfolio of risk-free bonds and equity (say an equity index). We also assume no debt. Then:

$$P_0^D = B_D^D + n_D^D S_D^D + B_F^D + n_F^D S_F^D$$

where $n_D S_D$ and $n_F S_F$ are the investment in two equity indexes—one domestic and the other foreign. Similarly, for the foreign country, we have (in the foreign country currency)

$$P_0^F = B_F^F + n_F^F S_F^F + B_D^F + n_D^F S_D^F$$

In the next period, the price of the portfolio is random and equal to

$$\tilde{P}_1^D = B_D^D (1 + r_d) + n_D^D S_D^D (1 + \tilde{R}_D) + \left(B_F^D (1 + r_f) + n_F^D S_F^D (1 + \tilde{R}_F) \right) \left(1 + R_{FD}^\xi \right)$$

where $\tilde{R}_D$ and $\tilde{R}_F$ are the domestic and the foreign indexes' RORs. For the foreign investor, we have

$$\tilde{P}_1^F = B_F^F (1 + r_f) + n_F^F S_F^F (1 + \tilde{R}_F) + \left(B_D^F (1 + r_d) + n_D^F S_D^F (1 + \tilde{R}_D) \right) \left(1 + R_{DF}^\xi \right)$$

The investors' expected utility of consumption in both countries over a two-period model are then

$$U_D \left(c_0^D, \tilde{c}_1^D \right) = u_D \left(c_0^D \right) + \beta E_0 u_D \left(\tilde{c}_1^D \right) = u_D \left(W_0^D - P_0^D \right) + \beta E_0 u_D \left(\tilde{P}_1^D \right)$$
$$U_F \left(c_0^F, \tilde{c}_1^F \right) = u_F \left(c_0^F \right) + \beta E_0 u_F \left(\tilde{c}_1^F \right) = u_F \left(W_0^D - P_0^F \right) + \beta E_0 u_F \left(\tilde{P}_1^F \right)$$

We consider first the domestic investor problem:

$$\underset{B_D^D, B_F^D, n_D^D, n_F^D}{\text{Max}} U_D \left(c_0^D, \tilde{c}_1^D \right) = u_D \left(W_0^D - P_0^D \right) + \beta E_0 u_D \left(\tilde{P}_1^D \right)$$

The necessary conditions for optimality are then:

$$\frac{\partial U_D}{\partial B_D^D} = -\frac{\partial u_D}{\partial P_0^D} \frac{\partial P_0^D}{\partial B_D^D} + \beta E_0 \left(\frac{\partial u_D}{\partial P_1^D} \frac{\partial \tilde{P}_1^D}{\partial B_D^D} \right) \quad \text{and} \quad \frac{\partial U_D}{\partial B_D^D} = -\frac{\partial u_D}{\partial P_0^D} + \beta (1 + r_d) E_0 \left(\frac{\partial u_D}{\partial P_1^D} \right) = 0$$

$$\frac{\partial U_D}{\partial B_F^D} = -\frac{\partial u_D}{\partial P_0^D} \frac{\partial P_0^D}{\partial B_F^D} + \beta E_0 \left(\frac{\partial u_D}{\partial P_1} \frac{\partial \tilde{P}_1^D}{\partial B_F^D} \right) \quad \text{and} \quad \frac{\partial U_D}{\partial B_F^D} = -\frac{\partial u_D}{\partial P_0^D} + \beta (1 + r_f) E_0 \left(\frac{\partial u_D}{\partial P_1^D} \left(1 + \tilde{R}_{FD}^\xi \right) \right) = 0$$

$$\frac{\partial U_D}{\partial n_D^D} = -\frac{\partial u_D}{\partial P_0^D} \frac{\partial P_0^D}{\partial n_D^D} + \beta E_0 \left(\frac{\partial u_D}{\partial P_1} \frac{\partial \tilde{P}_1}{\partial n_D^D} \right) \quad \text{and} \quad \frac{\partial U_D}{\partial n_D^D} = -S_D^D \frac{\partial u_D}{\partial P_0^D} + \beta E_0 \left(\left(1 + \tilde{R}_D \right) S_D^D \frac{\partial u_D}{\partial P_1} \right) = 0$$

$$\frac{\partial U_D}{\partial n_F^D} = -\frac{\partial u_D}{\partial P_0^D} \frac{\partial P_0^D}{\partial n_F^D} + \beta E_0 \left(\frac{\partial u_D}{\partial P_1} \frac{\partial \tilde{P}_1^D}{\partial n_F^D} \right) \quad \text{and} \quad \frac{\partial U_D}{\partial n_F^D} = -S_F \frac{\partial u_D}{\partial P_0^D} + \beta S_F E_0 \left(\frac{\partial u_D}{\partial P_1^D} \left(1 + \tilde{R}_F \right) \left(1 + \tilde{R}_{FD}^\xi \right) \right) = 0$$

And therefore, setting

$$\tilde{M}_0^D = \left(\beta \frac{\partial u_D / \partial \tilde{P}_1^D}{\partial u_D / \partial P_0^D} \right)$$

we have

$$\frac{1}{1 + r_d} = E_0^D \left(\tilde{M}_0^D \right), \quad \frac{1 + r_d}{1 + r_f} = E_0^D \left(\frac{\tilde{M}_0^D}{E \left(\tilde{M}_0^D \right)} \left(1 + \tilde{R}_{FD}^\xi \right) \right)$$

$$1 = \frac{1}{1 + r_d} E_0 \left(\frac{\tilde{M}_0^D}{E \left(\tilde{M}_0^D \right)} \left(1 + \tilde{R}_D \right) \right), \quad 1 = \frac{1}{1 + r_d} E_0 \left(\frac{\tilde{M}_0^D}{E \left(\tilde{M}_0^D \right)} \left(1 + \tilde{R}_F \right) \left(1 + \tilde{R}_{FD}^\xi \right) \right)$$

Assuming the Q probability measure for the domestic investor, we have

$$\frac{1}{1+r_{\mathrm d}}=E_0^Q(1), \quad \frac{1+r_{\mathrm d}}{1+r_{\mathrm f}}=E_0^Q\left(1+\tilde R_{\mathrm{FD}}^\xi\right)$$

$$1=\frac{1}{1+r_{\mathrm d}}E_0^Q\left(1+\tilde R_{\mathrm D}\right), \quad 1=\frac{1}{1+r_{\mathrm d}}E_0^Q\left(\left(1+\tilde R_{\mathrm F}\right)\left(1+\tilde R_{\mathrm{FD}}^\xi\right)\right)$$

These equations can be written conveniently with respect to the probability measure Q as follows:

$$\frac{r_{\mathrm d}-r_{\mathrm f}}{1+r_{\mathrm f}}=E_0^Q\left(\tilde R_{\mathrm{FD}}^\xi\right), \quad r_{\mathrm d}=E_0^Q\left(\tilde R_{\mathrm D}\right), \quad r_{\mathrm d}=E_0^Q\left(\tilde R_{\mathrm F}\right)+E_0^Q\left(\tilde R_{\mathrm{FD}}^\xi\right)+E_0^Q\left(\tilde R_{\mathrm F}\tilde R_{\mathrm{FD}}^\xi\right)$$

Replacing $E_0^Q\left(\tilde R_{\mathrm{FD}}^\xi\right)$, we have

$$\frac{r_{\mathrm d}-r_{\mathrm f}}{1+r_{\mathrm f}}=E_0^Q\left(\tilde R_{\mathrm D}\right)-E_0^Q\left(\tilde R_{\mathrm F}\right)-E_0^Q\left(\tilde R_{\mathrm F}\tilde R_{\mathrm{FD}}^\xi\right)$$

If $r_{\mathrm d}=r_{\mathrm f}$, then $-E_0^Q\left(\tilde R_{\mathrm F}\tilde R_{\mathrm{FD}}^\xi\right)=E_0^Q\left(\tilde R_{\mathrm F}\right)-E_0^Q\left(\tilde R_{\mathrm D}\right)$. Therefore, $E_0^Q\left(\tilde R_{\mathrm F}\right)-E_0^Q\left(\tilde R_{\mathrm D}\right)$, the difference between expected RORs from an investment in a domestic and foreign country (from the domestic investor's perspective), depends on the covariation of $\tilde R_{\mathrm F}$ and $\tilde R_{\mathrm{FD}}^\xi$. Explicitly, since

$$E_0^Q\left(\tilde R_{\mathrm F}\tilde R_{\mathrm{FD}}^\xi\right)=E_0^Q\left(\tilde R_{\mathrm F}\right)E_0^Q\left(\tilde R_{\mathrm{FD}}^\xi\right)+\rho_{\mathrm F,FD}^Q\sigma_{\mathrm F}^Q\sigma_{\mathrm{FD}}^Q$$

and

$$\begin{aligned}0&=E_0^Q\left(\tilde R_{\mathrm F}\right)\left[E_0^Q\left(1+\tilde R_{\mathrm{FD}}^\xi\right)\right]-E_0^Q\left(\tilde R_{\mathrm D}\right)+\rho_{F,FD}^Q\sigma_F^Q\sigma_{FD}^Q\\&=E_0^Q\left(\tilde R_{\mathrm F}\right)\frac{1+r_{\mathrm d}}{1+r_{\mathrm f}}-E_0^Q\left(\tilde R_{\mathrm D}\right)+\rho_{F,FD}^Q\sigma_F^Q\sigma_{FD}^Q\\&=E_0^Q\left(\tilde R_{\mathrm F}\right)-E_0^Q\left(\tilde R_{\mathrm D}\right)+\rho_{F,FD}^Q\sigma_F^Q\sigma_{FD}^Q\end{aligned}$$

As a result, if $\rho_{F,FD}^Q<0$, meaning that the greater the FX equity market, the stronger its currency in terms of its exchange for the domestic currency, we therefore have $E_0^Q\left(\tilde R_{\mathrm F}\right)=E_0^Q\left(\tilde R_{\mathrm D}\right)+\left(|\rho_{F,FD}^Q|\sigma_F^Q\sigma_{FD}^Q\right)$, which defines the required (FX) premium for a foreign investment. When the fixed-income RORs are not equal, $r_{\mathrm d}\neq r_{\mathrm f}$, we have

$$E_0^Q\left(\tilde R_{\mathrm F}\right)=\frac{1+r_{\mathrm f}}{1+r_{\mathrm d}}\left(E_0^Q\left(\tilde R_{\mathrm D}\right)-\rho_{F,FD}^Q\sigma_F^Q\sigma_{FD}^Q\right)-\frac{r_{\mathrm d}-r_{\mathrm f}}{1+r_{\mathrm d}}, \quad \rho_{F,FD}^Q<0$$

For example, if $r_{\mathrm d}<r_{\mathrm f}$, the required ROR $E_0^Q\left(\tilde R_{\mathrm F}\right)$ is increased due to a greater ROR in its (competing) fixed-income rate $r_{\mathrm f}$. Using a CAPM-like notation, we set

$$\beta_{\mathrm F,FD}^{\mathrm D}=-\rho_{\mathrm F,FD}^Q\frac{\sigma_F^Q}{\sigma_{FD}^Q}, \quad -\rho_{\mathrm F,FD}^Q\sigma_F^Q\frac{\left(\sigma_{FD}^Q\right)^2}{\sigma_{FD}^Q}=\beta_{\mathrm F,FD}^{\mathrm D}\left(\sigma_{FD}^Q\right)^2, \quad \beta_{\mathrm F,FD}^{\mathrm D}>0$$

And therefore

$$E_0^Q(\tilde{R}_F) = \frac{1+r_f}{1+r_d}\left(E_0^Q(\tilde{R}_D) + \beta_{F,FD}^D\left(\sigma_{FD}^Q\right)^2\right) - \frac{r_d - r_f}{1+r_d}, \quad \rho_{F,FD}^Q < 0$$

Again, if the fixed-income RORs are equal, then

$$E_0^Q(\tilde{R}_F) = E_0^Q(\tilde{R}_D) + \beta_{F,FD}^D\left(\sigma_{FD}^Q\right)^2$$

where $\beta_{F,FD}^D\left(\sigma_{FD}^Q\right)^2$ denotes the required RORs' premium. If this is not the case, then note that if $r_d > r_f$, the left-hand side of the equation will be greater, requiring a greater risk premium for investing in the foreign country, and vice versa if $r_d < r_f$.

Note that $E_0^Q(\tilde{R}_F)$, $E_0^Q(\tilde{R}_{FD}^\xi)$, and $E_0^Q(\tilde{R}_F\tilde{R}_{FD}^\xi)$ are expectations under the probability measure Q and can therefore be estimated on the basis of option prices (namely by calculating the implied risk-neutral probability distribution, as we shall see subsequently). This Q–beta CAPM differs from the standard CAPM, and therefore the $\beta_{F,FD}^D$ we have used here may be called a "forward beta."

Say that $E_0^Q(\tilde{R}_D) = 0.05$ and $E_0^Q(\tilde{R}_F) = 0.12$, then

$$\frac{1+r_d}{1+r_f}\left(0.12 + \frac{r_d - r_f}{1+r_d}\right) = 0.05 + \beta_{F,FD}^D\left(\sigma_{FD}^Q\right)^2$$

Thus, for the foreign country to reduce the premium that foreign investors require to invest in their country, they will have to increase their risk-free ROR. Say that $r_d = 0.04$, then

$$\frac{1.04}{1+r_f}\left(0.12 - \frac{r_f - 0.04}{1.04}\right) = 0.05 + \beta_{F,FD}^D\left(\sigma_{FD}^Q\right)^2 \quad \text{and} \quad r_f = \frac{0.11 - \beta_{F,FD}^D\left(\sigma_{FD}^Q\right)^2}{1.05 + \beta_{F,FD}^D\left(\sigma_{FD}^Q\right)^2}$$

This latter expression indicates the relationship between the required risk premium and the foreign risk-free rate. If risk-free rates are equal, $r_f = 0.04$, then $\beta_{F,FD}^D\left(\sigma_{FD}^Q\right)^2 = 0.15/1.04 = 0.1442$, which is the required risk premium. Say that the foreign country currency is appreciating at a rate of 6% (in repatriating invested funds in the foreign country), then $E_0^Q(\tilde{R}_{FD}^\xi) = 0.06$, and $1.12E_0^Q(\tilde{R}_{FD}^\xi) = 0.0672$. In this case, it is advantageous for the domestic investor to invest in the foreign country. However, if the currency depreciates at the same rate, we still have $-0.0672 > -0.07$, which continues to justify investing in the foreign country.

For a foreign investor, similar considerations are applied (but in reverse). In this case

$$\beta_{D,DF}^F = \frac{1}{\left(\sigma_{DF}^Q\right)^2}\left\{\left(E_0^V(\tilde{R}_F) - \frac{r_f - r_d}{1+r_d}\right) - E_0^V(\tilde{R}_D)\left(\frac{1+r_f}{1+r_d}\right)\right\}$$

or

$$\beta_{D,DF}^F = -\frac{1}{\left(\sigma_{DF}^Q\right)^2}\left\{E_0^V(\tilde{R}_F)\left(1 + E_0^V(\tilde{R}_{DF}^\xi)\right) - \left(E_0^V(\tilde{R}_D) - E^V(\tilde{R}_{DF}^\xi)\right)\right\}$$

Since, for a foreign investor, an appreciation of their currency is necessarily the inverse of that of the domestic currency (it is not necessarily true in this case, as the expectations are taken with respect to two different probability measures), we have $E_0^Q\left(\tilde{R}_{\text{FD}}^\xi\right) = 0.06$ and $E_0^Q\left(\tilde{R}_{\text{DF}}^\xi\right) = -0.06$, in which case

$$\beta_{\text{D,DF}}^{\text{F}} = -\frac{1}{\left(\sigma_{\text{DF}}^Q\right)^2}\left[0.12(1-0.06)-(0.05+0.06)\right] = -\frac{1}{\left(\sigma_{\text{DF}}^Q\right)^2}(0.1128-0.11) < 0$$

and, therefore, the foreign investor would invest in the foreign country.

3.6.6 Example: Rate of Returns in Foreign Equity Markets and the Foreign Exchange Rate

FX prices are, as stated earlier, relative prices. An FX rate is then measured relative to, say, the dollar—normally assumed to be a "strong" and reference currency. Suppose there are two countries (say the USA and China), then consider

$$\frac{1+r_d}{1+r_f}\left(E_0^Q\left(\tilde{R}_F\right) + \frac{r_d-r_f}{1+r_d}\right) = E_0^Q\left(\tilde{R}_D\right) + \beta_{\text{F,FD}}^{\text{D}}\left(\sigma_{\text{FD}}^Q\right)^2;$$

$$\frac{1+r_f}{1+r_d}\left(E_0^V\left(\tilde{R}_D\right) + \frac{r_f-r_d}{1+r_f}\right) = E_0^V\left(\tilde{R}_f\right) + \beta_{\text{D,DF}}^{\text{F}}\left(\sigma_{\text{DF}}^Q\right)^2$$

First, note that the correlation between the RORs in the foreign equity market and the FX rate from repatriating revenues from the foreign country is negative. This is the case because, as the FX rate increases, the investor would have to use more of the foreign currency to repatriate the income they made in that country. And conversely, when the foreign economy has a declining FX rate, the required ROR is smaller, as it is compensated by the increased currency exchange ROR. When there is no correlation, then $\beta_{\text{F,FD}}^{\text{D}} = \beta_{\text{D,DF}}^{\text{F}} = 0$, and therefore

$$E_0^Q\left(\tilde{R}_F\right) = \frac{1+r_f}{1+r_d}E_0^Q\left(\tilde{R}_D\right) - \frac{r_d-r_f}{1+r_d}; \quad E_0^V\left(\tilde{R}_D\right) = \frac{1+r_d}{1+r_f}E_0^V\left(\tilde{R}_f\right) - \frac{r_f-r_d}{1+r_f}$$

In other words, say that the risk-free rate in the domestic country is greater than in the foreign country. In this case, $r_d - r_f > 0$ and therefore the ROR in the foreign equity market is greater than that in the domestic market:

$$E_0^Q\left(\tilde{R}_F\right) = \frac{E_0^Q\left(\tilde{R}_D\right)(1+r_f)-(r_d-r_f)}{1+r_d} \quad \text{or} \quad E_0^Q\left(\tilde{R}_F\right) > E_0^Q\left(\tilde{R}_D\right)$$

If the risk-free RORs in both countries are equal, then $r_d = r_f$, and therefore

$$E_0^Q\left(\tilde{R}_F\right) = E_0^Q\left(\tilde{R}_D\right) + \beta_{\text{F,FD}}^{\text{D}}\left(\sigma_{\text{FD}}^Q\right)^2 \quad \text{and} \quad E_0^V\left(\tilde{R}_D\right) = E_0^V\left(\tilde{R}_f\right) + \beta_{\text{D,DF}}^{\text{F}}\left(\sigma_{\text{DF}}^Q\right)^2$$

Evidently, both the FX rate volatility and the foreign market equity index increase the required ROR on the foreign index. There are then two countervailing forces: on the one hand, stability of the FX rate reduces the required FX risk premium; and on the other hand, the strong (negative) correlation between the foreign equity index and FX leads to a growth in the index required ROR premium. These observations can be used to make the case for China's FX policy on the condition that there is no volatility in this exchange. Inversely, by maintaining equity prices in China's index to be far more in concordance with "world" RORs, the correlation between these returns and a free floating exchange rate would necessarily be smaller but with a greater volatility in China's FX rate.

3.7 Thought Experiments

Consider at present a risk premium for local investors to invest in their own country. Based on our conditions, for optimality we have

$$E_0^Q(\tilde{R}_D) - r_d = \left(\frac{1+r_d}{1+r_f}E_0^Q(\tilde{R}_F) - \frac{r_f(1-r_d)}{1+r_f} - \beta_{F,FD}^D\left(\sigma_{FD}^Q\right)^2\right)$$

$$E_0^V(\tilde{R}_f) - r_f = \left(\frac{1+r_f}{1+r_d}E_0^V(\tilde{R}_D) - \frac{r_d(1-r_f)}{1+r_d} - \beta_{D,DF}^F\left(\sigma_{DF}^Q\right)^2\right)$$

Since $E_0^Q(\tilde{R}_D) - r_d = E_0^V(\tilde{R}_f) - r_f = 0$, we have

$$E_0^Q(\tilde{R}_F) = \frac{1}{1+r_d}\left(r_f(1-r_d) + (1+r_f)\beta_{F,FD}^D\left(\sigma_{FD}^Q\right)^2\right);$$

$$E_0^V(\tilde{R}_D) = \frac{1}{1+r_f}\left(r_d(1-r_f) + (1+r_d)\beta_{D,DF}^F\left(\sigma_{DF}^V\right)^2\right)$$

If equity markets have the same ROR (priced by investors in their respective country), then

$$E_0^Q(\tilde{R}_F) = E_0^V(\tilde{R}_D)$$

And therefore the following relationship holds between the risk-free rates and the risk premiums:

$$\frac{(1+r_f)r_f(1-r_d)}{(1+r_d)^2} - \frac{r_d(1-r_f)}{1+r_d} + \frac{(1+r_f)^2}{(1+r_d)^2}\beta_{F,FD}^D\left(\sigma_{FD}^Q\right)^2 = \beta_{D,DF}^F\left(\sigma_{DF}^V\right)^2$$

Say that China "stabilizes" its FX rate by not letting it fluctuate. In this case, the propensity of investors in China will be to accept a smaller spread between investment in China's equity and bond markets. The implication of such a policy for China is that stability (assuming that the FX rate is a fair one rather than an artificially managed one) will contribute to foreign capital inflows, attracted by the risk-free returns and their conversion into the domestic currency. In this sense, foreign investors will buy China's obligations (rather than risk investment in China's equity markets), which would require an increase in China's foreign currency. When countries that are not as large or powerful as China are faced with such a situation, a potential for arbitrage arises with currency bets engineered to profit when the foreign country can no longer finance the stability of its currency. Such a situation arose when sterling was "attacked" by a group of hedge funds and resulting in a great loss to England's central bank a few decades ago. It was also in play in Hong Kong with a position taken by the Pershing hedge fund in the hope that the

Honk Kong dollar, which is "indexed" to the US dollar, be revalued (*The Economist*, September 26, 2011). If this were to happen, then Pershing would have realized an appreciable profit. However, it did not.

These thought exercises are of course biased because we considered relatively simple portfolios as well as one country at a time.

References

Arrow, K.J. (1951) Alternative approaches to the theory of choice in risk-taking situations. *Econometrica*, **19**: 404–437.

Chamberlain, G. (1983) Funds, factors and diversification in arbitrage pricing models. *Econometrica*, **51**: 1305–1324.

Connor, G. (1984) A unified beta pricing theory. *Journal of Economic Theory*, **34**: 13–31.

Constantinides, G.M. and Duffie, D. (1996) Asset pricing with heterogeneous consumers. *Journal of Political Economy*, **104**(2): 219–240.

Debreu, G. (1953) Une economie de l'incertain. Working Paper, Electricité de France, Paris.

Debreu, G. (1960) Une economie de l'incertain. *Economie Appliquée*, **13**(1): 111–116.

Eeckhoudt, L., Gollier, C., and Schlesinger, H. (1996) Changes in background risk and risk-taking behavior. *Econometrica*, **64**(3): 683–689.

Eichner, T. and Wagener, A. (2005) Measures of risk attitudes: correspondences between mean-variance and expected utility approaches. *Decisions in Economics and Finance*, **28**(1): 53–65.

Fama, E.F. and French, K.R. (1992) The cross-section of expected stock returns. *Journal of Finance*, **47**: 427–465.

Guetzkow, H. (1959) A use of simulation in the study of inter-nation relations. *Behavioral Science*, **4**(3): 183–191.

Guetzkow, H. (1962) *Simulation in Social Science: Readings*. Prentice-Hall: Englewood Cliffs, NJ.

Huberman, G. (1982) A simple approach to arbitrage pricing. *Journal of Economic Theory*, **28**: 183–191.

Ingersoll, J.E. (1984) Some results in the theory of arbitrage pricing. *Journal of Finance*, **39**: 1021–1039.

Kimball, M. (1990) Precautionary saving in the small and in the large. *Econometrica*, **58**: 53–78.

Lintner, J. (1965) The valuation of risk assets and the selection of risky investments in stock portfolios and capital budgets. *The Review of Economics and Statistics*, **47**(1): 13–37.

Markowitz, H.M. (1959) *Portfolio Selection: Efficient Diversification of Investments*. John Wiley & Sons, Inc.: New York.

Mehra, R. and Prescott, E.C. (1985) The equity premium: a puzzle. *Journal of Monetary Economics*, **15**: 145–161.

Merton, R.C. (1990) *Continuous Time Finance*. Blackwell: Cambridge, MA.

Munier, B. and Tapiero, C. (2008) Risk attitudes. In *Encyclopedia of Quantitative Risk Assessment*, B. Everitt and E. Melnick (eds). John Wiley & Sons.

Rencher, A.C. and Christensen, W.F. (2012) *Methods of Multivariate Analysis*. Wiley Series in Probability and Statistics. John Wiley & Sons.

Roll, R.R. and Ross. S.A. (1980) An empirical examination of the arbitrage pricing theory. *Journal of Finance*, **35**, 1073–1103.

Ross, S.A. (1976) The arbitrage theory of capital asset pricing. *Journal of Monetary Economics*, **13**(3): 341–360.

Ross, S.S. (1977) Return, risk and arbitrage. In *Risk and Return in Finance*, I. Friend and J. Bicksler (eds). Ballinger: Cambridge, MA; pp. 189–218.

Ross, S.S. (1978) The current status of the capital asset pricing model (CAPM). *Journal of Finance*, **33**: 885–901.

Rubinstein, M. (1973) The fundamental theorem of parameter-preference security valuation. *Journal of Financial and Quantitative Analysis*, **8**: 61–70.

Sharpe, W.F. (1964) Capital asset prices: a theory of market equilibrium under risk. *Journal of Finance*, **19**: 425–442.

Smith, A. (1994[1776]) *The Wealth of Nations*. Modern Library: New York, NY.

Stein, C. (1973) Estimation of the mean of a multivariate normal distribution. In *Proceedings of Prague Symposium on Asymptotic Statistics*, September.

Tapiero, C.S. (2015) A financial CCAPM and economic inequalities. *Quantitative Finance*, **15**(3): 521–534.

Walras, L. (1874–1877) *Elements d'Economie Politique Pure*. Corbaz: Lausanne (English translation by W. Jaffé, Allen and Unwin, London, 1954).

4

Macroeconomics, Foreign Exchange, and Global Finance

Motivation

This chapter reviews fundamental macroeconomic and international economic models from a global perspective. We discuss a number of linkages between geopolitics, risk finance, and macroeconomics. Two types of models are presented: (1) traditional closed-economy models based upon sovereign measurements of their own economy and (2) open-economy models, as originally extended by Keynes, emphasizing consumption and the interaction between domestic factors (including both private and public sectors), as well as interactions with foreign economies. These were originally extended by Mundell and Fleming. An economy is defined both by its monetary and by its real sectors, providing a macroeconomic relationship between real goods, money markets, and international transactions. We discuss the importance of balance of payments (BOP) in global finance along with its underlying principles and components, and analyze recent trends in macroeconomic policies and exchange rate movements that shape economic globalization. The sustainability of external debt and trends in foreign direct investment (FDI) are highlighted as well.

4.1   Introduction

Macroeconomics is an essential part of political governance. Its economic rationality and its application to sovereign policy are due, essentially, to John Maynard Keynes. Keynes defined an economy's aggregates in terms of three sectors:

- the goods market, consisting of the real economy and its associated fiscal policy;
- the money market—demand and supply of money, monetary policy and interest rates set by central banks;
- the asset market.

Consumption was introduced as a multiplier of macroeconomic growth by Keynes, providing policy-makers with a tool to affect prices. Mundell and Fleming's seminal contributions provided an extension to Keynes' framework by including foreign markets in national accounts—factors that relate the economic indicators of one country to others. In particular, they introduced BOP accounts to complete the Keynes model, thereby ushering an approach to international economics and exchanges. These have contributed to foreign exchange (FX) pricing and to the role and importance of FX markets based on the

Globalization, Gating, and Risk Finance, First Edition. Unurjargal Nyambuu and Charles S. Tapiero.
© 2018 John Wiley & Sons Ltd. Published 2018 by John Wiley & Sons Ltd.

parity of prices across national boundaries. From a macroeconomic perspective, FX rates are a derived asset class, a function of countries' macroeconomic statistics (e.g., BOP and demand and supply of foreign money). In a global environment, financial decisions assume many forms; for example, buying long or short, financing trades, lending or borrowing on a global scale, hedging, investing in foreign firms or international projects, and speculating on currencies' prices and sovereign debt. These set the foundations for diverse, large, and robust markets. At the same time, they contribute to the expansion of specialized and competing financial centers in an increasing number of countries.

Geopolitics and macroeconomics have empowered global finance as a means to pursue national agendas, set sovereign policies, and to search for financial opportunities, while at the same time gating one's sovereign economy. As a result, macroeconomics and finance and political agendas have evolved into a complex set of interdependent factors defining the evolution of globalization and gating.

Macroeconomic policies are derived from national statistics and geopolitical considerations, defining both national economic policies and their global implications. Questions include: How do global geopolitical events and competitive postures motivate and affect economic and financial policies? How do they alter the rationale and the complexity of theoretical and empirical financial and economic models? Their consequences are manifested in macroeconomic national accounts (e.g., gross domestic product (GDP), gross national income, consumption, and BOP). Their effects reverberate in sovereign expenditures, financial asset prices, commodity prices, financial regulation, trade incentives, and so on. The complexity of their interrelationships is debated in political, academic, and business circles, and results in complex models defined by their political and economic goals. In this context, global finance models differ from traditional economic and financial models. While international macroeconomics is based on the exchanges of countries' markets and their relationships to domestic economies, a globalized economy has open borders with free capital and goods flows across national boundaries. It is challenging academics, policy-makers, and the business world at large. As a result, economic, industrial, corporate, and financial interests that fuel and are fed by globalization assume many different forms, affecting and affected by geopolitical concerns.

For example, a plunge in commodity prices has important economic and political ramifications in emerging economies and for countries that depend entirely on commodity exports. Media and policies often characterize wars through the financial costs they entail. Similarly, macro-hedge funds respond to national political and financial policies, with their trade based on geopolitical opportunities. For example, in the 1990s, a group of macro-hedge funds, including Soros, the Tiger Hedge Fund, and others, forced a revaluation of the British pound, causing an extremely large loss to Britain's Treasury and earning extraordinary profits (over $1 billion profit in a day for Soros). In this chapter, we concentrate our attention to some fundamental macroeconomic models.

4.2 Fundamental Macroeconomic Models

Macroeconomic models may be classified in two categories: closed and open. The closed economy model is considered first.

4.2.1   The Keynes Model: Goods and Money Markets in a Closed Economy

The Keynes model is based on the supply of and demand for economic factors and their prices at equilibrium. The economic demand side consists of:

- Aggregate demand E for goods and services in an economy determined by private and government consumption expenditures C and G respectively, and investments I; that is, $E = C + I + G$. Each of these accounts is a function of other variables that make up the national economy.
- Consumption depends on income, $C(Y)$. It is set to be a function of disposable income Y^D, which is an income net of taxes $(Y - T)$. This relationship is defined by the marginal propensity to consume, denoted by the parameter b; that is, a proportion of disposable income consumed.
- Interest rate r (the cost of money) has an effect on investment $I(r)$, defined by $\partial I / \partial r < 0$ (i.e., the greater the interest rate, the lesser the investment and vice versa).

$$E = C(Y) + I(r) + G \text{ and } C(Y) = a + bY^D, a > 0, 0 < b < I, \text{ and } \partial C / \partial Y > 0, Y^D = Y - T$$

Aggregate supply is defined by total output or GDP, which is equal to national income Y. GDP can be measured in different ways: the expenditures approach, the income approach, and value added (i.e., a difference between total output and total intermediary goods).[1] In a closed economy, an equilibrium (short-run) is reached when the demand for goods and services is equal to the supply. In other words, an equilibrium level of output is determined when

$$\begin{cases} Y = C(Y) + I(r) + G \\ C(Y) = a + b(Y - T), \quad a > 0, 0 < b < 1, \text{ and } \partial C / \partial Y > 0 \end{cases}$$

This equilibrium in a real (goods) market provides then a relationship between the interest rate and output. Since an increase in interest rates causes investments to fall, it leads as a result to a fall in output. This is reflected in a downward-sloping curve called the IS curve. This curve shifts if any factor affecting demand changes, other than the interest rate. The effects of a fiscal policy on the real economy is then reflected in the shifts in the IS curve. For example, a fiscal expansion through an increase in government expenditure or a tax reduction shifts the IS curve to the right (or outward), as shown in Figure 4.1a, from IS_1 to IS_2. As a result, both the interest rate and output increase (r_1 to r_2 and Y_1 to Y_2). The real market should be defined together with the monetary (financial) market, depending on one another. Thus, in Figure 4.1, in addition to the goods market equilibrium, it points to the money market equilibrium, explained by the definition of money demand and money supply. These relationships are defined empirically in terms of macroeconomic statistics. International economic theories and sovereign economic policies are based on these relationships as well as their interactions with other economies, in which case a closed economy is "opened." "Openness," however, is relative, depending on how gating policies are defined. For example, the EU may be considered a "sovereign" region and its outreach by its gating policies across EU-member borders.

---

1 For details on how to measure GDP and national income and product accounts (NIPA) or national accounts, see BEA (2015).

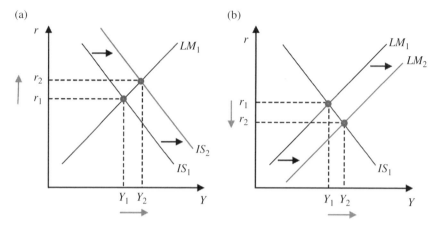

Figure 4.1 Fiscal and monetary policies under IS–LM model: (a) fiscal policy (expansionary); (b) monetary policy (expansionary).

4.2.1.1 Money Markets

Keynes' (1936) theory of liquidity preference determines the interest rate in the short run by analyzing the demand (MD) and supply (MS) of money, and the money market equilibrium in a closed economy. Money supply and financial "liquidity" of money fund and fuel the real market. Money supply is varied, consisting essentially of currency and checkable deposits.[2] The MS curve is a vertical line assuming that money supply, in terms of a currency, is controlled by the central bank. Money supply can be increased (or reduced) when the central bank buys (or sells) government bonds in the bond market through open market operations. Increasingly, technology, futures financial products, and currencies of "various sorts" are contributing to the supply and the liquidity of money. The demand side for money, however, consists of moneys held and used to pay for transactions, or for precautionary purposes, or for speculative purposes. Keynes (1936) explains these motives and how they determine an individual's demand or preference for liquidity. Higher income level encourages more spending, thus raising the demand for money. In contrast, higher interest rates on bonds provide incentives for investment, thus reducing the demand for money. The demand for money is then a function of nominal income Y^{nom} and the interest rate $\text{MD} = L(Y^{\text{nom}}, r)$ with $\partial L/\partial Y > 0$ and $\partial L/\partial r < 0$, as illustrated in Figure 4.2. In an equilibrium, money supply is equal to money demand, as shown by

$$\text{MS} = \text{MD} \rightarrow M = L(Y^{\text{nom}}, r)$$

The real money supply is defined by dividing both sides of the following equation by the price:

$$\text{MS}^{\text{real}} = \text{MD}^{\text{real}} \rightarrow \frac{M}{P} = M_R = L(Y, r)$$

where Y indicates real income and M_R is the real money stock.

---

2 The narrowest measure of money supply (the most liquid), known as M1, consists of currency, traveler's checks, demand deposits, and other checkable deposits. A broader definition of money supply, M2, includes M1 and savings deposits, small-denomination time deposits, and retail money funds (for more details on the composition of money aggregates and US historical data, see the Federal Reserve's H.6 statistical release).

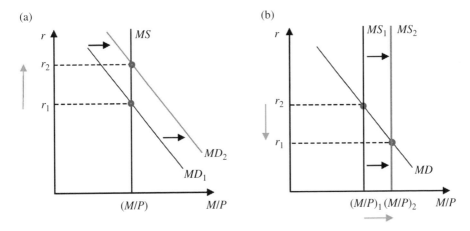

Figure 4.2 Money (financial) market: (a) a shift in money demand curve; (b) a shift in money supply curve.

The essential function of financial institutions is to "engineer and be the architects" that transfer "money" to real economic markets. This extremely broad definition has created derivative markets that have expanded future aggregate demand and future money supply. The growth of globalization has entitled and empowered financial institutions to trade globally, across national borders, all global currencies, and across time (with futures and forwards). Thus, financial institutions have become global enterprises, bridging macroeconomics and macro-finance.

Suppose that the real supply of money M_R declines and set $M_R = L(Y,r)$. Interest rates then increase since money becomes costlier to borrow and thus equity markets (stock markets and asset prices) decrease as they compete with a bond market that provides liquidity to borrowers (such as sovereign states through their treasury bills, government bonds, and corporate bonds). Inversely, an increase in the money supply has a negative effect on interest rates, as shown in Figure 4.2b. Therefore, it contributes to a growth in equity markets compared to bond markets. Assuming a money market equilibrium, total differentiation yields

$$dM_R = \frac{\partial L(Y,r)}{\partial Y}dY + \frac{\partial L(Y,r)}{\partial r}dr$$

If the real money supply is constant, $dM_R = 0$, and:

$$\frac{dY}{dr} = -\frac{\partial L(Y,r)/\partial r}{\partial L(Y,r)/\partial Y} > 0$$

Explicitly, this points to a rate of change in interest rates with increasing income as shown by the LM curve (derived from the short-run money market equilibrium). Namely, an increase in income leads to the outward shift in the money demand curve (see Figure 4.2a), resulting in turn in a rise in the interest rate. The LM curve thus points to the important effects of a monetary policy on output. For example, say that a central bank adopts an expansionary monetary policy, by increasing the money supply that reduces the interest rate. Expectedly, it will shift the LM curve to the right (or outward) as shown in Figure 4.1b (from LM_1 to LM_2). Interest rates will then fall from r_1 to r_2, whereas output will rise from Y_1 to Y_2. Practically, if we assume that the world is totally open and that sovereign states compete, would a reduction in interest rates in one country cause another to pursue a similar policy? Similarly, would a devaluation of the currency by one country be followed by another country doing the same? These questions are meant to highlight the importance of international macroeconomics and at the same time, consider the complexity of the global economy which, although open, remains competitive, defined by individual economic agendas.

In practice, sovereign states tend to use a mixture of fiscal and monetary policies in managing their economy. For a recovery from recession, both fiscal and monetary expansions play an important role. When both the IS and LM curves shift to the right, the output (income) Y increases. These results correspond to closed economies only. However, when economies' trade and exchange of goods and services are accounted for, they become interdependent, defining open economies as outlined in Section 4.2.2. Since effective policies are derived from national accounts (macroeconomic statistics), in open economies, sovereign agendas, and interdependency, gating, policy, and finance become geopolitical and strategic.

Questions and Problems 4.1

Using the IS–LM model, describe the effects of the following policies on interest rates, investment, consumption, and income. Illustrate the outcomes and analyze the effectiveness of these policies.

a) In order to stimulate the economy following a financial crisis and boost recovery, a sovereign policy provides a massive stimulus program while a central bank would reduce interest rates.
b) In order to curb an inflation, a central bank reduces money supply while the sovereign state reduces taxes on income to support an increase in consumption.
c) Describe the effects of a monetary policy that causes a liquidity trap. How can we escape a liquidity trap? Use the Japanese case to explain these effects, the causes, and avoidance of the liquidity trap.
d) How does a fiscal policy lead to a crowding out of investments? Refer to lessons from developing Asia.

4.2.2 Macroeconomic Accounting in Open Economies

Open economies, unlike closed economies, are complex and defined by their mutual interdependence, the terms of their exchange and their internal mechanisms, and by their gating policies (e.g., regulation and tariffs). They may be based on national policies such as trade and political considerations expressing national agendas. Exchanges assume many forms (e.g., exports, imports, capital flows, FDI). These and other factors provide signals of the trends in comparative political and economic policies, financial expectations about future performance, safety, stability, and geopolitical events in general. In this sense, FX traded in global financial markets contributes to a better appreciation of the openness of national economies and individual countries' economic and geopolitical strengths.

Open economies, both theoretically and practically, are, as already stated, relatively open while remaining relatively closed, reflecting countervailing costs and benefits of open economies. For example, are imports at lower prices increasing an export of jobs? Are such trends increasing supply and dependency risks of one sovereign state versus another? When all economies are completely open, the global economy is defined by one market with all goods and services flowing freely. Would enterprises, large and small, pursuing the maximization of their profits as well as reducing their financial obligations (on taxes, regulation, costs, etc.) contribute to the migration of wealth, knowledge, and know-how from one country to another? Would economic migrations, evading sovereign regulations and controls, contribute to higher or lower consumption prices as well? Gating financial flows and trade through regulation, trade barriers, trade incentives, quotas, control of consumption, taxes, and the protection of jobs leads in fact to hybrid-open. These define the current state of economic globalization and global finance. As a result, globalization and "hybrid-open economies" are contributing to countries increasingly adopting interdependent and complex domestic strategic policies with implicit conflicts seeking to expand globally while gating their own economies. These render the process of economic globalization to be defined by "push–pull" and contradictory forces.

To simplify a review of principles in open economies, we shall focus on fundamental precepts, emphasizing the basic differences between "open" and "closed," recognizing that, in fact, globalization has contributed to "hybrid-open economies," which from an academic viewpoint remains a work in process.

4.2.2.1 Open Economies and Finance

In a global, financially oriented, and tech-savvy world, currency is increasingly redefined in terms of derivative products, such as options, swaps (see Chapters 7–9), credit, and alternative money, all of which are traded with increased frequency and speed. In this sense, macroeconomic models that summarize aggregate indicators through their financial currency valuation may provide a partial, yet essential, picture of the economy. Further, a growing variety of financial products contributes to the facilitation of their exchange across national boundaries.

As an economy opens up to foreign trade and attracts foreign investments, domestic markets are affected by foreign economic performance, such as foreign income, foreign interest rate, and inflation. Fiscal and/or monetary policy changes have then an impact on domestic macroeconomic indicators (e.g., output, interest rates, consumption, and investments), but also on foreign investments based on their capital mobility. These interactions determine the price of FX rates, which in turn contribute to the determination of the balance of trade.

Macroeconomic financial and international accounting analyzes how countries finance their expenditures when domestic revenue sources and savings are insufficient.[3] In this context, the borrowing/lending relationship between private households, the public sector,

---

3 This occurs when savings are insufficient for investment $(S < I)$. Under the equilibrium, savings equal investments.

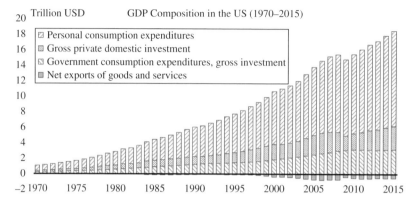

Figure 4.3 GDP Composition in the USA. *Source:* Data from the US Bureau of Economic Analysis.

and businesses defines a macro-finance economy embedded in a current account (CA).[4] An open economy model is therefore an extension of a closed economy model that adds and defines transactions of domestic and foreign economies in terms of their balance of trade BX; that is, the net exports of a country, EX − IM, where EX is exports and IM is imports. A country's trade surplus thus occurs when exports exceed imports (EX > IM).

To illustrate the composition of the GDP, historical data for the USA are given in Figure 4.3. This figure demonstrates that households' personal consumption is the major contributor to GDP, accounting for almost 70% of the GDP, followed by the government expenditures and private investments. The US trade balance has had persistent deficits since the late 1970s, due primarily to US imports that have contributed to economic globalization.

We consider next the relationships between private and public sectors, combined with expenditures and income sources. To do so, we first define consumption C in terms of net income (after taxes) and savings: $C = (Y - T) - S$ and substitute C into an output or GDP (Y) equation as shown next. As a result, the sum of government net flow $(G - T)$, private-sector net flow $(I - S)$, and trade balance BX is null. This relationship demonstrates interconnected transactions between the private and public sectors, as well as interactions between domestic and foreign sectors. Or, explicitly:

$$Y = C + I + G + \text{BX} \Rightarrow Y = (Y - T) - S + I + G + \text{BX} \Rightarrow$$

$$(G - T) + (I - S) + \text{BX} = 0$$

In other words, when the private sector of a sovereign state spends more than its income ($I > S$ or $G > T$), the CA (or trade balance) will indicate a deficit (BX < 0). A deficit is then compensated and financed by a net borrowing or by an increase in external debt.[5] This is, for example, exactly the case for the USA, with its high consumption expenditures and low savings rate, maintaining its economic balance by borrowing extensively from the rest of the world (including printing of money and treasury bills bought by foreign

---

4 The CA consists of mainly trade balance (exports and imports of goods and services), as well as receipts and payments of income, and transfers. More details about these transactions are discussed in Section 4.3.
5 This relationship between the CA and financial account (FA) is explained in Section 4.3 BOP accounting.

financial agents and countries such as China). The USA, in particular, has large twin deficits—a trade deficit $(BX < 0)$ and a government budget deficit $(G > T)$.

On the one hand, a growth of foreign debt reflects first the interest of foreign agents to invest in the USA, as well as their trust in the safety of their investments. On the other hand, the growth of debt, providing current access to "cheap money" by the USA (since it is also based on the printing by the US Treasury), also increases the future commitment of the USA to meet its financial obligations (see Chapter 8). In this sense, debt and mutual borrowing (see also the euro mutual debts obligations in Chapter 1) have reinforced trends in sovereign financial dependence and globalization. For example, the creation of the euro as a common currency has contributed to a financial dependence and to a partial political integration of European member states (these states have bulked a fiscal integration that has led to the euro being sustainable only with "difficulties as Brexit has shown").

Inversely, a CA or trade surplus $(BX > 0)$ corresponds to an accumulation of net foreign assets (or net lending through increased asset claims on foreign countries). This was the case in some Asian countries with high savings and/or government budget surplus.

$$\text{Twin deficits}: \ BX < 0, \text{Budget} < 0 \Rightarrow \underbrace{-BX}_{BX<0} = \underbrace{I-S}_{\text{Private } I-S} + \underbrace{G-T}_{\text{Budget} < 0}$$

$$\text{Twin surpluses}: \ BX > 0, \text{Budget} > 0 \Rightarrow \underbrace{BX}_{BX>0} = \underbrace{I-S}_{\text{Private } S-I} + \underbrace{G-T}_{\text{Budget} > 0}$$

These relationships provide a guideline to policymakers seeking to reduce trade deficits, at the same time increasing their dependence to sovereign states (such as the USA and China). For these reasons, a slowdown or an expansion of one's economy can have an important effect on the other. Trade deficits may then be reduced either by cutting budget deficits (Budget < 0), through a rise in taxes T and/or cutting expenditure G, and/or reducing net private borrowing by increasing private savings S. These decisions have dual consequences and are affected by geopolitical considerations. For example, increased terrorism and US military involvement will contribute to an increase rather than a decrease in G; inversely, a USA with a retreating and isolationist policy may in the short term reduce G rather than increasing it. In this context, open and in particular hybrid-open economies are far more sensitive to geopolitical considerations and events than closed economies.

4.3 Balance of Payments Accounts

4.3.1 The Structure of Balance of Payments

The BOP accounts summarize a country's flows of both private and official transactions; for example, trade in goods and services, and purchase/sale of financial assets, between residents and non-residents. It consists of inflows and outflows of the currency under the CA, and capital flows under the capital account (KA) and financial account (FA). The BOP, as indicated previously, has important implications for economic globalization and its derivatives, the demand and the supply of foreign currency, and FX markets. For example, payments for imported merchandises increase the demand for foreign currency or the supply of domestic currency. BOP trends also provide important signals to trade partners and may be used in setting economic and political measures to improve the BOP (in the presence of BOP deficits); for example, restrictions on imports and on capital outflows. Further, the BOP may also serve as an indicator of a country's economic performance; for example, pointing out whether domestic industries are internationally competitive or not. Thus, while BOP is an indicator of economic globalization, it also points to gating of some economies that experience an increase in imports at the expense of their own economic production (in industry, services, labor conditions, jobs, etc.). Although these contribute to the macroeconomic performance of national economies, they also stimulate geopolitical policies that sovereign states pursue in order to maintain and sustain their economic health and strategic positions.

Standard components of the BOP accounts described in *Balance of Payments Manual Sixth Edition (BPM6)* (IMF, 2009) are shown in Table 4.1 with examples of corresponding transactions. CA includes the balance on goods and services, primary income, and secondary income, including different current transfers. KA records acquisitions or disposals of

Table 4.1 Structure of the BOP accounts.

	Example transactions
I. CA	
1. Goods and services	Exports or imports of goods; receipts and payments for services
Goods	*General merchandise, non-monetary gold*
Services	*Maintenance, repair, transport, travel, construction, insurance, pension*
2. Primary income	Income from production process and financial assets, natural resource rents
Compensation of employees	*Wage and salaries, social contributions*
Investment income	*Dividends, interests, reinvested earnings*
Other primary income	*Production and imports taxes, subsidies, rent from natural resources*
3. Secondary income	Remittances, income and wealth taxes, social contributions, social benefits
II. KA	
1. Gross acquisitions/disposals of non-produced non-financial assets	Natural resources, contracts, leases, licenses, marketing assets, goodwill
2. Capital transfers	Debt forgiveness, capital taxes
III. FA	
1. Direct investment	Control of the voting power, new plant, real estate, reverse investment
2. Portfolio investment	Equity and investment fund shares, debt securities
3. Financial derivatives, employee stock options	Options, futures, swap contracts, employee stock options
4. Other investment	Currency and deposits, loans, insurance, pension, trade credit and advances
5. Reserve assets	Monetary gold, special drawing rights (SDR), reserve position in the IMF, currency and securities

Source: Data from IMF.

non-produced non-financial assets (e.g., licenses, trademarks) and capital transfers (such as debt forgiveness). FA records purchases or sales of financial assets, including FDI, portfolio investments, financial derivatives and employee stock options, and other investments involving changes to bank assets and liabilities, loans, trade financing, and reserve assets.

A firm becomes multinational when it undertakes FDI and an investor acquires a measured control of the foreign business. According to BPM6, cross-border direct investments are defined to exist if a resident direct investor has control (over 50% of the voting power) or a significant degree of influence (10% or more) of the management of a non-resident direct investment enterprise. A typical form of FDI occurs through the establishment of new production facilities in foreign countries, which is called greenfield investment. For example, German, Japanese, and Korean automakers, such as Mercedes, Honda, Hyundai, and Toyota, have built assembly plants in the USA, such as in Alabama. Another form of FDI is a global trend in mergers and acquisitions (M&A) of existing foreign businesses that acquire the firm for expansion and the control of their business. For example, one of the largest mergers was between Anheuser-Busch Inbev (Belgium) and SABMiller (UK) for around $100 billion in 2016. Other deals include Royal Dutch Shell's (Netherlands) acquisition of BG Group (UK) for $70 billion, and cross-border mergers, especially in pharmaceutical industry; for example, Teva Pharmaceutical Industries (Israel) and Allergan PLC-Generic Drug Business (US) for $39 billion, and Shire PLC (Ireland) and Baxalta Inc (US) for $31 billion.

Reserve assets consist of monetary gold, special drawing rights (SDR), and a reserve position in the International Monetary Fund (IMF) and other reserve assets.[6] The FA balance shows net lending/net borrowing (supply of funds from/into the country to/from the rest of the world) as well as a net acquisition of financial assets/net incurrence of liabilities (net changes in assets/liabilities).

4.3.2 Principles of Balance of Payments

Double-entry bookkeeping is used in BOP with both credit transactions (such as receipts of payments from non-residents) and debit transactions (such as payments to non-residents). Credit (cr) entries include transactions with FX inflows (e.g., exports of goods, receipts from services, interest or dividend payment receipts, inward investments by non-resident investors, including FDI inflow and portfolio investment). Debit (dr) entries then record transactions with FX outflows. Every transaction is recorded twice; once as a credit and once again as a debit. For example, a purchase of a foreign bond and its payment through a bank account is recorded as a credit (in FA) and again as a debit (in FA), both in FA but under different sub-accounts. Thus, the double-entry accounting implies that the BOP balance sums to zero: $CA + KA + FA = 0$.[7] This is shown in Figure 4.4, with

---

6 According to BPM6 (IMF, 2009: 113), monetary gold refers to "gold to which the monetary authorities (or others who are subject to the effective control of the monetary authorities) have title and is held as reserve assets." SDR was created in 1969 by the IMF and it can be exchanged or purchased from the members. Other reserve assets include currency and deposits, claims on monetary authorities and other entities, securities, financial derivatives, and other claims—see BPM6 (IMF, 2009).

7 In practice, BOP is often imbalanced due to problems associated with compilation, data coverage, classification, valuation, timing, quality of the reporting, and data collected from different agencies and organizations, as well as surveys and estimations. For example, in general, while trade data are obtained from customs, and/or banking transactions that are classified under international transactions reporting systems, other data are often based on surveys (workers' remittances, tourism expenditure, and direct investment). The imbalance is then balanced by "net errors and omissions" (NEO) (e.g., BOP + NEO = 0).

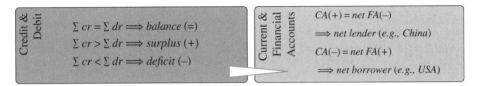

Figure 4.4 Credit and debit entries, and current account and financial accounts.

the balance (cr = dr), surplus (cr > dr), and deficits (dr > cr). In this context, CA surplus indicates net lending, whereas deficits show net borrowing from the rest of the world.[8]

Questions and Problems 4.2

Show how the following transactions are classified and recorded in the debit and credit of the US BOP.

a) Suppose the Boeing Corporation sold an airplane (Boeing 787) to Korean Airlines for $400 million and that Korean Airlines pays from its USD bank account kept with City Manhattan Bank in NYC.
b) Suppose that FedEx acquires the Dutch parcel company TNT Express for $5 billion. Suppose that TNT Express deposits the money in a bank in Amsterdam, which, in turn, uses the sum to purchase US Treasury notes.
c) A US engineer is hired by a Chinese company for consulting and gets paid from the US bank account maintained by the Chinese company.
d) Suppose that US government bonds with a value of $100 million were sold to the Chinese government and the payment was received through a US bank.

4.3.3 Global External Imbalances

Figure 4.5 shows the CA to GDP ratio as well as BOP accounts (CA and FA), where FA is found by adding the net acquisition and disposal of financial assets and liabilities for selected countries since 2005.[9,10] These data indicate large global external imbalances: while some developing and developed countries (e.g., China (CHN), Germany (DEU), Japan (JPN), and Switzerland (CHE)) have large CA surpluses, countries such as the UK, the USA, Brazil (BRA), and Turkey (TUR) have recorded CA deficits. Further, we observe a deterioration in CA for some countries with falling CA surpluses or rising CA deficits in the past decade. US trade deficits with some of its major trade partners, particularly China and the EU, as well as with Japan and Mexico, have increased dramatically. According to the US Bureau of Economic Analysis, US negative balances on goods with China surged from $69 billion in 1999 to $367 billion in 2015; similarly, US trade deficits with the EU surged from $45 billion to $157 billion during the same period. As for the net FA in Figure 4.5, these data include not only the FDI, portfolio

---

8 Since KA transactions are relatively very low, for clarity KA is omitted in the equations and discussions.
9 BOP data (from 2005) published by IMF (2009) are based on BPM6, and data prior to 2005 are compiled from BPM5 (IMF, 1993).
10 The difference between the CA and FA is recorded as the NEO. We should note that when China had massive capital outflows in 2015–2016, its NEO was at record high (see Table 4.2).

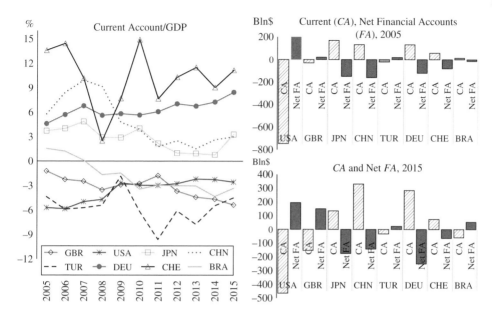

Figure 4.5 Trends in global imbalances (CA, net FA). *Source:* Data from The World Bank.

and other investments, and financial derivatives, but also reserve assets. Thus, depending on the changes in the FX reserves, FA excluding the reserve assets can be either positive or negative. This is explained in Table 4.2 using the breakdown of the FA data for China highlighting the massive capital outflows of 2015. These statistics, as well as trends in global imbalances, are associated necessarily with a migration of jobs, industrial, capacity in search of economic advantages and profits, as well as fluctuations in the currency, capital flows, and changes in FX reserves.

The capital outflows that were triggered by the sudden depreciation of the yuan continued to increase in 2016 with a further fall in FX reserves. We will explain this state of affairs using China's BOP accounts based on 2017 data from China State Administration of Foreign Exchange SAFE, as shown in Table 4.2. The KA and FA balance was $26 billion in 2016. Excluding the reserve assets, net capital outflows were –$417 billion due to reduced FX reserves by a record high amount (over $440 billion in 2016, which was much higher than the fall of $343 billion in 2015). The breakdown of data for these massive capital outflows indicates that major contributors resulting from a significant growth of direct investment abroad by Chinese, a very large increase in portfolio investment abroad, higher foreign assets, and a decrease in liabilities (including repayment of foreign debt by Chinese and withdrawal from Chinese banks).

The essential explanations for BOP imbalances may be due to economic (CA and FA accounts factors) as well as social and political factors, both domestic and abroad. In particular, CA imbalances are driven by forces pertaining to trade, such as relative prices, exchange rate, inflation, income level, trade competitiveness, and openness of trade. Major macroeconomic and institutional factors (e.g., financial market development) driving the CA in industrialized countries are examined by the IMF and other studies. As discussed previously, CA is affected by the government budget and private net

Table 4.2 China's BOP with selected sub-accounts (USD billion).

	1998	2005	2010	2011	2012	2013	2014	2015	2016
I. CA	**31**	**132**	**238**	**136**	**215**	**148**	**236**	**304**	**196**
II. KA and FA	**−13**	**−155**	**−185**	**−122**	**−128**	**−85**	**−169**	**−91**	**26**
Capital account	0	4	5	6	4	3	0	0	0
Financial account excl. reserve assets	−6	91	282	260	−36	343	−51	−434	−417
Direct investment	**41**	**90**	**186**	**232**	**176**	**218**	**145**	**68**	**−46**
Assets	−3	−14	−58	−48	−65	−73	−123	−174	−217
Liabilities	44	104	244	280	241	291	268	243	171
Portfolio investment	**−4**	**−5**	**24**	**20**	**48**	**53**	**82**	**−66**	**−62**
Assets	−4	−26	−8	6	−6	−5	−11	−73	−103
Liabilities	0	21	32	13	54	58	93	7	41
Financial derivatives	**0**	**0**	**0**	**0**	**0**	**0**	**0**	**−2**	**−5**
Other investments	**−44**	**6**	**72**	**9**	**−260**	**72**	**−279**	**−434**	**−304**
Assets	−35	−45	−116	−184	−232	−142	−329	−83	−334
Currency and deposits	1	−10	−58	−116	−105	−7	−186	−55	−44
Loans, trade credit & advances	−24	−36	−83	−116	−127	−92	−143	−93	−216
Other accounts receivable	−12	2	24	48	0	−42	−1	69	−74
Liabilities	−9	50	189	192	−28	214	50	−352	30
Currency and deposits	−5	16	60	48	−59	76	81	−123	10
Loans, trade credit & advances	−3	31	129	143	26	138	−36	−229	−3
Other accounts payable	0	3	−1	1	5	0	5	−2	24
Reserve assets	**−6**	**−251**	**−472**	**−388**	**−97**	**−431**	**−118**	**343**	**444**
III. NEO	**−19**	**23**	**−53**	**−14**	**−87**	**−63**	**−67**	**−213**	**−223**

Source: Data from China State Administration of Foreign Exchange SAFE.

savings. Bernanke (2005) points to the US CA deficits explained by the global saving glut (due to excessive Asian savings). Empirical findings in favor of the government budget are discussed in Chinn and Prasad (2003) and Chinn and Ito (2008) and others. Global issues on CA imbalances, sustainability of US CA and its trade deficits are examined by, for example, Obstfeld and Rogoff (1996, 2005, 2007), Bernanke (2005), Blanchard *et al.* (2005), Salvatore (2007, 2011), and Eichengreen (2006). Further we note that external imbalances are affected not only by private financial flows, but also by official financial flows depending on the degree of capital mobility. Large effects of FX intervention (through changes in FX reserves) on CA are found in studies by, for example, Bayoumi and Saborowski (2014), Gagnon (2012, 2013), and Bayoumi *et al.* (2015).

Questions and Problems 4.3

Study China's FX intervention in 2015 and its FX policy implications. Assess the impact of the fall in FX reserves on CA as well as FA. Discuss the motivation of such measure in terms of the exchange rate and capital flight. Were the government measures to curb the capital flows effective? How does the opening of the Chinese capital market affect lending and borrowing?

4.4 The Mundell and Fleming Model: IS–LM–BOP Model

Closed economies in equilibrium are defined, as noted earlier, by their equilibriums in both goods and money markets shown by the IS–LM curves. In an open economy, the BOP equilibrium provides a mechanism to express the dependency of a country with its trading and exchange partners. In this case, following the principles of the BOP discussed earlier, the BOP equilibrium is reached when the sum of the CA, KA, and FA is equal to zero. Mundell and Fleming have contributed to such an expansion of the basic Keynes model which we consider next. First, we define the exchange rate and its underlying factors. This analysis will be used to explain the effects of macroeconomic policies on the equilibrium in markets of goods, money, and external balance.

4.4.1 Equilibrium Exchange Rate in the Foreign Exchange Market

Exchange rates in FX markets can be defined simply by the demand and the supply of the currency that serves global exchanges. Technically, such a price is expressed by a parity between countries, defining their respective exchange rate. For example, let the price of a currency be calculated by how many euros can be exchanged for a US dollar, or inversely how many US dollars can be exchanged for one euro. Bilateral trade and capital flows between the USA and the EU determine the demand and the supply of the corresponding currencies, implying their need for mutual exchanges. On the one hand, changes in the exchange rate can affect exports/imports through changes in the prices of domestic/foreign goods in terms of domestic/foreign currency for foreign/domestic consumers. For example, a stronger dollar may make the US goods more expensive for foreign consumers, causing the US exports to decline. This would be associated with less demand for the USD or less supply of the foreign currency. At the same time, this appreciation of the USD makes foreign goods cheaper for US customers, raising the demand for imported goods. This situation may increase the demand for foreign currency or the supply of domestic currency. On the other hand, differentials in the macroeconomic factors between domestic and foreign countries may affect the exchange rate in the following ways:

- *Income ($Y^{US} > Y^{EU}$):* Increased demand for imports by US consumers due to, say, a growth in their income Y^{US} (assuming that the price of goods remains unchanged) leads to a higher demand for EU goods, increasing the demand for euros. This may cause the value of the euro to rise, which means that the euro is now worth more in US dollars (euro appreciation). On the other hand, equivalently the US dollar value becomes lower (US dollar depreciation) due to a higher supply of US dollars in exchange for the euro.

- **Inflation ($\pi^{US} > \pi^{EU}$):** Let inflation π be greater in the USA than in the EU. Reduced US exports to the EU (due to lower EU demand for US goods) leads to a lower EU supply of euros (lower demand for US dollars). Simultaneously, an increase in US imports from the EU (due to a greater US demand for EU goods) leads to a higher US demand for the euro. These changes contribute to the rise of the value of the euro.
- **Interest rate ($i^{US} > i^{EU}$):** Assume that the US interest rate rises compared with that in the EU. Investments in the USA thus become more attractive for EU investors. This increases the supply of the euro for exchange with the US dollar (higher demand for US dollars) resulting in a lower value of the euro (or higher value for the US dollar). Instead of a nominal interest rate, a real interest rate (inflation-adjusted rate) then ought to be considered when an investment decision is to be contemplated. Given the paramount importance of real rates, their implications will be expanded in later sections.
- **Expectations ($\pi_{t+1}^{EU} > \pi_t^{EU}$):** Anticipated movement of macroeconomic variables (e.g., inflation, interest rates, credit rating, debt payments, economic conditions, and political and security factors) may have an impact on future exchange rates as well. For example, an expected rise in EU inflation due to a series of monetary easing policies could lead to downward pressures on the euro with a greater supply of euros affecting future exchange rates.

These elements affect FX prices and are part of a complex set of factors acting at a global scale with sovereign states increasingly assuming an important gating role, whether direct or indirect through economic, financial, and geopolitical policies. These result in a simultaneous equilibrium across the global financial landscape placing gating and globalization into a complex globalization process. They render the prediction of FX prices challenging, combining macroeconomic and microeconomic considerations, geopolitical issues, environmental and political trends into a complex problem. From a practical financial viewpoint, FX pricing models are therefore both an art and theory based on the understanding of international relations and global economic and political trends.

Questions and Problems 4.4

Show graphically through shifts in the demand and supply curves for the currency and explain the change in the equilibrium exchange rate as a result of the following financial and economic conditions:

a) Suppose that the current interest rate is now higher in the USA while it remains low in Japan. In addition, suppose that Japan is struggling with deflation, but inflation suddenly has risen in the USA.
b) Owing to the improvement in the job market and a boost in economic growth in the USA, say that US consumers' income has increased at a greater pace than those in Japan.
c) Assume that Japan (a car manufacturing leader) increases tariffs on imports of automobile products. What are their consequences on the price of their exports and the yen?

d) Say that Brazil is experiencing an economic downturn with high inflation and concerns for a debt crisis combined with corruption scandals at Petrobras (the state-owned oil company) that led to its rating to be downgraded by Moody's. How would such an environment affect the demand and the supply of the Brazilian real? What would be their effects on capital flows (capital flight)?

4.4.2 IS–LM–BOP Model

Mundell (1963, 1968) and Fleming (1962) extended the closed economy models by including foreign trade and countries' BOPs. As noted previously, trade balance or net exports (EX−IM) is defined by BX, while its financial account is denoted by FA (an increasing function of the interest rate, $\partial FA/\partial r > 0$). A surplus in FA occurs when there is a net capital inflow due to a higher domestic interest rate compared with a foreign one. In this case, under a flexible FX rate regime, an equilibrium exchange rate ξ is defined by simultaneous adjustments across real (IS), monetary (*LM*), and foreign (BOP)[11] accounts, converting imports from foreign currency into the domestic currency. These lead to the following relationships:[12]

$$\text{Real equilibrium (IS)}: \ Y = C(Y) + I(r) + BX, \text{ where } BX = EX(\xi) - \xi \times IM(r, Y, \xi)$$

$$\text{Monetary equilibrium (LM)}: \frac{M}{P} = L(r)Y$$

$$\text{BOP equilibrium}: \ BX + FA = 0, \ EX(\xi) - \xi \times IM(r, Y, \xi) + FA(r) = 0$$

Prior to assessing these three markets graphically, a new curve for the BOP is described (see Gandolfo (2001)). The BOP curve shows a positive relationship between the interest rate and income, as demonstrated in Figure 4.6. Its slope depends on the degree of capital

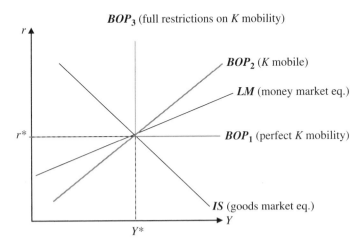

Figure 4.6 IS–LM–BOP model under fixed FX Rate (different capital *K* mobility).

11 Since the trade balance BX makes up most of the CA, for modeling purposes the trade balance (instead of the current account) is used for the BOP equilibrium. In addition, since the size of the KA is very small compared with FA, FA is used in the model. In other words, BX + FA = 0.
12 For details on the Mundell–Fleming model under fixed and flexible FX rates, see Gandolfo (2001).

mobility, as capital movement is a function of interest rate FA(r). A relatively flat BOP curve implies higher capital mobility. The BOP curve becomes a horizontal line, BOP_1, when the assets are perfectly substitutable and capital moves perfectly across countries, which in turn implies that domestic and foreign interest rates are equal.

4.4.2.1 An Open Economy under a Fixed Foreign Exchange Regime

We consider first the IS–LM–BOP model under the fixed FX rates as illustrated in Figure 4.6. Exports are assumed to be exogenous ($\overline{EX}$), but imports vary with changes in income and interest rates, $\partial IM/\partial Y > 0$, $\partial IM/\partial r < 0$. They do not depend on exchange rates since the FX rates are fixed. When domestic residents' income rises, imports from abroad would increase, leading to trade deficits. In order to ensure BOP equilibrium, these deficits must be financed by FA surplus, where $\partial FA/\partial r > 0$, thereby requiring interest rates to be higher to attract foreign investors and raise capital inflows to the domestic economy.

4.4.2.2 An Open Economy under a Flexible Foreign Exchange Regime

We consider next an open economy model under a flexible FX rate regime, where IS and BOP curves depend directly on the FX rate.[13] The effects of fiscal and monetary policies on r, Y, and ξ can be demonstrated using the Mundell–Fleming model. We analyze these policies' effects under the IS–LM–BOP model with an assumption of perfect capital mobility, implying a horizontal BOP line with $r_D = r_F$, under the flexible FX rate. Any shifts in IS or LM curves would lead to a BOP surplus/deficit (above/below BOP line) and affect both FA (through effects of interest rate on capital flows) and BX (through effects of exchange rate on exports or imports). Assuming that the initial equilibrium in the three markets we consider is at point A as shown in Figure 4.7, then the expansionary macroeconomic policy effects would be:

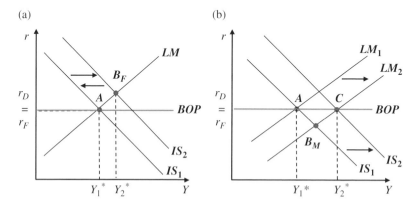

Figure 4.7 Macroeconomic policies' effects under floating FX rate (perfect capital mobility): (a) fiscal policy; (b) monetary policy.

---

13 Shifts in the IS and BOP curves due to changes in the exchange rate occur under the assumption pertaining to the critical elasticities, with FX elasticity of exports ε_{ex} and of imports ε_{im} to changes in the exchange rate, where the Marshall–Lerner condition must meet $\varepsilon_{ex} + \varepsilon_{im} > 1$ (see Gandolfo (2001)).

1) **Fiscal expansion.** It shifts the IS curve to the right, resulting in both a higher Y and r, at point B_F, which is above the BOP curve, where $r_D > r_F$. This ought to attract foreign investors and lead to a capital inflow that brings about a BOP surplus. Under a floating FX rate regime, it will lead to an exchange rate appreciation, which, in turn, reduces net exports, shifting the IS curve back to the left (Figure 4.7a).

2) **Monetary expansion.** An increase in money supply shifts the LM curve to the right, causing the r to fall ($r_D < r_F$) and output Y to increase (at point B_M). As a result, BOP has deficits (below the BOP curve) as capital outflow occurs, which, in turn, leads to an exchange rate depreciation. This raises net exports, shifting the IS curve to the right and sets an equilibrium finally at point C (Figure 4.7b).

Questions and Problems 4.5

Discuss the expansionary monetary policy implications of the Mundell–Fleming model with flexible exchange rate. Compare the results of a high and low capital mobility. Use the IS–LM–BOP mathematical model and shift the curves by graphs. What is the effect of this policy on exchange rate, output, and interest rate?

4.4.3 Two-Country Model with Mundell–Fleming

Consider two countries, with two dependent equations, defined by the accounting principle $BX_D + BX_F = 0$. This implies that a positive BOP in one country is a negative one for the other, or:

$$Y_D = C_D(Y_D) + I_D(r_D) + G_D + BX_D$$
$$Y_F = C_F(Y_F) + I_F(r_F) + G_F + BX_F$$
$$BX_D + BX_F = 0$$

The BOP is, however, a function of many economic factors, as shown by the IS–LM–BOP model. They essentially depend on relative prices denoted in a country's currency (and, therefore, their FX rates) as well as interest rates (and, therefore, on the flow of money for capital and credit investments). While imports are a function of an importing country's income, interest rates, and FX rates, exports are a function of foreign income, interest rates, and FX rates:

$$BX_D = EX_D - IM_D, \quad IM_D = IM_D(Y_D, r_D, \xi), \quad EX_D = EX_D(Y_F, r_F, \xi)$$

As a result, BX equations of two countries summarize a set of interconnected statistics that capture some of the complexity of international (open) economics. These relationships are summarized by

$$BX_D = BX_D(Y_D, Y_F, r_D, r_F, \xi_{FD}, \xi_{DF})$$

and

$$BX_F = BX_F(Y_F, Y_D, r_F, r_D, \xi_{DF}, \xi_{FD})$$

with $\xi_{DF} = 1/\xi_{FD}$ and $BX_D + BX_F = 0$ indicating that one country is exporting less than its imports and is therefore incurring an external debt. In this sense, the growth of such an imbalance contributes to the growth of indebtedness, with some nations being borrowers and others creditors.

Introducing the Mundell–Fleming extension into the Keynes model and assuming that purchasing power parity (PPP) holds:

$$\begin{cases} Y_D = C_D(Y_D) + I_D(r_D) + G_D + BX_D(Y_D, Y_F, r_D, r_F, \xi_{FD}, \xi_{DF}) \\ Y_F = C_F(Y_F) + I_F(r_F) + G_F + BX_F(Y_F, Y_D, r_F, r_D, \xi_{DF}, \xi_{FD}) \\ \text{with the real FX rate assumed to be } \xi_{FD} = P_F/P_D, \xi_{DF} = P_D/P_F \end{cases}$$

The relative values of these variables for both countries lead to both risks and arbitrage opportunities for foreign ventures (both real and financial). Such risks and opportunities underlie much of the activities seen in FX spot markets and their derivatives (such as forwards and options). As a result, both the FA and the CA have to be considered in these equations. As discussed earlier, CA consists of the trade balance BX, net factors exported abroad RX (expressing the net income flows from foreign-held assets and investments), and the unilateral transfers UT:

$$\begin{cases} CA_D = BX_D + RX_D^F + UT_D \\ BX_D = EX_D - IM_D, \quad RX_D^F = EX_D^F - IM_D^F \end{cases}$$

As a result:

$$\begin{cases} Y_D = GNE_D + CA_D, \quad GNE_D = C_D(Y_D) + I_D(r_D) + G_D \\ Y_F = GNE_F + CA_F, \quad GNE_F = C_F(Y_F) + I_F(r_F) + G_F \end{cases}$$

The FA consists of the KA as the net addition to domestic assets plus the net addition to foreign assets, since

$$\begin{cases} KA_D = KA_D^{IN} - KA_D^{OUT} \quad \text{and} \quad FA_D = FA_D^D - FA_D^F \\ FA_D^D = EX_D^A - IM_D^A, \quad FA_D^F = EX_D^{A,F} - IM_D^{A,F} \end{cases}$$

where $IM_D^{A,F} - EX_D^{A,F}$ is net imports of assets and $EX_D^A - IM_D^A$ is its net exports of assets. These statistics then define the BOP identity with

$$\begin{cases} CA_D + KA_D + FA_D = 0 \\ CA_F + KA_F + FA_F = 0 \end{cases}$$

Intricate relationships of open economies are further complicated through an intertemporal framework that would account for future FX rates' expectations, future trades, foreign investment, debt, and so on. Most modern international economic and financial models recognize the importance of these variables and therefore define these models as dynamic ones.

4.4.4 Extension of the Mundell–Fleming Model: Trade

We return to the Keynes–Mundell–Fleming model with M^S/P^i, the real supply of money is defined by the nominal money supply M^S adjusted by a price index P^i, and E, the demand (domestic expenditures), while Y, the income, represents the supply, or $E = C + I + G$ and $Y = C + I + G + BX$. Let L be an actual money balance (demand for money), which may be greater or smaller than the real supply of money. Mundell and Fleming define an adjustment mechanism based on the assumption that the difference between income and expenditures is proportional to the difference between the real stock of money balance and the real money supply (in terms of a domestic country):

$$Y_D - E_D = \lambda_D \left(L_D - \frac{M_D^S}{P_D^I} \right) \quad \text{or} \quad BX_D = \lambda_D \left(L_D - \frac{M_D^S}{P_D^I} \right)$$

with λ denoting the rate at which money holders adjust the actual money balance to the supply of real money. However, as indicated earlier, an equilibrium in a domestic money market indicates that money supply is equal to money demand:

$$\frac{M_D^S}{P_D} = L_D(Y_D, r_D) \quad \text{and therefore} \quad M_D^S = P_D L_D(Y_D, r_D)$$

Assume that $M_D^S/P_D = k_D(Y_D)^{\nu_D} e^{\varepsilon_D r_D}$, where k_D accounts for other factors that have become increasingly relevant such as complex credit markets and the velocity of money amplified by electronic exchanges. Similarly, for a foreign country, $M_F^S/P_F = k_F(Y_F)^{\nu_F} e^{\varepsilon_F r_F}$. The FX rate is then defined as

$$\xi_{FD} = \frac{P_F}{P_D} = \frac{M_F^S k_D(Y_D)^{\nu_D}}{M_D^S k_F(Y_F)^{\nu_F}} e^{\varepsilon_D r_D - \varepsilon_F r_F}$$

Combining this model with the Mundell–Fleming model, the following simultaneous equations result:

$$BX_D = \lambda_D \left(L_D(Y_D, r_D) - \frac{M_D^S}{P_D^I} \right), \quad BX_D = BX_D(\xi_{DF}, \xi_{FD}, Y_D, Y_F), \quad \xi_{DF} = 1/\xi_{FD}$$

$$BX_F(\xi_{DF}, \xi_{FD}, Y_D, Y_F) = \lambda_F \left(L_F(Y_F, r_F) - \frac{M_F^S}{P_F^I} \right)$$

$$M_F^S = P_F^I \left(L_F(Y_F, r_F) - \frac{BX_F(\xi_{DF}, \xi_{FD}, Y_D, Y_F)}{\lambda_F} \right)$$

$$M_D^S = P_D^I \left(L_D(Y_D, r_D) - \frac{BX_D(\xi_{DF}, \xi_{FD}, Y_D, Y_F)}{\lambda_D} \right)$$

If PPP holds:

$$\xi_{FD} = \frac{P_F^I}{P_D^I} = \frac{M_F^S}{M_D^S} \frac{\left(L_D(Y_D, r_D) - \dfrac{BX_D(\xi_{DF}, \xi_{FD}, Y_D, Y_F)}{\lambda_D} \right)}{\left(L_F(Y_F, r_F) - \dfrac{BX_F(\xi_{DF}, \xi_{FD}, Y_D, Y_F)}{\lambda_F} \right)}$$

The Mundell–Fleming model is thus an extension of the closed IS–LM model that considers the effects of trade with an external (BOP) equilibrium. It assumes (unlike the monetary model) that prices are flexible and preset in the short run. One of the most important forecasts of the model is the so called trilemma, which states that perfect capital mobility, monetary policy independence, and the fixed FX rate regime cannot be achieved simultaneously. In the long run, the FX rate level is perfectly correlated with the level of money supply, and monetary policy may only play a trivial role in economic growth.

4.5 Macroeconomic Factors Reshaping Global Outlook

4.5.1 Foreign Direct Investment

Globalization has contributed appreciably to the growth of both FDI and BOP transactions globally since the 1980s. In addition to the rapid growth in trade, financial transactions have accelerated at their fastest pace in advanced economies, followed by developing and emerging markets. With capital flows contributing to the capital stocks of host countries. Additionally, greenfield FDI has created employment in host economies. For example, US corporations have moved production facilities to Mexico and China, to profit from lower costs of production driven by lower wages. There are many other factors that tend to support or prevent such investments with factors driving FDI. These may include trade barriers, intangible assets, imperfect goods, capital, and labor market forces. Because of trade barriers, firms may locate production overseas rather than exporting; for example, mineral ores, coal, and cement may not be suitable for exporting due to high transportation costs.

FDI host (FDI inflow) and home (FDI outflow) regions are shown in Figure 4.8. For most developed countries, particularly in North America, FDI abroad has exceeded FDI inflows for most of the year. FDI composition and the trends of host countries are also evolving. Developing countries, especially in Asia, are not only hosting FDI, but also investing abroad more than ever. This trend shows that Asia remains an attractive destination for foreign investments driven by equity investments and infrastructure needs. In Figure 4.8, Asia includes Japan, which has large FDI ouflows. Besides Asia, Europe and North America are also large investment recipients as well as investor regions. Divestments, such as of Verizon by Vodafone in 2014 ($130 billion), cause the FDI inflows to the USA to decline significantly. Major industries for the FDI in the USA are in manufacturing, finance and insurance, and wholesale. The US direct investment abroad is dominated by holding of non-bank companies, finance and insurance, and manufacturing.

Cross-border M&A financial valuations have been rising significantly since the early 2000s, hitting a peak of $1 trillion in 2007. Major deals were made by the USA, Canada, and European countries. For example, deals with Ireland have shown a significant increase, as many companies have their tax domicile in Ireland (see Figure 4.9). Besides services in finance and business sectors, deals in information and communication dominated in early 2000, but in recent years pharmaceuticals are taking the lead. The share of top five industries in total M&A deals are shown in Table 4.3. The acquisition of Allergan (USA) by Actavis (Ireland) for almost $70 billion was the largest deal in 2015. Other deals with Ireland include Shire's (Ireland) acquisitions of Baxalta (USA) as well as Dyax Corp (USA), and a merger between Tyco International (Ireland) and Johnson Controls (USA) in 2016. M&A provides opportunities for companies in emerging markets to expand. However, sovereign states' policymakers are justifiably concerned over the acquisition of foreign enterprises that leads to increased market concentration, excessive controls over their local markets and strategic economic sectors, or has an adverse impact on

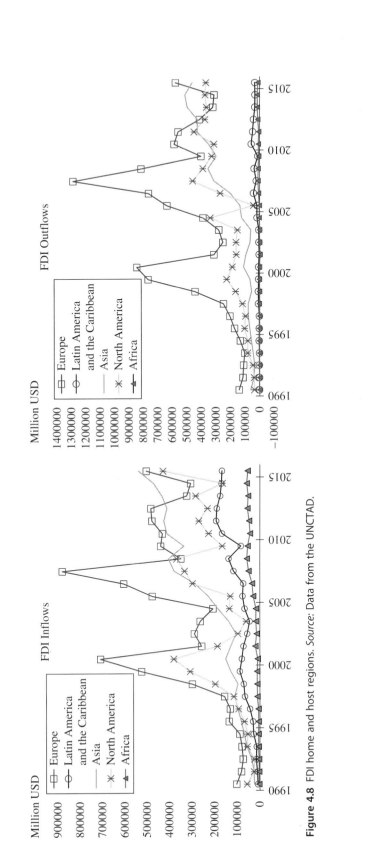

Figure 4.8 FDI home and host regions. *Source: Data from the UNCTAD.*

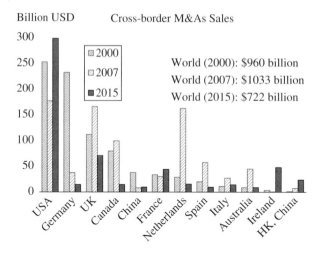

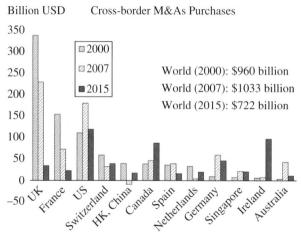

Figure 4.9 Cross border M&A by country (sales and purchases). *Source:* Data from the UNCTAD.

domestic production, labor, sovereign states' revenues and activities, in addition to the impact on their national security and culture. For example, owing to tightened tax rules by the US Treasury Department, a record high volume of M&A deals were withdrawn in 2016 (including $160.0 billion bid by Allergan and Pfizer).

China's investments abroad have, in recent years, increased significantly; outflows ($183 billion) have already exceeded inflows ($134 billion), and the value of M&A net purchases almost doubled and reached $92 billion in 2016.[14] Chinese companies' investments in the USA reached a cumulative value of almost $120 billion from 2000

14 Cross-border acquisitions by Chinese companies include Anbang Insurance Group (China) and Strategic Hotels & Resorts (USA), Tianjin Tianhai Investment (China) and Ingram Micro (USA), Qingdao Haier (China) and General Electric Co-Appliances Business (USA), and Investor Group (China) and Playtika Ltd (Israel) in 2016. Previous large acquisitions include China's MicroPort Scientific and the OrthoRecon division of the US Wright Medical Group (RTT News, 2014).

Table 4.3 Cross-border M&A (top five industries).

2000		Share (%)	2007	Share (%)	2015	Share (%)
Purchases						
1	Information, communications	38	Finance	54	Finance	38
2	Finance	20	Mining, quarrying, petroleum	12	Pharmaceuticals	21
3	Electricity, gas, water	8	Pharmaceuticals	6	Electrical, electrical equipment	5
4	Business services	6	Business services	5	Business services	4
5	Food, beverages, tobacco	5	Electricity, gas, water	4	Food, beverages, tobacco	4
Sales						
1	Information, communications	44	Finance	24	Pharmaceuticals	16
2	Finance	15	Electricity, gas, water	11	Finance	14
3	Business services	6	Mining, quarrying, petroleum	9	Business services	13
4	Food, beverages, tobacco	5	Business services	8	Chemicals, chemical products	7
5	Electricity, gas, water	5	Metals, metal products	7	Transportation, storage	5

Source: Data from UNCTAD.

to 2007 (first quarter). However, most investments have been made in recent years, with a total $46.2 billion (178 deals) in 2016 alone, according to 2017 data from the China Investment Monitor by Rhodium Group (n.d.). Almost all deals were in acquisitions and the rest in greenfield projects; around one-third of the overall investment is in real estate and hospitality, while around 12% is in information communication technology, followed by energy and other sectors. As the IMF's 2013 Spillover Report (IMF, 2013a) suggests, China's investment in the USA can expand further with the lifting of capital controls in China; this would promote investments in financial assets (securities) abroad, with a net foreign assets' increase of about 11–18% of GDP. Similarly, a study by the Hong Kong Institute for Monetary Research projects that the net investment income in China will reach 1.3% of GDP in 2020 compared with 0.5% in 2010 (He *et al.*, 2012). Further opening of the capital and financial accounts would also promote the usage of the yuan as an investment currency, making more Chinese assets available for foreign investors.

Questions and Problems 4.6

Study the BOP of the chosen economy.

a) Describe whether there is a CA surplus or deficit. Analyze the volatility of exports earnings/imports and discuss whether the BOP is sustainable.
b) Does the composition of capital inflows/outflows change? Discuss their effects on the economy and financial market. What factors drive capital inflows to the country?
c) Study exchange rate movements over time, analyze current trends, volatility, and their impact on trade, investment, and debt. Discuss how the central bank intervenes in the FX market.

4.5.2   External Debt and Sustainability

BOP accounts' flow data are used to construct stock data for analyzing cumulative investment positions, such as international investments position, and *creditor* or *debtor* status. For example, the USA became a net debtor nation in 1986 mainly because of large BX deficits which were financed by the FA, with increased claims on US assets. But for other countries, in particular developing countries with external debt denominated in foreign currency (e.g., in USD), it may be challenging to reduce their external debt due to their exposure to an FX risk. Interest burden and issues of debt may also have to be reckoned with. External debt increases due to consumption (e.g., Mexico), or investment (e.g., Indonesia), and/or debt service. However, debt used to finance long-term productive investments (e.g., infrastructure) may contribute to future economic growth, and may thus be more sustainable compared with consumption financing.

IMF (2012) showed that countries with rising debt-to-GDP ratios, but with no debt burden, had a weaker performance compared with highly indebted countries with decreasing debt ratios. In addition, the report demonstrated a low growth for countries whose debt ratios to GDP were in excess of 100% (see Figure 4.10). Some countries failed to service their debt and defaulted: Mexico in 1982, Argentina in 1998 and 2001, Chile in 1983, Nigeria in 1983 and 1986, Indonesia in 1998, and Russia in 1991 and 1998.

During the 1970s, many resource-rich countries borrowed extensively in international capital markets using their resources–assets as collateral. When commodity prices subsequently fell in the 1980s, the resource revenue's contribution fell significantly. These countries were not able to continue borrowing and, as a result, struggled to repay their debt. Debt burden is thus a major external disturbance for sustained development and may cause critical macroeconomic instability. The modeling of the resource export's contribution to economic growth distinguishes between resource-rich and resource-poor countries, and numerically analyzed using nonlinear model predictive control (NMPC). Using this method, Nyambuu (2017) confirms empirically observed long-run patterns and shows the typical boom/bust cycle phenomena, where economic growth may be strangled by excessive debt. The NMPC is further explained with its application in economics in Nyambuu and Semmler (2017a).

Debt crisis signals include not only budget deficits, inflation, and CA deficits, but also over-indebtedness. In this context, an excessive external debt may serve as a warning signal of impending debt crises, and a prime indicator for financial health, where optimal debt ratios may be used to define a "distance from default" (Nyambuu and Bernard, 2015). Further, assessing the sustainability of external debt and probability of default

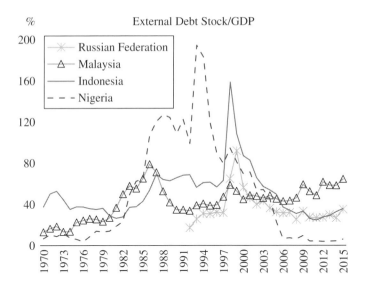

Figure 4.10 External debt stock-to-GDP ratios. *Source:* Data from The World Bank.

in Latin America, Africa, and Asia points to an overdependence on external debt that may lead to a debt crisis. Empirical findings suggest that a higher default probability as well as a greater risk premium are associated with large deviations from optimality, making the country more vulnerable to external shocks that affect the return on investment and long-term real interest rates (Nyambuu and Semmler, 2017b). For debt issued in a foreign currency; empirical studies have shown that credit default risk increases with greater fluctuations in exchange rates, particularly in fragile emerging countries such as Brazil, Indonesia, and Turkey (Nyambuu, 2016).

There is an extensive literature on the modeling of sovereign debt and its sustainability. An impact of high external debt (e.g., debt overhang) on economic performance was examined by Krugman (1988: 254–255) stressing "the presence of an existing, 'inherited' debt sufficiently large that creditors do not expect with confidence to be fully repaid" and "when their expected present value and/or when potential future resource transfers are less than the debt." A number of studies show that, after a certain period, external debt's positive impact may turn into a negative one. As discussed in IMF (2013b), empirical studies by Caner *et al.* (2010) and Ursua and Wilson (2012) indicate that, when the threshold reaches 95%, annual economic growth can fall by 0.15–0.20 percentage points due to an increase of 10 percentage points in debt-to-GDP ratio. Similarly, Cecchetti *et al.* (2011) found a threshold of 85% of GDP for public debt and 90% of GDP for corporate debt. Clements *et al.* (2003) studied 55 highly indebted poor countries and showed that debt reduction can be associated to an annual increase of per capita income by 1 percentage point. In contrast, no negative debt effect was found by Warner (1992) for middle-income countries or by Hansen (2001) for developing countries. Cohen (1993, 1997) showed that, at a debt-to-exports ratio in excess of 200% as well as debt-to-GDP ratios of 50%, the probability of rescheduling the debt increases substantially. Pattillo *et al.* (2002) found that debt impact became adverse at debt-to-GDP ratios above 35–40% and debt-to-exports ratios above 160–170%.

4.5.3 Government Bonds and Macroeconomic Factors

The US dollar strengthens due to an improved US economic growth, the Fed's monetary policy, and weaknesses in the eurozone and in Asia (slowing growth in China) as in 2014–2016. This is shown by the Federal Reserve's trade weighted US dollar index (broad index) against major currencies that rose from around 75 in 2014 to 95 in 2016. It grew further with the election of President Trump based on the expectation of a relief of the US financial regulation. In this sense, in global finance the strength of the currency is defined comparatively and politically. In order to stimulate the economy, central banks in the USA, Europe, and Japan have implemented monetary easing policies, maintaining the interest rate very low or near zero, to increase liquidity and spending, also known as QE. Easing policies, both conventional and unconventional, lower the borrowing costs and motivate investments. However, sovereign state policies do not always result in favorable outcomes. Investors' demand for risk-free (free of default risk) government bonds in countries, such as the USA, the UK, and Germany, drives these bonds' prices higher, which in turn lowers their bond yields (see Figure 4.11).[15] The yield on 10-year government bonds turned negative in Germany in June 2016, reflecting concerns of global investors driven by a rising uncertainty in global markets and Brexit (Britain's exit from the EU). Previously, Swiss and Japanese governments' bonds had negative yields.

Figure 4.10 shows an inverse relationship between the sovereign bond price and yield by considering a coupon bond with bond value or price *P*, with *C* coupon payment (annual or semi-annual) and *F* face (par) value or principal to repay when the bond matures in *T* years, which is shown by the following equation based on present value

---

15 Monthly average data for 10-year US treasury (constant maturity rate), British Government securities (zero coupon), and German Federal securities.

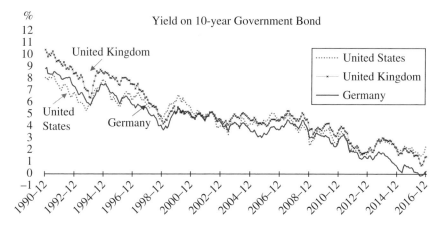

Figure 4.11 Yield on 10-year government bonds. *Source*: Data from the Federal Reserve Bank of St. Louis, Bank of England, and Deutsche Bundesbank.

of coupon and face value. In addition, maturity of the bond affects the sensibility of price to changes in the interest rate: the sensitivity increases with longer maturity.

$$\text{Price} = \sum_{t=1}^{T} \frac{C}{(1+i)^t} + \frac{F}{(1+i)^T}$$

In addition to falling yields in the EU as in 2014–2015, their negative deposit rates have led to capital outflows to other European countries and to the USA with investors seeking higher yields. This means that higher yields do not need to price the risk of currencies and state finances. Investment decisions based on the anticipation of the interest rate rise in the USA fuel a capital inflow to the USA, driving the value of the US dollar higher. A demand for US dollar denominated assets has in turn exerted pressure on the US dollar to grow even further. Table 4.4 points to multivariate and dependent factors that affect the domestic state as well as other states.

4.5.4   The Impact of a Strong US Dollar

US dollar fluctuations affect not only the domestic US economy and businesses, but also foreign economies, markets, consumers and firms as most of the commodities traded and international debt (issued bonds) are priced in US dollars. Consider the impact of the strong US dollar. Owing to a rise of the US dollar against almost all other currencies (including euros and Japanese yen) since mid-2014, US exporters and US-based multinational companies incurred large losses. This has occurred because of several factors, including:

- overseas profits converted back into US dollars;
- costs priced in US dollars (e.g., consumer products);
- rendering the US products less competitive and exports more expensive for foreign buyers.

Table 4.4 Macroeconomic factors shaping global economy and finance (2014–2015).

Europe	USA	Emerging markets
Easing monetary policy (QE in EU; interest rate cuts)	Easing monetary policy (QE1, QE2, QE3)	Easing monetary policy (e.g., China)
Negative deposit rate (e.g., EU, Denmark, Switzerland)	Strong US dollar	Currency depreciation (e.g., Mexico, Turkey, Russia)
Euro falls to record low	Downward pressure on inflation	High inflation (e.g., Brazil)
Economic stagnation	Economic growth	Slow growth (e.g., China, Brazil)
Deflation pressure	Expected interest rate rise	Unemployment (e.g., South Africa)
Record low bond yield (as bond prices rise)	Unemployment	International reserves depletion (e.g., Russia)
Unemployment	Shale oil boom, oversupply, oil price plunge	Debt default risk (e.g., Venezuela, Nigeria)
Swiss franc ceiling ended		Capital flight, stock sell-off (e.g., China, Russia)

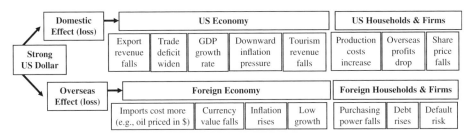

Figure 4.12 Effects of the strong US dollar on the US and world economy.

However, the net effect depends on the international exposure of the firms' costs and revenues, besides the fact of whether they are priced in US dollars or foreign currency. To reduce costs, certain US manufacturers have shifted their production overseas to countries like China and India due to a strong US dollar. Similarly, mining companies with operations overseas that benefit from the rising US dollar can reduce their losses from low commodity prices (due to mining profits in US dollars and costs in foreign currencies). Thus, imports growth due to increased global competitiveness, a strong US dollar, coupled with declining exports, has widened US trade deficits. Although oil imports and their price (in terms of US dollars) have declined, the strong US dollar is maintaining its global price (in local currencies, still costly). Potential losses due to the rising US dollar and their domestic and overseas effects are illustrated in Figure 4.12.

4.5.5 The US Dollar and Commodity Prices

Data trends in Figure 4.13 indicate an inverse relationship between the USD and commodity prices. In the global market, most commodities are priced in USD. This suggests a negative correlation between the USD index (DXY) (which reflects the performance of

Figure 4.13 USD index and commodity index movements. *Source:* Data from Bloomberg.

the USD against major currencies in the basket—EUR, JPY, GPB, CAD, SEK, CHF), and Bloomberg Commodity Index (BCOM), for the movement of commodity futures price. Sample daily data show that the correlation between the DXY and BCOM is–0.9 during the period of June 2, 2014–January 27, 2017.

4.5.6 Globalization and Economic Inequalities

The functional distribution of national income between wages, rents, and profits, which are indicated as factor shares, plays an essential and fundamental role in determining income inequality, a major political and policy concern (Glyn, 2009). Wealth distribution, in particular in the USA, is uneven. Relevant data and analysis, including Saez (2015), Piketty and Saez (2007), and CBO (2011), show that, in the USA, income inequality has risen sharply compared with other industrialized countries (e.g., the UK and France). From 1913 to early 1970s, these countries had a similar pattern of decreasing trend of income shares for the top income shares. However, since the 1970s the economic elite share has remained stable in France but increased sharply in the USA. As Piketty and Saez (2007) argue, a major source of high wage earners' income in France includes dividend income, and they further stress that for the USA "the coupon-clipping rentiers have been overtaken by the working rich" (Piketty and Saez, 2007: 167).

Empirical studies found that openness (i.e., globalization), for example, in terms of trade volume or Sachs–Warner openness index, is positively associated with higher inequality measured by the Gini coefficient—see Barro (2000) and Lundberg and Squire (2000). We refer to a Gini coefficient based on the distribution of households' income, where an increase in the index indicates higher inequality.[16] Figure 4.14 illustrates the

---

16 Data on income inequality (Gini coefficient) is estimated by the UN-WIDER World Income Inequality Database (WIID) as well as the World Bank's World Income Inequality Database. The World Wealth and Income Database (http://www.wid.world) on the world distribution of wealth and income provides the Pareto–Lorenz coefficient for the measurement of wealth concentration. For the estimation of the Pareto–Lorenz coefficient, see Atkinson (2006).

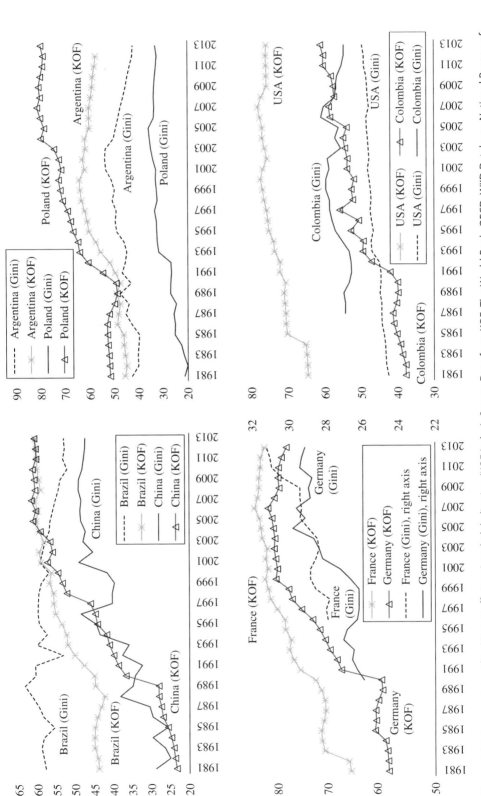

Figure 4.14 Income inequality (Gini coefficients) and globalization (KOF index). *Source:* Data from KOF, The World Bank, OECD, WIID Database, National Bureau of Statistics of China and U.S. Census Bureau.

Gini index and the KOF overall globalization index for different countries. The correlation between the KOF and Gini indexes is as follows: China (0.97), Poland (0.93), the US (0.83), Germany (0.68), France (0.64), Argentina (0.64), Colombia (0.52), Brazil (−0.5). For most of these countries, we observe a positive as well as a very high correlation between these two indexes; that is, a higher income inequality associated with a higher income inequality. Inequality in many developing economies had increased since the 1980s when they became more open to globalization. Inequality continues to rise not only in developed countries (in particular in the USA, France, and Germany), but also in some developing countries (in particular China). These trends, however, have been reversed in some countries in the last decades.

Households at the very top of the income distribution contribute significantly to the evolution of US inequality (Saez, 2015). Similarly, Piketty (2014: 326–327) shows that since the 1980s income inequality in emerging economies has increased significantly with a growing share for the 1% highest incomes. These shares in 2010 compared with the late 1980s were Argentina 17% (increased from 7%), China 11% (increased from 4%), India 12% (increased from 6%), Indonesia 13% (increased from 8%), and South Africa 17% (increased from 10%). In his study, fundamental inequality is defined by the excess rate of return on capital r compared with the rate of economic growth g (or $r > g$)—see Piketty (2014: 25). He states that "the process by which wealth is accumulated and distributed contains powerful forces pushing toward divergence, or at any rate toward an extremely high level of inequality" (Piketty, 2014: 27). Here, the destabilizing force of divergence "associated with the process of accumulation and concentration of wealth when growth is weak and the return on capital is high" (Piketty, 2014: 23).

This rise in inequality can be attributable to globalization, which led to increased international trade, labor migration, offshoring, and international investment. A number of studies, including Richardson (1995), Stiglitz (2012), Irwin (2008), Katz (2008), and Krugman (2008), emphasize the role of trade in explaining a rise in inequality. Globalization, which affected labor's bargaining position especially through specialization and factor mobility, has partly contributed to the rise in inequality in the USA. Globalization, apparently, may have strengthened capital but weakened labor. Further, the immobility of labor combined with flexible labor markets reinforced this process. Rebalancing of the world economy will depend on redistribution of income (Nayyar, 2011). Other explanations can be related to factors that have weakened the bargaining position of labor, like technological change, and a deregulation of capital, labor, and capital markets (Glyn, 2009). Daudey and Garcia-Penalosa (2007) covered OECD and developing countries and regressed the Gini coefficient of personal income on the labor's share (share of wages and salaries in the GDP) and the level of income. They showed that a large labor share, in particular in the manufacturing sector, is associated with a lower Gini coefficient of personal income. They found that the long-run labor share has a strong negative and significant effect on income inequality.

Stiglitz (2012) discusses competition of workers in the global marketplace as well as changes in labor-saving technologies and how these factors depress wages. Similarly, Guscina (2006: 5) stresses that "globalization pressures might have pushed industrial countries to adopt labor-saving technologies, further squeezing labor's share" (Glyn, 2009). A rise in the international trade in the late 1960s led to a rise in labor's share and profit squeeze. According to Kalecki's (1965) argument, this happened because of greater competition that eroded monopolistic positions. Impact of openness to the global trade and investment on productivity and wage shares (e.g., in eastern European countries) is analyzed by Bernard and Nyambuu (2016). A rapidly growing international trade has contributed to a fall in relative demand for unskilled labor (Blau and Kahn, 2009). However, Borjas *et al.* (1997) show that low-skilled workers that were replaced by trade did not have a large impact on wage inequality in the USA between 1980 and 1990. But Wood (1998) argues that, to some extent, the trade threat could reduce wages of low-skilled workers (Blau and Kahn, 2009). Other related factors include offshoring, purchases of intermediate inputs from foreign countries, large flows of FDI, openness of KA, and higher level of immigration (Glyn, 2009). Blinder (2007) stresses that offshoring of jobs in both manufacturing and services can reduce demand for certain kinds of skilled and unskilled labors and this displacement of workers would put a downward pressure on wages and facilitating technologies, leading to a greater wage inequality (Blau and Kahn, 2009).

4.6 Conclusion

All FX models are a simplification of a growing and unfolding complexity that defines global and macroeconomic finance. In this chapter we reviewed such models emphasizing macroeconomic factors and specific effects associated with finance and globalization. Various models and quantitative approaches are considered in subsequent chapters, all seeking to define the "how" and the "why" of the exchange rates, their mechanism, and their effects on countries' trade, financial exchanges, and global finance. Generally, these models fall into three categories integrated in a process of economic globalization and gating:

- macroeconomic models;
- risk-based and rational financial models;
- country risk models and geopolitical events.

We studied an open-economy model as an extension of the closed-economy model, emphasizing the external balance such as net exports and their implications for globalization. We also briefly discussed the development of hybrid-open economies to present economies in a process of economic globalization. Cross-border transactions involving inflows or outflows are made for different purposes. These are transactions in goods and services recorded under the CA, and purchases or sales of assets recorded under KA and FA, and reserve assets. We discussed how a country finances its CA deficit with foreign currency through its FA. When a BOP problem arises the central bank can intervene by selling or buying foreign reserve currency, which in turn affects the value of the domestic currency. We discussed the sustainability of external debt, highlighting its impact on the economic performance and the threshold of debt-to-GDP ratio. Furthermore, we outlined key determinants of FDI and emphasized its structural change from manufacturing to services, and from a labor intensive to a capital (technology)- intensive sector. Finally, we have also drawn some conclusions regarding economic globalization and domestic economic inequalities. Stiglitz (2012: 59–64, 277–278) highlights the reshaping or tempering of globalization addressing the problem of "race to the bottom," and discusses how globalization of trade and capital markets contributes to an increase in inequality. Other empirical findings in IMF studies, by Ostry *et al.* (2014), suggest that inequality has a negative impact on economic growth. These aspects of the "push-pull" effects of globalization and gating will be expanded further in this book (Chapters 5, 7, 8, 9).

Additionally, this chapter analyzed the relationship between the private sector, government, and the external sector based on national accounts and the equilibrium of national savings and investments. We studied an open-economy IS–LM–BOP model describing the interaction between the real economy, financial markets, and international trade. Subsequently, we addressed their macroeconomic policy effects under the Mundell–Fleming framework. In an open and interdependent world, international macroeconomic models are subject to economic and financial variables, as well as to other forces (such as the economic agenda pursued by individual countries and technological development redefining the means of money and its circulation). Therefore, macroeconomic models are important and still used as policy tools, but these are only partial guidelines to model global economic and financial exchanges that involve a far more complex and networked world as well as geopolitical and strategic issues and problems. In Chapter 5 we will present macroeconomic FX pricing models; subsequently, financial asset pricing (based on rational financial models), portfolio management, and options and swaps traded in domestic and foreign markets are considered in Chapters 7–8.

References

Atkinson, A.B. (2006) Concentration among the rich. Research Paper No. 2006/151. United Nations University–World Institute for Development Economics Research.

Bank of England. http://www.bankofengland.co.uk/boeapps/iadb/NewInterMed.asp.

Barro, R.J. (2000) Inequality and growth in a panel of countries. *Journal of Economic Growth*, **5**: 5–32.

Bayoumi, T. and Saborowski, C. (2014) Accounting for reserves. *Journal of International Money and Finance*, **41**: 1–29.

Bayoumi, T., Gagnon, J., and Saborowski, C. (2015) Official financial flows, capital mobility, and global imbalances. *Journal of International Money and Finance*, **52**: 146–174.

Bernanke, B.S. (2005) The global saving glut and the U.S. current account deficit. Speech at the Sandridge Lecture, March 10, Virginia Association of Economists, Richmond, VA.

Bernard, L. and Nyambuu, U. (2016) Financial Flows and Productivity in Eastern Europe: Implications for Growth and Policy. In: Financial Deepening and Post-Crisis Development in Emerging Markets, O. Canuto and A. Gevorkyan (eds). Palgrave-Macmillan.

Blanchard, O., Giavazzi, F., and Sa, S. (2005) The U.S. current account and the dollar. NBER Working Paper No. 11137.

Blau, F.D. and Kahn, L.M. (2009) Inequality and earnings distribution. In *The Oxford Handbook of Economic Inequality*, W. Salverda, B. Nolan, and T.M. Smeeding (eds). Oxford University Press; pp. 177–203.

Blinder, A.S. (2007) How many U.S. jobs might be offshorable? CEPS Working Paper No. 142, Princeton University.

Bloomberg. Bloomberg Indices. https://www.bloombergindices.com/.

Borjas, G., Freeman R., and Katz, L. (1997) How much do immigration and trade affect labor market outcomes? *Brookings Papers on Economic Activity*, **28**(1): 1–90.

Caner, M., Grennes, T., and Koehler-Geib, F. (2010) Finding the tipping point—when sovereign debt turns bad. World Bank Policy Research Working Paper No. 5391. World Bank: Washington DC. doi: 10.1596/1813-9450-5391.

CBO (2011) Trends in the Distribution of Household Income between 1979 and 2007. Publication No. 4031. Congressional Budget Office: Washington, DC.

Cecchetti, S.G., Mohanty, M.S., and Zampolli, F. (2011) The real effects of debt. Bank for International Settlements Working Paper No. 352. http://www.bis.org/publ/work352.pdf (accessed May 19, 2017).

China State Administration of Foreign Exchange. SAFE. 2017. http://www.safe.gov.cn/wps/portal/english/Data/Payments. Accessed on June 15, 2017.

Chinn, M.D. and Ito, H. (2008) Global current account imbalances: American fiscal policy versus east Asian savings. *Review of International Economics*, **16**(3): 479–498.

Chinn, M.D. and Prasad, E.S. (2003) Medium-term determinants of current accounts in industrial and developing countries: an empirical exploration. *Journal of International Economics*, **59**: 47'76.

Clements, B., Bhattacharya, R., and Nguyen, T.Q. (2003) External debt public investment, and growth in low-income countries. IMF Working Paper No. 03/249. International Monetary Fund: Washington, DC. https://www.imf.org/external/pubs/ft/wp/2003/wp03249.pdf (accessed May 19, 2017).

Cohen, D. (1993) Low investment and large LDC debt in the 1980s. *American Economic Review*, **83**(3): 437–449.

Cohen, D. (1997) Growth and external debt: a new perspective on the African and Latin American tragedies. Discussion Paper No. 1753. Centre for Economic Policy Research (CEPR): London.

Daudey, E., and Garcia-Penalosa, C. (2007) The Personal and the factor distributions of income in a cross-section of countries. *Journal of Development Studies*, **43**(5): 812–829.

Deutsche Bundesbank. http://www.bundesbank.de/Navigation/EN/Statistics/statistics.html.

Eichengreen, B. (2006) Global imbalances: the new economy, the dark matter, the savvy investor, and the standard analysis. *Journal of Policy Modeling*, **28**: 645–652.

Fleming, J.M. (1962) Domestic financial policy under fixed and under floating exchange rate. *IMF Staff Papers*, **9**: 369–379.

FRED, Federal Reserve Bank of St. Louis. https://fred.stlouisfed.org/.

Gagnon, J. (2012) Global imbalances and foreign asset expansion by developing-economy central banks. Working Paper No. 12e5, Peterson Institute for International Economics, Washington, DC.

Gagnon, J. (2013) The elephant hiding in the room: currency intervention and trade imbalances. Working Paper No. 13-2, Peterson Institute for International Economics, Washington, DC.

Gandolfo, G. (2001) *International Finance and Open-Economy Macroeconomics*. Springer.

Glyn, A. (2009) Functional distribution and inequality. In *The Oxford Handbook of Economic Inequality*, W. Salverda, B. Nolan, and T.M. Smeeding (eds). Oxford University Press; pp. 101–126.

Guscina, A. (2006) Effects of globalization on labor's share in national income. IMF Working Paper /06/294.

Hansen, H. (2001) The impact of aid and external debt on growth and investment: insights from cross-country regression analysis. Presented at *WIDER Conference on Debt Relief*, United Nations University, Helsinki. http://www.eldis.org/go/home&id=29565&type=Document#.WR7t9261u9J (accessed May 19, 2017).

He, D., Cheung, L., Zhan, W., and Wu. T. (2012) How would capital account liberalization affect China's capital flows and the renminbi real exchange rates? *China &World Economy*, **20**(6): 29–54.

IMF (1993) *Balance of Payments Manual (BPM5)*. International Monetary Fund: Washington, DC. http://www.imf.org/external/np/sta/bop/bopman.pdf (accessed May 19, 2017).

IMF (2009) *Balance of Payments and International Investment Position Manual (BPM6)*. International Monetary Fund: Washington, DC. https://www.imf.org/external/pubs/ft/bop/2007/pdf/bpm6.pdf.

IMF (2012) *Global Financial Stability Report: Restoring Confidence and Progressing on Reforms*. International Monetary Fund: Washington, DC. https://www.imf.org/External/Pubs/FT/GFSR/2012/02/pdf/text.pdf.

IMF (2013a) *IMF Multilateral Policy Issues Report: 2013 Spillover Report*. International Monetary Fund: Washington, DC. https://www.imf.org/external/np/pp/eng/2013/070213.pdf (accessed May 19, 2017).

IMF (2013b) *World Economic Outlook: Hopes, Realities, Risks*. International Monetary Fund: Washington, DC. http://www.imf.org/external/pubs/ft/weo/2013/01/pdf/text.pdf (accessed May 19, 2017).

Irwin, D. (2008) Trade and wages, reconsidered: comments and discussion. *Brookings Papers on Economic Activity*, **38**(1): 138–143.

Kalecki, M. (1965) *The Theory of Economic Dynamics*. George Allen and Unwin: London.

Katz, L. (2008) Trade and wages, reconsidered: comments and discussion. *Brookings Papers on Economic Activity*, **38**(1), 143–149.

Keynes, J.M. (1936) *The General Theory of Employment, Interest and Money*. Macmillan: London.

Krugman, P. (1988) Financing vs. forgiving a debt overhang. *Journal of Development Economics*, **29**: 253–268.

Krugman, P. (2008) Trade and wages, reconsidered. *Brookings Papers on Economic Activity*, **39**(1): 103–137.

KOF Index of Globalization. http://globalization.kof.ethz.ch/.

Lundberg, M. and Squire, L. (2000) The simultaneous evolution of growth and inequality. World Bank Working Paper. World Bank, Washington, DC

Mundell, R.A. (1963) Capital mobility and stabilization policy under fixed and flexible exchange rates. *Canadian Journal of Economics and Political Science*, **29**: 475–485.

Mundell, R.A. (1968) *International Economics*. Macmillan, New York.

National Bureau of Statistics of China. http://www.stats.gov.cn/.

Nayyar, D. (2011) The financial crisis, the great recession and the developing world. Global Policy. **2**(1):20–32.

Nyambuu, U. (2016) Foreign exchange volatility and its implications for macroeconomic stability: an empirical study of developing economies. In *Dynamic Modeling, Empirical Macroeconomics, and Finance: Essays in Honor of Willi Semmler*, L. Bernard and U. Nyambuu (eds). Springer International Publishing: Basel; pp. 163–182

Nyambuu, U. (2017) Financing sustainable growth through energy exports and implications for human capital investment. In *Inequality and Finance in Macrodynamics*, B. Bökemeier and A. Greiner (eds). Dynamic Modeling and Econometrics in Economics and Finance, Volume 23. Springer International Publishing: Basel; pp. 191–219.

Nyambuu, U. and Bernard, L. (2015) A quantitative approach to assessing sovereign default risk in resource-rich emerging economies. *International Finance and Economics Journal*, **20**(3): 220–241.

Nyambuu, U. and Semmler, W. (2017a) The Challenges in the Transition from Fossil Fuel to Renewable Energy. In *Industry 4.0 Entrepreneurship and Structural Change in the New Digital Landscape*, T. Devezas, J. Laitao, A, Sarygulov. Springer International Publishing: Basel; pp. 157–181.

Nyambuu, U. and Semmler, W. (2017b) Emerging markets' resource booms and busts, borrowing risk and regime change. *Structural Change and Economic Dynamics*, **41**: 29–42.

Obstfeld, M. and Rogoff, K. (1996) *Foundations of International Macroeconomics*. The MIT Press.

Obstfeld, M. and Rogoff, K. (2005) Global current account imbalances and exchange rate adjustments. *Brookings Papers on Economic Activity*, **1**: 67–146.

Obstfeld, M. and Rogoff, K. (2007) The unsustainable US current account position revisited. In *G7 Current Account Imbalances: Sustainability and Adjustment*, R.H. Clarida (ed.). University of Chicago Press/National Bureau of Economic Research.

OECD. OECD Stat. http://www.oecd.org/.

Ostry J.D., Berg A., and Tsangarides, C.G. (2014) Redistribution, inequality, and growth. IMF Staff Discussion Note 14/02.

Pattillo, C., Poirson, H., and Ricci, L. (2002) External debt and growth. IMF Working Paper 02/69. International Monetary Fund: Washington, DC. https://www.imf.org/external/pubs/ft/wp/2002/wp0269.pdf (accessed May 19, 2017).

Piketty, T. (2014) *Capital in the Twenty-First Century*. Harvard University Press: Cambridge, MA.

Piketty, T. and Saez, E. (2007) Income and wage inequality in the USA. In *Top Incomes over the Twentieth Century*, A. Atkinson and T. Piketty (eds). Oxford University Press.

Rhodium Group (n.d.) China Investment Monitor. http://rhg.com/interactive/china-investment-monitor (accessed May 19, 2017).

Richardson, D.J. (1995) Income inequality and trade: how to think, what to conclude. *Journal of Economic Perspectives*, **9**: 33–55.

RTT News (2014) MicroPort Scientific closes acquisition of Wright Medical's OrthoRecon business. January 13. http://www.rttnews.com/2250414/microport-scientific-closes-acquisition-of-wright-medical-s-orthorecon-business.aspx (accessed May 19, 2017).

Saez, E. (2015) Striking it richer: the evolution of top incomes in the United States (updated with 2013 preliminary estimates). https://eml.berkeley.edu/~saez/saez-UStopincomes-2013.pdf (accessed May 19, 2017).

Salvatore, D. (2007) U.S. trade deficits, structural imbalances, and global monetary stability. *Journal of Policy Modeling*, **29**: 697–704.

Salvatore, D. (2011) Editorial. *Journal of Policy Modeling*, **33**: 679–681.

Stiglitz, J.E. (2012) *The Price of Inequality: How Today's Divided Society Endangers Our Future*, 1st edn. W.W. Norton: New York.

The Federal Reserve. H.6 statistical release. Money Stock and Debt Measures. https://www.federalreserve.gov/releases/h6/current/default.htm.

The United Nations Conference on Trade and Development (UNCTAD). FDI/MNE database. HYPERLINK "http://www.unctad.org/fdistatistics" www.unctad.org/fdistatistics

The World Bank. World DataBank. World Development Indicators. http://databank.worldbank.org/data/home.aspx. Accessed on Jan. 3, 2017.

U.S. Bureau of Economic Analysis. BEA. 2015. Measuring the Economy: A Primer on GDP and the National Income and Product Accounts. https://www.bea.gov/national/pdf/nipa_primer.pdf.

U.S. Bureau of Economic Analysis. http://www.bea.gov/.

U.S. Census Bureau. https://www.census.gov/.

Ursua, J. and Wilson, D. (2012) Risks to growth from build ups in public debt. *Global Economics Weekly*, No. 12/10, Goldman Sachs: New York.

Warner, A.M. (1992) Did the debt crisis cause the investment crisis. *Quarterly Journal of Economics*, **107**(4): 1161–1186. doi: 10.2307/2118384.

Wood, A. (1998) Globalisation and the rise in labour market inequalities. *Economic Journal*, **108**(450): 1463–1482.

World Income Inequality Database (WIID). United Nations University – World Institute for Development Economics Research. http://www.wider.unu.edu/wiid/wiid.htm. Accessed on February 13, 2016.

5

Foreign Exchange Models and Prices

Motivation

This chapter outlines the macroeconomic foundations of foreign exchange (FX) markets and FX pricing. Purchasing power parity (PPP) is explained based on the law of one price (LOOP). In addition to asset-based and monetary approaches to exchange rate determination, various models (e.g., Frenkel–Mussa, Balassa–Samuelson, Dornbusch overshooting, and present value models) are outlined and discussed in light of the empirical evidence used to justify these models. Unlike the currency and FX pricing models to be considered in Chapter 7, the macroeconomic approach provides a broad perspective on the economic factors that determine FX rates.

5.1   Introduction

FX rates, their models, and pricing can be approached from two perspectives. First, a macroeconomic perspective based on the factors that define the economic exchanges between countries; and second, a financial perspective based on exchanges in currency markets, and financial and macroeconomic expectations (see also Chapter 7). In this sense, the market for currencies and the price of FX are both determined by macroeconomic and microeconomic factors. Their integration as a unified model is not usually assessed theoretically, although currency speculators do account for the interactions of macroeconomic and trade-trend factors, as well as the uncertainties of financial currency markets and their many derivatives and swaps.

Fundamental macroeconomic FX pricing models are based on two assumptions: PPP and interest rate parity. The first emphasizes that real prices for real goods (and in some cases services), once adjusted for the FX, ought to be the same. The latter points to interest rates as the essential factor motivating capital flows. The greater the interest rate, the greater the propensity of capital inflows. In this sense, FX results from countries' monetary policies and their internal inflation rates. Unfortunately, empirical evidence does not support these models in the short run. They are therefore primarily useful for estimating long-run trends. Financial currency markets are far more oriented to short-term estimates of FX price variations. Both approaches are supported by different data sets; the former by macroeconomic statistics and the latter by higher frequency, daily and at most weekly data.

Globalization, Gating, and Risk Finance, First Edition. Unurjargal Nyambuu and Charles S. Tapiero.
© 2018 John Wiley & Sons Ltd. Published 2018 by John Wiley & Sons Ltd.

FX rates, those based on macroeconomic models, are determined by international macroeconomic factors as well as by production outputs. They are also fed by financial and statistical data and economic news; thus, they maintain their coherence with fundamental economic theory and observed currency prices. Consider the USD; its strength/weakness is derived from the strength/weakness of the US economy relative to other economies as well as future expectations relative to other countries. Economic factors defining macroeconomic status include inflation, interest rates, political and economic gating, country risks, income differentials, and other factors that contribute to the aggregate supply and demand for currencies and their relative strengths/weaknesses (as discussed in Chapter 4). When a country has poor economic prospects, demand for its currency is reduced and its price is adversely affected. Currencies' prices can also be affected by sovereign credit risk, which implies the real interest rate for sovereign treasuries, and a broad number of factors based on markets' expectations (see also Chapter 8). For example, if the holder of US Treasury bills believes that the USA is faced with a potential default, this belief not only can have an important impact on the price of its Treasury bills, but also contribute to a flight from the USD to other currencies (see Chapter 8, where we address credit and debt denominated in a foreign currency). The price of the USD is then based on its public debt, the strength of the US economy; that is, its risks, demand, and supply. The trillions of US dollars held by China may affect a USD risk if China were to pursue a political agenda in conflict with the USA and unload its extensive USD holdings. Of course, if this had been the case, the cost of such a policy would have been sustained by both countries. In this sense, mutual debt, mutual interests, economic development, and growth contribute to economic and financial globalization as they create natural common interests. Similarly, trends and volatility of FX prices, and related macroeconomic indicators such as trade balances, as well as financial products (e.g., derivatives), provide important information for policy-makers and global investors, both of which have a mutual interest in global economic well-being. Their interactions, cross-border trades, capital flows, currencies exchanges, together with their derivatives are part of an increasing number of financial products, sold and owned globally, that have become pillars of the global financial system.

5.2 Macroeconomic Models of Foreign Exchange Rates

5.2.1 Underlying Factors for Modeling Foreign Exchange Prices

The strength of a currency is measured relative to a country's economic performance, and to the acceptance of the currency as a medium of exchange by the global financial community. As mentioned earlier, the strength of the dollar is derived from the performance of its economy, the size of its nontradable assets, and the risks implied in holding the US currency compared with other currencies. Political clout and sovereign stability further contribute to the willingness of the world to accept a currency as a medium of exchange. As long as the USA maintains its status as a "safe" economy and a leading political power, the US dollar will continue to serve as a reference currency. The Chinese yuan and the euro aspire to such a status, and their growth provides liquidity for international exchanges and denomination of international debt. As a result, the strength/weakness of a currency contributes to the demand and the flight to/from a currency. However, the opening and the expansion of China's economy, an increased use of the yuan in global trade, and an extensive globalized regulation in the hand of US regulators have led to some concerns over the status of the US dollar as a unique currency for financing trade and economic exchanges. The price of an FX rate, therefore, reflects:

- the underlying macroeconomic fundamentals of a country;
- the degree to which a currency is accepted and is used as a reference asset in trades;
- the "world" belief and acceptance of a currency reflecting a country's political "clout";
- the underlying financial credit risks associated with a country's currency.

These factors underlie macroeconomic and financial models for pricing FX currencies. The development of currencies' financial markets has further financialized currencies, making them an extremely important part of the financial products being traded globally. This was not always the case. Currency as a medium of exchange is embedded in the long history of money. As discussed earlier, prior to the Breton Woods agreement, exchange rates were formally fixed. Namely, five French francs were worth one US dollar, regardless of countries' economic and financial conditions, and the degree of openness to global trade, while $33 would buy an ounce of gold. Over time, fixed FX markets contributed to economic dislocations due to currencies mispricing sovereign states' economic statistics and their inefficiencies stifling growth. This led to insular economies stifling globalization and economic growth while encouraging arbitrage profiting from mispricing. In some cases, as indicated previously, this also led to immense arbitrage profits by macro-hedge funds speculating on a country's ability to sustain their FX rates. Currently, although economies may or may not be in turmoil, trends are set for a global financial market in all currencies, all of which are competing to be accepted globally and, if possible, become a reference currency.

5.2.2 Classification of Foreign Exchange Models

A non-exhaustive classification and typology for FX models (most of which are based on the Keynes–Mundell–Fleming framework) include:

- monetary macroeconomic models;
- real macroeconomic models;
- macroeconomic models based on expenditure functions;
- rational (financial) expectations (no arbitrage) models (see Chapter 7);
- implied rational expectations models based on FX futures and options (see Chapter 7)
- financial models based on econometric (macroeconomic) hypotheses to predict FX rates;
- FX models based on currencies (credit) risk (see Chapter 8);
- multivariate and dependency models—dealing with networked countries—including multivariate stochastic systems, FX tracking models (see Chapter 7), and copulas[1] (see Chapters 2 and 7) to model the cross-covariations of FX;
- long-run memory models, based on FX data granularity and data analytic models.

---

1 A copula is a multivariate probability distribution function which takes into account interdependencies between random variables.

Macroeconomic models based on economic factors include:

- Relative supply and demand for money in each country.
- Relative domestic and foreign debt reflecting sovereign states' risk exposures (in particular to foreign debt) and the ability of sovereign states to control their fiscal policies.
- The balance of payments of countries fueling demand and supply of their currency.
- The relative interest rates on sovereign debt (bonds). The higher the relative interest rate in a country, the greater the amount of funds invested in its treasury bills. At the same time, greater interest rates are dampening inflationary forces and economic growth.
- The countries' monetary policies, usually implemented by the Fed or central bank. For example, QE (QE1, QE2, QE3) in the USA between 2011 and 2014 for augmenting liquidity and economic expansion (combined with lower interest rates in treasury bills).
- Countries' political systems and their economic policies. In particular, pertaining to issues such as whether economic and financial markets are free or controlled, the political stability of a country, political and social unrest, security and corruption, terror, and so on.
- Volatile FX markets due to capital flights caused by challenging geopolitical events. For example, heavy intervention in the FX market in Russia in 2015.
- Fundamental economic statistics, such as GDP, GNP, public and private consumption, investments, employment, foreign and domestic debt, balance of payments, and retail sales, all of which provide indicators to an economic well-being, development, and sustainability.
- The evolution of a country's price level and inflationary pressures. For example, investors are more concerned with the real interest rates adjusted for inflation than with nominal interest rates. In other words, the FX rate ought to express the relative inflationary pressures between countries.
- FX option prices, expressing market beliefs about future FX prices. Derivatives and future prices not only provide direct information on markets' sentiments and beliefs regarding future prices, but are also used as a medium to price risk factors such as volatility implied by future prices (see Chapter 3).

While these are complex factors, each of these may have intricate and contradictory effects on a country's FX rate. These factors are nonetheless important and motivate theoretical and empirical financial studies that seek to capture their essential effects. In the following sections, we shall consider a number of cases that emphasize the impact of specific economic factors.

5.3 Exchange Rates and Purchasing Power Parity

5.3.1 Purchasing Power Parity and the Law of One Price

Traditional FX pricing models are essentially based on macroeconomic statistics and parity principles. These principles are based on a defined equivalence and the LOOP for all real goods across currency areas. Consider the principle of PPP, where D denotes a domestic country and F denotes a foreign country. The real price of consuming a real good, under the PPP principle, should be the same in both countries. If this were the case, currency denomination would merely reflect a financial FX price prevalent between these two countries. Since countries consume a very large portfolio of goods, both real and financial, any specific good is thus a partial reflection of the FX price. For this reason, instead of a single good, economists use a basket of goods to represent aggregate consumption. In a global and networked world, such models are naturally difficult to define; therefore, a rising number of tools, both model (theoretical) and data (empirical) based, are increasingly used by financial investors, hedge funds, and in general by traders and global A-National enterprises, as well as by the sovereign state policymakers.

PPP is then based on several assumptions based on the index or the basket of goods that FX prices are based on and its compatibility with a foreign basket. These include identical goods (such as McDonald's Big Mac), free competitive markets, no price constraints, adjustments or limitations, no trade frictions or trade barriers (no quotas or tariffs), no transportation costs, and no transaction costs. To maintain this equivalence, the parity with implied absolute PPP states

$$P_F = \xi_{FD} P_D \Rightarrow \xi_{FD} = \frac{P_F}{P_D} \quad \text{or} \quad P_D = \xi_{DF} P_F \Rightarrow \xi_{DF} = \frac{P_D}{P_F}$$

where P_D and P_F are the nominal prices in domestic and foreign countries, and ξ_{FD} and ξ_{DF} are the FX rates, the foreign currency for one unit of domestic currency, or the FX rate for the domestic currency in foreign currency. If there is a parity, then $\xi_{FD} = 1/\xi_{DF}$. Assume that the USA is the domestic country and Europe is the foreign country and consider a particular item sold in Europe for €100 and for $135 in the USA. If the LOOP holds for such an item, then the FX rate ought to be $1.35 per euro or €0.74 per US dollar. If prices differ in two locations, a market arbitrage occurs where buyers purchase at a lower price and sell in the other country at a higher price. However, this neglects some factors that affect prices. These factors differ across national boundaries, such as transaction costs, money transfers, taxes, controls, and so on. When the differences are appreciable, they may also entail illegal transfers; for example, a stealth transfer of tax due to income from one country to another. Practically, we refer to the PPP condition as a no-arbitrage requirement.

Similarly, suppose that the interest rate in the USA for treasury bills is 3% while in China it is 5% for a similar government bond. If a parity exists for the interest rate charged, such an equivalence will define the FX rate between the USA and China. Explicitly, if two bonds in two different countries with maturities at time T bear interest rates r_D and r_F, their initial prices in their respective currency are:

$$B_D(0) = B_D(T)e^{-r_D T} \quad \text{and} \quad B_F(0) = B_F(T)e^{-r_F T}$$

Suppose that at time $t = 0$ the FX rate between two equivalent bonds is $\xi_{FD}(0) = B_F(0)/B_D(0)$. In this case, since at time T, such an equivalence is also maintained, we have $\xi_{FD}(T) = B_F(T)/B_D(T)$, implying

$$\xi_{FD}(0) = \frac{B_F(0)}{B_D(0)} = \left(\frac{B_F(T)}{B_D(T)}\right)e^{-(r_F - r_D)T} = \xi_{FD}(T)e^{-(r_F - r_D)T}$$

Setting $\xi_{FD}(0) = \xi_{FD}(T)e^{-(r_F - r_D)T}$, the logarithm of the FX prices yields an equivalence in national bonds' rates:

$$r_D = r_F + \frac{1}{T}(\ln \xi_{FD}(0) - E_0 \ln \xi_{FD}(T)) \quad \text{and} \quad r_F = r_D + \frac{1}{T}(\ln \xi_{DF}(0) - E_0 \ln \xi_{DF}(T))$$

Such equivalence is far more complex than presumed by these simple examples as there are many additional economic, financial, and political factors, as well as national policies, that account for national treasury bills' rates. These differences have been used for trading, for instance, on interest rates differentials—that is, borrowing immensely in one country and depositing in another. For individual firms trading FX or assets denominated in FX, these factors cause the parity (or the LOOP) not to hold and create opportunities for arbitrage. This might lead a domestic sovereign state to act and remove the exercise of such opportunities either by new regulation or taxation. In Section 5.4 we discuss the arbitrage and the interest rate parity in terms of covered/uncovered interest parity.

Currency spreads may exist as a function of many factors, including local conditions, sovereign state's regulations, and potential and hidden taxation on all foreign transactions. To profit from currency spreads and benefit from trade, speculations and investment opportunities, financial products are designed to suit investors' tastes. For example, aggregate indexes are sought to summarize the state of national economies and their FX by financially traded products. Today, there are many such products, including exchange traded funds on commodity prices (oil, gold, etc.), which are particularly important for some countries' financial state.

A consumer price index (CPI) consists of a weighted portfolio or a basket of goods. Weighting each good would be particularly important, providing savvy investors the ability to assess how relevant such an index is. In the following, we define a CPI with N goods in two countries, each with good priced and weighted nominally in each country:

$$\text{CPI}_D = \sum_{i=1}^{N} w_i^D P_i^D, \quad \text{CPI}_F = \sum_{i=1}^{N} w_i^F P_i^F \quad \text{and} \quad \xi_{FD} = \frac{\text{CPI}_F}{\text{CPI}_D}$$

Practically, these models play an important role in providing policy guidelines to sovereign states, as well as signals to investors and international firms how to manage of their FX risks. These are a part of a complex system of endogenous and exogenous signals with many additional geopolitical factors that contribute to the intense and large financial exchanges in currency markets. In Chapter 7, a quantitative analysis of such models is provided with theoretical models that may be tested empirically to predict and price FX.

5.3.2 Application of the Law of One Price and Purchasing Power Parity

PPP may be used to compare the real GDP across countries; to compare the price level index (PLI), which is a ratio of a PPP and a nominal exchange rate. An international comparison program for 2011 by the World Bank (2014) estimated PPP data across 199 countries. Among the reported indicators, Switzerland, Norway, and Bermuda have the highest PLIs (in GDP terms) in the world, while the USA was placed 25th. By the same token, EC Eurostat provides PPP data for 37 countries. The Penn World

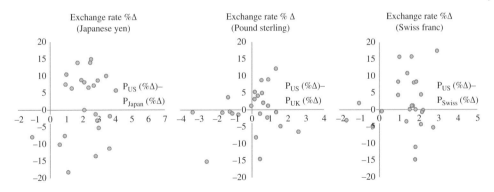

Figure 5.1 Exchange rate and inflation differentials, annual (1991–2014). *Source:* Data from IMF.

Table (version 9.0) by Feenstra *et al.* (2015) provides another data source based on a price survey for international comparisons of income, prices, and production with time-series data covering 167 countries since 1950. In addition, the OECD provides a methodology for cross-country data on PPP.

Besides nominal FX rates, baskets' relative prices (of commodities or financial products) provide important data sources used for financial and policy analysis. Relative PPP can be easily derived by using rates of change instead of absolute values. In this context, a percentage change in exchange rates equals the difference in inflation between domestic and foreign countries (with inflation defined as a percentage change in CPI). The relationship between inflation (using consumer prices) differentials and percentage changes in the exchange rate for the USA and other industrial countries (Japan, the UK, Switzerland) is shown in Figure 5.1. For all countries in this sample, the rates of change in the exchange rates are much larger than the differentials in the inflation rates for most years. This may indicate that relative PPP does not hold for certain FX rates. We will further study this observation empirically for major currencies.

The relationship between the inflation differentials (ID) for consumer prices and the rate of growth of exchange rates $\xi,\%\Delta$ for more countries and longer time series based on IMF data (1971–2014) taking the USA as home and another country as foreign (Australia, Canada, Japan, Switzerland, or the UK) is shown in Table 5.1. Results show that the correlation between these two variables (between the USA and most foreign countries) is very low; the highest is of Australia, which is 23%, compared with other countries.

Using these data, we ran the following regressions (with and without a constant) and estimated the relationship between the countries' FX rates and their prices:

regression with a constant $\xi_{\%\Delta,t} = \alpha + \beta\left(\pi_t^{US} - \pi_t^{F}\right) + e_t$

regression without a constant $\xi_{\%\Delta,t} = \beta\left(\pi_t^{US} - \pi_t^{F}\right) + e_t$

where $\xi_{\%\Delta,t}$ is a percentage change in spot exchange rate at t period, π_t^{US} and π_t^{F} are inflation rates in terms of percentage changes in consumer prices in the USA and foreign country respectively. The α parameter is the constant, β is a slope coefficient, and e_t is an error term (disturbance with a zero mean).

Table 5.1 Summary statistics for relative PPP.

	USA–Australia		USA–Canada		USA–Japan		USA–Switzerland		USA–UK	
	ID[a]	ξ,%Δ	ID	ξ,%Δ	ID	ξ,%Δ	ID	ξ,%Δ	ID	ξ,%Δ
Mean	−1.40	−0.09	−0.03	−0.01	1.50	3.38	1.69	4.15	−0.03	−0.07
Standard error	0.40	1.35	0.22	0.75	0.48	1.69	0.36	1.70	0.26	1.32
Median	−0.93	0.60	0.21	−0.37	2.23	2.65	1.65	1.94	0.28	−0.42
St. dev.	2.67	8.96	1.48	4.97	3.20	11.20	2.37	11.26	1.33	6.75
Sample var.	7.12	80.25	2.19	24.66	10.22	125.39	5.64	126.83	1.77	45.51
Kurtosis	0.00	−0.02	1.20	−0.32	7.12	2.02	2.80	1.16	0.39	0.48
Skewness	−0.74	0.25	−0.57	0.51	−2.05	0.86	0.94	0.89	−0.60	−0.56
Range	11.17	40.18	7.97	19.54	19.71	59.52	12.84	50.88	5.89	27.66
Min	−7.79	−20.33	−4.64	−7.23	−12.14	−18.17	−3.35	−14.88	−3.30	−15.58
Max	3.38	19.85	3.33	12.31	7.57	41.35	9.49	36.00	2.59	12.08
Correlation	0.23		0.10		0.03		0.04		0.04	

Source: Data from IMF.
[a] ID: inflation differential.

The results of these regressions, as demonstrated in Table 5.2, show positive slope coefficients that are generally less than 1; however, the coefficients are statistically insignificant, especially at 5% significance level. For the USA–Switzerland, a regression without a constant yields a statistically significant positive coefficient that is almost equal to 1 at the 10% level. This country pair may thus exhibit its relationship relative to its PPP. However, its R^2 is very low; only 5.5% of the variations in the ROR in exchange rate that may be explained by the change in the relative inflation rates between these two countries. The lack of a statistical significance reflects the complexity of FX and financial models and the interrelationships between real economic, financial, and other variables (besides the inflation differentials). Other problems arise due to simplifications implied in the aforementioned regression models.

These findings (in Table 5.2) show that there is little empirical evidence in support of PPP. This is particularly the case in the short run, due perhaps to restrictions and limitations of the underlying assumptions, as well as lag effects in the regression variables. Early studies (e.g., Frenkel, 1981) showed that PPP does not hold in the short run as the coefficient, expressing the relationship between the exchange rate and relative prices, differs from unity. Frenkel's (1981) reestimation included lags in variables and instrumental variables. Other studies, such as by Mishkin (1984) and Cumby and Obstfeld (1984), also found little evidence supporting the relative PPP especially in the short run. Froot and Rogoff (1995) argue that these tests failed to consider the nonstationarity of variables in the regression. Commonly used methods for testing the PPP include the unit root test (Dickey–Fuller (DF) and augmented DF (ADF)), as in Meese and Rogoff (1988), and cointegration for equilibrium relationship (long-run—see Engle and Granger (1987)).

Table 5.2 Regression results of relative PPP.

		With constant					No constant				
		Coeff.	SE	t	$P > \|t\|$	R^2		Coeff.	SE	t	$P > \|t\|$	R^2
Australia	α	1.00	1.5	0.66	0.51						
$n = 44$	β	0.77	0.50	1.53	0.13	0.053	β	0.61	0.44	1.39	0.17	0.043
Canada $n = 44$	α	0.00	0.75	0.00	1.00						
	β	0.33	0.52	0.65	0.52	0.010	β	0.33	0.51	0.65	0.52	0.010
Japan $n = 44$	α	3.24	1.89	1.72	0.09						
	β	0.09	0.54	0.17	0.87	0.001	β	0.49	0.50	0.98	0.33	0.219
Switzerland	α	3.83	2.12	1.81	0.08						
$n = 44$	β	0.19	0.73	0.26	0.80	0.002	β	0.98	0.61	1.59	0.12	0.055
UK $n = 26$	α	−0.05	1.34	−0.04	0.97						
	β	0.71	1.02	0.69	0.50	0.020	β	0.71	1.00	0.71	0.49	0.020

Instead of nominal FX rate, we may consider a real FX rate q, defined by the nominal exchange rate ξ adjusted for a ratio of domestic and foreign prices (P^D/P^F), which would be equal to 1 if the PPP holds absolutely. The real FX rate would then point to two baskets that trade between two countries, defined by $q = \xi/(P^D/P^F)$. Following Froot and Rogoff (1995), we ought to test whether the logarithm of the real exchange rate, $\log(q) = \log(\xi) - \log(p^D) + \log(p^F)$, is stationary or has a unit root ($H_0: \theta = 1$) against the long run PPP ($H_1: \theta < 1$) using the unit root test with the following AR(1) model with a lag:

$$\log(q_t) = \vartheta + \theta \log(q_{t-1}) + e_t$$

The DF test is constructed by deducting the $\log(q_{t-1})$ from both sides of the aforementioned model. The slope coefficient then becomes $\gamma = \theta - 1$, and the growth in the real exchange rate is $\Delta \log(q_t)$:

$$\Delta \log(q_t) = \vartheta + \gamma \log(q_{t-1}) + e_t$$

Furthermore, the ADF regression may be augmented with p lags of $\Delta \log(q_t)$, as shown in the following regression equation. A time trend (t) variable can be added to the regression as well.

$$\Delta \log(q_t) = \vartheta + \gamma \log(q_{t-1}) + \sum_{j=1}^{p} \varphi_i \Delta \log(q_{t-j}) + \delta t + e_t$$

As stated earlier, empirical evidence suggests that price differences do exist between different countries. Besides the factors mentioned earlier, this can be associated with the restricted assumptions of the PPP because in practice transaction costs, along with large transportation costs and trade tariffs, increase the cost of products and limit the mobility of goods internationally. In addition, some goods (e.g., labor and rent) are not tradable. In this regard, wages paid to employees and workers, as well as labor market structure, can differ across countries, implying different production costs.[2] This is reflected in the Big Mac Index published by *The Economist*,[3] which is based on PPP for McDonald's Big Mac. The PPP may also fail to hold due to price discrimination for differentiated goods when competition is imperfect. In this sense, the PPP assumption underlies a theoretical price model which assumes that global markets are complete, when, in fact, they may be incomplete.

Questions and Problems 5.1

Apply the unit root test with a trend to the real exchange rate data on USA/Australia and USA/Switzerland. Explain whether PPP holds in the long run. Analyze whether the relative prices for nontraded goods in these countries have changed considerably and how this would affect the tests of PPP.

5.4 Foreign Exchange Rates and Interest Rates: The Assets Approach

5.4.1 Covered Interest Arbitrage

The pricing of forward and spot FX contracts can be determined by interest rate parity. This is based on the presumption that the financial price of risk is unique across assets and across all countries. Specifically, a risk-free investment in a bond in the domestic country, with an interest rate r_H, ought to provide the same return as in the foreign country with an interest rate r_F. As the return on an investment abroad is usually in foreign currency, it is converted by the FX spot rate ξ. An investor may also employ a forward contract and sell the foreign currency forward to hedge the FX risk, removing the potential for arbitrage. In this case, when the investor is indifferent between two investments, covered interest parity (CIP) is said to hold. Then returns on investments at home and abroad are equalized using the forward FX rate ξ^{FR} to eliminate FX risks:

$$1 + r_H = \frac{\xi^{FR}}{\xi}(1 + r_F)$$

Interest rates affect FX trades (in particular rates set by central banks) as they represent expectations underlying inflation and therefore provide a signal to creeping currency devaluation. By the same token, when interest rates are reduced, financial liquidity is increased (as was the case following the 2007–2009 financial crisis), which may point to the policy a central bank adopts to combat financial duress. GDP, GNP, national and foreign debt, commercial and industrial sectors' transactions, and other indicators provide signals for basic trends that affect the FX market as well.

---

2 For empirical results of PPP and detailed discussion on shortcomings of the PPP in particular with regard to nontradable services, see Kravis and Lipsey (1983) and Obstfeld and Rogoff (1996).
3 http://www.economist.com/content/big-mac-index.

Table 5.3 Example on covered interest arbitrage.

	$t=0$		$t=1$					
EU borrow (€)	1000	Repay (€)	1010	r (EU)	0.01	ξ^S	1.2
USA invest ($)	1200	Earn ($)	1236	r (USA)	0.03	ξ^{FR}	**1.2**
Hedge	€1010	Convert (ξ^{FR})	$1212				
		Arbitrage	**24**				
	$t=0$		$t=1$					
EU borrow (€)	1000	Repay (€)	1010	r (EU)	0.01	ξ^S	1.2
USA invest ($)	1200	Earn ($)	1236	r (USA)	0.03	ξ^{FR}	**1.2238**
Hedge	€1010	Convert (ξ^{FR})	$1236				
		No arbitrage	**0**				

5.4.1.1 Example of Arbitrage (Covered Interest)

Assume that the interest rate in the EU ($r_€ = 1\%$) is lower than the interest rate in the USA ($r_\$ = 3\%$). Spot and forward exchange rates are the same: $\xi^S = \$1.2$ and $\xi^{FR} = \$1.2$ per euro. You can borrow in the EU and invest euro funds (€1000) in the USA seeking a higher yield. At first, you convert your euro funds to US dollars and invest it ($\xi^S \times 1000$) in the USA. At the same time, the forward exchange rate is hedged (€1000$(1 + r_€)$) since funds need to be repaid to the EU after 1 year. Thus, the future/ forward contract guarantees the conversion of this amount to euros at ξ^{FR}. After 1 year you will receive $\xi^S 1000(1 + r_\$)$ in the USA, but repay debt in the EU, €1000$(1 + r_€)$. Since the difference is positive in this example, interest arbitrage is feasible. As shown later, this will continue until the difference is zero indicating no arbitrage or CIP when $\xi^{FR} = \$1.2238$. Calculations are summarized in Table 5.3.

Questions and Problems 5.2

Assume that the annual interest rate is 2% in the USA and 3% in the EU, and the spot rate is $1.1/euro and the forward rate is $1.12/euro. Based on this information, show whether there is an arbitrage opportunity through hedging against the FX risk and find the yield that results from such an arbitrage. Determine whether the interest rate parity holds. If interest rate parity does not hold, how would you carry out covered interest arbitrage? What forward exchange rate will lead to no arbitrage?

5.4.2 Uncovered Interest Parities

When the FX risk is uncovered, an investor forecasts the future FX rate ξ^c and defines an expected FX rate (where the superscript "c" indicates expected variables). The uncovered interest rate parity (UIP) equation with no arbitrage arises from an asset-based approach to FX rates, where the home currency's domestic return equals the expected home currency return on foreign investments. Investments can be made in two sovereign states' risk-free bonds in their respective currencies, where the spot FX rate at time t is ξ_t, with nominal rates in the USA and the EU being $r_{US,t}$ and $r_{EU,t}$ respectively. Then the UIP condition can be approximated and defined as follows:

$$1 + r_{US,t} = \frac{\xi_t^c}{\xi_t}(1 + r_{EU,t}) \quad \text{or} \quad r_{US,t} = r_{EU,t} + \frac{\xi_t^c - \xi_t}{\xi_t}$$

Here, the interest rate on USD assets equals the sum of interest rates on the EUR-denominated asset and the expected FX rate of depreciation.

5.4.3 Real Interest Parity

Under relative PPP, the expected inflation differential at the $t + 1$ period determines an expected change in the exchange rate. Simultaneously under UIP, the expected change in the exchange rate is equal to the interest rate differential in two countries. We can then derive a relationship between the inflation and the interest rate, known as the Fisher effect (nominal interest rate increases due to a rise in the expected inflation rate). Thus, the real interest rate is defined by the difference between the nominal interest rate and inflation:

$$\text{relative PPP} \qquad \dot{e}_{\$€,t+1} = \pi^c_{\$,t+1} - \pi^c_{€,t+1}$$

$$\text{UIP} \qquad \dot{e}_{\$€,t+1} = r_{\$,t} - r_{€,t}$$

$$\text{Fisher effect} \qquad r_\$^{real} = r_{\$,t} - \pi^c_{\$,t+1} = r_{€,t} - \pi^c_{€,t+1} = r_€^{real} \Rightarrow$$

$$\text{real interest parity (RIP)} \quad r_\$^{real} = r_€^{real}$$

These relationships define the RIP between two countries. If the conditions for PPP and UIP hold, expected interest rates are the same across countries and equal a world (real) interest rate. This relationship is used by some investors able to calculate the real interest rates in several countries and bet on their differences, or buying bonds from a sovereign state with an inordinately high real interest rate. In practice, countries' real rates vary and a risk premium is often paid to compensate for risk. Empirical results have failed to show support for RIP however. Early empirical studies, attributable to Mishkin (1984), rejected the RIP and suggested that the real domestic interest rate varies from the world rate. Similarly, a study by Chinn and Frankel (1995) on real rates in the Pacific Rim examined how the domestic rates are affected by the real rates in the USA and Japan. They show that RIP does not hold for most countries, with evidence of cointegration of real interest rates.

5.4.4 Testing Uncovered Interest Parity

In order to account for the risk of holding assets by a risk-averse investor, the UIP model is modified by adjusting foreign returns for their risk. The right side of the UIP equation in Section 5.4.2 is then extended by adding a risk premium; for example, FX risk premium and default risk premium (see Chapter 3). Risk of loss can arise due to restrictions related to changes such as capital control, taxes, and regulations. Interest rate parity may not hold perfectly because of transaction costs between markets, transaction fees, differences in taxation of interest earnings and FX rate earnings, government controls, and political risk; for example, regime changes.

Real-world data show that the conditions for the UIP hypothesis might not hold in practice. For the UIP hypothesis, government controls over financial capital flows in a country can cause problems when equalizing returns. Similarly, empirical studies' findings indicate that UIP may not hold due to issues, including, for example, carry trade. Profits on carry trade are made by borrowing (going short) in a country with a lower interest rate in the domestic currency (e.g., Japan) and investing (going long) in a country with a higher interest rate (e.g., Australia) with a foreign currency, assuming that FX rate remains unchanged. Making the investment in emerging countries such as India can be more profitable as it can be inspired by India's positive growth outlook; the US Treasury bills can be more attractive if its interest rate is expected to rise while the US dollar strength increases.

Engel (2014), referring to the following regression equation, presents a development stemming from empirical studies on UIP a focus on how it fails to hold by testing the null hypothesis $H_0 : \beta = 1$. A number of empirical studies found that the sign of the estimated slope coefficient is negative and less than 1:

$$\Delta \xi_t = \alpha + \beta (r_{D,t} - r_{F,t}) + e_{t+1}$$

Furthermore, whether the current rates (difference between the forward and spot rates) can predict changes in a future rate or not can be studied using

$$\Delta \xi_t = \alpha - \beta \left(1 - \frac{\xi_t^{FR}}{\xi_t} \right) + e_{t+1}$$

Studies by Fama (1984) and Burnside *et al.* (2006) using such a regression model have found a negative slope coefficient (and thus different from 1) for nine countries (Belgium, Canada, France, Germany, Italy, Japan, Netherlands, Switzerland, and the USA) against the pound sterling, using exchange rate data between 1976 and 2005.

Questions and Problems 5.3

Describe the forward-premium puzzle by referring to its connection to the UIP and explain the underlying factors such as risk premium and peso problems. Discuss strategies pertaining to currency speculation (e.g., carry trade).

5.5 Demand and Supply of Money and Exchange Rates: Monetary Approach

If both domestic and foreign macroeconomic factors are involved in determining the supply and demand for money, a model comprising these factors is used to predict the FX rate, as Figure 5.2 indicates. Models vary by their factors and how they are applied in selecting the relevant country's FX price.

Figure 5.2 Macro factors driving FX prices.

$$MD(p) = MS(p) \Rightarrow \begin{matrix} \text{Money} \\ \text{Supply} \end{matrix} \Leftrightarrow \begin{matrix} \text{Money} \\ \text{Demand} \end{matrix} \Rightarrow \begin{matrix} \text{Domestic Price} \\ \text{Foreign Price} \end{matrix} \Rightarrow \text{FX rate through PPP}$$

Figure 5.3 Derivation of the FX rate from the money market.

A basic economic approach considers two countries, each has a demand for money and employs a policy to meet this demand. In this case, the equilibrium price $p*$ is determined by Say's law, where it is defined by equating the money demand $MD(p)$ and its supply $MS(p)$, which depends on the price (see Figure 5.3).

5.5.1 The Frenkel–Mussa Model

The monetary exchange rate model was pioneered by Frenkel (1976) and Mussa (1976, 1979). Frenkel (1976) adopted PPP, assuming perfectly flexible prices, where the exchange rate is determined by domestic and foreign prices, used to derive the price by the money market equilibrium. Assuming that PPP holds, Bilson (1978: 51–52) used the following money demand function by Cagan (1956) to derive the relative demand function between two countries solved for the exchange rate. Consider the money market equilibrium in countries D and F with money demand defined as follows, where elasticities of the money demand with respect to Y and r are ε and ς respectively:

$$\frac{M_D}{P_D} = K_D Y_D^\varepsilon e^{-\varsigma r_D} \quad \text{and} \quad \frac{M_F}{P_F} = K_F Y_F^\varepsilon e^{-\varsigma r_F}$$

PPP yields

$$\xi_{DF} = \frac{P_D}{P_F} = \frac{M_D}{M_F} \frac{K_F}{K_D} \left(\frac{Y_F}{Y_D} \right)^\varepsilon e^{-\varsigma(r_F - r_D)}$$

A logarithmic transformation of this equation provides a linear equation that can also be used for obtaining linear regression estimates:

$$\ln \xi_{DF} = \ln \left(\frac{P_D}{P_F} \right) = \ln \left(\frac{K_F}{K_D} \right) + \ln \left(\frac{M_D}{M_F} \right) + \varepsilon \ln \left(\frac{Y_F}{Y_D} \right) - \varsigma(r_F - r_D)$$

We can set $\vartheta(t) = \ln \xi_{DF}(t)$, $k(t) = \ln(K_F/K_D)$, $m(t) = \ln(M_F/M_D)$, and $y(t) = \ln(Y_F/Y_D)$, then consider two subsequent instants of time:

$$\vartheta(t) = k(t) + m(t) + \varepsilon y(t) - \varsigma(r_F(t) - r_D(t))$$

The financial approach to FX pricing states that under an assumption of rational expectations, we have:

$$\vartheta(t) = \frac{1 + r_F}{1 + r_D} E^Q \vartheta(t+1 | \mathfrak{I}_t)$$

where Q is a probability measure, appropriately selected (see also Chapter 7). In other words, the current FX rate is expressed as an expectation over the macroeconomic factors that are used to model the FX rate:

$$\vartheta(t) = \frac{1+r_F}{1+r_D} E^Q(k(t+1) + m(t+1) + \varepsilon y(t+1) - \varsigma(r_F - r_D)|\mathfrak{I}_t)$$

5.5.2 Foreign Exchange Prices and Inflation

Consider the US dollar and the euro, and set $(M_\$, M_\mathchar'26\mkern-9mu e)$ and $(Y_\$, Y_\mathchar'26\mkern-9mu e)$ to be the money supply and income for the two currency zones. The demand for real money is then assumed proportional to the country's interest rate and the real income, and therefore the real money stock is $M_\$/P_\$ = L_\$ Y_\$$ and $M_\mathchar'26\mkern-9mu e/P_\mathchar'26\mkern-9mu e = L_\mathchar'26\mkern-9mu e Y_\mathchar'26\mkern-9mu e$ (see Chapter 4). For a flexible FX regime, prices between countries are self-adjusting through the countries' FX. Then, assuming a PPP holds, the exchange rate is determined by $\xi_{\$/\mathchar'26\mkern-9mu e} = P_\$/P_\mathchar'26\mkern-9mu e = (M_\$/L_\$ Y_\$)/(M_\mathchar'26\mkern-9mu e/L_\mathchar'26\mkern-9mu e Y_\mathchar'26\mkern-9mu e)$.

If prices are fixed, the FX rate would be adjusted to reflect the fact that prices are not fluctuating freely according to the currency zones' supply of money and income. Thus, when the FX rate is fixed or manipulated, such actions will have an effect on prices. The rationality of these statements is based on the LOOP, which underlies the concept of parity (or unique price) as discussed earlier. Regardless of LOOP's validity, these prices might be defined in different terms reflecting a number of parities that can be verified empirically.

A logarithmic transformation of the price equation in the USA yields

$$\ln P_\$ = \ln\left(\frac{M_\$}{L_\$ Y_\$}\right) \Rightarrow \ln P_\$ = \ln M_\$ - \ln L_\$ - \ln Y_\$$$

A time difference of this model establishes an equivalence in terms of RORs, or

$$\Delta(\ln P_\$) = \Delta(\ln M_\$) - \Delta(\ln L_\$) - \Delta(\ln Y_\$) \quad \text{or} \quad \frac{\Delta P_\$}{P_\$} = \frac{\Delta M_\$}{M_\$} - \frac{\Delta L_\$}{L_\$} - \frac{\Delta Y_\$}{Y_\$}; \quad \frac{\Delta L_\$}{L_\$} = 0$$

Setting $m_{\$, t}$ as the growth rate of money supply $(\Delta M_{\$, t}/M_{\$, t})$, $y_{\$, t}$ as the growth rate of real income $(\Delta Y_{\$, t}/Y_{\$, t})$, and $\pi_{\$, t}$ as the inflation rate $(\Delta P_{\$, t}/P_{\$, t})$, the inflation rate is shown to be a difference between the growth rates of money supply and real income for the two currency zones:

$$\pi_{\$,t} = m_{\$,t} - y_{\$,t} \quad \text{and} \quad \pi_{\mathchar'26\mkern-9mu e,t} = m_{\mathchar'26\mkern-9mu e,t} - y_{\mathchar'26\mkern-9mu e,t}$$

Setting the rate of change in the exchange rate as $\dot{e}_{\$\mathchar'26\mkern-9mu e} = \Delta\xi_{\$\mathchar'26\mkern-9mu e}/\xi_{\$\mathchar'26\mkern-9mu e}$ yields a relative PPP:

$$\dot{e}_{\$\mathchar'26\mkern-9mu e,t} = \pi_{\$,t} - \pi_{\mathchar'26\mkern-9mu e,t} = (m_{\$,t} - y_{\$,t}) - (m_{\mathchar'26\mkern-9mu e,t} - y_{\mathchar'26\mkern-9mu e,t})$$

In other words, $\dot{e}_{\$/\mathchar'26\mkern-9mu e,t}$ is defined by the countries' relative inflation rates, which are calculated in terms of the rates of change in the money supply and the real income in these countries. An introduction of countries' debts and other macroeconomic factors alters the above equation. In this case, FX variations may be due to real and monetary macroeconomic factors (in our case monetary supply and real income).

Case Study and Discussion 5.1

Suppose that the inflation rate is higher in China than in the USA. The USD ought then to appreciate according to the inflation-adjusted parity under the relative PPP. Also, assume that the CNY is currently undervalued with respect to the USD. If inflation accelerates in China, it will, in effect, be a mechanism of self-correction/self-adjustment in the FX market for the USD if the latter FX is not altered. Such situations arise when a country intervenes in the FX market to maintain its undervalued currency, providing an FX trade support for exports. Inflation in China, resulting in more expensive products to export to the USA, may contribute, in the short run, to an improvement in the trade deficit with China, as Chinese goods in the USA will be necessarily more expensive and thereby less demanded. In the longer term, however, the US deficit would not improve since importers will switch to markets where similar goods can be acquired at a lower price and therefore maintain the trade deficit.

Case Study and Discussion 5.2

Inflation in a foreign country may have countervailing forces both in the short run and in the long run. Suppose that China is a strategic exporter of some raw materials, such as rare earth metals needed for electronic items and special military gear. If inflation sets in, the price of such materials will increase, contributing to an appreciating FX rate; yet, at the same time, it can also contribute to its exports as foreign (non-Chinese) firms will tend to hedge by augmenting the stocks in such material for future use. Similar observations are seen in the crude oil market with countries building strategic inventories to meet future needs at acceptable prices. Alternatively, future and option markets might point to such beliefs by FX traders. This case thus highlights some of the effects of multiple economic policies on FX and trade.

Questions and Problems 5.4

Suppose that the annual money supply growth is 5% in the USA and 11% in India. GDP growth is 2.4% in the USA and 7.4% in India. What is the expected rate of change in the exchange rate (USD/INR)? Find the inflation rates based on the given information. Describe the impact of an increase in money supply in the USA on the inflation rate and the exchange rate.

Questions and Problems 5.5

Study and present an empirical evidence for the relationship between inflation rates, the rate of change in the money supply, and the rate of change in exchange rates of major industrial countries relative to the USA from 1980. Does your findings support the monetary model? Discuss the hyperinflation and its impact on your results.

5.5.3 The Unified Asset/Monetary Approaches

While the asset approach determines the spot FX rate by employing UIP, a monetary approach defines the FX rate through the money market equilibrium. These are unified in the following manner. An equilibrium model in the short-term money market determines nominal interest rates in home and foreign currencies. The monetary approach instead defines the FX rate of two countries based on their prices PPP and long-term equilibrium in the money market. A combination of these approaches for setting the exchange rate in terms of money demand and supply was developed in Frenkel (1976) and Bilson (1978) with the Cagan-type money demand function. These are also specified in Frankel (1979, 1984). As a result, the exchange rate $\ln(\xi_{\$\epsilon})$ depends on the relative supply of money $M_\$/M_\epsilon$, relative income $Y_\$/Y_\epsilon$, and expected inflation differential $\pi_\$^c - \pi_\epsilon^c$ between two countries. For example, for each of these approaches, considering the USA ($) and Europe (€), we have the models given in Table 5.4.

5.5.4 Empirical Evidence on the Monetary Model of Exchange Rate

Frenkel (1976) applied the monetary approach to the determination of an exchange rate in a hyperinflationary period based on pre-World War II data in Germany. Frenkel assumed that the demand for real money is a function of expected inflation, and a fixed foreign price ($P_F = 1$). An estimate of the effect of the nominal money stock M and inflation expectations π^c on the exchange rate ξ using a log-linearized equation was derived from Equation A in Table 5.4 (Frenkel, 1976) with an error term e: $\ln \xi = \alpha + \beta \ln(M) + \gamma \ln(1 + \pi^c) + e$. Empirical findings were then shown to be consistent with the monetary exchange rate model. Similarly, assuming flexible prices, Bilson

Table 5.4 Asset and monetary approaches for the FX determination.

Asset approach	Monetary approach
USA: $\dfrac{M_\$}{P_\$} = L^\$(r_\$)Y_\$$	USA: $P_\$ = \dfrac{M_\$}{L^\$(r_\$)Y_\$}$
EU: $\dfrac{M_\epsilon}{P_\epsilon} = L^\epsilon(r_\epsilon)Y_\epsilon$	EU: $P_\epsilon = \dfrac{M_\epsilon}{L^\epsilon(r_\epsilon)Y_\epsilon}$
UIP: $r_\$ = r_\epsilon + \dot{e}_{\$\epsilon}$	PPP: $\xi_{\$\epsilon} = \dfrac{P_\$}{P_\epsilon}$ or $\ln(\xi_{\$\epsilon}) = \ln P_\$ - \ln P_\epsilon$
	Expected changes: $\dot{e}_{\$\epsilon} = \pi_\$^c - \pi_\epsilon^c$

Combined

Equation A: $\ln(\xi_{\$\epsilon}) = \ln(M_\$/M_\epsilon) - \beta \ln(Y_\$/Y_\epsilon) + \alpha(\pi_\$^c - \pi_\epsilon^c)$ (as in Frenkel (1976))

Equation B: $\ln(\xi_{\$\epsilon}) = \ln(M_\$/M_\epsilon) - \beta \ln(Y_\$/Y_\epsilon) + \alpha(r_\$ - r_\epsilon)$ (as in Bilson (1978))

Money demand: $\dfrac{M_\$}{P_\$} = (Y_\$)^\beta e^{-\alpha r_\$}$ and $\dfrac{M_\epsilon}{P_\epsilon} = (Y_\epsilon)^\beta e^{-\alpha r_\epsilon}$

(1978: 55) tested the monetary approach by estimating the following equation assuming that "an actual exchange rate adjusts toward the equilibrium rate":

$$\ln \xi_t = \alpha + \beta \ln\left(M_t^D - M_t^F\right) + \gamma(r_D - r_F) - \delta \ln\left(Y_t^D - Y_t^F\right) + \varepsilon \ln(\xi_{t-1}) + e$$

where M is money demand, r is interest rate, and Y is real income. He also claimed that the monetary approach can also be used for a short-term analysis.

Empirical studies of the FX rate based on the monetary approach have pointed to a cointegration between exchange rate movements and their driving forces on fundamental macroeconomic variables.[4] These variables (e.g., money supply M and output Y) were shown to be nonstationary. Using panel data for 14 countries between 1973 and 1994, Groen (2000) studied a long-run monetary and exchange rate model. His findings show that residuals are stationary, indicating the presence of cointegration (a stationary linear combination of variables). Cointegration tests by the panel data provided support for the validity of the long-run PPP. However, a study conducted by Cerra and Saxena (2010) based on a very large sample covering 98 countries relative to the USA for the period 1960–2004 has pointed to cointegration in their data, thus linking exchange rates and monetary variables. Both these studies apply the following econometric steps.

Step 1. Ordinary least squares (OLS) regression on the panel data:

$$\ln(\xi_{it}) = \alpha_i + \beta_i\left[\ln\left(M_{it}^D\right) - \ln\left(M_{it}^F\right)\right] + \theta_i\left[\ln\left(Y_{it}^D\right) - \ln\left(Y_{it}^F\right)\right] + e_{it}$$

Step 2. ADF test on the residuals from the step 1:

$$\Delta \hat{e}_{it} = \gamma \hat{e}_{i,t-1} + \sum_{j=1}^{p} \varphi_{ij} \Delta \hat{e}_{i,t-j} + \omega_{it}$$

An alternative econometric approach to FX estimates and predictions focuses on factors that affect sovereign states' demand for money for domestic (D) and foreign countries (F) when the money market is in equilibrium. For example, one may consider the following (and empirically testable) model:

$$\frac{M_D}{P_D} = f_D(Y_D, BOP_D, em_D, r_D, \ldots)$$

where Y_D is national income, BOP is the balance of payments, em_D is employment, and r_D is the interest rate. Other factors, such as input or output macroeconomic factors, can also be considered.

5.6 Extensions of the Models

5.6.1 The Balassa–Samuelson Model

The Balassa–Samuelson model is based on Balassa (1964) and Samuelson (1964) and seeks to explain the relationship between productivity and the real FX rate. The model considers tradable goods (which includes industrial goods produced in one country that

---

4 These studies are based on the cointegration testing procedure by Engle and Granger (1987).

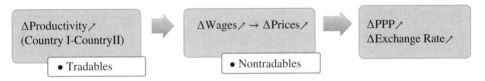

Figure 5.4 Relative productivity, wages, prices, and exchange rates.

can be sold in another) and nontradable goods (which are local services that cannot be traded).[5] Its empirical observations imply that countries with higher productivity in tradables compared with nontradables tend to have higher price levels. Additionally, assumptions of this model indicate that productivity gains in the tradable sector allow real wages to increase commensurately. Since wages are assumed to link the tradable and the nontradable sectors, wages and prices also increase in the nontradable sector. This leads to an increase in the overall price level, which in turn results in an appreciation of the real FX rate, as shown in Figure 5.4.[6]

5.6.1.1 The Model

The simpler model consists of two countries, two goods (tradable (T) and nontradable (N)), and one factor of production (wages). Suppose that the logarithmic prices of a domestic and foreign tradable good are given by the weighted prices of nontradable (N) and tradable (T) goods for both countries D and F, and denoted by p_T^D and p_T^F (see Gandolfo, 2001):

$$P^D = \left(P_N^D\right)^{\kappa_N^D} \left(P_T^D\right)^{1-\kappa_N^D} \quad \text{and} \quad P^F = \left(P_N^F\right)^{\kappa_N^F} \left(P_T^F\right)^{1-\kappa_N^F}$$

In logarithmic terms we have

$$p^D = \kappa_N^D p_N^D + \left(1-\kappa_N^D\right)p_T^D \quad \text{and} \quad p^F = \kappa_N^F p_N^F + \left(1-\kappa_N^F\right)p_T^F$$

When PPP holds for tradable goods, we have $p_T^F = e_{FD} + p_T^D$, with $e_T^{FD} = \ln\xi_T^{FD}$, $\ln\xi_T^{FD}$ for tradable goods from the foreign to the domestic country. Thus:

$$p^D = \kappa_N^D p_N^D + \left(1-\kappa_N^D\right)\left(p_T^F - e_T^{FT}\right) \quad \text{and} \quad p^F = \kappa_N^F p_N^F + \left(1-\kappa_N^F\right)p_T^F$$

Letting $\ln\xi_T^{FD}$ be $e_{Nom}^{FD} = p^F - p^D$, we have

$$e_{Nom}^{FD} = p^F - p^D = \kappa_N^F p_N^F + \left(1-\kappa_N^F\right)p_T^F - \kappa_N^D p_N^D - \left(1-\kappa_N^D\right)\left(p_T^F - e_T^{FT}\right)$$

Therefore:

$$e_{Nom}^{FD} = \left(1-\kappa_N^D\right)e_T^{FD} + \kappa_N^F p_N^F - \kappa_N^D p_N^D + \left(\kappa_N^D - \kappa_N^F\right)p_T^F.$$

which can be written explicitly by:

$$\xi_{Nom}^{FD}\left(\xi_T^{FD}\right)^{\kappa_N^D-1} = \left(P_N^F\right)^{\kappa_N^F} \left(P_N^D\right)^{-\kappa_N^D} \left(P_T^F\right)^{\kappa_N^D-\kappa_N^F}$$

---

5 Tradable sectors include agriculture, mining, manufacturing, and transport; nontradable industries are construction, wholesale, retail, hotel, real estate, electricity, and so on.

6 The Balassa–Samuelson model is sketched in a number of books, including Gandolfo (2001: chapter 15) and Obstfeld and Rogoff (1996: chapter 4).

By the same token:

$$\xi_{\text{Nom}}^{\text{DF}} \left(\xi_{\text{T}}^{\text{DF}}\right)^{\kappa_{\text{N}}^{\text{F}} - 1} = \left(P_{\text{N}}^{\text{D}}\right)^{\kappa_{\text{N}}^{\text{D}}} \left(P_{\text{N}}^{\text{F}}\right)^{-\kappa_{\text{N}}^{\text{F}}} \left(P_{\text{T}}^{\text{D}}\right)^{\kappa_{\text{N}}^{\text{F}} - \kappa_{\text{N}}^{\text{D}}}$$

Assuming that for nominal rates, $\xi_{\text{Nom}}^{\text{DF}} = 1/\xi_{\text{Nom}}^{\text{FD}}$, we have

$$\left(\xi_{\text{T}}^{\text{DF}}\right)^{1 - \kappa_{\text{N}}^{\text{F}}} \left(\xi_{\text{T}}^{\text{FD}}\right)^{1 - \kappa_{\text{N}}^{\text{D}}} = \left(\frac{P_{\text{T}}^{\text{F}}}{P_{\text{T}}^{\text{D}}}\right)^{\kappa_{\text{N}}^{\text{D}} - \kappa_{\text{N}}^{\text{F}}}$$

$$\left(\xi_{\text{T}}^{\text{DF}}\right)^{\kappa_{\text{N}}^{\text{F}} - 1} \left(\xi_{\text{T}}^{\text{FD}}\right)^{\kappa_{\text{N}}^{\text{D}} - 1} = \left(\frac{P_{\text{T}}^{\text{F}}}{P_{\text{T}}^{\text{D}}}\right)^{\kappa_{\text{N}}^{\text{D}} - \kappa_{\text{N}}^{\text{F}}}$$

Note that, in such a case, while there may exist a nominal PPP, the PPP need not be in trade. If $\kappa_{\text{N}}^{\text{F}} = \kappa_{\text{N}}^{\text{D}}$, we then have $\left(\xi_{\text{T}}^{\text{DF}} \xi_{\text{T}}^{\text{FD}}\right)^{\kappa_{\text{N}} - 1} = 1$ and therefore $\xi_{\text{T}}^{\text{DF}} = 1/\xi_{\text{T}}^{\text{FD}}$. In other words, the economic structure, between tradable and nontradable sectors does matter.[7] The Ballasa–Samuelson model addresses this problem as follows. Suppose that ξ is the FX rate, and let the tradable price of a good be $P_{\text{T}}^{\text{D}} = 1$ and $\xi P_{\text{T}}^{\text{F}} = 1$. Next, assume that the labor production function is given by the quantity of nontradable products it can produce per hour, or $w^{\text{D}} = Q^{\text{D}}$ and $\xi w^{\text{F}} = Q^{\text{F}}$. Finally, prices for nontradable goods are defined by wages or by $P_{\text{N}}^{\text{D}} = Q^{\text{D}}$ and $\xi P_{\text{N}}^{\text{F}} = Q^{\text{F}}$. Then the inflation rate in each country, expressed by the rate of change in prices, is $p_{\text{N}}^{\text{D}} = \ln P_{\text{N}}^{\text{D}} = \ln Q^{\text{D}}$ and $\ln \xi P_{\text{N}}^{\text{F}} = \ln \xi + p_{\text{N}}^{\text{F}} = \ln Q^{\text{F}}$. Next, let $(\kappa^{\text{D}}, \kappa^{\text{F}})$ be the proportions of nontradable goods and $(1 - \kappa^{\text{D}}, 1 - \kappa^{\text{F}})$ be the proportions of tradable goods in each of the domestic and foreign countries. As a result, a derivative yields:

$$\frac{\Delta P^{\text{D}}}{P^{\text{D}}} = \left(1 - \kappa^{\text{D}}\right) \frac{\Delta P_{\text{T}}^{\text{D}}}{P_{\text{T}}^{\text{D}}} + \kappa^{\text{D}} \Delta \frac{P_{\text{N}}^{\text{D}}}{P_{\text{N}}^{\text{D}}} = \kappa^{\text{D}} \frac{\Delta Q^{\text{D}}}{Q^{\text{D}}}$$

$$\frac{\Delta (\xi P^{\text{F}})}{(\xi P^{\text{F}})} = \left(1 - \kappa^{\text{F}}\right) \left(\frac{\Delta (\xi P_{\text{T}}^{\text{F}})}{(\xi P_{\text{T}}^{\text{F}})}\right) + \kappa^{\text{F}} \left(\frac{\Delta (\xi P_{\text{N}}^{\text{F}})}{(\xi P_{\text{N}}^{\text{F}})}\right) = \kappa^{\text{F}} \frac{\Delta Q^{\text{F}}}{Q^{\text{F}}}$$

The rate of change in the real FX rate is therefore

$$\frac{\Delta q}{q} = \frac{\Delta (\xi P^{\text{F}})}{(\xi P^{\text{F}})} - \frac{\Delta P^{\text{D}}}{P^{\text{D}}} = \kappa^{\text{F}} \frac{\Delta Q^{\text{F}}}{Q^{\text{F}}} - \kappa^{\text{D}} \frac{\Delta Q^{\text{D}}}{Q^{\text{D}}}$$

And the rate of change in the nominal FX rate is equal to the rate of real FX rate depreciation plus the inflation differential between the domestic and the foreign country:

$$\frac{\Delta \xi}{\xi} = \frac{\Delta q}{q} + \left(\frac{\Delta P^{\text{D}}}{P^{\text{D}}} - \frac{\Delta P^{\text{F}}}{P^{\text{F}}}\right)$$

5.6.1.2 Discussion: Empirical Evidence on Balassa–Samuelson Model

A number of empirical studies have examined tradables and nontradables sectors, and their implication for the PPP and real exchange rate. Various approaches to the Balassa–Samuelson model were addressed in studies by, for example, Rogoff (1992), Obstfeld

---

7 Gandolfo (2001) shows that PPP does not hold either for nontradable goods or for an aggregate price index (CPI).

(1993), Backus and Smith (1993), and De Gregorio *et al.* (1994). A definition of the tradable sector is based on different factors. Tradables can be sectors with a ratio of total export to total production greater than 10% as in De Gregorio *et al.* (1994); alternatively, it can use locational Gini coefficients as in Jensen and Kletzer (2005). Using OECD data (1970–1985), De Gregorio *et al.* (1994) show that the most tradable sector is manufacturing (45% of its production exported), followed by mining (31%), and agriculture (24%); the least tradables are overall services (4%). However, transportation is treated as tradables in their study because it has a very high export share in production (28%). We would expect these ratios to increase from the 1980s due to accelerated trade between countries and technological progress in the traded and nontraded industries.

Balassa (1964) tested the relationship between a ratio of PPP to the exchange rate, and GNP per capita. Based on industrial country data, Balassa (1964: 589) found a positive correlation coefficient (0.92) in favor of his hypothesis that "the higher level of service prices at higher income levels leads to systematic differences between purchasing-power parities and equilibrium exchange rates." Furthermore, a positive correlation (0.91) is also shown for the productivity growth in tradables (manufacturing) and the ratio of the general price index (GNP deflator) to the index of the prices of tradables (manufactured goods).

The vast majority of the literature has pointed to a positive correlation between the relative productivity (in tradables compared with nontradables) and relative price of nontradables ($\ln P = \ln P_N - \ln P_T$). In this context, Gregorio *et al.* (1994) show that nontradables have higher inflation than the tradables mainly due to both demand- and supply-side factors, including demand for nontradable goods and productivity growth in tradables. The weight of nontradables and their effects on the economy and international exchanges and currency remain a topic for further study, however.

Questions and Problems 5.6

Using the latest EU KLEMS Database (http://www.euklems.net/), collect data on sectoral prices, wages, value added, and employment from 1970 for the EU member states and the USA.

a) Classify the sectors into tradables and nontradables using the 10% threshold (export/ production). How did these ratios change from the ratios in Gregorio *et al.* (1994)? Are there any services with a ratio of more than 10%? Emphasize the contribution of an increased trade since the 1980s.

b) Calculate the productivity in different sectors. Analyze the trends in relative prices (of nontradable sector), relative wages, and relative productivity.

c) Calculate the change in relative prices $\Delta(P_N/P_T)$ for the EU and the USA (find the mean).

d) Calculate the correlation of the tradable goods' inflation rates. Find the correlation for the nontradables. Does it suggest a comovement of the prices? Find correlations for the growth rates of productivity.

5.6.2 The Dornbusch Overshooting Model

The FX rate-overshooting model, suggested by Dornbusch (1976), seeks to explain why FX rates have high variances. Dornbusch's insights were based on the assumption that lags in some parts of the economy can induce a compensating volatility in others. This model is based on an extension of the Mundell–Fleming model with FX rate dynamics.

Dornbusch argued that volatility is in fact a far more fundamental property than presumed. His model states that one permanent change in the money supply must lead to a proportionate change in the price level and the FX rate in the long run. However, in the short run, the price level is fixed and the nominal FX rate must overshoot its long-run equilibrium. Any initial disturbance of money supply will cause an even larger unanticipated rise in the instant FX rate than in the long-term FX rate. The assumptions of the model are:

- Aggregate demand is determined by the standard open economy IS–LM mechanism.
- Financial markets are able to adjust to shocks instantaneously, and investors are risk neutral.
- In contrast to Frenkel (1976) and Bilson (1978), goods prices are "sticky" in the short run.
- Aggregate supply is horizontal in the short run, though it is positively sloped in the long run.
- Adjustment process is faster for asset markets and exchange rates compared with the goods market.

5.6.2.1 The Dornbusch Model

The Dornbusch monetary model loosens the condition that prices must be preset, but allows for slow price adjustments. An important insight for policy implications is the overshooting of the nominal FX rate over its long-run equilibrium when an economic system is shocked by monetary supply. This model shows that, once a real economic shock occurs, markets may move to an equilibrium either through a flexible FX rate or a change in prices.

In the following, we briefly outline its foundation and the effects of a monetary policy through adjustment processes based on Dornbusch (1976). The following two approaches previously introduced are applied: (1) UIP under perfect capital mobility and money market equilibrium, as shown in the following equations. (2) In addition, it is assumed that PPP holds in the long run instead of the short run; thus, the long-run exchange rate is determined by long-run prices in domestic and foreign countries ($\xi^l = P_D^l / P_F^l$). Thus, for UIP:

$$r_D = r_F + \frac{\xi_{DF}^c - \xi_{DF}}{\xi_{DF}} \quad \text{or} \quad r_D = r_F + \dot{e}_{DF}$$

where the exchange rate's expected rate of change is $\dot{e}_{DF} = \Delta \xi_{DF}/\xi_{DF}$, with $e_{DF} = \ln \xi_{DF}$. Alternatively, assuming rational expectations, an adjustment coefficient φ is introduced by the difference of long-run e_{DF}^l and its log short run e_{DF} exchange rates: $\dot{e}_{DF} = \varphi(e_{DF}^l - e_{DF})$. Thus, for money market equilibrium:

$$\frac{M_D}{P_D} = L(Y_D, r_D), \quad \text{where} \quad L(Y_D, r_D) = (Y_D)^\beta e^{-\alpha r_D}$$

Using natural logarithm prices, with $p_D = \ln P_D$, we set

$$\ln(M_D) - p_D = \beta \ln(Y_D) - \alpha r_D, \quad \alpha > 0, \ \beta > 0$$

A combination of these two models (UIP and money market) yields

$$\ln(M_D) - p_D = \beta \ln(Y_D) - \alpha r_F - \alpha \varphi(e_{DF}^l - e_{DF})$$

In a long-run equilibrium, we assume a stationary money supply, equal interest rates ($r_D = r_F$), and a given output at full employment. Then, letting a zero rate of change in the exchange rate ($e_{DF}^l - e_{DF} = 0$), the long-term price as $p_D^l = \ln(M_D) - \beta \ln(Y_D) + \alpha r_F$ is determined.[8]

Based on these relationships and definitions, an exchange rate dynamic model for a long-run equilibrium is defined as a function of price as follows:

$$\dot{e}_{DF} = \frac{p_D - p_D^l}{\alpha} \quad \text{or} \quad \varphi(e_{DF}^l - e_{DF}) = \frac{p_D - p_D^l}{\alpha} \quad \text{or} \quad e_{DF} = e_{DF}^l - \frac{p_D - p_D^l}{\alpha\varphi}$$

Introducing the goods market, the following domestic demand function is used:

$$\ln D = \gamma + \varrho(e - p_D) + \tau \ln Y_D - \eta r_D$$

where D denotes the domestic output demand, γ is a shift parameter, e is the exchange rate, p_D is the price for domestic goods, r_D is the domstetic interest rate, Y_D is the real income, and a parameter ϱ is used to highlight the effect of the difference in exchange rate and demand price. The rate of change in the price is defined as $\dot{p} = \lambda \ln(D/Y_D)$ and equals to zero in the long run. Substituting the $\ln D$ function into $\dot{p} = \lambda \ln(D/Y_D) = 0$ provides the long-run equilibrium exchange rate assuming of $r_D = r_F$, whose model is defined as follows:

$$e_{DF}^l = p_D^l + (1/\varrho)[\eta r_F + (1-\tau)\ln Y_D - \gamma]$$

Overshooting of the exchange rate in the short run results in an expansionary monetary policy shown by the impact of the changes in $\ln(M)$ on e as follows, depending on an expectation coefficient φ and interest response of money α:[9]

$$\frac{de}{d\ln(M)} = 1 + \frac{1}{\varphi\alpha}$$

5.6.2.1.1 Adjustment Process

Following Dornbusch (1976), we present the adjustment process of the country and the effect of the monetary policy on the exchange rate movements as illustrated in Figure 5.5. It is based on the relationship between the exchange rate e and price p derived from the aforementioned dynamics of the exchange rate, where e_{DF} is a function of e_{DF}^l, p_D, and p_D^l. The asset market equilibrium (arbitrage of expected yields and money market equilibrium) is shown by a downward-sloped N curve in Figure 5.5. We assume that an economy is initially at point A_1, which represents the equilibrium in the long run with long-run p_{D1}^l and e_{DF1}^l. While the asset market clears in the short run through instant adjustment of the FX rates, the goods equilibrium is reached only in the long run through changes in prices.

We consider an expansionary monetary policy. When money supply increases, the N curve shifts to the right to maintain the equilibrium in the asset market. As a result, a new equilibrium (long run) is set at point A_3 with higher price and FX rate (with

---

8 For extension of the model with goods market, and illustration of the exchange rate overshooting under rational expectations and sticky prices, refer to Gandolfo (2001: chapter 15).

9 For further discussion of the overshooting with rational expectations and the extent of the overshooting depending on the coefficients is provided in Dornbusch (1976: 1169–1170).

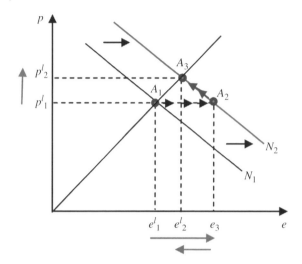

Figure 5.5 Monetary policy under Dornbusch overshooting model.

long-run p'_{D2} and e'_{DF2}) compared with the point A_1. Note that in this analysis an increase in e shows depreciation, whereas a decrease in e indicates appreciation. The adjustment process involves movements from A_1 to A_2 (market equilibrium in the short run), then from A_2 to A_3 (market equilibrium in the long run). We consider the first adjustment where an increase in money supply leads to a fall in the interest rate as well as expected depreciation of the long-run exchange. As a result, capital outflow increases and causes the FX rate to depreciate. These changes in turn cause the relative price to decline and demand to exceed supply of goods. The next adjustment occurs with the need to reduce this excess demand through a cut in the price. This would reduce the real money stock and increase the interest rate, which in turn would attract more capital into the economy. As a result, exchange rate appreciation occurs and the net expected yield is maintained. These causal relationships between the underlying variables of the adjustments, where M is money supply, r_D is domestic interest rate, K is capital, e is exchange rate, p is price, and D is demand, are outlined as follows:

1st adjustment $(A_1 \text{ to } A_2)$

$M \uparrow \; \to r_D \downarrow \; \to$ expectation of $e \uparrow \; \to K$ outflow $\uparrow \; \to e \uparrow$ (depreciation)

$r_D \downarrow$ and $e \uparrow \; \to$ relative $p \downarrow \; \to$ excess D (goods)

2nd adjustment $(A_2 \text{ to } A_3)$

$P \uparrow \; \to (M/P) \downarrow \; \to r_D \uparrow \; \to K$ inflow $\uparrow \; \to e \downarrow$ (appreciation)

$\to$ net expected yield is maintained

Questions and Problems 5.7

Show, using a graph, the effect of the tight monetary policy on the exchange rate under the Dornbusch model of the exchange rate overshooting. Explain the adjustment process.

5.6.2.2 Discussion: Empirical Evidence on the Overshooting Model

There is a vast literature on the Dornbusch overshooting model, as reviewed in Obstfeld and Rogoff (1995, 2000). A few empirical studies have found results consistent with the Dornbusch overshooting hypothesis for the exchange rate. However, a number of studies regarding interactions between monetary policy and exchange rate were not able to substantiate the overshooting hypothesis. Two puzzles arose in these empirical studies: forward discount bias puzzle (delayed overshooting) and exchange rate puzzle. Eichenbaum and Evans (1995) showed the first puzzle (the forward rate is a biased predictor) using an unrestricted vector autoregressive (VAR) methodology: the USD showed a persistent and long overshooting of 2–3 years following monetary contraction in the USA. The second puzzle occurs when the real exchange rate depreciates in response to tight monetary policy shocks (see Sims (1992)).

Recent studies use a further development of the VAR approach imposing different restrictions on the exchange rate. A structural VAR (with non-recursive contemporaneous restrictions) is used in an open economy study by Kim and Roubini (2000). In their study of six countries (Germany, Japan, the UK, France, Italy, Canada), the exchange rate puzzle was not found. Furthermore, they showed that the exchange rate appreciates first as a result of the tight monetary policy, but a few months later the exchange rate depreciates (following the UIP).

5.6.3 The Real Interest Differential Theory

Frankel (1979) developed a real interest differential model of the exchange rate combining the assumptions of theories by Frenkel and Bilson, and Dornbusch (1976); namely, monetary equilibrium in the long run, "secular rates of inflation," and "sticky price." In addition to the assumptions that the UIP and the long-run PPP conditions hold, this model assumes that expected change in the exchange rate is determined not only by the difference between its current exchange rate and its equilibrium rate (as in Dornbusch), but also by the expected inflation differential in the long term:

$$\dot{e}_{DF} = \varphi\left(e_{DF}^l - e_{DF}\right) + \left(\pi_D^c - \pi_F^c\right)$$

In Frankel (1979), the exchange rate is explained by the relative money supply, relative income, a differential in the interest rates (with a negative coefficient), and a differential in the expected inflation in the long run (with a positive coefficient) between the two countries (as shown by the next equation). Empirical results of the model using monthly data for mark/dollar exchange rate between 1974 and 1978 show a significantly negative coefficient of ϑ and a significantly positive coefficient of μ.

$$\ln(\xi_{DF}) = \ln(M_D/M_F) - \beta \ln(Y_D/Y_F) - \vartheta(r_D - r_F) + \mu\left(\pi_D^c - \pi_F^c\right)$$

5.6.4 Present-Value Models: Complete and Incomplete Markets

Present-value models are based on rational expectations of FX prices, using a number of economic factors and an expectation of future FX rates. These factors are called FX rate fundamentals as they presumably define basic determinants of FX rates. These models are also tailored to provide tools and rules for central banks to better manage monetary policy and FX rates. The Taylor rule provides an interface between short-term (nominal and real) interest rates and macroeconomic conditions. A similar rule was applied recently in the USA to justify its use of a quantitative easing policy and to augment financial liquidity. These rule-models recognize the interdependency between countries' interest rates differentials and their macroeconomic factors. There are a number of variations of these models, based on their usage of the nominal and real FX rates. Some of these models are summarized in the following.[10]

These models are derived from the basic equation

$$M_t^D = P_t^D \left(Y_t^D\right)^\gamma e^{-ar_t^D + \tilde{v}_t^D} \quad \text{and} \quad M_t^F = P_t^F \left(Y_t^F\right)^\gamma e^{-ar_t^F + \tilde{v}_t^F}$$

where, by PPP, the FX rate is $\tilde{\xi}_{DF}(t) = \left(P_t^D / P_t^F\right) e^{\tilde{\varepsilon}_t^D}$, with $\tilde{\varepsilon}_t^D$ a normally distributed error term. By symmetry, we also have $\tilde{\xi}_{FD}(t) = \left(P_t^F / P_t^D\right) e^{\tilde{\varepsilon}_t^F}$. A logarithm transformation yields

$$e_{DF}(t) = \ln\left(\tilde{\xi}_{DF}(t)\right) = \ln\left(P_t^D\right) - \ln\left(P_t^F\right) + \tilde{\varepsilon}_t^D$$

$$e_{FD}(t) = -e_{DF}(t) = \ln\left(\tilde{\xi}_{FD}(t)\right) = \ln\left(P_t^F\right) - \ln\left(P_t^D\right) + \tilde{\varepsilon}_t^F$$

Thus, $\tilde{e}_{DF}(t) = \tilde{e}(t) = p_t^D - p_t^F + \tilde{\varepsilon}_t$, where $\tilde{\varepsilon}_t = \tilde{\varepsilon}_t^D = -\tilde{\varepsilon}_t^F$. As a result, for two consecutive periods, we have

$$\tilde{e}(t) = p_t^D - p_t^F + \tilde{\varepsilon}_t$$

$$\tilde{e}(t+1) = p_{t+1}^D - p_{t+1}^F + \tilde{\varepsilon}_{t+1}$$

$$\Delta\tilde{e}(t+1) = \tilde{e}(t+1) - \tilde{e}(t) = \left(p_{t+1}^D - p_t^D\right) - \left(p_{t+1}^F - p_t^F\right) + \left(\tilde{\varepsilon}_{t+1} - \tilde{\varepsilon}_t\right)$$

And therefore

$$\Delta\tilde{e}(t+1) = \Delta p_{t+1}^D - \Delta p_{t+1}^F + \Delta\tilde{\varepsilon}_{t+1}$$

Note that $\Delta\tilde{e}(t+1)$ is a ROR in the FX rate, since

$$\Delta\tilde{e}(t+1) \approx d\ln\xi(t) = \frac{d\xi(t)}{\xi(t)} = R_{t+1}^\xi,$$

$$\text{as well as } \Delta p_{t+1}^k \approx d\ln P_t^k = \frac{d P_t^k}{P_t^k} = r_t^k \quad (k = D \text{ and } F)$$

Thus, under rational expectations (namely, complete markets), we have with a filtration $\mathfrak{I}_t$ at time t of

$$E_t(\Delta\tilde{e}(t+1)|\mathfrak{I}_t)) = E_t\left(R_{t+1}^\xi|\mathfrak{I}_t\right) = r_t^D - r_t^F - \tilde{\delta}_t$$

Next take the natural logarithm of $M_t^D = P_t^D\left(Y_t^D\right)^\gamma e^{-ar_t^D + \tilde{v}_t^D}$ and $M_t^F = P_t^F\left(Y_t^F\right)^\gamma e^{-ar_t^F + \tilde{v}_t^F}$:

$$m_t^D = \ln\left(M_t^D\right) = \ln\left(P_t^D\right) + \gamma\ln\left(Y_t^D\right) - ar_t^D + \tilde{v}_t^D = p_t^D + \gamma y_t^D - ar_t^D + \tilde{v}_t^D$$

$$m_t^F = \ln\left(M_t^F\right) = \ln\left(P_t^F\right) + \gamma\ln\left(Y_t^F\right) - ar_t^F + \tilde{v}_t^F = p_t^F + \gamma y_t^F - ar_t^F + \tilde{v}_t^F$$

Subtracting one from the other, we have

$$m_t^D - m_t^F = p_t^D - p_t^F + \gamma\left(y_t^D - y_t^F\right) - \alpha\left(r_t^D - r_t^F - \frac{\tilde{v}_t^D - \tilde{v}_t^F}{\alpha}\right), \quad \tilde{\delta}_t = \frac{\tilde{v}_t^D - \tilde{v}_t^F}{\alpha}$$

---

10 For further study, see Obstfeld and Rogoff (1996).

Or:

$$\alpha\left(r_t^{D} - r_t^{F} - \tilde{\delta}_t\right) = \left(p_t^{D} - p_t^{F}\right) + \gamma\left(y_t^{D} - y_t^{F}\right) - \left(m_t^{D} - m_t^{F}\right)$$

In other words:

$$e(t) = \ln\left(\frac{P_t^{D}}{P_t^{F}}\right) = E_t\left(R_{t+1}^{\xi}|\mathfrak{T}_t\right) - \gamma\left(y_t^{D} - y_t^{F}\right) + \left(m_t^{D} - m_t^{F}\right)$$

In other words, we obtain the external balance model:

$$e(t) = E_t\left(R_{t+1}^{\xi}|\mathfrak{T}_t\right) + f_t, \quad f_t = -\gamma\left(y_t^{D} - y_t^{F}\right) + \left(m_t^{D} - m_t^{F}\right)$$

This model prices the logarithm of FX rate by the expected future ROR in the FX rate plus the macroeconomic factors defined by $f_t = \ln F_t$, with

$$F_t = \left(\frac{M_t^{D}}{M_t^{F}}\right)\left(\frac{Y_t^{D}}{Y_t^{F}}\right)^{-\gamma}$$

An explicit price for the current FX is thus

$$\xi_{DF}(t) = \left(\frac{M_t^{D}}{M_t^{F}}\right)\left(\frac{Y_t^{D}}{Y_t^{F}}\right)^{-\gamma} e^{E_t\left(R_{t+1}^{\xi}|\mathfrak{T}_t\right)}$$

These models allow us to focus greater attention on the requirements of international solvency and international portfolio choices as they relate to FX rates. Extensions of these models provide a weighting scheme between the FX expectations' future rates of returns and the effects of the macroeconomic factors:

$$e(t) = bE_t\left(R_{t+1}^{\xi}|\mathfrak{T}_t\right) + (1-b)f_t, \quad b = \lambda/(1+\lambda)$$

Iterating this model, we have

$$e(t) = (1-b)E_t\left(\sum_{i=0}^{k-1} b^i f_{t+i}|\mathfrak{T}_t\right) + b^k E_t\left(R_{t+1}^{\xi}|\mathfrak{T}_t\right)$$

Assuming an infinite past, this is reduced to

$$e(t) = (1-b)E_t\left(\sum_{i=0}^{\infty} b^i f_{t+i}|\mathfrak{T}_t\right)$$

5.7 Conclusions

In this chapter we have outlined and assessed both the theoretical and empirical implications of PPP to determine the exchange rate, and showed their empirical applications and their analysis performed by numerous authors. As these studies indicate, price differentials may not explain a large proportion of changes in exchange rates. In practice, the principle of parity is viewed as a long-term relationship rather than a short one, reflecting the necessary economic adjustments that countries have to implement to reach a state of economic equilibrium. As this is often the case in reality, the presumption that FX currency markets are complete (in a financial sense, and therefore in economic equilibrium) is often criticized. Interventions, wage and price controls, transaction costs, incentives, rare and unpredictable events, as well as political and other risks, render such markets incomplete (at least in the short run) and therefore difficult to price. However, the PPP model is still applied within economic theories, and there is some empirical validation, especially for significantly long time horizons. A deviation from PPP is explained with a Balassa–Samuelson effect: higher prices in industrial countries compared with emerging economies.

FX models, especially the asset approach based on the interest rate parity, were examined. While CIP considers a pricing of forward and spot FX contracts, UIP assumes that expected changes in the FX rate are determined by the interest rate differential in two countries. If both the UIP and PPP conditions hold, we could then derive the RIP through the Fisher equation; real interest rate is determined by the nominal interest rate and inflation rate. We discussed empirical evidence on how parities fail to hold while analyzing the monetary approach by referring to the Frenkel–Mussa model, as well as Bilson's (1978) approach, where money market equilibrium with money demand and supply set the exchange rate. Very often, in empirical testing, both asset and monetary approaches are unified. We looked at empirical studies on the relationship between the exchange rate movement and the economic fundamental variables in this chapter.

Finally, we noted that, in international macroeconomic and financial models, prices of both tradable goods and nontradable ones play an important role in determining the real exchange rate and international competitiveness. We referred to the early studies by Balassa (1964) and Samuelson (1964), where relative prices were emphasized. Variants of these models, both in the supply side (total factor productivity corresponding to technological changes) and demand approaches were used. The empirical literature provides ample evidence on the relative price of nontradables as one of the fundamental determinants of the real exchange rate and highlight their comovements. We also discussed the Dornbusch exchange rate overshooting model, which is described as one of the most influential work (see Rogoff (2002)), and its empirical testing for the explanations of the high variances of the FX rates.

Appendix 5.A: Suggested Empirical Work for Econometric and Statistical Analysis

1) Calculate RORs for exchange rate (nominal and real) and prices (CPI) for different countries.
2) Do the statistical summary of macroeconomic, financial, international indicators for different countries.
3) Calculate correlations between macroeconomic, international, and financial variables.
4) Using OLS estimation, test hypotheses for PPP and test whether absolute and relative PPPs hold.
5) Use lags, instrumental variables, and trending variables to explain the PPP.
6) Conduct a unit root test (ADF) for stationarity of real exchange rate.

7) Use cointegration model (Engle–Granger test) to test the validity of PPP in the long term.

8) Analyze trends and seasonality of FX rates, trending variables, detrending of the high-frequency FX rates, and conduct multifractal detrended fluctuation analysis for FX rates.

9) Forecast exchange rates using autoregressive (AR) models, conduct threshold AR, AR–moving average model.

10) Using time series test for serial correlation (using t-test for AR(1), the Durbin–Watson test).

11) Test for heteroscedasticity (the White tests); weighted least square estimates.

12) Conduct autoregressive conditional heteroscedasticity (ARCH), generalized ARCH (GARCH), and their extensions.

13) Using panel data, conduct Chow test for structural change.

14) Using OLS estimation, test hypotheses for FX models: test whether interest parity holds for CIP and UIP.

15) Determine stationary and nonstationary time series using macroeconomic variables, including money supply, output, inflation, and exchange rate.

16) SUR estimation: using data on tradable/nontradable sectors assess the Ballasa–Samuelson model.

17) Conduct a unit root test (ADF) for monetary approach of the exchange rate.

18) Cointegration model: use Engle–Granger test for monetary approach of the exchange rate.

19) Using generalized least squares (GLS) technique, estimate monetary model by Frenkel–Bilson.

20) Use maximum likelihood estimation for cointegration in monetary model of exchange rate.

21) Use VAR approach for testing the Dornbusch exchange rate overshooting model.

22) Using system-generalized method of moment (GMM) method and panel data, forecast exchange rate dynamics and its volatility.

23) Estimate a logit or probit model (probability model) for currency crisis.

References

Backus, D. and Smith, G. (1993) Consumption and real exchange rates in dynamic economies with non-traded goods. *Journal of International Economics*, **35**(3–4): 297–316.

Balassa, B. (1964) The purchasing power parity doctrine: a reappraisal. *Journal of Political Economy*, **72**: 584–596.

Bilson, J.F.O. (1978) The monetary approach to the exchange rate: some empirical evidence. *Staff Papers (International Monetary Fund)*, **25**(1): 48–75.

Burnside, C., Eichenbaum, M., Kleshchelski, I., and Rebelo, S. (2006) The returns to currency speculation. National Bureau of Economic Research, Working Paper No. 12489.

Cagan, P. (1956) The monetary dynamics of hyperinflation. In *Studies in the Quantity Theory of Money*, M. Friedman (ed.). University of Chicago Press: Chicago, IL; pp. 25–117.

Cerra, V. and Saxena, S.C. (2010) The monetary model strikes back: evidence from the world. *Journal of International Economics*, **81**: 184–196.

Chinn, M.D. and Frankel, J.A. (1995) Who drives real interest rates around the Pacific Rim: the USA or Japan? *Journal of International Money and Finance*, **14**: 801–821.

Cumby, R.E. and Obstfeld, M. (1984) International interest rate and price level linkages under flexible exchange rates: a review of recent evidence. In *Exchange Rate Theory and Practice*, J. Bilson and R.C. Marston (eds). University of Chicago Press, Chicago, IL; pp. 121–151.

De Gregorio, J., Giovannini, A., and Wolf, H. (1994) International evidence on tradables and nontradables inflation. *European Economic Review*, **38**: 1225–-1244.

Dornbusch, R. (1976) Expectations and exchange rate dynamics. *Journal of Political Economy*, **84**: 1161–1176.

Eichenbaum, M. and Evans, C. (1995) Some empirical evidence on the effects of shocks to monetary policy on exchange rates. *Quarterly Journal of Economics*, **110**: 975–1010.

Engel, C. (2014) Exchange rates and interest parity. In *Handbook of International Economics*, vol. 4, G. Gopinath, E. Helpman, and K. Rogoff (eds). Elsevier; pp. 453–522.

Engle, R.F. and Granger, C.W.J. (1987) Co-integration and error correction: representation, estimation and testing. *Econometrica*, **55**: 251–276.

Fama, E.F. (1984) Forward and spot exchange rates. *Journal of Monetary Economics*, **14**: 319–338.

Feenstra, R.C., Robert I., and Timmer M.P. (2015) The next generation of the Penn World Table. *American Economic Review*, **105**(10): 3150–3182. (See www.ggdc.net/pwt.)

Frankel, J.A. (1979) On the mark: a theory of floating exchange rates based on real interest differentials. *American Economic Review*, **69**: 610–622.

Frankel, J.A. (1984) Tests of monetary and portfolio balance models of exchange rate determination. In *Exchange Rate Theory and Practice*, J.F.O. Bilson and R.C. Marston (eds). University of Chicago Press.

Frenkel, J.A. (1976) A monetary approach to the exchange rate: doctrinal aspects and empirical evidence. *Scandinavian Journal of Economics*, **78**(2): 200–224.

Frenkel, J.A. (1981) The collapse of purchasing power parities during the 1970's. *European Economic Review*, **16**: 145–165.

Froot, A.K. and Rogoff, K. (1995) Perspectives on PPP and long-run real exchange rates. In *Handbook of International Economics*, vol. 3, G.M. Grossman and K. Rogoff. Elsevier; pp. 1647–1688.

Gandolfo, G. (2001) *International Finance and Open-Economy Macroeconomics*. Springer.

Groen, J.J.J. (2000) The monetary exchange rate model as a long-run phenomenon. *Journal of International Economics*, **52**: 299–319.

IMF. International Financial Statistics. http://elibrarydata.imf.org/finddatareports.aspx?d=33061&e=169393. Accessed May 18, 2014.

Jensen, B. and Kletzer, L. (2005) Tradable services: understanding the scope and impact of services offshoring. *Brookings Trade Forum, Offshoring White-Collar Work*, 75–133.

Kim, S. and Roubini, N. (2000) Exchange rate anomalies in the industrial countries: a solution with a structural VAR approach. *Journal of Monetary Economics*, **45**: 561–586.

Kravis, L. and Lipsey, R. (1983) *Toward an Explanation of National Price Levels*. Princeton Studies in International Finance, No. 52. Princeton University Press.

Meese, R. and Rogoff, K. (1988) Was it real? The Exchange rate interest differential relation over the modern floating exchange rate period. *Journal of Finance*, **43**: 933–948.

Mishkin, F.S. (1984) Are real interest rates equal across countries? An empirical investigation of international parity conditions. *Journal of Finance*, **39**: 1345–1357.

Mussa, M. (1976) The exchange rate, the balance of payments and monetary and fiscal policy under a regime of controlled floating. *Scandinavian Journal of Economics*, **78**(2): 229–248.

Mussa, M. (1979) Empirical regularities in the behavior of exchange rates and theories of the foreign exchange market. *Carnegie-Rochester Conference Series on Public Policy*, **11**: 9–57.

Obstfeld, M. (1993) Modeling trending real exchange rates. Working Paper No. C93-011, Center for International and Development Economics Research, University of California, Berkeley.

Obstfeld, M. and Rogoff, K. (1995) Exchange rate dynamics redux. *Journal of Political Economy*, **103**: 624–660.

Obstfeld, M. and Rogoff, K. (1996) *Foundations of International Macroeconomics*. The MIT Press.

Obstfeld, M. and Rogoff, K. (2000) New directions for stochastic open economy models. *Journal of International Economics*, **50**: 117–153.

OECD. Prices and purchasing power parities (PPP). http://www.oecd.org/std/prices-ppp/.

Rogoff, K. (1992) Traded goods consumption smoothing and the random walk behavior of the real exchange rate. *Bank of Japan Monetary and Economic Studies*, **10**: 1–29.

Rogoff, K. (2002) Dornbusch's overshooting model after twenty-five years. IMF Working Paper. 02/39.

Samuelson, P. (1964) Theoretical notes on trade problems. *Review of Economics and Statistics*, **46**: 145–164.

Sims, C.A. (1992) Interpreting the macroeconomic time series facts: the effects of monetary policy. *European Economic Review*, **36**: 975–1011.

The World Bank. 2014. International Comparison Program (ICP). World Bank: Washington DC. http://icp.worldbank.org/. Accessed June 28, 2014.

6

Asia

Financial Environment and Risks

Motivation

Asia's economies have fueled the expansion of globalization and are assuming an ever larger role in global finance. This chapter provides an overview and a perspective on Asia's financial and economic development, emphasizing the structures underlying its growth and its contribution to global finance. These include increased trade, currency usage, foreign investment, and the development of a banking sector and bond and stock markets. In this chapter, we feature Asian capital and equity markets and outline different approaches to measure and evaluate the investment and the risks that Asia's financial industry is facing. Additionally, a detailed discussion of China and Japan is presented. For China, we highlight the importance of the banking sector, the role of state-owned enterprises, and the challenges facing equity and bond markets, with an emphasis on rising debt. For Japan, in addition to the banking sector, issues related to the effectiveness of corporate governance, the importance of industrial companies, and the volatility of its government bonds are discussed.

6.1   Introduction

Asia's nations differ broadly in their degree of economic and financial development, as well as in their social, political, religious, cultural, ethnic, linguistic, and geographical properties. Their combined economic activities have contributed to an increase in a global output, trade, consumption, and demand, and supply by providing new sources of raw material, labor, and capital. These elements have underwritten a substantial financial activity, innovation in financial products, and the expansion of global financial markets. Beyond their growth, we address questions such as: What does it mean for investors? What are the risk implications for businesses investing in Asia? What risk measures and models we may use?

Asian economic expansion emerged in the 1960s, when Asia's economic growth pace outperformed the Western industrial economies. For example, in Japan, a GDP growth rate of 10%, which occurred between 1955 and 1973, was typical. Further, the emergence of Newly Industrialized Asian Economies (NIAEs) consisting of Hong Kong (SAR), South Korea, Singapore, and Taiwan (also known as the "Four Tigers" or "Little Dragons") has added a dynamic and changing economic environment. Their development involved large foreign direct investment (FDI) inflows, active mergers and acquisitions

Globalization, Gating, and Risk Finance, First Edition. Unurjargal Nyambuu and Charles S. Tapiero.
© 2018 John Wiley & Sons Ltd. Published 2018 by John Wiley & Sons Ltd.

(M&A) activities, and an economic and financial restructuring, maturing in 2001. These changes led to the emergence of Hong Kong (SAR) as a hub of global business and a bridge to China's huge economic potential. Economic liberalization grew hand in hand with trade and foreign investment policies. Further, domestic rules were made to attract investments in sustainable development. Capitalizing on its geographical proximity to Asia's emerging "Tigers," Japan has become both a major trade partner of Asian economies and concurrently leveraged its new economic and financial clout as a viable competitor in global markets. Simultaneously, a gradual political and economic liberalization in China has allowed it to become the second largest economy in the world, and thereby a global economic and financial powerhouse to be reckoned with. The implication of these developments point to the importance of:

- macroeconomic and financial factors defining the economic positioning of Asia;
- management of economic and financial risks necessary to assure the safety of exchanges, sustainability of trade, and the gradual liberalization of Asia's economies;
- economic size, currency, and the entities defining global finance and the emergence of selective and gated exchanges.

Asia's industrial and labor productivity, spearheaded by global outsourcing and free exchange across national boundaries, have further contributed to a realignment of the global economy growing now out of industrial upheavals, networked trade, and developments in international supply chain management. In addition, it has promoted a multipolar and interdependent economic and financial landscapes. This has, in turn, generated not only global growth, but also global financial entities with contagion risks it is subject to. For example, the demise of Lehman Brothers, a sprawling global investment bank, in September 2008, almost brought down the world's financial system by affecting the US economy and mutating the financial crisis into a European crisis. The effects of this crisis were global and, ex-post, contagious and with global risks which could have been predicted (and may have been known). The complacency of financial regulators, the misplaced trust in financial engineering and lack of attention to risk assessment, and the expansion of global liquidity through low borrowing costs (interest rates) are but some of the factors that led to the global financial meltdown. At the same time, it has allowed Asia's economic influence to assume new and global proportions, and acquire a new role in the world financial system.

Asia's economic clout, expressed by its volume of trade and financial flows, is now meaningful on a global scale. FDI inflows to Asia have accounted for more than two-thirds (68%) of the total FDI inflows in developing economies, in contrast to other parts of the world; for example, Africa accounts for only 9% (although increasing quickly), and Latin America and Caribbean countries 22% in 2016 (UNCTAD, 2017). Expansion rates in recent years also point to more aggressive investments in these countries originating in Asia's economies. As a result:

- Asian economies have matured, and have thus expanded their global presence, replacing and competing with developed economies long settled into their own parts of the world. Current attempts to institute currency baskets as an alternative to the US dollar dominance in trade constitute an example.
- Economic inflows and outflows are expanding, in tune with Asia's global trade and political outreach; for example, massive investments by China in Africa, in Latin America, in the USA, and in the rest of the world.

- Financial-capital markets in Asia have expanded hand in hand with their need for capital investments and financial liquidity. In politically stable regions, newly found economic and self-serving financial hubs and markets have emerged. These trends are, in some cases, confronted by protection and tax policies in developing economies. However, in some cases (e.g., US tariffs and China's dollar holdings) they are actually ushering in an era of gated economies in a globalized world, with preferential and reciprocal agreements, that raise future uncertainties and the prospects of currency and trade wars.

For Asia's development, the liberalization of its financial markets, a stronger banking system, and better control of all forms of debt are needed to boost competitiveness and efficiency. Learning from the consequences of the recent slowdown in developing economies, together with rising debt (especially in China between 2015 and 2017 and the downgrading of China's and Hong Kong's ratings by Moody's in May 2017), risk management is seen to be an essential part of the process. The high yields demanded for sovereign bonds issued by emerging markets constitute further evidence of Asia's increased default risk. Thus, China intends to highlight its financial market reforms, liberalized interest and exchange rate policies, and internationalization of the yuan as a global payment and reserve currency (inclusion of yuan in special drawing rights in October 2016). In addition, a gradual opening of the capital account, accelerated a bond market development, and deregulation in support of greater private sector participation in the economy are all being debated. These policies are likely to contribute to the integration of Asian economies into the world financial system. Previously mentioned intentions were further promulgated in 2017 following the election of the US President, who was calling for US gating policies to be strengthened. These and other factors are underlying the future evolution of global finance, its profitability, and the risk spectrum of world trade.

In order to simplify this chapter's presentation, we will focus our attention on the financial sector, feature diverse capital and equity markets in both developed and developing Asia, and emphasize the particular importance of both China and Japan.

6.2 Driving Engines of Economic Growth in Asia

The rapid economic growth in Asia since the 1990s was due to its openness to trade and investments in the global economy, a high level of savings, export-led growth emphasizing manufacturing, a dynamic agricultural sector, human capital investments, macroeconomic stability, as well as the comparative advantage of low wages and a disciplined labor force. Further, it has also emphasized a gradual shift from labor-intensive or resource-intensive industrial policy to capital-intensive industries.

As a result, Asia's GDP share in the world increased rapidly since the 1970s, while advanced countries' and the EU's GDP shares have declined. Explicitly, an emerging and developing Asia's GDP share has surged from around 7% in 1991 to 21% in 2015, and it is expected to rise to 26% in 2021 (IMF, 2016a). Further, living standards of Asian residents have improved dramatically in terms of GDP per capita. For example, from around $100 in China,[1] $300 in South Korea, and $400 in Malaysia in 1970 to almost $8000, $27 000, and $10 000 respectively in 2015 (The World Bank, 2016).

---

1 Data for China throughout the chapter indicate mainland China. Data for Hong Kong SAR are shown separately.

Asia's economies, according to the KOF index of globalization (http://globalization. kof.ethz.ch/) released in 2016, have become more globalized economically, socially, and politically. For example, Singapore is placed 20th, Malaysia 31st, Japan 39th, and China 71st by the overall globalization index in year 2014. However, their index of economic globalization, measured by cross-border trade, investment and income flows, and restrictions on capital flows and trade, is higher for some Asian economies but lower for others: Singapore is ranked 1st, Malaysia 35th, but Japan is 78th and China 121st.

6.2.1 International Trade

Intra-trade of Asian economies, as well as trade with the USA and the EU, has also increased significantly. The trade matrix in Table 6.1 shows the size and the direction of foreign trade in 2015 and in 1990 (the upper right triangle of the matrix represents exports, whereas the lower left triangle shows imports). For example, China's (mainland) exports have increased significantly (to the USA $410.8 billion, to the EU $356.6 billion, to Asian developing countries $310.2 billion, and to Japan $135.9 billion). The USA has massive trade deficits, especially with Asian developing countries.

China's trade with other Asian countries exceeds its trade with the USA or the EU (see Table 6.1). This is also the case for Japan and South Korea. An increased interdependence of Asian countries in terms of trade highlights the need for more cooperation. For example, the role of the Asian Infrastructure Investment Bank (AIIB), recently set to finance infrastructure that will lead to higher regional economic growth, improve living standards in many Asian countries, facilitate trade and its financing among Asian countries, and reduce cross-border trades' logistic costs through an advanced infrastructure and transportation networks such as the high-speed Silk Road.

6.2.2 Exchange Rate

As trade and financial exchanges grow, sovereign states' FX rates assume a growing importance. Many Asian countries have adopted a managed floating system mainly to solve the problem of exchange rate volatility. In other words, by their interventions in FX markets, they seek to stabilize and correct overvalued or undervalued currencies. Similarly, some Asian economies conduct auctions for selling or buying FX in a transparent framework to manage their foreign reserves and risks, and to influence the price of their FX rates. A general trend engages Asian economies toward an FX liberalization, however. A weakening of their BOP in the last few years has led to an increased pressure to depreciate their currencies, resulting in FX mutual interventions to deal with capital flows and volatility.[2] The majority of Asian currencies pegged to a single currency (e.g., USD) or a basket of currencies limits their abilities to affect their FX, however. For this reason, Asian countries may practice alternative exchange rate regimes, as summarized in the following.

- Advanced Asian countries (e.g., Japan) exercises *free floating* arrangements by allowing their currencies to float freely against other currencies.

---

2 See Chapter 1 for further discussion on fragile five economies, including Asian economies such as Indonesia, as well as devaluation of the Chinese yuan in August 2015.

Table 6.1 Asia's trade within Asia, with the EU, and with the USA; 1990 versus 2015 (billion USD).

Imports from	China (mainland)	Hong Kong, SAR	Japan	South Korea	India	Asia (developing)	EU	USA
						Exports to		
2015								
China (mainland)		332.7	135.9	101.4	58.3	310.2	356.6	410.8
Hong Kong, SAR	8.2		15.9	7.0	13.1	292.9	43.3	44.3
Japan	142.7	2.7		44.0	8.1	197.7	66.0	126.4
South Korea	174.3	0.1	26.8		12.0	219.2	48.6	70.1
India	13.4	0.006	4.9	4.2		43.8	44.9	40.4
Asia (developing)	181.5	0.03	260.1	132.6	8.7			669.5
EU	209.0	0.00005	71.2	57.2	0.01			426.1
USA	144.9	0.0006	68.3	44.2	5.4	186.3	274.1	
1990								
China (mainland)		27.2	9.2	0.4	0.2	2.6	6.6	5.3
Hong Kong, SAR	14.6		4.7	1.9	0.3	24.8	15.4	19.8
Japan	7.7	0.002		17.5	1.7	32.3	59.8	91.1
South Korea	0.2	0.0	11.7		0.4	4.3	10.2	19.4
India	0.1	0.01	2.1	1.6		0.9	5.1	2.7
Asia (developing)	2.4	5.6	41.5	4.7	1.0			39.5
EU	9.8	35.6	38.3	9.1	8.1			104.6
USA	6.6	0.0	52.8	0.01	2.6	18.8	104.7	

Source: Data from IMF.

The upper right triangle of each matrix shows exports; the lower-left triangle shows imports. *Exports* of a country (fixed row) to a counterparty country are shown in the corresponding column. For example, in 2015, China exported to Hong Kong, SAR (332.7), Japan (135.9), South Korea (101.4), India (58.3), Asia (developing) (310.2), EU (356.6), and the USA (410.8). *Imports* of a country (fixed column) from a counterparty country are shown in the corresponding row. For example, China imported from Hong Kong, SAR (8.2), Japan (142.7), South Korea (174.3), India (13.4), Asia (developing) (181.5), EU (209), and the US (144.9) in 2015.

- Indonesia, South Korea, Philippines, and Thailand have adopted a *floating* exchange rate as they only intervene in their FX market exceptionally and only for short, controlled periods, mainly to avoid undue volatility.
- Hong Kong (SAR) maintains a national currency, but its currency is permanently pegged to the USD.

- Remaining Asian countries adopt a mixture of fixed and floating exchange rate regimes. For example, Singapore features the BBC system—band, basket, and crawl (slope).

6.2.2.1 Global Economic Indexes and Market Volatility

The impact of global financial indexes and market volatility (e.g., the CBOE volatility index (VIX)) on Asia's exchange rates differs across countries depending on their exchange rate regimes and the degree of financial market liberalization. Exchange rates in fully liberalized financial markets (e.g., Japan and Singapore) are affected by global economic indexes and macro-statistics such as US Treasury yield rate and VIX. As shown in Figure 6.1, most Asian currencies have become considerably volatile, moving in response to changes in global markets. In particular, the currencies of Indonesia and Malaysia reached their lowest levels in 2015 since the Asian financial crisis of 1997 (following the collapse of resource prices and lower commodity demand concurrent with a slower growth in China). Although a weak currency boosts exports, it increases the debt burden of the sovereign and corporate borrowings denominated in foreign currency.

To mitigate excessive currencies' volatility and their departing from an inter-currencies differences, sovereign states have in some cases adopted a reference currencies basket and an anchor to their own currency (see also Chapter 7). For example, Singapore uses a trade-weighted exchange rate or nominal effective exchange rate (NEER) as an effective instrument for their monetary policy. In December 2015, China's Foreign Exchange Trade System (CFETS) introduced a new CFETS RMB index referencing the yuan to a basket of 13 trade partners' currencies with the largest weights on USD (26.4%) and EUR (21.4%). Trends in exchange rates in trade-weighted terms demonstrate gradual movements, especially for China.

According to the Bank for International Settlements (BIS)[3], the Japanese yen is set relative to the weight of its major trade partners, including China (29.5%), the USA (16.6%), and the euro area (14%). NEER, in Figure 6.2, shows the changes in terms of trade (TOT) in Asian countries, which is also measured relative to other currencies. These figures point out that some FX rates move in tandem, appreciating and depreciating together, while others follow opposite trajectories.

NEER for Chinese, Singaporean, and South Korean currencies showed an upward trend compared with the 2010 level. However, NEER for Japan with worsening trade deficits has fallen rapidly since mid-2012, indicating a deterioration of TOT and higher costs for imported goods and services (e.g., energy imports), with increased external sources from abroad affected by the shutdown of the Fukushima nuclear plant. The Japanese economy has been experiencing slow growth, very low inflation, massive public debt, and widening current account deficits. These approaches to FX prices, therefore, provide an implied departure from purchasing power parity (PPP) embedded in the law of one price (LOOP) (see Chapter 5 for details). Rather than FX prices defined in international financial markets by buyers and sellers of currencies, some with the ability to sway FX prices by either sovereign policies, extraordinary natural and political events, or by economic trends reversals.

Further, it is noteworthy to state that real effective exchange rates (REERs) are in fact NEERs adjusted by relative prices between a sovereign state and its trading partners.

---

3 NEER is calculated as a weighted average of the bilateral exchange rate with the currencies of the major trading partners, with an increase indicating an appreciation (trade based on 2008–2010). The BIS used 42 currencies for calculating the effective exchange rate of a particular country's currency ("broad-based" rates).

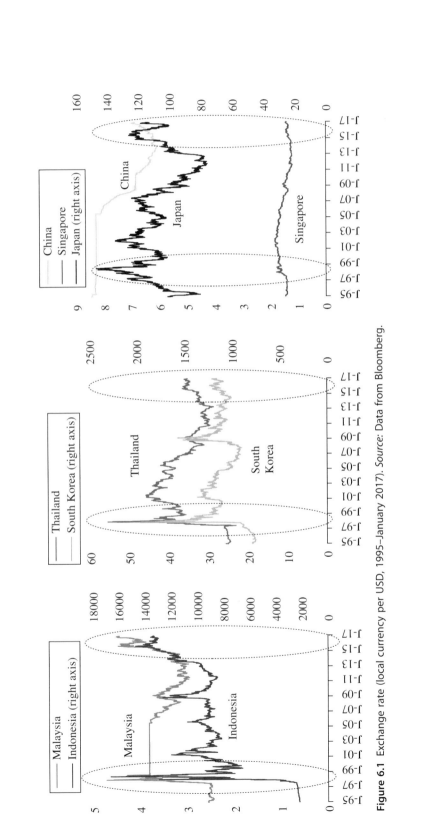

Figure 6.1 Exchange rate (local currency per USD, 1995–January 2017). *Source: Data from Bloomberg.*

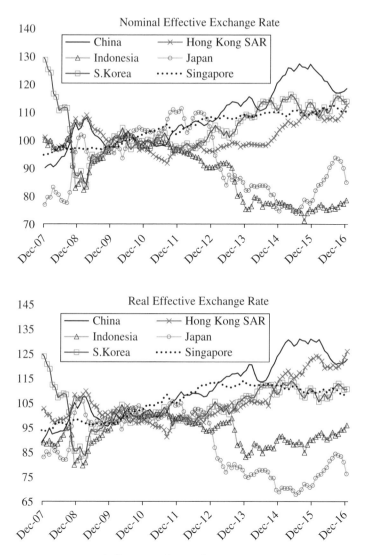

Figure 6.2 Nominal effective and real effective exchange rates in Asia (2007–2016).
Source: Data from BIS.

A comparison of REERs for some Asian countries demonstrates improvement for some, but a deterioration in international competitiveness for others. REERs are then affected not only relative to external FX rates, but also relative to economic factors such as net foreign assets, commodity-based TOT, government expenditures, and consumer price changes.

Questions and Problems 6.1

a) China's central bank's devaluation of the yuan on August 11, 2015 (by around 2% against USD), was the largest daily movement of the yuan since 2005. Examine its effect and implication for the Chinese economy as well as for global finance. Assess the changes in the trade-weighted index.

b) Since the slowdown in the Chinese economy in 2014–2015, around $300 billion "hot money" left the economy (according to Bloomberg). What types of financial flows are defined by "hot money" and how does it connect to a property bubble? How did China counter capital outflows?

c) How does the weak Asian currency spur exports and growth? Take a particular Asian country as an example and analyze the currency devaluation in recent years by comparing the pros and cons. How does it aggravate the debt burden for both corporate and sovereign debt denominated mostly in USD?

d) The Dow Jones Industrial Average index plunged more than 500 points (daily change) and by more than 1000 points from 17 500 in August 18, 2015, to less than 16 500 in August 21, 2015. How did the slowdown in the Chinese economy and devaluation of the yuan in 2015 affect the stock market in the USA?

e) Devaluation of the yuan may trigger competitive devaluations of other emerging market currencies. Discuss possible outcomes and a global currency war.

6.2.3 Foreign Investments Expansion

Since the 1970s, Asia has opened up to the global market through trade and investments, resulting in increased net private and official financial flows, contributing to its position in global finance. Asia's net FDI inflows increased from $46 billion in 2000 to almost $270 billion in 2014, while its net portfolio investments and net financial derivatives amounted to $125 billion in 2014 (IMF, 2016a). Compared with 1990, FDI inflows increased almost 20 times in 2016 with major countries, including China, Hong Kong SAR, and Singapore (see Table 6.2). These FDI inflows have contributed to a structural transformation of Asia

Table 6.2 FDI and value of cross-border M&As in Asia (billion USD).

| | FDI | | | | M&A (net) | | | |
| | Inflow | | Outflow | | Sales | | Purchases | |
	1990	2016	1990	2016	1990	2016	1990	2016
Developing Asia	23	442.7	11.1	363.1	0.5	41.9	6.1	143.2
China	3.5	133.7	0.8	183.1	—	5.9	1.3	92.2
Hong Kong, SAR	3.3	108.1	2.4	62.5	0.3	7.6	0.6	0.1
South Korea	1	10.8	1.1	27.3	—	−0.4	0.04	4.8
Singapore	5.6	61.6	2	23.9	0.5	4.5	0.1	6.2
Thailand	2.6	1.6	0.2	13.2	0	−1.9	0.01	4.5
Indonesia	1.1	2.7	0	−12.5	—	−1.2	0.2	0.2
Malaysia	2.6	9.9	0.1	5.6	−0.2	3.9	0.01	1.6
Japan	1.8	11.4	50.8	145.2	0.01	20.1	13.5	80.7

Source: Data from the UNCTAD.

and its economies. This occurred hand in hand with technology transfers shifting Asia from primary, low-technology and labor-intensive industries to high-technology, export-oriented sectors. Managerial, industrial, and service skills, and education and training opportunities delivered by large Western corporations have amplified and further equalized the competitive posture of Asia's economies in the world. Furthermore, regional integration, expanded markets, and new emerging opportunities have contributed to a coalescent Asia, one that is increasingly independent and competitive.

Asia's global expansion occurred through international investments, cross-border M&As in particular (see Table 6.2). Japan has been a traditional source of FDI for Asian economies; its huge investments in Asia are attributable to its domestic high wages and prices, which has amplified the need to reduce costs and thereby their need for Asian outsourcing and investment strategies (particularly in the electrical and electronics sectors). By the same token, foreign expansion of Chinese corporate and national enterprises contributed to an exit of FDI by investing in transportation, real estate, resource exploration, tourism, services, and manufacturing on a global scale. FDI outflows from China have already exceeded its inflows. In addition, China's net purchases in terms of M&As reached a historical peak of $92 billion in 2016. Major M&A deals involved Chinese transnational corporations such as China National Chemical Corp, Huawei Technologies, Wanxiang Group, Zheng Tai Group, and other large Chinese state-owned enterprises (SOEs). These trends are contributing to both the dependence of Asian national entities among themselves and their independence from the developing and Western economies (USA and Europe). At the same time, it is creating an economic and financial group, potentially politically inclined and on a collision course with Western economies.

According to UNCTAD (2017), there are a large number of state-owned MNEs in Asia: China (257 companies), Malaysia (79), Singapore (29), and Japan (6). These MNEs play an important role in the expansion of investment abroad. Chinese state-owned financial MNEs (The Industrial and Commercial Bank of China (ICBC), which is 34.6% state-owned, followed by other big banks) were ranked at the top, worldwide, in terms of foreign assets in 2016. In non-financial industries, China National Offshore Oil Corp (100% state owned) was ranked eighth, while Malaysia's Petronas (60.6% state owned) was ranked 13th.

Questions and Problems 6.2

In recent years, Chinese investors have diversified their foreign by purchasing of properties abroad. These include the Waldorf Astoria hotel in New York, the Sheraton Hotel in Sydney, and an office building on Sydney's Circular Quay. Discuss the motivations for China's investment shifts toward real estate from the energy sector.

6.3 Financial Sector Development in Asia

Globalization opened its doors to the Asian banking sector in the 1980s and 1990s, leading to improved investment opportunities, pooling of savings, resources and trade financing efficiency, and reduced transaction costs, as well as risk management and financial innovation. The Asian financial systems are typically characterized by:

- A deep banking sector with dominant banking products. Asian banks have maintained higher profitability ratios (e.g., earning a return on equity (ROE)[4] of over 20%) compared with some Western developed economies, with more stable capital ratios.
- Increased financial assets with a greater participation of non-banking financial institutions and capital markets (e.g., stock and government and corporate bond markets).
- Rapidly developing asset markets (e.g., stock and real estate markets).

Commercial banks are an essential part of the financial system of both developing and developed Asia (see Figure 6.3). Beyond Japan's large financial markets, it also has a large non-banking financial sector and bond markets. These markets remain relatively undeveloped in "in-development" Asia compared with their own banking sector. In Asia's bank-dominated financial systems, such as in Japan and NIAEs, financial repression was used as an industrial policy instrument in its early development stages. These included a control of credit allocation by the government and setting interest rates on both deposits and loans below the market clearing rates.

Although these have contributed to the expansion of financial markets, they have entailed risks such as the following:

- Shadow banking involving lending through entrusted and trust loans. Bankers' acceptances have been growing fast, especially in China, with massive credit expansion but

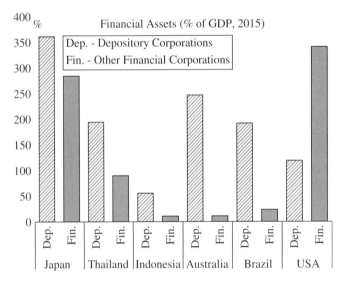

Figure 6.3 Financial assets in deposit-taking and non-bank financial corporations (excluding central bank). *Source:* Data from IMF.

---

4 ROE = net income/equity. International Monetary Fund (IMF) data for ROE is calculated as net income/ average value of capital. The Du Pont system shows the relationship between balance sheet ratios (operating profit margin ratio, asset turnover ratio, and equity multiplier).

with little transparency and close ties with banks. These factors pose significant risks for the banking system and its financial stability.

- Bond markets have been weak. Local currency-denominated bond markets, in particular corporate bonds, were not well developed, while short-term bonds have assumed the lion's share of bond issues. In China, in particular, SOEs issue the dominant share of corporate bonds, and the majority of government bonds are held by the state-owned banks instead of private investors. Furthermore, the issue of bonds denominated in (or indexed to) a foreign currency has entailed FX risks.
- There are still a large number of SOEs in Asia that are often technologically inefficient, overstocked, heavily indebted, and lack competition with respect to private companies. These SOEs hinder economic growth and challenge financial market structure.
- Stock market performance has been volatile. For example, the crash of China's stock market at the end of August 2015.

Asia's debt is also at risk. It has emerged as the largest debt market for non-financial corporations, accounting for almost half (or $24.2 trillion) of the world's total debt at the end of 2013 according to S&P (2014). China has the largest corporate debt ($14.2 trillion) in the world. There is also a significant corporate debt demand in other Asian countries: Japan ($5 trillion) and South Korea ($1.4 trillion) (see S&P (2014)). Credit has expanded rapidly in Asia, and with higher leverage since the Asian financial crisis. In China, for example, to curb a rapidly rising credit, restrictions were imposed on deposit rates in the banking system, which contribute to the expansion of its shadow banking. For example, IMF (2014) showed that, in terms of financial assets, more than one-third of the total is investment funds, with the major subsectors being shadow banking, followed by money market mutual funds and finance companies.

6.3.1 Fast-Growing Banking Sector

Profitability ratios (particularly ROE) in Asia have, typically, been close to 20%, with an exception of South East Asian banks,[5] especially in Malaysia with ROE of almost 30% according to IMF's Financial Soundness Indicator Database (see Figure 6.4). This led to Asian banks growing rapidly with increased revenues and expanding globally by M&A. For example, Singapore's DBS Bank purchased private banking giant Société Générale in Asia (Singapore and Hong Kong (SAR)) in 2014. In addition, the acquisition of certain Asia-Pacific activities of Britain's Royal Bank of Scotland by CIMB of Malaysia in 2012 helped to boost their own operations to an all-Asia banking system. Their earnings are based on interest margins, which account for more than half of their gross income (since most Asian banks are traditionally commercial banks). These banks have a very high return on assets (ROA)[6] (see Figure 6.4, left-hand side), with Chinese and Japanese banks ranked world largest in terms of assets, tier-1 capital (core capital used to assess capital adequacy), and net interest income. Thus, most indicators of Asian banks' financial soundness have shown large positive changes since the 1990s. The asset quality has increased, with fewer non-performing loans (NPLs), and capital reserves have become more adequate to cover existing risks. Figure 6.4 (right-hand side) shows the capital adequacy as measured by the regulatory capital to risk-weighted assets ratio;

---

5 Singapore's DBS Bank is Southeast Asia's largest bank, and CIMB is Malaysia's second largest bank by assets.
6 ROA = net income/average value of total assets.

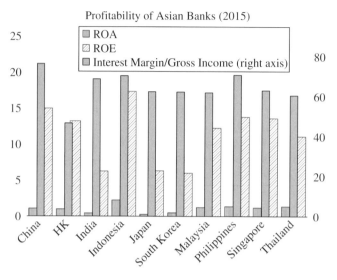

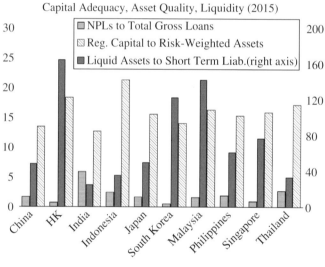

Figure 6.4 Profitability, capital adequacy, asset quality, and liquidity of deposit taking institutions in Asia. *Source:* Data from IMF.

the asset quality of NPLs to total gross loans ratio, and the liquidity of current assets to short-term liabilities (i.e., the current ratio).

According to the ranking of banks by the magazine *Global Finance* (2016), the DBS Bank is the "Safest Bank in Asia," the third safest global commercial bank, and the 12th safest bank internationally, based on total assets and long-term credit ratings by major international rating agencies, such as Fitch, Moody's, and S&P. The number of Asian banks considered safe has increased; Singaporean banks dominate in almost all categories (Table 6.3).

Table 6.3 Ranking of Asian banks in the world's safest banks (2016).

Rank	World's Safest Banks	Rank	World's Safest Commercial Banks	Rank	The Safest Banks in Asia
#12	DBS Bank (Singapore)	#3	DBS Bank (Singapore)	#1	DBS Bank (Singapore)
#14	OCBC (Singapore)	#5	OCBC (Singapore)	#2	OCBC (Singapore)
#15	Korea Development Bank	#6	United Overseas Bank (Singapore)	#3	Korea Development Bank
#16	United Overseas Bank (Singapore)	#17	Hang Seng Bank (Hong Kong)	#4	United Overseas Bank (Singapore)
#17	Export–Import Bank of Korea	#42	Shinhan Bank (South Korea)	#5	Export–Import Bank of Korea
#25	Industrial Bank of Korea	#49	Bank of Tokyo–Mitsubishi UFJ	#6	Industrial Bank of Korea
#31	Hang Seng Bank (Hong Kong)			#7	Hang Seng Bank (Hong Kong)
#36	China Development Bank			#8	China Development Bank
#39	Agricultural Development Bank of China			#9	Agricultural Development Bank of China
#42	Export-Import Bank of China			#10	Export–Import Bank of China

Source: Data from Global Finance Magazine 2016.

6.3.2 Bond Market Development

Asian countries have issued bonds in both foreign and local currencies. For example, Indonesia issued sovereign bonds denominated in USD ($4 billion in 2014 and $3.5 billion in 2015); Chinese SOE Sinopec raised USD- as well as EUR-denominated bonds ($5 billion and €1.5 billion); China Development Bank issued USD- and EUR-denominated bonds worth $6.3 billion in 2016. At the same time, bonds issued in local currencies have expanded fast across Asia to avoid currency risks, especially for the highly leveraged companies. Figure 6.5 illustrates the trends and composition of outstanding local currency-denominated bonds as a share of GDP in Asian economies.

Japan has the largest bond market in Asia with massive government borrowing,[7] whereas South Korea has dominant corporate bond issues. Bond markets have expanded in the whole region: in the fourth quarter of 2015, Japan's bond market in local currency more than doubled compared with that of December 2000; in China and in Thailand the market tripled, and it almost doubled in Singapore and South Korea. In particular, local currency corporate bonds became a popular instrument for raising capital in emerging countries, reaching a record high of 20% of GDP (2015 quarter 4) from only 0.3% in (2000

---

7 As defined by ADB, government bonds consist of obligations of the government, central bank, and state-owned companies. Corporates include public and private companies.

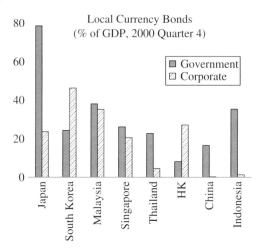

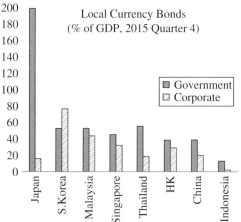

Figure 6.5 Expansion of local currency bond markets in Asia (as percentage of GDP). *Source:* Data from Asian Development Bank.

quarter 4) in China. Constrained by limited domestic credit, Asian corporations, in particular Chinese companies, have also issued bonds with a value of billions of dollars to foreign investors. Emerging East Asia's foreign currency bonds, almost all denominated in USD, and some in EUR and JPY, increased from $182.6 billion in 2015 to $215.6 billion in 2016 with dominance of China ($120 billion) followed by Hong Kong SAR ($29.2 billion) and South Korea ($28.6 billion) according to the Asian Development Bank (ADB, 2017) (see Figure 6.6). The values expressed in USD cover total amount of issued bonds denominated in USD, Euro, and Yen. We should note that sovereign bonds dominate in countries such as Indonesia and Philippines.

Owing to the inefficiency and the limitations of financial sectors (weak bank regulations, deficiencies in risk and corporate management, etc.), Asia was vulnerable to the external shocks that led to the financial crisis of 1997–1998. Asia also had problems relating to large foreign currency-denominated liabilities and a dependency on external demand and credit. When the financial crisis migrated to Asia, asset prices rose, capital flight occurred, and bank balance sheets collapsed. Post-crisis policies and reforms have focused on the development of a strong domestic financial system, such as promoting

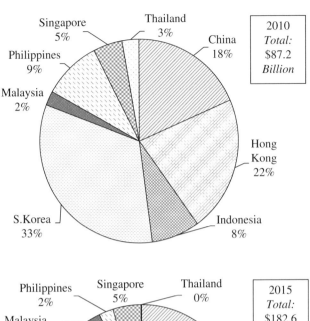

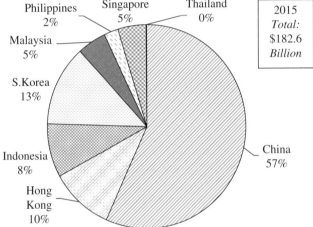

Figure 6.6 Foreign currency bond markets in Asia. *Source:* Data from Asian Development Bank.

domestic currency denominated corporate bond markets. These measures helped to resist and cope with the subsequent crisis. However, the effects of the 2007 financial crisis on Asia had different consequences to Asian countries, depending on their degree of economic and financial openness, their dependency on external demand, and credit. In other words:

- Financial systems in Asia have been relatively resilient to external shocks (e.g., limited exposure to toxic assets).
- They recovered faster from the crisis due to successful financial reforms.
- Financial reforms were applied to financial regulation and macroeconomic policies, strengthening their sustainability and reducing their vulnerability.

- Reforms focused on restructuring the financial sector through bank recapitalization. Asian banks' balance sheets have improved with lower NPLs and higher capital adequacy ratios (as recommended by Basel III regulation proposals).

Questions and Problems 6.3

a) This past decade, Asian economies, including China and Malaysia, issued and sold an appreciable amount of bonds denominated in USD, especially, sold to US mutual fund companies. In contrast to bonds in local currency, these bonds involve FX risks that have increased with a prospective stronger US economy and currency. What are the implications for US mutual investments? What are the implications for the Malaysian economy?

b) Foreign investors hold a large share of local currency denominated bonds in Asian countries (e.g., Malaysia and Indonesia). What are the risks associated with its capital outflow? Discuss how it affects the volatility of the fixed income market.

c) Discuss an increase in US interest rates and how it affects the Asian bond market, particularly borrowing costs. What would be the outcomes of raising domestic interest rates to attract investors? How can capital outflow be prevented?

d) Daimler AG was the first foreign non-financial corporation that issued yuan bonds (panda bonds) on the domestic bond market. Discuss the advantages for the firm (in particular its cost savings and its avoidance of FX risk). How does this sale promote the internationalization of the yuan?

6.3.3 Stock Market Development

The expansion of Asian financial markets, relative to bond markets, has grown rapidly since the early 1990s and pointed to Asia's appetite for risk. As a result, equity investments were preferred to fund development. However, stock markets have different degrees of development, such as:

- developed stock exchanges in Tokyo and Hong Kong (SAR);
- recently growing stock exchanges in Shanghai and Shenzhen in China—these are developing under financial and capital reforms.

Emerging markets offer selective opportunities to both domestic and foreign investors (with some restrictions imposed on foreigners, such as new equity offerings), providing extended pathways for diversification. While the US share of the world market capitalization was almost 41%, East Asia and the Pacific accounted for 35%, with China (mainland), Japan, and Hong Kong (SAR) dominating in 2015 Asian holdings.[8] This is attributable to the Shanghai and Hong Kong exchanges attracting global investors to securities listed in China. However, stock markets in some Asian countries lack transparency compared with developed stock exchanges. Certain issues relating to the real estate sector in China pose additional challenges as well. Market capitalization in

---

8 The World Bank (World Development Indicators): http://databank.worldbank.org/data/home.aspx.

GDP is compared in Figure 6.7. In addition, regional comparisons of stock market capitalization, value of traded stocks, and turnover ratios are illustrated in Figure 6.8. The ratio of the traded domestic shares' value to the market capitalization is highest for the developing East Asian and Pacific region compared with the all-income level East Asian and Pacific region as well as South Asia.

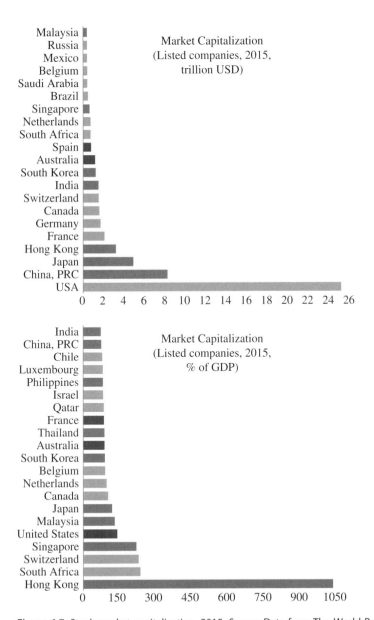

Figure 6.7 Stock market capitalization, 2015. *Source:* Data from The World Bank.

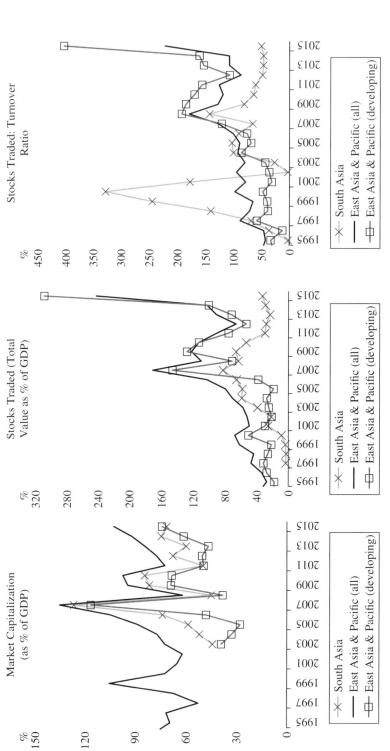

Figure 6.8 Stock market development in Asia (market capitalization, total value of stocks traded as % of GDP, stocks traded turnover ratio). *Source:* Data from The World Bank.

Questions and Problems 6.4

Following the stock market crash at the end of August 2015, the Chinese government intervened to stabilize stock prices. Discuss these measures, including the buy-back of shares (in particular SOEs) and their impact on the shares and investors.

6.4   Risks of Investing in Asia

Bonds and credit default risks apart, investments in both developed and developing Asia are exposed to FX and country-specific risks. As expected, bonds issued by Asian companies with attractive yields involve higher levels of risk exposure compared with those with lower returns. Even if investors are able to mitigate default and country risks, FX rates remain important.

According to the ranking of international country risk provided by the PRS Group, Japan and China are considered low risk, whereas countries like Indonesia and India are moderately risky. Factors that have a positive impact on political risk include a stable government, a favorable socioeconomic environment, a low corruption, an investment profile, effective and well-designed regulations and laws, less religious and ethnic conflict, more democracy, and less bureaucracy.[9]

In China, while cumulative real returns on bonds have had a positive trend since the early 1990s, equities have demonstrated a very volatile real return. In Japan, both equities' and bonds' cumulative real returns have increased steadily over time since the 1950s. Annualized real returns of the capital markets, including equities and bonds, in China and Japan in comparison with Australia, the USA, and the world are presented in Dimson *et al.* (2016). Their report shows that equity risk premiums relative to long-term government bonds as well as to treasury bills are positive in Japan, Australia, the USA, and world, but negative in China.

6.4.1   Foreign Exchange Risk

FX developments, during 2014–2015, characterized by strong USD and weaker Asian currencies,[10] pushed Asian dollar-denominated returns lower; some even turned negative. The importance of FX risks cannot be understated. Thus, we analyze it by using the standard deviations of USD : Asian currencies (monthly percentage changes); see Table 6.4. There are high currency risks across countries and across time in Asia with the exception of the JPY, which seems stable during the periods covered. Volatility was highest during the period between 1991 and 2000 for most Asian countries because of the Asian financial crisis in 1997–1998. Some examples include Indonesia 11%, South Korea 4.8%, China 4.6%, Thailand 4%, and Malaysia 3%.

Correlation coefficients of the rate of change in FX rates differ across countries as well. For example, Table 6.5 outlines their correlations over the period 2011–2015. In particular, currency movements in South East Asian countries are shown to be highly

---

9 For more information, see http://www.prsgroup.com/.
10 Exchange rate was 120 JPY/USD in 2015, which used to exchange with around 80 JPY in 2012. Other currencies also depreciated: over 60 INR/USD in 2015 from 45 INR in 2011; 13 000 IDR/USD in 2015 from 8500 IDR in 2011.

Table 6.4 Standard deviation of FX (%, monthly percentage changes).

	China	Hong Kong, SAR	India	Indonesia	Japan	South Korea	Malaysia	Singapore	Thailand
	RMB/$	HKD/$	INR/$	IDR/$	JPY/$	KRW/$	MYR/$	SGD/$	THB/$
1970–1980	1.67	1.30	1.52	3.11	2.38	2.23	1.57	1.47	0.26
1981–1990	2.47	1.51	1.14	4.38	2.97	0.77	1.05	1.14	1.70
1991–2000	4.57	0.06	1.58	11.10	2.89	4.80	2.97	1.50	3.93
2001–2010	0.37	0.13	1.71	2.69	2.26	2.81	1.11	1.20	1.61
2011–2015	0.48	0.05	2.23	1.84	2.38	1.46	1.65	0.99	1.25

Source: Data from Bloomberg.

Table 6.5 Correlation of exchange rate of Asian currencies (percentage monthly change), 2011–2015.

	RMB/$	HKD/$	INR/$	IDR/$	JPY/$	KRW/$	MYR/$	SGD/$	THB/$
RMB/$	1.00								
HKD/$	0.00	1.00							
INR/$	0.01	0.09	1.00						
IDR/$	−0.05	−0.02	0.41	1.00					
JPY/$	0.03	0.00	−0.17	0.12	1.00				
KRW/$	0.06	0.17	0.47	0.02	0.07	1.00			
MYR/$	0.33	0.04	0.62	0.42	0.07	0.56	1.00		
SGD/$	0.26	0.08	0.55	0.38	0.28	0.67	0.82	1.00	
THB/$	−0.04	−0.01	0.61	0.43	−0.12	0.30	0.57	0.49	1.00

Source: Data from Bloomberg.

correlated.[11] While most correlation coefficients are positive, there are several negative coefficients. This is a potential opportunity used by investors to reduce their portfolio volatility (see Chapter 2 and also Chapter 7).

The RORs on Asian stock market indexes indicate that returns in Indonesia, China, India, and Thailand are higher than other Asian stocks (Table 6.6). However, these stocks have much higher risks than stocks with lower returns (Japan, Hong Kong (SAR), and Malaysia) because of their exchange rate fluctuations. Consider a US investor who invests in Asian assets in Asian currency by converting USD for a year. At the end of the investment period, the investor exchanges Asian local currency back to USD. If

---

11 A rapid depreciation of Thai baht (THB) had a contagious effect on other countries during the Asian financial crisis in 1997–1998.

Table 6.6 Average returns and standard deviations on Asian indexes.

		Japan	Hong Kong	Shanghai	Shenzhen	South Korea	India	Indonesia	Malaysia	Thailand	Singapore
		NKY	HSI	SHCOMP	SZCOMP	KOSPI	NIFTY	JCI	FBMKLCI	SET	FSSTI
Annual (2000–2014)											
R (%)	In LCU	2.8	5.9	17.0	22.0	8.8	17.9	21.0	7.3	14.5	5.6
	In USD	0.8	5.9	19.2	24.5	11.2	17.7	20.4	8.5	17.5	7.8
SD (%)	In LCU	27.0	27.6	53.5	62.0	30.1	35.9	37.7	20.6	40.8	27.7
	In USD	22.0	27.5	55.3	64.9	35.0	42.4	47.5	23.7	47.2	30.5
Monthly (2000–2015 March)											
R (%)	In LCU	0.2	0.4	0.9	1.2	0.6	1.2	1.4	0.5	0.9	0.3
	In USD	0.1	0.4	1.0	1.4	0.8	1.1	1.2	0.6	1.0	0.5
SD (%)	In LCU	5.7	6.2	7.9	8.7	6.8	7.2	6.7	4.4	6.9	5.6
	In USD	5.4	6.2	7.9	8.7	8.5	8.5	9.0	5.1	8.0	6.4

Source: Data from Bloomberg.
R: average returns; SD: standard deviation; LCU: local currency; USD: US dollars.

Table 6.7 Correlation between Asian indexes (monthly returns denominated in USD, 2000–2015 March).

	NKY	HSI	SHCOMP	SZCOMP	KOSPI	NIFTY	JCI	FBMKLCI	SET	FSSTI
NKY	1									
HSI	0.57	1								
SHCOMP	0.21	0.44	1							
SZCOMP	0.20	0.34	0.89	1						
KOSPI	0.62	0.69	0.29	0.25	1					
NIFTY	0.57	0.68	0.30	0.25	0.63	1				
JCI	0.47	0.51	0.18	0.15	0.60	0.61	1			
FBMKLCI	0.35	0.55	0.32	0.33	0.51	0.55	0.57	1		
SET	0.53	0.52	0.16	0.17	0.65	0.60	0.62	0.49	1	
FSSTI	0.54	0.77	0.28	0.22	0.71	0.71	0.68	0.62	0.66	1.00

Source: Data from Bloomberg.

the FX rate had not changed much (e.g., USD/HKD), the investor would have received the same return (HKD return = USD return). Depending on FX movements, USD returns can be higher or lower than returns in local currencies. In order to eliminate this risk, covered interest rate parity (CIP), introduced in Chapter 5, can be used for hedging FX risk through derivative instruments; for example, FX swaps, plain vanilla options (European or American options), or "zero-cost structures." In addition, uncovered interest rate parity (UIP) can be applied as well (see Chapters 5, 7, and 8).

Asian assets' returns are highly correlated, as shown in Table 6.7. But the correlation between Japanese and Chinese currencies is lower than others, so investors would prefer to keep both these assets in their portfolio.

6.4.2 Foreign Exchange Option

Derivative markets, particularly the options market, have assumed a greater importance in Asia (see Chapter 7 for their quantitative development).[12] An option provides a right (not obligation) to purchase (call option) or sell (put option) an asset (e.g., stocks, bonds, FX, commodities) to its holder with a specified expiration date. These contracts serve as essential hedging tools benefiting Asian financial markets against investment risks. In particular, for an international investment, hedging against the volatility in FX is necessary as investments are made in different currencies. Thus, foreign currency option contracts are used for sale or purchase of foreign currency in exchange for domestic currency at specified quantity. The payoff is determined by the strike price and exchange rate (at date of maturity). Besides the payoff (i.e., value of call or put), we should also consider a premium or cost of the option to assess net profits of the option holder. For example, the

---

12 Stock index options and stock options have been actively traded in South Korea since the late 1990s. In India, trading of index options was launched in 2001. China introduced stock options based on exchange-traded funds (ETFs) on the Shanghai Stock Exchange in February 2015 and approved credit default swap trading in September 2016.

won–yuan currency option (South Korean and Chinese currencies) was signed in November 2014. This direct trading of Asian currencies promotes the internationalization of yuan and reduces the cost of currency conversions. The pricing of these instruments and their application to financial exchanges and transactions are varied, priced both in financial markets and over-the-counter transactions. More common transactions are engineered through swaps; some are securitized, and thus traded in financial markets (such as the VIX), while others are set through financial intermediaries (see Chapters 7 and 8).

6.4.3 Portfolio with Asian Assets

Consider a portfolio consisting of US equities, commodities, and Asian equities. For example, a portfolio with annual returns based on the S&P 500 (SPX) Index, Oil (CO1) and Copper (HG1), Japanese Nikkei 500 (NKY) Index and Chinese Shanghai Composite Index (SHCOMP) between 2000 and 2014. A summary of their statistics is shown in Table 6.8. Although investment in SPX or NKY has a very low risk, they offer a very low return compared with commodities and assets in Asia. High returns in China may be very attractive to investors, but they may assume more risk than other assets in the portfolio.

Table 6.9 shows that returns in SPX and NKY are highly correlated as expected ($\rho = 0.81$). But the correlation of Japanese and Chinese stocks is very low; including these assets would make the portfolio more diversified and reduce the portfolio risk with the assets that have low correlation.

The portfolio's expected returns and portfolio volatility are shown in Table 6.10 for different (weighted) portfolios. Although portfolio 3 (Port 3) is of equal weights, it provides an expected return of 4.5%, with a volatility of 6.6%. Solving for the optimal value for minimum volatility results in 3.1%, but this investment with only US stocks and oil, shown as portfolio 1, has the lowest return (2.7%). An investor would then need to keep Chinese stock and copper to increase their returns, but with an appropriate weight to maintain lower volatility. In order to reduce the risk (non-market) of the portfolio, we can add another security to the portfolio as long as the beta is less than one.

Table 6.8 A summary statistics of portfolio assets denominated in USD.

	USA	Oil	Copper	Japan	China
	SPX Index	CO1 Comdty	HG1 Comdty	NKY	SHCOMP
Mean	4.1	11.6	15.6	0.8	19.2
Standard deviation	18.8	35.0	44.6	22.0	55.3
Sample variance	352.4	1221.7	1987.4	483.3	3054.1
Kurtosis	0.5	−0.3	3.2	−0.7	0.2
Skewness	−0.8	−0.2	1.3	−0.2	0.9
Range	68.1	122.4	191.0	72.6	201.2
Minimum	−38.5	−51.4	−53.6	−34.9	−63.0
Maximum	29.6	70.9	137.3	37.7	138.3

Source: Data from Bloomberg.

Table 6.9 Correlation.

	SPX	CO1 Comdty	HG1 Comdty	NKY Index	SHCOMP Index
SPX Index	1				
Oil: CO1 Comdty	0.30	1			
Copper: HG1 Comdty	0.59	0.71	1		
Japan: NKY Index	0.81	0.41	0.60	1	
China: SHCOMP Index	0.41	0.29	0.44	0.11	1

Table 6.10 Portfolio's expected returns and portfolio volatility.

			Weights							
		Expected returns	Port. 1	Port. 2	Port. 3	Port. 4	Port. 5	Port. 6	Port. 7	Port. 8
US	SPX Index	2.3	86.8	40.0	20.0	41.5	20.0	11.9	13.2	1.0
Oil	CO1 Comdty	5.7	13.2	20.0	20.0	26.3	21.7	17.6	13.6	0.0
Copper	HG1 Comdty	8.2	0.0	20.0	20.0	0.0	38.2	53.7	37.4	97.3
Japan	NKY Index	−1.6	0.0	20.0	20.0	0.0	9.8	6.6	0.0	1.7
China	SHCOMP	8.0	0.0	0.0	20.0	32.2	10.4	10.3	35.8	0.0
Portfolio's expected returns			2.7	3.4	4.5	5.0	5.5	6.4	7.0	8.0
Portfolio volatility (variance)			3.1	4.9	6.6	6.7	8.2	10.6	11.7	17.8

The expected portfolio return $E(R^p) = \sum_{j=1}^{N} \alpha_j E(R_j)$, with weight α and portfolio volatility $\sigma_P^2 = \sum_{j=1}^{N} \sum_{k=1}^{N} \alpha_j \alpha_k \sigma_{j,k}$, is illustrated together with Pearson's correlation coefficient (ranging from −1 to +1) in Figure 6.9 with three dimensions. It shows the evolution from the "straight line" (when correlation $\rho = 1$) through the "bend" shape, to the final "check mark" shape (when $\rho = -1$).

Questions and Problems 6.5

Derive the relationship between expected return and beta using the risk premium for an Asian security and SPX Index. Explain the systematic risk premium. Determine this security's systematic risk and unsystematic (firm-specific) risk. Show how adding an Asian security can affect a portfolio's standard deviation.

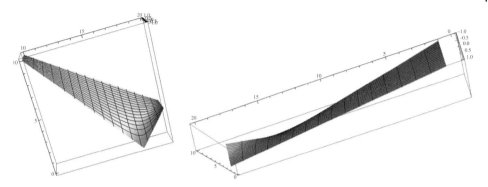

Figure 6.9 Portfolio's expected return, portfolio volatility, and correlation.

6.5   Financial Development in China

China has expanded its cooperation with other countries to promote foreign investments and increase trading in yuan and bonds. To do so, agreements have been signed to expand exchanges. For example, China contracted Britain to be a main offshore hub and to promote global financial markets and capital flows. Further, owing to relaxed banking regulations, China, instead of setting up bank subsidiaries in the UK, set up their own bank branches in the UK, supervised by China's banking regulation. As a result of a growing economy in both production and services, total lending in China surged to almost 90 trillion yuan, at the end of 2013 (up from around 20 trillion yuan in 2002); see *The Economist* (2014a). The outstanding credit has increased further and exceeded 200% of GDP, according to the central bank of China. Bloomberg Intelligence reports that this ratio reached almost 260% in 2016 (Bloomberg, 2017). Lending in other financial markets has also risen: while bond markets' lending increased to almost 10 trillion yuan, non-bank financial institutions' credits reached almost 20 trillion yuan. S&P (2014) also confirms the surge in Chinese corporate debt, which is mostly (more than 60%) financed with bank loans. These debt levels have contributed to a growth in China's credit default risk. To mitigate this risk, it approved the launching of credit default swap trading for the first time in late 2016, providing an opportunity for investors to buy a market insurance. Further, an increase in NPLs and the recent boom in its domestic and foreign stock market investments may cause FX risks. According to a joint report by the World Bank and the Development Research Center of the State Council, P. R. China (WB and DRCSC, 2013), the financial system in China:

- is still "unbalanced, costly to maintain, and potentially unstable" (WB and DRCSC, 2013: 115) and vulnerable to potential risks;
- lacks an effective regulatory framework;
- has a dominant state-owned banking sector, with a government intervening in the financial sector;
- has massive bank credits as its main source of corporate fund raising;
- has an expanding shadow banking;
- has unbalanced capital markets with an underdeveloped corporate bond market.

6.5.1 Importance of the Banking Sector in China

The structure of the Chinese banking system has been reshaped by financial reforms since the 1980s while expanding its outreach over financial markets. The two-tier banking sector with the People's Bank of China (PBC—central bank) and state-owned specialized commercial banks was introduced in 1978 when the economy opened up. China has 4262 banking institutions, with policy banks (3), large commercial banks (5), joint stock commercial banks (12), city commercial banks (133), postal savings bank (1), private banks (5), asset management banks (4), foreign banking institutions that operate locally (40), hundreds of rural banks and credit cooperatives, and many other companies as of the end of 2015, that were regulated by the China Banking Regulatory Commission (CBRC, 2016). Its largest state-owned bank (the world's biggest according to the 2016 ranking), ICBC, with $274 billion[13] tier 1 capital, is now deemed a global bank, with subsidiaries and a partner in M&A, is contributing to the expansion of Chinese global business.

The regular banking sector dominates financial markets in China, with significant growth and global reach over the past decade, including:

- ICBC's extension of its global service network and active acquisitions abroad; the first Chinese bank acquiring a controlling stake in a US commercial bank (80% stake in the Bank of East Asia).
- Increased engagement of ICBC in the repo market on Wall Street (compared with 2010, when it bought the Prime Dealer Services unit, Fortis Securities, from BNP Paribas SA).
- ICBC FS (Financial Services) is a registered US investment adviser since July 2016. It became a member of the New York Stock Exchange in 2013.
- ICBC's expansion through the acquisition of small banks in Argentina, Thailand, and elsewhere.
- ICBC's acquisition of the London-based Standard Bank global markets business in 2014 that has expanded its commodity trading.
- Branching of the Agricultural Bank of China abroad, including a New York branch in 2012, Dubai in 2013, Sydney in 2014, and subsidiaries in London and Hong Kong (SAR).

Total assets of banking institutions surged to 232 trillion yuan and stood at around 310% of GDP by the end of 2016. It is expected to expand further.

Commercial banks' assets account for almost 80% of China's banking institutions. This expanding banking sector, growing with the debt it assumed, has also raised risk concerns regarding an asset quality deterioration attributable to a rise in NPLs and a decline in provision coverage in 2015 and 2016 (see Table 6.11). NPLs of commercial banks have been increasing significantly, with outstanding balance of 1.5 trillion yuan by the end of 2016 from 0.4 trillion yuan in 2011. They consist of three NPL categories: substandard, doubtful, and loss, which excludes an enormous amount of "special mention"[14] loans (amounting to 3.3 trillion yuan at the end of 4th quarter (Q4) of 2016 compared with 2.9 trillion yuan in 2015Q4). With an increasing number of defaults in the slower

---

13 The Banker Database: http://www.thebankerdatabase.com/.
14 According to CBRC (2014), "special mention loan means the borrower has ability to repay the loan currently but may be affected by some unfavorable factors."

Table 6.11 Indicators at end of fourth quarter of commercial banking institutions in China.

	2010	2011	2012	2013	2014	2015	2016
NPL ratio (%)	1.1	1.0	0.95	1.0	1.25	1.67	1.74
Provision coverage ratio (%)	217.7	278.1	295.51	282.70	232.06	181.18	176.4
Liquidity ratio (%)	42.2	43.2	45.83	44.03	46.44	48.01	47.55
Loan/deposit ratio (%)	64.5	64.9	65.31	66.08	65.09	67.24	67.61
ROA (%)	1.1	1.3	1.28	1.27	1.23	1.10	0.98
ROE (%)	19.2	20.4	19.85	19.17	17.59	14.98	13.38
Capital adequacy ratio (%)	12.2	12.7	13.25	12.19	13.18	13.45	13.28
Core capital adequacy ratio (%)	10.1	10.2	10.62	9.95	10.56	10.91	10.75
Net profit (annual, trillion yuan)	0.76	1.04	1.24	1.42	1.55	1.59	1.65

Source: Data from China Banking Regulatory Commission.
Note: capital adequacy ratio from the third quarter in 2014 was calculated using a changed methodology. Net profit shows the cumulative annual amount.

economy, concerns are raised over the quality of banks' assets and the potential for an increase in distressed assets. IMF (2016b) suggests a growing vulnerability of China's corporate sector, as the estimated bank loans potentially at risk (with a borrower who is unable to cover the interest payments) may have reached $1.3 trillion.

Participation of foreign investors in Chinese banks rose as well. Since the end of 2006, both foreign banks and their Chinese counterparts operate under the same regulatory environment. Foreign bank branches are conducting businesses in yuan, engaged in derivative transactions, issuing financial bonds in yuan, and issuing credit cards. Foreign banks' activities in China are also becoming increasingly liberalized, providing foreign currency services to Chinese residents and local currency operations (e.g., HSBC China), and serving small and micro-sized enterprises.

Questions and Problems 6.6

a) China's internet giants Alibaba, Baidu, and Tencent are now competing with commercial banks by offering online finance services with higher yields. Discuss the advantages and challenges associated with these online investment funds and compare such banking with the banking regulations on banks' required reserves. How do these funds invest in domestic interbank and bond markets and connect to the overall banking system?

b) China launched a deposit insurance in May 2015 and issued guidelines for large-scale certificates of deposit. What is the implication for the interest rate liberalization reform? How does this affect the margins of the state-owned large banks?

c) In 2015, the Chinese central bank implemented a series of easing policies in the banking sector, including lower reserve requirement ratios and interbank rates, lifting the ceiling on deposit rates (over 1 year), and revising bank lending rules. In addition, a series of steps has been taken toward tightening shadow-banking regulations. Discuss the effects of these measures.

6.5.1.1 Shadow Banking

The rapid credit growth of the China's financial system has also increased risks due to informal banking deals in financial products (e.g., trust loans swaps) with a high risk of default. FSB (2011) defines shadow banking as "credit intermediation involving entities and activities outside the regular banking system." They also indicate that shadow lending in the last decade has increased from $26 trillion to $71 trillion for 20 major countries and expanded 42% in China in 2012. IMF (2014) warns about the acceleration of the shadow banking phenomenon in emerging economies. One of the major concerns raised in shadow banking involved the mismatch of maturity.

In a special report by *The Economist* (2014a), a "regulatory arbitrage" in China with a government able to intervene through its state-owned banks is highlighted. Trusts in China offer high returns on investments and lend to industries that have limited access to bank loans. Products of shadow banking firms and banks, such as Jilin Trust and China Credit Trust, were distributed through Chinese state-owned banks (e.g., China Construction Bank and ICBC). Non-standard credit has expanded in all banks, especially in medium-sized banks.

When the Chinese banking system's regulation was tightened, bank loans declined, but financial flows through trusts and entrusted have risen since 2010. Banks issue large amounts of wealth management products offering high yields that reached 25% of GDP in May 2014. According to the qualitative risk scoring system in IMF (2014, 2016b), shadow banking in China has a higher risk than in other emerging markets (e.g., South East Asian non-banking sector and Mexico's real estate investment trust), as well as advanced economies, accounting for all factors, including size, maturity, liquidity, credit, and leverage.

Bank loans are still the dominant channels for Chinese firms to raise funds. Banks' lending share has declined, however, as corporate bonds have increased in value in recent years. A broad measure of aggregate financing in the real economy introduced by the PBC measures new credit and liquidity. Traditional bank loans accounted over 90% of the total social financing in 2002 (see Figure 6.10), but the share has declined to around 60% with access to other financing sources, particularly shadow banking. Shares of shadow banking investment products, such as short-term wealth management products and long-term trust products, in GDP have increased significantly, especially since 2012. These trusts are supervised by the CBRC. Chinese regulators have tightened the conditions to better manage shadow banking and prevent some accounting tricks from being used in trust products. These include restrictions on off-balance-sheet activities, limits on lending of trust's funds, as well as limits on trust beneficiary rights products for banks and trusts.

6.5.2 State-Owned Enterprises

Sovereign states (particularly in emerging economies) are the dominant shareholders in the world's biggest companies, both industrial and financial. Some of these corporate entities include PetroChina (China), China Mobile (Hong Kong (SAR)), Sinopec (China), NTT (Japan), and Oil & Natural Gas (India). Industrial development in sectors such as steel, iron, coal, and cement, as well as in the green energy sector, has both large

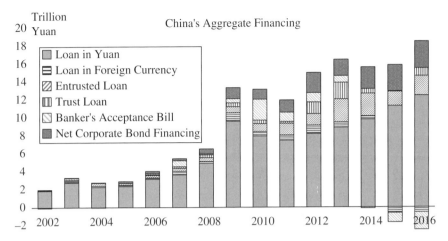

Figure 6.10 Credits in China (funds raised, newly increased aggregate financing). *Source:* Data from The People's Bank of China.

output and sales, and serves as an engine of economic growth in China. There are about 155 000 SOEs in China diversified into sectors ranging from big banks to energy companies with strategic and political agendas that contribute to economic growth. However, only less than half of the SOEs are companies operating in strategic sectors. SOEs in China have the advantage over private companies due to their access to easier and cheaper financing terms and their access to state-owned banks, real estate locations, and other resources.

Reforms in SOEs since the 1990s have shown progress in privatization with a declining number of SOEs and an increasing number of other types of enterprises, especially private firms and HMT (Hong Kong, Macao, and Taiwan) and foreign enterprises, whose industrial output has been surging (Figure 6.11, Table 6.12). In recent years, SOEs' management practices have improved, private stakes have increased, and more SOEs are listed on the stock market with initial public offering (IPO) pioneers such as the CITIC Group. Chinese SOEs still face inefficiencies and competition with their private companies that have expanded rapidly since the early 2000s. According to Gavekal Dragonomics, as discussed in *The Economist* (2014b), ROA for Chinese industrial private firms reached 9% in 2014, whereas it declined for SOEs to 5% in 2014 from 7% in 2006, indicating a fall in profitability. Similarly, Chinese official sources show that industrial state-owned and holding companies have earned lower profits than shareholding and private firms (Figure 6.11), and the ratio of SOEs' profits to total costs has fallen (Table 6.12).

Questions and Problems 6.7

a) China's central bank reduced finance companies' reserve requirement in 2015 to support funding of SOEs. Discuss the concerns over the SOE sector in China and the impact of the Chinese government's measures on these enterprises.

b) Discuss the massive foreign investment in China's SCE (CITIC) by Itochu Corporation (Japan) and Charoen Pokphand Group (Thailand). How does the private capital investment create opportunity in businesses in China?

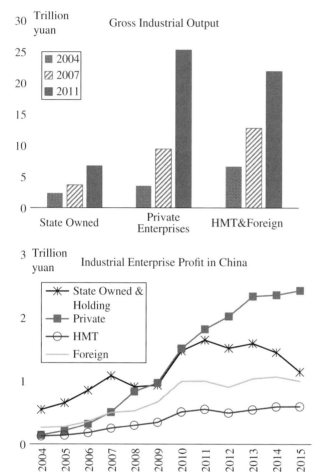

Figure 6.11 Growing industrial enterprises in China (gross industrial output and industrial profit). *Source:* Data from National Bureau of Statistics of China.

Table 6.12 Performance of industrial enterprises in China.

	Number of industrial enterprises (thousand)			Profits-to-costs ratio		
	1999	2007	2016	1999	2007	2014
State-owned & Holding	61	21	19	2.89	9.9	5.82
Private	15	177	215	4.4	6.08	6.77
HMT & Foreign Funded	27	67	52	4.39	6.45	6.93

Source: Data from National Bureau of Statistics of China

6.5.3   Challenges in Equity Markets in China

The Chinese corporate debt market plays a central role in global finance: corporate borrowing of $14.2 trillion in China overtook the USA, which had $13.1 trillion (S&P, 2014). China's bond market has expanded with a total outstanding bond value of almost 30 trillion yuan in 2013, which has tripled since 2006. According to the Wind Financial Terminal, financial bonds account for one-third of the total bond market. This followed a rapid growth in the corporate bond market by almost 8 trillion yuan in 2013. However, a significant rise in Chinese corporate borrowing (parts of which are financed by shadow banking) adds a large credit risk to the global market while increasing the pool of players who invest in the Chinese economy.

   The first default on a corporate bond (coupon payment) was by Shanghai Chaori Solar Energy Science and Technology Co Ltd. In October 2014, it announced a debt restructuring through a joint venture of nine Chinese firms, and the Great Wall Asset Management (state-owned bank for bad loans). Together with the Shanghai Eternal Sunshine Investment Management Centre, they issued a guarantee worth 880 million yuan (Reuters, 2014). Prior to this announcement, analysts expected that the government would not bail out the private company. Fitch Ratings has pointed out that this default and involvement of the government showed that the Chinese corporate bond market was and is probably immature and ineffective (*Financial Times*, 2014). In the following years, the number of defaults on bonds has increased, with 21 in 2015 and 32 in the second half of 2016, including the 400 million yuan default by the Evergreen Holding Group Co., according to the Wind Info (http://www.wind.com.cn/en/). This list was dominated by the energy and steel SOEs, such as Sichuan Coal Industry Group, Dongbei Special Steel Group, and Non-ferrous Metal Group, that were affected by several factors, including the SOE reforms, slowdown of Chinese economy, and collapse of resource prices.

6.5.4   Stock Market Development in China

The stock market in China, with several thousand listed companies and a massive turnover value, has a large total market capitalization. Previously (with the exception of FDI), only qualified foreign investors could invest in short-term instruments in China (with limited access to the stock market). UBS Group AG was the first foreign group to be approved to purchase yuan-denominated "A shares"[15] in 2003. This development was part of a financial opening, including:

- Launching of the Shanghai Stock Exchange as well as the Shenzhen Stock Exchange in 1990. And a listing of H-shares by Chinese mainland companies on the Hong Kong Stock Exchange starting with Tsingtao Brewery Co. in 1993. The number of traded shares and market capitalization on each stock exchange have grown significantly.
- The launch of the Qualified Foreign Institutional Investor (QFII) program in 2002. There was an increase in the quota for foreign investments and the number of

---

15 According to the Shanghai Stock Exchange, "A-shares, or the RMB-denominated common shares, refer to any ordinary shares issued by the domestic companies in China and to be subscribed and traded in RMB by domestic institutions, organizations or individuals (excluding investors from Taiwan, Hong Kong and Macao). B-shares refer to the RMB-denominated special shares with their par values marked in RMB in their circulation and to be subscribed and traded in foreign currencies." (http://english.sse.com.cn/products/equities/overview).

institutions with approved investment funds under the QFII. As of December 2016, a total of 278 foreign institutions were approved for total QFII quotas of $87 billion.[16] Besides QFII, the quota for the Offshore Renminbi QFII or RQFII program (established in 2011) was increased significantly (528 billion yuan as of December 2016). Furthermore, a new rule for QFII with much greater flexibility was released in February 2016.

- A greater access to foreign investors in stocks and bonds, especially under the QFII. This includes, for example, an investment quota (over $1 billion) granted to Fidelity Investments Management Ltd and to other companies. And an increase of the investment cap by $10 billion for foreign investors, such as the Australian arm of Vanguard Group and sovereign wealth fund of Singapore in 2015 (WSJ, 2015).
- Lifting of limitations with the launch of a program called "Shanghai–Hong Kong Stock Connect" between the Shanghai and Hong Kong stock exchanges (October 2014) to provide all foreign investors, including small trading firms, a direct access to A-shares listed on the Shanghai Stock Exchange. Trading in Shanghai is settled only in yuan. This scheme is intended to facilitate investment procedures and lower costs. Furthermore, the overall quota was abolished on August 16, 2016 (The Securities & Futures Commission of Hong Kong, 2016).
- Launch of "Shenzhen–Hong Kong Stock Connect"—a link between the Shenzhen and Hong Kong stock exchanges (December 2016)—providing global investors access to many new stocks of Chinese tech firms in particular.
- New equity options (China 50 ETF) were traded on the Shanghai Stock Exchange in 2015. Before this, the CSI 300 Index futures were traded in 2010. This Shanghai Stock Exchange 50ETF (exchange-traded funds) is a European-style option.

The total market capitalization, which includes stocks (A-shares quoted in CNY and B-shares in USD), funds, ETFs, and different bonds, has grown significantly since 2006 (93.3 trillion yuan as of November 2016), as shown in Figure 6.12. Capital raised on both Chinese stock exchanges has shown a record high in recent years, underscoring an increased role of the securities market. The number of listed companies combined in both stock exchanges has increased (over 3200 companies as of April 2017); the monthly combined turnover reached a record high of 50.3 trillion yuan in June 2015 based on both stock exchanges' data.

Trends in the SHCOMP and shares of Chinese firms listed in Hong Kong (Hang Seng China Enterprises Index (HSCEI)) illustrated in Figure 6.13 demonstrate a volatile performance. In 2015–2016, a series of investigations were implemented by the China Securities Regulatory Commission to improve the stock exchange: focusing on insider trading, dividends paid by firms, delisting of suspect companies, pricing of IPOs, encouraging foreign investors, and more listing of better companies at better prices.

Questions and Problems 6.8

a) Trading volume has surged in Hong Kong since the launch of Shanghai–Hong Kong Stock Connect, with massive equity purchases by Chinese mainland investors: on some days, the quota of 10.5 billion yuan was reached. Discuss the turnover (purchases and sales) and how it affects the Hang Seng Index and Hang Seng China

---

16 State Administration of Foreign Exchange of China (SAFE): http://www.safe.gov.cn/.

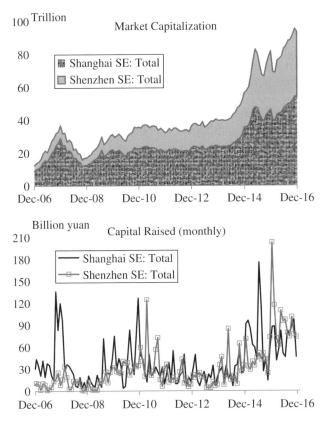

Figure 6.12 Stock market in China (market capitalization and capital raised). *Source:* Data from Shanghai Stock Exchange and Shenzhen Stock Exchange.

Figure 6.13 Stock market performance in China (daily indexes, 2006–January 2017). *Source:* Data from Shanghai Stock Exchange and Hang Seng Indexes.

Enterprises Index (dominated by SOEs). How do global investors contribute to the stock market compared with "mom-and-pop" investors?

b) Assess the impact of China's stock market volatility on financial stability in China. What risks does this volatility entail and how can it be prevented? One particular concern relates to a growing number of Chinese investors involved in highly leveraged stocks using borrowed money.

c) Assess the price-to-earnings ratios of Chinese companies listed on the Shanghai Stock Exchange. Are the stock prices inflated? Examine the relationship between the stock and economic growth in China.

6.6 Finance in Japan

6.6.1 Banking Sector in Japan

Japan's banking system is defined by a *keiretsu* (Hoshi and Kashyap, 2001; Morck and Nakamura, 2004), integrating banking, industrial, and business activities across Japan. These are large economic enterprises with extremely large assets, as discussed in Section 6.3. In Japan, low interest on deposits has allowed local large banks to significantly profit from net interest margins, providing loans mainly to corporations. ROE in Japanese banking system almost reached 6% in 2014[17] from 1% in 2009 (see Figure 6.16). A summary of the main operations of the Japanese banking sector based on all 116 banks, including 5 city banks and 64 regional banks, is shown in Figure 6.14.

Most banks, however, still practice traditional commercial banking, accepting large deposits and providing loans to firms or trade financing. More than half of investment securities in financial assets are government bonds: their total securities investment shares doubled since 1997. City banks, regional banks, postal savings, trust accounts, and financial institutions for small and medium-sized businesses are the major sources of fund raising in Japan. Since the late 1990s, as a result of financial reforms aimed at promoting economic performance, the role of banks has declined, and the importance of shareholders and corporate governance has been redefined.

6.6.2 Effectiveness of Corporate Governance

One of the factors associated with a relatively poor economic performance in the last two decades has been the topic of extensive discourse. Morck and Nakamura (2001) suggested that this is due to poor shareholders relationships with earnings retained rather than paying shareholders dividends. Such policies were used to explain the growth of enterprise cash accounts to almost 44% of GDP, compared with firms in South Korea (34%), Germany (19%), and the USA (11%) (*The Economist*, 2014d). Figure 6.15 illustrates booming retained earnings in all industries. A dividend yield, calculated by dividing dividend by the share price, has also been volatile with a downward trend. The Japanese government has thus encouraged its firms to spend more through reforms of dividend policy, expansion of shareholders' rights, and an increase in salary. As a result, dividend yields started rising again, as shown in Figure 6.15.

---

17 Note that annual data for Japan ends on March of each year.

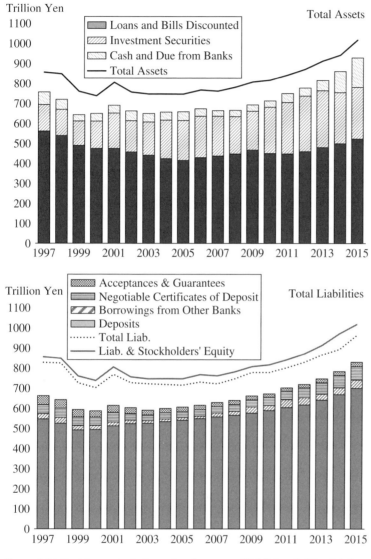

Figure 6.14 Banking sector in Japan (total assets and liabilities of all banks). *Source:* Data from Japanese Bankers Association.

Without dividends, in a stagnant equities market, investors have little incentive to invest. Further, hoarding cash in the form of retained earnings might not be a stimulating policy and provide a disincentive to investors and consumers.

6.6.3 The Importance of Industry

The economic engine of Japan has been its industrial exports, rather than consumption. ROE in Japanese industries, in both manufacturing and non-manufacturing, has shown increasing trends since the financial crisis in 2007 (Figure 6.16). However, financial

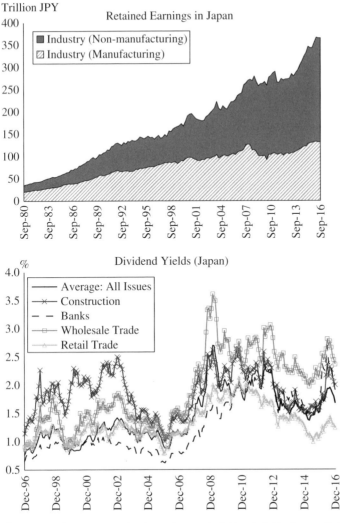

Figure 6.15 Corporate retained earnings and dividend yields. *Source:* Data from Ministry of Finance Japan and from Tokyo Stock Exchange.

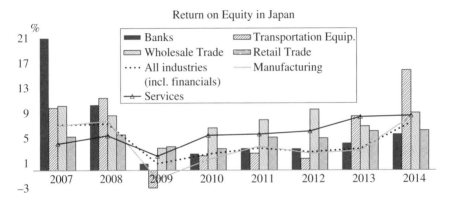

Figure 6.16 Return on equity in Japan. *Source:* Data from Tokyo Stock Exchange.

performance of different firms within the same industry can have significant variations. Thus, ROE ought to be compared in firms of the same group.

While trade balances of intermediate goods have persistently shown large surpluses, the export promotion of final consumer goods has recorded continuous deficits since 2009. According to the Japan Foreign Trade Council, the lion's share of final products exported were cars, followed by steel, parts, and organic chemicals, with large drops in consumer durable goods. The share in total exports declined to 15.7% in 2013—almost returning to its original share in the 1960s. However, Japanese companies, especially in the automobile industry, have moved some of their production potential to foreign countries, both to reduce their production costs and access to foreign markets more easily. WSJ (2014), for example, emphasized the increased profits of manufacturers of intermediate goods exporters, contributing to record high profits by Japanese corporations, with net income surging from a loss in the fiscal year of 2009 to a profit of 25.3 trillion yen in fiscal year of 2014 (SMBC Nikko Securities).

Changes in the exchange rate (JPY per USD) together with a stock market performance and government bond yields are illustrated in Figure 6.17. With depreciation of the yen, investors were motivated to invest in Japanese industrial export companies and contribute to a revival of the Japan stock market. The Nikkei Stock (Nikkei 225) closed in 2015 at its highest price, over 20 000, since 2000. Exports revenues and corporate profits benefiting from the weak yen and cheap oil have contributed to this surge. In addition, reforms on Japanese corporate governance and the prospects of higher dividend payments and stock buy-backs have motivated investors—both domestic and global—to invest in Japanese stocks with a foreign share of ownership of 31% in 2014 compared to 5% in 1990. Of course, it was reflected in a rise of the Nikkei.

6.6.4 Bond Market Volatility in Japan

Starting in March 2000, the Bank of Japan[18] (BOJ) implemented several rounds of quantitative easing (QE) (QE1), using massive asset purchases to boost liquidity by increasing the monetary base of Japan. This was followed by QE2 in October 2010, and QE3 in April 2013. The latest round of monthly purchases of Japanese government bonds was worth 7 trillion yen. As a result, the yen was devalued, largely to boost exports and smooth the negative effects caused by the previous rise in the consumption tax (from 5% to 8% in April 2014), implemented to support fiscal revenues (*The Economist*, 2014c).

The BOJ monetary intervention, aimed at a reduction of bond yields with an increase in bond prices, led to higher volatility in yields. At the same time, the BOJ has been trying to increase inflation with a target of 2%. Thus, the expectation of a future rise in inflation has encouraged investors to sell more government bonds, which resulted in higher bond yields. Large upward spikes in the bond yield would cause serious problems in the economy with massive public debt (almost 250% of GDP), affecting Japanese businesses by raising borrowing costs and causing large losses in the financial sector since banks own these government bonds. Generally speaking, an upward-sloped yield curve is predictive of a healthy economy only if investors are anticipating higher interest rates. The upward slope comes from an anticipation that relatively short-term bonds will command a high coupon and/or will be sold at a discount in financial markets. For bond investors,

---

18 https://www.boj.or.jp/en/.

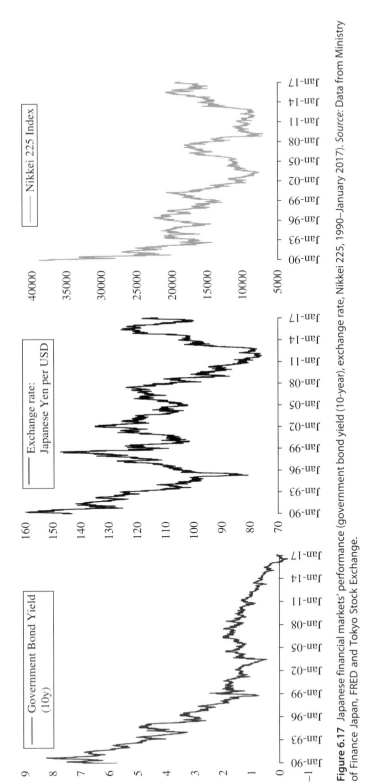

Figure 6.17 Japanese financial markets' performance (government bond yield (10-year), exchange rate, Nikkei 225, 1990–January 2017). *Source*: Data from Ministry of Finance Japan, FRED and Tokyo Stock Exchange.

however, volatility is what they seek to avoid. Thus, spikes in bond yields are what policy-makers ought to have stayed clear of.

Some economists and investors were even predicting a government bond crisis during the period of increased yields. However, later, in mid-2014, bond yields were reduced to their lowest since 2013, and Japanese stock market performance improved (Figure 6.17). Subsequently, in February 2016, the BOJ introduced a negative rate on its government bonds to lower the borrowing cost and to boost the economy. Driven by the demand for safe investment due to increased uncertainty in the global economy and events such as Brexit, the negative yield on 10-year government bonds fell further.

Questions and Problems 6.9

a) Discuss Japan's debt trap and effectiveness of the government strategies to reduce the public debt. Does an increase in consumption tax contribute to the economic growth?

b) Assess the volatility in Japanese bond prices. What is an estimated capital loss from a 1 percentage point increase in government bond yield? Refer to the calculations made by the BOJ.

c) Study the balance sheet of the BOJ. What are the risks (such as interest rate risk) of holding a large share of Japanese government bonds (10% held by BOJ)? BOJ has increased the purchase of exchange traded funds. How does it affect Japanese shares?

d) How does a negative yield affect the profitability of the banking sector in Japan?

6.7 Conclusion

Asia's role in global finance has grown over time as its GDP has become a major con-tributor to the world GDP. Fixed capital asset investment has been the primary driver for this. Savings in excess of investments (net saving) in Asia have led to net exports of capital (especially to advanced countries). Although economic growth in Asia is largely attributed to investments and exports, countries like China have shifted toward a con-sumption-led economy as its urbanization policy has expanded appreciably its consum-ing middle class, 25% of the total, which possesses a greater disposable income than the rest of the population. The Chinese economy is nonetheless largely fueled by exports, but it is also supported by imports of raw materials, particularly from countries such as Brazil and Australia. Thus, a slowdown in the Chinese economy necessarily results in a slowing growth of trade and globalization.

Asian economies' industrial and economic growth faces challenges due to their dependence on exports. However, unlike the "tiger" economies, developing Asian coun-tries have large populations that, under appropriate wealth transfer and greater eco-nomic equalities, may lead to consumption as an additional and important growth engine. Following the 2008 financial crisis, such an awareness has contributed to faster growth of the real sector in Asia, although its financial markets were lagging. A pressing problem in China includes a surge of lending, named "credit equal gold," and the devel-opment of shadow banking. Rising overall debt in China, together with increased default risks, especially during the slowdown of its economy, led to a credit rating downgrade by Moody's from Aa3 to A1 for the first time since 1989. Thus, a balanced approach to risk management is essential. Underlying any sensible approach to the future of financial markets in Asia are well-structured and efficient, which are this able to contribute to a sustainable development and growth. In other words, an economic environment rendering change feasible. For example, these include:

- transparent and liquid capital markets;
- stability and investment safety;
- rule of property and law;
- increased privatization of government-controlled sectors, particularly public banks;
- improvement of corporate credit quality and credit risk management and pricing;
- effective corporate governance with strengthened roles of shareholders.

There are increasing economic, financial, and geopolitical risks and vulnerabilities, not only from global financial changes, but also from domestic, social, and market conditions in some Asian economies. These are associated to projected lower economic growth, higher costs of capital, and financial market volatility, as well as a legacy of economic inequalities. China is dealing with problems in its financial sector. These include large increases in the use of credit, massive corporate debt, the expansion of shadow banking, the efficiency of SOEs, development of the corporate bond market, volatile stock market performance, and asset quality-related balance sheet issues.

Some regional initiatives include ASEAN+3, Economic Review and Policy Dialogue, Chiang Mai Initiative, Asian Bond Market Initiative, AIIB, and the Asian Bond Fund Initiative. However, underscoring China's financial development has been the creation of the Asian Infrastructure Investment Bank (AIIB), which China hopes will rival the World Bank and provide greater political independence from Western-led international economic organizations. The AIIB's intent would then be to finance infrastructure projects ranging over rail, ports, high-speed trains, and a massive Silk Road Fund that will expand trade by connecting China, Central Asia, and the Middle East. East Asian economies promoted regional financial integration to improve financial cooperation and to prevent spillovers from global market instability, to develop regional financial market development, and to promote sustainable economic growth.

References

ADB (2016a) ADB Asian Bonds Online. Bond Market Indicators. Asian Development Bank. https://asianbondsonline.adb.org/regional/data/bondmarket.php?code=LCY_in_GDP_Local (accessed July 11, 2017).

ADB (2016b) Asian Bonds Online. Asia Bond Monitor March 2016. Asian Development Bank. https://asianbondsonline.adb.org/documents/abm_mar_2016.pdf (accessed July 11, 2017).

ADB (2017) Asian Bonds Online. Asia Bond Monitor March 2017. Asian Development Bank. https://asianbondsonline.adb.org/documents/abm_mar_2017.pdf (accessed July 11, 2017).

Bank for International Settlements. BIS Effective Exchange Rate Indices. http://www.bis.org/statistics/eer/.

Bloomberg (2017) China credit growth exceeds estimates despite regulatory curbs. *Bloomberg News*, May 12. https://www.bloomberg.com/news/articles/2017-05-12/china-credit-growth-exceeds-estimates-despite-regulatory-curbs (accessed July 11, 2017).

CBRC (2014) Supervision statistics of Q2, 2014. China Banking Regulatory Commission. http://www.cbrc.gov.cn/EngdocView.do?docID=403BCC3E340949998F9A87A3CAA8E023 (accessed May 22, 2017).

China Banking Regulatory Commission. CBRC. Statistics. http://www.cbrc.gov.cn/chinese/home/docViewPage/110009.html.

China Banking Regulatory Commission. CBRC (2016) China Banking Regulatory Commission 2015 Report. http://www.cbrc.gov.cn/chinese/files/2016/6C1DEC063D6442B289B7C24F662D2E52.pdf.

Dimson, E., Marsh, P., and Staunton, M. (2016) *Credit Suisse Global Investment Returns Sourcebook 2016*. Credit Suisse Research Institute: Zurich.

FRED. Federal Reserve Bank of St. Louis. Board of Governors of the Federal Reserve System. https://fred.stlouisfed.org/categories/95.

FSB (2011) Shadow banking: strengthening oversight and regulation. Financial Stability Board, October 27. http://www.financialstabilityboard.org/publications/r_111027a.pdf (accessed May 22, 2017).

Financial Times (2014) China landmark bond default heads towards bailout: state-owned bad-loan bank shields investors from losses. October 8. https://www.ft.com/content/10adc7be-4ebe-11e4-b205-00144feab7de (accessed May 22, 2017).

Global Finance (2016) *Global Finance* names worlds safest banks 2016. https://www.gfmag.com/awards-rankings/best-banks-and-financial-rankings/global-finance-names-worlds-safest-banks-2016.

Hang Seng Indexes. Statistics. https://www.hsi.com.hk/HSI-Net/HSI-Net.

Hoshi, T., and Kashyap, A.K. (2001) *Corporate Financing and Governance in Japan: The Road to the Future*. The MIT Press: Cambridge, MA.

IMF (2014) *Global Financial Stability Report (GFSR), Risk Taking, Liquidity, and Shadow Banking: Curbing Excess While Promoting Growth*. International Monetary Fund: Washington, DC.

IMF (2016a) *World Economic Outlook, April 2016. Too Slow for Too Long*. International Monetary Fund: Washington, DC. http://www.imf.org/external/pubs/ft/weo/2016/01/pdf/text.pdf (accessed May 20, 2017).

IMF (2016b) *Global Financial Stability Report. Potent Policies for a Successful Normalization*. International Monetary Fund: Washington, DC. http://www.imf.org/~/media/Websites/IMF/imported-flagship-issues/external/pubs/ft/GFSR/2016/01/pdf/_text_v2.ashx (accessed May 22, 2017).

IMF (2016c) Direction of Trade Statistics (DOTS). http://data.imf.org/?sk=9D6028D4-F14A-464C-A2F2-59B2CD424B85 (accessed July 11, 2017).

IMF (2016d) Financial Soundness Indicator. FSI. fsi.imf.org/.

IMF (2016e) International Financial Statistics (IFS). http://data.imf.org/?sk=5DABAFF2-C5AD-4D27-A175-1253419C02D1.

Japanese Bankers Association Statsitics. http://www.zenginkyo.or.jp/en/stats/.

KOF (2016) Index of Globalization. http://globalization.kof.ethz.ch/.

Ministry of Finance Japan. Statistics. http://www.mof.go.jp/english/statistics/index.html.

Morck, R., and Nakamura, M. (2001) Japanese corporate governance and macroeconomic problems. In *The Japanese Business and Economic System—History and Prospects for the 21st Century*, M. Nakamura (ed.). Palgrave, Houndmills, UK; pp. 325–349.

Morck, R., and Nakamura, M. 2004. A frog in a well knows nothing of the ocean: A history of corporate ownership in Japan. In *A Global History of Corporate Governance*, R. Morck (ed.). University of Chicago Press: Chicago; pp. 367–466.

National Bureau of Statistics of China. Statistics. http://www.stats.gov.cn/tjsj/.

PBC (2016) Aggregate Financing to the Real Economy. The People's Bank of China. http://www.pbc.gov.cn/diaochatongjisi/116219/116225/index.html (accessed January 23, 2017).

Reuters (2014) Chaori bailout shows Beijing's desire to protect bond market. October 9. http://www.reuters.com/article/china-chaori-solar-bondholders-idUSL3N0S43EP20141009 (accessed May 22, 2017).

S&P (2014) Credit shift: as global corporate borrowers seek $60 trillion, Asia-Pacific debt will overtake U.S. and europe combined. Standard & Poor's Ratings Services, June 15.

Shanghai Stock Exchange. http://english.sse.com.cn/.

Shanghai Stock Exchange. Market Data, http://www.sse.com.cn/market/overview/.

Shenzhen Stock Exchange. Market Data. https://www.szse.cn/main/marketdata/.

State Administration of Foreign Exchange of China. SAFE (2016). http://www.safe.gov.cn/.

The Banker Database. https://www.thebankerdatabase.com/index.cfm/featured_ranking.

The Economist (2014a) China: a question of trust. May 10. http://www.economist.com/news/special-report/21601622-or-not-case-may-be-question-trust (accessed May 22, 2017).

The Economist. (2014b) State-owned enterprises: fixing China Inc. August 30. http://www.economist.com/news/china/21614240-reform-state-companies-back-agenda-fixing-china-inc (accessed May 22, 2017).

The Economist (2014c) Japan's economy: slings and arrows. September 13. http://www.economist.com/news/finance-and-economics/21617031-harmful-tax-hike-and-reticent-employers-take-their-toll-slings-and-arrows (accessed May 22, 2017).

The Economist (2014d) Corporate savings in Asia: a $2.5 trillion problem. September 27. http://www.economist.com/news/leaders/21620203-japanese-and-south-korean-firms-are-worlds-biggest-cash-hoarders-hurts-their (accessed May 22, 2017).

The Securities & Futures Commission of Hong Kong (2016) Joint announcement of the China Securities Regulatory Commission and the Securities and Futures Commission on 16 Aug 2016. https://www.sfc.hk/edistributionWeb/gateway/EN/news-and-announcements/news/doc?refNo=16PR80.

The World Bank (2016) World Development Indicators. http://databank.worldbank.org/data/home.aspx.

The World Bank and the Development Research Center of the State Council, P. R. China (2013) China 2030: Building a Modern, Harmonious, and Creative Society. World Bank: Washington, DC.

Tokyo Stock Exchange. Japan Exchange Group. Statistics. http://www.jpx.co.jp/english/markets/.

WSJ (2014) What's behind Japan's profit rebound? Unsexy companies like Toray. *The Wall Street Journal*, October 5.https://www.wsj.com/articles/whats-behind-japans-profit-rebound-unsexy-companies-like-toray-1412562603 (accessed July 11, 2017).

WSJ (2015) China raises investment cap for foreign investors. *The Wall Street Journal*, April 30. https://www.wsj.com/articles/china-raises-investment-cap-for-foreign-investors-1430384460 (accessed May 22, 2017).

UNCTAD (2017) *World Investment Report 2017*. United Nations: Geneva. http://unctad.org/en/PublicationsLibrary/wir2017_en.pdf (accessed July 11, 2017).

7

Financial Currency Pricing, Swaps, Derivatives, and Complete Markets

Motivation

FX time series and models, although generally available, are nevertheless complex and multivariate due to the many factors they entail. They span a wide range of economic factors that encompass sovereign financial, economic, and political factors and their interrelationships. To simplify, factors such as sovereign interest rates, the CPI, trade, macroeconomic statistics and their simultaneous and interactive effects define FX prices. As a result, theoretical FX pricing models are many and varied. Some models are derived from multiple economic and financial factors priced in sovereign currencies, others are defined relative to baskets of currencies, and some are defined by empirically tested models. The approaches that we consider in this chapter are essentially based on fundamental and market-based financial currency models, as well as on tracking models. In addition, we shall consider off-market financial exchange models and swaps, used profusely by corporate firms seeking protection from currency risks and by speculators (see also Chapter 8).

7.1 Introduction

FX prices are derived from real and financial assets as well as from macroeconomic policies and statistics, regulation, interest rates, and other factors; for example, off-market events such as political and natural and significant events. In many instances, they are also priced relative to a basket of currencies, tracking other currencies' prices to define their own. They are priced in markets, although they depend on central banks' interest rates and sovereign states' policies (when they intervene in currency markets and impose restrictions on FX transactions and prices). FX prices are thus defined by a plethora of financial factors and agents, anchored in fundamental economic statistics, trade, future expectations, perceived risk/safety, capital flows, and so on. Their complexity is reflected in the broad number of FX models that seek to replicate and forecast currency prices. Although FX is mostly derived by sovereign states' relative economic, governance, and future expectations (see Chapter 5), they are also an underlying asset for a multitude of financial products, such as options and swaps, thus allowing hedgers, investors, and speculators to bet on future FX prices. The former are traded in FX markets, and the latter are traded between willing domestic and foreign parties with or without intermediaries.

Globalization, Gating, and Risk Finance, First Edition. Unurjargal Nyambuu and Charles S. Tapiero.
© 2018 John Wiley & Sons Ltd. Published 2018 by John Wiley & Sons Ltd.

Conventional financial currency pricing models are varied. In Chapters 4 and 5 we have emphasized their pricing based on sovereign macroeconomic statistics such as interest rates, trade, capital flows, sovereign risks, investments, consumption, and so on. Many theoretical FX pricing models are based on a LOOP wherein similar assets or combined economic and financial statistics define an FX price as "a relative price." For example, the PPP principle is applied to countries' CPIs, their real price equivalencies defining a theoretical FX rate. These comparative prices include many additional factors, such as cross-border taxation and tariffs, import controls and quotas, central bank financial policies, and other factors that challenge the accurate prediction of FX rates. For these reasons, financial models used to predict FX prices are necessarily varied, complex, and can best be thought of as works in progress.

In this chapter, we shall consider stochastic models and financial approaches based on the principles of "parity" and "sovereign tracking." The former approach is based on fundamental finance, with prices defined by complete market models, set to imply observable FX future prices. The latter approach consists of "currency tracking models." For example, sovereign states track baskets of currencies or global indexes that reflect their own economic agenda (e.g., their trade policies). For example, an FX price may be defined relative to the global price of a basket of CPIs, or it may be defined relative to a basket of other currencies weighted to account for trade, or the weights of economic and financial exchanges they maintain with a group of other countries. There are in fact many models one may conceive to model, price, and predict FX prices. The extensive list of references at the end of this chapter provides only a few models compared with an extensive algorithmic development of FX models that seek arbitrage opportunities in FX markets. The models we consider are simplified, providing alternative formulations that presume unregulated FX markets may converge to complete markets, their complexity and their non-economic factors affect their evolution and can provide opportunities that FX traders seek to profit from. As a result, FX models are essentially multivariate, statistically dependent, and strategic (in the sense that they are subject to interventions by sovereign and large corporate and other entities). They should be thought of, therefore, only as reference models, their validity to be confirmed by extensive financial and econometric testing.

The financial models we consider in this chapter are not substitutes for the macroeconomic approaches pursued in Chapters 4 and 5. Rather, they complement them and are based on *derived* financial currency pricing models. For example, to illustrate the LOOP, we apply the principle of PPP to sovereign prices for the CPIs. The parities define the sovereign FX rates. Such an approach is extended to obtain a more realistic estimate of FX prices that account not only for global CPI, but also for other economic factors. As a result, in our era of globalization, financial and real assets' prices are also strategic; FX prices are strategic, reflecting the might and the policies that sovereign states are able to exercise to protect their interests. Capital flows, trade, and many other economic, political, and financial factors are then both consequences and causes to determining FX prices in financial markets. The financial models we consider are therefore relative. Some of them include the following.

- Financial and stochastic models that seek to price currencies based on rational expectations and data analysis. For example, multivariate and generalized lognormal (Black–Scholes model) and reverting to guidelines, prices, or baskets of currencies models.

There are a large number of such models published and implemented privately by traders and financial institutions. Some of these models are based on simulations and scenarios generating models that attest to their complexity. In strategy-based and competing sovereign economies, FX models may be inherently contagious or prone to generate "currency wars." For example, if the price of coffee in the USA is extremely high, while it is much lower in another country, we can expect a "migration of coffee" toward the USA. Over a large number of consumption assets, such a migration can lead to a change in FX prices. By the same token, in globalized economies, we may expect a "migration" of volatilities across financial markets. For example, a volatility index in the USA or in China, "migrating" to other countries' volatility indexes, all of which affect prices and, implicitly, their FX. Similar processes are observed in debt defaults when sovereign states very much depend on one another, as is the case in the eurozone, with countries being simultaneously lenders and borrowers to one another (see Chapter 8).

- FX pricing models may be of three sorts. As stated earlier, they may be derived from the LOOP principle, based on cross-border pricing of similar consumption baskets (their CPIs) as well as a function of their macroeconomic statistics (such as capital flows, interest rates and balance of payments). They are also volatility implied, defined by future and optional prices traded globally in global and sovereign financial markets. Given the volume of FX future markets, these markets are important sources of financial information. Finally, there are a multitude of "algorithmic" FX pricing models. For example, tracking models that seek to maintain a parity to a specific currency or to a basket of currencies. Also, keeping a parity to the US dollar will lead to a sovereign strategy of "dollarization." By the same token, letting one's FX track a basket of other FX prices with which a given sovereign state maintains extensive economic exchanges is also a tracking model that simplifies the modeling of FX pricing to be data compatible rather than theoretically defined. When all sovereign states pursue such FX policies, there are important consequences, such as FX contagions and currency wars (when basket prices are altered selectively).
- Financial econometric models based on estimates of trends defined by regression models and volatility estimates; for example, autoregressive conditional heteroscedasticity (ARCH) and generalized ARCH (GARCH) types of models, as discussed in Chapter 2, are often used. Unlike implied volatility and future pricing models, these models are based on past data and thus reflect past trends rather than intentional future changes as implied in future FX markets. In a globalized world, such models are necessarily multivariate, expressing the statistical dependence embedded in their FX time series.
- Strategic models, based on currency gaming by gated sovereign states explicitly and implicitly managing their FX (through trade policies, regulations, etc.). In other words, given the economic stakes associated with sovereign states' FX prices, sovereign agencies may be tempted to manipulate their currency, resulting in retaliations that lead to currency wars and theoretically to strategic currency markets defined by game theory models. Such an approach will be considered and used in Chapter 10, albeit in a regulatory framework.

Both the complexity and our ability to reconcile financial trade and markets data with macroeconomic factors, policies, and statistics, as well as political trends across national boundaries, render currency pricing models challenging.

7.2 The Consumption Price Index and Foreign Exchange in Complete Financial Markets

Assume two countries' CPIs, one domestic, $CPI_D(t)$, and the other foreign, $CPI_F(t)$. Again, for simplicity, say that their rate of change is normally distributed and defined by a lognormal stochastic process with μ_D the domestic statistical rate of return (ROR) and σ_D its volatility. We also assume that R_D is a domestic (sovereign) risk-free rate and $W_D(t)$ is a Brownian motion defining the domestic CPI's random noise. The domestic CPI is defined by the following P-stochastic model:

$$\frac{\Delta CPI_D(t)}{CPI_D(t)} = \mu_D \Delta t + \sigma_D \Delta W_D(t), \quad CPI_D(0) > 0$$

Consider instead the Q-pricing model, resulting from an application of Girsanov's theorem. In other words, it consists of a transformation of the CPI process to a martingale, by transforming the underlying price process to a relative price (e.g., the risk-free expectation of a martingale stochastic process; i.e., the Q-price process). Explicitly, let $\mu_D - R_D$ and $\mu_D > R_D$ be a risk premium. Without changing materially the CPI price process, we add and subtract a risk-free rate and define

$$\frac{\Delta CPI_D(t)}{CPI_D(t)} = R_D \Delta t + \sigma_D \left[\Delta W_D(t) + \left(\frac{\mu_D - R_D}{\sigma_D} \right) \Delta t \right], \quad CPI_D(0) > 0$$

where $\Delta W_D^Q(t) = \Delta W_D(t) + [(\mu_D - R_D)/\sigma_D]\Delta t$ defines the Q-probability measure. As a result:

$$\frac{d CPI_D(t)}{CPI_D(t)} = R_D\, dt + \sigma_D\, dW_D^Q(t), \quad CPI_D(0) > 0$$

By the same token, for a foreign CPI price with its risk-free rate R_F in continuous time we obtain

$$\frac{d CPI_F(t)}{CPI_F(t)} = R_F\, dt + \sigma_F\, dW_F^Q(t), \quad CPI_F(0) > 0$$

A relative PPP in terms of CPIs requires that the FX price is defined by the ratio of the CPIs, or $\xi_{DF}(t) = (CPI_D(t))(CPI_F(t))^{-1}$. Further, CPI's volatility "migrates to the FX stochastic model," thereby defining the FX model's volatility, while their future pricing models define optional prices and an implied volatility we define as "an index of FX fear" associated with the risk factors underlying FX markets. For generality, assume that CPI prices are defined by

$$\xi_{DF}(t) = \theta_{DF}(CPI_D(t))^{\mu_{DF}}(CPI_F(t))^{\nu_{FD}}$$

If $\mu_{DF} = 1$, $\nu_{DF} = -1$, and $\theta_{DF} = 1$, a PPP defines the FX. If this is not the case, there is no PPP (although there can be a partial PPP, depending on the evolution of consumption and FX prices).

Assume that θ_{DF} is constant and set $\xi_{DF} = \theta_{DF}f(x,y)$. A Taylor series expansion based on Itô's lemma (see Appendix 7A.1) yields

$$d\xi_{DF} = \theta_{DF}\left[\frac{\partial f(x,y)}{\partial x}dx + \frac{\partial f(x,y)}{\partial y}dy + \frac{1}{2}\frac{\partial^2 f(x,y)}{\partial x^2}(dx)^2 + \frac{1}{2}\frac{\partial^2 f(x,y)}{\partial y^2}(dy)^2 + \frac{\partial^2 f(x,y)}{\partial x \partial y}(dx\,dy) \right]$$

An elementary development results in a bivariate lognormal process for $\{\xi_{DF}(t), \xi_{FD}(t)\}$ defined by

$$\frac{d\xi_{DF}}{\xi_{DF}} = \mu_{DF}\frac{dCPI_D(t)}{CPI_D(t)} + \nu_{DF}\frac{dCPI_F(t)}{CPI_F(t)} - \frac{1}{2}\mu_{DF}(1-\mu_{DF})\left(\frac{dCPI_D(t)}{CPI_D(t)}\right)^2$$

$$- \frac{1}{2}\nu_{DF}(1-\nu_{DF})\left(\frac{dCPI_F(t)}{CPI_F(t)}\right)^2 + \mu_{DF}\nu_{DF}\left(\frac{dCPI_D(t)}{CPI_D(t)}\right)\left(\frac{dCPI_F(t)}{CPI_F(t)}\right)$$

and

$$\frac{d\xi_{FD}}{\xi_{FD}} = \mu_{FD}\frac{dCPI_F(t)}{CPI_F(t)} + \nu_{FD}\frac{dCPI_D(t)}{CPI_D(t)} - \frac{1}{2}\mu_{FD}(1-\mu_{FD})\left(\frac{dCPI_F(t)}{CPI_F(t)}\right)^2$$

$$- \frac{1}{2}\nu_{FD}(1-\nu_{FD})\left(\frac{dCPI_D(t)}{CPI_D(t)}\right)^2 + \mu_{FD}\nu_{FD}\left(\frac{dCPI_F(t)}{CPI_F(t)}\right)\left(\frac{dCPI_D(t)}{CPI_D(t)}\right)$$

Replacing the terms $dCPI_D(t)/CPI_D(t)$ and $dCPI_F(t)/CPI_F(t)$, the following bivariate process is obtained (with $\xi_{DF}(0) > 0$):

$$\begin{cases} \dfrac{d\xi_{DF}}{\xi_{DF}} = \left[\mu_{DF}R_D + \nu_{DF}R_F - \dfrac{1}{2}\mu_{DF}(1-\mu_{DF})\sigma_D^2 - \dfrac{1}{2}\nu_{DF}(1-\nu_{DF})\sigma_F^2 + \mu_{DF}\nu_{DF}\rho_{DF}\sigma_D\sigma_F\right]dt \\[2mm] \qquad\quad + \mu_{DF}\sigma_D\,dW_D^Q(t) + \nu_{DF}\sigma_F\,dW_F^Q(t) \\[3mm] \dfrac{d\xi_{FD}}{\xi_{FD}} = \left[\mu_{FD}R_F + \nu_{FD}R_D - \dfrac{1}{2}\mu_{FD}(1-\mu_{FD})\sigma_F^2 - \dfrac{1}{2}\nu_{FD}(1-\nu_{FD})\sigma_D^2 + \mu_{FD}\nu_{FD}\rho_{DF}\sigma_D\sigma_F\right]dt \\[2mm] \qquad\quad + \mu_{FD}\sigma_F\,dW_F^Q(t) + \nu_{FD}\sigma_D\,dW_D^Q(t) \end{cases}$$

At a PPP, $\mu_{DF} = 1$ and $\nu_{DF} = -1$, we have

$$\begin{cases} \dfrac{d\xi_{DF}}{\xi_{DF}} = \left(R_D - R_F + \sigma_F^2 - \rho_{DF}\sigma_D\sigma_F\right)dt + \sigma_D\,dW_D^Q(t) - \sigma_F\,dW_F^Q(t), \quad \xi_{DF}(0) > 0 \\[3mm] \dfrac{d\xi_{FD}}{\xi_{FD}} = \left(R_F - R_D + \sigma_D^2 - \rho_{DF}\sigma_D\sigma_F\right)dt + \sigma_F\,dW_F^Q(t) - \sigma_D\,dW_D^Q(t), \quad \xi_{FD}(0) > 0 \end{cases}$$

Note that the FX is then defined in terms of the sovereign reference risk-free rates, CPI volatilities, and their correlation, as well as the CPIs' respective Brownian motions. In order to price these FX, consider the $\ln \xi_{DF}$ transformation (an application of Itô's lemma):

$$d\ln\xi_{DF} = (\mu_{DF}R_D + \nu_{DF}R_F)dt - \frac{1}{2}\left(\mu_{DF}\sigma_D^2 + \nu_{DF}\sigma_F^2 - \rho_{DF}\mu_{DF}\nu_{DF}\sigma_D\sigma_F\right)dt$$

$$+ \mu_{DF}\sigma_D\,dW_D^Q(t) + \nu_{DF}\sigma_F\,dW_F^Q(t), \quad \xi_{DF}(0) > 0$$

Under Q-probability measures, FX prices in the general case, for both $\xi_{DF}(0)$ and $\xi_{FD}(0)$, are

$$\begin{cases} \xi_{DF}(0) = e^{-\Re_{DF}t}E^Q\xi_{DF}(t) \\[2mm] \xi_{FD}(0) = e^{-\Re_{FD}t}E^Q\xi_{FD}(t) \end{cases}$$

with discount factors

$$\begin{cases} \Re_{DF} = \mu_{DF}R_D + \nu_{DF}R_F - \frac{1}{2}\left[\mu_{DF}(1-\mu_{DF})\sigma_D^2 - \nu_{DF}(1-\nu_{DF})\sigma_F^2 + 2\rho_{DF}\mu_{DF}\nu_{DF}\sigma_D\sigma_F\right] \\ \Re_{FD} = \mu_{FD}R_F + \nu_{FD}R_D - \frac{1}{2}\left[\mu_{FD}(1-\mu_{FD})\sigma_F^2 - \nu_{FD}(1-\nu_{FD})\sigma_D^2 + 2\rho_{DF}\mu_{FD}\nu_{FD}\sigma_D\sigma_F\right] \end{cases}$$

By the same token, call options' prices on the FX with respective strikes K_{DF} and K_{FD} are

$$\begin{cases} C_{DF}(0) = e^{-\Re_{DF}t}E^Q\{\mathrm{Max}(\xi_{DF}(t) - K_{DF}, 0)\} \\ C_{FD}(0) = e^{-\Re_{FD}t}E^Q\{\mathrm{Max}(\xi_{FD}(t) - K_{FD}, 0)\} \end{cases}$$

Their implied volatilities are therefore defined by both an expectation of the future price and the discount factor that includes also the domestic and foreign volatilities and their correlation. Their computation is complicated further by the parameters μ_{DF} and ν_{DF} as well as μ_{FD} and ν_{FD}. Under a CPI parity, $\mu_{DF} = 1$ and $\nu_{DF} = -1$, we have explicitly:

$$\begin{cases} \xi_{DF}(0) = e^{-(R_D - R_F)t + \left(\sigma_F^2 - \rho_{DF}\sigma_D\sigma_F\right)t}E^Q\xi_{DF}(t) \\ \xi_{FD}(0) = e^{-(R_F - R_D)t + \left(\sigma_D^2 - \rho_{DF}\sigma_D\sigma_F\right)t}E^Q\xi_{FD}(t) \end{cases}$$

while call option prices under Q-probability measures are

$$\begin{cases} C_{DF}(0) = e^{-(R_D - R_F)t + \left(\sigma_F^2 - \rho_{DF}\sigma_D\sigma_F\right)t}E^Q\{\mathrm{Max}(\xi_{DF}(t) - K_{DF}, 0)\} \\ C_{FD}(0) = e^{-(R_F - R_D)t + \left(\sigma_D^2 - \rho_{DF}\sigma_D\sigma_F\right)t}E^Q\{\mathrm{Max}(\xi_{FD}(t) - K_{FD}, 0)\} \end{cases}$$

When the domestic sovereign state is independent of the foreign CPIs, then the correlation ρ_{DF} is null, although the discount factor remains dependent on the variance of the foreign CPIs. In this case, the presumption that an FX price is defined by $\xi_{DF}(0) = e^{-(R_D - R_F)t}E^Q\xi_{DF}(t)$ has to be reassessed. If an estimate of the FX parameters does not point to a PPP, that is, $\mu_{DF} \neq 1$, $\nu_{DF} \neq -1$ and $\mu_{FD} \neq 1$, $\nu_{FD} \neq -1$, then FX prices are incomplete and, therefore, far more complex to estimate and to price.

Remarks:
In this analysis, note that $\{\xi_{DF}(t), \xi_{FD}(t)\}$ defines a bivariate lognormal stochastic process. In a complete market, however, $\mu_{DF} = 1$, $\nu_{DF} = -1$, $\mu_{FD} = 1$, and $\nu_{FD} = -1$, and therefore $E^{Q_D}(\xi_{DF}(t))E^{Q_F}(\xi_{FD}(t)) = e^{(\Re_{DF} + \Re_{FD})t}$. Consider the general case $\xi(t) = \xi_{FD}(t)\xi_{DF}(t)$. Applying Itô's lemma:

$$\frac{d\xi}{\xi} = \frac{\xi_{FD}d\xi_{DF} + \xi_{DF}d\xi_{FD} + d\xi_{DF}d\xi_{FD}}{\xi}$$

or:

$$\frac{d\xi(t)}{\xi(t)} = (\mu_{DF} + \nu_{FD})\frac{d\mathrm{CPI}_D(t)}{\mathrm{CPI}_D(t)} + (\nu_{DF} + \mu_{FD})\frac{d\mathrm{CPI}_F(t)}{\mathrm{CPI}_F(t)}$$

$$- \frac{1}{2}[\mu_{DF}(1-\mu_{DF}) + \nu_{FD}(1-\nu_{FD}) - 2\nu_{FD}\mu_{DF}]\left(\frac{d\mathrm{CPI}_D(t)}{\mathrm{CPI}_D(t)}\right)^2$$

$$- \frac{1}{2}[\nu_{DF}(1-\nu_{DF}) + \mu_{FD}(1-\mu_{FD}) - 2\nu_{DF}\mu_{FD}]\left(\frac{d\mathrm{CPI}_F(t)}{\mathrm{CPI}_F(t)}\right)^2$$

$$+ (\mu_{DF}\nu_{DF} + \mu_{FD}\nu_{FD} + \mu_{DF}\mu_{FD} + \nu_{DF}\nu_{FD})\left(\frac{d\mathrm{CPI}_D(t)}{\mathrm{CPI}_D(t)}\right)\left(\frac{d\mathrm{CPI}_F(t)}{\mathrm{CPI}_F(t)}\right)$$

In the case of CPIs' parity, we have $d\xi(t)/\xi(t) = 0$, $\xi(0) = 1$, and therefore $\xi(t) = 1$; that is, $\xi_{DF}(t) = 1/\xi_{FD}(t)$ as expected. However, when this is not the case, a stochastic evolution of $\xi(t)$ as defined in the prior equation provides a model of FX "dis-parity." Replacing the CPIs' derived FX leads to a lognormal process that measures the FX "disparity." Explicitly:

$$\frac{d\xi(t)}{\xi(t)} = (\mu_{DF} + \nu_{FD})R_D\,dt + (\nu_{DF} + \mu_{FD})R_F\,dt$$

$$-\frac{1}{2}[\mu_{DF}(1-\mu_{DF}) + \nu_{FD}(1-\nu_{FD}) - 2\nu_{FD}\mu_{DF}]\sigma_D^2\,dt$$

$$-\frac{1}{2}[\nu_{DF}(1-\nu_{DF}) + \mu_{FD}(1-\mu_{FD}) - 2\nu_{DF}\mu_{FD}]\sigma_F^2\,dt$$

$$+[\mu_{DF}(\nu_{DF} + \mu_{FD}) + \nu_{FD}(\mu_{FD} + \nu_{DF})]\rho_{DF}\sigma_D\sigma_D\,dt$$

$$+(\mu_{DF} + \nu_{FD})\sigma_D\,dW_D(t) + (\nu_{DF} + \mu_{FD})\sigma_F\,dW_F(t), \quad \xi(0) = \xi_D(0)\xi_F(0)$$

In a global world, where CPIs are priced relatively to global indexes (such as the IMF global CPI), all CPIs are necessarily dependent. The estimation of FX parameters and their derivatives are therefore to be assessed carefully.

For example, say that an FX's call option whose strike is K_{DF} is priced by

$$C_{DF}(0) = e^{-\Re_{DF}t}E^Q\text{Max}\{\xi_{DF}(t) - K_{DF}, 0\}$$

Its discount rate $\Re_{DF}$ is a function of its future (implied) CPIs' volatilities and their statistical dependence, as stated earlier. An estimate of their implied volatilities would require a greater number of option prices (i.e., an options-rich FX market) to provide a system of equations to be inverted, to obtain a point estimate of implied volatilities. For example, solving for the volatilities implied in the following equations:

$$C_{DF}(0) = e^{-\Re_{DF}(\rho_{DF}\,\sigma_D,\sigma_F)t}E^Q\text{Max}\{\xi_{DF}(t) - K_{DF}, 0\}$$

$$C_{FD}(0) = e^{-\Re_{FD}(\rho_{DF}\,\sigma_D,\sigma_F)t}E^Q\text{Max}\{\xi_{FD}(t) - K_{FD}, 0\}$$

$$\xi_{DF}(0) = e^{-\Re_{DF}(\rho_{DF}\,\sigma_D,\sigma_F)t}E^Q(\xi_{DF}(t))$$

$$\xi_{FD}(0) = e^{-\Re_{FD}(\rho_{DF}\,\sigma_D,\sigma_F)t}E^Q(\xi_{FD}(t))$$

At a CPI parity, however, the discount factor is reduced to $R_D - R_F - \sigma_F^2 + \rho_{DF}\sigma_D\sigma_F$, and of course the expectation of the probability distribution of the FX $\xi_{DF}(t)$ is defined with respect to its probability measure. These results, therefore, differ from both the macro-economic approach to FX pricing (see Chapters 4 and 5) and the conventional univariate stochastic models approaches. The implications of these results are practically important to the extent that they reveal a greater complexity of FX models and their dependence on a multitude of economic, financial, and other factors. Further, they altered the implied volatility and the "Greeks," as will be seen subsequently.

Further, derived CPIs and other economic and risk factors in FX models may be manipulated by sovereign states. For example, if a CPI (or cost of living index) is an FX determinant factor, manipulated by its domestic country or if its volatility alters the FX, it may contribute to an increase or decrease in exports and imports. If two countries at cross-purposes proceed to affect each other's own CPI prices, a "currency war" results. Some of these issues are considered in the following.

7.3 A Generalized Consumption Price Index Foreign Exchange Pricing Model

In an era of globalization, FX prices and their models are multivariate, embedding the complexity and simultaneity of their global economic, financial, and political relationships. FX prices are thus derived from a multitude of economic factors. For example, for simplicity, we tested empirically the PPP of two countries' CPIs in this section (as well as in Chapter 5 for different currencies and longer time series) and found, expectedly, that they were insufficient to predict the FX. To obtain a better fit, augmenting the simultaneous effects of multiple sovereign CPIs and economic factors can be used (such as exports and imports and balance of payments). For demonstration purposes, consider a nonlinear CPI parity and let a sovereign state k define a set of economic factors as a geometric model:

$$Y_k(t) = \theta_k \prod_{i \neq k}^n [Y_i(t)]^{\mu_{k_i}} e^{\sigma_k W_k(t)}$$

with each factor noise statistically dependent due to the global interdependence of Ys. In this case, note that PPP is a more complex and simultaneous relationship that ought to hold across all sovereign states, or:

$$\xi_{kj}(t) = \frac{Y_k(t)}{Y_j(t)} = \frac{\theta_k \prod_{i \neq k}^n [Y_i(t)]^{\mu_{k_i}} e^{\sigma_k W_k(t)}}{\theta_j \prod_{i \neq j}^n [Y_i(t)]^{\mu_{j_i}} e^{\sigma_j W_j(t)}}, \quad k = 1,2,3,\ldots,n$$

For example, for a three-sovereign-state world, we have three equations:

$$\xi_{12}(t) = \frac{1}{\xi_{21}(t)} = \frac{\theta_1 [Y_2(t)]^{\mu_{12}} [Y_3(t)]^{\mu_{13}} e^{\sigma_1 W_1(t)}}{\theta_2 [Y_1(t)]^{\mu_{21}} [Y_3(t)]^{\mu_{23}} e^{\sigma_2 W_2(t)}}$$

$$\xi_{13}(t) = \frac{1}{\xi_{31}(t)} = \frac{\theta_1 [Y_2(t)]^{\mu_{12}} [Y_3(t)]^{\mu_{13}} e^{\sigma_1 W_1(t)}}{\theta_3 [Y_1(t)]^{\mu_{31}} [Y_2(t)]^{\mu_{32}} e^{\sigma_3 W_3(t)}}$$

$$\xi_{23}(t) = \frac{1}{\xi_{32}(t)} = \frac{\theta_2 [Y_1(t)]^{\mu_{21}} [Y_3(t)]^{\mu_{23}} e^{\sigma_2 W_2(t)}}{\theta_3 [Y_1(t)]^{\mu_{31}} [Y_2(t)]^{\mu_{32}} e^{\sigma_3 W_3(t)}}$$

And therefore, the ln(FX) rates are dependent due to both their measurements and by their definition in terms of other prices (which may include prices other than the factors considered). Dropping the $e^{\sigma_i W_i(t)}$ terms for convenience, we assume:

$$\xi_{12}(t) = \frac{\theta_1}{\theta_2} [Y_1(t)]^{-\mu_{21}} [Y_2(t)]^{\mu_{12}} [Y_3(t)]^{\mu_{13} - \mu_{23}}$$

$$\xi_{13}(t) = \frac{\theta_1}{\theta_3} [Y_1(t)]^{-\mu_{31}} [Y_2(t)]^{\mu_{12} - \mu_{32}} [Y_3(t)]^{\mu_{13}}$$

$$\xi_{23}(t) = \frac{\theta_2}{\theta_3} [Y_1(t)]^{-\mu_{31} + \mu_{21}} [Y_2(t)]^{-\mu_{32}} [Y_3(t)]^{\mu_{23}}$$

And therefore the FX and factors $Y_k(t)$, $k = 1, 2, 3$, define a system of three nonlinear equations. Their geometric parameters may be estimated by the simultaneous linear regressions

$$\ln \xi_{12}(t) = \ln \left(\frac{\theta_1}{\theta_2} \right) - \mu_{21} \ln[Y_1(t)] + \mu_{12} \ln[Y_2(t)] + (\mu_{13} - \mu_{22}) \ln[Y_3(t)] + \varepsilon_{12}$$

$$\ln \xi_{13}(t) = \ln \left(\frac{\theta_1}{\theta_3} \right) - \mu_{31} \ln[Y_1(t)] + (\mu_{12} - \mu_{32}) \ln[Y_2(t)] + \mu_{13} \ln[Y_3(t)] + \varepsilon_{13}$$

$$\ln \xi_{23}(t) = \ln \left(\frac{\theta_2}{\theta_3} \right) - (\mu_{31} - \mu_{21}) \ln[Y_1(t)] - \mu_{32} \ln[Y_2(t)] + \mu_{23} \ln[Y_3(t)] + \varepsilon_{23}$$

where $\varepsilon_{12} = \sigma_1 W_1(t) - \sigma_2 W_2(t)$, and similarly for ε_{13} and ε_{23}, leading necessarily to a system of ln-linear stochastic differential equations. An application of Itô's lemma to the ln(FX) and their solution will lead to a multivariate model defined by the factors' Ys of all sovereign states. Say (again for simplicity) that

$$\xi_{12}(t) = f(x_1, x_2, x_3, y) = \frac{\theta_1}{\theta_2} [Y_1(t)]^{-\mu_{21}} [Y_2(t)]^{\mu_{12}} [Y_3(t)]^{\mu_{13} - \mu_{23}}$$

Then after a Taylor series development (or, equivalently, the application of Itô's lemma)

$$d\xi_{12}(t) = \frac{\partial f}{\partial x_1} dx_1 + \frac{\partial f}{\partial x_2} dx_2 + \frac{\partial f}{\partial x_3} dx_3 + \frac{1}{2} \left[\frac{\partial^2 f}{\partial x_1^2} (dx_1)^2 + \frac{\partial^2 f}{\partial x_2^2} (dx_2)^2 + \frac{\partial^2 f}{\partial x_3^2} (dx_3)^2 \right]$$
$$+ \frac{\partial^2 f}{\partial x_1 \partial x_2} (dx_1 dx_2) + \frac{\partial^2 f}{\partial x_1 \partial x_3} (dx_1 dx_3) + \frac{\partial^2 f}{\partial x_2 \partial x_3} (dx_2 dx_3)$$

we obtain

$$\frac{d\xi_{12}(t)}{d\xi_{12}(t)} = -\mu_{21} \frac{dY_1(t)}{Y_1(t)} + \mu_{12} \frac{dY_2(t)}{Y_2(t)} + (\mu_{13} - \mu_{23}) \frac{dY_3(t)}{Y_3(t)} + \mu_{12}(\mu_{13} - \mu_{23}) \left(\frac{dY_2(t)}{Y_2(t)} \frac{dY_3(t)}{Y_3(t)} \right)$$
$$+ \frac{1}{2} \left[\mu_{21}^2 \left(\frac{dY_1(t)}{Y_1(t)} \right)^2 + \mu_{12}^2 \left(\frac{dY_2(t)}{Y_2(t)} \right)^2 + (\mu_{13} - \mu_{23})^2 \left(\frac{dY_3(t)}{Y_3(t)} \right)^2 \right]$$
$$- \mu_{21} \mu_{12} \left(\frac{dY_1(t)}{Y_1(t)} \frac{dY_2(t)}{Y_2(t)} \right) - \mu_{21}(\mu_{13} - \mu_{23}) \left(\frac{dY_1(t)}{Y_1(t)} \frac{dY_3(t)}{Y_3(t)} \right)$$
$$+ \mu_{12}(\mu_{13} - \mu_{23}) \left(\frac{dY_2(t)}{Y_2(t)} \frac{dY_3(t)}{Y_3(t)} \right)$$

Inserting the corresponding Ys and developing the FX processes for $\xi_{13}(t)$ and $\xi_{23}(t)$, we have a system of three simultaneous and dependent lognormal stochastic processes. The models' parameters may be estimated empirically by applying standard regression models as well as a capital asset pricing model (CAPM) and arbitrage pricing theory estimation techniques (see Chapters 2 and 3). Example 7.1 considers such an approach based on estimating FX CAPM models relative to the US dollar.

Example 7.1   Betas for Asian and US Indexes

The CAPM "beta" is a relative measure of systematic risk, which is the sensitivity or slope coefficient from regressing a return on a market return (or on a diversified portfolio). For a US investor, betas of Asian indexes against the USA may determine the sensitivity of an

Table 7.1 Asian and US indexes.

	Sensitivity to US Market (if US index increases by 1%)	Movement
$\beta = 1$	Asian index is predicted to increase by 1%	Tracking movement
$\beta > 1$	Asian index is predicted to increase by more than 1%	Amplified movement
$0 < \beta < 1$	Asian index is predicted to increase by less than 1%	Less movement

Asian index to US market movements (see Table 7.1). The equations below summarize a relationship between the Asian and US indexes.

$$r_t^{\text{Asia}} = \alpha + \beta r_t^{\text{US}} + e_t \ \text{ and } \ \beta^{\text{Asia}} = \rho_{\text{Asia, US}} \frac{\sigma^{\text{Asia}}}{\sigma^{\text{US}}} \ \text{ or } \ \beta^{\text{Asia}} = \frac{\sigma_{\text{Asia, US}}}{\sigma_{\text{US}}^2}$$

Table 7.2 summarizes calculations we have made for several indexes based on monthly return data for January 2000–March 2015. The results show that most Asian countries' betas are lower than unity except for South Korea and India. Almost all the betas are statistically significant as the t stat is very high (p value is very small). The correlation with the US index is also shown.

Example 7.2   Empirical Exercises on FX Parity
FX parity, although a theoretical concept and useful, is incomplete. Explicitly, using monthly data on the Chinese yuan/US dollar CPI and the US CPI Chinese yuan FX, for 2010–2016 ln-regressed on the yuan FX, we estimated the parameters (neglecting the volatility effects).

For the yuan FX: $\xi_{\text{FD}}(t) = \theta_{\text{F}} (\text{CPI}_{\text{F}})^{\mu_{\text{F}}} (\text{CPI}_{\text{D}})^{\nu_{\text{F}}}$, $\theta_{\text{F}} = 9.40$, $\hat{\mu}_{\text{F}} = 0.9852$, $\hat{\nu}_{\text{F}} = -2.233$, all of which are statistically significant with statistical t values 5.79, 2.61, and 3.64 respectively. The ln-regression yields $R^2 = 0.3922$, indicating the importance of CPIs in defining the FX, but also pointing to its insufficiency when referring to its CPIs. Other factors, such as the balance of trade, ought to be accounted for. Finally, it is important to note the disparity of $\hat{\mu}_{\text{F}} = 0.9852 < 1$ and $\hat{\nu}_{\text{F}} = -2.233 < -1$ from their reference (PPP) values $\hat{\mu}_{\text{F}} = 1$ and $\hat{\nu}_{\text{F}} = -1$ as they point to the insufficiency of CPIs' prices implied in the calculation of the FX rate.

Further, based on 63 months of CPI data, simple linear regressions were run on the ln(CPI) of the USA, China, Japan, India, Brazil, and the UK. The results, shown in Tables 7.3 and 7.4, were obtained for an FX of the USD to the CNY with parameter estimates, all of which are statistically meaningful.

7.4   Relative and Foreign Exchange Basket Price Tracking

FX, CPI, or other assets may be priced relative to a basket or financial indexes. For example, IMF devised a global index of CPIs prices, and Blackrock and other financial institutions defined and marketed specialized exchange-traded funds tracking a specific economic activity (such as the S&P 500, a representative index of sectorial economic activity and its like). Such an approach became increasingly popular and has developed

Table 7.2 Asian country betas (monthly returns in Asian indexes denominated in USD, 2000–2014).

	Japan	Hong Kong	Shanghai	Shenzhen	South Korea	India	Indonesia	Malaysia	Thailand	Singapore
	NKY	HSI	SHCOMP	SZCOMP	KOSPI	NIFTY	JCI	FBMKLCI	SET	FSSTI
Regression										
Intercept	−0.1	0.1	0.9	1.3	0.4	0.8	0.9	0.4	0.8	0.2
Beta	0.7	1.0	0.5	0.4	1.4	1.1	1.0	0.5	0.9	1.0
t stat (beta)	10.2	13.1	3.6	2.8	13.2	9.0	7.3	7.2	8.0	13.2
p value	0.00	0.00	0.00	0.006	0.00	0.00	0.00	0.00	0.00	0.00
Descriptive statistics										
Av. return	0.1	0.4	1.0	1.4	0.8	1.1	1.2	0.6	1.0	0.5
Stand. dev.	5.4	6.2	7.9	8.7	8.5	8.5	9.0	5.1	8.0	6.4
Corr. w/USA	0.6	0.7	0.3	0.2	0.7	0.6	0.5	0.5	0.5	0.7
Kurtosis	0.2	0.8	1.2	0.5	1.0	1.6	2.4	0.8	1.7	2.8
Skewness	−0.4	−0.3	−0.1	0.0	−0.1	0.0	−0.5	−0.2	−0.5	−0.5
Range	29.5	39.4	52.4	52.4	59.2	66.1	71.7	34.1	58.7	50.4
Minimum	−17.7	−22.3	−24.5	−23.2	−31.9	−29.8	−40.0	−17.6	−32.5	−26.4
Maximum	11.8	17.0	27.9	29.2	27.3	36.3	31.7	16.5	26.2	24.0

Source: Data from Bloomberg.

Table 7.3 Regression results for the USA and China (dependent variable: log(USDCNY)).

R^2	Coeff. var.	Root MSE	log(USDCNY) mean
0.8716	0.4604	0.0085	1.8381

Source: Data from IMF and The World Bank.

Table 7.4 Regression results for different countries.

Parameter	Estimate	Standard error	t value	$Pr > |t|$
Intercept	3.62794	1.3265	2.73	0.0083
log(USCPI)	0.72994	0.4363	1.67	0.0998
log(CNCPI)	−0.39360	0.1950	−2.02	0.0483
log(INCPI)	−0.14091	0.0759	−1.86	0.0687
log(BZCPI)	0.45541	0.0650	7.00	<0.0001
log(UKCPI)	−1.53117	0.3163	−4.84	<0.0001

Source: Data from IMF and The World Bank.

a variety of reference baskets and, as a result, a large and varied set of pricing models. In the following, we shall consider specific examples to highlight both the complexity and the diversity of such models. In particular, we shall define an FX based on its tracking of a basket of currencies (or CPIs, in which case an FX would be defined by the PPP of their baskets). FX baskets defined by sovereign states are designed to meet economic needs that reflect their economic priorities. When sovereign states manipulate their pricing baskets, currency wars can result. Whether a basket is manipulated (or not), any change in an FX price may lead to all or some FX changing, reflecting a functional dependence of their FX. For example, following Trump's election as the US president, the US dollar increased relative to other currencies, leading to FX perturbations almost everywhere (in particular in countries and investors with debt in US dollars). Defining FX in terms of an economic parity between sovereign states is thus far more complicated than presumed by the LOOP parity of CPIs or CPIs basket parity. The multiplicity of risk and economic factors underlying FX prices, compounded further by exogenous factors due to uncertain and unrelated events, thus contribute to complex and algorithmic approaches to FX pricing. Nonetheless, we necessarily simplify financial FX models to maintain their tractability, and maintain their usefulness for financial traders and financial advisors.

The FX models we consider in the following provide a simplistic basket pricing model (i.e., based on FX prices defined relative to a basket of currencies), all of which are priced relative to the USD (or relative to a global currencies' index). Further, since each sovereign state may track and price its currency based on the self-developed algorithm, both FX and its evolution are a function of "all" other states' basket prices. In this case, basket prices become tools that alter the economic balance of FX prices.

7.4.1 Currency Basket Design

Say that a currency is priced relative to a weighted sum of FX all of which are measured relative to a leading currency (such as the US dollar). Say that an FX $\xi_{12}(t)$ is equated to a weighted portfolio of $N-1$ other FX, $\xi_{12}(t) = \sum_{k \neq 1}^{N} w_{1k} \xi_{k2}(t)$, all of which are priced relative to country 2's currency (say the US dollar). Pricing an FX by sovereign state 1 is then a tracking problem consisting of defining a series of weights for a country, say country 1, that defines a series of weights w_{1k} providing a definition of their FX. For example, the *Wall Street Journal* dollar index is measured relative to 16 currencies pricing the US dollar. In general, weights w_{1k} are selected based on their importance. There are many ways to define these weights, as well as update continuously their definition to be coherent with financial market prices or to affect their own FX price. For tractability, we formulate a simple optimization problem to define the weights of a basket of currencies (or FX, defined relative to the US dollar).

Let there be a sovereign state 1. Given N FX time series of length n, a least-squares estimate of the tracking parameters (weights) of state 1 is defined by minimizing their expected squared deviation. Assuming for simplicity a deterministic system, the following Lagrange problem results:

$$\operatorname*{Min}_{k \neq 1} \frac{1}{n} \sum_{\tau=0}^{n} \left\{ \xi_{12}(\tau) - \sum_{k \neq 1}^{N} w_{1k} \xi_{k2}(\tau) \right\}^2 \quad \text{subject to} : w_{1k} \geq 0 \text{ and } \sum_{k \neq 1}^{N} w_{1k} = 1$$

If all other sovereign states proceed similarly, a "Cournot game-like" problem results defined by

$$\operatorname*{Min}_{w_{ij}, j \neq i} \frac{1}{n} \sum_{\tau=0}^{n} \left\{ \xi_{i2}(\tau) - \sum_{j \neq i}^{N} w_{ij} \xi_{j2}(\tau) \right\}^2 \quad \text{subject to} : w_{ij} \geq 0 \text{ and } \sum_{j \neq i}^{N} w_{ij} = 1, \ i = 1, 3, 4, ..., N$$

If the financial volume of trade, imports, and exports of country 1 with other countries is to be accounted for, a more inclusive tracking model may be defined. Since all countries proceed in the same manner, all N sovereign states selecting weights w_{ik}, $i = 1, 2, 3, ..., N$, would define their FX simultaneously.

For example, say that within a given period of time $[0, T]$ the FX basket weights are constants. The ith sovereign FX USD price is $FX_{iD}(t)$, $t \in [0, T]$, with baskets weights $[w_{ik}]$, $w_{ii} = 0 \, i, k = 1, ..., n, \ i \neq k$:

$$\operatorname*{Min}_{w_{ik}, i \neq k} E \sum_{t=0}^{T} \left(\xi_{iD}(t) - \sum_{k \neq i}^{N} w_{ik} \xi_{kD}(t) \right)^2 + \lambda_i \left(1 - \sum_{k \neq i}^{N} w_{ik} \right), t = 1, 2, 3, ..., T; i = 1, 2, ..., N$$

resulting in a system of simultaneous linear equations for an optimal vector w_{ik}:

$$w_{ik}: \ 2 \sum_{t=0}^{T} \left(\xi_{iD}(t) \xi_{kD}(t) - \sum_{j \neq i,}^{N} w_{ij} (\xi_{jD}(t))(\xi_{kD}(t)) \right) - \lambda_i = 0 \ t = 1, 2, 3, ..., T; i = 1, 2, ..., N$$

Thus, for four states, say, the following system of linear equations defines the weights to the basket of state 1, where $1 = w_{12} + w_{13} + w_{14}$:

$$w_{12}: \left(\sum_{t=0}^{T}(\xi_{1D}(t)\xi_{2D}(t)) - w_{12}\sum_{t=0}^{T}(\xi_{2D}(t))^2 - w_{13}\sum_{t=0}^{T}(\xi_{3D}(t)\xi_{2D}(t)) - w_{14}\sum_{t=0}^{T}(\xi_{4D}(t)\xi_{2D}(t)) \right) - \frac{\lambda_1}{2} = 0$$

$$w_{13}: \left(\sum_{t=0}^{T}(\xi_{1D}(t)\xi_{3D}(t)) - w_{12}\sum_{t=0}^{T}(\xi_{2D}(t)\xi_{3D}(t)) - w_{13}\sum_{t=0}^{T}(\xi_{3D}(t))^2 - w_{14}\sum_{t=0}^{T}(\xi_{4D}(t)\xi_{3D}(t)) \right) - \frac{\lambda_1}{2} = 0$$

$$w_{14}: \left(\sum_{t=0}^{T}(\xi_{1D}(t)\xi_{4D}(t)) - w_{12}\sum_{t=0}^{T}(\xi_{2D}(t)\xi_{4D}(t)) - w_{13}\sum_{t=0}^{T}(\xi_{3D}(t)\xi_{4D}(t)) - w_{14}\sum_{t=0}^{T}(\xi_{4D}(t))^2 \right) - \frac{\lambda_1}{2} = 0$$

$$1: \qquad w_{12} + w_{13} + w_{14} = 1$$

which is reduced to a 3×3 linear system when replacing $w_{14} = 1 - w_{12} - w_{13}$:

$$\left\{ \sum_{t=0}^{T}(\xi_{1D}(t)\xi_{2D}(t)) - \sum_{t=0}^{T}(\xi_{4D}(t)\xi_{2D}(t)) + w_{12}\left[\sum_{t=0}^{T}(\xi_{4D}(t)\xi_{2D}(t)) - \sum_{t=0}^{T}(\xi_{2D}(t))^2 \right] \right.$$
$$\left. + w_{13}\left[\sum_{t=0}^{T}(\xi_{4D}(t)\xi_{2D}(t)) - \sum_{t=0}^{T}(\xi_{3D}(t)\xi_{2D}(t)) \right] \right\} - \frac{\lambda_1}{2} = 0$$

$$\left\{ \sum_{t=0}^{T}(\xi_{1D}(t)\xi_{3D}(t)) - \sum_{t=0}^{T}(\xi_{4D}(t)\xi_{3D}(t)) + w_{12}\left[\sum_{t=0}^{T}(\xi_{4D}(t)\xi_{3D}(t)) - \sum_{t=0}^{T}(\xi_{2D}(t)\xi_{3D}(t)) \right] \right.$$
$$\left. + w_{13}\left[\sum_{t=0}^{T}(\xi_{4D}(t)\xi_{3D}(t)) - \sum_{t=0}^{T}(\xi_{3D}(t))^2 \right] \right\} - \frac{\lambda_1}{2} = 0$$

$$\left\{ \sum_{t=0}^{T}(\xi_{1D}(t)\xi_{4D}(t)) - \sum_{t=0}^{T}(\xi_{4D}(t))^2 + w_{12}\left[\sum_{t=0}^{T}(\xi_{4D}(t))^2 - \sum_{t=0}^{T}(\xi_{2D}(t)\xi_{4D}(t)) \right] \right.$$
$$\left. + w_{13}\left[\sum_{t=0}^{T}(\xi_{4D}(t))^2 - \sum_{t=0}^{T}(\xi_{3D}(t)\xi_{4D}(t)) \right] \right\} - \frac{\lambda_1}{2} = 0$$

In matrix notation we have

$$\begin{bmatrix} w_{12} \\ w_{13} \\ \lambda_1 \end{bmatrix} = \begin{bmatrix} \left(\sum_{t=0}^{T}(\xi_{4D}(t)\xi_{2D}(t)) - \sum_{t=0}^{T}(\xi_{2D}(t))^2 \right) & \left(\sum_{t=0}^{T}(\xi_{4D}(t)\xi_{2D}(t)) - \sum_{t=0}^{T}(\xi_{3D}(t)\xi_{2D}(t)) \right) & -\frac{1}{2} \\ \left(\sum_{t=0}^{T}(\xi_{4D}(t)\xi_{3D}(t)) - \sum_{t=0}^{T}(\xi_{2D}(t)\xi_{3D}(t)) \right) & \left(\sum_{t=0}^{T}(\xi_{4D}(t)\xi_{3D}(t)) - \sum_{t=0}^{T}(\xi_{3D}(t))^2 \right) & -\frac{1}{2} \\ \left(\sum_{t=0}^{T}(\xi_{4D}(t))^2 - \sum_{t=0}^{T}(\xi_{2D}(t)\xi_{4D}(t)) \right) & \left(\sum_{t=0}^{T}(\xi_{4D}(t))^2 - \sum_{t=0}^{T}(\xi_{3D}(t)\xi_{4D}(t)) \right) & -\frac{1}{2} \end{bmatrix}^{-1}$$
$$\times \begin{bmatrix} \sum_{t=0}^{T}(\xi_{1D}(t)\xi_{2D}(t)) - \sum_{t=0}^{T}(\xi_{4D}(t)\xi_{2D}(t)) \\ \sum_{t=0}^{T}(\xi_{4D}(t)\xi_{3D}(t)) - \sum_{t=0}^{T}(\xi_{1D}(t)\xi_{3D}(t)) \\ \sum_{t=0}^{T}(\xi_{4D}(t))^2 - \sum_{t=0}^{T}(\xi_{1D}(t)\xi_{4D}(t)) \end{bmatrix}$$

Statistically, we note that the basket parameters for "1" are a function of the variance, and the many correlations that FX are defined by our tracking objective:

$$E\sum_{t=0}^{T}\left(\xi_{iD}(t)-\sum_{k\neq i}^{N}w_{ik}\xi_{kD}(t)\right)^{2}$$

When a basket consists of more currencies, the problem's dimension and computational problems are more important. However, given the solutions w_{12}^{*}, w_{13}^{*}, and $w_{14}^{*}=1-w_{12}^{*}-w_{13}^{*}$, the FX based on such constant basket weights are at any time t random quantities defined by

$$\tilde{\xi}_{1D}(t)=w_{12}\tilde{\xi}_{2D}(t)+w_{13}\tilde{\xi}_{3D}(t)+w_{14}\tilde{\xi}_{4D}(t)\qquad 1=w_{12}\tilde{\xi}_{21}(t)+w_{13}\tilde{\xi}_{31}(t)+w_{14}\tilde{\xi}_{41}(t)$$

$$\tilde{\xi}_{2D}(t)=w_{21}\tilde{\xi}_{1D}(t)+w_{23}\tilde{\xi}_{3D}(t)+w_{24}\tilde{\xi}_{4D}(t)\quad\text{or}\quad 1=w_{21}\tilde{\xi}_{12}(t)+w_{23}\tilde{\xi}_{32}(t)+w_{24}\tilde{\xi}_{42}(t)$$

$$\tilde{\xi}_{3D}(t)=w_{31}\tilde{\xi}_{1D}(t)+w_{32}\tilde{\xi}_{2D}(t)+w_{34}\tilde{\xi}_{4D}(t)\qquad 1=w_{31}\tilde{\xi}_{13}(t)+w_{32}\tilde{\xi}_{23}(t)+w_{34}\tilde{\xi}_{43}(t)$$

$$\tilde{\xi}_{4D}(t)=w_{41}\tilde{\xi}_{1D}(t)+w_{42}\tilde{\xi}_{2D}(t)+w_{43}\tilde{\xi}_{3D}(t)\qquad 1=w_{41}\tilde{\xi}_{14}(t)+w_{42}\tilde{\xi}_{24}(t)+w_{43}\tilde{\xi}_{34}(t)$$

where $\tilde{\xi}_{43}(t)$ is the FX of state "4" and "3" for example. These equations may then provide a statistical estimate based on their means and variance (as well as their covariance) defined by the set of equations above, or

$$E\big(\tilde{\xi}_{1D}(t)\big)=w_{12}E\big(\tilde{\xi}_{2D}(t)\big)+w_{13}E\big(\tilde{\xi}_{3D}(t)\big)+w_{14}E\big(\tilde{\xi}_{4D}(t)\big)$$

$$E\big(\tilde{\xi}_{2D}(t)\big)=w_{21}E\big(\tilde{\xi}_{1D}(t)\big)+w_{23}E\big(\tilde{\xi}_{3D}(t)\big)+w_{24}E\big(\tilde{\xi}_{4D}(t)\big)$$

$$E\big(\tilde{\xi}_{3D}(t)\big)=w_{31}E\big(\tilde{\xi}_{1D}(t)\big)+w_{32}E\big(\tilde{\xi}_{2D}(t)\big)+w_{34}E\big(\tilde{\xi}_{4D}(t)\big)$$

$$E\big(\tilde{\xi}_{4D}(t)\big)=w_{41}E\big(\tilde{\xi}_{1D}(t)\big)+w_{42}E\big(\tilde{\xi}_{2D}(t)\big)+w_{43}E\big(\tilde{\xi}_{3D}(t)\big)$$

and

$$\text{var}\big(\tilde{\xi}_{1D}(t)\big)=\text{var}\big(w_{12}\tilde{\xi}_{2D}(t)+w_{13}\tilde{\xi}_{3D}(t)+w_{14}\tilde{\xi}_{4D}(t)\big)$$

$$\text{var}\big(\tilde{\xi}_{2D}(t)\big)=\text{var}\big(w_{21}\tilde{\xi}_{1D}(t)+w_{23}\tilde{\xi}_{3D}(t)+w_{24}\tilde{\xi}_{4D}(t)\big)$$

$$\text{var}\big(\tilde{\xi}_{3D}(t)\big)=\text{var}\big(w_{31}\tilde{\xi}_{1D}(t)+w_{32}\tilde{\xi}_{2D}(t)+w_{34}\tilde{\xi}_{4D}(t)\big)$$

$$\text{var}\big(\tilde{\xi}_{4D}(t)\big)=\text{var}\big(w_{41}\tilde{\xi}_{1D}(t)+w_{42}\tilde{\xi}_{2D}(t)+w_{43}\tilde{\xi}_{3D}(t)\big)$$

For example, $\text{var}\big(\tilde{\xi}_{1D}(t)\big)$ in the latter set of equations is a function defined by other states' FX variance and the many correlations the basket implies. Explicitly, following an elementary development, we have

$$\text{var}\big(\tilde{\xi}_{1D}(t)\big)=(w_{12})^{2}\text{var}\big(\tilde{\xi}_{2D}(t)\big)+(w_{13})^{2}\text{var}\big(\tilde{\xi}_{3D}(t)\big)+(w_{14})^{2}\text{var}\big(\tilde{\xi}_{4D}(t)\big)$$

$$+2w_{12}w_{13}\rho_{2,3}\sqrt{\text{var}\big(\tilde{\xi}_{2D}(t)\big)\text{var}\big(\tilde{\xi}_{3D}(t)\big)}$$

$$+2w_{12}w_{14}\rho_{2,4}\sqrt{\text{var}\big(\tilde{\xi}_{2D}(t)\big)\text{var}\big(\tilde{\xi}_{4D}(t)\big)}$$

$$+2w_{13}w_{14}\rho_{3,4}\sqrt{\text{var}\big(\tilde{\xi}_{3D}(t)\big)\text{var}\big(\tilde{\xi}_{4D}(t)\big)}$$

By the same token, a similar development leads to $\text{var}\big(\tilde{\xi}_{2D}(t)\big)$, $\text{var}\big(\tilde{\xi}_{3D}(t)\big)$, and $\text{var}\big(\tilde{\xi}_{4D}(t)\big)$. Further, to obtain tracking parameters relative to other FX, we also use transformations such as $\tilde{\xi}_{21}(t) = \tilde{\xi}_{2D}(t)/\tilde{\xi}_{1D}(t)$, which results in the following system of linear equations:

$$1 = w_{12}E(\tilde{\xi}_{21}(t)) + w_{13}E(\tilde{\xi}_{31}(t)) + w_{14}E(\tilde{\xi}_{41}(t))$$

$$1 = w_{21}E(\tilde{\xi}_{12}(t)) + w_{23}E(\tilde{\xi}_{32}(t)) + w_{24}E(\tilde{\xi}_{42}(t))$$

$$1 = w_{31}E(\tilde{\xi}_{13}(t)) + w_{32}E(\tilde{\xi}_{23}(t)) + w_{34}E(\tilde{\xi}_{43}(t))$$

$$1 = w_{41}E(\tilde{\xi}_{14}(t)) + w_{42}E(\tilde{\xi}_{24}(t)) + w_{43}E(\tilde{\xi}_{34}(t))$$

Similarly, their variance may be found, as calculated above for $\text{var}(\tilde{\xi}_{1D}(t))$. Thus, given the baskets' weights w_{ik}^*, defined over a given period of relative FX stability, we obtain FX normal tracking error terms $\varepsilon_{iD}(t)$, where

$$\varepsilon_{iD}(t) = \xi_{iD}(t) - \sum_{k \neq i}^{n} w_{ik}^* \xi_{kD}(t)$$

Assuming no such error term (i.e., $\varepsilon_{iD}(t) = 0$), an FX may be defined as well by the ratio of their tracking basket:

$$\frac{\xi_i(t)}{\xi_k(t)} = \xi_{ik}(t) = \frac{\left\{ \displaystyle\sum_{j \neq i}^{N} w_{ij}\xi_j(t) \right\}}{\left\{ \displaystyle\sum_{j \neq k}^{N} w_{kj}\xi_j(t) \right\}}$$

When $\varepsilon_{iD}(t) \neq 0$, the tracking process may imply a dynamic transformation of FX prices relative to each other. We consider such a dynamic framework in the following.

7.4.2 A Global Consumption Price Index, Reversion and Foreign Exchange Prices

Stochastic pricing models are tested both on the basis of their underlying rationality and the quality of their empirical results. Lacking appropriate risk-free global bonds, providing risk-free interest rates we may use instead global indexes (such as those defined earlier) relative to which one may price FX prices. Two approaches may be used. One may define for example a CPI lognormal model priced relative to its global index, thereby defining a probability measure relative to the global index. A domestic price (or a foreign one) may then be defined as tracking the global index price (such as the IMF's CPI). First assume a simple mean reversion model:

$$\begin{cases} d\text{CPI}_D = -\alpha_D(\text{CPI}_D - \text{CPI}_G)dt + \sigma_D dW_D(t) \\ d\text{CPI}_F = -\alpha_F(\text{CPI}_F - \text{CPI}_G)dt + \sigma_F dW_F(t) \end{cases}$$

When CPI_G is deterministic, $\text{CPI}_G = \overline{\text{CPI}}_G$; setting $\text{CPI}_{D1} = \text{CPI}_D/\overline{\text{CPI}}_G$ and $\text{CPI}_{F1} = \text{CPI}_F/\overline{\text{CPI}}_G$, we obviously have

$$\begin{cases} d\text{CPI}_D = -\alpha_D(\text{CPI}_D - \overline{\text{CPI}}_G)dt + \sigma_D dW_D(t) \\ d\text{CPI}_F = -\alpha_F(\text{CPI}_F - \overline{\text{CPI}}_G)dt + \sigma_F dW_F(t) \end{cases}$$

By the Girsanov theorem, let η_D and η_F be the risk premiums, and set the Q prices $dW_D^Q(t) = dW_D(t) + \eta_D\,dt$ as well as $dW_F^Q(t) = dW_F(t) + \eta_F\,dt$. As a result, under Q-pricing we have

$$\begin{cases} d\mathrm{CPI}_D = \left(\alpha_D\overline{\mathrm{CPI}}_G - \sigma_D\eta_D\right)dt - \alpha_D\mathrm{CPI}_D\,dt + \sigma_D\,dW_D^Q(t) \\ d\mathrm{CPI}_F = \left(\alpha_F\overline{\mathrm{CPI}}_G - \sigma_F\eta_F\right)dt - \alpha_F\mathrm{CPI}_F\,dt + \sigma_F\,dW_F^Q(t) \end{cases}$$

Defining $\eta_D = \alpha_D\overline{\mathrm{CPI}}_G/\sigma_D$, $\eta_F = \alpha_F\overline{\mathrm{CPI}}_G/\sigma_F$, a standard mean reversion model (an Ornstein–Uhlenbeck process) results:

$$\begin{cases} d\mathrm{CPI}_D = -\alpha_D\mathrm{CPI}_D\,dt + \sigma_D\,dW_D^Q(t) \\ d\mathrm{CPI}_F = -\alpha_F\mathrm{CPI}_F\,dt + \sigma_F\,dW_F^Q(t) \end{cases}$$

whose solution is

$$\mathrm{CPI}_D(t) = \mathrm{CPI}_D(0)e^{-\alpha_D t} + \sigma_D\int_0^t e^{-\alpha_D(t-\tau)}dW_D^Q(\tau)$$

$$\mathrm{CPI}_F(t) = \mathrm{CPI}_F(0)e^{-\alpha_F t} + \sigma_F\int_0^t e^{-\alpha_F(t-\tau)}dW_F^Q(\tau)$$

And in expectation: $\mathrm{CPI}_D(0) = e^{\alpha_D t}E(\mathrm{CPI}_D(t))$ and $\mathrm{CPI}_F(0) = e^{\alpha_F t}E(\mathrm{CPI}_F(t))$. The FX price, under a Q pricing expectation, is then found by setting $\mathrm{CPI}_D^*/\mathrm{CPI}_F^*$ and calculating its stochastic process and its expectations leads to an FX estimate. This is left as a simple Itô calculus exercise. In the following, we consider a generalized model, combining both the lognormal process and a basket pricing reversion model which is transformed to a multivariate lognormal pricing model.

Example 7.3 CPI Pricing Relative to a Basket of CPIs
We generalize further the aforementioned problem by considering a basket of CPIs, $\mathrm{CPI}_G = \sum_{i=1}^n w_k\mathrm{CPI}_k$, and set the following global index reversion model:

$$d\mathrm{CPI}_i = -\alpha_i(\mathrm{CPI}_i - \beta_i\mathrm{CPI}_G)dt + \sigma_i\mathrm{CPI}_i\,dW_i(t), \quad i = 1,2,\ldots,N$$

Therefore, it is defined by a matrix lognormal stochastic process. For simplicity, consider the FX between two countries defined by the ratio of two CPIs such as

$$d\mathrm{CPI}_D = -\alpha_D(\mathrm{CPI}_D - \beta_D\mathrm{CPI}_G)dt + \sigma_D\mathrm{CPI}_D\,dW_D(t)$$
$$d\mathrm{CPI}_F = -\alpha_F(\mathrm{CPI}_F - \beta_F\mathrm{CPI}_G)dt + \sigma_F\mathrm{CPI}_F\,dW_F(t)$$

For convenience, we define $\mathrm{CPI}_{GD} = \mathrm{CPI}_G/\mathrm{CPI}_D$ and $\mathrm{CPI}_{GF} = \mathrm{CPI}_G/\mathrm{CPI}_F$:

$$\frac{d\mathrm{CPI}_D}{\mathrm{CPI}_D} = -\alpha_D\left(1 - \beta_D\frac{\mathrm{CPI}_G}{\mathrm{CPI}_D}\right)dt + \sigma_D\,dW_D(t), \quad \mathrm{CPI}_D(0) > 0$$

$$\frac{d\mathrm{CPI}_F}{\mathrm{CPI}_F} = -\alpha_F\left(1 - \beta_F\frac{\mathrm{CPI}_G}{\mathrm{CPI}_F}\right)dt + \sigma_F\,dW_F(t), \quad \mathrm{CPI}_F(0) > 0$$

Note that when $\beta_D = 0$ and $\beta_F = 0$, we have two lognormal CPI prices. Assume that the global CPI is indeed defined by a lognormal process with an increasing global CPI:

$$\frac{dCPI_G}{CPI_G} = \alpha_G\,dt + \sigma_G\,dW_G(t), \quad CPI_G(0) > 0$$

And let $CPI_{DG} = CPI_D/CPI_G$. Assume $CPI_{DG}(t) = (CPI_D(t))^{\mu_D}(CPI_G(t))^{\nu_D}$, then CPI_{DG} has an underlying stochastic process given by

$$\frac{dCPI_{DG}}{CPI_{DG}} = \mu_D\frac{dCPI_D(t)}{CPI_D(t)} + \nu_D\frac{dCPI_G(t)}{CPI_D(t)} - \frac{1}{2}\mu_D(1-\mu_D)\left(\frac{dCPI_D(t)}{CPI_D(t)}\right)^2$$

$$- \frac{1}{2}\nu_D(1-\nu_D)\left(\frac{dCPI_G(t)}{CPI_G(t)}\right)^2 + \mu_{DF}\nu_{DF}\left(\frac{dCPI_D(t)}{CPI_D(t)}\right)\left(\frac{dCPI_G(t)}{CPI_G(t)}\right)$$

and therefore we substitute $\mu_D = 1$ and $\nu_D = -1$ into the following equation:

$$\frac{dCPI_{DG}}{CPI_{DG}} = \left[-(\alpha_D + \alpha_G) + \alpha_D\beta_D CPI_{GD}\right]dt + \sigma_G^2\,dt - \rho_{GD}\sigma_G\sigma_D\,dt$$

$$+ \sigma_D\,dW_D(t) - \sigma_G\,dW_G(t)$$

And by the same token:

$$\frac{dCPI_{GD}}{CPI_{GD}} = \mu_G\frac{dCPI_G(t)}{CPI_G(t)} + \nu_G\frac{dCPI_D(t)}{CPI_D(t)} - \frac{1}{2}\mu_G(1-\mu_G)\left(\frac{dCPI_G(t)}{CPI_G(t)}\right)^2$$

$$- \frac{1}{2}\nu_G(1-\nu_G)\left(\frac{dCPI_D(t)}{CPI_D(t)}\right)^2 + \mu_G\nu_G\left(\frac{dCPI_D(t)}{CPI_D(t)}\right)\left(\frac{dCPI_G(t)}{CPI_G(t)}\right)$$

At $\mu_D = 1$ and $\nu_D = -1$:

$$\frac{d\,CPI_{GD}}{CPI_{GD}} = \frac{dCPI_G(t)}{CPI_G(t)} - \frac{dCPI_D(t)}{CPI_D(t)} + \left(\frac{dCPI_D(t)}{CPI_D(t)}\right)^2 - \left(\frac{dCPI_D(t)}{CPI_D(t)}\right)\left(\frac{dCPI_G(t)}{CPI_G(t)}\right)$$

or

$$\frac{dCPI_{GD}}{CPI_{GD}} = (\alpha_G + \alpha_D - \alpha_D\beta_D CPI_{GD})dt + (\sigma_D^2 - \rho_{GD}\alpha_G\sigma_G\sigma_D)dt + \sigma_G\,dW_G(t) - \sigma_D\,dW_D(t)$$

These provide a system of three simultaneous stochastic differential equations:

$$\frac{dCPI_D}{CPI_D} = -\alpha_D(1 - \beta_D CPI_{GD})dt + \sigma_D\,dW_D(t), \quad CPI_D(0) > 0$$

$$\frac{dCPI_{DG}}{CPI_{DG}} = \left[-(\alpha_D + \alpha_G) + \alpha_D\beta_D CPI_{GD} + \sigma_G^2 - \rho_{GD}\sigma_G\sigma_D\right]dt + \sigma_D\,dW_D(t) - \sigma_G\,dW_G(t)$$

$$\frac{dCPI_{GD}}{CPI_{GD}} = (\alpha_G + \alpha_D - \alpha_D\beta_D CPI_{GD})dt + (\sigma_D^2 - \rho_{GD}\alpha_G\sigma_G\sigma_D)dt + \sigma_G\,dW_G(t) - \sigma_D\,dW_D(t)$$

Setting $\xi_{DF}(t) = (CPI_D(t))^{\mu_D}(CPI_F(t))^{\nu_D}$, Itô's lemma yields

$$\frac{d\xi_{DF}}{\xi_{DF}} = -\left[\alpha_D\mu_{DF}(1 - \beta_D CPI_{GD}) + \alpha_F\nu_{DF}(1 - \beta_F CPI_{GF})\right]dt - \frac{1}{2}\mu_{DF}(1 - \mu_{DF})\sigma_D^2\,dt$$

$$- \frac{1}{2}\nu_{DF}(1 - \nu_{DF})\sigma_F^2\,dt + \mu_{DF}\nu_{DF}(\rho_{DF}\sigma_D\sigma_F\,dt) + \mu_{DF}\sigma_D\,dW_D(t) + \nu_{DF}\sigma_F\,dW_F(t)$$

By symmetry, the lognormal processes for CPI_{GF} and CPI_{FG} may be derived, defining a multivariate lognormal process with six random variables. Assuming parity, we have

$$\frac{d CPI_D}{CPI_D} = -\alpha_D(1 - \beta_D CPI_{GD})dt + \sigma_D\, dW_D(t), \quad CPI_D(0) > 0$$

$$\frac{d CPI_F}{CPI_F} = -\alpha_F(1 - \beta_F CPI_{GF})dt + \sigma_F\, dW_F(t), \quad CPI_F(0) > 0$$

$$\frac{d CPI_{DG}}{CPI_{DG}} = \left[-(\alpha_D + \alpha_G) + \alpha_D\beta_D CPI_{GD}\right]dt + \sigma_G^2\, dt - \rho_{GD}\sigma_G\sigma_D\, dt + \sigma_D\, dW_D(t) - \sigma_G\, dW_G(t)$$

$$\frac{d CPI_{FG}}{CPI_{FG}} = \left[-(\alpha_F + \alpha_G) + \alpha_F\beta_F CPI_{GF}\right]dt + \sigma_G^2\, dt - \rho_{GF}\sigma_G\sigma_F\, dt - \sigma_D\, dW_D(t) + \sigma_G\, dW_G(t)$$

$$\frac{d CPI_{GD}}{CPI_{GD}} = (\alpha_G + \alpha_D - \alpha_D\beta_D CPI_{GD})dt + \left(\sigma_D^2 - \rho_{GD}\alpha_G\sigma_G\sigma_D\right)dt + \sigma_G\, dW_G(t) - \sigma_D\, dW_D(t)$$

$$\frac{d CPI_{GF}}{CPI_{GF}} = (\alpha_G + \alpha_F - \alpha_F\beta_F CPI_{GF})dt + \left(\sigma_F^2 - \rho_{GF}\alpha_G\sigma_G\sigma_F\right)dt + \sigma_G\, dW_G(t) - \sigma_F\, dW_F(t)$$

An FX, assuming the generalized model, yields (where the reference baskets of D and F are introduced)

$$\frac{d\xi_{DF}}{\xi_{DF}} = -\left(\alpha_D\mu_{DF} + \alpha_F\nu_{DF} - \mu_{DF}\nu_{DF}\rho_{DF}\sigma_F\sigma_D\right)dt$$

$$+ \left(\sum_{k \neq D}^{n} \alpha_D\mu_{DF}w_{Dk}CPI_{kD} + \alpha_F\nu_{DF}\sum_{i \neq F}^{n} w_{Fi}CPI_{iF} \right)dt$$

$$- \frac{1}{2}\left[\mu_{DF}(1 - \mu_{DF})\sigma_D^2 + \nu_{DF}(1 - \nu_{DF})\sigma_F^2 \right]dt + \mu_{DF}\sigma_D\, dW_D(t) + \nu_{DF}\sigma_F\, dW_F(t)$$

At a CPI PPP, with $\mu_{DF} = 1$ and $\nu_{DF} = -1$, the following process results:

$$\frac{d\xi_{DF}}{\xi_{DF}} = -\left[\alpha_D(1 - B_D) - \alpha_F(1 - B_F) + \sigma_F^2 + \rho_{DF}\sigma_F\sigma_D \right]dt + \sigma_D\, dW_D(t) - \sigma_F\, dW_F(t)$$

where $B_D = \sum_{k \neq D}^{n} w_{Dk}CPI_{kD}$ and $B_F = \sum_{i \neq F}^{n} w_{Fi}CPI_{iF}$ are the baskets of the domestic and the foreign CPIs. Note that $B_D = w_{D1}CPI_{1D} + w_{D2}CPI_{2D} + \cdots + w_{Dn}CPI_{nD}$ and $B_F = w_{F1}CPI_{1F} + w_{F2}CPI_{2F} + \cdots + w_{Fn}CPI_{nF}$. As a result, assuming the parity in all CPIs, we have instead

$$B_D = w_{D1}\xi_{1D} + w_{D2}\xi_{2D} + \cdots + w_{Dn}\xi_{nD} \quad \text{and} \quad B_F = w_{F1}\xi_{1F} + w_{F2}\xi_{2F} + \cdots + w_{Fn}\xi_{nF}$$

This extensive FX model requires the development of a system of codependent $2n$ lognormal stochastic processes.

In practice, these models may be of much greater dimensions. For example, a basket of 16 currencies as used by the *Wall Street Journal* would require 32 simultaneous lognormal processes. Pricing an FX is in this case theoretically and practically feasible (although it requires careful calculations, which are left for the motivated reader). However, computational methods that seek to estimate the implied volatilities are far more challenging.

7.4.3 Global Index Reversion and Foreign Exchange

We consider again the generalized lognormal process with a global price index. The model defined earlier is changed slightly:

$$\begin{cases} \dfrac{d\,CPI_D}{CPI_D} = -\alpha_D\left(1 - \dfrac{CPI_G}{CPI_D}\right)dt + \sigma_D\,dW_D(t) \\[3mm] \dfrac{d\,CPI_F}{CPI_F} = -\alpha_F\left(1 - \dfrac{CPI_G}{CPI_F}\right)dt + \sigma_F\,dW_F(t) \end{cases}$$

And the global index is given by a lognormal process:

$$\dfrac{d\,CPI_G}{CPI_G} = \beta_G\,dt + \sigma_G\,dW_G, \quad CPI_G(0) > 0$$

Under a Q probability measure we have

$$\dfrac{d\,CPI_G}{CPI_G} = R_G\,dt + \sigma_G\,dW_G^Q, \quad CPI_G(0) > 0$$

where $CPI_{DG} = CPI_D/CPI_G$ and $CPI_{FG} = CPI_F/CPI_G$, as well as $CPI_{GD} = CPI_G/CPI_D$, are given by Itô's lemma:

$$d\,CPI_{DG} = \dfrac{d\,CPI_D}{CPI_G} - \dfrac{CPI_D}{CPI_G}\dfrac{d\,CPI_G}{CPI_G} + \dfrac{CPI_D}{CPI_G}\left(\dfrac{d\,CPI_G}{CPI_G}\right)^2 - \dfrac{CPI_D}{CPI_G}\left(\dfrac{d\,CPI_D}{CPI_D}\dfrac{d\,CPI_G}{CPI_G}\right)$$

$$d\,CPI_{GD} = \dfrac{d\,CPI_G}{CPI_D} - \dfrac{CPI_G}{CPI_D}\dfrac{d\,CPI_D}{CPI_D} + \dfrac{CPI_G}{CPI_D}\left(\dfrac{d\,CPI_D}{CPI_D}\right)^2 - \dfrac{CPI_G}{CPI_D}\left(\dfrac{d\,CPI_G}{CPI_G}\dfrac{d\,CPI_D}{CPI_D}\right)$$

Or

$$d\,CPI_{DG} = \alpha_D\,dt - CPI_{DG}\left[\left(\alpha_D + R_G - \sigma_G^2 + \rho_{DG}\sigma_D\sigma_G\right)dt - \sigma_D\,dW_D(t) + \sigma_G\,dW_G^Q\right]$$

$$d\,CPI_{FG} = \alpha_F\,dt - CPI_{FG}\left[\left(\alpha_F + R_G - \sigma_G^2 + \rho_{FG}\sigma_F\sigma_G\right)dt - \sigma_F\,dW_F(t) + \sigma_G\,dW_G^Q\right]$$

Let $A_D = \alpha_D + R_G - \sigma_G^2 + \rho_{DG}\sigma_D\sigma_G$ and $A_F = \alpha_F + R_G - \sigma_G^2 + \rho_{FG}\sigma_F\sigma_G$; then

$$d\,CPI_{DG} = (\alpha_D - A_D CPI_{DG})\,dt + CPI_{DG}(\sigma_D\,dW_D(t) - \sigma_G\,dW_G)$$

$$d\,CPI_{FG} = (\alpha_F - A_F CPI_{FG})\,dt + CPI_{FG}(\sigma_F\,dW_F(t) - \sigma_G\,dW_G)$$

We define a probability measure by setting

$$\sigma_D\,dW_D^Q(t) = \sigma_D\left[dW_D(t) + \left(\dfrac{A_D - R_D}{\sigma_D}\right)\right]$$

and therefore

$$\sigma_D\left[dW_D^Q(t) - \left(\dfrac{A_D - R_D}{\sigma_D}\right)dt\right] = \sigma_D\,dW_D(t)$$

and so

$$d\,CPI_{DG} = (\alpha_D - A_D CPI_{DG})\,dt + \left\{\sigma_D CPI_{DG}\left[dW_D^Q(t) - CPI_{DG}(A_D - R_D)\,dt\right]\right. $$
$$\left. - \sigma_G CPI_{DG}\,dW_G\right\}$$

and

$$dCPI_{DG} = (\alpha_D - R_D A_D CPI_{DG})dt + CPI_{DG}\left(\sigma_D dW_D^Q(t) - \sigma_G dW_G\right)$$

and finally

$$\frac{dCPI_{DG}}{CPI_{DG}} = -R_D dt + \alpha_D CPI_{GD} dt + \sigma_D dW_D^Q(t) - \sigma_G dW_G^Q$$

However, since

$$dCPI_{GD} = \frac{dCPI_G}{CPI_D} - \frac{CPI_G}{CPI_D}\frac{dCPI_D}{CPI_D} + \frac{CPI_G}{CPI_D}\left(\frac{dCPI_D}{CPI_D}\right)^2 - \frac{CPI_G}{CPI_D}\left(\frac{dCPI_G}{CPI_G}\frac{dCPI_D}{CPI_D}\right)$$

elementary developments yield

$$\frac{dCPI_{GD}}{CPI_{GD}} = (R_D - \rho_{GD}\sigma_G\sigma_D)dt + \sigma_G dW_G^Q$$

And therefore the following simultaneous bivariate lognormal process under the probability measures $W_D^Q(t)$ and dW_G^Q results in a four-variate lognormal process:

$$\frac{dCPI_{DG}}{CPI_{DG}} = (-R_D + \alpha_D CPI_{GD})dt + \sigma_D dW_D^Q(t) - \sigma_G dW_G^Q, \quad CPI_D(0) > 0$$

$$\frac{dCPI_{FG}}{CPI_{FG}} = (-R_F + \alpha_F CPI_{GF})dt + \sigma_F dW_F^Q(t) - \sigma_G dW_G^Q, \quad CPI_F(0) > 0$$

$$\frac{dCPI_{GD}}{CPI_{GD}} = (R_D - \rho_{GD}\sigma_G\sigma_D)dt + \sigma_G dW_G^Q, \quad CPI_{GD}(0) = \frac{CPI_G(0)}{CPI_D(0)} > 0$$

$$\frac{dCPI_{GF}}{CPI_{GF}} = (R_F - \rho_{GF}\sigma_G\sigma_F)dt + \sigma_G dW_G^Q, \quad CPI_{GF}(0) = \frac{CPI_G(0)}{CPI_F(0)} > 0$$

Further, assuming a PPP, an FX ξ_{DF} is defined by $\xi_{DF} = CPI_{DG}/CPI_{FG}$, which can be calculated by the usual application of Itô's lemma and, subsequently, priced. Explicitly:

$$\frac{dCPI_{DG}}{CPI_{DG}} = (-R_D + \alpha_D CPI_{GD})dt + \sigma_D dW_D^Q(t) - \sigma_G dW_G^Q, \quad CPI_D(0) > 0$$

$$\frac{dCPI_{FG}}{CPI_{FG}} = (-R_F + \alpha_F CPI_{GF})dt + \sigma_F dW_F^Q(t) - \sigma_G dW_G^Q, \quad CPI_F(0) > 0$$

And therefore, $CPI_{DG} = CPI_D/CPI_G$. Assume $\xi_{DF} = (CPI_{DG})^{\mu_D}/(CPI_{FG})^{\nu_D}$, then its underlying stochastic process is given by

$$d\xi_{DF} = \mu_D \frac{dCPI_{DG}(t)}{CPI_{DG}(t)} + \nu_D \frac{dCPI_{FG}(t)}{CPI_{FG}(t)} - \frac{1}{2}\mu_D(1-\mu_D)\left(\frac{dCPI_{DG}(t)}{CPI_{DG}(t)}\right)^2$$

$$- \frac{1}{2}\nu_D(1-\nu_D)\left(\frac{dCPI_{FG}(t)}{CPI_{FG}(t)}\right)^2 + \mu_{DF}\nu_{DF}\left(\frac{dCPI_{DG}(t)}{CPI_{DG}(t)}\right)\left(\frac{dCPI_{FG}(t)}{CPI_{FG}(t)}\right)$$

Or

$$d\xi_{DF} = \mu_D(-R_D + \alpha_D CPI_{GD})dt + \nu_D(-R_F + \alpha_F CPI_{GF})dt$$

$$-\frac{1}{2}\mu_D(1-\mu_D)(\sigma_D^2 + \sigma_G^2 - 2\rho_{DG}\sigma_D\sigma_G)dt - \frac{1}{2}\nu_D(1-\nu_D)(\sigma_F^2 + \sigma_G^2 - \rho_{FG}\sigma_F\sigma_G)dt$$

$$+\mu_{DF}\nu_{DF}\left[\rho_{FD}\sigma_D(\sigma_F - \sigma_G) - \rho_{FG}\sigma_F\sigma_G + \sigma_G^2\right]dt + \mu_D\sigma_D\,dW_D^Q(t) + \nu_D\sigma_F\,dW_F^Q(t)$$

$$-(\nu_D\sigma_G + \mu_D\sigma_G)dW_G^Q$$

At parity, $\mu_D = 1$ and $\nu_D = -1$, the FX is

$$d\xi_{DF} = -(R_D - R_F)dt + CPI_{GF}(\alpha_D\xi_{DF} - \alpha_F)dt + \left[\sigma_F^2 + 2\sigma_G^2 - \rho_{FD}\sigma_D(\sigma_F - \sigma_G) + \rho_{FG}\sigma_F\sigma_G\right]dt$$

$$+\sigma_D\,dW_D^Q(t) - \sigma_F\,dW_F^Q(t), \quad \xi_{DF}(0) > 0$$

$$\frac{dCPI_{GF}}{CPI_{GF}} = (R_F - \rho_{GF}\sigma_G\sigma_F)dt + \sigma_G\,dW_G^Q, \quad CPI_{GF}(0) > 0$$

Note that the solution for $CPI_{GF}(t)$ is

$$CPI_{GF}(t) = CPI_{GF}(0)e^{\left[R_F - \rho_{GF}\sigma_G\sigma_F - (1/2)\sigma_G^2\right]t + \sigma_G\,dW_G^Q}$$

And therefore the FX price is a nonlinear stochastic differential equation:

$$d\xi_{DF} = -(R_D - R_F)dt + CPI_{GF}(0)(\alpha_D\xi_{DF} - \alpha_F)e^{\left[R_F - \rho_{GF}\sigma_G\sigma_F - (1/2)\sigma_G^2\right]t + \sigma_G\,dW_G^Q}dt$$

$$+\left[\sigma_F^2 + 2\sigma_G^2 - \rho_{FD}\sigma_D(\sigma_F - \sigma_G) + \rho_{FG}\sigma_F\sigma_G\right]dt + \sigma_D\,dW_D^Q(t) - \sigma_F\,dW_F^Q(t), \quad \xi_{DF}(0) > 0$$

Although an analytical solution is not easily found, its numerical solution is feasible. Note that in expectation:

$$dE(\xi_{DF}) = -\left[(R_D - R_F) - \sigma_F^2 - 2\sigma_G^2 + \rho_{FD}\sigma_D(\sigma_F - \sigma_G) + \rho_{FG}\sigma_F\sigma_G\right]dt$$

$$-\alpha_F CPI_{GF}(0)e^{(R_F - \rho_{GF}\sigma_G\sigma_F)t} + (CPI_{GF}(0)\alpha_D\Phi(t))dt, \quad \xi_{DF}(0) > 0$$

where $\Phi(t) = E\left(\xi_{DF}(t)e^{\left[-(1/2)\sigma_G^2\right]t + \sigma_G\,dW_G^Q}\right)$.

7.4.4 Q Pricing and Multiple Risks

FX models are multivariate, and therefore subject to multiple risk sources. Let the kth sovereign state's $CPI_k(t)$ be defined by

$$\frac{dCPI_k(t)}{CPI_k(t)} = \mu_k\,dt + \sigma_{kk}\,dW_k(t) + \sum_{i\neq k}^{n}\sigma_{ki}\,dW_i(t), \quad k = 1,2,...,n$$

Using the Girsanov theorem, we replace $dW_i(t) = dW_i^Q(t) + \eta_i\,dt$, and therefore

$$\frac{dCPI_k(t)}{CPI_k(t)} = \left(\mu_k + \sigma_{kk}\eta_k + \sum_{i\neq k}^{n}\sigma_{ki}\eta_i\right)dt + \sigma_{kk}\,dW_k^Q(t) + \sum_{i\neq k}^{n}\sigma_{ki}W_i^Q(t), \quad k = 1,2,...,n$$

To obtain a risk-neutral martingale, set $\left(\mu_k - R_k + \sigma_{kk}\eta_k + \sum_{i \neq k}^{n} \sigma_{ki}\eta_i\right) = R_k$. For example, consider the case $n = 3$, then in matrix notation we have

$$
\begin{bmatrix}
1 & 0 & 0 & 0 \\
\mu_1 - R_1 & \sigma_{11} & \sigma_{12} & \sigma_{13} \\
\mu_2 - R_2 & \sigma_{21} & \sigma_{22} & \sigma_{23} \\
\mu_3 - R_3 & \sigma_{31} & \sigma_{32} & \sigma_{33}
\end{bmatrix}
\begin{bmatrix}
1 \\ \eta_1 \\ \eta_2 \\ \eta_3
\end{bmatrix}
=
\begin{bmatrix}
1 \\ R_1 \\ R_2 \\ R_3
\end{bmatrix}
$$

The solution for the risk premiums is

$$
\begin{bmatrix}
1 \\ \eta_1^* \\ \eta_2^* \\ \eta_3^*
\end{bmatrix}
=
\begin{bmatrix}
1 & 0 & 0 & 0 \\
\mu_1 - R_1 & \sigma_{11} & \sigma_{12} & \sigma_{13} \\
\mu_2 - R_2 & \sigma_{21} & \sigma_{22} & \sigma_{23} \\
\mu_3 - R_3 & \sigma_{31} & \sigma_{32} & \sigma_{33}
\end{bmatrix}^{-1}
\begin{bmatrix}
1 \\ R_1 \\ R_2 \\ R_3
\end{bmatrix}
$$

and $dW_k(t) = dW_k^Q(t) + \eta_k^*\, dt$. As a result:

$$
\frac{d\mathrm{CPI}_k(t)}{\mathrm{CPI}_k(t)} = R_k + \sum_{i=1}^{n} \sigma_{ki}\, dW_i^Q(t), \quad k = 1, 2, \ldots, n
$$

And the FX $\xi_{kj}(t) = \mathrm{CPI}_k(t)/\mathrm{CPI}_j(t)$ is

$$
d\left(\frac{\mathrm{CPI}_k}{\mathrm{CPI}_j}\right) = \frac{d\mathrm{CPI}_k}{\mathrm{CPI}_j} + \mathrm{CPI}_k\, d\left(\frac{1}{\mathrm{CPI}_j}\right)
$$

$$
= \frac{d\mathrm{CPI}_k}{\mathrm{CPI}_j} + \mathrm{CPI}_k\left[-\frac{d\mathrm{CPI}_j}{\mathrm{CPI}_j^2} + \frac{1}{\mathrm{CPI}_j}\left(\frac{d\mathrm{CPI}_j}{\mathrm{CPI}_j}\right)^2 \right] - \left(\frac{d\mathrm{CPI}_k\, d\mathrm{CPI}_j}{\mathrm{CPI}_j^2}\right)
$$

Thus:

$$
d\ln\left(\frac{\mathrm{CPI}_k}{\mathrm{CPI}_j}\right) = (R_k - R_j)\, dt + \sum_{i=1}^{n} \sigma_{ki}\, dW_i^Q(t)\, dt - \sum_{i=1}^{n} \sigma_{ji}\, dW_i^Q(t)
$$

$$
+ \left(\sum_{i=1}^{n} \sigma_{ji}\, dW_i^Q(t)\right)^2 - \left(\sum_{i=1}^{n} \sigma_{ki}\, dW_i^Q(t)\right)\left(\sum_{i=1}^{n} \sigma_{ji}\, dW_i^Q(t)\right)
$$

We have then

$$
\frac{d\xi_{kj}}{\xi_{kj}} = (R_k - R_j)\, dt + \sum_{i=1}^{n} \sigma_{ki} W_i^Q(t) - \sum_{i=1}^{n} \sigma_{ji} W_i^Q(t) + \left(\sum_{i=1}^{n} \sigma_{ji} W_i^Q(t)\right)^2
$$

$$
- \left(\sum_{i=1}^{n} \sigma_{ki} W_i^Q(t)\right)\left(\sum_{i=1}^{n} \sigma_{ji} W_i^Q(t)\right)
$$

As a result, the discount factor is defined by the covariations of countries volatilities and their mutual effects. For example, for three sovereign states we have

$$\frac{d\xi_{12}}{\xi_{12}} = (R_1 - R_2)\,dt + \sigma_{11}\,W_1^Q(t) + \sigma_{12}\,W_2^Q(t) + \sigma_{13}\,W_3^Q(t) - \sigma_{21}\,W_1^Q(t) - \sigma_{22}\,W_2^Q(t)$$

$$- \sigma_{23}\,W_3^Q(t) + (\sigma_{21}\,W_1^Q(t) - \sigma_{22}\,W_2^Q(t) - \sigma_{23}\,W_3^Q(t))^2$$

$$- \Big(\sigma_{11}\,W_1^Q(t) + \sigma_{12}\,W_2^Q(t) + \sigma_{13}\,W_3^Q(t)\Big)\Big(\sigma_{21}\,W_1^Q(t) - \sigma_{22}\,W_2^Q(t) - \sigma_{23}\,W_3^Q(t)\Big)$$

Or

$$\frac{d\xi_{12}}{\xi_{12}} = \Omega_{12}\,dt + (\sigma_{11} - \sigma_{21})\,dW_1^Q(t) + (\sigma_{12} - \sigma_{22})\,dW_2^Q(t) + (\sigma_{13} - \sigma_{23})\,dW_3^Q(t), \quad \xi_{12}(0) > 0$$

where

$$\Omega_{12} = R_1 - R_2 + (\sigma_{21})^2 + (\sigma_{22})^2 + (\sigma_{23})^2 - \sigma_{11}\sigma_{21} + \sigma_{12}\sigma_{22} + \sigma_{13}\sigma_{23}$$

$$+ \rho_{12}(-2\sigma_{22}\sigma_{21} + \sigma_{11}\sigma_{22} - \sigma_{12}\sigma_{21})$$

$$+ \rho_{13}(-2\sigma_{23}\sigma_{21} + \sigma_{11}\sigma_{23} - \sigma_{13}\sigma_{21}) + \rho_{23}(2\sigma_{22}\sigma_{23} + \sigma_{12}\sigma_{23} + \sigma_{13}\sigma_{22})$$

Thus, pricing an FX is defined by multiple factors, their volatility, and their intricate correlations. To obtain the FX price, an ln transformation of the multi-risk lognormal process will define the complete FX market price.

7.5 Options Pricing: Applications and Examples

Options are contingent contracts, providing the holder (buyer) of an option the right to exercise the terms set by the contract while the issuer or seller of the option collects a premium with an obligation to maintain the option's contract terms. The simplest vanilla options are the call and put European options. The call option is a bet that a future price, set at an explicit future time, will exceed a traded strike, providing an opportunity to mitigate future losses due to mispricing (for a buyer and a seller of the call option). By the same token, a put option assumes the inverse position, betting that an underlying future price will fall below its traded strike. Options of various properties, although simple in principle, can be complex and engineered to define an alphabet soup providing an extremely large variety of optional alternatives traded in financial markets or traded over the counter (OTC). Exchanges occur, however, only when they respond to common needs that can be traded in financial markets. OTC swap contracts, however, are engineered by an agreement of specific parties and mostly an agreement reached through intermediaries.

Theoretically, options' future prices are defined relative to observable and related options prices currently traded. Under appropriate assumptions of, for example, no-arbitrage and uniqueness, options are defined as an expectation of future relative prices set relative to a probability measure. For example, a risk-neutral probability measure de facto accounts for a risk premium paid that renders the underlying process risk consequences to be "devoid of risk," and therefore their expectation is discounted at the risk-free rate. A foreign asset priced by a domestic agent or an option priced by a domestic investor has to account for the risk-free rates of foreign and domestic countries where the exchange is made. Both rates account for the risk each implies when the asset is priced under each country's probability measures (or equivalently, embedded in their currency FX). Both foreign and domestic risks are not removed by such a model, but their risks are mitigated by the premium implied in their probability measure. Risk consequences are thus abated by a risk premium when future price expectations are calculated.[1] Further, when FX options underlying processes are derived from other financial and economic assets, we saw that their statistical properties are to be considered as well (namely, their volatility and their correlation). A theoretical FX price depends then on its FX model. Since there are multiple models one may consider, predicted FX prices do not need to be the same. The complexity of FX markets, therefore, requires complex models, some of which we have considered.

Options are used for many purposes: some to facilitate the management of risks (of both domestic and foreign assets), some to build financial liquidity, some to trade on future prices of commodities and currency trends, some to speculate on current and future disparities of currencies, and so on. Options traded in financial markets are mostly standardized, and therefore market priced, providing a personal means of exchange (i.e., with the transaction settled in a financial market).

The utility and popularity of options have led to the expansion of optional markets both nationally and by OTC swaps (see Chapter 8) that are often based on optional pricing models. The problems we consider in the following highlight their diversity.

7.5.1 Pricing Currency Options

An option pricing model is based on a Q probability measure using a prediction of future prices. These predictions (based on the predictive model and its volatility, which is the only unobservable parameter) are discounted at a risk-free rate. Under their probability measures, CPI option prices and FX rate options can be calculated. For example, call and put options on the FX rate are given by

$$\frac{B_D(0)}{B_F(0)}C_{FD}(0:K_F) = \frac{B_D(T)}{B_F(T)}E^Q_{D,F}(C_{FD}(T)) = \frac{B_D(T)}{B_F(T)}E^Q_{D,F}\text{Max}\{\xi_{FD}(T)-K_F,0\},$$

$$\frac{B_D(0)}{B_F(0)}P_{FD}(0:X_F) = \frac{B_D(T)}{B_F(T)}E^Q_{D,F}(P_{FD}(T)) = \frac{B_D(T)}{B_F(T)}E^Q_{D,F}\text{Max}\{X_F-\xi_{FD}(T),0\}$$

In a complete market, under an appropriate probability measure, the option price is defined by a current expectation of the future FX price. For example, for an FX call option:

$$\frac{B_D(0)}{B_F(0)}C_{FD}(0:K_F) = \frac{B_D(T)}{B_F(T)}E^Q_{D,F}\text{Max}\{\xi_{FD}(T)-K_F,0\}$$

$$= \frac{B_D(T)}{B_F(T)}E^Q_{D,F}\text{Max}\left\{\xi_{FD}(0)e^{-(1/2)\left(\sigma_F^2+\sigma_D^2\right)T}e^{\sigma_F W^Q_F(T)-\sigma_D W^Q_D(T)}-K_F,0\right\}$$

1 For the detailed discussion on risk premium especially in the futures and forward contracts, see Cooper (1993).

The call option is in the money and $\left\{ \xi_{FD}(0)e^{-(1/2)\left(\sigma_F^2 + \sigma_D^2\right)T}e^{\sigma_F W_F^Q(T) - \sigma_D W_D^Q(T)} - K_F, 0 \right\} > 0$

or if

$$\sigma_F W_F^Q(T) - \sigma_D W_D^Q(T) > \ln K_F + \frac{1}{2}\left(\sigma_F^2 + \sigma_D^2\right)T.$$

Let $f_N\left(W_F^Q(t), W_D^Q(t)\right)$ be a joint normal probability distribution with known variances and correlation. As a result, $\sigma_F W_F^Q(t) - \sigma_D W_D^Q(t)$ has a normal probability distribution with zero mean and a variance: $\sigma_{FD}^2 = (\sigma_F)^2 + (\sigma_D)^2 - 2\rho\sigma_F\sigma_D > 0$; we denote by $f_N\left(Z : \sigma_{FD}^2\right)$, with its cumulative distribution $F_N\left(u : \sigma_{FD}^2\right)$.

Martingale pricing has to be used carefully, however, since only one martingale can define the unique market price model. When a foreign asset is priced by a domestic investor, each country has its own risk valuation (and thus each with its own probability measure). Their respective measures have to be accounted for as we have assumed here (for their correlation). Practically, since this is only money, we presume that it is valued equally across national boundaries and therefore their differences may be accounted for by their FX rate. If this was not the case, it may open arbitrage opportunities, which would invalidate the pricing model considered here.

A price, however, is the outcome of an exchange between buyers and sellers that have reached an agreement to exchange at a given price. Financial data may indicate that currency markets and foreign assets' prices do not comply with such theoretical models, however. Therefore, in practice, FX pricing consists in a large part to reconcile both theoretical models and observed prices with the complexity of global finance. In a global multi-currency world, these problems are far more complex for many reasons.[2] For example, valuations differ (and therefore probability measures may be country specific). Although, as already stated, when transformed into money, they ought to be equivalent for all countries, otherwise there would be a potential for arbitrage that would violate the theoretical assumptions of pricing models. The theoretical complexity of FX financial pricing has led financial practitioners to develop alternative "algorithmic approaches" as well as tracking baskets of currencies. We have considered such an approach which leads necessarily to extremely dependent models—functionally and statistically. They may be applied only if their predictions can be justified empirically.

Although we have used repeatedly the concept of "parity" across sovereign (financial) boundaries, empirical verifications would point out that parity is rather a convenient concept, simplifying the disparities of assets and services that are observed in global and complex economies. In a global economy defined as one complete globalized market, prices ought to be identical once their FX rates and many other factors that contribute to their friction (such as taxes, transportation, and logistic costs) are accounted for. Yet, their disparities render modeling and the financial analysis of foreign assets much more complex than presumed by financial models—albeit these models are anchors we need to better understand the underlying complexity of global economies and their markets. For these reasons, we are mostly using relatively simple models, including two commonly used reference models —the lognormal (as used earlier) and the mean reverting model (defined in Chapter 2)—which we have combined into a single model. These models, under appropriate assumptions, have provided FX

---

2 For FX rate determination and foreign currency derivatives, see, for example, Kallianiotis (2013).

future prices and therefore underlie optional financial products. Their development and their application, however, requires both theoretical and computational developments which were not expanded sufficiently. The problems we consider are merely examples to highlight some of the issues we encounter in global FX pricing and investment management.

7.5.2 Options and Martingale Pricing Relative to a Global Index

In the following, we consider an FX call option price whose strike is a given percentage of a global currency index, or $\text{Max}(\xi - kG, 0)$ where G defines the global index. In this case:

$$\text{Max}(\xi - kG, 0) = \xi \mathbf{1}_{\xi/G > k} - kG \mathbf{1}_{\xi/G > k} = U_1 - U_2$$

where $\mathbf{1}_{\xi/G > k}$ denotes the future price of the option in the money (otherwise it is null). Therefore, considering each function U_1 and U_2 priced relative to G:

$$\frac{U_1(0)}{G(0)} = E_\xi \left(\frac{\xi \mathbf{1}_{\xi/G > k}}{G} \right), \quad \frac{U_2(0)}{G(0)} = E_{\xi^G} \left(\frac{kG \mathbf{1}_{\xi/G > k}}{G} \right) = k E_{\xi^G} \left(\mathbf{1}_{\xi/G > k} \right)$$

Note that the probability measure is defined relative to the global index. Then:

$$\frac{U_1(0)}{\xi(0)} = E \left(\frac{\xi}{G} \mathbf{1}_{\xi/G > k} \right) = E_{\xi^G} \left(\xi^G \mathbf{1}_{\xi/G > k} \right)$$

$$\frac{U_2(0)}{G(0)} = k P_{\xi^G} \left(\frac{\xi}{G} > k \right) = k P_{\xi^*} \left(\xi^G > k \right)$$

Next, we introduce the price at T, the option exercise time, and obtain

$$\frac{U_1(0)}{\text{CPI}(0)} = E_\xi \left(\xi^G(0) e^{-(1/2)\sigma^2 T - (1/2)\theta^2 T - \rho\sigma\theta T + \sigma W_1{}^G(T) + \theta W_2{}^G(T)} \mathbf{1}_{\xi/G > k} \right)$$

$$\frac{U_2(0)}{G(0)} = k P_{\xi^G} \left(\xi^G(0) e^{-(1/2)\sigma^2 T - (1/2)\theta^2 T - \rho\sigma\theta T + \sigma W_1{}^G(T) + \theta W_2{}^G(T)} > k \right)$$

Letting

$$\mathbf{1}_{\xi/G > k} = P \left(\xi^G(T) > K \right) = 1 - P \left(\xi^G(T) \le K \right)$$

as well as

$$P \left(\xi^G(T) \le K \right) = P \left(\xi^G(0) e^{-(1/2)\sigma^2 T - (1/2)\theta^2 T - \rho\sigma\theta T + \sigma W_1{}^G(T) + \theta W_2{}^G(T)} \le K \right)$$

$$= P \left(\ln \left(\frac{\xi^G(0)}{K} \right) - \frac{1}{2} (\sigma^2 + \theta^2 + \rho\sigma\theta) T \le \sigma W_1{}^G(T) + \theta W_2{}^G(T) \right)$$

we obtain

$$\mathbf{1}_{\xi/G > k} = P \left(\sigma W_1{}^G(T) + \theta W_2{}^G(T) \le \ln \left(\frac{\xi^G(0)}{K} \right) - \frac{1}{2} (\sigma^2 + \theta^2 + \rho\sigma\theta) T \right)$$

$$\frac{U_1(0)}{\xi(0)} = E_{\xi^G}\left(\xi^G(0)e^{-(1/2)\sigma^2 T - (1/2)\theta^2 T - \rho\sigma\theta T + \sigma W_1{}^G(T) + \theta W_2{}^G(T)}\mathbf{1}_{\xi/G > k}\right)$$

$$\frac{U_2(0)}{G(0)} = KP_{\xi^G}\left(\sigma W_1{}^G(T) + \theta W_2{}^G(T) > \ln\left(\frac{K}{\xi^G(0)}\right) + \frac{1}{2}\left(\sigma^2 + \theta^2 + \rho\sigma\theta\right)T\right)$$

And therefore the price of this option is

$$C_K(\xi_0, kG, 0) = \frac{U_1(0)}{\xi(0)} - \frac{U_2(0)}{G(0)}$$

$$= E_{\xi^G}\left(\xi^G(0)e^{-(1/2)\sigma^2 T - (1/2)\theta^2 T - \rho\sigma\theta T + \sigma W_1{}^G(T) + \theta W_2{}^G(T)}\mathbf{1}_{\xi/G > k}\right)$$

$$- KP_{\xi^G}\left(\sigma W_1{}^G(T) + \theta W_2{}^G(T) > \ln\left(\frac{K}{\xi^*(0)}\right) + \frac{1}{2}\left(\sigma^2 + \theta^2 + \rho\sigma\theta\right)T\right)$$

7.6 Spread and Two-Factor Options

Spread options are two-factor option models written on two assets. When they are written on more than two assets, they are called multiple spread options. They are extensively used in global finance. Consider, for example, two currencies or two commodities traded globally; a spread call option of two assets is then written generally as $\max[aS_1(T) + bS_2(T) - K, 0]$, where K is the prespecified price known as the strike price, or the exercise price of the option; a and b are weights of the two assets in the payoff; $a > 0$, $b < 0$; usually, $a = 1$ and $b = -1$. The spread option has both call and put options. Payoffs at maturity are then

$$C(S_1(T), S_2(T)) = \max[S_1(T) - S_2(T) - K, 0]$$
$$P(S_1(T), S_2(T)) = \max[K - (S_1(T) + bS_2(T)), 0]$$

To price these options, a simple approach consists of modeling two assets' differences and then applying a standard option pricing formula (call or put, for example). Spread options are very popular and extensively traded in both OTC markets and exchanges such as the New York Mercantile Exchange (NYMEX) (from 1994). This popularity is explained by their multiple functions: investors/hedgers can use options on the spread between long-term and short-term treasuries or FX rates; corporations can hedge the risks of their gross profits (e.g., in the oil industry, we use options on the spread between crude and refined oil prices). The pricing of these options depends on the assets' underlying processes and on their relationships. Smith (1976), Garman (1992), Ritchken and Tapiero (1986), and Tapiero (2010, 2013a,b, 2015), for example, provide pricing models. Their pricing is often based on martingales-defined Q-pricing models relative to a global index rather than a risk-free bond. For example, pricing a currency relative to a basket of currencies or relative to a basket of CPIs.

Although spread options may be traded in a financial exchange market, the bulk comes from OTC trades, both national and international. They are designed to mitigate adverse movements of several indexes; hence their popularity. Because of their generic nature, spread options are used in markets as different as fixed income markets, the currency and FX markets, the commodity futures markets, and the energy markets. At the

NYMEX, spread options are traded on the spread/difference between heating oil and crude oil, as well as between gasoline and crude oil. These spreads are better known as crack spreads, and options on these spreads are known as crack spread options. Crack spread options are useful to refineries for hedging purposes. With the deregulation of the electricity/power markets around the world, hedgers and risk takers are now also using options on the price difference between oil and electricity. In the energy market, such options are known as spark spread options. When $K = 0$, these options are equivalent to the exchange options indicated and solved earlier.

7.6.1   Spread and Correlation Options

Spread and correlation options were initially priced by Garman (1992). The majority of pricing models for correlation options are based on the strong assumption that correlation between underlying assets is constant. FX time series have revealed however, that this is not the case. For example, it is a well-known fact that such an assumption could generate serious problems for pricing and hedging.[3] A simplistic approach to modeling the spread option is to consider the spread itself as a financial price, lognormally distributed, and apply the usual Black–Scholes-type lognormal formulas (Black and Scholes, 1973). These assume that the probability the spread will ever become negative is null (although a mean-reverting model may circumvent negative spreads). In addition, the lognormal assumption would suggest that spread fluctuations would increase for large spreads and decrease for small ones. These have implications often supported by neither evidence nor experience. Spread options are therefore nontrivial instruments. Traders of these instruments are called upon to manage multiple price risks, an array of gamma risks, correlation risks increasingly relevant in a global financial framework, and a host of similar challenges (some of which will be considered subsequently).

Questions and Problems 7.1

Let a domestic investor make a bet on two currencies. These bets assume many forms, such as buying the currency long and option (future) bets. To price these financial bets, assume a US investor, pricing their bet in US dollars, and let the investor distribute their assets across two other currencies, all of which are defined by a lognormal model. The ROR of such an investment in US dollars is then distributed in proportions to two foreign assets in their currencies, α_{F1} and α_{F2}, and its residual invested in risk-free US bonds (in dollars). In this case, the portfolio ROR is:

$$d\ln S_D = \alpha_{F1}(d\ln \xi_{F1D} + \ln S_{DF1}) + \alpha_{F2}d\ln \xi_{F2D} + (1 - \alpha_{F1} - \alpha_{F2})R_{fD}\,dt$$

Let $W_D(0)$ be the initial wealth of the investor. As a result, after funds are allocated to foreign investments, their costs are:

---

3 For detailed analysis on pricing and hedging of spread options, see, for example, Carmona and Durrleman (2003), and for currency hedging see Glen and Jorion (1993).

$$\frac{\alpha_{F1}}{\xi_{F1}(0)}S_{F1}(0) + \frac{\alpha_{F2}}{\xi_{F2}(0)}S_{F2}(0)$$

which results in the initial bond investment:

$$B_D(0) = S_D(0) - \frac{\alpha_{F1}}{\xi_{F1}(0)}S_{F1}(0) - \frac{\alpha_{F2}}{\xi_{F2}(0)}S_{F2}(0)$$

Using this information:

1) Construct a risk-neutral pricing model for each of these investments.
2) Price the portfolio in US dollars.
3) Using mean and variance objectives, select the optimal allocation of your initial funds.
4) Assume as an alternative that all the investor's funds are invested locally in the US stock exchange market (e.g., the S&P index) and compare such an alternative to the mean–variance optimal investment.
5) Explain why and when you would prefer to invest locally and when you would invest in the multi-country portfolio.

7.6.2 The Price and the Profit/Loss of a Foreign Investment

A foreign stock priced in a domestic currency has necessarily two sources of risk. The first associated with the stock price and the other associated with the exchange rate. For simplicity, say that $S_D(0) = S_F(0)/\xi^{FD}(0)$, while at time t the profit of the domestic investor is

$$1 + r_D = \frac{\left(S_F(t)\xi^{FD}(t)\right)}{S_F(0)\xi^{FD}(0)} - \tau_D\left(\frac{\left(S_F(t)\xi^{FD}(t)\right)}{S_F(0)\xi^{FD}(0)} - S_D(0)\right)$$

with τ_D the domestic tax on foreign profits and r_D its ROR. The problem we are concerned with is to define the price of this return when the investment is repatriated. Obviously:

$$1 + r_F = \frac{S_F(t)}{S_F(0)}, \quad 1 + r_\xi = \frac{\xi^{FD}(t)}{\xi^{FD}(0)}$$

and letting $S_D(0) = 1$ we have

$$1 + r_D = (1 + r_F)(1 + r_\xi) - (\tau_D)\text{Max}((1 + r_F)(1 + r_\xi) - 1, 0)$$

For example, let $\tau_D = 0.35$, $r_F = 0.15$, and $r_\xi = -0.1$, then

$$1 + r_D = (1.15)(0.9) - (0.35)\text{Max}((1.15)(0.9) - 1, 0)$$

$$= 1.035 - (0.35)(0.035) = 1.02275$$

which is 2.275% ROR for an investment that has two sources of risk. This simple calculation points to the power of taxing foreign profits heavily and gating firms that seek to invest in foreign countries. Gating, from a taxation viewpoint, contributes to globalization since the pursuit of profits at lower tax rates will lead to a greater flow of capital.

Questions and Problems 7.2

Based on the factors already noted:

a) Discuss the impact of domestic taxation on foreign income to the real rate of required ROR. In this case, an application of Itô's lemma yields

$$dS_{FD}(t) = d\left(S_F(t)\xi^{FD}(t)\right) = \xi^{FD}(t)\,dS_F(t) + S_F(t)\,d\xi^{FD}(t) + d\xi^{FD}(t)\,dS_F(t)$$

To price $S_{FD}(t)$, note that the discount rate factor applied is in this case equal to the foreign country risk-free rate plus the risk premium to remove the currency risk and their correlations. Let

$$\frac{dS_F(t)}{S_F(t)} = \mu_F\,dt + \sigma_F\,dW_F, \quad S_F(0) > 0$$

$$\frac{d\xi^{FD}(t)}{\xi^{FD}(t)} = \lambda_{FD}\,dt + \sigma_{FD}\,dW_{FD}, \quad \xi^{FD}(0) > 0$$

Then

$$\frac{dS_{FD}(t)}{S_{FD}(t)} = \left(\mu_F + \lambda_{FD} + \rho_{F,FG}\sigma_{FD}\sigma_F\right)dt + \sigma_F\,dW_F + \sigma_{FD}\,dW_{FD}, \quad S_{FD}(0) = S_F(0)\xi^{FD}(0) > 0$$

b) Assume risk-neutral pricing and calculate the real ROR (including taxation) as well as the ROR in case profits are not repatriated.

7.6.3 A Quanto Option

Quanto is an option on a foreign currency denominated asset, but the payoff is in a domestic currency. In this situation, the holder of the option has a double exposure: the asset price risk and the FX risk. Payoffs can then be determined in several manners. The following are a few cases where ξ_T^{FD} denotes the FX rate, while S_T^{FD} is the asset price in the foreign currency, and K_T^{FD} is the strike, which is also denominated in the foreign currency. The following call options result:

1) The foreign asset is defined in a foreign currency, and therefore the call option has a foreign return which is repatriated to the domestic currency, or $C^F\left(S_T^{FD}, \xi_T^{FD}, T\right) = \max\left(S_T^{FD} - K_T^F, 0\right)$ and $C^D = \tilde{\xi}_T^{DF}\max\left(S_T^{FD} - K_T^F, 0\right)$. The foreign asset is denominated in the domestic currency:

$$C_T^D(S_T, \xi_T, T) = \max\left(\xi_T^{FD}S_T^F - K_T^D, 0\right), \quad S_0^F = \xi_0^{DF}S_0^D, \quad S_T^F = \xi_0^{DF}S_0^D\left(1 + R_T^{SF}\right)$$

$$S_T^D = \xi_T^{FD}S_T^F = S_0^D\left(1 + R_T^{SF}\right)\left(\xi_T^{FD}\xi_0^{DF}\right) = S_0^D\left(1 + R_T^{SF}\right)\left(1 + R_T^{FD}\right)$$

or

$$C_T^D(S_T, \xi_T, T) = \max\left(S_0^D\left(1 + R_T^{SF}\right)\left(1 + R_T^{FD}\right) - K_T^D, 0\right)$$

where $\left(1+R_T^{\mathrm{SF}}\right)\left(1+R_T^{\mathrm{FD}}\right)$ are the ROR on the investment in the foreign country and the ROR on the currency (which is also a bet). As a result, there are two sources of risk, which can be compounded if these risks are dependent.

2) Exchange rates are fixed at a given level:

$$C\left(S_T^{\mathrm{D}},\bar{\xi}_T^{\mathrm{FD}},T\right)=\bar{\xi}_T^{\mathrm{FD}}\max\left(S_T^{\mathrm{F}}-K_T^{\mathrm{F}},0\right),\quad S_0^{\mathrm{F}}=\xi_0^{\mathrm{DF}}S_0^{\mathrm{D}},\quad S_T^{\mathrm{F}}=\left(1+R_T^{\mathrm{SF}}\right);$$

3) Asset linked to the FX call:

$$C\left(S_T^{\mathrm{D}},\xi_T^{\mathrm{FD}},T\right)=S_T^{\mathrm{F}}\max\left(\xi_T^{\mathrm{FD}}-\bar{\xi}^{\mathrm{FD}},0\right),\quad S_0^{\mathrm{F}}=S_0^{\mathrm{D}}\xi_0^{\mathrm{DF}},\quad S_T^{\mathrm{F}}=S_0^{\mathrm{D}}\xi_0^{\mathrm{DF}}\left(1+R_T^{\mathrm{SF}}\right),$$

which is in fact a call option of the currency with strike $\bar{\xi}^{\mathrm{FD}}$. Other versions can be constructed as well by combining hedging (optional) transactions on the underlying foreign asset and on the effective FX rate at the option's maturity.

When both the FX and the underlying asset are defined in terms of a stochastic process, these prices may be dependent on one another, while price in one or another currency can be determined by applications of stochastic calculus and techniques for risk-neutral pricing.

7.7 Optional Trading Strategies

Optional portfolios provide the means to price hedging strategies. Vanilla options strategies include the protective put and cover call. There are many others, each providing a particular approach to hedging. Strategic portfolios in FX have multiple purposes. They may be used to hedge currencies' risks; for a domestic investor they can be used to bet on foreign assets, and so on. A number of essential strategic optional strategies are considered in the following. These strategies are used profusely in domestic financial markets, but provide an increased set of hedging and betting opportunities on FX markets as the risks sustained by domestic investors are compounded by the foreign and currency risks they assume.

7.7.1 The Protective Put and Foreign Trading

A protective put is a trading strategy which acts as portfolio insurance (to be seen later on). It is based on a portfolio which consists of buying a security long and buying an option put with strike X and exercise at time T. The initial price is $\pi(0)=S(0)-P_{X,T}(0)=S(0)-P_{X,T}(0)$, where $P_{X,T}(T)=\mathrm{Max}(X-S(T),0)$, and at a future time t, $\pi(t)=S(t)-P_{X,T}(t)=S(T)-\mathrm{Max}(X-S(T),0)$ and $d\pi(t)=dS(t)-dP_{X,T}(t)$. The price of such a strategy can be valued in terms of the Greeks, which are discussed in Section 7.8. Its formulation in a foreign context is obviously more complex, as a domestic investor would be confronted by two risks: the FX and the stock risks (defining as well its put option price).

Assume that a domestic investor is investing in a foreign country. How would they apply a protective put to an investment in the foreign country? The initial price in the domestic currency is:

$$\pi(0)=\xi_{\mathrm{DF}}(0)S_{\mathrm{F}}(0)-\xi_{\mathrm{DF}}(0)P_{X,T}^{\mathrm{F}}(0)$$

where $S_F(0)$ is the stock price in the foreign currency, and therefore $\xi_{FD}(0)$ is the FX rate that the domestic investor uses to buy the foreign asset as well as to price the put option. At time t, we then have in the foreign currency

$$d\pi_F(t) = dS_F(t) - dP^F_{X,T}(0)$$

while in the domestic currency we have

$$d(\xi_{FD}(t)\pi_F(t)) = d(\xi_{FD}(t)S_F(t)) - d\left(\xi_{FD}(t)P^F_{X,T}(t)\right)$$

with

$$d(\xi_{FD}(t)\pi_F(t)) = \pi_F(t)\,d\xi_{FD}(t) + \xi_{FD}(t)\,d\pi_F(t) + d(\xi_{FD}(t))\,d(\pi_F(t))$$
$$d(\xi_{FD}(t)S_F(t)) = S_F(t)\,d\xi_{FD}(t) + \xi_{FD}(t)\,dS_F(t) + d(\xi_{FD}(t))\,d(S_F(t))$$
$$d\left(\xi_{FD}(t)P^F_{X,T}(t)\right) = P^F_{X,T}(t)\,d\xi_{FD}(t) + \xi_{FD}(t)\,d\left(P^F_{X,T}(t)\right) + d(\xi_{FD}(t))\,d\left(P^F_{X,T}(t)\right)$$

And therefore

$$\pi_F(t)\,d\xi_{FD}(t) + \xi_{FD}(t)\,d\pi_F(t) + d(\xi_{FD}(t))\,d(\pi_F(t))$$
$$= S_F(t)\,d\xi_{FD}(t) + \xi_{FD}(t)\,dS_F(t) + d(\xi_{FD}(t))\,d(S_F(t))$$
$$- P^F_{X,T}(t)\,d\xi_{FD}(t) - \xi_{FD}(t)\,d\left(P^F_{X,T}(t)\right) - d(\xi_{FD}(t))\,d\left(P^F_{X,T}(t)\right)$$
$$\pi_F(t)\,d\xi_{FD}(t) + \xi_{FD}(t)\,d\pi_F(t) + d(\xi_{FD}(t))\,d(\pi_F(t))$$
$$= S_F(t)\,d\xi_{FD}(t) + \xi_{FD}(t)\,dS_F(t) + d(\xi_{FD}(t))\,d(S_F(t))$$
$$- P^F_{X,T}(t)\,d\xi_{FD}(t) - \xi_{FD}(t)\,d\left(P^F_{X,T}(t)\right) - d(\xi_{FD}(t))\,d\left(P^F_{X,T}(t)\right)$$

Let the foreign price be defined by a lognormal process (under a risk-neutral probability measure):

$$\frac{dS_F(t)}{S_F(t)} = R_F\,dt + \sigma_F\,dW^{Qs}_F(t), \quad S_F(0) > 0$$

The FX price is then defined by the following process:

$$\frac{d\xi_{FD}(t)}{\xi_{FD}(t)} = (R_F - R_D)\,dt + \sigma_{FD}\,dW^Q_{FD} \quad \text{or} \quad \xi_{FD}(t) = \xi_{FD}(0)e^{(R_F-R_D)t - (1/2)(\sigma_{FD})^2 W^Q_{FD}}$$

Note that

$$d\xi_{FD}(t)S_F(t) = S_F(t)\,d\xi_{FD}(t) + \xi_{FD}(t)\,dS_F(t) + d(\xi_{FD}(t))\,d(S_F(t))$$
$$= S_F(t)\xi_{FD}(t)\left[(R_F - R_D)\,dt + \sigma_{FD}\,dW^Q_{FD}\right]$$
$$+ \xi_{FD}(t)S_F(t)\left(R_F\,dt + \sigma_F\,dW^{Qs}_F(t)\right) + \xi_{FD}(t)S_F(t)\left(\sigma_{FD}\sigma_F\,dW^{Qs}_F(t)\,dW^Q_{FD}\right)$$

Assuming that $dW^{Qs}_F(t)\,dW^Q_{FD} = \rho_{F,FD}\,dt$ and setting $U_{FD}(t) = \xi_{FD}(t)S_F(t)$, we have

$$\frac{dU_{FD}(t)}{U_{FD}(t)} = \left[(R_F - R_D) + R_F + \rho_{F,FD}\sigma_{FD}\sigma_F\right]dt + \sigma_{FD}dW_{FD}^Q + \sigma_F dW_F^{Q_S}(t)$$

By the same token, consider the put option price given by:

$$\frac{d\,P_{X,T}^F(t)}{P_{X,T}^F(t)} = R_F dt + \sigma_{P,F}dW_{P,F}^{Q_P}(t) \quad \text{or} \quad P_{X,T}^F(t) = P_{X,T}^F(0)e^{R_F t - (1/2)(\sigma_{P,F})^2 t + \sigma_{P,F}W_{P,F}^{Q_P}(t)}$$

In this case, we can also use

$$V_{X,T}^F(t) = \xi_{FD}(t)P_{X,T}^F(t) = P_{X,T}^F(0)\xi_{FD}(0)e^{R_F t - (1/2)(\sigma_{P,F})^2 t + \sigma_{P,F}W_{P,F}^{Q_P}(t)}e^{(R_F - R_D)t - (1/2)(\sigma_{FD})^2 W_{FD}^Q}$$

Setting $V_{X,T}^F(t) = \xi_{FD}(t)P_{X,T}^F(t)$, we obtain

$$\frac{d\,V_{X,T}^F(t)}{V_{X,T}^F(t)} = \left[(R_F - R_D) + R_F + \rho_{P,FD}\sigma_{FD}\sigma_{P,F}\right]dt + \sigma_{FD}dW_{FD}^Q + \sigma_{P,F}dW_{P,F}^{Q_P}(t)$$

In this case:

$$dZ(t) = dU_{FD}(t) - dV_{X,T}^F(t)$$

$$= \left\{\left[(R_F - R_D) + R_F + \rho_{F,FD}\sigma_{FD}\sigma_F\right]U_{FD}(t)dt + \sigma_{FD}U_{FD}(t)dW_{FD}^Q\right\}$$

$$+ \sigma_F U_{FD}(t)dW_F^{Q_S}(t)\bigg\}$$

$$- \left\{\left[(R_F - R_D) + R_F + \rho_{P,FD}\sigma_{FD}\sigma_{P,F}\right]V_{X,T}^F(t)dt + \sigma_{FD}V_{X,T}^F(t)dW_{FD}^Q\right.$$

$$+ \sigma_{P,F}V_{X,T}^F(t)dW_{P,F}^{Q_P}(t)\bigg\}$$

$$Z(t) = \pi_F(t)\xi_{FD}(t), \quad Z(0) = \pi(0)\xi_{DF}(0) = U_{FD}(0) - V_{X,T}^F(0)$$

where

$$U_{FD}(0) = \xi_{DF}(0)S_F(0), \quad V_{X,T}^F(0) = \xi_{DF}(0)\text{Max}(X - S_F(T),0)$$

whose solution is the solution of systems of three linear stochastic differential equations.

Questions and Problems 7.3

Let $P_{X,T}(t)$ be the price of a put option; that is $P_{X,T}(t) = e^{-R_f(T-t)}\text{Max}(X - S(T),0)$. Define the Greeks (explained in Section 7.8 in detail). What are the implications of the Delta and the Vega of the price of such a strategy?

7.7.2 The Covered Call

A covered call is a portfolio which consists of owning long both a currency bet and its call option. In this case $\pi(0) = \xi(0) - C(0)$, and at maturity (with strike X) we have

$$\pi(T) = \xi(T) - C(T) = \xi(T) - \text{Max}(\xi(T) - X,0)$$

Therefore, $\pi(T) = \text{Min}[\xi(T),X]$, which assures the holder of the portfolio at least the strike (in case the underlying currency price falls below the strike). Such strategies are therefore used as an insurance against market price risk. At any time T we then have the price of the currency less the option price (acting as an insurance):

$$\pi(T) = \xi(T) - C(T) = \xi(T) - \text{Max}(\xi(T) - X, 0)$$

As a result, the price of the covered call (under a risk-neutral probability measure) is

$$\pi(0) = \xi(0) - e^{-R_f T} \text{Max}(\xi(T) - X, 0)$$

A covered call strategy in a foreign country requires that we consider the FX effects as done here. This is left as an exercise.

7.8 The Greeks and Financial Risk Management

A portfolio or an option price is a function of a number of parameters that define the portfolio or the option. Some of these parameters are contracted; therefore, once they are selected, they no longer change as long as the option is alive. Some of the parameters change in time and due to random events reflecting economic and other conditions. In such conditions, option prices change in tandem with their parameters, providing important information that can be used to assess their effects on prices and manage the risk they imply. In the following, we measure their effects by their price sensitivity to these parameters based on, for simplicity, a lognormal process. We call these measures the Greeks. Defining the Greeks based on the option prices of FX as calculated here is, of course, much more difficult. For a common domestic option on a stock price Black–Scholes model, an option (say call), is defined by its parameters $C \equiv C(S, \tau, \sigma, R_f | T, K)$, $\tau = T - t$, where S, τ, σ, and R_f are the stock price, the current time, the volatility, and the risk-free discount rate, while T and K are the option maturity and its strike. Assuming marginal parametric variations, a Taylor series expansion, based on the first- and second-order terms for randomly varying parameters, yields

$$dC = \frac{\partial C}{\partial S} dS + \frac{\partial C}{\partial \tau} dt + \frac{\partial C}{\partial \sigma} d\sigma + \frac{\partial C}{\partial R_f} dR_f + \frac{1}{2} \frac{\partial^2 C}{\partial S^2} (dS)^2$$

We can rewrite in terms of Greek letters, each expressing the option price sensitivity to the parameter defining the price of the option:

$$\Delta = \frac{\partial C}{\partial S}, \quad \theta = \frac{\partial C}{\partial t}, \quad \nu = \frac{\partial C}{\partial \sigma}, \quad \rho = \frac{\partial C}{\partial R_f}, \quad \Gamma = \frac{\partial^2 C}{\partial S^2}$$

And in terms of "Greek letters"

$$dC = \Delta \, dS + \theta \, dt + \nu \, d\sigma + \rho \, dR_f + \frac{1}{2} \Gamma (dS)^2$$

Each of these letters is a measure of sensitivity based on the option pricing model. For an FX pricing model, the risk-free rate would be the differential between the risk-free rates in both domestic and foreign country, or $R_f = r_d - r_f$. Further, when an FX is derived from other financial or economic factors, then an option with an underlying such FX involves the parameters in a more complex function, and therefore its "Greeks" are to be defined appropriately. In the following, we consider the standard approach to the Greeks. Further study is needed to adapt and develop Greeks to complex optional FX models.

The Greeks are as follows:

- The Delta, $\Delta = \partial C / \partial \xi$. It measures a variation in the call option price relative to a variation in its underlying stock or currency price.
- The Theta, $\theta = -\partial C / \partial \tau$. This measures the variation in the FX call option relative to a time-to-maturity increment. We generally expect that options will become less valuable with the passage of time (although this assumption turns out not to be always true, as expectation and the volatility of future prices are changing continuously with new information). With the option's remaining time to maturity, we set θ equal to the negative of the derivative of the option price.
- The Vega, $\nu = \partial C / \partial \sigma$. The Vega measures the sensitivity of the option price to a standard deviation of the underlying return to the volatility σ (the FX volatility or the stock price volatility). Given the Black–Scholes formula, calls and puts have the same Vega. In the FX models we considered in this chapter, FX prices were also a function of the volatilities the FX derived factors may be considered as well.
- The Gamma, $\Gamma = \partial^2 C / \partial \xi^2$. The Gamma is the second derivative (acceleration) of the option's price with respect to the underlying FX or stock prices. Gamma gives the convexity of the option price with respect to its underlying stock or currency price. For options priced by Black–Scholes formula, the call and the put have the same Gamma.
- The Rho, $\rho = -\partial C / \partial R_f$. The Rho measures the change in an option price when the rate changes.

The Greeks are therefore marginal changes in an option price and are valid for small deviations in the economic parameters. The Greeks are in practice extremely important, both in domestic and foreign markets. Their development and uses are broadly included in standard textbooks, and therefore we shall not cover them here in detail.

FX stochastic models are extensively developed and used by financial institutions, academics, and professionals. The references we list in this chapter are therefore a partial list of academic and other publications that have recognized the complexity and multivariability of FX models. They are listed to motivate the reader to pursue their development.

Appendix 7.A: Mathematical Review

Global (and multi-country) pricing of financial assets models is multivariate. In the following, we review a number of mathematical tools we use in this chapter. For further reviews, refer to Tapiero (1978, 2010, 2013a,b), Bensoussan and Tapiero (1982), and Malliaris and Brock (1982).

7.A.1 Itô Calculus

In the following, we review briefly elements of Itô's multivariate calculus. Such models are useful in global financial models.

Addition

Let x_1 and x_2 be two processes satisfying the following stochastic differential equations:

$$dx_i = f_i(x_i,t)\,dt + \sigma_i(x_i,t)\,dW_i; \quad i = 1,2$$

where dW_1 and dW_2 are standard Wiener processes f_i, σ_i, $i = 1,2$. f_i are assumed independent of future Wiener processes (i.e., these are non-anticipating or adapted processes). Define the sum process

$$y = x_1 + x_2, \quad \text{then} \quad dy = dx_1 + dx_2$$

Or

$$dy = (f_1(x_1,t) + f_2(x_2,t))\,dt + \sigma_1(x_1,t)\,dW_1 + \sigma_2(x_2,t)\,dW_2; \quad i = 1,2$$

Note that if $E(dW_1\,dW_2) = \rho\,dt$, these two random variables are correlated. In this case, special attention ought to be given to the treatment of these equations and to the risks that statistical dependence implies. Further, since $y = x_1 + x_2$, we can replace $x_2 = y - x_1$ and obtain a system of correlated stochastic differential equations. Subsequently, we shall consider (when appropriate) approaches to reducing these models to their being statistically independent in order to simplify their treatment. For example, considering y rather than x_2, we have

$$dy = (f_1(x_1,t) + f_2(y - x_1,t))\,dt + \sigma_1(x_1,t)\,dW_1 + \sigma_2(y - x_1,t)\,dW_2$$
$$dx_1 = f_1(x_1,t)\,dt + \sigma_1(x_1,t)\,dW_1$$

The Differential Rule

We consider first Itô's lemma for a single variate stochastic differential equation. Let $F(x,t)$ be a continuous (twice differentiable) function in x and t, with continuous derivatives $\partial F/\partial t$, $\partial F/\partial x$, and $\partial^2 F/\partial x^2$, then $y = F(x,t)$ has a stochastic differential equation which is given by a Taylor series expansion of the function to include all terms in the infinitesimal interval of order dt (which in this case includes the second-order term):

$$dF = \frac{\partial F}{\partial t}\,dt + \frac{\partial F}{\partial x}\,dx + \frac{1}{2}\frac{\partial^2 F}{\partial x^2}(dx)^2$$

and therefore

$$dF = \left(\frac{\partial F}{\partial t} + \frac{\partial F}{\partial x}f(x,t) + \frac{1}{2}\sigma^2\frac{\partial^2 F}{\partial x^2}\right)dt + \frac{\partial F}{\partial x}\sigma\,dW(t)$$

A two-variable process is given by $y = F(x_1,x_2,t)$. A Taylor's series expansion of this function keeps terms of order dt as well. Furthermore, owing to the potential correlation of these processes, their correlated random variables ought to be accounted for as well. This yields

$$dy = \frac{\partial F}{\partial t}\,dt + \frac{\partial F}{\partial x_1}\,dx_1 + \frac{\partial F}{\partial x_2}\,dx_2 + \frac{1}{2}\sigma_1^2\frac{\partial^2 F}{\partial x_1^2}(dW_1)^2$$

$$+ \frac{1}{2}\sigma_2^2\frac{\partial^2 F}{\partial x_2^2}(dW_2)^2 + \sigma_1\sigma_2\frac{\partial F}{\partial x_1 \partial x_2}(dW_1)(dW_2)$$

$$[dW_k]^2 = dt, \quad k = 1,2, \quad \text{and} \quad dW_1\,dW_2 = \rho_{12}\,dt$$

which we can rewrite as follows:

$$dy = \left(\frac{\partial F}{\partial t} + \frac{\partial F}{\partial x_1} f_1(x_1, t) + \frac{\partial F}{\partial x_2} f_2(x_2, t) + \frac{1}{2}\sigma_1^2\frac{\partial^2 F}{\partial x_1^2} + \frac{1}{2}\sigma_2^2\frac{\partial^2 F}{\partial x_2^2} + \rho\sigma_1\sigma_2\frac{\partial^2 F}{\partial x_1 \partial x_2} \right) dt$$

$$+ \sigma_1 \frac{\partial F}{\partial x_1} dW_1 + \sigma_2 \frac{\partial F}{\partial x_2} dW_2$$

where ρ is the correlation between the two Wiener processes.

When x is an n-vector stochastic process, f an m-vector, σ an $n \times m$ matrix, and $dW(t)$ an m-vector Wiener process with $E(dW^{\mathrm{T}}dW) = Q(t)dt$, the correlation matrix. Then for: $F(x_1, x_2, ..., x_m, t)$, Itô's vector differential rule is given by

$$dF = \frac{\partial F}{\partial t} + \frac{\partial F^{\mathrm{T}}}{\partial x}dx + \frac{1}{2} \ \mathrm{trace} \ \sigma Q \sigma^{\mathrm{T}} \frac{\partial^2 F}{\partial x^2}dt$$

where

$$\frac{\partial F}{\partial t} = \frac{\partial F}{\partial t}; \ \frac{\partial F^{\mathrm{T}}}{\partial x} = \left\{ \frac{\partial F}{\partial x_1}, \frac{\partial F}{\partial x_2}, ..., \frac{\partial F}{\partial x_n} \right\}, \ \frac{\partial^2 F}{\partial x^2} = \begin{bmatrix} \frac{\partial^2 F}{\partial x_1^2} & \cdots & \frac{\partial^2 F}{\partial x_n^2} \\ \vdots & & \vdots \\ \frac{\partial^2 F}{\partial x_1 \partial x_n} & \cdots & \frac{\partial^2 F}{\partial x_n^2} \end{bmatrix}$$

Multiplication of Functions

Consider two twice continuously differentiable real scalar functions $F(x_1, t)$ and $G(x_2, t)$ and consider the product of these two functions:

$$H(x_1, x_2, t) = F(x_1, t)G(x_2, t)$$

Then, the stochastic differential equation of the product is

$$dH = FdG + GdF + \frac{\partial F}{\partial x_1}\frac{\partial G}{\partial x_2}dx_1 dx_2$$

with dG and dF given by the following differential rule. In particular when $x_1 = x_2$ (i.e., these are the same process), then

$$dH = FdG + GdF + \sigma^2\frac{\partial F}{\partial x}\frac{\partial G}{\partial x}dt$$

This arises directly from Itô's differential rule, since by definition

$$dH = (F + dF)(G + dG) - FG = FdG + GdF + (dF)(dG)$$

Division of Functions

Let $G(x_2, t) > 0$ and consider again the twice continuously differentiable function $F(x_1, t)$ and $G(x_2, t)$. Define the quotient:

$$H(x_1, x_2, t) = \frac{F(x_1, t)}{G(x_2, t)}$$

And let x_1 and x_2 be two stochastic differential equations with $E(dW_1 dW_2) = \rho dt$. Then by Itô's differential rule we have

$$H(x_1(t),x_2(t)) = H(x_1(0),x_2(0)) + \int_0^t \frac{\partial H(s)}{\partial s}\,ds$$

$$+ \int_0^t \frac{\partial H(s)}{\partial x_1}\sigma_1(x_1(s),s)\,dW_1(s) + \int_0^t \frac{\partial H(s)}{\partial x_2}\sigma_2(x_2(s),s)\,dW_2(s)$$

$$+ \int_0^t \left\{ \frac{\partial H(s)}{\partial x_1}f_1(x_1(s),s) + \frac{\partial H(s)}{\partial x_2}f_2(x_2(s),s) + \frac{1}{2}\frac{\partial^2 H(s)}{\partial x_1^2}\sigma_1^2(x_1(s),s) \right.$$

$$\left. + \frac{1}{2}\frac{\partial^2 H(s)}{\partial x_2^2}\sigma_2^2(x_2(s),s) + \frac{\partial^2 H(s)}{\partial x_1 \partial x_2}\rho\sigma_1(x_1(s),s)\sigma_2(x_2(s),s) \right\}ds$$

where $E(dW_1(s)\,dW_2(s)) = \rho\,ds$. Since $H(x_1,x_2,t) = F(x_1,t)/G(x_2,t)$, we can calculate the partial derivatives, leading to

$$\frac{\partial H}{\partial x_1} = \frac{F_1}{G}; \quad \frac{\partial H}{\partial x_2} = -\frac{FG_1}{G^2}; \quad \frac{\partial H}{\partial s} = -\frac{F_0 G - G_0 F}{G^2};$$

$$\frac{\partial^2 H}{\partial x_1^2} = \frac{F_2}{G}; \quad \frac{\partial^2 H}{\partial x_2^2} = -FG_2 G - 2\frac{G_1^2}{G^3}; \quad \frac{\partial H}{\partial x_1 \partial x_2} = -\frac{F_1 G_1}{G^2}$$

where F_i and G_i denote the ith derivative of the functions F and G with respect to the states, while F_0 and G_0 denote the time derivatives. Inserting these terms in the previous equation for $H(x_1, x_2, t)$, we obtain the Itô calculus rule for a ratio of two random variables with known stochastic differential equations, or:

$$H(x_1(t),x_2(t)) = H(x_1(0),x_2(0)) + \int_0^t \frac{\partial F}{G\partial s}\,ds - \int_0^t \frac{F\partial F}{G^2 \partial s}\,ds$$

$$+ \int_0^t \frac{\partial F}{G\partial x_1}\sigma_1(x_1(s),s)\,dW_1(s) - \int_0^t \frac{F\partial G}{G^2 \partial x_2}\sigma_2(x_2(s),s)\,dW_2(s)$$

$$+ \int_0^t \left\{ \frac{\partial F}{G\partial x_1}f_1(x_1(s),s) - \frac{F\partial G}{G^2 \partial x_2}f_2(x_2(s),s) + \frac{1}{2}\frac{\partial^2 F}{G\partial x_1^2}\sigma_1^2(x_1(s),s) \right.$$

$$-\frac{1}{2}F\frac{G(\partial^2 G/\partial x_2^2) - 2(\partial G/\partial x_2)^2}{G^3}\sigma_2^2(x_2(s),s)$$

$$\left. - \frac{\partial F(s)}{\partial x_1}\frac{\partial G(s)}{\partial x_2}\frac{1}{G^2}\rho\sigma_1(x_1(s),s)\sigma_2(x_2(s),s) \right\}ds$$

If x_1 and x_2 are the same process, and if H is independent of time, this is reduced to

$$d\left[\frac{F}{G}\right] = \left[\frac{1}{G}\right]dF - \left[\frac{F}{G^2}\right]dG - \left[\frac{\sigma^2\dfrac{\partial F\,\partial G}{\partial x\,\partial x}}{G^2}\right]dt + \left[\frac{F\sigma^2\dfrac{\partial F\,\partial G}{\partial x\,\partial x}}{G^3}\right]dW$$

If both F and G are both functions of x_1 and x_2, we compute the partial derivatives of H and insert them in the previous equation. This problem is left as an exercise for the reader to work with. Finally, it should be noted that both c and d are special cases of b.

The Derivative Rule

Let $F(x)$ be a twice continuously differentiable function of the real variable x; then, $G(x) = \partial F / \partial x$.

Let the Wiener process $\{w, t > 0\}$ with variance σ^2. Then, for $t_0 < T$:

$$\int_{t_0}^{T} G(W) \, dW = F(W(T)) - F(W(t_0)) - \frac{1}{2} \int_{t_0}^{T} \frac{\partial^2 F(W)}{\partial x^2} \sigma^2 \, dt$$

These rules will be used repeatedly in applications. The derivative rule can also be written as

$$\int_{0}^{t} G(W(s)) \, dW(s) = \int_{0}^{w(t)} G(s) \, ds - \frac{1}{2} \int_{0}^{t} \frac{\partial G(W(s))}{\partial W} \, ds$$

Girsanov's Theorem

Girsanov's theorem is important for many applications in finance. Essentially, it shows how to change the drift of an Itô stochastic differential equation by changing its probability measure to obtain a process without drift (and thereby define a martingale). The theorem states that the stochastic function

$$L(t) = \exp\left(\int_{0}^{t} h(s) \, dw(s) - \frac{1}{2} \int_{0}^{t} h^2(s) \, ds \right)$$

where $h(s)$, $0 < s < T$, is both a bounded and adapted function and is the unique solution of

$$\frac{dL(t)}{L(t)} = h(t) \, dW(t); \quad L(0) = 1; \quad E(L(t)) = 1, \ \forall t \in [0, T]$$

and $L(t)$ is a martingale since it satisfies all the mathematical properties of martingales. The solution of Girsanov's differential equation can be determined by application of Itô's differential rule by using the transformation $y = \log L$; then:

$$dy = \frac{dL}{L} - \frac{1}{2L^2} (dL)^2 = h(t) \, dw(t) - \frac{1}{2} h^2(t) \, dt$$

whose integration leads directly to

$$y(t) = \int_{0}^{t} h(s) \, dW(s) - \frac{1}{2} \int_{0}^{t} h^2(s) \, ds$$

Substituting for $L(t)$, we have

$$L(t) = L(0)\exp\left(\int_0^t h(s)\,dW(s) - \frac{1}{2}\int_0^t h^2(s)\,ds\right), \quad L(0) = 1$$

In this case, note that $y(t)$ is a process with drift while that of $L(t)$ has no drift.

7.A.2 The Feynman–Kac Formula

Consider a price process of the type

$$dS(t) = R(t,S)\,dt + \Lambda(S,t)\,dW(t), \quad S(0) > 0$$

with $W(t)$ a standard and adapted Brownian motion. $R(t, S)$ is the process drift and $\Lambda(S, t)$ its volatility. Let R_f be a risk-free rate and let $C(t, S)$ be a continuous function of time and stock price. Finally, we have the following pricing martingale under a Q probability measure:

$$dS(t) = R_f\,dt + \Lambda(S,t)\,dW(t), \quad S(0) > 0$$

The Feynman–Kac Formula, a measure-independent formula, defines the derived process $C(t, S)$ with boundary $C(T,S) = V(S)$, by the Fokker–Planck equation:

$$\frac{\partial C(t,S)}{\partial t} + \frac{1}{2}\frac{\partial^2 C}{\partial S^2}\Lambda^2(S,t) + R(t,S)\frac{\partial C}{\partial S} - R_f C(t) = 0 \quad \text{with} \quad C(T,S) = V(S)$$

Under its Q probability measure and the conditional filtration $\Im_t$, we have

$$C(t,S) = e^{-R_f(T-t)}E^Q(V(S(T)|\Im_t)$$

This formula is extremely useful as it allows us to move from one expression to another and use Monte Carlo simulation techniques to calculate the expected terminal value. For example, if we set

$$R(t,S) = R_f S \quad \text{and} \quad \Lambda(S,t) = \sigma S \quad \text{with} \quad C(T,S) = V(S(T)) = \text{Max}[S(T) - K, 0]$$

with its underlying process

$$dS(t) = R_f S(t)\,dt + \Lambda(S,t)\,dW(t), \quad S(0) > 0, \quad \text{and} \quad V(S(T)) = \text{Max}[S(T) - K, 0]$$

then, as a result:

$$C(t,S) = e^{-R_f(T-t)}E^Q(\text{Max}[S(T) - K, 0]|\Im_t)$$

7.A.3 Stochastic Integral and Quadratic Variations (Benhamou, 2007)

Stochastic integrals assume various computational forms. Define the time interval $[0, T]$, which we reduce in the time intervals $\left[t_{i+1}^H - t_i^H\right]$, where H is parameter defining time intervals of various size. If $H < 1$, time intervals are greater. Let $M(t)$ be a martingale with

$\left[M\left(t_{i+1}^{H}\right) - M\left(t_{i}^{H}\right)\right]$, and at the limit when $\left[t_{i+1}^{H} - t_{i}^{H}\right] \to 0$ a quadratic variation martingale $M(t)$ is defined for a Brownian motion we then have $H = 1$, and therefore a limit of the integral of $f(\tau)$ is defined by

$$\int_{0}^{T} f(\tau) \, dM(\tau) \approx \sum_{i=1}^{n} f(\tau_{i}) \left[M(\tau_{i+1}) - M(\tau_{i})\right]$$

and for a Brownian motion

$$\int_{0}^{T} f(\tau) \, dW(\tau)$$

Letting $\sigma(\tau)$ be the process volatility, then $M(t) = \int_{0}^{t} \sigma(\tau) \, dW(\tau)$, while the quadratic variation is

$$\langle M(t) \rangle = \int_{0}^{t} \sigma^{2}(\tau) \, d\tau$$

In this case, a Brownian motion stochastic process such as the following is well defined:

$$\frac{\Delta S}{S} = \mu_{S} \Delta t + \sigma_{S} \Delta W(t)$$

In the multivariate case, with n and dependent Brownian motions $W_{1}(t), \dots, W_{n}(t)$:

$$\frac{\Delta S_{i}}{S_{i}} = \mu_{S_{i}} \Delta t + \boldsymbol{\sigma}_{S_{i}} \Delta \mathbf{W}_{i}(t)$$

where $\boldsymbol{\sigma}_{S_{i}} \Delta \mathbf{W}_{i}(t) = \sigma_{S_{i1}} \Delta W_{1}(t) + \sigma_{S_{i2}} \Delta W_{2}(t) + \cdots + \sigma_{S_{in}} \Delta W_{n}(t)$ is a vectors product with quadratic variation:

$$\left\langle \int_{0}^{T} \boldsymbol{\sigma}_{S}(\tau) \, d\mathbf{W}(\tau), \int_{0}^{T} \boldsymbol{\nu}_{S}(\tau) \, d\mathbf{W}(\tau) \right\rangle = \int_{0}^{T} \boldsymbol{\sigma}_{S}(\tau) * \boldsymbol{\nu}_{S}(\tau) \, d\tau$$

In this case, we can define the risk premium:

$$\mu_{S_{i}} - R_{f} = \lambda_{1} \sigma_{i1} + \lambda_{2} \sigma_{i2} + \cdots + \lambda_{n} \sigma_{in} \quad \text{or} \quad \mu_{S_{i}} - R_{f} = \boldsymbol{\lambda} * \boldsymbol{\sigma}_{i}$$

and

$$\frac{dS_{i}}{S_{i}} = \mu_{S_{i}} \, dt + \boldsymbol{\sigma}_{S_{i}} \Delta \mathbf{W}(t) = \left(R_{f} + \boldsymbol{\lambda} * \boldsymbol{\sigma}_{i}\right) + \boldsymbol{\sigma}_{i} * d\mathbf{W}(t)$$

Application of the Girsanov theorem yields the Q probability measure (which is similar to an application of the Sharpe ratio as seen in Chapter 3). Thus, under the Q probability measure, we set

$$\mathbf{Z}(t) = \mathbf{W}(t) + \int_{0}^{t} \lambda(\tau) \, d\tau \quad \text{or} \quad \frac{dS}{S} = R_{f} \, dt + \boldsymbol{\sigma}_{S} \, d\mathbf{Z}(t) \quad \text{or} \quad \frac{dS}{S} = R_{f} \, dt + \boldsymbol{\sigma}_{S} \, d\mathbf{Z}(t)$$

and finally

$$\frac{dS}{S} = R_f \, dt + \boldsymbol{\sigma}_S \, d\mathbf{W}^Q(t)$$

7.A.4 Pricing, the Radon–Nykodim Derivative and Girsanov Theorem

The choice of a financial asset relative to another asset is particularly important in FX and global finance. For example, should a CPI be priced relative to the dollar? Should a financial transaction in a foreign country be priced relative to the euro, to the US dollar, or other financial assets? A conventional wisdom would state that each sovereign state and its financial agents would seek to price its economic and financial assets with respect to their own. In a global environment, it is conceivable that a price is determined and thus valued based on a reference currency or even a basket of currencies. The Radon–Nykodim derivative provides a means to change probability measures. We noted earlier that a complete market model for a country's CPI could be defined (for a lognormal model) by

$$E^Q\left(\frac{CPI_F(t)}{B_F(t)}\right) - \frac{CPI_F(0)}{B_F(0)} = 0 \text{ and therefore } \frac{CPI_F(0)}{B_F(0)} = E^Q\left(\frac{CPI_F(t)}{B_F(t)}\right)$$

where expectation is taken with respect to a risk-neutral probability measure. The underlying transformed risk-neutral process is then a martingale.

The Girsanov theorem is a pricing approach that defines a probability measure that transforms an underlying price process into a martingale; namely, all future expected measures have the same mean. Therefore, the current price is necessarily an expectation (under the appropriate probability measure) of a future price. This particular property implies as well that current prices embed all the information regarding future expected prices. Given a probability measure, we can also look for an alternative measure with respect to which prices will be set. To do so, we use the Radon–Nykodim derivative, which we outline simply in the following.

Assume that a CPI is priced relative to a risk-neutral probability measure (i.e., a risk-free bond) and consider two successive instants of time, say t and $t + dt$, during which the CPI and bond prices change from $CPI(t) \rightarrow CPT(t) + dCPI(t)$ and $B(t) \rightarrow B(t) + dB(t)$. Since prices under the risk-neutral probability measure are well defined, we have

$$E^Q\left(\frac{CPI(t)}{B(t)}\right) = E^Q\left(\frac{CPI(t) + dCPI(t)}{B(t) + dB(t)}\right) \text{ or } E^Q\left(\frac{CPI(t)}{B(t)} - \frac{CPI(t) + dCPI(t)}{B(t) + dB(t)}\right) = 0$$

And therefore

$$E^Q\left(\frac{CPI(t)[B(t) + dB(t)] - B(t)[CPI(t) + dCPI(t)]}{B(t)[B(t) + dB(t)]}\right) = 0$$

$$E^Q(CPI(t)[dB(t)] - B(t)[dCPI(t)]) = 0$$

As a result:

$$E^Q\left(\frac{\mathrm{CPI}(t)}{B(t)} - \frac{\mathrm{dCPI}(t)}{\mathrm{d}B(t)}\right) = 0 \rightarrow \mathrm{CPI}_0 = \frac{\mathrm{CPI}(0)}{B(0)} = E^Q\left(\frac{\mathrm{CPI}(t)}{B(t)}\right) = E^Q\left(\frac{\mathrm{dCPI}(t)}{\mathrm{d}B(t)}\right)$$

To change the probability measure, from say a risk-neutral probability measure to one far more representative of a global market index, consider the following global measure $G(t)$ and say

$$\mathrm{CPI}_0 = \frac{\mathrm{CPI}(t)}{G(t)} = \frac{\mathrm{dCPI}(t)}{\mathrm{d}G(t)}$$

while with the risk-neutral measure is

$$\mathrm{CPI}_0 = \frac{\mathrm{CPI}(t)}{B(t)} = \frac{\mathrm{dCPI}(t)}{\mathrm{d}B(t)}$$

Thus, $\mathrm{d}B(t)(\mathrm{CPI}(t)/B(t)) - \mathrm{d}S(t) = 0$ or $\mathrm{dCPI}(t) = \mathrm{d}B(t)(\mathrm{CPI}(t)/B(t))$, which is replaced in the global probability measure, which yields

$$\frac{\mathrm{CPI}(t)}{B(t)}\left(\frac{B(t)}{G(t)} - \frac{\mathrm{d}B(t)}{\mathrm{d}G(t)}\right) = 0, \quad \frac{\mathrm{CPI}(t)}{B(t)} \neq 0, \quad \text{or} \quad \frac{B(t)}{G(t)} - \frac{\mathrm{d}B(t)}{\mathrm{d}G(t)} = 0$$

Finally:

$$\frac{\mathrm{d}B(t)}{\mathrm{d}G(t)} = \frac{B(t)}{G(t)}$$

Namely, if the bond is a deflator providing a risk-neutral measure, another measure can be determined if it solves the Radon–Nikodim derivative. For example, consider a bond process:

$$\frac{\mathrm{d}B}{B} = R_F\,\mathrm{d}t$$

Then, another risk-neutral probability measure can be determined if

$$\frac{\mathrm{d}B(t)}{\mathrm{d}G(t)} = \frac{B(t)}{G(t)} \Rightarrow \frac{R_F B(t)\,\mathrm{d}t}{\mathrm{d}G(t)} = \frac{B(t)}{G(t)} \Rightarrow \frac{\mathrm{d}G(t)}{G(t)}$$

$$= R_F\,\mathrm{d}t\,\frac{\mathrm{CPI}(t)}{B(t)}\left(\frac{B(t)}{G(t)} - \frac{\mathrm{d}B(t)}{\mathrm{d}G(t)}\right) = 0, \quad \frac{\mathrm{CPI}(t)}{B(t)} \neq 0$$

7.A.5 Reducing a Dependent Vector to be Independent

Define two random vectors $\mathbf{w}$ and $\mathbf{v}$ and let $\mathbf{Q}$ be their correlation matrix, which is both a square and invertible matrix; thus, one random vector can be defined in terms of the other (and vice versa). Set $\mathbf{w} = \mathbf{Q}\mathbf{v}$, and then solving for $\mathbf{v}$, we have $\mathbf{Q}^{-1}\mathbf{w} = \mathbf{v}$. For example, for two sources of risks and a matrix:

$$\mathbf{Q} = \begin{pmatrix} q_{11} & q_{12} \\ q_{21} & q_{22} \end{pmatrix}; \quad \begin{pmatrix} w_1 \\ w_2 \end{pmatrix} = \begin{pmatrix} q_{11} & q_{12} \\ q_{21} & q_{22} \end{pmatrix}\begin{pmatrix} v_1 \\ v_2 \end{pmatrix} \quad \text{and} \quad \begin{pmatrix} v_1 \\ v_2 \end{pmatrix} = \begin{pmatrix} q_{11} & q_{12} \\ q_{21} & q_{22} \end{pmatrix}^{-1}\begin{pmatrix} w_1 \\ w_2 \end{pmatrix}$$

Say that $\mathbf{Q}$ is a correlation matrix, with $q_{ii} = 1$, $\rho = q_{12} = q_{21}$, $i = 1, 2$, and therefore

$$w_1 = v_1 + q_{12}v_2 \quad \text{and} \quad w_2 = q_{12}v_1 + v_2, \quad \text{or} \quad v_1 = \frac{w_1 - w_2\rho}{1 - \rho^2}, \quad v_2 = \frac{w_2 - w_1\rho}{1 - \rho^2}$$

We determine next the matrix $\mathbf{Q}$ eigenvalues λ_j, $j = 1, 2$, by solving the determinant equation

$$|\mathbf{Q} - \lambda I| = 0, \quad \text{with} \quad \mathbf{Q} - \lambda I = \begin{pmatrix} q_{11} - \lambda & q_{12} \\ q_{21} & q_{22} - \lambda \end{pmatrix}$$

and

$$\begin{vmatrix} q_{11} - \lambda & q_{12} \\ q_{21} & q_{22} - \lambda \end{vmatrix} = (q_{11} - \lambda)(q_{22} - \lambda) - q_{12}q_{21} = 0$$

The solution yields a quadratic equation whose solution are the eigenvalues λ_i, $i = 1, 2$:

$$\lambda_1 = \frac{q_{22} + q_{11}}{2} + \sqrt{\left(\frac{q_{22} + q_{11}}{2}\right)^2 - q_{11}q_{22} + q_{12}q_{21}},$$

$$\lambda_2 = \frac{q_{22} + q_{11}}{2} - \sqrt{\left(\frac{q_{22} + q_{11}}{2}\right)^2 - q_{11}q_{22} + q_{12}q_{21}}$$

$\lambda_1 = 1 + \rho$, $\lambda_2 = 1 - \rho$.

To determine the eigenvectors associated with each eigenvalue of this matrix, we solve the following matrix equation:

$$\mathbf{Q}\boldsymbol{\beta}_j = \lambda_j \boldsymbol{\beta}_j, \quad j = 1, 2, \ldots, n$$

or explicitly for eigenvectors λ_1 and λ_2

$$\begin{pmatrix} q_{11} & q_{12} \\ q_{21} & q_{22} \end{pmatrix} \begin{pmatrix} \boldsymbol{\beta}_1 \\ \boldsymbol{\beta}_2 \end{pmatrix} = \begin{pmatrix} \lambda_1 & 0 \\ 0 & \lambda_1 \end{pmatrix} \begin{pmatrix} \boldsymbol{\beta}_1 \\ \boldsymbol{\beta}_2 \end{pmatrix}; \quad \begin{pmatrix} q_{11} & q_{12} \\ q_{21} & q_{22} \end{pmatrix} \begin{pmatrix} \boldsymbol{\beta}'_1 \\ \boldsymbol{\beta}'_2 \end{pmatrix} = \begin{pmatrix} \lambda_2 & 0 \\ 0 & \lambda_2 \end{pmatrix} \begin{pmatrix} \boldsymbol{\beta}'_1 \\ \boldsymbol{\beta}'_2 \end{pmatrix}$$

Generally, since the matrix $\mathbf{Q}$ is symmetric non-negative definite, the eigenvalues are all non-negative and the eigenvectors are all orthogonal to each other. In our case, for a correlation matrix, we have

$$\begin{pmatrix} 1 & \rho \\ \rho & 1 \end{pmatrix} \begin{pmatrix} \boldsymbol{\beta}_1 \\ \boldsymbol{\beta}_2 \end{pmatrix} = \begin{pmatrix} 1 + \rho & 0 \\ 0 & 1 + \rho \end{pmatrix} \begin{pmatrix} \boldsymbol{\beta}_1 \\ \boldsymbol{\beta}_2 \end{pmatrix}, \quad \text{eigenvector for } \lambda_1$$

$$\begin{pmatrix} 1 & \rho \\ \rho & 1 \end{pmatrix} \begin{pmatrix} \boldsymbol{\beta}'_1 \\ \boldsymbol{\beta}'_2 \end{pmatrix} = \begin{pmatrix} 1 - \rho & 0 \\ 0 & 1 - \rho \end{pmatrix} \begin{pmatrix} \boldsymbol{\beta}'_1 \\ \boldsymbol{\beta}'_2 \end{pmatrix}, \quad \text{eigenvector for } \lambda_2$$

Or

$$\boldsymbol{\beta}_1 + \rho\boldsymbol{\beta}_2 = (1 + \rho)\boldsymbol{\beta}_1 \quad \text{and} \quad \rho\boldsymbol{\beta}_1 + \boldsymbol{\beta}_2 = (1 + \rho)\boldsymbol{\beta}_2, \quad \text{and therefore} \quad \boldsymbol{\beta}_2 = \boldsymbol{\beta}_1$$

$$\boldsymbol{\beta}'_1 + \rho\boldsymbol{\beta}'_2 = (1 - \rho)\boldsymbol{\beta}'_1, \quad \text{and} \quad \rho\boldsymbol{\beta}'_1 + \boldsymbol{\beta}'_2 = (1 - \rho)\boldsymbol{\beta}'_2, \quad \text{and therefore} \quad \boldsymbol{\beta}'_1 = -\boldsymbol{\beta}'_2$$

References

Benhamou, E. (2007) *Global Derivatives: Products, Theory and Practice*. World Scientific: Singapore.

Bensoussan, A. and Tapiero, C.S. (1982) Impulsive control in management: prospects and applications. *Journal of Optimization Theory and Applications*, **37**: 419–442.

Black, F., and Scholes, M. (1973) The pricing of options and corporate liabilities. *Journal of Political Economy*, **81**: 637–659.

Carmona, R. and Durrleman, V. (2003) Pricing and hedging spread options. *SIAM Review*, **45**: 627–685.

Cooper, R. (1993) Risk premia in the futures and forward markets. *Journal of Futures Markets*, **13**(4): 357–371.

Garman, M. (1992) Spread the load. *Risk*, **5**: 68–69.

Glen, J. and Jorion, P. (1993) Currency hedging for international portfolios. *Journal of Finance*, **48**(5): 1865–1886.

Kallianiotis, J.N. (2013) *Exchange Rates and International Financial Economics: History, Theories, and Practices*. Palgrave Macmillan: London.

Malliaris, A.G. and Brock, W.A. (1982) *Stochastic Methods in Economics and Finance*. North Holland: Amsterdam.

Ritchken, P. and Tapiero, C.S. (1986) Contingent claim contracts and inventory control. *Operations Research*, **34**: 864–870.

Smith, C.W. (1976) Option pricing: a review. *Journal of Financial Economics*, **3**: 3–51.

Tapiero, C.S. (1978) Time, dynamics and the process of management modeling. *TIMS Studies in Management Science*, **9**: 7–31.

Tapiero, C.S. (2010) *Risk Finance and Asset Pricing*. John Wiley & Sons, Inc.: Hoboken, NJ.

Tapiero, C.S. (2013a) *Engineering Risks and Finance*. Springer: New York.

Tapiero, C.S. (2013b) The multi-agent CCAPM and debt pricing. Working paper, New York University Tandon School of Engineering, Department of Finance and Risk Engineering.

Tapiero, C.S. (2015) A financial CCAPM and economic inequalities. *Quantitative Finance*, **15**(3): 521–534.

8

Credit Risk and International Debt

Motivation

Credit and capital flows, together with trade (Chapter 9), underlie the expansion of financial globalization by providing liquidity and the capital required for economic development. Banks, financial markets, insurance firms, and a multitude of other financial institutions increasingly use innovative products that have contributed to the expansion of global credit and finance. This chapter provides an overview of credit risk and debt pricing. We introduce multi-country credit risk and its models from a number of perspectives. Technically, we define credit from three points of view: (1) a personal utility-based approach to credit prices and bipartite lender–borrower exchanges, (2) fundamental finance, option-based, and structured approaches to securitized risks based on Merton's model, synthetic instruments, and securitized credit and insurance products (e.g., credit default swaps (CDSs)), and (3) central bank's policy regarding interest rates and liquidity. Lenders and banks are intermediaries for central banks. They manage liquidity through interest rates and monetary policy (e.g., QE). Thus, globalization and credit growth are mutually dependent, and causally contribute to the expansion of global finance.

8.1 Introduction

A credit between two parties is a trust that one bestows on the other to meet previously negotiated commitments. For example, a lender trusting that a borrower will meet a contractual commitment. In a foreign environment, for a domestic lender, granting credit may be more profitable, but it may also be more risky. It may include credit risks, compounding foreign exchange (FX) risks, and legal, political, and other risks. In this context, "credit" need not only refer to default, but also to changes in assessments (e.g., Moody's or S&P's credit ratings). This is important because a change in creditworthiness can trigger a sell-off by funds with certain minimal standards. Thus, complexity is implicit, and difficulties in structuring, securitizing, and pricing risks have contributed to the popularity of standardized products. At the same time, the high demand for individual transactions has led to a demand for OTC financial products such as swaps (see Chapter 7 and later this chapter). The global financial credit industry has thus grown, expanding its outreach through a complex apparatus to lend and borrow globally, in multiple time zones, and in multiple currencies. In its wake, it has contributed to a transformation of banking into global institutions, networked with technological and organizational apparatus to

Globalization, Gating, and Risk Finance, First Edition. Unurjargal Nyambuu and Charles S. Tapiero.
© 2018 John Wiley & Sons Ltd. Published 2018 by John Wiley & Sons Ltd.

meet global demand. These include a broad variety intermediaries, dealers, and financial markets that are adapted to global trades, as well as financially engineered products to meet the very large variety of needs in many countries. Concurrently, global banking has allowed investors greater flexibility in managing their investments, some to profit legitimately, others seeking to avoid taxation or regulations, albeit faced with compounded credit risks, including currency risks, domestic borrowing and lending regulations, inflation, legal issues, taxation, and so on.

The size of national debts, relative to an economy's wealth and health, provides a measure of the sovereign credit risk, normally priced by rated sovereign bonds. For example, the Greek debt crisis in 2015 (although all euro denominated) and its related sovereign default threats were shown to be a financial, political, and contagious crisis with important repercussions for the euro. Similarly, Argentina's debt to hedge funds it had refused to pay for 15 years led to a willingness to lend to Argentina only at exorbitant rates—the cost of a lack of trust. It led to Argentina's global liquidity strangulation, which was resolved after a change in its political governance and a settlement of its debt. Credit risks are therefore a common part of normal functions in sovereign treasuries, in banking and lending financial institutions, and in consumers' and investors' transactions. The latter affects the health of the mortgage industries, insurance, and their respective prices. In international exchanges, option-based products have been engineered with the goals of providing insurance to currency transactions and for exchanges across national boundaries, typically using swap contracts; some swaps, (e.g., CDSs,) have been securitized. For example, the VIX (volatility index) prices defined as an "index of fears."

The ease and the flexibility of OTC swaps have led to an exponential increase in their use. Both financial options markets and swaps are now found in financial markets throughout the world. As they are more developed and believed to be fairly priced, advanced economies typically use market-priced (standardized) options; elsewhere, such as in Africa and Asia, OTC products are used. Securitized and structured products, such as collateralized debt obligations (CDOs) have provided both opportunities to investors seeking greater yields everywhere and for those interested in greater diversification and lower overall risks. Their excessive use also led, in some measure, to the 2007 financial crisis and to a vigorous financial regulation (see Chapter 10) that followed. They remain, nevertheless, a fixture of credit finance. Today, CDSs, unlike other credit risk products, are mostly securitized and serve as risk *insurance*. These financial products are now used for many risk management purposes.[1] These products, as well as treasury bonds issued by sovereign states and their interest rates, have been a major engine for debt growth, and have raised consumption and investments globally.

Financial institutions have labored to define guiding and standardized pricing principles, to grant loans, and to manage risks globally. The Basel Committee defined a country or a sovereign risk as a spectrum of risks arising from economic, political, and social environmental factors. A foreign country risk is then defined by these (and other) factors, including foreign debt, equity, and other investments priced by financial institutions. The growing interdependence of countries' economies and their financial systems hand in hand with globalization has created a bigger, resilient, and "free" banking system. Yet, at the same time, it is a fragile system and is less responsive to sovereign regulation. This has led to sovereign authorities to design regulatory policies that are far more stringent

---

1 For the analysis of risk management, see Cox and Tait (1991); and for management of interest rate and currency risks, refer to the handbook by Schwartz and Smith (1990).

(see Chapter 10). The US regulation system, for example, based on the preeminence of the US dollar as the preferred exchange currency, has applied its regulatory principles globally, to both corporate firms (big and small) and investors everywhere. Currency wars, taxation, trade, and other fundamental activities are a result of gating and anti-globalization policies. For example, the promise by President Trump to gate the USA physically and financially (e.g., by imposing a 5% tax on all imports) would add to the challenges of the global economy and global finance.

8.2   Growth of Debt and Debt Dependency

An overly grown debt has a credit risk that may threaten an enterprise or an individual to bankruptcy. For a country, an excessive debt imposes difficulties in running its affairs and to become dependent when its debt is mostly held by foreign interests or states. Previously, we discussed Argentina's debt. However, the US debt to China and Japan in trillions of dollars may, in specific circumstances, be also threatening. Dependency of foreign banks on debtor countries can be shown using the Bank of International Settlements (BIS) data to track the outstanding amount of banks' foreign claims (see Table 8.1). For example, the UK owes countries such as the USA, Germany, Spain, and France, but at the same time these countries owe the UK billions of dollars. This interdependence indicates how a default by one country may induce a financial stress on others, especially in the banking sector. For example, the debt of Greece was essentially due to the national bank's champions of France, Germany, and others and threatening the robustness of their balance sheets. Issues were raised that demanded (for political and economic reasons) for sovereign states to intervene and support a rescue package to assure Greece's ability to meet its financial needs (or perhaps assure their own banks of due payments). The political alternative to a Grexit (a Greek exit from the euro and the EU) was an additional political demand from the EU to prevent a Greek financial meltdown. The consequences of such a possibility were proved by the Brexit (Britain voting to exit the EU) to be in fact extremely costly and politically consequential.

The expansion of business, trade, and economic activities in general is derived from credit, its availability, and its price. It underlies and fuels trade, globalization, and the purchasing power of currencies. For example, following the 2007–2008 financial crisis, global liquidity was fed by low interest rates (by central banks) and by national treasuries printing money. The demand for the US dollar to infuse a global economic activity augmented its national debt, but at the same time, due to its status as a secured and trusted currency, it has maintained the price of currency. However, the increased indebtedness of sovereign states and their dependence (see Figure 8.1 and Tables 8.1 and 8.2) point to the mutual relationship and a dependency that debt and its interconnectedness have in the euro currency region and its associated partners (e.g., the UK and Switzerland). Central government debt stock in Figure 8.1 highlights outstanding domestic and foreign liabilities and their growing shares of GDP.

Table 8.2, for example, is a matrix outlining debt correlations between European countries. Thus, if one country falters in its payments, its effect on other countries may be important. Such a dependence naturally increases sovereign credit risks. As already stated, when the Greek financial debt crisis was at its worst, European banks financing

Table 8.1 Foreign claims of reporting banks on counterparty country (outstanding amount as of end of 2015, in billion USD).

Reporting country	Austria	Belgium	France	Germany	Greece	Ireland	Italy	Japan	Netherlands	Spain	UK	USA
Austria		1.7	6.2	37.7	0.2	0.9	6.9	0.1	4.6	3.5	12.3	8.5
Belgium	1.1		17.8	7.8	0.0	15.1	8.7	0.7	22.6	9.5	18.1	11.0
France	14.5	183.3		148.3	1.2	34.7	294.4	150.1	94.2	101.6	220.5	434.2
Germany	56.4	25.5	169.9		23.1	46.9	86.7	34.6	114.2	78.8	389.8	433.4
Greece	0.3	0.6	0.7	2.1		0.2	0.2	0.02	0.3	0.1	9.7	0.9
Ireland	0.0	0.8	4.5	0.9			1.3		1.8	2.4	67.3	6.0
Italy	78.7	7.4	39.9	178.2	0.7	7.1		6.3	18.0	43.4	46.5	36.4
Japan	4.4	21.9	153.0	98.4	0.2	40.1	31.2		84.6	21.8	198.2	1414.1
Netherlands	11.2	0.0	73.7	150.6	0.9	12.2	28.5	10.5		40.8	98.6	172.6
Spain		4.8	54.5				58.6		15.6		378.6	263.3
UK	6.5	12.2	146.1	143.2	5.4	86.7	27.7	98.8	93.5	19.4		740.3
USA	12.0	21.8	153.8	157.1	2.9	68.6	49.1	284.5	79.3	44.8	461.4	
Total	220	433	1011	1216	40	365	673	774	648	435	2576	5381

Source: Data from BIS.

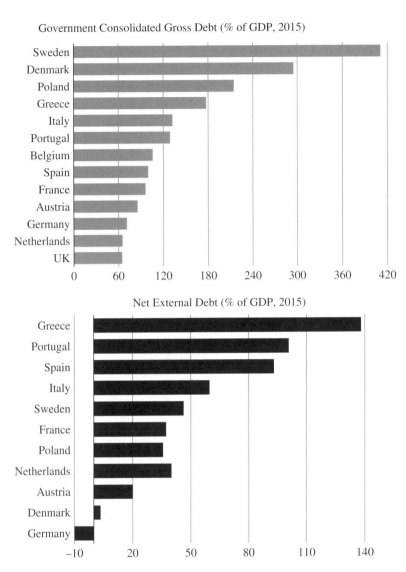

Figure 8.1 Growth of debt in the EU and globalization (government consolidated gross debt and net external debt). *Source:* Data from EUROSTAT.

Greece's debt were threatened by their risk exposure, pleading their sovereign government to seek a solution and prevent the threat of a local debt crisis in other EU member countries (such as Spain, Portugal, and Italy). The debt of Greece was 165% of its GDP, signaling a potential future default. The debt crisis of Mexico in the 1980s ending in 1994, the Asian crisis in 1997, the Russian crisis in 1998, and the mega-crisis of 2007–2008 in the USA (that has migrated globally over a decade) have reinforced the expectations that excessive leverage, debt, and dependence have created a debt-liquidity and credit risks that can a threaten global economic stability. A similar situation exists in Asia, where trade and finance are increasingly dependent on global markets. These risks have increased with the growth of global debt, dependence, and correlation-contagious

Table 8.2 Government consolidated gross debt in the EU and correlation.

	Belgium	Germany	Greece	Spain	France	Italy	Hungary	Netherlands	Austria	Poland	Portugal	UK
Belgium	1.00											
Germany	0.95	1.00										
Greece	0.88	0.97	1.00									
Spain	0.99	0.91	0.82	1.00								
France	0.97	0.99	0.95	0.95	1.00							
Italy	0.97	0.98	0.95	0.94	1.00	1.00						
Hungary	0.92	0.98	0.98	0.86	0.97	0.98	1.00					
Netherlands	0.99	0.95	0.89	0.96	0.97	0.96	0.92	1.00				
Austria	0.97	0.98	0.96	0.94	0.99	0.99	0.98	0.96	1.00			
Poland	0.95	1.00	0.97	0.91	0.99	0.99	0.99	0.95	0.99	1.00		
Portugal	0.98	0.99	0.94	0.95	1.00	0.99	0.97	0.97	0.99	0.99	1.00	
UK	1.00	0.96	0.89	0.98	0.98	0.97	0.93	0.99	0.98	0.96	0.99	1

Source: Data from EUROSTAT.

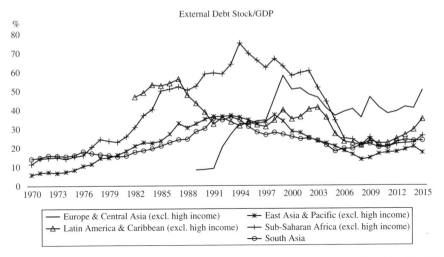

Figure 8.2 Growth of regional external debt as share of GDP. *Source:* Data from The World Bank.

omnipresent risks. Many Latin American, Eastern European, and some Asian countries have a significant debt burden (see figures in Chapter 4). Regional external debt (excluding high-income countries) for developing countries shows that Europe and Central Asia have a very high relative debt, whereas East Asia–Pacific has the lowest relative debt measured by their debt-to-GDP ratios (see Figure 8.2). For example, concerns regarding the US debt that China holds in trillions of dollars (although it has been reduced to just over $1 trillion) have both political and economic implications to their dependence and to the gating of their currency's holders. These sovereign high levels of debt have created markets of their own being traded for profit and loss with financial institutions and hedge funds specializing in trading these debts and their obligations.

8.3   Foreign Exchange is a Credit Bestowed to a Sovereign Entity

Currency holders are also credit holders, granting their trust to a sovereign state to sustain the value of its currency in domestic and foreign exchanges and in meeting the terms of its debt. Its price is paid by the currency holder for the liquidity it provides as well as for the inflation of that currency. In this sense, currency is broadly associated with states' fixed income (treasury bills) and their alternative investment in equity markets and the liquidity that the currency provides (i.e., to the extent it is negotiable). These prices reflect the needs and the means of exchange between global investors, speculators, and governments as well as the trust one has in a particular currency. For example, the US dollar reserves of China have a number of advantages, including, among others, liquidity, relative currency safety, and potentially a political power over the currency issuer.

Paper currencies conclude a long history of money anchored in a human history of trade and credit based on a variety of means to store and exchange value. Technology and e-finance are contributing to a change of wealth denominators, with electronic transactions and credit assuming an important role. Prior to the Renaissance, currency was defined by minted metals, granting a great deal of power to those wielding the supply of gold (e.g., Spain). The limited capacity of these currencies to provide financial liquidity has contributed to minted metals falling as the main medium of exchange. To provide such liquidity, banking families in Italy as well as traders in Holland and subsequently England introduced paper obligations as a means to trade, which in effect defined a currency and provided liquidity in the form of promissory notes (in fact credit papers). Thus, a new financial system arose based on the implicit fiduciary (credit) trust in a banking system that has provided a required liquidity and guarantees to paper money—the bank's currency. This has been the case ever since. In the USA, at the beginning of the last century. over a thousand banks were able to print their own currency, ending with the collapse of the US financial system and the need to seek a reliable guarantor. The exchange between these currencies was embedded in a currency holder trust in the banks printing money. Today, the printer and the guarantor of a currency is the sovereign state. In the USA, this is assumed by the Federal Reserve Bank (which monitors, regulates, and manages the financial end of the economy through its financial policies) and the US government (which sets the fiscal policy of the country—defining its expenditures, its revenues through taxation, debt, etc.). Currently, however, a technological currency revolution is seeking to devise a currency which is sovereign free. Electronic and internet-traded currencies such as bitcoins seek to be used as alternative moneys where exchanges can be made independently and free from sovereign controls.

The predictability and relative stability of FX prices (most of which are presumed on the basis of currencies' parity using macroeconomic, financial and geopolitical factors), as well as currencies mutually tracking each other (see Chapters 5 and 7), have allowed the use of currencies to exchange and trade. At the same time, increasingly nations that are well aware of the advantages they acquire in manipulating their FX rates have also contributed to a strategic pricing of currencies and to potential risks resulting from tinkering in off-markets agreements. The strength of a currency is an indicator of the trust one has in its economic well-being, strength, political stability, and the power of its economic and financial institutions. Sovereign states with a weak currency and no credit may jeopardize their standing, which is reflected in both the volatility and the decline of their currency as an acceptable means of exchange. It also contributes to their costs of borrowing. In light of the financial crisis of 2007–2008 and the rise of Asia as a strong currency area, as well as weaknesses in the euro as a competing alternative to the US dollar, the US dollar has maintained its dominance. Based on its strength and advantages, the USA prints money and increases its debt sold and exchanged globally. This has also led to an increased determination by China and other countries to seek alternative means to a reference FX (preferably using their own currency) for international currency exchanges. As stated in Chapter 1, these lead to "multi-polar" financial and currency markets, each vying for a strategic advantage. Since all currencies are merely the prices of promissory notes, guaranteed by sovereign states, financial transactions are necessarily *credit* transactions.

FX also has other options, providing FX financial markets rich information and opportunities to hedge and to speculate (see also Chapter 7). Their strength is based on the strength of their currency contracts and the enrichment that facilitates the business of trade, investment, diversifications, and the flow of moneys across national boundaries. Given the dependence of countries' economies, in order to maintain a stable and trading world environment, sustainable and stable currencies are needed (or at least define an anchor currency agreed on globally that can provide both liquidity and minimize currency credit risk). To a large extent, the US dollar has been used ever since the end of World War II as the anchor currency, allowing it to incur debt at preferential rates due to a global demand for the US dollar. A recent realignment of competing economies in Asia provides an important challenge to the future of a "single currency anchor."

8.4 Credit and Global Risks

Global risks are due to a complex set of factors that are both country and intercountry specific (exchange, credit–debt, politics, environment, social, etc.). They may relate to trade, to wars, or to exchanges that sustain the global economy. They may also be related to natural causes, such as an earthquake or a catastrophe. Global credit finance, however, is resilient as it is a necessity to global trades and to an extensive network of interdependent relationships, agreements, resources, and capacities, all of which affect domestic economic and financial sectors. Global credit risks are therefore both important and strategic. These entail significant risks, many of which are not accounted for (and therefore not priced, or uncertain). They include, for example, country-specific risks, FX, trading, regulation, and macroeconomic risks, sovereign debt default, foreign and interest (bonds), foreign credit, investment, legal, political, and external (natural and wars) risks, international oprisks, and others (neglected or unknown). In the following, we consider a partial review of these risk factors.[2]

8.4.1 Country-Specific Risks

Country risks are defined by macroeconomic, legal, regulatory, and geopolitical factors (e.g., overleveraged debt, persistent negative balance of payments, country's treasury bonds rating, bubbles, legal reliabilities, regulatory biases, corruption, and strategic risks). It also includes a sovereign state's political climate, wars, revolutions, its power structure, legal framework, and governance. Country risks affect investments (such as ownership of firms, land, and infrastructure), the country's borrowing rates, and so on. To quantify a country's financial risk, rating firms such as S&P, Fitch, and Moody's rate sovereign treasury bonds. Other independent agencies, such as Business Monitor International (BMI Research), *The Economist* Intelligence Unit's (EIU) Country Risk Service,[3] and PRS,[4] provide country risks data, their analysis, rankings, and forecasts of different risks (e.g., political, economic, liquidity, and operational risk) for over 100 countries. For example, the BMI country risk index[5] and its components are described in Figure 8.3, which seeks to summarize country risks in terms of political, economic and financial market vulnerabilities, and operational risks. Operational risks cover logistics

---

2 See Bonfim (2009) for drivers of credit risk emphasizing not only the firm-level information, but also macroeconomic dynamics. Also, Ganguin and Bilardello (2004) provide analysis of different credit risks covering corporate credit risks (including sovereign and credit risks, industry risks, business risk) and credit risk of debt instruments (including debt structure, insolvency regimes).

3 http://www.eiu.com/home.aspx.

4 International Country Risk Guide: http://www.prsgroup.com/about-us/our-two-methodologies/icrg. Political Risk Yearbook: http://epub.prsgroup.com/customer/pry/. CountryData: http://epub.prsgroup.com/the-countrydata-gateway/.

5 http://www.bmiresearch.com/.

Country Risk	=	Political Risk	Economic Risk	Operational Risk
1. Switzerland 2. Norway 3. Sweden 4. Singapore 5. Denmark 6. Canada 7. Hong Kong 8. Austria 9. Luxembourg 10. United States		Policy-making; Social stability; Security/ external threats; Policy continuity; Characteristics of polity and society	Structure; Economic growth; Monetary & Fiscal policies; External factors; Financial markets (local debt markets; capital control risk; external borrowing)	Labor market risk; Logistics risk; Trade, Investment; Crime, Security

Figure 8.3 Country risk indicators and ranking (2015) by Business Monitor International Ltd (http://www.bmiresearch.com).

risks, labor markets' risks, trade and investment, crime, and security risks. Similarly, EIU rates the country risk based on sovereign risk (sovereign default on debt), currency risk, banking sector risk, political risk, and economic structure risk. The top ten countries are listed in order of their country risk index with Switzerland ranked the lowest.

8.4.2 Foreign Exchange Risks

FX risks are priced in various ways, including, for example, currency spreads, currency volatility, currency options and other derivatives and their dependence. Financial risks then arise from unexpected variations in currency prices, from a lack of liquidity, and adverse events in FX markets due to sovereign gating policies, geopolitical events, and so on. Currency risks reflect mostly financial risks that affect both financial capital flows and trade (and thus affect states' imports and exports) and sovereign states' reserve currencies. An alternative definition to currency risks is embedded in their deviation from the parity that may be due to mispricing of a CPI and default models that fail to account for all the relevant factors that define an FX through PPP. Currency spreads are due to several factors embedded in investors' expectations of economic statistics, sovereign states' ability to meet their commitments, demand and supply of the currency, and sovereign states' political and economic policies (e.g., the direct and indirect support of their currency or currencies' regulations).

FX risk measures based on unexpected variations in exchange rates consist of two elements: internal and external. Internal elements depend on the flow of funds associated with FX, investments, and related economic activities. External elements include extreme events as well as the systemic dependence of FX in all other countries (since FX is necessarily measured and defined relative to other countries). Risks are then defined as already stated by the financial exposure to a currency, such as the spread of exchange rates, their swap markets' prices, and their derivatives. And not least, defined by what the other sovereign states do to their currency. To mitigate these risks, first a currency exposure ought to be denominated in terms of factors that define the price of the currency being considered. Second, it ought to be associated with any asset or liability, physical or financial, investors might own or owe, and be practical from an investor's point of view. From a short-term viewpoint, FX variability, its predictability, and its growth are also considered.

In Figure 8.4 we plot the evolution of daily FX rate relative to the US dollar for the yuan (China), the yen (Japan), Mexican peso, Australian dollar, euro, and pound (UK) from

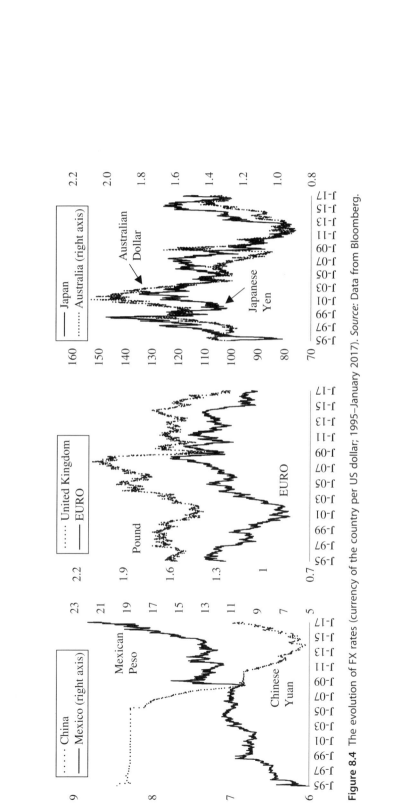

Figure 8.4 The evolution of FX rates (currency of the country per US dollar; 1995–January 2017). *Source:* Data from Bloomberg.

1995 to January 27, 2017. We observe that flexible FX rates (e.g., yen and pound), determined by market forces, are more volatile than FX, which tend to be relatively more fixed to the US dollar (e.g., management of the yuan by China).

FX credit risks resulting from FX by other sovereign states as well as their economic factors (such as macroeconomic and trade taxation and regulatory policies) render FX credit risks strategic; that is, depending on "others' policies and their realization." These lead to FX being the outcome of sovereigns' skirmishes and, at times, to an all-out currency war. For example, the US president announcing his intent to free exports from taxation and impose a tax on imports may be interpreted as a trade war resulting either in a realignment of trade and exchanges globally or in an open trade and financial credit war. Politics and conflicts, normally neglected in defining assets' prices (such as nationalization, selective actions assumed by governments against or in favor of foreign investors), may cause strategic risks to both trade and FX credit risks. A number of examples and simple models to price credit and FX risks are considered in the following and considered subsequently in greater quantitative detail.

8.4.3 Credit Trading and Currency, Sovereign Bond Risks, Currency Stability

8.4.3.1 Credit Trading Risks

These are defined by a violation of exchange trading terms, their direct and derived costs, and reputation. Most sovereign states provide export support through export banks or through other means (e.g., foreign delegations). In some cases, such supports are deemed illegal, providing incentives to exporters that counter reciprocal sovereign agreements. For example, the European Commission (EC) found that Huawei Technologies and the ZTE Telecommunications Corporation—the largest equipment maker in China —profits from significant government support, including massive credit lines from the state-owned bank (WSJ, 2011). Such an incentive has made it possible for ZTE to assume an "unfair" competitive advantage compared with European champion firms in telecommunications (such as Alcatel and Nokia). Sanctions, dumping, and other trading practices involve trading risks.

8.4.3.2 Currency Credit Risks

Currency holders may be interpreted as creditors to the issuer of the sovereign state currency who may indulge in the mismanagement of its currency. For the currency holder, credit risk may then be due to inflation, and to an over-QE financial policy, downgrading of the buying power of its currency, etc. For example, the trillions of US dollars held by Japan and China, may face an appreciable credit loss if a US president would at one time decide to devalue the US dollar.

8.4.3.3 Sovereign and Foreign Bonds' Risks and Prices

Rating firms, such as Moody, Fitch, S&P, and others, provide a rating scale that provides a risk guidance to investors and to currency traders and holders. Their assessment of a sovereign credit risk (at best a probabilistic assessment) provides a rating scale that may be downgraded or upgraded during a yearly period. A strong, safe, and stable economy and its currency may be given a high rating, while a weak or unstable economy may be at risk of a downgrade. This threat implies an increased default risk and thereby a greater risk premium it assumes to cover the credit risk of both its currency and the cost of issuing more treasury bills (i.e., printing money). These prospects have important financial implications. For example, a sovereign state may have to pay more for borrowing (i.e., issuing treasury bonds with higher interest rates). This is not always the case, however. When S&P downgraded long-term US Treasury bills in 2011, it was ignored by financial markets, expressing their trust in the US economy relative to other economies. More importantly, the political clout and the inventory of the US nontradable assets contributed probably to the strength of the US dollar—providing lenders (i.e., holders of the currency) an additional security that may be recognized only implicitly in financial currency trades. In the 2016–2017, the US dollar strengthened due to a revival of the US economy combined with a weakness of other economies. Whether the US dollar continues to appreciate or not may depend on the state of the US presidency (i.e., political factors) and its economy.

The rating of bonds (e.g., treasury bills) and their price thus underlie a very broad assessment of sovereign state economic and future prospects, as well as a judgement of its policies. It is therefore, primarily, a financial statement, albeit influenced by political and environmental economic factors. The rating of sovereign currency (both foreign and local currencies) is summarized in S&P (2017) (see Table 8.3 for selected defaults), indicating sovereign foreign- and local-currency defaults. Some countries, such as Argentina, defaulted twice: in 2001 (November) and in 2014 (July); the ratings 1 year before each default were BB and B– respectively. Argentina failed to pay bond interest payments of $539 million in 2014 (June 30) and eventually defaulted on its sovereign debt on July 30,

Table 8.3 Selected sovereign currency defaults.

	Foreign currency			Local currency	
Default year	Country	Rating (1 year before)	Default year	Country	Rating (1 year before)
1999	Russia	BB–			
1999; 2000; 2002	Indonesia	B–; CCC+; B–			
2001; 2014	Argentina	BB; B–	2001	Argentina	BBB–
2003	Uruguay	BB–			
2005	Venezuela	B–			
2008	Ecuador	B–	2001	Ecuador	B–
2010, 2013	Jamaica	B, B–	2010, 2013	Jamaica	B, B–
2012 (Feb; Dec)	Greece	BB+; CCC	2012 (Feb, Dec)	Greece	BB+
2013	Cyprus	CCC+	2013	Cyprus	CCC+
2015	Ukraine	CCC			
2016	Mozambique	B			
2016	Republic of Congo	B			

Source: Data from S&P 2015.

2014. Subsequently, in 2016, Argentina had to reckon with its past failings to meet its obligations by paying (with embedded additional payments) the holders of its debt. Such an action followed a political change that was motivated by its need to turn again to foreign lenders to meet its national economic needs. Factors considered in the S&P ratings of sovereign credit are shown in Figure 8.5.

In the following we summarize a sample of government bonds by country based on the financial market pricing of their economy. Sovereign credit ratings by S&P with the effective date and 10-year government bond yields on June 16, 2017, are shown in Table 8.4 with notes on their economic and political condition. Note in particular the yield of bonds reflecting both their rating and other factors, such as the weight of external debt compared with the debt held by the national banks and investors. As a result, the price of sovereign bonds could be considered as a derivative of many factors and policies that define a sovereign state, both summarized by financial and economic data and geopolitical events and their valuation in financial markets. The models we use to price these bonds (as well as other assets) are therefore simple compared with their real complexity.

Ratings by financial rating agencies are not without error; nor are these ratings always reliable. Agencies' ratings of mortgage-backed securities portfolios (such as CDOs) were rated as almost risk free when they were not. The 2007–2008 financial meltdown has proved that rating firms being paid credit to rate portfolios were, mostly, misleading. By the same token, as stated earlier, S&P's downgrade of the US AAA bonds rating to AA+ in August 2011, prior to the US Obama presidential election due to a high debt burden, a budget deficit, and a political stalemate between the Democrat President of the USA and a house controlled by Republicans, was in fact ignored by financial markets. It proved that when there are few financial and political alternatives to the US relative stability, such a downgrade can be meaningless. In this sense, ratings, just as market financial prices, are in fact relative. Another example of the downgraded industrial economy is the UK, whose rating was cut from AAA to AA in June 2016 due to an increased risk in external financing caused by their decision to exit the EU, which is referred to as Brexit. Since the Brexit vote, it seemed that a downgrading was due to markets' uncertainty rather than actual facts. The future of the UK pound thus depends on its negotiations with the EU as well as on how it will fare economically and financially following the Brexit (if at all, if it chooses to remain in the EU). Sovereign bond prices are therefore affected by the following essential factors:

Sovereign Rating =	Institutional	Economic	External	Monetary	Fiscal
	Governance & institutional effectiveness; Accountability Transparency; Security risks	Economic Structure; Growth; Income; Economic diversity, volatility	External liquidity; External indebtedness, International investment position	Monetary flexibility; Monetary policy credibility; Monetary mechanism	Fiscal flexibility; Performance; Sovereign deficits; Debt structure; Debt burden

Figure 8.5 Sovereign credit rating factors used by S&P.

Table 8.4 Sovereign credit ratings (long term) and government bonds.

Country	Rating (S&P)	Outlook	Effective date	10-year gov't bond yield (%)	Comments
Germany	AAA	Stable	1/13/2012	0.27	Euro concerns; aging population; strong external balance; public finance
Singapore	AAA	Stable	2/25/2011	2.06	Perceived as current safe haven
Switzerland	AAA	Stable	2/17/2011	−0.20	Perceived as current safe haven
USA	AA+	Stable	8/5/2011	2.51	Debt crisis, budget and trades imbalances
UK	AA	Negative	6/27/2016	0.61	Brexit
Japan	A+	Stable	8/5/2011	0.05	Tsunami and recovery; high budget deficits
Mexico	BBB+	Negative	8/23/2016	6.84	Governance and local upheavals
Spain	BBB+	Positive	3/31/2017	1.44	Debt crisis
Portugal	BB+	Stable	9/18/2015	2.88	Debt crisis; improved budget deficits; gradual recovery
Brazil	BB	Negative watch	5/22/2017	10.43	Political uncertainty; economic challenges with high inflation, fiscal deterioration
Italy	BBB−	Stable	12/5/2014	1.98	Debt and issues of governance
India	BBB-	Stable	2/25/2011	6.49	Fiscal improvements; positive growth prospects
Greece	B−	Stable	1/22/2016	5.55	Debt crisis; euro support; possibility of leaving eurozone; improved liquidity

Source: Data from Bloomberg, Ratings and 10 year government bond yields on Aug. 8, 2016.

- The sovereign commitment through its central banks and monetary policy to institute a price for risk through the interest paid on its treasury bills.
- Financial markets' exchanges trading in sovereign bonds and their many derivatives.
- The nontradable assets of a sovereign country including its real nontradable assets, its political clout, and stability.

The first factor is policy motivated and based on macroeconomic and geopolitical considerations (see Chapters 4, 5, and 6), while the second is based on global financial market forces expressing their demand and supply of sovereign bonds. Finally, the last one is (as in astrophysics) a "black hole," not seen (i.e., not traded) but influential and at time the dominant factor. Further, when a currency is relatively stable, compared with others, its demand will increase, allowing it to print more money and issue its treasury bills at a very low interest rate that others would buy even at a real loss (if, subsequently, devaluations and inflation set in) which they perceive to be smaller than current alternatives.

8.4.3.4   Investment, Transparency and Legal Risks, and Currency Stability

Investing in countries where their laws and their applications are subject to multiple interpretations is very risky. In Ukraine, for example (but also in other post-communist countries), the laws defining private property were not clear or did not exist. As a result, trades, attracting foreign capital, and investment needed for economic development may be lagging in such countries. Of course, such constraints are weighted against the profits that credit and trade may provide. Another example is ownership in China, which is not always well defined; for example, a 50-year government lease on land is only a partial ownership—see *The Economist* (2011). Chinese industries, such as mining and steel, need foreign capital investments, but the law does not permit foreign ownership and therefore foreign ownership can be implemented only through intermediate ownership associations that expand the network of risk. Similarly, conflicting interpretations of the laws of two countries, submitted to judicial proceedings in one country, may lead to penalties. This was the case for China's exporter of vitamin C to the USA, penalized in one court and overturned in another (WSJ, 2016b) on the basis of a regulatory conflict.

8.4.3.5   Stability, Volatility of Foreign Exchange, and Credit

These also have important implications for trade and foreign investments. For example, the European fiscal crisis has raised investors' concerns about how much foreign exposure to have, but also about how bets (and hedging) should be made (NYT, 2011).[6] Traditionally, US investors faced with the prospect of a falling price for the dollar have profited from their foreign investments (in dollar terms) and therefore had no need to hedge their foreign income and holdings. In a mundane way, financial volatility in currency markets may be a symptom of a currency instability, reflecting financial investors' and speculators' bets of the future on the currency (relative) price. For a Chinese investor in the USA, however, hedging US dollar returns may be essential if the yuan were to appreciate (or depreciate if submitted to international pressures). Such an instability in FX markets can lead to an increase in the FX price and to sovereign states seeking to redefine a reference and stable currency more amenable to their needs (instead of the current dominance of the US dollar in trade and credit markets).

8.5   Credit Risk, Credit Derivatives, and Credit Default Swaps

Credit risk and its price increase when distrust increases (such as political interventions in foreign countries, nationalization, and instability of countries). In such cases, financial loss, disappointment, and a misuse of trust occur, requiring increasingly complex contracts to account for ex-post events that are a priori ill-defined or uncertain. In insurance and financial markets, these are reflected in their insurance premiums and prices. A traditional definition to credit risk thus covers a set of multiple risks, including essentially:

- Default risks that can result in extremely large penalties for financial institutions.
- Recovery and loss risks, as well as reputation risks. These differ from country to country and are applied according to the laws of domestic and foreign lenders and borrowers.

---

6 For hedging credit risk, see Bielecki and Rutkowski (2002).

- Collateral risks mitigated by the assets used to secure contract risks and default.
- Third-party's guarantee risk. For example, insurance coverage risks such as sovereign state trading banks insuring their exporters and providing a coverage to trade insurance risks.
- Legal risk for legal fees and recoveries. These differ as well from country to country.
- Risk capital exposure for capital set aside for losses.
- Macroeconomic and sovereign risks as well as systemic risks.
- Counterparty risk or the risk inherent in trade and political conflicts, information and power asymmetries, and regulatory compliance within a sovereign state and across national boundaries.

Credit risks may be mitigated by pre-posterior steps taken to predict and assure that the terms of the contract agreed are respected (e.g., Reyniers and Tapiero, 1995a,b). One may do so by penalties for specific violations of agreements combined by buying and selling credit derivatives and insurance contracts. Their prices and valuations are difficult to assess as there are few (if any) financial markets that can account for their consequences. Their prices are therefore set by swaps.

The tools used to manage credit risks are also varied. For example, in both domestic and foreign countries, limiting or insuring the level of obligations, seeking collaterals, netting, recouponing, syndication, diversification, and optional swaps are some of the tools that financial credit services firms or banks might use. Securitization (i.e., packaging portfolios with assets and financial contracts) and exchange traded funds (ETFs) have, on the one hand, expanded their liquidity, but on the other hand they have reduced the transparency of these assets' risk exposure. Namely, the securitization of common credit contracts (such as mortgages and life insurance) allocating risks and payments according to an ordered schedule and parties has contributed to an "explosion" of named financial products and their derivatives that has, on the one hand, increased the availability of credit and, on the other hand, increased the latent risks their buyers and sellers were faced with. Investors seeking higher yields have led to the creation of specialized ETFs focused on globalization and geo-sectorial and country ETFs where yields may be expected to be greater. ETFs are today extremely popular with trillions of dollars in investments. They, too, are aggregates that harbor domestic and foreign risks, far more subject to news and volatility risks than by data risks. CDOs compared with tracking ETFs are portfolios packaging a large number of, say, mortgages, life insurance, or other less liquid assets and sold as credit derivatives, with payment schedules set in a manner to meet buyers' preferences. Their complex structure has rendered them difficult to assess stealth risks. Prior to the financial crisis of 2007–2008, they were sold globally through an alphabet soup of portfolios. These portfolios have both distorted debt markets and their regulation. For example, municipal bonds issued by states and cities have been leveraged by using these bonds as collaterals to other debt in order to increase their yield.

In some sovereign states, an overregulation of such instruments (through an increase in capital adequacy ratio in banks) has hampered liquidity and economic activity and thereby the creation of wealth, while "underregulation" (in particular in emerging markets with cartels and few economic firms managing the economy) has led to speculative markets and financial distortions. The financial profession has been marred with such problems, to account for their compliance as applied both domestically and in foreign countries (see Chapter 10). Their manifestations are commonly noted by the daily media by cross-border capital flows and the number of firms changing their legal economic origins (e.g., from high US taxes to low-taxed and less-regulated countries). They have also contributed to the launch of financial markets all over Africa and Asia that may, on the one hand, be less restrictive and, on the other hand, bear greater credit risks. For these reasons, regulated systemic and credit risks are important, leading to a mismatch between financial and macroeconomic factors. In a global environment, these factors are increasingly interdependent.

8.6 Swaps

8.6.1 A Definition and Types of Swaps

Swaps are exchange products tailored to meet the needs of individual traders, contracted as bipartite agreements, or through intermediaries and tripartite agreements. Swaps in global finance are increasingly important as a means of economic and financial exchange. In their simple form, they entail an exchange between, say, two parties or entities that have a common interest to engage in an exchange. As discussed in Chapter 1, trade between countries may be interpreted as a swap. Although swaps assume many forms, a swap transaction occurs if there are apparent reasons for the parties involved to be engaged in such a transaction. These may include:

- The advantage each of the parties derives from the transaction (if they have a choice).
- The swaps market mechanism set to bring parties to exchange or intermediaries that can contribute to the transparency and the opportunity to exchange.
- Externalities expressed in particular reasons to trade off financial and regulated markets that are not part of a swap contract.

Each of these, in any of their combinations, may be treated in its appropriate setting to be packaged and priced and render their valuation and parties' pricing challenging. Given the complexity of global financial transaction, swaps have assumed an increasing importance in servicing businesses and providing a trading extension to financial markets. Swaps' diversity may be due to the multitude of wants and needs that parties have, as well as the financial and logistical problems encountered in cross-boundaries transactions. Their numbers are extremely large, and therefore we shall summarize a few examples in the following—see also Hull (2014), Tapiero (2004, 2010, 2013), and de Weert (2008):

- **Barter is an exchange** between two countries with the terms defined as a swap contract. Such an exchange implies both country-specific factors and currency and agendas underlying the exchanging countries' parts of the swap.
- **Cross-currency swaps** are tailored to meet the needs of two firms or international financial traders. For example, a payment in a domestic currency receiving in exchange a payment forward in foreign currency. It may be defined by a current exchange of cash flows between two financial traders for a predetermined time period (defined as the length of the contract time) for a future and specified future cash flow.
- **Swaps may be "back-door financial products"** that render them stealth transactions; that is, difficult to supervise or regulate. For example, regulatory controls of traders in China unable to acquire foreign currency (unless through an appropriate intermediary

in Hong Kong) may have led to creative contracts that allow an indexation or a stealth transfer of yuan funds in a foreign currency to be collected elsewhere. If the Chinese party is buying dollars or currency options in FX markets, paid for a personal transaction in China, then it may be defined as a contractual agreement which may or may not be priced as an option of some sort, exchanged in a financial market. While such transactions may be motivated by a stealth cross-border transfer of funds, it may also be legitimate if motivated by currency risk management concerns. Their additional and broker costs are thus a price paid due to regulators gating cross-border financial transactions.

- **Industrial acquisition**. For example, if a French industrialist has euros but needs dollars to acquire a firm in the USA, they may enter in a swap contract with a US bank or with an industrialist that has dollars but needs euros for other transactions in France, thereby avoiding both transaction costs from country to country.

OTC contracts have the advantage that they may be engineered and tailored to meet the exact needs of clients. As a result, unlike traded and securitized swaps such as CDSs, OTC meets the demand of financial clients better than standardized swaps would. However, OTCs assume a credit counterparty risk, as experienced during the 2007 financial crisis when counterparties were not able to assume their contractual commitments. These risks are amplified in a global environment due to different legal rights and discrimination against parties in some countries if these are foreign. OTCs as swaps can be implemented through brokers, and they too assume various forms:

- **Standardized OTC:** trades that are standardized are transparent and based on a clear definition of what they purport to deliver in terms of quantity, quality, and identity, which is defined by the exchange and remains identical for all transactions. Although useful, these are not required in OTC trades.
- **OTC derivative markets:** these are significant in some asset classes, such as interest rates, FX, stocks, and commodities. Prior to the financial crisis (2007–2008), secondmarket.com created a financial platform where exchanges that would not be carried in financial markets were able to find partners for their trades (e.g., owners of options on a startup going to an initial public offering).

Although swaps have risks difficult to price, there are many reasons (in particular in global finance) to use swaps in exchanges. These may include:

- The OTC swap has a direct and implied advantage.
- Swaps may promise relatively high financial gains, based either on personal or institutional information (or misinformation) in the hands of brokers and dealers.
- The increased simplicity of investing in institutionalized swap shops and also dealerships acting through financial advisors and financial salesmen compared with individuals investing in financial markets.
- Particular needs and personal reasons to trade OTC; that is, off-financial and regulated markets.

Each of these reasons and in any of their combinations, treated in their appropriate setting, are engineered and packaged, rendering their valuation and their pricing challenging to individual parties and to managed financial markets.

8.6.2 The Theoretical Q-Price of Spread Options

This example provides a Q-pricing approach for a spread option. Such options provide a pricing model to the spread of say one contract and another. Swaps can of course be more complex than spread options. For simplicity, we consider these options as an exercise by pricing the spread of two currencies or two stocks, or two assets. Say that a contract (whether in a currency or supplies' commodity prices) is set in the following term. You pay $S_1(T)$ if $S_1(T) < S_2(T)$ and $S_2(T)$ if $S_1(T) > S_2(T)$. That is:

$$\text{Min}(S_1(T), S_2(T)) = S_1(T) - \text{Max}(0, S_1(T) - S_2(T))$$

which defines the price as a portfolio consisting of its underlying price less the price of the call option on the spread. Such options are commonly used in international exchange contracts, whether traded in organized markets or assessed in swap contracts. A martingale approach to price a spread option consists of defining the probability measure which is appropriate to each part of the option contract. For example, let

$$\text{Max}(0, S_2(T) - S_1(T)) = S_2(T)\mathbf{1}_{S_2(T) \geq S_1(T)} - S_1(T)\mathbf{1}_{S_2(T) \geq S_1(T)} = V_1(T) - V_2(T)$$

The option price is then given by its initial price $V(0) = V_1(0) - V_2(0)$. We can price separately $V_1(0)$ and $V_2(0)$. To do so, we price $V_1(0)$ relative to a probability measure $S_2(t)$ and $V_2(0)$ may be priced relative to $S_1(t)$. Explicitly, we have

$$\frac{V_1(0)}{S_2(0)} = E_{S_2}^{Q_2}\left(\frac{V_1(T)}{S_2(T)}\right) \quad \text{and} \quad \frac{V_2(0)}{S_1(0)} = E_{S_1}^{Q_1}\left(\frac{V_2(T)}{S_1(T)}\right)$$

In the first case, we have

$$V_1(0) = S_2(0)E_{S_2}^{Q_2}\left(\frac{V_1(T)}{S_2(T)}\right) = S_2(0)E_{S_2}^{Q_1}\left(\frac{S_2(T)\mathbf{1}_{S_2(T) \geq S_1(T)}}{S_2(T)}\right) = S_2(0)E_{S_2}^{Q_2}\left(\mathbf{1}_{S_2(T) \geq S_1(T)}\right)$$

$$= S_2(0)\Pi_{S_2}^{Q_2}(S_2(T) \geq S_1(T)) = S_2(0)\Pi_{S_2}^{Q_2}\left(\frac{S_1(T)}{S_2(T)} \leq 1\right)$$

We proceed by symmetry with the second term and obtain

$$V(0) = V_1(0) - V_2(0) = S_2(0)\Pi_{S_2}^{Q_2}\left(\frac{S_1(T)}{S_2(T)} \leq 1\right) - S_1(0)\Pi_{S_1}^{Q_1}\left(\frac{S_2(T)}{S_1(T)} \geq 1\right)$$

The first term is priced relative to S_2 (its probability measure); the random variable $S_1(T)/S_2(T)$ is then a martingale given by

$$\frac{S_1(T)}{S_2(T)} = \frac{S_1(0)}{S_2(0)}e^{-(1/2)\sigma^2 T + \sigma W(T)}$$

where σ^2 is the returns' variance of the difference (S_1, S_2) given by $\sigma^2 = \sigma_1^2 + \sigma_2^2 - 2\rho\sigma_1\sigma_2$. The proof of this result is a straightforward application of Itô's calculus to the ratio of stock prices we used earlier, where $y(t) = f(S_1(t), S_2(t)) = S_1(t)/S_2(t)$, leading to

$$dy(t) = \frac{\partial f}{\partial S_1}dS_1 + \frac{\partial f}{\partial S_2}dS_2 + \frac{1}{2}\frac{\partial^2 f}{\partial S_1^2}(dS_1)^2 + \frac{1}{2}\frac{\partial^2 f}{\partial S_2^2}(dS_2)^2 + \frac{\partial^2 f}{\partial S_1 \partial S_2}(dS_1)(dS_2)$$

or

$$dy(t) = \frac{1}{S_2(t)}dS_1 - \frac{S_1(t)}{S_2{}^2(t)}dS_2 + \frac{S_1(t)}{S_2{}^3(t)}\frac{\partial^2 f}{\partial S_2{}^2}(dS_2)^2 + \frac{\partial^2 f}{\partial S_1 \partial S_2}(dS_1\,dS_2)^2$$

And therefore

$$dy(t) = \frac{1}{S_2(t)}dS_1 - \frac{S_1(t)}{S_2{}^2(t)}dS_2 + \frac{1}{2}\frac{S_1(t)}{S_2{}^3(t)}(dS_2)^2 - \frac{1}{S_2{}^2(t)}(dS_1\,dS_2)^2$$

As a result:

$$\frac{dy(t)}{y(t)} = \left(\mu_1 - \mu_2 + \frac{1}{2}\sigma_1{}^2 + \frac{1}{2}\sigma_2{}^2 - \rho\sigma_1\sigma_2\right)dt - \sigma_1\,dW_1 + \sigma_2\,dW_2$$

Thus:

$$\Pi_{S_2}^{Q_2}\left(\frac{S_1(T)}{S_2(T)} \leq 1\right) = \Pi_{S_2}^{Q_2}\left(\frac{S_1(0)}{S_2(0)}e^{-(1/2)\sigma^2 T + \sigma W(T)} \leq 1\right) = \Pi_{S_2}^{Q_2}\left(e^{-(1/2)\sigma^2 T + \sigma W(T)} \leq \frac{S_2(0)}{S_1(0)}\right)$$

$$= \Pi_{S_2}^{Q_2}\left[-\frac{1}{2}\sigma^2 T + \sigma W(T) \leq \ln\left(\frac{S_2(0)}{S_1(0)}\right)\right] = \Pi_{S_2}^{Q_2}\left[W(T) \leq \frac{1}{\sigma}\ln\left(\frac{S_2(0)}{S_1(0)}\right) + \frac{1}{2}\sigma T\right]$$

Furthermore, note that $W(T)$ is a Brownian motion and therefore a normal probability distribution with zero mean and variance T, which can therefore be written as

$$\Pi_{S_2}^{Q_2}\left(\frac{S_1(T)}{S_2(T)} \leq 1\right) = \Phi\left[\frac{1}{\sigma\sqrt{T}}\ln\left(\frac{S_1(0)}{S_2(0)}\right) + \frac{1}{2}\sigma\sqrt{T}\right]$$

Again, by symmetry, we have

$$\Pi_{S_1}^{Q_1}\left(\frac{S_2(T)}{S_1(T)} \geq 1\right) = \Phi\left[\frac{1}{\sigma\sqrt{T}}\ln\left(\frac{S_2(0)}{S_1(0)}\right) - \frac{1}{2}\sigma\sqrt{T}\right]$$

As a result, the price of the exchange option is

$$V(0) = V_1(0) - V_2(0) = -\Pi_{S_1}^{Q_1}\left(\frac{S_2(T)}{S_1(T)} \geq 1\right) - \Pi_{S_2}^{Q_2}\left(\frac{S_1(T)}{S_2(T)} \leq 1\right)$$

$$= \Phi\left[\frac{1}{\sigma\sqrt{T}}\ln\left(\frac{S_2(0)}{S_1(0)}\right) + \frac{1}{2}\sigma\sqrt{T}\right] - \Phi\left[\frac{1}{\sigma\sqrt{T}}\ln\left(\frac{S_1(0)}{S_2(0)}\right) - \frac{1}{2}\sigma\sqrt{T}\right]$$

In conclusion, the spread option price depends only on the volatilities of both stocks and their correlation.

8.6.3 A Swaps Pot-pourri

- **Interest rate swaps.** These swaps involve a counterparty paying a floating rate based on an agreed floating interest rate or index and another paying a fixed rate for a defined contract time. Such contracts are used by firms (such as insurance firms) that have a stable income in order to manage their assets and liabilities. As a result, such swaps have "two legs," that is, interest rate swaps are an exchange of two bonds. In other words, one receiving a bond with a fixed rate and paying a floating (Libor) rate. The price of such a swap is then the price difference of these two bonds: $P_S = P_{BFixed} - P_{BLibor}$.

- **Forward (time) swaps.** They combine two swaps with two different durations; a forward swap may be constructed meeting the needs of the swaps' parties. For example, when Boeing sells to Air France and JetBlue Airplanes, a delivery schedule is set. Airlines then engage in exchanging their positions in the delivery schedule. Such exchanges involve an exchange of time position and money. In many cases, financial firms acquire a large number of airplanes positioned advantageously in a delivery schedule which they subsequently sell at a great profit to needy airlines. Forward swaps thus provide borrowers and investors a financial exchange mechanism for locking a time of delivery, a future interest rate, and managing interest rate risk for fixed-income positions as well as speculating on future rates. Johnson (2010: 667) explains that

  > Financial and non-financial institutions that have future borrowing obligations can lock in a future rate by obtaining forward contracts on fixed-payer swap positions. For example, a company wishing to lock in a rate on a five-year, fixed-rate $100 million loan to start two years from today, could enter a two-year forward swap agreement to pay the fixed rate on a 5-year 9%/LIBOR swap

(which may lead some banks setting the Libor interest rate to manipulate it to their own ends). Interest rates swaps would involve then a counterparty paying a floating rate based on an agreed on index and another paying a fixed rate for a defined contract time. Such contracts are used by firms (such as insurance) that have a stable income in order to manage their assets and liabilities.

- **Equity swaps.** A party pays the returns on a stock index, the other pays at a benchmark interest rate; for more, see Johnson (2004). These transactions can be made in any of the parties' currency. Such a swap allows a party exposure to the equity market in another country without owning the equity securities.
- **Credit swaps.** These are essentially currency or interest rates swaps. They also include liability swaps and assets swaps.
- **FX or currency swaps.** These provide a currency liquidity to two parties that both will need for their foreign obligations and transactions. Based on the agreement with predetermined conditions, cash flows in two different currencies are exchanged between two parties. Currency swaps assume many forms. For example, for FX transactions, tom-next (or tomorrow next) swaps may be used to avoid transaction costs as well as to hedge FX risk—see Kallianiotis (2013) for further discussion and numerical examples. Suppose that a Chinese firm may be long in USD from business in the USA but its primary operations are conducted in yuan in China. But after a certain time (say 3 months) they must make payments in the USA. Their strategy would consists of two steps: (a) to pay for their domestic expenses in China (by selling (spot) their USD and buying CNY); and then (b) to pay their business partners in the USA in 3 months (by buying (spot) USD and selling CNY). **Cross-currency swaps** involve three cash flows: an initial simultaneous spot capital exchange (such as debt each of the parties assumes in its own currency); an interest swap during the effective time of the contract; and a forward reexchange for the same initial sums at the contract

maturity date. As a result, such swaps have two legs. A cross-currency derivative is a simultaneous purchase and sale of an identical amount of one currency for another with two different value dates.

- **Swaptions.** Options on swap; these grant the holder the right to enter into the swap. As Johnson (2004: 482) explains:

> Swaptions are similar to interest rate options or options on debt securities. They are, however, more varied: they can range from options to begin a 1-year swap in 3 months to a 10-year option on an 8-year swap (sometimes referred to as a 10 × 8 swaption); the exercise periods can vary for American swaptions; swaptions can be written on generic swaps or non-generic ones. ... Swaptions can be used for speculating on interest rates, hedging debt and asset positions against market risk, and ... be used in combination with other securities to create synthetic positions. ... For swaptions, the underlying instrument is a forward swap and the option premium is the up-front fee.

He further states the right of the swaption buyer "to start an interest rate swap with a specific fixed rate or exercise (strike) rate, and with a maturity at or during a specific time period in the future," and how the "seller [is] obligated to take the opposite counterparty position" in the case if the swaption is exercised (see Johnson (2004: 482)). There can be a receiver or a payer swaption depending on whether the holder has the right to receive or pay the fixed rate. For example, a *receiver swaption* has the right to receive a fixed rate.

- **Commodity swaps.** Commodity swaps consist of the exchange of cash flows based on the price of a commodity. For example, such an exchange may be based on one paying a fixed price for the commodity and the other paying a floating price (e.g., the average price over a given time period). These swaps are common in agricultural settings. For example, in the Philippines an investor may provide a farmer funds needed to seed tracts of land for a proportional sharing of the agricultural goods resulting at the time they are obtained.
- **Credit swaps and CDSs.** These include a large variety of swaps. For example, liability swaps and assets swaps. CDSs have expanded into many (single-name) derivatives. A CDS buyer or holder through a bilateral contract with a seller of the CDS obtains a future right to be compensated upon an event happening or an (binary) event triggered by some other event. If no event occurs, no compensation is paid to the holder and the CDS expires—it is then worthless. A CDS is therefore a financial insurance providing a financial market for risk exchange. It may also be an option when put options are used to mitigate future risks. In Chapter 9 we shall consider credit risks and credit derivatives that are defined as swaps as well as options used to share and mitigate credit risks (whether institutionalized or market based). There is a large family of swaps used for debt and risk management, some of which are outlined in the following. CDSs, however, have been securitized and are traded in the Chicago Mercantile Exchange (see Section 8.7 on securitized CDSs).
- **Total returns swap (TRS).** In this bilateral financial contract, one party (TR payer) pays the total positive return of a bond, loan, or other financial obligation (i.e., a reference asset), while the other party (TR receiver) pays a fixed or floating rate payment plus any negative total returns on the reference asset. Some of the issues to address

then include the default exposure versus premium rate volatility. These premiums are extensively used based on volatility and variance swaps products that are derivatives of VIXs or used to construct such indexes that are commonly traded in financial markets. For a TRS, we have the following relationships:
- Total return = Interest flows + (Final value – Original value)
- Reference asset: can be a bond, loan, an index, an equity, a commodity.
- TR receiver: is long both for the price and the default risk of the reference asset
- TR payer: is the legal owner of the reference asset
- TRS: is then the total rate of return.

Thus, a TRS allows one to transfer the risk underlying an economic asset or activity.
- **Variance swap.** Volatility is an essential statistical characteristic used in financial models, and therefore its pricing is important. In some models a risk premium is assumed to account for the price of volatility; and an asset with no volatility has, under the no arbitrage assumption, a risk-free price. For these reasons, there are various measures and pricing models that measure volatility, including historical volatility, implied volatility (in future contracts), the VIX factor based on future and implied volatilities of the S&P 50 and variance swaps. The latter, variance swap is an additional measure of volatility which is priced in some financial markets. Such a swap pays the difference between annualized variance of an underlying σ_S^2 and the annualized strike σ_K^2 agreed on when a trade is reached. As a result, the price of the swap is $(\sigma_S^2 - \sigma_K^2)N$, where N is the notional of the variance swap. To price such a swap, replicating options can be constructed (e.g., see de Weert (2008: 140–141)).
- **Volatility and variance swaps and the VIX factor.** These define a payout and explore its associated risks properties (a derivative or signaled by volatility or assets financial variance). For example, a variance swap attempts to replicate the VIX fear factor, which has an appreciable effect on stock prices and credit risks. Variance swaps may be related to different optional portfolios, including, for example, straddles and strangles that attempt to replicate the swap payout. Generally, variance swaps seek to replicate an implied volatility for a given maturity and thereby better manage volatility risks.

8.7 Credit Default Swaps and Securitized Volatility

CDSs and their derivatives are, as indicated earlier, bilateral financial contracts that isolate specific aspects of a credit risk from an underlying instrument and transfer that risk between two parties. The CDS consists of an individual negotiating; namely, an OTC transaction or a note structure between two parties (protection buyer and protection seller), the value of which is based on the credit of the third party for which obligations are triggered by the occurrence of a specific credit event. This event, a "trigger event," is linked to the reference entity for which there is an objective and available information stated as standard International Swaps and Derivatives Association terms. When a loss event occurs, its settlement is sought and may be achieved in a number of ways, including a cash settlement and/or a physical settlement. The price is then defined by seeking an equivalent exchange. Such an approach differs from insurance, which is actuarially based compared with a market price for a CDS. CDSs are important signals to the well-being of sovereign bonds and sovereign ratings. When crisis hit, the CDS prices surge to a record high level, as was the case in the global financial crisis with global CDS markets, measured by their outstanding $58 trillion at the end of 2007.[7] Observing CDS prices that protect bond holders against corporate or sovereign default is an indicator of the credit risk attached to these bonds. For example, in light of the dramatic fall in oil prices, S&P downgraded a number of oil-producing countries, such as Saudi Arabia, Bahrain, and Kazakhstan, while maintaining Qatar, an energy oil and gas producer (WSJ, 2016a). Their difference was Qatar's policies on subsidies, their economic diversification, and so on. As a result, CDS prices for Qatar were smaller, implying its greater stability and ability to weather potential economic storms. Another example is the significant increase in insurance costs against the default of major financial firms and bank debt, including Goldman Sachs and Deutsche Bank. When the CDS prices of the lenders rose to a high level, especially for Deutsche Bank, their shares fell substantially, as occurred in early 2016.

The advantages of CDSs are that they are managed by banks under loan underwriting standards as well as being a risk diversification across different borrowers. There are limits in banks' liabilities to reduce credit risk, as well as a potential lack of diversification's opportunities. Credit derivatives may also provide insurance against credit-related losses. These contracts separate ownership and the management of credit risk from other qualitative and quantitative aspects of ownership of financial assets.[8] A credit derivative may then be structured as a swap, an option, or as a collateral security. If the credit obligations are triggered by the occurrence of a credit event, it is called a default product. There are, of course, many sorts of such products.

Figure 8.6 shows 5-year CDSs referring to the default probability in different regions, namely Latin America, Europe, Asia, Africa, and others. While CDS spreads are very low and stable for most developed countries, such as Australia, Germany, and the UK, it has been volatile in most emerging economies (not only during the financial crisis of 2007–2008, but also in recent years, especially for Latin American countries). The risk of sovereign default has risen in these countries due to deteriorating macroeconomic indicators, such as weak growth, fiscal budget deficits, and the escalation of political risk. Venezuela remains the region's highest sovereign risks. Brazil has had an upward pressure in default probability since 2013 due to depreciation in exchange rate and deficits in current account and fiscal budgets, which causes the risk premium to rise even further. If the commodity prices do not rebound and demand from China does not strengthen in the near future, credit risk will persist in many resource-exporting emerging countries.

In addition to 5-year CDSs, we compared CDS spreads (on different countries' USD denominated sovereign debt) for different maturities, as shown in Figure 8.7. This illustration of CDS term structure shows which country has positively sloped curves and which has inverted curves indicating rising default future risks. A CDS spread curve for a bond issuer with a good rating indicates low CDS spreads for the short maturities with less likelihood of risk deterioration. In this case, the CDS spread increases as maturity rises. However, other cases with inverted curves (e.g., Greece and Venezuela) occur for the sovereign bond issuer with low ratings, and very high credit risks in the short run (widened spreads with an immediate future) compared with the long run. Owing to a deterioration in both macroeconomic instability in its political environment, Venezuela's CDS curve has been inverting. In addition, its 5-year CDS spread increased by 4000bps

---

7 See BIS OTC derivatives statistics: http://www.bis.org/statistics/derstats.htm.
8 For the risk valuation of CDSs, see Blanchet-Scalliet and Patras (2008).

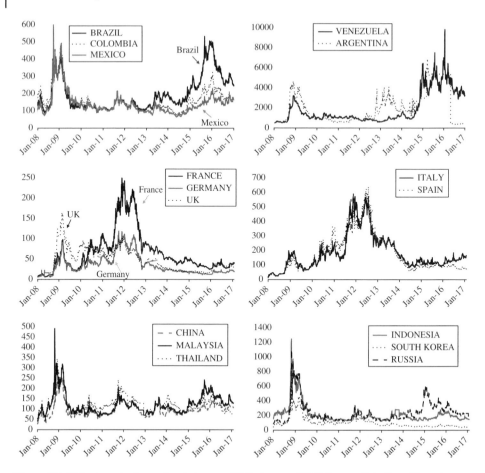

Figure 8.6 CDSs spreads, 5-year (bps), January 2008–January 2017. *Source:* Data from Bloomberg.

over 1 year and 2000bps from the beginning of 2015, indicating a significant increase in the protection cost (risk premium) for credit default.

8.8 Pricing Credit Risk

We may approach credit pricing from several points of view. The common approach to price default risks is based on reduced-form models. Such an approach provides a modeling framework to bet on the price of these bonds. In other words, prices are defined by a financial market with prices predicted based on such models. When these are foreign bonds issued in their foreign currency, then for a buyer of such bonds the risk of the bond is compounded by an FX risk. This market pricing approach is then defined as indicated in Chapter 7 in terms of a pricing martingale. A specific case will be defined by a mitigated credit risk based on collaterals used as a partial insurance against default payments. Finally, credit pricing may be based on kernel pricing with parties' utility functions to the

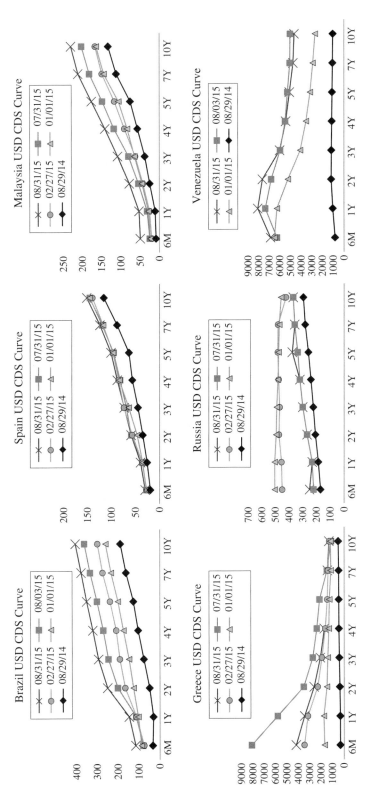

Figure 8.7 CDS spread curves (term structure). *Source:* Data from Bloomberg.

credit transactions defining the credit price (see also Chapter 3). We consider reduced-form models in the following. For different approaches on credit pricing, credit risk, and credit derivatives models, see Jarrow (1988), Bluhm *et al.* (2003), Duffie and Singleton (2003), Schönbucher (2003), Lando (2004), and Pykhtin (2005), but for more advanced analysis of assessing and pricing the credit risk refer to Jarrow and Rudd (1982), Das and Tufano (1996), and Cossin and Pirotte (2001). In addition, for the pricing of default risk, see Hull and White (1992, 1995) and Duffie (1999).

8.8.1 Reduced-Form Models

Exogenous or reduced-form models make no attempt to define default as an endogenous event (arising from a low level of firm value or cash flow or a loss of its collateral). Instead, these models specify default as an exogenous event that does not incorporate explicitly the firm leverage and its value. As a result, these models are essentially market-based and define a debt risk in terms of a risk premium accounting for the risk perceptions of buyers and sellers of debt. These models were studied by numerous financial economists, such as Jarrow *et al.* (1997), Jarrow and Turnbull (1995), and Schönbucher (2003). For example, assume a default-free zero-coupon bond, paying \$1 at maturity T. The price of a foreign bond denominated in its foreign currency is, from a domestic viewpoint, a currency risk. In other words, it is a risk-free bond in the foreign currency but bearing an FX risk in the domestic US dollar currency. Let $B(t, T)$ be the risk-free bond price, or $B(t, T) = e^{-R_f(t, T)(T-t)}$, $B(T, T) = 1$, where $R_f(t, T)$ is the risk-free rate at time t. For a foreign bond, whose risk-free rate is $R_F(t, T)$, its price $B_F(t, T)$ at time T is random and given by $\tilde{\xi}_{FD}(t, T)B_F(t, T)$, where $\tilde{\xi}_{FD}(T)$ is the random estimate of the FX at the bond's maturity. The price of this bond is then, under a Q-pricing model for the FX, given by $B_F(t, T)E^Q\left(\tilde{\xi}_{FD}(t, T)\right)$. Next assume a default bond, whose value at its maturity is either \$1 or nothing at all. Or:

$$\mathbf{1}_{\tau > t} = \begin{cases} 1 & \text{If default occurs in } (t, T) \\ 0 & \text{If no default occurs} \end{cases}$$

Let $f_D(\tau|\mathfrak{I}_t)$ be the probability of the bond defaulting under the current conditional filtration $\mathfrak{I}_t$, and therefore $[1 - F_D(T)|\mathfrak{I}_t)]$ be the probability of no default at T. Its hazard rate is thus

$$h_D(\tau|\mathfrak{I}_t) = \frac{f_D(\tau|\mathfrak{I}_t)}{1 - F_D(\tau|\mathfrak{I}_t)} \quad \text{and} \quad 1 - F_D(\tau|\mathfrak{I}_t) = e^{-\int_0^\tau h_D(\tau|\mathfrak{I}_t)\,d\tau}$$

For example, assume that the default probability distribution is exponential with mean μ, then its hazard rate equals μ. Its expected price is $B_D(t, T) = E(B(t, T)\mathbf{1}_{\tau > T}) = B(t, T)[1 - F_D(T|\mathfrak{I}_t)]$. Replacing these terms by their discount rates, we have

$$B_D(t, T) = e^{-R_f(t, T)(T-t)}e^{-\int_t^T h_D(\tau|\mathfrak{I}_t)\,d\tau} = e^{-[R_f(t, T) + \mu](T-t)}$$

In particular, for a constant risk-free rate $R_f(t, T) = R_f(T-t)$ we have $B_D(t, T) = e^{-[R_f + \mu](T-t)}$, and μ defines a spread (the risk premium price) for the default bond. In other words, the transformed no-default probability of the bond was translated into a risk-implied premium insurance which is added to the risk-free discount rate. The rationality of such an approach is that it allows us to express the money effects of a default as a traded single parameter financial discount rate amplifying the risk-free discount applied to future (and random) payments. The actual financial price of this premium is then defined by the exchange of the default bond buyer and bond seller. When FX risk is compounded, we expect that the price set by the market will be greater or smaller according to the market expectations of FX rate increasing or decreasing. In the following, we price a foreign bond using utility arguments as introduced in Chapter 3.

8.8.2   Credit Price and Debt Leverage: An Example

In many cases, borrowing costs may be smaller in one country compared with another. Investors prefer then to incur debt in one country to invest in the other. Such transactions of course imply FX risks. Let the domestic party be the credit holder and the foreign party be the debt holder (e.g., borrowing in yen (JPY) and investing in USD). Let the initial funds available for both consumption and investment in USD be $\hat{W}_0^{\mathrm{D}}$, with

$$\hat{W}_0^{\mathrm{D}} = W_0^{\mathrm{D}} + D_{\mathrm{D}}^{\mathrm{D}} + \xi_{\mathrm{FD}}^0 D_{\mathrm{F}}^{\mathrm{D}}(1 - \delta_{\mathrm{FD}})$$

or

Available funds = Initial wealth + Domestic debt + Foreign borrowing

where the domestic investor's initial wealth is W_0^{D} in USD. Assume a debt $D_{\mathrm{D}}^{\mathrm{D}}$ contracted locally (in USD) and $D_{\mathrm{F}}^{\mathrm{D}}$ contracted in a foreign country (in JPY). Given the current FX rate and its transaction cost, the debt assumed in yen is $D_{\mathrm{F}}^{\mathrm{F}}$ and $D_{\mathrm{F}}^{\mathrm{D}} = D_{\mathrm{F}}^{\mathrm{F}} \xi_{\mathrm{FD}}^0 (1 - \delta_{\mathrm{FD}})$ for the domestic country. Consider a period later and let R_{D} be the domestic risk free rate and R_{F} be the foreign Japanese risk-free discount rate. Assuming all funds are invested, then

$$\widetilde{W}_1^{\mathrm{D}} = W_0^{\mathrm{D}}\left(1 + \widetilde{R}_{\mathrm{D}}\right) + D_{\mathrm{D}}^{\mathrm{D}}\left(\widetilde{R}_{\mathrm{D}} - R_{\mathrm{D}}^{\mathrm{B}}\right) + \xi_{\mathrm{FD}}^0 D_{\mathrm{F}}^{\mathrm{D}}(1 - \delta_{\mathrm{FD}})\left(1 + \widetilde{R}_{\mathrm{D}}\right)$$
$$- \left[\widetilde{\xi}_{\mathrm{DF}}^1 D_{\mathrm{F}}^{\mathrm{D}}(1 + \delta_{\mathrm{DF}})\left(1 + R_{\mathrm{F}}^{\mathrm{B}}\right)\right]$$

where $\widetilde{R}_{\mathrm{D}}$ is the domestic rate of return (ROR) on investment, $R_{\mathrm{D}}^{\mathrm{B}}$ is the domestic cost of borrowing in USD (and therefore $\widetilde{R}_{\mathrm{D}} - R_{\mathrm{D}}^{\mathrm{B}}$ is the net return in USD). Then, $\xi_{\mathrm{FD}}^0 D_{\mathrm{F}}^{\mathrm{D}}$ is the net foreign debt invested locally (in USD), whose transaction cost is $\xi_{\mathrm{FD}}^0 D_{\mathrm{F}}^{\mathrm{D}} \delta_{\mathrm{FD}}$. Its ROR is thus $\xi_{\mathrm{FD}}^0 D_{\mathrm{F}}^{\mathrm{D}}(1 - \delta_{\mathrm{FD}})\left(1 + \widetilde{R}_{\mathrm{D}}\right)$. A period later, the debt including its interest rate (in JPY) is $D_{\mathrm{F}}^{\mathrm{D}}(1 + R_{\mathrm{F}}^{\mathrm{B}})$. However, to repatriate, an FX $\widetilde{\xi}_{\mathrm{DF}}^1$ and a transaction cost δ_{DF} are paid to reimburse the foreign debt. As a result, the domestic ROR is

$$\frac{\widetilde{W}_1^{\mathrm{D}} - W_0^{\mathrm{D}}}{W_0^{\mathrm{D}}} = \widetilde{R}_{\mathrm{D}} + \frac{D_{\mathrm{D}}^{\mathrm{D}}}{W_0^{\mathrm{D}}}\left(\widetilde{R}_{\mathrm{D}} - R_{\mathrm{D}}^{\mathrm{B}}\right)$$
$$+ \frac{D_{\mathrm{F}}^{\mathrm{D}}}{W_0^{\mathrm{D}}}\left[\xi_{\mathrm{FD}}^0(1 - \delta_{\mathrm{FD}})\left(1 + \widetilde{R}_{\mathrm{D}}\right) - \left(1 + \widetilde{R}_{\mathrm{DF}}\right)(1 + \delta_{\mathrm{DF}})\left(1 + R_{\mathrm{F}}^{\mathrm{B}}\right)\right]$$

where D_D^D/W_0^D is the initial wealth proportion assumed in domestic borrowing and $\xi_{FD}^0 D_F^D/W_0^D$ is its proportion in foreign borrowing. Note that $\tilde{\xi}_{DF}^1/\xi_{DF}^0 = 1 + \tilde{R}_{DF}$, which is an FX loss due to an increase in the JPY FX if $\tilde{R}_{DF} < 0$ and a gain if $\tilde{R}_{DF} > 0$ (in such a case, the JPY is cheaper than the USD). A foreign debt is then contributing to the domestic ROR if

$$\frac{1 - \delta_{FD}}{(1 + \delta_{DF})(1 + R_F^B)} > \frac{1 + \tilde{R}_{DF}}{1 + \tilde{R}_D}$$

In other words, transaction costs and the foreign debt payment rate are measured relative to the JPY FX growth (or loss) rate relative to the prospective ROR in USD.

8.8.3 Utility and Credit, Debt Leverage and Reimbursement at the Second Period

Consider two parties and their utility functions. The domestic party is assumed to have the following decision variables: B_D^D, B_F^D, D_D^D, and D_F^D, denoting the bonds it invests domestically and internationally for future consumption, as well as the debts it assumes, contracted domestically and internationally, and its lending to the second foreign party (at the party request). Current consumption is then defined by its current wealth, the debt it assumes domestically, the debt it assumes in the foreign party less the credit (debt for the foreign party) it gives to the foreign party, and its investment in the foreign bond:

$$c_0^D = W_0^D + D_D^D + \xi_{FD}^0 D_F^D (1 - \delta_{FD}) - D_D^F - B_D^D - B_F^D (1 - \delta_{DF})$$

By the same token, for the foreign party, we have

$$c_0^F = W_0^F + D_F^F + \xi_{DF}^0 D_D^F (1 - \delta_{DF}) - D_F^D - B_F^F - B_D^F (1 - \delta_{FD})$$

A period later (the last period, since it is a two-period problem), residual wealth is consumed. As a result, the following utilities of consumption are obtained (where ν_d and ν_f are two parameters discounting future consumption relative to current one):

$$U^D(.) = \begin{cases} \underset{B_D^D, B_F^D, D_D^D, D_D^F}{\text{Max}} u_0^D \left[W_0^D + D_D^D + \xi_{FD}^0 D_F^D (1 - \delta_{FD}) - D_D^F - B_D^D - B_F^D (1 - \delta_{DF}) \right] \\ + \mu E u_1^D \left[(1 - \nu_d) B_D^D (1 + r_d) + (1 - \nu_d) B_F^D (1 + r_f)(1 - \delta_{DF})(1 - \delta_{FD}) \left(1 + \tilde{R}_{FD}^\xi \right) \right. \\ \left. - (1 - \nu_d) D_D^D \left(1 + \tilde{R}_{DD} \right) (1 - \nu_f) \xi_{FD}^0 D_F^D \left(1 + \tilde{R}_{DF} \right) (1 - \delta_{DF}) \tilde{\xi}_{DF}^1 \right. \\ \left. + (1 - \nu_d) D_D^F \left(1 + \tilde{R}_{FD} \right) \right] \end{cases}$$

$$U^F(.) = \begin{cases} \underset{B_F^F, B_D^F, D_F^F, D_F^D}{\text{Max}} u_0^F \left[W_0^F + D_F^F + \xi_{DF}^0 D_D^F (1 - \delta_{DF}) - D_F^D - B_F^F - B_D^F (1 - \delta_{FD}) \right] \\ + \mu E u_1^F \left[(1 - \nu_f) B_F^F (1 + r_f) + (1 - \nu_f) B_D^F (1 + r_d)(1 - \delta_{FD})(1 - \delta_{DF}) \left(1 + \tilde{R}_{DF}^\xi \right) \right. \\ \left. - (1 - \nu_f) D_F^F \left(1 + \tilde{R}_{FF} \right) - (1 - \nu_d) \xi_{DF}^0 D_D^F \left(1 + \tilde{R}_{FD} \right) (1 - \delta_{FD}) \tilde{\xi}_{FD}^1 \right. \\ \left. + (1 - \nu_f) D_F^D \left(1 + \tilde{R}_{DF} \right) \right] \end{cases}$$

We consider the case of the domestic party first:

$$\frac{\partial U^D(.)}{\partial D_D^D} = \frac{\partial u_0^D\left(c_0^D\right)}{\partial c_0^D} - \mu E\frac{\partial u_1^D\left(c_1^D\right)}{\partial c_1^D}(1-\nu_d)\left(1+\tilde{R}_{DD}\right) = 0$$

$$\frac{\partial U^D(.)}{\partial D_D^F} = -\frac{\partial u_0^D\left(c_0^D\right)}{\partial c_0^D} + \mu E\frac{\partial u_1^D\left(c_1^D\right)}{\partial c_1^D}(1-\nu_d)\left(1+\tilde{R}_{FD}\right) = 0$$

$$\frac{\partial U^D(.)}{\partial B_D^D} = -\frac{\partial u_0^D\left(c_0^D\right)}{\partial c_0^D} + \mu E\frac{\partial u_1^D\left(c_1^D\right)}{\partial c_1^D}(1-\nu_d)(1+r_d) = 0$$

$$\frac{\partial U^D(.)}{\partial B_F^D} = -\frac{\partial u_0^D\left(c_0^D\right)}{\partial c_0^D}(1-\delta_{DF})$$

$$+ \mu E\frac{\partial u_1^D\left(c_1^D\right)}{\partial c_1^D}(1-\nu_d)(1+r_f)(1-\delta_{DF})(1-\delta_{FD})\left(1+\tilde{R}_{FD}^\xi\right) = 0$$

And therefore, setting

$$\tilde{M}^D = \mu\frac{\partial u_1^D\left(c_1^D\right)/\partial c_1^D}{\partial u_0^D\left(c_0^D\right)/\partial c_0^D}$$

these are reduced to the kernel pricing equations:

$$E\left(\tilde{M}^D\right) = \frac{1}{(1-\nu_d)(1+r_d)}, \quad 1 = \frac{1}{1+r_d}E\left(\frac{\tilde{M}^D}{E\left(\tilde{M}^D\right)}\left(1+\tilde{R}_{DD}\right)\right) = \frac{1}{1+r_d}E^D\left(1+\tilde{R}_{DD}\right)$$

$$1 = \frac{1}{1+r_d}E\left(\frac{\tilde{M}^D}{E\left(\tilde{M}^D\right)}\left(1+\tilde{R}_{FD}\right)\right) = \frac{1}{1+r_d}E^D\left(1+\tilde{R}_{FD}\right)$$

$$1 = \frac{(1+r_f)(1-\delta_{FD})}{1+r_d}E\left(\frac{\tilde{M}^D}{E\left(\tilde{M}^D\right)}\left(1+\tilde{R}_{FD}^\xi\right)\right) = \frac{(1+r_f)(1-\delta_{FD})}{1+r_d}E^D\left(1+\tilde{R}_{FD}^\xi\right)$$

By the same token, for the foreign party, under a probability measure F we have

$$E\left(\tilde{M}^F\right) = \frac{1}{(1-\nu_f)(1+r_f)}$$

and therefore

$$1 = \frac{1}{1+r_f}E\left(\frac{\tilde{M}^F}{E\left(\tilde{M}^F\right)}\left(1+\tilde{R}_{FF}\right)\right) = \frac{1}{1+r_f}E^F\left(1+\tilde{R}_{FF}\right)$$

$$1 = \frac{1}{1+r_f}E\left(\frac{\tilde{M}^F}{E\left(\tilde{M}^F\right)}\left(1+\tilde{R}_{DF}\right)\right) = \frac{1}{1+r_f}E^F\left(1+\tilde{R}_{DF}\right)$$

$$1 = \frac{(1+r_d)(1-\delta_{DF})}{1+r_f}E\left(\frac{\tilde{M}^F}{E\left(\tilde{M}^F\right)}\left(1+\tilde{R}_{DF}^\xi\right)\right) = \frac{(1+r_d)(1-\delta_{DF})}{1+r_f}E^F\left(1+\tilde{R}_{DF}^\xi\right)$$

These lead to six pricing equations, which we summarize as follows using their probability measures (alternatively, we could use their kernel prices):

$$1 = \frac{1}{1+r_d}E^D\left(1+\tilde{R}_{DD}\right), \quad 1 = \frac{1}{1+r_d}E^D\left(1+\tilde{R}_{FD}\right), \quad 1 = \frac{(1+r_f)(1-\delta_{FD})}{1+r_d}E^D\left(1+\tilde{R}_{FD}^{\xi}\right)$$

$$1 = \frac{1}{1+r_f}E^F\left(1+\tilde{R}_{FF}\right), \quad 1 = \frac{1}{1+r_f}E^F\left(1+\tilde{R}_{DF}\right), \quad 1 = \frac{(1+r_d)(1-\delta_{DF})}{1+r_f}E^F\left(1+\tilde{R}_{DF}^{\xi}\right)$$

Note that the probability measures D and F are not similar, as they account for a variety of factors that are specific to the two countries. In addition, $E^D\left(1+\tilde{R}_{DD}\right) = E^F\left(1+\tilde{R}_{FD}\right)$ means only that the price of debt domestically (if it is not constrained locally or externally) and in the foreign country is equal. For example, set $\bar{R}_{DD}$ as the price of debt in USD (assumed to be riskless), then the probability measure indicates that $\bar{R}_{DD} = E^D\left(\bar{R}_{FD}\right)$ and $\bar{R}_{FD}$ equals some ROR which includes a risk premium for the risk of this debt. Considering again the domestic party only, we have

$$1 = \frac{1+r_d}{(1+r_f)(1-\delta_{FD})}E^D\left(1+\tilde{R}_{FD}^{\xi}\right) \quad \text{or} \quad \xi_{FD}^0 = \frac{1+r_d}{(1+r_f)(1-\delta_{FD})}E^D\left(\tilde{\xi}_{FD}^1\right)$$

which indicates that the FX rate under the D measure is debt free. This is, of course, not the case, since the effects of debt are embedded in the kernel price which defines the probability measure D. Similarly, for the foreign country:

$$1 = \frac{1+r_f}{(1+r_d)(1-\delta_{DF})}E^F\left(1+\tilde{R}_{DF}^{\xi}\right) \quad \text{or} \quad \xi_{DF}^0 = \frac{1+r_f}{(1+r_d)(1-\delta_{DF})}E^F\left(\tilde{\xi}_{DF}^1\right)$$

The following two pricing equations express what each party considers the current FX price ought to be. Therefore, it is not the FX market rate unless $\xi_{FD}^0 = 1/\xi_{DF}^0$:

$$\xi_{FD}^0 = \frac{1+r_d}{(1+r_f)(1-\delta_{FD})}E^D\left(\tilde{\xi}_{FD}^1\right) \quad \text{and} \quad \xi_{DF}^0 = \frac{1+r_f}{(1+r_d)(1-\delta_{DF})}E^F\left(\tilde{\xi}_{DF}^1\right)$$

And

$$\xi_{FD}^0 = \frac{1}{\xi_{DF}^0} \quad \text{iff} \quad E^D\left(\tilde{\xi}_{FD}^1\right)E^F\left(\tilde{\xi}_{DF}^1\right) = (1-\delta_{DF})(1-\delta_{FD})$$

For example, let there be call options on the following FX rates:

$$C_{FD}\left(\xi_{FD}^0, K_{FD}\right) = \frac{1+r_d}{(1+r_f)(1-\delta_{FD})}E^D\text{Max}\left(\tilde{\xi}_{FD}^1 - K_{FD}, 0\right)$$

$$C_{DF}\left(\xi_{DF}^0, K_{DF}\right) = \frac{1+r_f}{(1+r_d)(1-\delta_{DF})}E^F\text{Max}\left(\tilde{\xi}_{DF}^1 - K_{DF}, 0\right)$$

And say that $\widetilde{\xi}^1_{\text{FD}} = \left(\widetilde{\xi}^+_{\text{FD}}, \widetilde{\xi}^-_{\text{FD}}\right)$ and $\widetilde{\xi}^1_{\text{DF}} = \left(\widetilde{\xi}^+_{\text{DF}}, \widetilde{\xi}^-_{\text{DF}}\right)$; thus, the implied probabilities are

$$C_{\text{FD}}\left(\xi^0_{\text{FD}}, K_{\text{FD}}\right) = p^D \frac{1+r_d}{(1+r_f)(1-\delta_{\text{FD}})} \left(\widetilde{\xi}^+_{\text{FD}} - K_{\text{FD}}\right) \quad \text{and} \quad p^D = \frac{C_{\text{FD}}\left(\xi^0_{\text{FD}}, K_{\text{FD}}\right)(1+r_f)(1-\delta_{\text{FD}})}{(1+r_d)\left(\widetilde{\xi}^+_{\text{FD}} - K_{\text{FD}}\right)}$$

$$C_{\text{DF}}\left(\xi^0_{\text{DF}}, K_{\text{DF}}\right) = p^F \frac{1+r_f}{(1+r_d)(1-\delta_{\text{DF}})} \left(\widetilde{\xi}^+_{\text{DF}} - K_{\text{DF}}\right) \quad \text{and} \quad p^F = \frac{C_{\text{DF}}\left(\xi^0_{\text{DF}}, K_{\text{DF}}\right)(1+r_d)(1-\delta_{\text{DF}})}{(1+r_f)\left(\widetilde{\xi}^+_{\text{DF}} - K_{\text{DF}}\right)}$$

In which case:

$$\xi^0_{\text{FD}} = \frac{1+r_d}{(1+r_f)(1-\delta_{\text{FD}})} \left[p^D \widetilde{\xi}^+_{\text{FD}} + \left(1-p^D\right)\widetilde{\xi}^-_{\text{FD}}\right]$$

$$= \frac{1+r_d}{(1+r_f)(1-\delta_{\text{FD}})} \left\{ \left[\frac{C_{\text{FD}}\left(\xi^0_{\text{FD}}, K_{\text{FD}}\right)(1+r_f)(1-\delta_{\text{FD}})}{(1+r_d)\left(\widetilde{\xi}^+_{\text{FD}} - K_{\text{FD}}\right)}\right] \left(\widetilde{\xi}^+_{\text{FD}} - \widetilde{\xi}^-_{\text{FD}}\right) + \widetilde{\xi}^-_{\text{FD}} \right\}$$

$$\xi^0_{\text{DF}} = \frac{1+r_f}{(1+r_d)(1-\delta_{\text{DF}})} \left[p^F \widetilde{\xi}^+_{\text{DF}} + \left(1-p^F\right)\widetilde{\xi}^-_{\text{DF}}\right]$$

$$= \frac{1+r_f}{(1+r_d)(1-\delta_{\text{DF}})} \left[\frac{C_{\text{DF}}\left(\xi^0_{\text{DF}}, K_{\text{DF}}\right)(1+r_d)(1-\delta_{\text{DF}})}{(1+r_f)\left(\widetilde{\xi}^+_{\text{DF}} - K_{\text{DF}}\right)} \left(\widetilde{\xi}^+_{\text{DF}} - \widetilde{\xi}^-_{\text{DF}}\right) + \widetilde{\xi}^-_{\text{DF}}\right]$$

Therefore, the market price for the FX rate is defined if $\xi^0_{\text{FD}} = 1/\xi^0_{\text{DF}}$ or

$$\frac{1+r_d}{(1+r_f)(1-\delta_{\text{FD}})} \left\{ \left[\frac{C_{\text{FD}}\left(\xi^0_{\text{FD}}, K_{\text{FD}}\right)(1+r_f)(1-\delta_{\text{FD}})}{(1+r_d)\left(\widetilde{\xi}^+_{\text{FD}} - K_{\text{FD}}\right)}\right] \left(\widetilde{\xi}^+_{\text{FD}} - \widetilde{\xi}^-_{\text{FD}}\right) + \widetilde{\xi}^-_{\text{FD}} \right\}$$

$$= \left\{ \frac{1+r_f}{(1+r_d)(1-\delta_{\text{DF}})} \left[\frac{C_{\text{DF}}\left(\xi^0_{\text{DF}}, K_{\text{DF}}\right)(1+r_d)(1-\delta_{\text{DF}})}{(1+r_f)\left(\widetilde{\xi}^+_{\text{DF}} - K_{\text{DF}}\right)} \left(\widetilde{\xi}^+_{\text{DF}} - \widetilde{\xi}^-_{\text{DF}}\right) + \widetilde{\xi}^-_{\text{DF}}\right] \right\}^{-1}$$

These results allow us to compare the prices of call options' prices (as well as put options) to test whether FX prices are in equilibrium or they provide arbitrage opportunities.

8.9 Debt, The Merton Model, and Default

Default, or the propensity to default, results from an imbalance between the debt and its collateral equity (equivalently, from a debt that cannot be met by the price of its collateral or the debtor's ability to service the debt). Default may occur when equity is insufficient to meet the requirements of the bond-holders. Such an approach, based on a seminal paper by Merton (1974), has also been used to price the first generation of credit derivatives. In this example, we assess the price of a bond and its collateral as a two-state model and extend it to its international framework. For example, we will assume that

China is the holder of US Treasury bonds, which it holds in USD in China but revalued in its domestic currency—the yuan. To do so, it has first converted yuans into US dollars and provided the USA with the credit it has assumed. The price of China's credit and the price the USA pays for its credit is compounded by the FX. In the following, we consider for simplicity a two-state preference model with no FX, and subsequently we consider the same problem with currency risk added.

Merton's approach consists of letting the price of equity be equivalent to that of a call option. Explicitly, let a firm value be V and its bond obligation be B. Equity is thus defined by (since bond-holders have priority on the firm's assets)

$$E = \begin{cases} V - B & V > B \\ 0 & V < B \end{cases} \quad \text{or} \quad E = \text{Max}(V - B, 0) \text{ at time } T = 1$$

From the bond-holder's point of view, we note that the price of the firm's obligation at time $T = 1$ is then

$$V_B = \begin{cases} B & V > B \\ V & V < B \end{cases} \quad \text{or} \quad V_B = \text{Min}(B, V) = V - E = V - \text{Max}(V - B, 0)$$

For example, say that in a binomial model the values in the next period are given by (V^+, V^-). Thus, equity and bond prices are

$$(E^+, E^-) = \{(V^+ - B)^+, (V^- - B)^+\} \quad \text{and} \quad (V_B^+, V_B^-) = \{\min(V^+, B), \min(V^-, B)\}$$

To price corporate firm liabilities V_B, construct a portfolio consisting of the firm's leverage and borrowing. Let the firm leverage be N and let b be the amount borrowed at the risk-free rate. Then, a replication of corporate liability priced at time $T = 0$ is given by $V_B = NV - b$. One period later, at time $T = 1$, we have

$$\text{Time } T = 0: V_B = NV - b \Leftrightarrow \begin{cases} NV^+ - b = V_B^+ = \min(V^+, B) \\ NV^- - b = V_B^- = \min(V^-, B) \end{cases} \text{Time } T = 1$$

A solution for the replicating portfolio parameters is

$$N = \frac{V_B^+ - V_B^-}{V^+ - V^-}, \quad b = \frac{V^- V_B^+ - V^+ V_B^-}{(V^+ - V^-)(1 + R_f)}$$

For no arbitrage, we have

$$V_B = NV - b = \left(\frac{V_B^+ - V_B^-}{V^+ - V^-}\right) V - \frac{V^- V_B^+ - V^+ V_B^-}{(V^+ - V^-)(1 + R_f)}$$

or

$$V_B = \left(\frac{V_B^+ - V_B^-}{V^+ - V^-}\right) \left\{ V - \frac{V^- \min(V^+, B) - V^+ \min(V^-, B)}{(V_B^+ - V_B^-)(1 + R_f)} \right\}$$

For example, assume that the debt principal is $B = 100$, the risk-free rate is 0.08, and the firm value is 110, which may increase or decrease to 125 and 75 respectively, corresponding to RORs of 13.63% and −31.18%. Then we can calculate $NV - B$ as replicating the corporate liabilities and subsequently calculate the corporate equity, as previously indicated, by $E = V - V_B$. Specifically, we have

$$V_B = \left(\frac{100-75}{125-75} \right) \left[110 - \frac{75(100)-125(75)}{(100-75)(1+0.08)} \right] = 89.7; \quad E = 110 - V_B = 110 - 89.7 = 20.3$$

If we have 100 equity shares, the price per share without debt is $e_0 = 10/100 = 0.1$, while with debt it equals $e_1 = 20.3/100 = 0.203$. This gain is acquired at the expense of the bond-holders who have invested \$100 million and are left after such an investment with a value of \$89.7 million (a loss of \$10.3 million). In other words, equity holders have more than doubled their equity price by incurring a \$100 million debt. They have done so, however, at the price of an increased risk of default and loss of equity. These simple observations explain the amount of debt that certain speculative investors assume in order to make as much money as possible.

8.9.1 The Merton Debt Model and Foreign Exchange

We consider next the same problem with FX risk. Unlike the conventional Merton problem, let the US debt be taken in a foreign country, say China. As a result, US equity at time $t = 0$, when the bond is contracted to China, is

$$E_0^D = \begin{cases} V_0^D - \xi_{FD}^0 B_F^D & V_0^D > \xi_{FD}^0 B_F^D \\ 0 & V_0^D < \xi_{FD}^0 B_F^D \end{cases}; \quad E_0^D = \text{Max}\left(V_0^D - \xi_{FD}^0 B_F^D, 0 \right)$$

where B_F^D is the debt in foreign currency (yuan), converted to a domestic currency at the current FX rate ξ_{FD}^0. From the foreign bond-holder's viewpoint, we note that the price of the US obligation at time $t=0$ is in the creditor currency V_0^F (note that $\xi_{DF}^0 V_0^D$ is the value of the US holdings in the creditor's yuan currency at that time):

$$V_0^F = \begin{cases} B_F^D & \xi_{DF}^0 V_0^D > B_F^D \\ \xi_{DF}^0 V_0^D & \xi_{DF}^0 V_0^D < B_F^D \end{cases} \quad \text{or} \quad \xi_{DF}^0 V_0^F = \text{Min}\left(B_F^D, \xi_{DF}^0 V_0^D \right)$$

$$= \xi_{DF}^0 V_0^D - \xi_{DF}^0 E_0^D = \xi_{DF}^0 V_0^D - \text{Max}\left(\xi_{DF}^0 V_0^D - B_F^D, 0 \right)$$

An instant of time later, we then have

$$\tilde{E}_1^D = \begin{cases} \tilde{V}1D - \tilde{\xi}_{FD}^1 B_F^D (1+r_{FD}) & \tilde{V}_1^D > \tilde{\xi}_{FD}^1 B_F^D (1+r_{FD}) \\ 0 & \tilde{V}_1^D < \tilde{\xi}_{FD}^1 B_F^D (1+r_{FD}). \end{cases}$$

$$= \text{Max}\left(\tilde{V}_1^D - \tilde{\xi}_{FD}^1 B_F^D (1+r_{FD}), 0 \right)$$

$$\tilde{V}_1^F = \begin{cases} B_F^D & \tilde{\xi}_{DF}^1 \tilde{V}_1^D > B_F^D (1+r_{FD}) \\ \tilde{\xi}_{DF}^1 \tilde{V}_1^D & \tilde{\xi}_{DF}^1 \tilde{V}_1^D > B_F^D (1+r_{FD}) \end{cases} \quad \text{or} \quad \tilde{V}_1^F = \text{Min}\left(B_F^D (1+r_{FD}), \tilde{\xi}_{DF}^1 \tilde{V}_1^D \right) = \tilde{\xi}_{DF}^1 \left(\tilde{V}_1^D - \tilde{E}_1^D \right)$$

$$= \tilde{\xi}_{DF}^1 \left(\tilde{V}_1^D - \text{Max}\left(\tilde{V}_1^D - \tilde{\xi}_{DF}^1 B_F^D (1+r_{FD}), 0 \right) \right)$$

To price such a credit, we shall use an approach consisting of replicating its price by a portfolio $V^F = NV^D - b + c\xi_{FD}$, where N, b, and c are parameters we seek to define. We assume that the value of the firm an instant later can assume two values: $\left(\bar{V}_1^D, \bar{V}_2^D \right)$;

therefore, the price of its equity also assumes two values: $(\bar{E}_1^D, \bar{E}_2^D)$. Further, FX rates also assume two values: (ξ_{DF}^+, ξ_{DF}^-). As a result:

$$\bar{E}_{1+}^D = \text{Max}\left(\bar{V}_1^D - \xi_{FD}^+ B_F^D(1+r_{FD}),0\right) \quad \text{and} \quad \bar{E}_{1-}^D = \text{Max}\left(\bar{V}_1^D - \xi_{FD}^- B_F^D(1+r_{FD}),0\right)$$

$$\bar{E}_{2+}^D = \text{Max}\left(\bar{V}_2^D - \xi_{FD}^+ B_F^D(1+r_{FD}),0\right) \quad \text{and} \quad \bar{E}_{2-}^D = \text{Max}\left(\bar{V}_2^D - \xi_{FD}^- B_F^D(1+r_{FD}),0\right)$$

$$\bar{V}_{1+}^F = \xi_{DF}^+ \bar{V}_1^D - \tilde{\xi}_{DF}^+ \text{Max}\left(\bar{V}_1^D - \xi_{FD}^+ B_F^D(1+r_{FD}),0\right) = \frac{\bar{V}_1^D}{\xi_{FD}^+} - \frac{\text{Max}\left(\bar{V}_1^D - \xi_{FD}^+ B_F^D(1+r_{FD}),0\right)}{\xi_{FD}^+}$$

$$\bar{V}_{1-}^F = \xi_{DF}^- \bar{V}_1^D - \tilde{\xi}_{DF}^- \text{Max}\left(\bar{V}_1^D - \xi_{\div D}^- B_F^D(1+r_{FD}),0\right) = \frac{\bar{V}_1^D}{\xi_{FD}^-} - \frac{\text{Max}\left(\bar{V}_1^D - \xi_{FD}^- B_F^D(1+r_{FD}),0\right)}{\xi_{FD}^-}$$

$$\bar{V}_{2+}^F = \xi_{DF}^+ \bar{V}_2^D - \xi_{DF}^+ \text{Max}\left(\bar{V}_2^D - \xi_{FD}^+ B_F^D(1+r_{FD}),0\right) = \frac{\bar{V}_2^D}{\xi_{FD}^+} - \frac{\text{Max}\left(\bar{V}_2^D - \xi_{FD}^+ B_F^D(1+r_{FD}),0\right)}{\xi_{FD}^+}$$

$$\bar{V}_{2-}^F = \xi_{DF}^- \bar{V}_2^D - \xi_{DF}^- \text{Max}\left(\bar{V}_2^D - \xi_{FD}^- B_F^D(1+r_{FD}),0\right) = \xi_{DF}^- \frac{\bar{V}_2^D}{\xi_{FD}^-} - \frac{\text{Max}\left(\bar{V}_2^D - \xi_{FD}^- B_F^D(1+r_{FD}),0\right)}{\xi_{FD}^-}$$

As a result, the price of this portfolio is found by setting

$$\bar{V}_{1+}^F = N\bar{V}_1^D - b + c\xi_{FD}^+, \quad \bar{V}_{1-}^F = N\bar{V}_1^D - b + c\xi_{FD}^-$$

$$\bar{V}_{2+}^F = N\bar{V}_2^D - b + c\xi_{FD}^+, \quad \bar{V}_{2-}^F = N\bar{V}_2^D - b + c\xi_{FD}^-$$

These define a system of three variables (N, b, and c) with four equations (one of which is redundant, as we shall see shortly) and which we can solve. First, note that $N = (\bar{V}_{1+}^F - \bar{V}_{2+}^F)/(\bar{V}_1^D - \bar{V}_2^D)$, and further that $c = (\bar{V}_{1+}^F - \bar{V}_{1-}^F)/(\xi_{FD}^+ - \xi_{FD}^-)$, as well as $c = (\bar{V}_{2+}^F - \bar{V}_{2-}^F)/(\xi_{FD}^+ - \xi_{FD}^-)$, implying that one of these equations is redundant. Given N and c, we can calculate

$$b = \bar{V}_1^D \frac{\bar{V}_{1+}^F - \bar{V}_{2+}^F}{\bar{V}_1^D - \bar{V}_2^D} + \xi_{FD}^+ \frac{\bar{V}_{1+}^F - \bar{V}_{1-}^F}{\xi_{FD}^+ - \xi_{FD}^-} - \bar{V}_{1+}^F$$

The price of the foreign creditor option is therefore $V_0^F = NV_0^D - b + c\xi_{FD}^0$, or

$$V_0^F = \bar{V}_{1+}^F \frac{\bar{V}_{1+}^F - \bar{V}_{1-}^F}{\xi_{FD}^+ - \xi_{FD}^-} - \frac{(\bar{V}_1^D - \bar{V}_0^D)(\bar{V}_{1+}^F - \bar{V}_{2+}^F)}{\bar{V}_1^D - \bar{V}_2^D} - (\xi_{FD}^+ - \xi_{FD}^0)\frac{\bar{V}_{2+}^F - \bar{V}_{2-}^F}{\xi_{FD}^+ - \xi_{FD}^-}$$

which provides a clear statement on the effects of future FX prices and their effects on the value of the debt.[9]

8.9.2 Market Pricing Debt and Credit Risk

Two types of models are commonly used to price bonds. These include, as considered earlier, the structural no-arbitrage approach due to Merton and the reduced-form

---

9 For a review on valuing risky debt with fixed and floating rates, see Longstaff and Schwartz (1995) for example.

models. These models attempt to cope simultaneously with default and interest-rate risk. The former model is based on a collateral maintained to meet the contracts' obligations, and the latter model is based on a risk premium determined by the exchange in a risk market. Subsequently, we shall also provide a utility (and therefore "personal") approach to the pricing of credit risks and debt. These models are therefore far more appropriate to swap prices defined for specific exchanges rather than standardized swaps priced by financial market models.

Typically, structural default models specify a value process with default occurring when values cross an explicit threshold at which default is deemed likely (e.g., default defined by a debt-to-equity ratio). For example, a debt secured by a collateral may indicate a default if the debt price becomes greater than its collateral price. This is particularly the case when the cost of a mortgage increases over the cost of the home used as a collateral. Default may also arise when regulatory interventions limit the use of bonds as leverage to other financial transactions, contributing to its price falling appreciably, or when some events lead to the bond being worthless. Default is then a "stopping time" or an event defined by the evolution of a representative firm process expressing both its states and its policies (investments, speculation, etc.). In these terms, the price of debt is measured in terms of an option that represents the debt default risk based on the presumption that default is internal, expressed by the imbalance of debt and its collateral. In an international framework, default and the price of default vary from country to country due to countries' legal frameworks, industrial policies, and other factors. A theoretical and seminal model was suggested by Merton (1974) (see Chapter 3 for its development). It consists of a firm's stakeholders holding its equity (the collateral) and its bond-holders. In case of default, bond-holders have prior claim to the residual wealth of the company. In its simplistic form, it defines a firm's price in terms of its value V and its bond B. Equity is thus defined by an option (since bond-holders have priority on the firm's assets): $E = \text{Max}(V - B, 0)$. However, from the bond-holder's viewpoint, we note that the price of the firm's obligation is also an option, with $V_B = \text{Min}(B, V) = V - E = V - \text{Max}(V - B, 0)$. To price corporate firm's liabilities, for example, a replicating "priceable" portfolio is constructed consisting of the firm's leverage and borrowing. A price of debt is then determined based on the assumptions that there is a unique price for all portfolios with the same risk-returns (see Chapter 7). This is not the case, however, for endogenous multi-agent pricing (i.e., sovereign states that can affect both collateral and bond prices) as we shall subsequently see in this chapter. When a foreign bond is priced from a domestic viewpoint, we also account for the currency risk, and therefore its price ought to account for the multiple risks such bonds imply. In Chapter 7, a specific example to that effect was treated. We now consider a simple and introductory numerical example.

8.9.3 Debt and Options: A Merton Continuous-Time Model

Let an investor's equity be $E(t)$ and let $V(t)$ be its value, while $D(t)$ is its debt. The bond-holder (who owns the debt) collects either the amount due or the residual value, while the equity holder obtains nothing or the residual value after bond-holders have been paid. In this case, we have

Bond-holder's collection at T : $\text{Min}(V(T), D(T))$

Equity holder's collection at T : $\text{Max}(V(T) - D(T), 0)$

Assume now that the firm value is defined by a lognormal model, which we write with Q probability measure as

$$\frac{dV}{V} = R_f \, dt + \sigma \, dW^Q, \quad V(0) = V_0 + D(0)$$

Note that, once a debt is granted, the investor value increases based on its self-capital and debt it presupposes. Assume first that the debt plus its bank interest rate is to be repaid only at some time T and equals $D(T) = D(0)e^{R_B T}$. Default can occur only at the time the debt is to be paid and occurs if $D(T) = D(0)e^{R_B T} > V(T)$. The creditor-bond-holder then collects $\mathrm{Min}(V(T), D(T))$, while the equity holder collects $\mathrm{Max}(V(T) - D(T), 0)$. As a result, at any time t, under a Q probability measure, the debt (creditor's) and the equity holder prices are the option prices given by

$$D(0) = e^{-R_f T} E^Q \{ \mathrm{Min}(V(T), D(T)) \} = e^{-R_f T} E^Q (D(T) - \mathrm{Max}(D(T) - V(T), 0))$$

or

$$\left[e^{(R_B - R_f)T} - 1 \right] D(0) = e^{-R_f T} E^Q \left(\mathrm{Max} \left(D(0)e^{-R_B T} - V(T), 0 \right) \right)$$

while the equity's price is given by the call option:

$$E(0) = e^{-R_f T} E^Q \left\{ \mathrm{Max} \left(V(T) - D(0)e^{R_B T}, 0 \right) \right\}$$

The investor's leverage, given by its equity to debt ratio, is thus

$$\frac{E(0)}{D(0)} = e^{-R_f T} E^Q \left\{ \mathrm{Max} \left(\frac{V(T)}{D(0)} - e^{R_B T}, 0 \right) \right\}$$

An investor seeking to leverage the value of their holdings will then ask for a loan that maximizes their equity, while the bank would seek to maximize the value of its loan. This results in a game where the firm seeks to leverage its equity to increase its value while the bank seeks to maximize the price of the investor value:

$$\underset{R_B}{Max} \left(e^{(R_B - R_f)T} - 1 \right) D(0) - e^{-R_f T} E^Q \left(\mathrm{Max} \left(D(0)e^{-R_B T} - V(T), 0 \right) \right) = 0$$

$$\underset{D(0)}{Max} E(0) = e^{-R_f T} E^Q \left\{ \mathrm{Max} \left(V(T) - D(0)e^{R_B T}, 0 \right) \right\}$$

Let $(R_B^*, D^*(0))$ be the Nash solution to the bank and the firm game. We shall assume then that this solution defines the term of the debt and its size. Given such a solution, the probability of default and collecting the investor value is $P^Q(T) = P(V(T) < D)$, which we can write explicitly as

$$P^Q(T) = P \left(V(t)e^{[R_f - (1/2)\sigma^2](T-t) + \sigma W^*(T-t)} < D(T) \right)$$

and with $\varepsilon^Q(0,1) \sim N(0,1)$:

$$P^Q(T) = P \left(\varepsilon^Q(0,1) \le Z^* \right), \quad Z^* = \frac{\ln \dfrac{D(t)}{V(t)} - \left(R_f - R_B - \dfrac{1}{2}\sigma^2 \right)(T-t)}{\sigma \sqrt{T-t}}$$

where $\varepsilon^Q(0, 1)$ is a standard normal random variable whose probability function is $f_n(.)$. As a result:

$$\frac{\partial P^Q(T)}{\partial R_B} = \frac{\sqrt{T-t}}{\sigma(1+R_B)} f_n(Z^*) > 0, \quad 0 < \frac{\partial Z^*}{\partial \sigma} = \sqrt{T-t} - \frac{1}{\sigma} Z^* \text{ if } \sigma > \frac{Z^*}{\sqrt{T-t}}$$

The values to the debt holder and to the equity holder are thus dependent on one another and can be summarized by the following conditions:

1) If there is no default by the investor, the debt holder collects $D(T)$ and the equity holder collects $V(T) - D(T)$ with probability $1 - P^Q(T)$.
2) If the investor defaults with probability $P^Q(T)$, the debt holder collects the investor holdings value and the equity holder collects nothing.

These collections have, as indicated earlier, option values that allow one to price the investor holdings (and by extension the price of its holdings traded in financial markets). These are given by

$$\text{Min}(V(T), D(T)) = D(0)e^{R_B^* T} - \text{Max}(D(0)e^{R_B^* T} - V(T), 0) \quad \text{for the debt holder:}$$

$$\text{Max}(V(T) - D(0)e^{R_B^* T}, 0) \quad \text{for the equity holder}$$

The calculation of the price of these options using the martingale method is then a straightforward exercise. For example, consider a Black–Scholes option with a firm paying a dividend rate q. The payout at the exercise time T is $\text{Max}(\psi(V(T) - K), 0)$, where $\psi = +1$ if it is a call option and $\psi = -1$ if it is a put option. The stock the firm value is

$$\frac{dV}{V} = (\mu - q) dt + \sigma dW$$

With a Q probability measure it is

$$\frac{dV}{V} = (R_f - q) dt + \sigma dW^Q, \quad V(0) > 0$$

whose solution is

$$V(T) = V(0)\exp\left[\left(R_f - q - \frac{1}{2}\sigma^2\right)(T-t) + \sigma(W(T) - W(t))\right].$$

For a call option $\psi = 1$, we have

$$C(t) = e^{-R_f(T-t)} E^Q(\text{Max}(V(T) - D(T), 0))$$

$$= e^{-R_f(T-t)} E^Q V(T) 1_{V(T) > D(T)} - D(T)e^{-R_f(T-t)} E^Q 1_{V(T) \le D(T)} = V_1 - V_2$$

Let $E^Q 1_A = Q(A)$, then $V_2 = e^{-R_f(T-t)} D(T) Q(V(T) > D(T))$, where

$$Q(V(T) > D(T)) = P\left[V(t)e^{[R_f - q - (1/2)\sigma^2](T-t) + \sigma(W(T) - W(t))} > D(T)\right]$$

$$= P\left[W(T) - W(t) > \ln\left(\frac{D(T)}{V(t)}\right)^{1/\sigma} - \frac{1}{\sigma}\left(R_f - q - \frac{1}{2}\sigma^2\right)(T-t)\right]$$

And

$$V_2(t) = e^{-R_f(T-t)}D(T)P\left[W(T) - W(t) > \frac{\ln\left(\dfrac{D(T)}{V(t)}\right) - \left(R_f - q - \frac{1}{2}\sigma^2\right)(T-t)}{\sigma}\right]$$

We compute V_1 in the same manner. Explicitly, let $V_1 = V(T)1_{V(T)>D(T)}$ and define the following measure:

$$\frac{V_1(t)}{V(t)} = \frac{V(T)}{V(t)}1_{V(T)>D(T)}$$

The rationale for our seeking a measure, say U, is that at time T

$$\frac{V_1(T)}{V(T)} = E^U\left(\frac{V(T)}{V(T)}1_{V(T)>D(T)}\right) = E^U\left(1_{V(T)>D(T)}\right)$$

To do so, consider the $y = 1/V$; then, by Itô's calculus, we have

$$dy = \frac{\partial y}{\partial V}dV + \frac{1}{2}\frac{\partial^2 y}{\partial V^2}(dV)^2 = -\frac{1}{V^2}dV + \frac{1}{V^3}(dV)^2 = -\frac{1}{V^2}dV + \frac{\sigma^2 V^2}{V^3}dt$$

$$= -\frac{(\mu - q)V\,dt + \sigma V\,dW}{V^2}dV + \frac{\sigma^2 V^2}{V^3}dt$$

Therefore, the following results:

$$\frac{dy}{y} = -\left(\mu - q - \sigma^2\right)dt + \sigma dW$$

To determine the measure, we set

$$\frac{dy}{y} = -\left(\mu - q - \sigma^2\right)dt + \sigma dW + R_f dt - R_f dt = \left(-R_f - q + \sigma^2\right)dt + \sigma\left(dW + \frac{R_f - \mu}{\sigma}dt\right)$$

$$\frac{dy}{y} = \left(-R_f - q + \sigma^2\right)dt + \sigma dW^U$$

And since $\ln(1/V) = -\ln V$, by Itô's calculus

$$d(\ln V(t)) = \left(R_f - q + \frac{\sigma^2}{2}\right)dt + \sigma dW^U$$

$$V_1(t) = V(t)e^{-q(T-t)}E^U\left(1_{V(T)>D(T)}\right)$$

and since

$$d(\ln V(t)) = \left(R_f - q + \frac{\sigma^2}{2}\right)dt + \sigma dW^U$$

$$V(T) = V(t)e^{[R_f - q + (\sigma^2/2)](T-t) + \sigma(W^U(T) - W^U(t))}$$

In this case:

$$E^U\left(1_{V(T)>D(T)}\right) = E^U\left(V(t)e^{[R_f-q+(\sigma^2/2)](T-t)+\sigma(W^U(T)-W^U(t))} > D(T)\right)$$

$$= E^U\left((W^U(T)-W^U(t)) > \ln\left(\frac{D(T)}{V(t)}\right)^{1/\sigma} - \frac{1}{\sigma}\left(R_f-q+\frac{\sigma^2}{2}\right)(T-t)\right)$$

$$= E^U\left(\varepsilon(0,1) > \frac{\ln\left(\dfrac{D(T)}{V(t)}\right) - \left(R_f-q+\dfrac{\sigma^2}{2}\right)(T-t)}{\sigma\sqrt{T-t}}\right)$$

And

$$V_1(t) = V(t)e^{-q(T-t)}P^U\left(\varepsilon(0,1) < \frac{\ln\left(\dfrac{V(t)}{D(T)}\right) + \left(R_f-q+\dfrac{\sigma^2}{2}\right)(T-t)}{\sigma\sqrt{T-t}}\right)$$

The price of the call option (i.e., the price of equity) is thus

$$V_1(t) - V_2(t) = V(t)e^{-q(T-t)}P^U\left(\varepsilon(0,1) < \frac{\ln\left(\dfrac{V(t)}{D(T)}\right) + \left(R_f-q+\dfrac{\sigma^2}{2}\right)(T-t)}{\sigma\sqrt{T-t}}\right)$$

$$-e^{-R_f(T-t)}D(T)P\left[\varepsilon(0,1) > \frac{\ln\left(\dfrac{D(T)}{V(t)}\right) - \left(R_f-q-\dfrac{1}{2}\sigma^2\right)(T-t)}{\sigma\sqrt{(T-t)}}\right]$$

Since the strike is $D(T) = D(0)e^{R_B T}$, then at time $t = 0$ we have $e^{-R_B T}D(T) = D(0)$. The game of the equity holder would be to select for a given interest payment the debt they seek. The option price is then

$$\underset{D(0)}{\text{Max}} = V(0)e^{-qT}P^U\left(\varepsilon(0,1) < \frac{\ln\left(\dfrac{V(0)}{D(0)e^{R_B T}}\right) + \left(R_f-q+\dfrac{\sigma^2}{2}\right)T}{\sigma\sqrt{T}}\right)$$

$$-e^{-R_f T}D(0)e^{R_B T}P\left[\varepsilon(0,1) > \frac{\ln\left(\dfrac{D(0)e^{R_B T}}{V(0)}\right) - \left(R_f-q-\dfrac{1}{2}\sigma^2\right)T}{\sigma\sqrt{T}}\right]$$

References

Bank for International Settlements. BIS. Consolidated Banking Statistics. http://www.bis.org/statistics/consstats.htm.

Bielecki, T. and Rutkowski, M. (2002) *Credit Risk: Modeling, Valuation and Hedging.* Springer Verlag: New York.

Blanchet-Scalliet, C. and Patras, F. (2008) Counterparty risk valuation of a CDS. link https://arxiv.org/abs/0807.0309.

Bluhm, C., Overbeck, L., and Wagner, C. (2003) *Introduction to Credit Risk Modeling*. Chapman and Hall: London.

Bonfim, D. (2009) Credit risk drivers: evaluating the contribution of firm level information and of macroeconomic dynamics. *Journal of Banking & Finance*, **33**(2): 281–299.

Cossin, D. and Pirotte, H. (2001) *Advanced Credit Risk Analysis: Financial Approaches and Mathematical Models to Assess, Price and Manage Credit Risk*. John Wiley & Sons, Ltd: Chichester.

Cox, J.J. and Tait. N. (1991) *Reliability, Safety and Risk Management*. Butterworth-Heinemann: Oxford.

Das, S. and Tufano, P. (1996) Pricing credit sensitive debt when interest rates, credit ratings and credit spreads are stochastic. *The Journal of Financial Engineering*, **5**(2): 161–198.

De Weert, F. (2008) *Exotic Options Trading*. John Wiley & Sons.

Duffie, D. and Singleton, K.J. (2003) *Credit Pricing, Measurement and Management*. Princeton University Press: Princeton, NJ.

Duffie, G.R. (1999) Estimating the price of default risk. *Review of Financial Studies*, **12**: 197–226.

EUROSTAT. http://ec.europa.eu/eurostat.

Ganguin, B. and Bilardello, J. (2004) *Standard & Poor's Fundamentals of Corporate Credit Analysis*. McGraw-Hill: New York.

Hull, J.C. (2014) *Options, Futures, and Other Derivatives*, 9th edn. Pearson.

Hull, J.C. and White, A. (1992) The price of default risk. *Risk*, **5**: 101–103.

Hull, J.C. and White, A. (1995). The impact of default risk on the prices of options and other derivatives securities. *Journal of Banking and Finance*, **19**: 299–322.

Jarrow, R.A. (1988) *Finance Theory*. Prentice Hall: Englewood Cliffs, NJ.

Jarrow, R.A. and Rudd, A. (1982) Approximate option valuation for arbitrary stochastic processes. *Journal of Financial Economics*, **10**: 347–369.

Jarrow, R. and Turnbull, S. (1995) Pricing derivatives on financial securities subject to credit risk., *Journal of Finance*, **50**: 53–86.

Jarrow, R.A., Lando, D., and Turnbull, S. (1997) A Markov model for the term structure of credit spreads. *Review of Financial Studies*, **10**: 481–523.

Johnson, R.S. (2004) *Bond Evaluation, Selection, and Management*. Wiley-Blackwell.

Johnson, R.S. (2010) *Bond Evaluation, Selection, and Management*, 2nd edn. Wiley-Blackwell.

Kallianiotis, I. (2013) *International Financial Transactions and Exchange Rates Trade, Investment, and Parities*. Palgrave Macmillan.

Lando, D. (2004.) *Credit Risk Modeling*. Princeton University Press: Princeton, NJ.

Longstaff, F. and Schwartz, E. (1995) A simple approach to valuing risky fixed and floating rate debt. *Journal of Finance*, **50**: 789–819.

Merton, R.C. (1974) On the pricing of corporate debt: the risk structure of interest rates. *Journal of Finance*, **29**: 449–470.

NYT (2011) Those euro bets have many ifs. *The New York Times*, December 3. http://www.nytimes.com/2011/12/04/your-money/currency-hedging-has-many-ifs-for-investors.html.

Pykhtin, M. (ed.) (2005) *Counterparty Credit Risk Modeling*. Risk Books: London.

Reyniers, D.J. and Tapiero, C.S. (1995a) The delivery and control of quality in supplier–producer contracts. *Management Science*, **41**(10): 1581–1589.

Reyniers, D.J. and Tapiero, C.S. (1995b) Contract design and the control of quality in a conflictual environment. *European Journal of Operations Research*, **82**(2): 373–382.

S&P (2017) *Default, Transition, and Recovery: 2016 Annual Sovereign Default Study and Rating Transitions*. http://media.spglobal.com/documents/SPGlobal_Ratings_Article_3 +April+2017_201+Annual+Sovereign+Default+Study+and+Rating+Transitions.pdf (accessed July 14, 2017).

Schönbucher, P.J. (2003) *Credit Derivatives Pricing Models: Models, Pricing and Implementation*. John Wiley & Sons, Ltd: Chichester.

Schwartz, R. and Smith, C.W. (1990) *The Handbook of Currency and Interest Rate Risk Management*. New York Institute of Finance.

Tapiero, C.S. (2004) *Risk and Financial Management: Mathematical and Computational Methods*. John Wiley & Sons.

Tapiero, C.S. (2010) *Risk Finance and Asset Pricing*. John Wiley & Sons, Inc.: Hoboken, NJ.

Tapiero, C.S. (2013) *Engineering Risks and Finance*. Springer: New York.

The Economist (2011) China's murky ownership rules. Who owns what? July 9. http://www.economist.com/node/18928526.

The World Bank, Word Databank. http://data.worldbank.org/.

WSJ (2011) EU finds China gives aid to Huawei, ZTE. *The Wall Street Journal*, February 3.

WSJ (2016a) S&P downgrades Kazakhstan, Oman, Bahrain, Saudi Arabia on oil slump. *The Wall Street Journal*, February 17. http://www.wsj.com/articles/s-p-downgrades-kazakhstan-oman-bahrain-saudia-arabia-on-oil-slump-1455734291 (accessed May 26, 2017).

WSJ (2016b) U.S. court throws out price-fixing judgment against Chinese vitamin C makers. *The Wall Street Journal*, September 20. http://www.wsj.com/articles/u-s-court-throws-out-price-fixing-judgment-against-chinese-vitamin-c-manufacturers-1474391092 (accessed May 25, 2017).

9

Globalization and Trade

A Changing World

Motivation

This chapter outlines the importance of trade in globalization and how it contributes to sovereign policies and gating. We provide an overview of the evolution of trade, based on conventional approaches as well as its financial and gating aspects and analyze their underlying risks and related issues. These include inversion, outsourcing, risk externalities, strategic trade, and trade barriers. Trade models emphasizing Ricardo's theory are outlined. We define trade models using three approaches: (1) the relative industrial and economic efficiency (2) the strategic approach to trade based on game theoretic models, and (3) a market-based approach that reflects consumers' demand and prices for goods, whether produced domestically or abroad. We contribute to trade modeling by introducing a strategic global and financial pricing approach to heterogeneous (and competing) agents based on dependent utilities, as well as competing suppliers. We outline a multi-country financial consumption approach beginning with a one-period utility–consumption–demand model, extended to a Cournot multi-period financial consumption model accounting for both current and future consumption.

9.1 Introduction

Economic trade theory was advanced by Adam Smith, who rationalized the efficiency of free economic exchange in 1776. Subsequently, David Ricardo, in 1817, advocated the economic efficiency of trade based on nations' comparative advantages. Gough (2002) noted:

> In the early 1800s, British landowners controlled Parliament; import and export of grain had been controlled by the Corn Laws, a collection of tariffs, subsidies, and restrictions intended to reduce imports, boost exports, and keep the price of grain high. Newly wealthy factory owners emerged wanting cheap food so that they could keep the wages they paid low. The debate lasted for years, resulting in the eventual repeal of the Corn Laws in 1848. The British economist David Ricardo supported repeal and developed the argument for free trade that still

Globalization, Gating, and Risk Finance, First Edition. Unurjargal Nyambuu and Charles S. Tapiero.
© 2018 John Wiley & Sons Ltd. Published 2018 by John Wiley & Sons Ltd.

remains the central point today: that specialization and free trade will benefit all trading parties, even when some are "absolutely" more efficient producers than others.

These historical postulates for trade theory are now being challenged for numerous reasons, including political agendas and the realization that globalization has not profited all. Not least are the evolution of industrial technologies, and fragmentation of industry, and political and domestic economic agendas. For example, today a typical product is mostly assembled out of hundreds, and in some cases thousands, of globally produced parts, contributing to a loss of jobs for some and profits for others. Apple computers may be considered as "American" computers, but they are in fact tested, produced, and assembled primarily by Foxconn in China. GM and Ford, well-known American automobile brands, may be partially assembled in the USA, with other parts and subassemblies imported from Mexico, Germany, Brazil, Argentina, and dozens of other countries. In his classic book *Les Mots et les Choses*, the French thinker Michel Foucault (1966) explained how human knowledge (including economics) is rooted, in part, in taxonomy. Thus, the fundamental category of "nation" or "sovereign state," at least as far as trade is concerned, is rather ambiguous. Consequently, in our modern industrial world, the measurement of trade is far more difficult to define. By the same token, global enrichment has contributed to emerging economies, increasing their technological and economic capacities, and equalizing their abilities to compete. This has allowed them to assume a more respectable position in world affairs. In other words, modern logistical software and supply chain management have allowed world trade to consist of a multitude of parts and assemblies imported from many origins in (and from) many countries. Their net effects have led to a growing industrial specialization and to a far greater migration of jobs, both in and out of traditionally leading industrial and commercial countries. For example, in the USA, the expansion of high-tech innovation and industrialization has increased the demand for qualified manpower; this has led to an influx of talent into the USA at the expense of other countries. Given the US opportunities and pay for know-how and knowledge that are more than in other countries, a talent migration from India, Europe, China, and elsewhere has enriched the technological might of the USA, and thereby of important segments of its economy. However, this migration has recently been hampered as part of a policy to gate migration and protect high-value domestic jobs for local candidates.

These claims, although supported by statistical data, are far more complex than presumed by trade theory. Technology, the increased need for intelligence, the increased complexity of robotic assembly and manufacturing, as well as the complexity of products and services has led to increased regulation and tariffs on trade, thus redefining sovereign trade policies. A similar situation arises in global finance, with liquidity and borrowing sought and delivered globally, yet delivered across international boundaries and lending to the financialization of industrial and business policies. As a result, technological infrastructure, technical know-how, software, trade, industrial inversion, and real activities have been and are orchestrated by financial valuation and management. Capital investments, costs, sovereign subsidies, and special economic advantages have contributed to a transformation of demand for manpower and intelligence, as well as to a structural change in the demand and the supply of employment. Globalization has opened the gates and the means to meet demand for imports and exports that are fueling trade as well as technology migration. It is a second business and industrial revolution, one which has swept the world into a global transition. The growth of trade in all regions (as shown in Figure 9.1) has provided economic and social benefits, a relative political stability, and the freedom of movement across national boundaries. This process has intensified global competition between sovereign states seeking to equalize their

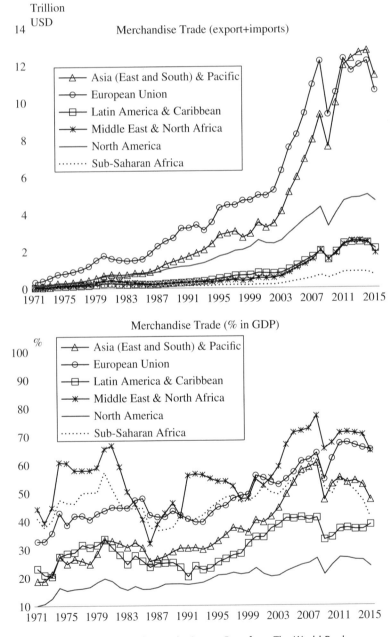

Figure 9.1 Merchandise trade trends. *Source:* Data from The World Bank.

relative economic well-being. In this context, globalization has contributed to the growth of economic and social entropy among sovereign states; that is, leading toward a greater equalization of know-how, industrial capacity, and wealth, albeit also to an increase in economic inequalities within Western sovereign states. In sum, entropy growth is leading to the concurrent growth of globalization and sovereign gating, "seeking" to engineer and maintain sovereign economic and social advantages while, at the same time, profiting from globalization. In this environment, trade in its broader definition is a fundamental and strategic aspect of globalization.

The economic justifications of trade are, as already stated, both simple and complex. On the one hand, the principle of comparative advantage is both rational and meaningful when trades can be balanced by a partner's needs and their exchange. When partners have equal capabilities, trade has social, economic, but also development risk implications that are far more confusing and complex to assess. For example, producing cars in the USA, in Brazil, or in any other country no longer has any particular technological advantage (such advantages remain in agriculture because of land and weather conditions). By the same reason, some sovereign states expand industrial activities at the expense of a migration of pollution with long-run risks assumed. For these reasons, trade is no longer motivated by barters, but is motivated by "financialization" and by financial agendas. In this context, demand for consumption, competing supplies, FX, tariffs, and regulation are some of the factors that define trade, albeit their real risks are often short-changed by myopic financial considerations. In this chapter, we consider such problems from a financial viewpoint, while maintaining that such problems are far more important and complex than what financial valuation surmises. Some elements include:

- the financial utility of sovereign consumption and global prices (defined by global demand);
- the wealth of nations competing for consumption goods;
- trade and financial gating policies (or anti-globalization) considered further in Chapter 10;
- geopolitics in a world in conflict.

The models we consider are, necessarily, very simple, but they provide a preliminary and rational assessment of the evolution of trade and its financial consequences. In the following, we review conventional approaches to trade and the evolution of its financial and gating aspects.

9.1.1 Trade and Globalization: A Gated and Changing World

Trade arises for a number of essential reasons:

- economic—embedded in industrial and business specialization and efficiency;
- self-serving altruistic—embedded in the mutual interest of engaging in an exchange;[1]
- political—reflecting the political "rapprochement" of national interests.

Globalization has redefined trade by providing a new, free, and friendly economic and social environment for its expansion. It is globally acquiescent with each party pursuing economic and financial objectives. Politically, trade is a global "Genghis Khan" economic strategy, namely, conquering markets and profiting from trade while sharing know-how

---

1 See Nyambuu (2017) for a definition of self-serving altruism and its implications for trade.

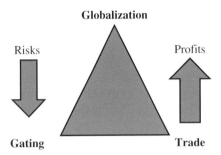

Figure 9.2 The business of trade: many factors, many challenges.

and resources over a constantly expanding region. However, in a gated environment, trade is also fueled by the pursuit of profits and the need to cut costs, to seek fewer regulatory controls, less taxation, greater diversification, and to access new economic and financial markets. This relationship is summarized in Figure 9.2. In other words, trade *is* a self-serving financial and economic policy, based on an increased mutual advantage. Its global outreach is amplified by technology, an economic rationality, and global logistics and technological systems bridging the divide of consumers and suppliers everywhere. The media abound with pronouncements and problems concerning the opportunities and the risks of global and trade finance.

Events recorded and analyzed in media pertaining to global finance, discussed in Chapter 1 and covered in this chapter, attest to the broad outreach and to the importance of financial trade. Most governments' policies today, whether explicit by the decisions they make or by their regulations, tariffs, political agreements, and so on, are meant to assure the claims they can extract from the financial returns of trade. Since all countries engaged in trade seek the same advantages, they may work at cross-purposes, and therefore their cross-border trades may be based on temporary comparative advantages. Trade and sovereign gating thus became strategic, as well as increasingly competitive when globalization allows for demand and supply from everywhere and everything to be freely traded. In other words, as stated earlier, a trade entropy is growing since trade competition is increasingly being pursued by trade partners progressively equal and subject to gating policies that equalize the opportunities and the profits of trade. When this is not the case, explicit and implicit manipulations of incentives and tariffs, in international corporate taxation, and in interventions in currencies, interest rates, FX markets, and so on are used to confront the trade advantages that one party may have over the others. Global "equalization and gating," combined with competitive trade, is thus altering the nature and approach to trade anchored in Ricardo's theory of comparative advantage. Rather, it is increasingly embedded in imperfect competition models of trade and financialization that recognizes the inherent markets' incompleteness and imperfections due to a heterogeneous world as well as sovereign states' trade repression, incentives and support policies.

The public press is full of examples that point to manipulations of import and export markets, as well as direct and indirect interventions on their FX. They may point to changing corporate national "loyalties" and to changing sovereign policies. For example, Apple Inc., with a market value of $753.7 billion as of March 2017,[2] called itself a US company a decade ago when it was producing and selling mostly in the USA. Today, with

---

2 Apple was placed third in the Fortune 500 (http://beta.fortune.com/fortune500/apple-3) ranking by its total revenue of $215.6 billion in 2016.

major parts of its production and economic activity (as well as the market for its products) outside the USA, it can hardly be called "American." Such a process, with over trillions of dollars held externally by firms (initially treated as national champions), has fueled a growth of outsourcing, the export of jobs through foreign investments and the growth of A-National enterprises operating in global markets and responding to the advantages and risks that result from both natural hazards and sovereign states' policies.

To maintain trade advantages, some sovereign states have managed their currency. For example, officials from Germany, Brazil, China, and South Africa have expressed a concern that quantitative easing by the Federal Reserve Bank of the USA has contributed to a weakening of the dollar and thereby to a competitive advantage in exports for US products (NYT, 2010). There are persistent claims against China's intervening in its FX markets by underpricing the renminbi (yuan) against the US dollar and thus providing an edge to its exporting firms. Similar concerns have been expressed by Switzerland following the extreme rise in the Swiss Franc that has contributed to a drastic decline in its exports. These claims are part of a global trend in resource competitions as well as protectionist policies by countries counter to the G20 pledges to keep markets open and set a framework within which firms operate and seek advantages to profit from—whether to block their markets to trade or to open foreign markets. Global Trade Alert (http://www.globaltradealert.org/), a website on which economists monitor and rate trade measures, points to an increase in harmful protectionist measures taken by countries (in particular the G20) who are increasingly acting to close their markets to foreign competition. These developments are amplified further by news highlighting an economic environment where national agendas dominate economic policy. For example, Hotten (2010), a reporter for BBC News, points to currencies manipulations as economic "weapons," where countries from Brazil, Columbia, Switzerland, and many others are trying to devalue their currency, leading to a global state of "competitive currencies devaluation" motivated by domestic economic, trade, and political agendas. Such problems, of course, affect FX prices as developed in Chapter 7, based on the mutual FX tracking of sovereign states.

Further, export incentives and import tariffs are mostly set by sovereign states to alter the terms of economic exchanges and therefore provide advantages to some and hardships to others. For example, export insurance firms such as COFACE (French Company for Insurance of Foreign Business), as well as national trade and foreign ministries, support national firms and provide economic support to national champions in foreign markets. In some cases, such actions target commodities (e.g., oil and rare earths) where sovereign states have a particular control. For example, China's overt refusal to supply Japan with rare mineral earth metals needed to fuel its electronic industry (extended to a global control of supply), the supply of lithium in the hand of China and Bolivia, are just another manifestation of sovereign states' interventions in global economic exchanges that promises to lead to greater economic conflicts. These actions, some taken overtly and others covertly, underlie political and domestic policies and imply strategic motivations that transcend traditional economic and financial rationalities.

9.1.2 Trade and Comparative Risks

The conventional wisdom states that consumers benefit from trade by paying lower prices and access to a greater variety of products. At the same time, especially in developed economies, trade has led to the migration of jobs, to greater specialization, a weakened industrial infrastructure, greater internal financial inequalities, a weakened capacity of sovereign states to manage their economy and regulation, a greater economic interdependence, as well as to an increase in an alienation of national identity, with the latter challenging the definition of an economic national identity. These elements are contributing in some sovereign states to the rise of political conflicts, to the rise of counter-globalization political reforms, sovereign gating policies, and to internal and political conflicts (as if is the case in the USA, Europe, and other countries in 2016–2017). For example, the technological comparative advantages of the USA that has in the past contributed to the growth of advanced (and well-paid) jobs in the USA is now confronting a far greater technological competition from China and other countries. By the same token, trade has allowed many countries to create jobs and economic opportunities to attract corporate firms (in particular when global networking and freedom of movement and business allow them to operate globally). Trade in an open world, however, has risk consequences that are both new and differ from country to country, providing advantages to one and challenging another. For example:

- Increased specialization by countries to be trade efficient renders countries far more dependent and therefore far more subject to economic and geopolitical pressures and blackmail. Efficiency, gained at the expense of diversity and industrial economies of scope, renders such sovereign states ever more dependent. For example, in the USA, the number of smaller industrial enterprises (capable to compete) has declined; instead, financial services are dominated by global financial enterprises.
- Financial globalization and the domestic importance of trade have led to prices that are competitive (and therefore globally efficient) but, at the same time, from a social viewpoint, they may have risk consequences that are not accounted for.
- Trade incentives, such as exports insurance, are part of an extensive array of policy tools, both financial and political, that are used to strengthen countries' exports. The financial advantages of acquiring externally at a low price to sell at a higher price internally have also led some countries to assume greater debt through their trade imbalances. This has contributed to a greater financial dependence, with countries assuming credit risks they cannot maintain (see Chapter 8). For example, Greece in 2008–2015 assumed debt that has in fact rendered it dependent on foreign financial powers. By the same token, the US trade imbalance and its associated debt have increased significantly and at the same time has weakened the USA to exercise its potential political clout. The net result of such trade and financial (debt) imbalances contributes to weaker national economies and to the gradual transfer of national assets from domestic ownership to foreign ownership. For example, foreign ownership of US assets reached around 40% of GDP (or $7.3 trillion) at the end of 2015 (WSJ, 2016b).
- The combination of free trade and globalization has facilitated industrial and corporate inversion as well as the massive migration of talent, the loss of jobs from one country to another, greater cultural diversity, and increased economic inequalities, in particular in advanced and rich countries. This also contributes to greater risks and burdens in attending to those countries' needy and job-seeking citizens and, as a result, to greater political uncertainty.

In the long run, globalization and trade are contributing de facto to cross-boundary equalization, and at the same time it raises national challenges leading to sovereign states resorting to a broad set of taxations and protectionist-gating policies to protect their trade and their economic interest. The current evolution of global finance is therefore squeezed between centrifugal globalization forces and centripetal gating ones.

9.1.3   Inversion and Outsourcing

Outsourcing is essentially a transfer of previously in-state activities to an external (foreign) state. Such a transfer may contribute to corporate firms' numerous advantages, as well as to access to new markets and lower taxation. For a sovereign state, it is a loss of both jobs and revenues. Furthermore, it contributes to a loss of control, rendering a sovereign state's gating policies weaker. These elements generate risks. The presumption that these risks are mitigated by direct advantages arises from a collaboration and stable exchanges between domestic and foreign partners. Outsourcing (a form of inversion, delegated to a foreign corporate firm), for example, might imply not only a focus on core competencies and cost-efficient policies, but also on risks. The main risks (ex ante and ex post) include the outsourcing of critical activities and the risks assumed ex post once planned supply and associated terms are not met. As a result, in a globalized world, outsourcing ought to be conceived in numerous ways, based on model relationships which involve entirely or partly arm's-length contractual and conflicting partnerships. These associations are therefore an evolution that leads to a corporate entity being redefined as a networked set of corporate entities operating with common (complete or partial) interests. These entities are, of course, far more complex to manage and challenge the modeling of their operation and their strategic decisions. They are therefore "risk factories," providing the prospect of far greater profits. For example, Apple's growth is (and was) supported by the industrial capacity and costs of Foxconn in China. At the same time, it risks a future and global competition by Foxconn, as is becoming evident through Foxconn strategic diversification of its industrial and technological capacities. To manage these risks, a number of approaches are suggested in the literature, requiring a greater understanding of competitive advantages "going international and global," recognizing the importance of cultural, material, and human resources and their heterogeneity, as well as the effects of a natural imperfect mobility and its internal alignment in a global environment. Obviously, elements to mitigate these risks include:

1) Maintaining flexibility and the resources that provide a competitive advantage (e.g., for Apple, design and technology are their two essential advantages).
2) Avoiding monopolistic or oligopolistic markets. Both these markets are politically and economically regulated. For this reason, outsourcing agreements signed in China and in Ireland are not necessarily similar.
3) Managing the risks of post-contractual dependency, including prices, security, and backup alternatives.[3]

9.1.4   Trade and Risk Externalities

Financial risk externalities are the costs or benefits that are experienced by someone who is not a party to the transaction that produced it. Risk externalities can therefore be either

---

3 For further discussion, see Kogan and Tapiero (2007).

positive or negative. Externalities are important because they can create incentives to engage in too much or too little of an activity, from an efficiency perspective. When all of the costs and benefits of a transaction are internal, meaning that all they are experienced by someone directly involved, we expect the transaction to take place only if the benefits are greater than the costs. These benefits and costs are also important in trade. Say, for example, that a good is produced locally and exported to a foreign country at a price which is extremely competitive in the foreign country. While it may benefit the employees of the exporting firm in the domestic country, it may contribute to a loss of jobs in the foreign country that substitute an internal and real economic activity (e.g., producing jobs) by a financial activity (e.g., paying the exporter or assuming debt to do so). In this case, trade has both real economic and financial consequences. For example, it may lead to lower consumption prices, contributing to a greater demand for consumption. The exporting country, however, while profiting financially from its real economic activity, incurs costs such as local pollution. In that case, the fact that a product was produced and sold does not necessarily imply that wealth was created because of such an exchange. To know for sure, we would have to find out the economic value of the pollution damage, the risk consequences of importing combined with the risk consequences of exporting. Their profits therefore have cost and risk consequences, both of which are to be accounted for in corporate and sovereign policies.

Measurements of trade profits and their risks are thus both complex and essential and ought not only to emphasize their advantages, but also their implied consequences (see Section 9.2).

9.1.5 Globalization, Gating, and Strategic Trades

Gating, as stated previously, has emerged hand in hand with an expanding globalization. For example, the G20 continues to take more protectionist actions with new restrictions (145 more measures between October 2015 and May 2016) dominated by anti-dumping measures, especially in the metal industry (e.g., steel), as shown in WTO (2016a). These are gating policies in the hand of sovereign states that seek to protect both the capacity to export and hinder their imports. Some of the measures, including the EU's anti-dumping duties on steel imports, were discussed in Chapter 1. Another example is a series of anti-dumping duties imposed by the EU on imports from China on solar panel glass (due to unfair prices) during the period of 2013–2016. Other cases include Brazil's anti-dumping investigation on the imports of polyester film from Peru; a series of anti-dumping duties imposed by China, especially in 2015–2016 (on unbleached sack paper imported from the EU, Japan, and the USA; on electrical steel from the EU and Japan; on optical fiber preform from Japan and the USA). Such measures ranging from import tariffs and non-tariff trade barriers imply deviations in foreign trade practices.

The business of trade and gating policies and their associated risks are thus a function of the trade environment and its derivatives. A cursory summary include:

- The macroeconomic environment; that is, the health of national economies, both with a capacity to produce and the demand for greater consumption as well as their evolving needs.
- The economic comparative advantage a country has over another. This may include the comparative industrial and manufacturing base of exporters and importers, their labor costs, natural resources, technology, and economic and political trade

agreements. These are advantages and disadvantages that may change over time and hand in hand with the evolution of globalization.

- Economic growth contributing to the increase in total production capacity, employment, output, and relative costs.
- International business and the growth of global and A-National firms. These firms contribute to the growth of cross-border trade both in process products (i.e., based on manufacturing components) and in final products. For example, car manufacturing and computers everywhere have an immense trade system associated with them, with parts fabricated globally but assembled, branded, distributed, and serviced in specific states. These firms are, however, increasingly difficult to control or regulate.
- The strength of the country's currency (e.g., the strength of the US dollar and its global use as a reference currency support the negative balance of payments the USA maintains thanks to the willingness of sovereign states to earn US financial dollars in exchange for real traded goods). Inversely, the ability to borrow and spend, say in US dollars, provides a mechanism to expanding global growth and trade.
- FX and trade. Traditionally, macroeconomic variables such as interest rates and national income are used to define FX rates (as discussed in Chapters 1, 4, and 5). FX, however, is also manipulated in some countries to support or hinder trade and thus are a strategic policy when it is exercised (see also Chapter 7). Indirectly, it assumes a greater importance due to its effects on employment, outsourcing, and their like—all of which are essential ingredients of sovereign national and international policies. These considerations underlie both explicit and implicit interventions in FX markets by sovereign states. For example, in some cases, an exchange rate might be tailored to the transaction—whether of exports or imports. China, for example, has considered applying a tax on transactions made in a foreign currency (to reduce the outflow of capital). By the same token, in some markets, what may be conceived as a single currency market is in fact a market with several currency prices tailored to accommodate the economics of trade.

These elements are changing finance and its global business, being an essential engine of globalization. They contribute to the evolution of open frontiers (although with a gating policy to counter some sovereign risks); the evolution of multinationals; international trade agreements such as the General Agreement on Tariffs and Trade (GATT) and the World Trade Organization (WTO); in their wake, they contribute to the design of competing international monetary systems. These agreements are both economic and political. As discussed in chapter 1, GATT has had eight rounds of international trade negotiations, all aimed at reducing trade barriers to support both economic development and political stability. In the grim post-war atmosphere of 1947, the average import tariff in industrialized countries was around 40%. Today it is around 5%. In the 1960s, the "Kennedy" round of GATT achieved an average cut of around 30%, reducing manufacturers' costs by about 10% by 1972. In the late 1970s, the "Tokyo" round also achieved tariff cuts of approximately a third, with greater cuts for trade between the most developed countries and smaller cuts for trade between developed and newly industrialized countries. Each tariff cut represented another path toward globalization, whereas each gating policy represented another path to counter-globalization.

As of July 2016, the WTO has 164 member countries accounting for almost 98% of total world trade. According to WTO (2016b), within 20 years of the establishment of the WTO the average of applied tariffs was reduced to 8% from 15%, and the share of tariff-free world trade volume increased to 60%. In particular, one of the most significant tariff liberalization deals covering enormous trade volume was the expansion of WTO's Information Technology Agreement in December 2015. The original IT agreement was concluded in 1996 by 29 participants (the EU counted as one country) and increased to 82 members; however, its product coverage was not changed during all these years. Thus, expansion of this agreement acknowledges the massive technological change and need to lower its cost. Under this expanded deal by 53 members (including Australia, Canada, China, the EU, Hong Kong SAR, Japan, Singapore, the USA, and others), tariffs on an additional 201 IT products (with annual trade value of $1.3 trillion) were to be eliminated immediately (with participants such as Hong Kong, Japan, Norway, and Singapore) or progressively within several years. These zero tariffs will benefit all 164 members of the WTO and lead to an increase in both exports and imports of IT products and further contribute to the cost of the products as many IT products are used as production inputs. The Director General of the WTO, Roberto Azevêdo, stated that this deal is the "first major tariff-cutting deal at the WTO since 1996" (WTO, 2016b: 21). Other trade-promoting events include the approving of the multilateral Trade Facilitation Agreement in 2014.

9.2 Tracking Trade and Globalization

Trade is measured and tracked by research institutes, economic organizations (such as the International Monetary Fund (IMF)), national agencies, and others, all of which provide an abundance of indexes, statistics, and predictions of the evolution of trade and globalization. These statistics express a partial domestic assessment of globalization and its contribution to economic development in both advanced and emerging economies. Globalization indexes, seeking to capture many aspects of globalization and their economic, financial, social, safety, migration and environmental implications, are difficult to assess, however. For example, the KOF index of globalization (published by the Swiss Economic Institute) has maintained a database of 207 countries since 1970. In this section we emphasize the economic aspect of the KOF globalization index, which is defined by two sub-indexes (in equal weights) including actual economic flows in GDP (trade, foreign direct investment (FDI), portfolio investment, income payments to foreign nationals) and economic restrictions (hidden import barriers, mean tariff rate, international trade taxes (tariff revenues), capital account restrictions). This index can therefore serve as an index of "global openness and attractiveness" of a country to facilitate the flow of jobs, money, and global exchanges. The historical data on this index, together with its sub-indexes, as illustrated in Figure 9.3, points to a growing trend of economic globalization since 1970 which is attributable to a growth of actual flows and less restrictions.[4] However, we also observe a reversed trend in trade restrictions since the late 1990s for some countries and in the early 2000s for European countries and the USA which contributed to a decline in globalization. This also occurred in many

---

4 Note that higher values of the sub-indexes imply more globalization. But higher values of the restrictions index in Figure 9.3 refer to less barriers and limitations on trade and capital. For example, KOF index data show that for Singapore, after the Asian financial crisis (1997), although economic flows continued to increase, its economic globalization did not increase much because of trade- and capital-related restrictions between 1997 and 2002.

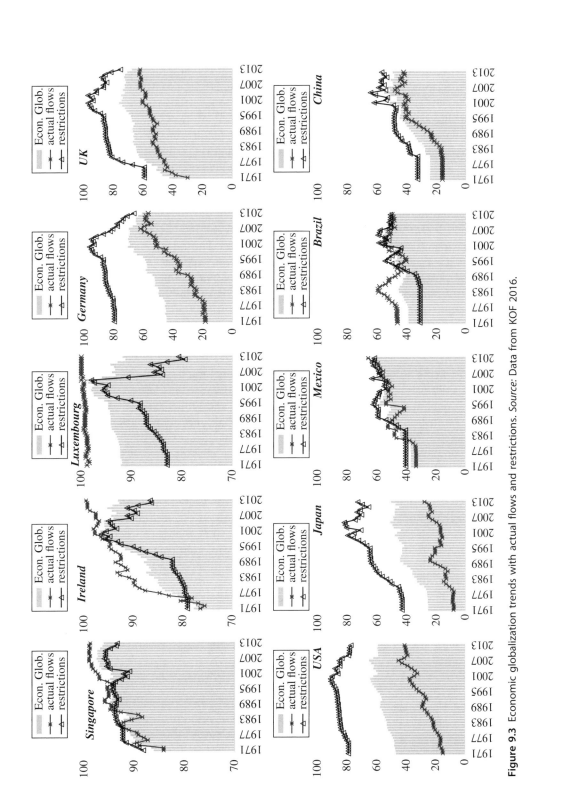

Figure 9.3 Economic globalization trends with actual flows and restrictions. *Source:* Data from KOF 2016.

countries following the financial crisis of 2008, mostly as an outcome from increased concerns about the state of domestic economies and a strategic gating by sovereign states. According to the KOF Globalization Index released in December 2016,[5] the world's most economically globalized country is Singapore, followed by Ireland, Luxembourg, Netherlands, and Malta. Ireland, for example, is globalized due to the open-border policy and taxation policies it has used to attract industrial investments. The economic benefits and terms Ireland offers and a lack of excessive regulation (see Chapter 10) have contributed also to a dynamic inversion process by firms seeking greater accessibility to foreign markets, less regulation, less taxation, and greater yields.

The KOF sub-indexes on restrictions are based on a method introduced by Gwartney *et al.* (2015). They constructed sub-indexes for barriers of hidden imports, cost of compliance, mean tariff rates, and tax revenues from trade using data from the *Global Competitiveness Report* by the World Economic Forum (2016), *Doing Business* by the World Bank, *World Tariff Profiles* by the WTO, and the IMF's *Government Finance Statistics Yearbook* and *International Financial Statistics*. The indexes on capital account restrictions are based on the IMF's Annual Report on Exchange Arrangements and Exchange Restrictions. In their annual report on Economic Freedom of the World, countries are ranked on the scale of 1–10 based on an index of Freedom to Trade Internationally. Using their data we illustrate the historical trend in this overall index for selected countries as well as its sub-indexes, including tariff, regulatory trade barriers (non-tariff and compliance cost of trade), and capital and people movement control in Figure 9.4. These indexes also show the fall in the ratings (since early 2000), which can be explained in terms of increased non-tariff trade barriers[6] and growth of regulations on businesses and investments (especially in the USA).

From national and political points of view, trade and globalization have in some countries contributed to an awareness that global and free markets may be "double-edged": for one increasing exports, the other decreasing imports; for one increasing employment, the other may also be losing jobs; for greater global wealth, greater social and economic inequalities may ensue. Further, in a globalized world, with greater and homogeneous industrial and technological capacities, increasingly competitive exchanges and gated economies may have altered the fundamental and conventional assumptions that have defined open economies and free trade as well as their contribution to the national common good. In such an environment, economics and finance are increasingly assessed from social and political perspectives: trade, economic specialization, global industrial services, and technology-intensive and in (some cases stealth) financial services. These are both challenging with new opportunities and new risks. These issues are attended to below based on simple models to highlight the intricate complexity that global trade and globalization are confronted by. Financial and risk perspectives based on utility and fundamental financial and pricing models are used (see also Chapters 4 and 5 for macroeconomic models).

---

5 http://globalization.kof.ethz.ch/.

6 According to International Classification of Non-tariff Measures by UNCTAD (2015: 2–3), non-tariff trade barriers include "technical measures, such as sanitary or environmental protection measures, as well as others traditionally used as instruments of commercial policy, e.g. quotas, price control, exports restrictions, or contingent trade protective measures, and also other behind-the-border measures, such as competition, trade-related investment measures, government procurement or distribution restrictions."

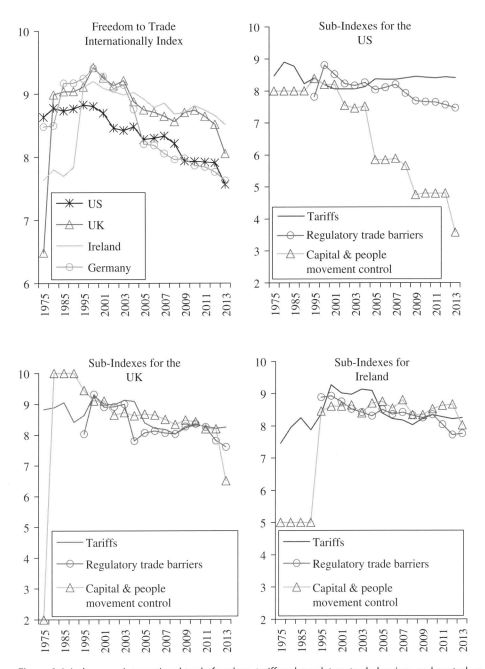

Figure 9.4 Indexes on international trade freedom, tariff and regulatory trade barriers, and control on capital and people movements. *Source:* Data from The Economic Freedom of the World: 2015 Annual Report by Gwartney *et al.* 2015.

Measurement of globalization and trade is thus based on extensive macroeconomic statistical data and socioeconomic and financial indexes. For example, the human development index (HDI) is a measure of health, education, and income, reported by the United Nations Development Programme (UNDP) (which reports numerous other statistics and indexes). Its measures provide social developments as to whether globalization is expanding or receding. For example, UNDP (2015) highlights a major progress in human development and living standards. This is important for both geopolitical and economic reasons. HDI indicators such as life expectancy at birth, mean years and expected years of schooling, and gross national income (GNI) per capita (all important for prospective importers and exporters) also provide a ranking of countries in a globalized world. In 2014, the top 10 countries in HDI-based ranking were Norway, Australia, Switzerland, Denmark, Netherlands, Germany, Ireland, the USA, Canada, and New Zealand. In terms of regional ranking, HDI is the highest for Latin America and the Caribbean (0.75) and Europe and Central Asia (0.75), followed by East Asia and the Pacific (0.71), Arab states (0.69), South Asia (0.61), and the lowest for sub-Saharan Africa (0.52) (see UNDP (2015)). Whether globalization improves and equalizes these and other countries is presumed to be reflected in the evolution of HDIs. A large number of institutions and agencies—for example, the United Nations, the World Bank, the IMF, and the Organisation for Economic Co-operation and Development (OECD)—provide additional and abundant data sources that pertain to trade and its effects on globalization. The OECD, for example, defines the degree of globalization in terms of FDI and investment flows, aggregate trade, countries' R&D, activities of multinationals, and internationalization of technology. These data complement macroeconomic data provided by both international institutions and countries' national statistical agencies. For financial markets trading in stocks, commodities, and goods and their derivatives, the trades that are made are set in prices in all currencies. As a result, assets and their terms of exchange across national boundaries are also priced and contribute to setting FX rates between countries. Such markets, together with bond markets, are the largest and most liquid financial markets. These statistics and indexes provide the foundations for testing and estimation of trade models.

HDIs are of course part of the extensive databases regarding globalization. Figure 9.3, for example, points to an increasing trend in the KOF index trade volume for all the regions (defined in terms of total merchandise traded, priced for exports and imports in current US dollars). In such a case, the mutual and increasing trends in HDIs and KOF trade indexes may indicate the correlation of both social improvements and global trade. A rapid trade growth in emerging and developing economies, in particular Asia, observed since the 1970s with its opening up to global trade would therefore suggest that it was concurrent with a social development. These developments are also prevalent in China surpassing the USA as the world's largest goods trading country in 2012 (measured by total trade). Further, the expansion of trade in developing economies, as manifested in their accounting of the share in world trade (merchandise exports and imports), almost doubled from 23% in 1990 to 44% in 2015, attesting to a growing economic globalization. This is calculated using the United Nations Conference on Trade and Development (UNCTAD) statistics and shown in Table 9.1 with an increasing share of trade of developing economies (dominated by Asian countries) in world trade compared with a decreasing share of developed economies' trade since 1990.

As WTO members, individual countries are committed to reduce customs tariffs. According to the World Bank,[7] the world average applied tariff rate that was almost at 10% in the late 1990s dropped to less than 7% in the 2010s. Similarly, the EU tariff rate was cut from 6% in 1995 to only 2% in 2015. Related observations illustrated in

---

7 http://databank.worldbank.org/data/home.aspx.

Table 9.1 Evolution of trade shares of developed, developing, and transition economies.

	Share in world trade (%)											
	1990	1995	2000	2005	2010	2011	2012	2013	2014	2015	2016
Developed economies	73	70	66	61	54	53	51	51	51	52	53
Transition economies	3	2	2	3	4	4	4	4	4	3	3
Developing economies	24	28	32	36	42	42	43	45	45	45	44
Developing Africa	3	2	2	3	3	3	4	3	3	2	2
Developing America	4	4	6	6	6	6	6	6	6	6	6
Developing Asia	17	21	24	28	33	34	35	35	36	37	36

Source: Data from UNCTAD.

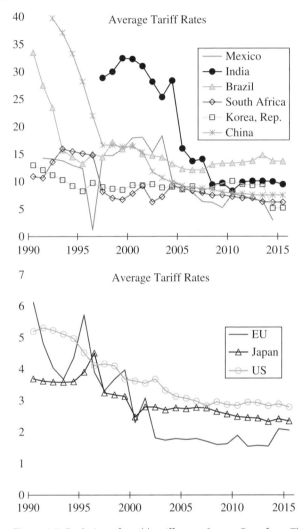

Figure 9.5 Evolution of world tariff rates. *Source:* Data from The World Bank.

Figure 9.5 attest to a decline in tariff barriers through a fall of average tariff rates in almost all countries, which in turn encourages more trade. For example, since the implementation of the North American Free Trade Agreement in 1994, trade between the countries covered has surged. According to IMF (2017) data for US merchandise trade with Mexico, imports stood at $41 billion in 1993 and $294 billion in 2016, while exports were $42 billion in 1993 and $231 billion in 2016, with widening trade deficits (at the same time, raising concerns in the USA of the migration of US jobs to Mexico). A pronouncement by President Trump following his election in 2016 has raised some concerns regarding the NAFTA agreements and trade agreements in general. As a result, free-trade deals are being challenged by politicians, labor unions, and environmental groups opposing these deals due to their potential effects on wages, labor standards, income inequality, and environmental standards. These concerns generate, in their wake, gating policies applied by all sovereign states to protect their national interests.

In the following, we shall consider specific models that are based on the modeling approaches we have developed in Chapters 2, 3, 7, and 8.

9.3 Strategic Trade and Gating

9.3.1 Strategic Trade

In the 1980s, a strategic approach to trade, relaxing the assumption of unhindered competing firms and economies, was advanced by Brander and Spencer (1985). Their approach suggested that trade occurs in imperfect (competition) markets. Models were based on monopolistic competition and oligopoly and expanded in a number of papers published between 1983 and 1995.[8] The assumptions of these models are:

- Each firm maximizes its profit independently and reaches its production (or pricing) decision independently.
- Firms are too small to affect the market as a whole (an assumption increasingly challenged by the scale and the power of A-National enterprises).
- Firms enter and leave markets due to new technologies, costs, regulations, and new profit opportunities or losses. In a dynamic, free, and global economy, monopoly profits are thus not sustainable. In other words, when firms' profit margins increase, the number of entering competing firms increases, leading to price fluctuations converging to an equilibrium price.
- Equilibrium is reached when marginal profits are null.

Oligopoly models based on an incongruence of firms' agendas have been recognized as another element in trade to be concerned with (Brander and Spencer, 1985). In this context, entry barriers to trade, a finite number of competing firms, each of which can affect the market mechanism, the supply and price of goods, and trade have provided a renewed justification to a strategic trade policy in favor of domestic champions. These include a broad set of policy tools such as export incentives that engineer a competitive advantage and concurrent with economic political agendas. Tools such as tax repression on imports and direct and indirect barriers to trade are being used to augment domestic jobs and sovereign states' revenues. The consequences of such policies are usually complex and require fine tuning as they tend to have unintended outcomes and can favor some at the expense of others. For these reasons, numerous advocacy groups lobbying for or against a policy usually financed by interest groups, to influence representatives to support or hinder particular aspects of a trade policy. These trends have reinforced further the power of large and well-endowed firms and industries and have thus become essential parties in the processes of globalization and gating.

Technically, trade policies, pitting one set of interests against another, have led to gaming models. Different situations arise when specific economic goals are pursued. Collie and De Meza (2003: 279) summarized that:

> According to de De Meza (1986), countries with the lowest production costs choose the highest export subsidies. The principle involved is that since the

---

8 In particular, see the surveys in the *Handbook of International Economics*, the second volume edited by Jones and Kenen (2003) and the third volume edited by Grossman and Rogoff (2003).

motivation to subsidize is to shift profits to home firms, the location with the most profitable firms (i.e. country where costs are the lowest) will set the highest subsidies.

Extensions and developments of this approach are numerous and include, among others, those by Neary (1994) and Collie and De Meza (2003). Similarly, as already stated, some sovereign states support their home industries by taxing imports to establish a source of government revenues and to protect local industries.

The strategic approach to trade is thus a departure from a "laissez faire trade policy" and a counter-globalization policy. Morasch (2000) points out that "strategic trade theory" alters the behavior of oligopolistic firms in international markets, challenging governments to implement such policies to appropriate rents. For example, a policy to tax foreign revenues leads firms to maintain their revenues in foreign lands where profits are stealth and nontaxable. As a result, these firms accumulate economic and financial foreign bases that alter their own character from domestic to A-National firms (as discussed previously). In the USA, this situation leads, in some extreme cases, to firms shifting their industrial might to foreign countries while maintaining their marketing and consumer bases in the USA. Apple Inc. and the inversion policy (countered by new US legalities) used by a number of pharmaceutical companies are such blatant cases. For example, to curb tax avoidance and promote fair competitive posture among firms, sovereign states have been examining foreign companies' tax practices. Some companies were scrutinized in the USA, France, the UK, and Italy, including Google Inc., Amazon.com Inc., Microsoft Corp., and Hewlett-Packard Co. (see Bloomberg (2014)). One of the formal investigations by the European Commission (EC) within EU member states inquired about the US companies' tax deals of firms such as Apple Inc., Fiat SpA, and Starbucks Corp. in Ireland, Luxembourg, and the Netherlands respectively. Such a scrutiny examined whether these firms received "illegal aid by governments," also referred to as "state aid" (see WSJ (2014)).[9] The EU estimates that the tax evasion costs annual losses (potential tax revenues) of €1 trillion.[10] By the same token, corporate relocation, also called corporate inversion, has captured broad attention in particular in the USA with accelerating inversion deals. This occurs through reincorporation, where the large corporation merges with a small company overseas where there is a lower corporate tax (e.g., Ireland). According to NYT (2014), 22 companies have announced inversions since 2011, with completed deals of around $76 billion. Data in this New York Times article refers to Thomson Reuters. Since then, measures have been taken to slow the rate of inversion, and in some cases to render inversion extremely costly for firms to do so. For example, US pharmaceutical company AbbVie abandoned the $54 billion merger deal with Irish company Shire in 2014.

To assess trade policies in such a strategic environment, games can provide cursory means to evaluate strategic alliances based on collaborative game solutions or contribute to evasive policies of control (see Eaton and Grossman (1986)). Morasch (2000: 38), for example, states that problems that sovereign states' policy-makers face include:

---

9 For details, see EC (2014).
10 See European Parliament (2013).

(i) Governments lack relevant information about firms and markets and thus do not know whether to impose a subsidy or a tax. (ii) Social costs of public funds may yield a negative net welfare effect of the policy. (iii) Since strategic trade policy usually has adverse effects on foreign countries, foreign governments may retaliate which leads to a prisoners' dilemma.

Despite their limitations, these policies remain important to control trade selectively. For example, in the 1990s, France sought to limit the import of Japanese electronic goods by subjecting them to a very tight quality control with one person allocated to test incoming imports from Japan. Similarly, Holland may stifle new and efficient balance technologies by submitting them to controls for over a year (some say to allow their domestic champion to test and develop a competing balance to the new and technologically more advanced balance). Not least, western Europe was in the not too distant past stifling finished product competition from African countries by a broad set of regulations, keeping Africa as exclusive raw material exporters, and so on. International trade is replete with "unfair" policies designed to protect domestic firms, on the one hand, and to provide an international competitive advantage to its firms on the other hand (see Neary (1994)).

The pursuit of strategic policies (fiscal or financial) is not new. At a macroeconomic level, some sovereign states have also turned to currency wars, with FX rates manipulated to provide a "blanket" trade advantage to its domestic champions. In other cases, export subsidies are implied in insurance of foreign trade transactions as well as loans and financial advantages to the exporting firm. These policies may collide. For example, a currency policy to support exports can also lead to domestic market inefficiencies by contributing to inflationary and employment dependence on foreign demand. Globalization has revealed that trade, based on the demand from foreign consumers, need not be robust and therefore can in some cases be counter-productive. For example, China has overtly sought to maintain an FX rate to keep a foreign competitive advantage, but has also faced greater dependence on foreign demand (therefore rendering China's domestic economy to be dependent on foreign wants). Similarly, the USA (as well as Europe) provides direct and indirect subsidies to maintain big-item industries (such as Boeing and Airbus) as a focus of its trade policy while remaining idle in confronting the outsourcing of its industrial infrastructure. These are some partial examples among many others pointing out that strategic actions or inactions by sovereign states are far more the rule than the exception. These elements alter both the economic modeling of trade and the policy models sovereign states use to support selectively and hinder trade.

9.3.2 Trade Models

Trade models are varied, extensively studied, and have changed over time with the evolution of globalization, economic and industrial enterprises, financial markets, and sovereign policies. These models are, therefore, a priori complex. Fundamental references to such models include Ricardo (1817), Dixit and Norman (1980), Dixit (1984, 1987), Johnson (1953), Leontief (1953), Balassa (1967), Gros (1987), Krugman (1979, 1980, 1981, 1990), Helpman and Krugman (1985), Park (2000), Samuelson (2001), Opp (2010), and Gandolfo (2014), and many others. For example, Dixit (1987) brought attention to the microeconomic and competitive aspects of trade (and therefore strategic exchanges between firms). Johnson (1953) raised the issue of retaliation and its implications for game theory based on models for collaboration, competition, and currency wars—see Nash (1950), Gros (1987), Opp, (2010), and Gould and Woodbridge (1998). Park (2000) analyzes trade agreements between small and large countries and their effects on the efficient frontier of self-enforcing agreements (and hence the negotiation outcomes).

The Krugman model of monopolistic competition emphasizes the importance of the economies of scale for trade and shows that "trade, and gains from trade, will occur, even between countries with identical tastes, technology, and factor endowments" (Krugman, 1979: 469). In addition, products differentiation was incorporated in Krugman (1980). Further, an empirical relationship between intra-industry specialization and trade, in particular "trade among similar countries, of two-way trade in similar products," was explained in Krugman (1981: 960) using empirical and theoretical research indicating that "the index of intra-industry trade equal to the index of similarity in factor proportions." The strategic trade policy and its empirical studies are presented in a book edited by Krugman and Smith (1994). In addition, a large number of books, such as Obstfeld and Rogoff (1996) and Gandolfo (2014), have summarized both past contributions and the effects of incentives on trade. Brander and Spencer in a series of seminal papers expanded these studies to Cournot models for trade and therefore contributed to a strategic approach to trade models. Exports–imports to a country are then determined by simultaneous country prices (determined by their dependent inverse demand functions) and by the countries' supply-side economics (an approach we shall consider later). Industry-wide approaches to trade have subsequently been devised to explain some elements and factors that determine the evolution of trade and the important role of FX rates and their manipulation in managing trade advantages.

The multiple approaches to trade highlight the economic and political contradictions that trade generate in a global world. Some seeking to pay lower prices for goods, but having to contend with a migration of jobs and capital to foreign countries and vice versa. Trade, therefore, has many lessons to contend with. The models we shall be concerned with will highlight some of these elements as well as the implications of trade.

As technology and capital migrate from country to country, the balance of comparative advantages will also shift. Empirically, trade models have focused on two broad themes.

- One approach seeks to explain the terms of trade (i.e., the quantitative relative prices of exports and imports): (1) examine how prices are affected by changes by factor supplies or technology as well as the effects of national policies on trade (such as tariffs, macroeconomic variables, jobs); (2) determining exchange rates, and balance of payments resulting from trade patterns.
- Another approach is more qualitative and is concerned with the patterns of trade (products) between countries.

These approaches are essentially macroeconomic and were discussed in Chapters 4, and 5.

9.4 A Multi-Country Utility of Financial Consumption

Financial decisions are based on wealth, money, currencies, and many assets that are priced and traded. Priced consumption requires financial commitments to buy (for consumers) and to sell (for suppliers). In a multi-country and aggregate environment, these decisions are differentiated by:

1) global world prices, and sovereign state prices set by multiple factors relative to the global price;
2) a distinction between what a country can and will dispose to pay for consumption;
3) a disposable wealth to consume now and invest for future consumption and risk preferences;
4) a competitive or collaborative environment between countries as well as their financial regulation defining a geopolitical financial environment.

For convenience, we maintain a utility rationale. Consumption defined by consumers' utility defining the price they are willing to pay for consumption and the price they actually pay for consumption based on suppliers' and markets' economic interests and costs. Further, although the financial models we construct are essentially n-person games and potentially infinite (see Aumann (1964)), we reduce our models to be of the Cournot type reduced to n games of two persons each. These simplifications will provide tractable financial and game models which we believe also define the trading environment; namely, all being—one against all. The treatment we consider next expands on our results in Chapter 3 and includes examples and simplifications to obtain tractable results.

9.4.1 A One-Period Utility Model: The Consumption Demand Side

Assume that wealth commitments to consumption are heterogeneous and let a sovereign state k compete globally for consumption by allocating W_0^k in a global or reference currency (for the moment we ignore FX rates). The price being necessarily dependent on other parties' allocations is necessarily a random function $\tilde{\pi}_0^k\left(\tilde{C}^G\right)$ of aggregate demand $\tilde{C}^G$, a priori unknown. The net utility of consumption for an individual sovereign k is defined by maximizing $u_0^k(c_0^k) - \tilde{\pi}_0^k c_0^k$, where $\tilde{\pi}_0^k(c_0^k)$ defines the price of consumption the sovereign state would be willing to pay which equals its marginal utility $\tilde{\pi}_0^k(c_0^k) = \partial u_0^k(c_0^k)/\partial c_0^k$, a function of consumption c_0^k. In a multi-country model, the price of consumption in a sovereign state is a function of the aggregate demand for consumption, which is $\tilde{\pi}_0^K\left(\tilde{C}^G\right)$. Consumption of sovereign k is then defined by its marginal utility set at a price $\tilde{\pi}_0^K\left(\tilde{C}^G\right)$ the sovereign will pay; that is, a solution of $\tilde{\pi}_0^K\left(\tilde{C}^G\right) = \partial u_0^k(c_0^K)/\partial c_0^K$ defines the consumption of sovereign k. Assume a unique price $\tilde{\pi}_0\left(\tilde{C}^G\right)$ (i.e., the price of consumption imports available to all sovereign states in the same currency), then the ratio of prices $\tilde{\pi}_0\left(\tilde{C}^G\right)/\tilde{\pi}_0^K(c_0^k)$ defines what the consumer will pay in a sovereign state k relative to the price they would pay had its consumption level been optimal (i.e., maximizing its net utility of consumption). For example, paying \$2.30 per gallon for gasoline relative to the \$1.30 price defined by a consumption optimal utility. This ratio is greater than unity as it may include additional costs, such as logistic and tariffs costs imposed on imports as well as a price to a competing global demand for consumption. Alternatively, aggregate demand reduces the global consumption price, and then $\tilde{\pi}_0\left(\tilde{C}^G\right) < \tilde{\pi}_0^k(c_0^k)$ in which case sovereign k would be induced to consume more.

In this case, imports from a global supply source depend on its price and the sovereign utility marginal utility of consumption. This approach to a financialization of consumption thus indicates that consumption is defined by the global price of consumption while imports are defined by the differences inherent in the sovereign marginal utility set at the global price and its optimal marginal utility consumption.

The price, consumption, and trade relationships we may outline are partial, neglecting many factors that account for prices and trade. Nonetheless, they point to one of the essential questions that sovereign states are confronted by in an era of globalization. Namely, provide consumption at the least price through imports, control consumption through tariffs and taxation, loss of domestic jobs, and so on. Or, inversely, gate imports, prevent imports and provide incentives for domestic suppliers.

9.4.2 A One-Period Utility Model: The Supply Side

We consider again the simple demand model $u_0^D \left(c_0^D \right) - \tilde{\pi}_0^D c_0^D$ (note that the price of consumption is random), where we set $c_0^D = S_0^D + S_0^{FD}$ with S_0^D as a domestic supply and S_0^{FD} defines imports from a foreign country. Similarly, $c_0^F = S_0^F + S_0^{DF}$. Furthermore, we set the domestic price to be a function of global supply, or $\tilde{\pi}_0^D \left(S_0^{DD} + S_0^{FF} \right)$, given by $S_0^{DD} = S_0^D + S_0^{DF}$ and $S_0^{FF} = S_0^F + S_0^{FD}$. The intent of this problem is to highlight some basic relationships defining the propensity to import and export. In our approach, imports from a foreign country (which are exports for such a country) are set by the domestic country, and vice versa. For simplicity, we assume that each supplier measures its profits and costs in its local currency. Further, we also assume that prices are set by suppliers in their currency and defined by equilibrium price equal to the marginal cost of the supplier. For a domestic supplier, for example, total consumption and supply, c_0^D and S_0^{DD}, are inclusive, as already stated, of the domestic imports (increasing consumption) and exports (increasing supply). For a domestic supplier, the following problem is defined, where the price in the domestic country is a function of the aggregate supply:

$$\underset{S_0^{DD}}{\text{Max}} \prod_0^{DD} = S_0^{DD} \tilde{\pi}_0^D \left(S_0^{DD} + S_0^{FF} \right) - C_0^{DD} \left(S_0^{DD} \right), \quad S_0^{DD} = S_0^D + S_0^{DF}$$

Therefore:

$$\frac{\partial \prod_0^{DD}}{\partial S_0^{DD}} = 0 \quad \text{or} \quad \tilde{\pi}_0^D \left(S_0^{DD} + S_0^{FF} \right) + S_0^{DD} \frac{\partial \tilde{\pi}_0^D}{\partial S_0^{DD}} = \frac{\partial C_0^{DD}}{\partial S_0^{DD}}$$

And by symmetry we have

$$\tilde{\pi}_0^F \left(S_0^{DD} + S_0^{FF} \right) + S_0^{FF} \frac{\partial \tilde{\pi}_0^F}{\partial S_0^{FF}} = \frac{\partial C_0^{FF}}{\partial S_0^{FF}}$$

Since $c_0^D = S_0^D + S_0^{FD}$ and $c_0^F = S_0^F + S_0^{DF}$, the demand for consumption and the price each will be willing to pay are defined by the utility of consumption, $U_0^D = u_0^D \left(c_0^D \right) - c_0^D \tilde{\pi}_0^D \left(c_0^D + c_0^F \right)$, where total supply equals total consumption, $S_0^{DD} + S_0^{FF} = c_0^D + c_0^F$. As a result:

$$\frac{\partial u_0^D\left(c_0^D\right)}{\partial c_0^D} = \pi_0^D\left(c_0^D + c_0^F\right) + c_0^D \frac{\partial \pi_0^D\left(c_0^D + c_0^F\right)}{c_0^D}$$

Thus, noting that $\pi_0^D\left(c_0^D + c_0^F\right) = \pi_0^D\left(S_0^{DD} + S_0^{FF}\right)$ and $\partial \tilde{\pi}_0^D / \partial S_0^{DD} = \partial \pi_0^D / \partial c_0^D$, the following system of equations results:

$$\tilde{\pi}_0^D + \left(S_0^D + S_0^{DF}\right)\frac{\partial \tilde{\pi}_0^D}{\partial S_0^{DD}} = \frac{\partial C_0^{DD}}{\partial S_0^{DD}}, \quad S_0^{DD} = S_0^D + S_0^{DF}; \quad \pi_0^D + \left(S_0^D + S_0^{FD}\right)\frac{\partial \tilde{\pi}_0^D}{\partial S_0^{DD}} = \frac{\partial u_0^D\left(c_0^D\right)}{\partial c_0^D}$$

Solving these two equations, we have

$$\tilde{\pi}_0^D = \frac{\partial u_0^D\left(c_0^D\right)}{\partial c_0^D}\left(\frac{S_0^D + S_0^{DF}}{S_0^{DF} - S_0^{FD}}\right) - \frac{\partial C_0^{DD}}{\partial S_0^{DD}}\left(\frac{S_0^D + S_0^{FD}}{S_0^{DF} - S_0^{FD}}\right);$$

$$\frac{\partial \tilde{\pi}_0^D}{\partial S_0^{DD}} = \frac{1}{S_0^{DF} - S_0^{FD}}\left(\frac{\partial C_0^{DD}}{\partial S_0^{DD}} - \frac{\partial u_0^D\left(c_0^D\right)}{\partial c_0^D}\right)$$

By symmetry, in the foreign country it is

$$\pi_0^F = \frac{\partial u_0^F\left(c_0^F\right)}{\partial c_0^F}\left(\frac{S_0^F + S_0^{FD}}{S_0^{FD} - S_0^{DF}}\right) - \frac{\partial C_0^{FF}}{\partial S_0^{FF}}\left(\frac{S_0^F + S_0^{DF}}{S_0^{FD} - S_0^{DF}}\right);$$

$$\frac{\partial \tilde{\pi}_0^F}{\partial S_0^{FF}} = \frac{1}{S_0^{FD} - S_0^{DF}}\left(\frac{\partial C_0^F}{\partial S_0^{FF}} - \frac{\partial u_0^F\left(c_0^F\right)}{\partial c_0^F}\right)$$

Assuming a PPP, and the FX as a function of trade, the marginal utilities of consumption, and the marginal costs of supply are given by

$$\xi_0^{DF} = \frac{\pi_0^D}{\pi_0^F} = \frac{\dfrac{\partial u_0^D\left(c_0^D\right)}{\partial c_0^D}\left(\dfrac{S_0^D + S_0^{DF}}{S_0^{DF} - S_0^{FD}}\right) - \dfrac{\partial C_0^{DD}}{\partial S_0^{DD}}\left(\dfrac{S_0^D + S_0^{FD}}{S_0^{DF} - S_0^{FD}}\right)}{\dfrac{\partial u_0^F\left(c_0^F\right)}{\partial c_0^F}\left(\dfrac{S_0^F + S_0^{FD}}{S_0^{FD} - S_0^{DF}}\right) - \dfrac{\partial C_0^{FF}}{\partial S_0^{FF}}\left(\dfrac{S_0^F + S_0^{DF}}{S_0^{FD} - S_0^{DF}}\right)}$$

Further elementary manipulations yield

$$\frac{\partial \tilde{\pi}_0^D}{\partial S_0^{DD}} = \frac{\partial}{\partial S_0^{DD}}\left[\left(\frac{\partial u_0^D\left(c_0^D\right)}{\partial c_0^D} - \frac{\partial C_0^{DD}}{\partial S_0^{DD}}\right)\left(\frac{S_0^{DD}}{S_0^{DF} - S_0^{FD}}\right) + \frac{\partial C_0^{DD}}{\partial S_0^{DD}}\right]$$

$$= \frac{1}{S_0^{DF} - S_0^{FD}}\left(\frac{\partial C_0^{DD}}{\partial S_0^{DD}} - \frac{\partial u_0^D\left(c_0^D\right)}{\partial c_0^D}\right)$$

Or

$$S_0^{DD}\frac{\partial}{\partial S_0^{DD}}\left(\frac{\partial u_0^D\left(c_0^D\right)}{\partial c_0^D} - \frac{\partial C_0^{DD}}{\partial S_0^{DD}}\right) + \frac{\partial^2 C_0^{DD}}{\partial\left(S_0^{DD}\right)^2}\left(S_0^{DF} - S_0^{FD}\right) = -2\left(\frac{\partial u_0^D\left(c_0^D\right)}{\partial c_0^D} - \frac{\partial C_0^{DD}}{\partial S_0^{DD}}\right)$$

And by symmetry we have

$$
S_0^{FF} \frac{\partial}{\partial S_0^{FF}} \left(\frac{\partial u_0^F(c_0^F)}{\partial c_0^F} - \frac{\partial C_0^{FF}}{\partial S_0^{FF}} \right) + \frac{\partial^2 C_0^{FF}}{\partial (S_0^{FF})^2} \left(S_0^{FD} - S_0^{DF} \right) = -2 \left(\frac{\partial u_0^F(c_0^F)}{\partial c_0^F} - \frac{\partial C_0^{FF}}{\partial S_0^{FF}} \right)
$$

A number of special cases arise. Suppose that exports and imports are equal (i.e., $S_0^{FD} = S_0^{DF}$) and let

$$
\frac{\partial}{\partial S_0^{DD}} \ln \left(\frac{\partial u_0^D(c_0^D)}{\partial c_0^D} - \frac{\partial C_0^{DD}}{\partial S_0^{DD}} \right) = -\frac{2}{S_0^{DD}} \quad \text{or} \quad \ln \left(\frac{\partial u_0^D(c_0^D)}{\partial c_0^D} - \frac{\partial C_0^{DD}}{\partial S_0^{DD}} \right)
$$

$$
= -2 \int_1^{S_0^{DD}} \frac{dx}{x} = \ln \left(S_0^{DD} \right)^{-2}
$$

And therefore (by symmetry) we have

$$
\frac{\partial u_0^D(c_0^D)}{\partial c_0^D} - \frac{\partial C_0^{DD}}{\partial S_0^{DD}} = e^{-2\ln(S_0^{DD})} \quad \text{and} \quad \frac{\partial u_0^F(c_0^F)}{\partial c_0^F} - \frac{\partial C_0^{FF}}{\partial S_0^{FF}} = e^{-2\ln(S_0^{FF})}
$$

In other words, the net marginal utility of consumption and its marginal cost of production are equal when the volume produced is extremely large. Namely, size matters, since

$$
\frac{\partial u_0^D(c_0^D)}{\partial c_0^D} = \frac{\partial C_0^{DD}}{\partial S_0^{DD}} \quad \text{if } S_0^{DD} \to +\infty \quad \text{(as well as for the foreign party)}
$$

When the supply volume of one or both parties is relatively smaller, then the willingness to pay for consumption (i.e., the marginal utility of consumption) is greater than the marginal costs of production (the least price to pay for consumption) since

$$
\frac{\partial u_0^D(c_0^D)}{\partial c_0^D} > \frac{\partial C_0^{DD}}{\partial S_0^{DD}}
$$

with their difference increasing the smaller the supply. This abbreviation has an implication for globalization, since with increasing supply (at the global level) the price that consumers pay will be increasingly smaller due to the increased efficiency arising from the smaller difference between the marginal utility of consumption and the marginal production cost (itself increasingly small due to supplies' economies of scale). When imports and exports are asymmetric, we note that this relationship is perturbed by the second derivative of supply costs.

Similarly, we note that the relative prices of consumption are important. Namely, allowing elementary manipulations, we have

$$
\xi_0^{DF} = \frac{\dfrac{\partial C_0^{DD}}{\partial S_0^{DD}} + \left(\dfrac{\partial u_0^D(c_0^D)}{\partial c_0^D} - \dfrac{\partial C_0^{DD}}{\partial S_0^{DD}} \right) \left(\dfrac{S_0^{DD}}{S_0^{DF} - S_0^{FD}} \right)}{\dfrac{\partial C_0^{FF}}{\partial S_0^{FF}} - \left(\dfrac{\partial u_0^F(c_0^F)}{\partial c_0^F} - \dfrac{\partial C_0^{FF}}{\partial S_0^{FF}} \right) \left(\dfrac{S_0^{FF}}{S_0^{FD} - S_0^{DF}} \right)} > 0
$$

Let $0 < E_0^D = \left(S_0^{DF} - S_0^{FD}\right)/S^{DD}$ be a positive export balance for the domestic party, per unit, produced by the domestic supplier and $E_0^F < 0$. Further, we set the domestic marginal utility and marginal consumption MU_0^D and MC_0^D respectively:

$$MU_0^D = \frac{\partial u_0^D\left(c_0^D\right)}{\partial c_0^D} \quad \text{and} \quad MC_0^D = \frac{\partial C_0^{DD}}{\partial S_0^{DD}}$$

then the FX is

$$\xi_0^{DF} = \frac{E_0^F}{E_0^D}\left[\frac{MU_0^D - \left(1 - E_0^D\right)MC_0^D}{MU_0^F - \left(1 - E_0^F\right)MC_0^F}\right] > 0$$

Suppose that the domestic party is a net exporter to the foreign party. Then $0 < E_0^D$ and $E_0^F = -E^D < 0$ and

$$\frac{MU_0^D - \left(1 - E_0^D\right)MC_0^D}{E_0^D} > 0 \quad \text{and} \quad MU_0^D > \left(1 - E_0^D\right)MC_0^D$$

$$\frac{\left(1 + E_0^D\right)MC_0^F - MU_0^F}{E_0^D} > 0 \quad \text{and} \quad MU_0^F < \left(1 + E_0^D\right)MC_0^F$$

$$\text{and} \quad \xi_{DF} = \frac{MU_0^D - \left(1 - E_0^D\right)MC_0^D}{\left(1 + E_0^D\right)MC_0^F - MU_0^F}$$

As a result, we have

$$E_0^D = \frac{\left(MU_0^D - MC_0^D\right) - \xi_{DF}\left(MU_0^F - MC_0^F\right)}{\xi_{DF}MC_0^F - MC_0^D}$$

And therefore the propensity to export (i.e., at the request of the foreign country demand for imports) is a function of the marginal profit $MP_0^D = MU_0^D - MC_0^D$ less that of the foreign country (accounting for its FX rate) divided by the FX-adjusted differences in marginal costs of production. Further, it is easy to verify that $\partial \xi_{DF}/\partial E_0^D > 0$, and therefore the propensity to export by D leads as well to an increase in its FX rate. In other words, an increase in exports by China ought to be associated with an increase in the price of the yuan. In other words, for an exporter (say China) its marginal utility is greater than the marginal production cost, whereas for the foreign party (say the USA) the marginal utility of consumption is smaller than the marginal cost of production. And as the exports increase, the FX, the price of the foreign currency in its local currency, increases as well if

$$\frac{\partial \xi_0^{DF}}{\partial E_0^D} > 0 \quad \text{if} \quad MC_0^D < \frac{1}{2}MU_0^F\left(\frac{MU_0^D}{MU_0^F} + \frac{MC_0^D}{MC_0^F}\right)$$

An inverse conclusion is reached if

$$\frac{\partial \xi_0^{DF}}{\partial E_0^D} < 0 \quad \text{if} \quad MC_0^D > \frac{1}{2}MU_0^F\left(\frac{MU_0^D}{MU_0^F} + \frac{MC_0^D}{MC_0^F}\right) \qquad \xi_0^{DF} := \frac{\dfrac{\partial u_0^D\left(c_0^D\right)}{\partial c_0^D} - \dfrac{\partial C_0^{DD}}{\partial S_0^{DD}}S_0^{DD}}{\dfrac{\partial C_0^{FF}}{\partial S_0^{FF}} - \dfrac{\partial u_0^F\left(c_0^F\right)}{\partial c_0^F}S_0^{FF}}$$

9.4.3 A One-Period Financialized Utility Cournot Model

Let W_0^k be the wealth of a sovereign state expended on consumption. Wealth-endowed countries with a large population commit greater wealth to consumption while others commit less. In this case, the utility of consumption and the policies associated with consumption are financial. The net utility of financial consumption for a consumption party k is

$$\underset{W_0^k}{\text{Max}}\, u_0^k\left(\frac{W_0^k}{\pi_0^k}\right) - W_0^k \quad \text{and} \quad \frac{\partial u_0^k}{\partial c_0^k}\frac{\partial c_0^k}{\partial W_0^k} = 1 \quad \text{or} \quad \pi_0^k = \frac{\partial u_0^k}{\partial c_0^k}$$

In this section, we consider a one-period problem, meaning that a sovereign consumes all its wealth to current consumption, while in Section 9.4.4 we expand the financial consumption problem to two periods. In such a case, financial consumption is defined by both the price of aggregate demand and supply as well as by the financial savings and investment strategies of sovereign consumers. This problem is developed in detail in Tapiero (2014).

In a global environment with multiple sovereign consumers, prices are random as they depend on what each sovereign state will commit to consumption. Setting $\tilde{C}^G = \tilde{c}_0^k + \tilde{C}_0^{nk}$ to be the aggregate demand for consumption, with $\tilde{C}_0^{nk}$ the aggregate demand of other sovereign states, the optimal financial consumption of a sovereign state k is defined by "one sovereign k" gaming all other sovereign consumers "nk" (i.e., not k):

$$\underset{W_0^k}{\text{Max}}\, E u_0^k\left(\frac{W_0^k}{\tilde{\pi}_0^K\left(\tilde{c}_0^k + \tilde{C}_0^{nk}\right)}\right) - W_0^k \quad \text{and} \quad \frac{\partial u_0^k}{\partial c_0^k}\frac{\partial \tilde{c}_0^k}{\partial W_0^k} = 1$$

In this particular case:

$$\frac{\partial c_0^K}{\partial W_0^k} = \frac{1}{\tilde{\pi}_0^K\left(\tilde{c}_0^K + \tilde{C}_0^{nk}\right)} - \frac{W_0^k}{\left[\tilde{\pi}_0^K\left(\tilde{c}_0^K + \tilde{C}_0^{nk}\right)\right]^2}\frac{\partial \tilde{\pi}_0^K}{\partial \tilde{c}_0^k}\frac{\partial c_0^K}{\partial W_0^k}$$

And therefore

$$E\left(\frac{\partial u_0^k}{\partial c_0^k}\frac{\partial \tilde{c}_0^k}{\partial W_0^k}\right) = 1$$

is reduced to

$$E\frac{\partial u_0^k}{\partial c_0^K} = E\left(\tilde{\pi}_0^K\left(\tilde{c}_0^K + \tilde{C}_0^{nk}\right) + W_0^k\frac{\partial \ln \tilde{\pi}_0^K}{\partial \tilde{c}_0^K}\right)$$

As a result, the marginal utility of consumption is indeed the price of consumption plus a quantity proportional to the wealth committed to consumption, which reduces the price it will pay if the greater the consumption the smaller the price (this need not be always the case, however). Of course, if $\partial \tilde{\pi}_0^K/\partial \tilde{c}_0^K$ is negligible, all sovereign states will pay the same price adjusted per country to pay for tariffs and other transaction trade costs. When this is not the case, the wealth committed may increase or decrease the marginal utility of consumption (and thus the willingness to pay for consumption). For example, if an increase in demand for oil raises the global price of oil, the price of consumption that, say, sovereign state k will be willing to pay for consumption will increase the greater the wealth committed to consumption. Since all sovereign states are confronted with the same terms, the solution of the game that sovereign states are engaged in is given by the simultaneous solution of a system of equations given by (where we neglected the randomness implied in the consumption game that the sovereign states are in fact invested in)

$$\frac{\partial u_0^k}{\partial c_0^K} = \tilde{\pi}_0^K \left(\tilde{c}_0^K + \tilde{C}_0^G \right) + W_0^k \frac{\partial \ln \tilde{\pi}_0^K}{\partial \tilde{c}_0^K}, \quad K = 1, 2, \ldots, n, \quad \tilde{C}_0^G = \sum_{K=1}^{n} \tilde{c}_0^K$$

For example, for a world of two major and competing consumers, we have

$$\frac{\partial u_0^1}{\partial c_0^1} = \pi_0^1 \left(c_0^1 + c_0^2 \right) + W_0^1 \frac{\partial \ln \pi_0^1 \left(c_0^1 + c_0^2 \right)}{\partial c_0^1}$$

$$\frac{\partial u^2}{\partial c_0^2} = \pi_0^2 \left(c_0^1 + c_0^2 \right) + W_0^2 \frac{\partial \ln \pi_0^2 \left(c_0^1 + c_0^2 \right)}{\partial c_0^2}$$

Say that there is one price for consumption: $\pi_0 = \pi_0^1 = \pi_0^2$; since $\partial u^k / \partial c_0^k = \partial u^k / \partial C_0^G$, we have

$$\frac{W_0^1}{W_0^2} = \frac{\left(\partial u_0^1 / \partial C^G \right) - \pi_0}{\left(\partial u^2 / \partial C^G \right) - \pi_0}$$

In other words, the greater the wealth committed to consumption by a sovereign state, the greater the net benefit it derives from globalization of trade (i.e., paying the global price as every other state).

By including the supply side, results similar to those derived here lead to similar conclusions.

In the following, we consider a multi-period pricing case where consumption is financial; namely, consumption is defined by the allocation of financial resources to consumption rather than deciding how much to consume.

9.4.4 The Cournot Multi-Period Financial Consumption

The multi-period problem differs from the single period as consumption expenditures account for both current and future consumptions. Suppose that a sovereign state has wealth W_t^k and invests Λ_t^k for future consumption. Current financial consumption is then $W_t^k - \Lambda_t^k$, while savings are invested in a portfolio with rate of return $\tilde{R}_1^k \left(a_0^k \right)$ (with $0 \leq a_0^k \leq 1$ denoting the proportional investment in bonds at a known risk-free rate). The next period's wealth is then $W_{t+1}^k = \Lambda_t^k \left(1 + \tilde{R}_{t+1}^k \left(a_0^k \right) \right)$, $W_0^k > 0$. If the next period is an end period, where all invested savings are consumed, then current and future (random) consumptions are

$$W_t^k - \Lambda_t^k; \quad W_{t+1}^k = \Lambda_t^k \left(1 + \tilde{R}_{t+1}^k \left(a_t^k \right) \right), \quad W_0^k > 0$$

Consumption in both periods is random, however, since initially the price of consumption is random (as it depends on other consumers), while in the second period it depends on both a random disposable income and the price of consumption. In this case, consumption at both periods is given by

$$\tilde{c}_t^k = \frac{W_t^k - \Lambda_t^k}{\tilde{\pi}_t\left(\tilde{c}_t^k + \tilde{C}_t^{nk}\right)}$$

and at a final time $t + 1$ by

$$\tilde{c}_{t+1}^k = \frac{\tilde{W}_{t+1}^k}{\tilde{\pi}_{t+1}\left(\tilde{c}_{t+1}^k + \tilde{C}_{t+1}^{nk}\right)} = \frac{\Lambda_t^k\left(1 + \tilde{R}_{t+1}^k\left(a_t^k\right)\right)}{\tilde{\pi}_{t+1}\left(\tilde{c}_{t+1}^k + \tilde{C}_{t+1}^{nk}\right)}$$

Assuming, for simplicity, that in a global world all sovereign states pay the same price, the following game results with its stopping time at $t + 1$ when financial wealth is fully committed to consumption:

$$EU_t^k\left(W_t^k\right) = \operatorname*{Max}_{\Lambda_t^k, a_t^k} Eu_k\left(\frac{W_t^k - \Lambda_t^k}{\tilde{\pi}_t\left(\tilde{c}_t^k + \tilde{C}_t^{nk}\right)}\right) + \beta EU_{t+1}^k\left(\frac{\Lambda_t^k\left(1 + \tilde{R}_{t+1}^k\left(a_t^k\right)\right)}{\tilde{\pi}_{t+1}\left(\tilde{c}_{t+1}^k + \tilde{C}_{t+1}^{nk}\right)}\right), \quad W_0^k > 0$$

Considering a sovereign state k, we have the first-order condition

$$E\frac{\partial U_t^k\left(\tilde{c}_t^k\right)}{\partial c_t^k}\frac{\partial c_t^k}{\partial \Lambda_t^k} + \beta E\frac{\partial U_{t+1}^k\left(\tilde{c}_{t+1}^k\right)}{\partial c_{t+1}^k}\frac{\partial c_{t+1}^k}{\partial \Lambda_t^k} = 0$$

where

$$\frac{\partial c_t^k}{\partial \Lambda_t^k} = -\frac{1}{\tilde{\pi}_t + \left(W_t^k - \Lambda_t^k\right)\dfrac{\partial \ln \tilde{\pi}_t}{\partial c_t^k}} \quad \text{and} \quad \frac{\partial c_{t+1}^k}{\partial \Lambda_t^k} = \frac{1 + \tilde{R}_{t+1}^k\left(a_t^k\right)}{\tilde{\pi}_{t+1} + \Lambda_t^k\left(1 + \tilde{R}_{t+1}^k\left(a_t^k\right)\right)\dfrac{\partial \ln \tilde{\pi}_{t+1}}{\partial c_{t+1}^k}}$$

And therefore, the following pricing formula is obtained:

$$1 = \beta E\left\{M_{t+1}\frac{\left(1 + \tilde{R}_{t+1}^k\left(a_t^k\right)\right)\left[\tilde{\pi}_t + \left(W_t^k - \Lambda_t^k\right)\dfrac{\partial \ln \tilde{\pi}_t}{\partial c_t^k}\right]}{\tilde{\pi}_{t+1} + \Lambda_t^k\left(1 + \tilde{R}_{t+1}^k\left(a_t^k\right)\right)\dfrac{\partial \ln \tilde{\pi}_{t+1}}{\partial c_{t+1}^k}}\right\}$$

where

$$M_{t+1} = \frac{\partial U_{t+1}^k\left(\tilde{c}_{t+1}^k\right)/\partial c_{t+1}^k}{\partial U_t^k\left(\tilde{c}_t^k\right)/\partial c_t^k}$$

is a probability measure, defined as a ratio of future and current marginal utilities. Or following elementary manipulations, defining $1 + \tilde{\eta}_{t+1} = \tilde{\pi}_{t+1}/\tilde{\pi}_t$ as the ratio of the future to current price of consumption (i.e., the inflation rate), we have

$$1 = \beta E\left\{\frac{M_{t+1}}{1 + \tilde{\eta}_{t+1}}\left(\frac{\left(1 + \tilde{R}_{t+1}^k\left(a_t^k\right)\right)\left[\tilde{\pi}_t + \left(W_t^k - \Lambda_t^k\right)\dfrac{\partial \ln \tilde{\pi}_t}{\partial c_t^k}\right]}{\tilde{\pi}_t + \Lambda_t^k\left(1 + \tilde{R}_{t+1}^k\left(a_t^k\right)\right)\dfrac{\partial\left(1 + \tilde{\eta}_{t+1}\right)^{-1}}{\partial c_{t+1}^k}}\right)\right\}; \quad \tilde{\pi}_{t+1}/\tilde{\pi}_t = 1 + \tilde{\eta}_{t+1}$$

Of course, if there is no inflation, then $\tilde{\pi}_{t+1}/\tilde{\pi}_t \equiv 1$:

$$1 = \beta E \left\{ M_{t+1} \left(\frac{\left(1 + \tilde{R}^k_{t+1}(a^k_t)\right)\left[1 + \left(W^k_t - \Lambda^k_t\right)\frac{\partial \pi_t}{\pi_t^2 \partial c^k_t}\right]}{1 + \Lambda^k_t \left(1 + \tilde{R}^k_{t+1}(a^k_t)\right)\frac{1}{\pi_t^2}\frac{\partial \pi_t}{\partial c^k_{t+1}}} \right) \right\}; \quad \tilde{\pi}_{t+1}/\tilde{\pi}_t = 1$$

and

$$\left\{ \frac{\left(1 + R^f_{t+1}\right)\left[1 + \left(W^k_t - \Lambda^k_t\right)\frac{\partial \pi_t}{\pi_t^2 \partial c^k_t}\right]}{1 + \Lambda^k_t \left(1 + R^f_{t+1}\right)\frac{1}{\pi_t^2}\frac{\partial \pi_t}{\partial c^k_{t+1}}} \right\}^{-1} = \beta E\{M_{t+1}\}$$

And the pricing formula in case $\tilde{\pi}_{t+1}/\tilde{\pi}_t \equiv \pi_t$ is

$$1 = \frac{1}{1 + R^f_{t+1}} E^{M_{t+1}} \left\{ \frac{\left(1 + \tilde{R}^k_{t+1}(a^k_t)\right)\dfrac{\left[1 + \left(W^k_t - \Lambda^k_t\right)\frac{\partial \pi_t}{\pi_t^2 \partial c^k_t}\right]}{1 + \left(W^k_t - \Lambda^k_t\right)\frac{\partial \pi_t}{\pi_t^2 \partial c^k_t}}}{\dfrac{1 + \Lambda^k_t \left(1 + \tilde{R}^k_{t+1}(a^k_t)\right)\frac{1}{\pi_t^2}\frac{\partial \pi_t}{\partial c^k_{t+1}}}{1 + \Lambda^k_t \left(1 + R^f_{t+1}\right)\frac{1}{\pi_t^2}\frac{\partial \pi_t}{\partial c^k_{t+1}}}} \right\}; \quad \tilde{\pi}_{t+1}/\tilde{\pi}_t = 1$$

Of course, if prices are independent of the volume of consumption, then we have the usual risk-neutral pricing model for the price of future returns consisting of an investment strategy a^k_t:

$$1 = \frac{1}{1 + R^f_{t+1}} E^{M_{t+1}} \left(1 + \tilde{R}^k_{t+1}(a^k_t)\right)$$

The solution of this consumption problem results in a pricing model far more adapted to global finance which is well defined in terms of sovereign states' financial consumption. Of course, if

$$\frac{\partial \ln \tilde{\pi}_t}{\partial c^k_t} = \frac{\partial \ln \tilde{\pi}_{t+1}}{\partial c^k_{t+1}} = 0$$

then letting $\tilde{\pi}_{t+1}/\tilde{\pi}_t = 1 + \eta_{t+1}$, with η_{t+1} an inflation rate, we have

$$1 = \beta E \left\{ M_{t+1} \frac{1 + \tilde{R}^k_{t+1}(a^k_t)}{1 + \eta_{t+1}} \right\}$$

which is a kernel pricing CCAPM with inflation-adjusted rates of returns. In this sense, as seen earlier, "poorly endowed sovereign states" are price takers, while large consumption-endowed sovereign states have a "power" over the market by their own decisions and thus are partly price makers. If a sovereign agent invested in risk-free rate treasury inflation-protected security (i.e., inflation index bonds), then $a_t^k = 1$ and therefore $\tilde{R}_{t+1}^k(1) = R_f$, the risk-free rate, in which case

$$\frac{1}{1 + R_f^{\text{TIPS}}} = E_t^k\left(M_{t+1}^k | \mathfrak{I}_t^k\right)$$

Therefore, setting an inflation-adjusted probability measure, we have

$$M_{t+1}^{*k} = \frac{\left(M_{t+1}^k\right)}{E_t^k\left(M_{t+1}^k | \mathfrak{I}_t^k\right)}$$

Therefore:

$$1 = \frac{1}{1 + R_f^{\text{TIPS}}} E_t^{M_{t+1}^{*k}}\left(\frac{1 + \tilde{R}_{t+1}^k\left(a_t^k\right)}{1 + \eta_{t+1,t}} | \mathfrak{I}_t^k\right)$$

which defines a probability measure based on the kth party pricing kernel. Essential questions we may be concerned with are to what extent wealth inequalities increase or whether the rich are getting richer. First, these depend on the growth rate of a sovereign state wealth. Second, they depend on the effects of savings. Is the propensity to save greater for the richer state? The model considered here has essentially pointed to the effect of financial consumption changes over time but not to wealth (albeit, both depend on one another). Third, is there a relationship between a party k wealth, their propensity to save and their investment strategy $\left(a_t^k\right)$? A tentative answer is embedded in the rate of growth in financial consumption expenditure. These are complex issues that are a function of numerous factors, but their integration in a financial pricing model of consumption may provide some insights on these fundamental economic, financial, and social issues. Owing to the complexity of these game pricing models, a solution is necessarily numerical.

9.5 The Demand Sector and its Supply

The demand sector consists of numerous consumers seeking to consume a basket of goods. Each consumer is assumed to have a utility of consumption $u_i(Q_{iC})$. Let $u_i(Q_{iC}) - \pi_i Q_{iC}$ be its net utility, and therefore the price that the consumer is "willing to pay" for an optimal consumption is its marginal utility, or $\pi_i(Q_{iC}) = \partial u_i(Q_{iC})/\partial Q_{iC}$. The price one wants to pay and the price what one actually pays need not be the same, however. If the price that one actually pays is greater than $\pi_i(Q_{iC})$, then of course the consumer will adapt by consuming less, and vice versa if the price is less than the marginal utility price $\pi_i(Q_{iC})$ set above, then the consumer will profit by consuming more. Let the price a consumer pays in country i be $p_i(Q)$, with $Q = \sum_{i=1}^{n} Q_{iC}$ expressing the local price and its relationship to the global demand (and hence global supply when it is plentiful). The price differences between countries are therefore a financial incentive for exports and imports between countries. This occurs when (neglecting the effects of

FX) all prices equal, $p_i(Q) = p(Q)$, $i = 1, 2, ..., n$, and there is no trade arbitrage (and thus no trade). In this case, the utility of consumption is financial defined by the expenditure allocated to consumption by the consumer, and the (equilibrium) price each country will have to pay is a solution of the Cournot game:

$$\operatorname*{Max}_{Q_{iC}} U_{iC} = u_i(Q_{iC}) - p(Q)Q_{iC}, \quad Q = \sum_{i=1}^n Q_{iC}; \quad i = 1, ..., n$$

or

$$p(Q) = \frac{\partial u_i}{\partial Q_{iC}} - \frac{\partial p(Q)}{\partial Q} Q_{iC} \quad \text{or} \quad \frac{\partial p(Q)}{\partial Q} = \frac{\pi_i(Q_{iC}) - p(Q)}{Q_{iC}}$$

As a result, from a consumer's point of view, they profit from a lower price if the price they are willing to pay is greater than the price they will pay; that is, $\pi_i(Q_{iC}) > p(Q)$. However, the greater the "price premium" consumers derive, the greater the selling price rate of change when aggregate consumption increases. Subsequently, we shall see that these relationships are more complex as they also involve the countries' supply embedded in their propensity to export and to import. In particular, we shall subsequently see that consumers would be willing to pay less (and thus will pay less) when imports increase. In other words, assuming that globalization is based on a greater level of exchange, it is thus based necessarily on the lower prices consumers demand. Since, in a single-currency world, all consumers have the same marginal price, we have

$$\frac{\pi_i(Q_{iC}) - p(Q)}{Q_{iC}} = \frac{\pi_j(Q_{jC}) - p(Q)}{Q_{jC}}$$

Therefore, for all i and j, the price is defined by the relative consumption "price premium" they derive. In this case, the greater the number of consumers, the smaller the consumer premium. Of course, for a single and global consumer, at the limit we have $\pi_j(Q_{jC}) = p(Q)$. In this case, there are no price fluctuations and $\partial p(Q)/\partial Q = 0$ or $p(Q) = \bar{p}$ is an equilibrium price. Of course, if $\partial p(Q)/\partial Q \neq 0$, then

$$\frac{\pi_i(Q_{iC}) - p(Q)}{\pi_j(Q_{jC}) - p(Q)} = \frac{Q_{iC}}{Q_{jC}}$$

And therefore

$$p(Q) = \pi_i(Q_{iC}) \frac{1 - \dfrac{Q_{iC}\,\pi_j(Q_{jC})}{Q_{jC}\,\pi_i(Q_{iC})}}{1 - \dfrac{Q_{iC}}{Q_{jC}}}$$

For example, let utilities be logarithmic; then $\pi_j(Q_{jC}) = 1/Q_{jC}$, and therefore

$$p(Q) = \frac{1}{Q_{iC}} \frac{1 - \left(\dfrac{Q_{iC}}{Q_{jC}}\right)^2}{1 - \dfrac{Q_{iC}}{Q_{jC}}} = \frac{1}{Q_{iC}} \frac{\left(1 - \dfrac{Q_{iC}}{Q_{jC}}\right)\left(1 + \dfrac{Q_{iC}}{Q_{jC}}\right)}{1 - \dfrac{Q_{iC}}{Q_{jC}}} = \frac{Q_{jC} + Q_{iC}}{Q_{iC}Q_{jC}}, \quad \forall i, j, \quad i \neq j$$

Elementary manipulations based on a summation of these equations yield

$$p(Q) = \frac{Q_{jC} + Q_{iC}}{Q_{iC} Q_{jC}} \quad \text{or} \quad p(Q) \sum_{i=1}^{n} Q_{iC} = n + \frac{1}{Q_{jC}} \sum_{i=1}^{n} Q_{iC} \quad \text{and} \quad p(Q)Q = n + \frac{1}{Q_{jC}} Q$$

And subsequently to

$$p(Q)QQ_{jC} = nQ_{jC} + Q \quad \text{as well as} \quad p(Q)Q \sum_{j=1}^{n} Q_{jC} = n \sum_{j=1}^{n} Q_{jC} + Q$$

And finally, we note that prices decline as aggregate demand increases, or

$$p(Q) = \frac{1+n}{Q} \quad \text{if} \quad \frac{\pi_i(Q_{iC}) - p(Q)}{\pi_j(Q_{jC}) - p(Q)} = \frac{Q_{iC}}{Q_{jC}} > 0$$

In this simple case, when

$$\frac{\partial p(Q)}{\partial Q} = \frac{\pi_i(Q_{iC}) - p(Q)}{Q_{iC}}$$

holds, we have

$$-\frac{1+n}{Q^2} = \frac{\pi_i(Q_{iC}) - \dfrac{1+n}{Q}}{Q_{iC}} \quad \text{and} \quad (1+n)Q_{iC} = (1+n)Q - \pi_i(Q_{iC})Q^2$$

However, since $\pi_j(Q_{iC}) = 1/Q_{iC}$, we obtain a direct relationship between the consumption of a consumer i, the number of consumers, and the aggregate demand:

$$(Q_{iC})^2 - Q_{iC}Q + \frac{Q^2}{1+n} = 0 \quad \text{and} \quad Q_{iC} = Q\left(\frac{1}{2} - \sqrt{\frac{1}{4} - \frac{1}{1+n}}\right)$$

Note that when n is very large, the consumption of i is very small. Suppose that there are 15 consumers; we then have

$$Q_{iC} = Q\left(\frac{1}{2} - \frac{1}{4}\sqrt{3}\right)$$

9.6 Conclusions

There is a vast economic and financial literature on trade. Some of its elements were introduced at the beginning of this chapter, as well as in Chapters 4 and 5. Subsequently, we used a very simple one-period utility consumption demand model as well as defined a financial consumption problem. The former was integrated with a supply problem with imports and exports between two parties. These led to results that have allowed a number of observations pertaining to trade, prices defined as a function of aggregate supply, as well as FX, and a number of trade factors that affect their price. There are, of course, a number of factors that did not consider, for example, changes in interest rate, inflation, and expectations.

The intent of this chapter was to provide another approach to trade models as discussed in Chapters 4 and 5, which is based on the financialization of consumption. In particular, our approach differs from FX models based on the asset and monetary approaches as the Frenkel–Mussa model suggests, based on absolute parity of prices across sovereign states and a risk-neutral FX rate, resulting from endogenous market forces. In practice, the principle of parity is viewed as a long-term relationship rather than a short one, reflecting the necessary economic adjustments that countries have to come through to reach a state of economic equilibrium. Thus, the presumption that FX currency markets are complete (in a financial sense, and therefore in economic equilibrium) is often criticized. Interventions, transaction costs, incentives, and rare and unpredictable events, as well as political and other risks, render such markets incomplete (at least in the short run) and therefore difficult to price. These elements are far more privy of financial considerations. Furthermore, since observed FX prices are mostly short-term FX data, estimation of rate-of-return models may be more appropriate for econometric analysis.

In international macroeconomic and financial models, prices are sought for both tradable goods and nontradables. The latter play an important role in determining the real exchange rate and international competitiveness. In Chapter 5 we referred to early studies such as by Balassa (1964) and Samuelson (1964) where the relative price and real FX rates were emphasized in a model with tradable goods. Variants of these models, both on the supply-side (total factor productivity corresponding to technological changes) and demand-side approaches, are used. Empirical literature on PPP was addressed in Chapter 5. These provide evidence for a relative price of nontradables as one of the fundamental determinants of the real exchange rate and highlight their comovements. Furthermore, we considered in Chapter 5 other important models, in particular the Dornbusch exchange rate overshooting model with its empirical evidence. The Cournot game approach (and therefore strategic) was used in this chapter to reconcile both the demand and the supply factors. These issues are fundamental to trade models as FX is the dominant factor in both pricing imports and exports and thereby the price of consumption. In this sense, the financial approach to consumption set in this chapter is a complement to the important and extensive economic literature on this subject.

References

Aumann, R.J. (1964) Markets with a continuum of traders. *Econometrica*, **32**: 39–50.

Balassa, B. (1964) The purchasing power parity doctrine: a reappraisal. *Journal of Political Economy*, **72**: 584–596.

Balassa, B. (1967) *Trade Liberalization among Industrial Countries: Objectives and Alternatives*. McGraw-Hill: New York.

Bloomberg (2014) Apple, Starbucks tax deals with Irish, Dutch probed by EU. June 11.

Brander, J.A. and Spencer, B.J. (1985) Export subsidies and international market share rivalry. *Journal of International Economics*, **18**: 83–100.

Collie, D. and de Meza, D. (2003) Comparative advantage and the pursuit of strategic trade policy. *Economic Letters*, **81**: 279–283.

De Meza, D. (1986) Export subsidies and high productivity: cause or effect? *Canadian Journal of Economics*, **19**: 347–350.

Dixit, A. (1984) International trade policy for oligopolistic industries. *Economic Journal*, **94** (Suppl): 1–16.

Dixit, A. (1987) Strategic aspects of trade policy. In *Advances in Economic Theory, Fifth World Congress*, T. Bewley (ed.). Cambridge University Press, New York.

Dixit, A. and Norman, V. (1980) *Theory of International Trade: A Dual, General Equilibrium Approach*. Cambridge University Press.

Eaton, J. and Grossman, G.M. (1986) Optimal trade and industrial policy under oligopoly. *Quarterly Journal of Economics*, **101**: 383–406.

EC (2014) State aid: Commission investigates transfer pricing arrangements on corporate taxation of Apple (Ireland) Starbucks (Netherlands) and Fiat Finance and Trade (Luxembourg). European Commission: Brussels. http://europa.eu/rapid/press-release_IP-14-663_en.htm (accessed May 29, 2017).

European Parliament (2013) Motion for a European Parliament resolution on fight against tax fraud, tax evasion and tax havens. http://www.europarl.europa.eu/sides/getDoc.do?pubRef=-//EP//TEXT%20REPORT%20A7-2013-0162%200%20DOC%20XML%20V0//EN accessed May 29, 2017).

Foucault, M. (1966) *Les Mots et les Choses: Une Archéologie des Sciences Humaine*. Éditions Gallimard: Paris.

Gandolfo, G. (2014) *International Trade Theory and Policy*. Springer.

Gough, L. (2002) *Global Finance*. Capstone Publishing.

Gould, D.M. and Woodbridge, G.L. (1998) The political economy of retaliation, liberalization and trade wars. *European Journal of Political Economy*, **14**(1): 115–137.

Gros, D. (1987) A note on the optimal tariff retaliation and the welfare loss from tariff wars in a framework with intra-industry trade. *Journal of International Economics*, **23**: 357–367.

Grossman G.M. and Rogoff, K. (eds) (2003) *Handbook of International Economics, Volume 3*, 5th edn. Handbooks in Economics **3**. North Holland: Amsterdam.

Gwartney, J.D., Hall, J.C., and Lawson, R. (2015) *Economic Freedom of the World: 2015 Annual Report*. Fraser Institute: Vancouver. https://www.fraserinstitute.org/sites/default/files/economic-freedom-of-the-world-2015.pdf (accessed May 29, 2017).

Helpman, E. and Krugman, P.R. (1985) *Market Structure and Foreign Trade*. MIT Press: Cambridge, MA.

Hotten, R. (2010). Currency wars threaten global economic recovery. *BBC News*, October 7. http://www.bbc.com/news/business-11484532 (accessed May 29, 2017).

IMF (2017) Direction of Trade Statistics. http://data.imf.org/?sk=9D6028D4-F14A-464C-A2F2-59B2CD424B85 (accessed June 14, 2017).

Johnson, H.G. (1953) Optimal tariffs and retaliation. *Review of Economic Studies*, **21**: 142–143.

Jones W.J. and Kenen, P.B. (eds) (2003) *Handbook of International Economics, Volume 2, International Monetary Economics and Finance*, 5th edn. Handbooks in Economics **3**. North Holland: Amsterdam.

Kogan, K. and Tapiero, C. (2007) *Supply Chain Games: Operations Management and Risk Valuation*. Springer.

Krugman, P.R. (1979) Increasing returns, monopolistic competition, and international trade. *Journal of International Economics*, **9**: 469–479.

Krugman, P.R. (1980) Scale economies, product differentiation, and the pattern of trade. *The American Economic Review*, **70**(5): 950–959.

Krugman, P.R. (1981) Intraindustry specialization and the gains from trade. *The Journal of Political Economy*, **89**(5): 959–973.

Krugman, P.R. (1990) *Rethinking International Trade*. MIT Press: Cambridge, MA.

Krugman, P.R. and Smith, A. (eds) (1994) *Empirical Studies of Strategic Trade Policy*. University of Chicago Press.

Leontief, W.W. (1953) Domestic production and foreign trade: the American capital position re-examined. *Proceedings of the American Philosophical Society*, **97**: 332–349.

Morasch, K. (2000) Strategic alliances: a substitute for strategic trade policy? *Journal of International Economics*, **52**(1): 37–67.

Nash, Jr., J.F. (1950) The bargaining problem. *Econometrica*, **8**: 155–162.

Neary, J.P. (1994) Cost asymmetries in international subsidy games: should governments help winners or losers? *Journal of International Economics*, **37**(3): 197–218.

Nyambuu, U. (2017) Self-serving altruistic behavior and its implications for consumption, trade, and foreign exchange rates. *Risk and Decision Analysis*, **6**(2): 137–149. doi: 10.3233/RDA-170119.

NYT (2010) Countering China, Obama backs India for U.N. Council. *The New York Times*, November 8. http://www.nytimes.com/2010/11/09/world/asia/09prexy.html?_r=0 (accessed May 29, 2017).

NYT (2014) White House weighs actions to deter overseas tax flight. *The New York Times*, August 5.

Obstfeld, M. and Rogoff, K. (1996) *Foundations of International Macroeconomics*. The MIT Press: Cambridge, MA.

Opp, M.M. (2010) Tariff wars in the Ricardian model with a continuum of goods. *Journal of International Economics*, **80**: 212–225.

Park, J.-H. (2000) International trade agreements between countries of asymmetric size. *Journal of International Economics*, **50**: 473–495.

Ricardo, D. (1817) *On the Principles of Political Economy and Taxation*. John Murray: London. http://socserv2.socsci.mcmaster.ca/econ/ugcm/3ll3/ricardo/prin/index.html.

Samuelson, P. (1964) Theoretical notes on trade problems. *Review of Economics and Statistics*, **46**: 145–164.

Samuelson, P. (2001) A Ricardo–Sraffa paradigm comparing gains from trade in inputs and finished goods. *Journal of Economic Literature*, **39**(4): 1204–1214.

Tapiero, C. (2014) A financial CCAPM and economic inequalities. *Quantitative Finance*, **15**(3): 521–534.

The World Bank. World Development Indicators. http://databank.worldbank.org/data/home.aspx. Accessed on December 20, 2016.

UNCTAD (2015) *International Classification of Non-tariff Measures, 2012 Version*. United Nations: New York. http://unctad.org/en/PublicationsLibrary/ditctab20122_en.pdf (accessed on May 29, 2017).

UNCTAD, UNCTADSTAT, http://unctadstat.unctad.org/wds/ReportFolders/reportFolders.aspx?

UNDP (2015) *Human Development Report 2015: Work for Human Development*. United Nations Development Programme: New York. http://hdr.undp.org/sites/default/files/2015_human_development_report.pdf (accessed May 29, 2017).

World Economic Forum (2016) The Global Competitiveness Report 2016–2017. http://www3.weforum.org/docs/GCR2016-2017/05FullReport/TheGlobalCompetitivenessReport2016-2017_FINAL.pdf (accessed May 29, 2017).

WSJ (2014) U.S. firms probed on taxes. *The Wall Street Journal*, June 12. http://online.wsj.com/public/resources/documents/print/WSJ_-B001-20140612.pdf (accessed May 29, 2017).

WSJ (2016a) U.S. imposes 266% duty on some Chinese steel imports. *The Wall Street Journal*, March 1. http://www.wsj.com/articles/u-s-imposes-266-duty-on-some-chinese-steel-imports-1456878180 (accessed May 29, 2017).

WSJ (2016b) World trade today isn't what it used to be. *The Wall Street Journal*, March 21. http://www.wsj.com/articles/world-trade-today-isnt-what-it-used-to-be-1458599472 (accessed May 29, 2017).

WTO (2016a) Report on G20 Trade Measures. https://www.wto.org/english/news_e/news16_e/g20_wto_report_june16_e.pdf (accessed May 29, 2017).

WTO (2016b) Annual Report 2016. https://www.wto.org/english/res_e/booksp_e/anrep_e/anrep16_e.pdf (accessed May 29, 2017).

10

Compliance and Financial Regulation

Motivation

In this chapter we stress the increased complexity of both the regulatory environment and compliance risk in an increasingly global, gated, and strategic financial marketplace. In particular, markets are influenced by political concerns as well as by technology and information. In such an environment, compliance is both strategic and statistical. This chapter examines both aspects, highlighting regulatory risks and their controls. At the same time, we introduce relatively simple quantitative models to estimate compliance probabilities and their risks using audit games and strategic controls. The models we consider include (1) Bernoulli compliance models and their derivatives, (2) statistical compliance and statistical risks, (3) multivariate statistical approaches, and (4) regulation and compliance games.

10.1   Introduction

Globalization, gating, and regulation by multiple agencies, regulatory bodies, and sovereign entities have led to a regulatory maze with extreme economic consequences. These, in turn, have led to a systemic transformation of financial institutions at both national and international levels, challenging globalization, and forcing firms and investors everywhere to be compliant with a plethora of complex requirements and certifying organizations (Kim and Santomero, 1994; Alexander *et al.*, 1996; Barth *et al.*, 2001, 2004, 2008; Ai and Sappington, 2002; Roubini, 2008; Macey, 2013; C.S. Tapiero, 2013a,b). Aggressive regulatory systems have at the same time embraced bipolar policies that, on the one hand institute control mechanisms on banking and financial institutions, and on the other hand gate finance both domestically and across national boundaries. For examples, see Armstrong and Sappington (2005), as well as numerous publications of the Basel Committee (e.g., Basel Committee on Banking Supervision, 2009) and Basel III.

Financial regulators around the world (with the USA as an exception) have shied away from developing globe-spanning rules in favor of shoring up the financial systems under their local purview (Carney, 2016). They did and do so "discriminately." For example, while European countries seek to impose greater controls on US banks, the USA imposes greater controls on European banks and global finance in general, by the use of US dollars in financial and economic transactions as a means to articulate a global regulation.

Globalization, Gating, and Risk Finance, First Edition. Unurjargal Nyambuu and Charles S. Tapiero.
© 2018 John Wiley & Sons Ltd. Published 2018 by John Wiley & Sons Ltd.

As a result, strategies coined "ring-fencing," and more generally "gating," have sought to roll back elements of globalization and global finance. These bipolar and (at times) conflictual processes (i.e., regulatory gating and domestic financial regulation) do not have the same agenda. While regulatory gating seeks to be more protective of domestic markets, domestic regulation is far more invested in the control of financial institutions and systemic risks, although both domestic and global finance are increasingly dependent on one another.

The complexity and growing reach of regulations everywhere have thus moved compliance (both domestic and global) from a back office function to be a front office one. Some companies feel that they are held hostage and forced to pay out huge settlements rather than risk trial. As a result, many corporations are concurrently setting up an internal infrastructure to comply with regulation and in some cases migrate the legal residence to countries where regulation is less invasive (also called an inversion strategy). For example, in a recent case, Deutsche Bank AG, in order to avoid potential and greater damages, reached a $7.2 billion settlement to resolve a years-long US investigation into its dealings in mortgage-backed securities, removing a legal hurdle that fueled investors' angst. It agreed to pay a $3.1 billion civil penalty and provide $4.1 billion for consumers' relief (Foerster and Onaran, 2016). In another case, Goldman-Sachs agreed to pay $5.1 billion to end an investigation into its packaging of residential mortgage-backed securities in the run-up to the financial crisis (Schaefer, 2016).

Compliance is both statistical and strategic. In complex and extensive regulatory systems with thousands of often incompatible and inconsistent regulatory items, it is practically impossible to be fully compliant. Instead, it might be reasonable to use statistical metrics to establish a statistical definition of compliance or a lack of it. Further, since regulation is then strategic, involving well-defined agents (players or financial firms and regulatory agencies) with different agendas, agents' decisions, although consequential, are also random games (due to the unknown games consequences). For example, whether a regulator will audit or not, as well as whether the audit if carried out has any financial or other consequence. Furthermore, these decisions may be based on public information and/or political agendas, news and/or inside informants, and/or other (or previously unknown) reasons. These, and other factors, lead to financial institutions being targeted, rightly or wrongly, with regulatory compliance audits best represented by complex "random payoff games," that is, games of strategy where outcomes are also random.

In summary, in such a challenging regulatory environment, all financial institutions are, to a greater or in a lesser degree, noncompliant; audits and compliance are strategic activities, based on information and control games models, and defined by established relationships of law, public and investor relations, and, of course, profits. Theoretical underpinnings to these games may be found, for example, in Maschler (1966), Harsanyi (1967, 1968a,b), Harsanyi and Selten (1987), Russell (1990), Ruckle (1992), Avenhaus *et al.* (1995), Reyniers and Tapiero (1995a,b), Aumann and Hart (2002), and Camerer (2003). These sources provide audit gaming approaches.

Aggressive financial regulation and the increased costs of compliance following the Dodd–Frank Act have led further to a greater concentration of financial firms with far greater powers, reducing financial competition, and increasing the cost of entry and innovation. A new presidential financial policy suggested by the US president in 2017, calling for a repeal of the Dodd–Frank regulation, has, as a result, contributed to an appreciable rise in financial stock markets. Large banks, such as J.P. Morgan,

Goldman Sachs, Independent Community Bankers of America, and others are, however, concerned that an easing deregulation would lead to a greater banking competition in which they see a disadvantage. For example, Goldman Sachs, while expressing its concerns that regulation costs have increased appreciably, said they were also aware that these costs are affordable to big banks compared with the prospective benefits they may derive from a global dominance of finance. Further, with a globalized and costly financial regulation, financial institutions are amending their financial strategy to be more defined by a few "players" with particular agendas, rather than a "markets finance" defined by many and independent financial agents.

The fundamental intent of financial regulation, to mitigate financial inefficiencies has its own risks and adverse consequences; some are unintended and potentially anti-competitive, while others may counter the beneficial effects of a globalized finance and the systemic risks that uncontrolled financial institutions can take on. The economist and Nobel Prize winner George Stigler, years ago, pointed out that regulation may in fact "serve the interests of the industry they regulate" (as stated in Owen and Braeutoigam (1978: 11)). It does so by gating new entrants and innovation, and maintains the dominance and the power of regulated industries. The increased use of "too big to fail" (TBTF) designation may be an implicit recognition that the regulatory reforms of 2014–2016 have actually led to greater systemic risks. For example, Macey (2013) points out that regulation has engendered numerous theories of "regulatory risk," claiming that regulations contribute to a standardization of financial institutions and financial risk management that itself increases systemic risk (compared with a heterogeneous and diversified financial system). Globalization, sovereign gating, regulations, and the transformation of financial institutions and the financial system render compliance and regulatory systems far more complex and costly than the systems they are trying to control. For example, see Aubert and Reynaud (2005) on cost efficiency, Beck *et al.* (2006) on addressing corruption in lending and regulation, Keppo *et al.* (2010) and C.S. Tapiero (2014) on risks and unintended consequences of banks regulation, May and Arinaminpathy (2010) on the systemic risks of banking systems models, both Bird and Kortanek (1974) and Laffont (1995) on games and pollution regulation (also see C.S. Tapiero (1995, 2005a–c)), and Gonzalez (2005) and Koehn and Santomero (1980) on the effects of regulation on risk incentives. In addition to an extensive literature on financial regulation, regulatory systems in industries, in the environment, in utilities, health trade, and so on, and a broad background and approaches to regulation and to the risks and uncertainty they entail, see O.J. Tapiero (2013a–c).

The purpose of this chapter, however, is not to review and present a comprehensive analysis and assessment of regulation and financial compliance. Rather, we provide a limited view that emphasizes compliance in light of regulatory risks and their potential consequences. The financial regulatory and compliance literature (both academic and professional) has increased appreciably since the 2008 financial crisis. For example, among many others, see Shahin and Feiger (2013) on risk management in financial institutions, Macey (2013) on theories of regulatory risk, the surprise theory, the arbitrage theory, and the regulatory mistake theory, C.S. Tapiero (2013a) on reengineering risk and the future of finance, and Jackson and Walter (2013) on the future of financial regulation.

10.1.1 Regulation, Politics, and Geopolitics

Political and geopolitical concerns have increased the importance of regulatory laws as means required to protect sovereign social and economic interests and affirm far greater controls on financial institutions and financial products and markets. Furthermore, increased regulation has been justified as follows:

- To compensate and prevent financial risk externalities and their consequences (e.g., financial institutions contributing to markets' distortions without assuming any of their consequences; overleveraged institutions with TBTF risks that, eventually, may have to be assumed by taxpayers).
- To protect financial positive externalities based on fair and efficient financial markets and institutions (e.g., providing the mechanisms and the exchanges that contribute to market liquidity; "fair access" to trade for all rather than for a select few insiders; economic development, and an efficient economic allocation of resources).
- To mitigate the consequences of information and power asymmetries prevalent in financial systems, and thereby regulate, control, and penalize excesses.
- To protect sovereign interests and institute an offshore regulatory legitimacy. For example, regarding capital flight, money laundering, and tax evasions as legitimate areas of concern to regulators.

Regulation is therefore in a continuous transition, motivated by sovereign policies and their socioeconomic agendas, as well as by the consequence of an unfolding globalization and the mitigating factors that sovereign states apply to gate their economies. It is mostly applied domestically, but it is increasingly in search of a global regulatory framework to protect sovereign interests—financial, political, and others. For example, US regulation is, in principle, motivated by the integrity and the functionality of financial markets, by investors' access "equality" to markets, in information and "fairness," and so on. These elements led to a complex jurisdiction to keep pace with the growth of a global technological and financial complexity, financial loopholes, and the stealth movements of capital across national boundaries. For example, only recently have regulators acted against the stealth transfer of international funds through law firms. These transfers were found to be very hard to detect and contributing to financial laundering (summing to over a trillion dollars!). Sovereign states' purviews of these challenges have led to regulatory jurisdictions and regulatory apparatus that can differ appreciably from the US regulation viewpoint. These elements underlie a gated global finance, each country defining its own regulatory vantage point and agenda.

Regulation and economic gating are also political agendas—some in the hands of sovereign agencies with conflicting purposes leading to the growth of a global dark market. For example, *The Economist* (1999) estimated that the world's shadow economy was $9 trillion, evading both sovereign tax and regulations set by other authorities. They referred to an early study by Schneider in the late 1990s that covered 76 countries and pointed out that the underground economy's (or stealth economy's) shares in GDP were approximately 15% in developed countries and around 33% in emerging economies! In a more recent study based on 162 countries, Schneider (2012) estimated that the share of the shadow economy in GDP (weighted average) was 16% for the world, 13% for OECD countries, 26% for developing economies, and 34% for transition economies in 2007. Underground (shadow) economies are therefore "dark matter," unseen, undetectable, and yet omnipresent. The existence of such matter has numerous causes and effects; for example, relatively high tax rates increase the propensity to evade taxes, shadow economies increase as well with sovereign states' gating and the stringency of laws they apply. Schneider's (2012) estimation shows that many developing and less developed countries have a very large share of a black market in GDP. For example, Zimbabwe

(62%), Bolivia (64%), Peru (54%), and Thailand (48%). In contrast, EU member states and other developed economies have a much smaller informal sector with a falling trend. For example, the shadow economy to GDP ratio has dropped respectively from 2003 to 2015 from 23% to 18% in the EU (average of 28 countries), 9% to 6% in the USA, and from 11% to 8% in Japan—see Schneider (2015). In emerging economies, where taxes are generally lower, the stealth economy is larger due to an evasion from the laws of the land. Inversion, resulting from firms moving their corporate legal identity from high- to low-level taxation areas is a legal framework that is applied institutionally. By the same token, the expansion of political conflicts, terrorism, and war in the Middle East and elsewhere contribute to the growth of the shadow economy.

In this sense, financial regulation has a far greater role than just assuring the compliance of a financial entity. By its actions, and not only its principles, it implies a broad sociopolitical and economic agenda. It may however contribute in some extreme cases to a "factory of dark matter;" namely, a financial activity that is omnipresent but not to be seen or understood.

Such risks underlie the aggressive–reactive actions taken by regulators to gate economies and assert sovereign controls over financial institutions, the flow of capital, and the legitimacy of domestic and foreign financial transactions needed for economic growth. In its quest, financial regulation has evolved, defining "legitimacy" and "financial compliance" to be in states of continuous change, much more complex with thousands of rules, some nuanced and subject to various interpretations by regulatory authorities. World markets fueled by a changing economic environment, sovereign agendas, and not least sovereign states in collision have increased the pursuit of gating and geopolitical strategies to protect long-acquired economic controls and now questionable advantages.

In such an environment, compliance is more difficult and costly to implement, and transforms financial institutions from "agents of risks" to "agents of risk avoidance." Their implications to finance are immense, unfolding over time and leading to a mutating finance, relatively focused on concerns of compliance and risk aversion rather than managing efficiently the risk–returns opportunities of financial and real resources.

10.1.2 Regulatory Risks, Finance, and Compliance

An extensive regulatory finance (with many thousands of regulations to comply with, a far greater power assumed by regulators, with the power to interpret financial jurisdictions) has contributed to financial firms' priority to comply. It has also mutated financial institutions to seek greater simplicity, less risk, less prone to regulation and finance and far more equipped to meet the costly challenges of compliance. Or, alternatively, migrate to shores that are more regulation tolerant. Further, financial size and power have become a dominant strategy to pursue (rather than lending and profits). For example, "simplicity and less risk" have led to a reduction of bank services and limited their strategic focus, stifling new initiatives, and lending more to large corporate entities and less to smaller ones. Such a transformation has also contributed to a far greater concentration of oligopolistic banking in the hands of a few leaders (some TBTF and "happy to be such"), to the growth of apparently simpler products (such as exchange-traded funds compared with selective investments, to more passive investment and far less active investments), and stifling financial innovation. By the same token, an unbridled regulation has induced a systemic change into domestic gated banks faced with greater operations and financial costs. For example, numerous financial institutions had to hire at great expense in-house regulators (often to be vetted by regulatory agencies) that have altered both the governance structure of financial institutions and in some cases the ability of financial investors to assume the risks that fuel the creation of liquidity and the health of financial markets. Penalties imposed on noncompliance to small and large financial institutions have also led to retaliation that also has systemic consequences. Their effects are the migration of industrial enterprises (not to avoid taxes but to avoid omnipresent and intervening regulatory powers). This also lead to an anti-competitive concentration of economic powers and thereby to the increased prominence of TBTF firms (i.e., firms defined as inducing potentially systemic risks).

Examples regarding regulatory risks and compliance abound. We consider a number of typical examples in the following:

- Globalization and national agendas are fueling a regulatory environment that is far more strategic (i.e., with regulatory systems that may be incoherent and/or competing, and thus impossible to comply with).
- Global imposition of a sovereign jurisdiction has consequences if it is defined within legally agreed and negotiated agreements.
- Asymmetric regulatory systems and their applications appeal to economic retaliation and migration of national enterprises.
- Regulatory complexity increases self-sustaining regulation costs and compliance costs.
- Regulation has stealth systemic and noncompliance risks, such as the growth of dark markets, migration, and technological developments to render regulation ineffective. For example, OTC trades and IT systems designed to avoid regulatory audits.

Financial technology and financial products innovation combined with creative financial logistics have, for example, challenged both financial regulators and the emergence of financial compliance as a front office activity within large corporate financial firms.

In a global financial environment, regulation is then necessarily strategic, defined by the "game that nations and their governments play." Thus, although regulation is clearly needed to counter markets' departing from fair and efficient market principles, the following questions remain: How much regulation is really needed? What are the "risks of regulation and the costs of compliance"? Are regulations counter-productive to both the regulatory system and the compliant financial system?

Financial firms, individual investors, and traders have become far more technology savvy, aided by new networking and stealth technologies, electronic markets, robotized trading and trades launched on a variety of time scales and from varied information sources, leading to a mutated finance and and an increase in its complexity. A technological competitiveness between financial institutions and regulators may then set a parallel to Ashby's 1951 law of requisite variety. This implies that regulatory controls are functioning effectively if they maintain their ability to audit and control the complexity of "real finance." Inversely, real finance can overcome regulatory powers as long as it maintains its complexity greater than that it may be dealt with by regulators' technological capacities. These two countervailing processes render the regulatory system and compliance continually a changing dynamic process. In other words, it is in a perpetual imbalance, confronted both by compliance and regulations risks. For example, attempts to impose a tractable and simple regulation on the "living will" of a bank (i.e., constraining bank losses to its own—such as hedging risk externalities, resulting in losses to others that the bank will not sustain) is a valiant purpose that might not be regulated by augmenting a percentage of banks' safe capital. In other words, if a tsunami hits the beach, the survival of "beach-goers" cannot be guaranteed.

Examples in finance, economics, and in industrial and environmental sectors abound. Peter Eavis (2016: B1) in *The New York Times* points out that implementing the Dodd–Frank Act directives to shield taxpayers and the economy from bank failures is "eye-numbingly complex."

10.1.3 Regulation and Risks: Economic Literature

Global risks are many and varied. We consider four essential risk. (1) Risks exchanged, potentially priced when they can be traded. These risks underlie fundamental models in finance (such as option pricing models, swaps, macrofinance and trends strategies). (2) Sovereign compliance risks. In a global world with financial transactions involving several sovereign states, a financial entity may comply with one state and not comply with another state. Thus, a firm producing goods in the USA that has some of its products sold in other countries may have to comply with the multiple regulations of other countries. By the same token, a financial transaction across national boundaries is faced with compliance in all states where the transactions were made or occurred. (3) Global uncertainty defined by unknown unknowns or neglected knowns. They may, for example, be derived from geopolitical realities, or neglected due to oversimplification of financial models, ignoring dependence, contagions, and the complexity of exchanges that underscore global finance. (4) Strategic risks, resulting from strategic and international and economics confrontations, as well as gating confrontations and regulations and their implications for risk compliance. For example, while market risks are expressed in terms of random events (i.e., using Brownian motion), regulation risks are due to:

- What we know, do, and others do to us. These may be the risk of being audited, the risk of a regulator finding a regulated compliant while the regulated is actually noncompliant.
- The risk of not knowing the regulations we ought to comply with, the political risks we were not aware of, and so on. Global finance harbors "factories of compounded risks and uncertainty." For example, faced with a clear statement that insider trading is illegal, some sovereign states may choose to ignore its existence or call it by another name (Knight, 1921; Langlois and Cosgell, 1993; O.J. Tapiero, 2013a–c).

Neglecting risks knowingly or unknowingly facing future and consequential events leads to a statistical approach to compliance and therefore to risk models of regulation and compliance that are bounded by our own rationality defined by:

- what we know
- what others know
- what we know about others and vice versa
- what others know about us
- what we do to each other.

These elements underlie the extensive literature on what financial regulation does and its consequences have focused essentially on the effects of regulation on risk-taking by regulated firms and systemic risks. Following the Dodd–Frank legislation, greater concern was given to the systemic risks that TBTF banks may harbor, that the financial systems may create through contagion, a lack of global controls, and other factors—for example, see Bisias, *et al.* (2012). These concerns are an add-on to an extensive economic literature on the theory of the regulated firm that has provided an economic framework to study the policies of regulated firms, the pricing of their services, and their propensity to assume risks.

TBTF banking systems and regulation provide important and strategic challenges, both in theory and in practice to both regulators and complying banks. From a regulatory viewpoint, bank failures are "risk externalities" manifested in the costs assumed by their clients and an erosion of trust in the financial systems. For example, *The Economist* (2012a,b) has pointed in particular to the limits of regulation, the costs of complexity, and an overreaching regulation. Excessive regulation, or a lack of it, has its own risk consequences.

In summary, regulation risks examples abound, including among others (C.S. Tapiero, 2013b: 413):

- the migration of economic agents to areas where regulation is less pronounced (at a cost of a loss of jobs, downsizing of firms, outsourcing);
- the rise of stealth and virtual financial entities with a global economic activity;
- counter-cyclicality leading to the accelerated demise of corporate entities in a down economic cycle;
- the complexity effects of regulation and their costs to regulated firms;
- the effects of a self-financing regulation (by penalties imposed, and leading to excessive controls and "out-of-court settlements");
- the risks of certainty implied in penalizing financial firms avoiding risks at all costs;
- increased systemic risks due to a standardized (rather than diversified) financial system subject to a common risk, and so on.

In other words, while regulation is needed to protect markets' integrity and sustainability, it is mitigated by the implications of its effects on markets efficiency. On theoretical grounds, the role of regulators and regulation, as well as the propensity for financial institutions to be increasingly larger, renders the underlying foundation of a theoretical finance to be far more strategic in the sense that an overly complex regulation might not lead to full compliance but rather to a "statistical compliance," and inversely a "statistical noncompliance," with consequences defining the risk of compliance.

For example, the Dodd–Frank regulation initiated in 2011 has expanded into a complex regulation book consisting of 5000 pages, continuously adapting to its own experience and regulatory agendas, and therefore in a state of constant change. This is challenging both compliance and regulators alike, with many regulations yet to be understood and integrated in financial firms' systems (except, perhaps, for a few lawyers who have articulated these regulations). The controls of such regulations and their noncompliance are thus, commensurably, far more difficult to assess. For example, given 300 regulations there are 300 controls a regulator or a regulated may pursue. If a regulator was to control only 10 of the 300 regulations, the number of alternative controls is then $\begin{pmatrix} 300 \\ 10 \end{pmatrix}$

and therefore practically unwieldy. The same applies, of course, to large or even small financial institutions that have diverted significant resources to comply with an abundant legal and financial regulation. These render a "total control" of financial compliance a practical impossibility.

The current tendency of regulation agency to insert an intra-firm regulator, financed by the firm as part of financial and legal settlement, may have costs and systemic consequences that have not yet been assessed. A statistical definition of compliance may in such cases provide a theoretical and practical alternative to an overreaching total compliance in an unwieldy and complex regulation system. A "zero-default compliance" in a complex regulatory system is therefore self-defeating. For example, Posner (2013) rightly points out that:

> Judges (in finance and regulation) are confronted with (financial and regulation) complexity…bewildered by a changing world distinguish between two kinds of complexity: external complexity not created by judges and internal complexity created by the law (regulation) such as intricate rules of interpretation, bloated conventions or citations or vague poorly written opinions.
>
> While the judiciary cannot do much about the former (external) complexity, it and addresses the later…but how? The rise of external complexity has increased internal complexity… judges escape from the external complexity by augmenting internal complexity … The greater the complexity (read uncertainty) they cannot control…they seek refuge in the control of internal convexity which increases further internal complexity (my words). If you cannot control what is important, you make important what you can control. Judges … like others, do not want to be transparent to the laity. They want their calling to be a mystery and one way to make it is to make it is complexity. As a result, complexity, centralization, information asymmetry, power asymmetry, … all converge to a greater complexity.
>
> In a complex political world, financial agents are selective, seek impermeable walls by erecting gates or changing homes (Global capital flows fell from $11 Trillions in 2007 to a third in 2012 … many reasons but also national measures to regulate and gate capital flows … Money as rivers have continue to flow to countries where they are least hindered). CFC is a recent manifestation of sovereign states who view these gates as an opportunity.
>
> Negation of Complexity and the cult of Regulation … A risk of certainty in an uncertain world and in a domain where risk primes. What are the alternatives: Total regulation or backdoor nationalization; Simplify the regulation process; Statistical regulation.

In a gated world (*The Economist*, 2013), with a proliferation of regulators, regulation agencies, and a dynamic set of rules and laws to comply with, both regulation and compliance can be self-defeating, distorting both financial markets and the rationalities they pursue. These open a family of unintended arbitrage opportunities. Regulation's intent regarding the financial playing field, where financial markets are complete or at least provide to all their participants equal access, information, and change, may also falter due to excessive regulation.

10.2   Regulation Risks

Regulation is a two-edged sword: both seeking to remove markets and behavioral risks, and at the same time introducing regulatory risks. For example, regulation stifles risk-taking and innovation. In a closed economy, these are issues compensated by the sovereign states' policies, while in an open and global economy the potential ability of a nation to counter the regulatory risk consequences is limited. In some cases, regulators may even contribute to regulation wars, leading to a counter-regulatory cycle.

Regulation in a global world is also interactive. Suppose that a regulation introduced in a country "A" leads to a regulation in country "B" to be altered to meet the risk consequences that country A implies to country B. Such a recipe leads necessarily to a "battle of regulators," where the regulated are obviously assuming the consequences. Large banks, for example, have been subject to such threats. These exchanges may occur within a national regulation system. For example, what if multiple agencies' regulators oversee a financial enterprise for its noncompliance, with one agency claiming a violation and the other not? Or, what if an audit by a regulator in one agency is contagious, leading to competitive audits by other agencies. This has the effect of stifling economic activity and reducing economic development, the creation of jobs, and a game in financial regulation. As Nocera (2012) wrote:

> One reason is that the more complex the rules are, the greater the likelihood that smart bankers will find ways to game them. Another is that contradictory regulations, however well meaning, simply don't make the system safer. But the most important reason is that complexity risk is having an effect on business.

Competing regulations may bear important risk consequences and contradict the intent of regulation as they affect the economy adversely, induce potential social costs, and affect labor markets (through the migration of jobs and the downsizing of regulated enterprises) as well as the markets for goods and services.

Attempts to increase international regulation by The Basel Committee sought to put together new norms to reduce banks' risks. However, these norms harbor risks that have reduced and contributed to credit starvation across the Western world at times that credit was badly needed for economic expansions. Central bank policies of quantitative easing (QE) were a last resort applied to supply the required liquidity. For Europe it is also a competitive disadvantage relative to the USA. While in the USA firms are mostly financed through financial markets at a 70% rate (the remaining 30% through banks), in Europe the percentages are the inverse (30% through financial markets and 70% through banks). Banks, therefore, are not in fact just business firms. Unlike firms producing goods or providing a service, banks by lending money are creating money, expanding its quantity and its uses. By their actions, they assume, therefore, a public responsibility to provide liquidity, which justifies their regulation.

The media is fueled with pronouncements and problems in global finance. A synopsis of selected articles was provided in Chapter 1. Additional examples are given in the following.

Current financial and other regulations set by the USA and applied globally will have to be amended to account for the Eurogroup—a partner, rather than being a party subjugated to the US regulation system. These will require revisions of the Volcker rule as well as the Dodd–Frank regulation, and international negotiations to define the guiding elements of a global financial regulation.

Financial institutions are particularly affected by the complexity and the global outreach of US regulation. For example, when regulations across national boundaries are not coordinated, meeting potentially contradictory regulation rules renders the process of compliance extremely difficult. As a result, foreign or domestic banks are preventively gating themselves by cutting off customers and retreating from businesses and markets for fear that they will not be able to comply—a preemptive strategy in the face of American regulation (*The Economist*, 2014). These policies are complex and double-edged. For instance, the Red Cross transfers funds to help the displaced and alleviate tragedies; and other countries are crossing the US financial regulation and thus becoming noncompliant, running the risks of extremely large penalties. From an entirely different perspective, while a market's expansion may provide opportunities, it also opens domestic markets to intensive competition.

These elements are evidently to be accounted for by financial advisors and financial traders when the decision to invest in what and where is to be pursued.

10.3 Regulation, Technology, and Compliance

The surge in financial regulation and compliance arose following the 2007–2009 financial crisis, increasing an awareness that the financial system has changed and is far more interdependent and complex than previously assumed and regulated. A preliminary response was formulated by the Dodd–Frank Act, resulting in thousands of new regulations, far more aggressively applied. It has also created a new financial environment, less free and increasingly subject to audits and compliance risks. Compliance and regulatory avoidance have also motivated new IT and financial IT software. In an ever-expanding and technology-based finance, regulation's intents to protect "the social contract" between financial institutions, consumers of financial institutions, and the public at large, while seeking a riskless sustainable financial environment, have become far more difficult to articulate and difficult to meet—both for the regulated and the regulators. As a result, removing risks from finance has also led to other risks, as pointed out by Ashby's cybernetic law of "requisite variety," with complexity beckoning complexity, leading to an endless spiral where one or the other—regulation or the financial system—overwhelmed, will cease to function as expected.

10.3.1 Importance of Technology and Information

Technology has expanded both the scope and the outreach of regulators and the ability to evade it, increasing the complexity and the business of finance. Technological expansion through IT, networking, and algorithmic-robotized technologies is a two-edged sword. On the one hand, it provides new opportunities and financial vistas; on the other hand, it increases competing alternatives to conventional banking and money and the transparency of a financial system that profited immensely from the information asymmetry it always had. For example, the Uberization of money, assisted by an internet infrastructure, global and instantaneous outreach, has overcome the constraints of both time and space and thereby the availability of information and its use. At the same time, it has empowered individuals to trade, to exchange with peer-to-peer software a broad variety of products (financial or not). It leads, however, to a "financial tyranny" by the few who profit from cyber-financial risks, or by technologies that disguise and/or hide their transactions, leveraged by the increasing power of networking technologies. The increased "democratization" of technology and its financial uses has altered the institutional financial world. Peer-to-peer debt, for example, and the broad variety of outsourcing software have and are bypassing financial transactions traditionally managed by brokers or banks. Similarly, financial products are redesigned to be more accessible to meet individual needs (e.g., OTC swaps assisted by IT). These have gradually changed the banking system, with currencies and liquidity becoming far more varied and stealth, and therefore providing tools to evade regulatory audits (i.e., developing the tools of stealth noncompliance). Digital and alternative currencies, cyber and digital crypto risks, trading technologies, algorithmic trading (already accounting for one-third of total currencies trading in 2016), the use of intelligent and learning algorithms, strategic taxation and arbitrage across national boundaries, and so many others are new manifestations of a changing financial environment. These raise challenges of all sorts—to regulators, to the effectiveness of sovereign regulation, and of course to the ability to evade and to comply with a dynamic regulatory environment. In this environment, upended by globalization, financial risks have mutated, challenging "regulatory and compliance systems." These systems are currently in a constant evolution, responding to new regulatory dynamics confronted daily with new manifestations of noncompliance and the complexity to gate it.

Financial markets theories have overall neglected the importance of scale in financial markets, where the big overwhelms the small, as well as the treatment of peer-to-peer financial exchanges. It has also neglected the interactive effects of sovereign and retaliatory regulations at cross-purposes that create more volatility, instabilities with bubbles, and chaos. In this environment, increased dependence and contagion have rendered real global finance far more sensitive to a geopolitical approach to regulation such as the creation of common regulatory areas hand in hand with common economic trading areas and able to maintain and control cross-national financial exchanges.

Increasingly, globalization, while opening the world to new freedoms and new markets, also lays bare and far more transparent national markets to foreign competition, migration, and clashes of cultures. In this environment, uncertainty and complexity prevail, and global risks and their management are far more complex, often misunderstood, mispriced, and country and culture specific. The one imbued with lack of knowledge or the unknown-unknown, the other imbued with a lack of know-how to decipher the intricate and dependent elements that define the complexity of financial markets and technology-intensive financial transactions. Financial regulation and its compliance, based on standards and rules and proven measurements, are far more difficult to define and assess their risk consequences.

Regulation and compliance, by contrast, are essentially based on data and risk measurements, basically measuring what we know and what we can and choose to observe, rather than what we need the most—the unpredictable risks, occurring due to many causes, such as natural, operational, technological, systemic, geopolitical, macroeconomic, and strategic reasons. Cultural and traditional values, a physical and changing natural and business environment (whether due to climatic and populations growth and migrations as well as different political and regulatory systems), are also to be accounted for. As noted in Chapter 2, risk measures are constructed to confront predictable events and the likelihoods of their losses. The measurements of their ex-post consequences and their risk externalities are, as a result, and mostly, guess-estimates. Risks are then defined within a known system of rules, regulations, and predictable behaviors. In an increasingly complex, dependent, strategic, and contagious global financial world, these risks are far more difficult to identify, to measure, to evaluate, and to price. Therefore, practically, for IT-intensive finance, uncertainty reigns and regulation has yet to be articulated. Policies that seek to prevent systemic risks by regulating TBTF firms are then incomplete, since an IT finance is oblivious to size. It can have systemic effects without being large. In this sense, the family of TBTF "agents" is far greater than presumed, and therefore its risks are far greater. These lead regulation and compliance to be a "work in progress" attuned to many factors that steer globalization and IT finance and IT gating regulations in both collaborative and conflicting environments.

10.3.2 Regulation, Technology, and Complexity Risks

Technology expands our capacities to do more, to do better, and to construct self-organizing (robotized and intelligent) systems. It also induces a spiraling growth of "complexity" and the need to control its potential risk consequences (Ashby, 1952; C.S. Tapiero, 1994). Because of complexity, controls are needed based on more advanced technologies inducing higher levels of risk and complexity, thereby leading to a dynamic forward growth of risks. Managing the risks of complexity may then be pursued by more complex control systems or by seeking a system simplification. Ohno, the famed Japanese production guru, for example, has launched an industrial manufacturing approach based on a radical simplification of processes—"only simple processes can be efficient"— as a means to institute greater controls over these processes. Similar problems arise in taxation, regulation, health care, and in the banking sector. For example, can a complex tax and regulation policy attain its purpose or merely provide employment to accountants and lawyers to entangle the many problems and risks that wage and investment earners have to contend with? By the same token, can overly complex organizations implode when they can no longer be controlled (e.g., implosion of the banking sector in 2008, the lack of internal controls at J.P. Morgan Chase that led to a loss of $3 billion in 2012)? The technological evolution of industrial processes has been beset by its march toward an increased complexity, leading such processes from being artisanal to complex and technology intensive. With globalization and the migration-outsourcing of basic and fundamental functions to Asia, networked complexity has assumed new dimensions and new challenges in the creation and in the operation of complex networks of enterprises. These are redefining the role of technology in an ever-changing financial "logistics."

10.4 Statistical and Compliance Risks

Regulators depend on "whistle-blowers" and on statistical information and signals provided by statistical outliers. For example, a compliance detection based on tracking financial institution's sectorial or aggregate trading profits, and their deviations from statistical standards. Compliance and audit prevention, their costs, and the breadth and the complexity of regulating and complying domestically and in foreign countries have become daunting.

Traditionally, sovereign and sectoral regulating agencies (e.g., regulating financial transactions, commodity trades, banks) have been challenged by "what it means to be compliant," "what they can do to be compliant," and "the implications of compliance for their business model." For example, technology, data tracking, insiders' reports (whether well intended or bearing personal agendas) empowered by reports through social media have introduced new and challenging dimensions to regulatory and compliance transparency. These have led to data sharing by collaborating regulators and internationally to (lacking a global regulation) the application of a domestic jurisdiction spanning foreign financial and other activities that can be justified or are in the national interest. These new-found powers of regulation have led to a transformation of both regulation and compliance.

Diverse regulating agencies, state, federal, and in some cases international, each with responsibilities and agendas, have provided a sovereign regulation, each with a global outreach and each pursuing its national interest. The decision to audit a financial activity or a bank is then both a matter of the sovereign's jurisdiction, political considerations, and costs mitigated by potential revenues from penalties imposed on a noncompliant bank. These elements have led to a regulation system which is political, economic, extensive, and far more complex. In this environment, compliance is transformed, becoming both strategic and statistical—in other words, given the complexity and the extent of a regulatory jurisdiction, compliance is conditional on regulators audits and defined as a probability prospect.

For example, if a hedge fund is unusually and consistently successful compared with a basket of hedge funds' rates of returns, its (Bayesian) prior estimate of noncompliance may be greater than expected, providing a signal to regulation—for applications of Bayesian games in finance, see, for example, Bassan (2003), Bassan and Natoli (2003), and Bassan *et al.* (2003).

Consequences of the new regulatory environment have led, therefore, to what we defined earlier as regulatory risks expressed by standardization, risk avoidance, less financial competition, substantial new corporate finance costs, and, in some cases, to the migration of economic entities. In this sense, in overly good or bad times, deviating unduly from average performance may provide signals for noncompliance, and therefore to a regulator's audit. Statistical estimates of noncompliance based on data that logistic regression estimates (or other probability models we shall consider later) contribute further to regulators' prior pre-posterior estimates of noncompliance, and therefore to predicting the probability of noncompliance and its audit (for a mathematical development of pre-posterior control games, see Reyniers and Tapiero (1995a,b)).

The greater the complexity, the greater the number of regulations a financial agent has to comply with, the greater the prior probability of noncompliance. Explicitly, if a regulation jurisdiction is spread over a 5000-page document that only lawyers understand and only mathematicians can calculate, the prior expected probability of noncompliance may be very small (in case of a presumed compliance) and yet with an extremely large variance rendering its estimate useless. In this case, a regulator need only be persistent, regulating till a noncompliance is detected and then penalizing the regulated as a function of the regulation costs that justify regulatory efforts expended. In a statistical sense, all regulated are then presumed noncompliant and all may be penalized when/if audited. For these reasons, the prospect of an extensive audit has led financial firms to agree to a financial settlement and avoid greater costs spanning years of controls. These issues are particularly acute for mid-size and small banks and financial institutions due to the extremely high legal and accounting services that audits entail.

The implications of the new regulation and its compliance are necessarily extremely complex and require much research—for related game theory problems, see, for example, Nash (1950, 1951), Aumann (1976, 1988), Nau and McCardle (1990), Banks *et al.*, (2011), and Brandenburger and Dekel (1987). Nonetheless, in order to highlight the rationality of the arguments raised, we shall consider in the following a number of quantitative games and statistical problems that highlight the diversity and the challenges of a statistical and a game-like compliance. These models and the problems we consider are meant to provide a motivation to assess compliance as a statistical and strategic problem. This approach differs in fact from the common view that a financial institution ought to be compliant with all the elements of a regulatory jurisdiction as interpreted by regulatory courts.

10.4.1 Statistical Regulation and Compliance

In this section, we lay out a quantitative formulation for a regulation/compliance probability problem to highlight its complexity. Suppose that a bank's regulatory profile in, say, country k consists of a vector N_k, $\mathbf{r}_k = \{r_{1k}, r_{2k}, r_{3k}, \ldots, r_{N_k k}\}$ of random variables, each with a probability of being compliant or not compliant. We set $R_k(t, \mathbf{r}_k)$ to be an explicit probability model defining the probability of compliance at time t when subjected to an audit in country k. To simplify, we consider the following approaches in the subsequent sections:

- Bernoulli compliance models and their derivatives;
- statistical compliance and statistical risks;
- a multivariate statistical approach;
- regulation and compliance games.

10.4.2 Bernoulli Audits and Noncompliance

In its simplest definition, a financial agent may or not be compliant with a specific regulatory jurisdiction. Let compliance be defined by a probability $p \in [1, 0]$. Estimates of compliance by a financial risk manager and by a regulator may, however, be random: $\tilde{p}_A \in [1, 0]$ and $\tilde{p}_R \in [1, 0]$ respectively, as well as derived from numerous factors providing noncompliance signals. For example, suppose that regulators define compliance as a quantile risk (i.e., value-at-risk capital holding regulation). Let $\tilde{W}_A(t)$ be a bank capital state at time t, a function of its investments, loans, and so on. And say that regulators specify that at all time a percentage α of this average capital $\hat{W}_A(t, T)$ that is defined over a period $(t - T, t)$ is invested in risk-free assets (or liquid assets with negligible rates of returns); then, since the capital value is a function of wealth held at time t, we have $p(t | \tilde{W}_A(t)) = P(\tilde{W}_A(t) > \alpha \hat{W}_A(t, T))$. Thus, the probability of compliance is a function of the requirement to set aside a rolling capital $\alpha \hat{W}_A(t, T)$. In other words, the probability of compliance is a random time variable given by $\tilde{p}(t) = \tilde{p}(t | \alpha, t - T, \hat{W}_A(t, T), \tilde{W}_A(t))$. Thus, in a volatile financial environment, if a bank is subject to sudden losses. It may become necessarily noncompliant. By the same token, noncompliance is counter-cyclical—a greater probability in "hard times" and a smaller one in good times—and thereby lead to the sale of assets at a loss to cover regulatory requirements.

For a sovereign regulator, noncompliance is necessarily a statistical estimate due to incomplete financial statistics (or whistle-blowers that provide insider information) with a propensity to audit more in "bad times" when the expected probabilities of noncompliance would be much greater. For these reasons, both regulators and financial agents (such as banks) engage in model building that allows the definition of statistical estimates that assess compliance states and serve as "proofs of intent" when noncompliance payments and penalties are set or resolved in courts of law. In such an environment, regulation and compliance are both strategic and probabilistic.

10.4.3 A Beta Probability Distribution of Noncompliance

A random probability of noncompliance has important effects to both regulation and the risks of noncompliance. Suppose that the probability of noncompliance at time t of any financial agent is a random variable $x(t)$ which we assume for discussion purposes to be defined by a Beta probability distribution with parameters α_t and β_t:

$$b(x(t)|\alpha_t,\beta_t) = \frac{x(t)^{\alpha_t - 1}[1 - x(t)]^{\beta_t - 1}}{B(\alpha_t,\beta_t)}, \quad E(x(t)) = \frac{\alpha_t}{\alpha_t + \beta_t},$$

$$\text{var}(x(t)) = \frac{\alpha_t \beta_t}{(\alpha_t + \beta_t)^2(\alpha_t + \beta_t + 1)}$$

where $B(\alpha_t,\beta_t) = \Gamma(\alpha_t)\Gamma(\beta_t)/\Gamma(\alpha_t + \beta_t)$. Assume for simplicity that a regulator estimate of current market conditions implies an expected noncompliance estimate $E(x(t))$ and say that m independent financial institutions are selected at random for audits. The number of noncompliant firms detected would then have a mixture (Lexis) binomial probability distribution:

$$E\{\text{PNC}(i|m,x(t))\} = E\left(\binom{m}{i}(x(t))^i(1 - x(t))^{m-i}\right)$$

where its mean and variance are

$$E(i) = mE(x(t)) \quad \text{and} \quad \text{var}(i) = mE(x(t))(1 - E(x(t))) + m(m-1)\ \text{var}(x(t))$$

The expected number of noncompliant financial institutions is therefore a function of its number (in the thousands for the USA) and the expected probability distribution of non-compliant. The variance, however, may be much greater since it is proportional to $m(m-1)$. For example, if the variance of noncompliance is very small (say 0.001) in a sample of 1000 banks, and with the expected probability of noncompliance 0.1, then $E(i) = 100$ and $\text{var}(i) = 1090$, which points to a relatively great uncertainty (even though the number assumed here is probably better than would be the case in reality due to the extreme complexity of the regulatory jurisdiction).

10.4.4 Auditing a Bank for Compliance

Suppose that 50 banks are selected at random from a population of 1500 for an audit and let the probability of a noncompliant bank have a Beta probability distribution. Let $\alpha_t = 1.1$ and $\beta_t = 2.5$. The noncompliance mean and its variance estimates are then

$$E(i|m,E(x(t))) = 50\left(\frac{1.1}{6}\right) = 50(0.1833) = 9.16$$

$$\text{var}E(i|m,E(x(t))) = 9.16\left(\frac{4.9}{6}\right) + \frac{50(49)(1.1 \times 4.9)}{(6)^2(7)} = 59.88$$

which increases appreciably the noncompliance variance.

A similar exercise applied by the regulator to the number of regulations to be controlled or to the regulated to be audited leads to an extremely high level of uncertainty, defined by the variance of the noncompliance probability. For example, say that a regulatory jurisdiction has 7000 regulations, and let the expected probability and its variance of noncompliance to an item be extremely small with $E(x(t)) = 0.001$ and $\text{var}(x(t)) = 0.0001$. The expected number of noncompliances and their variance are then $E(n) = 7000 \times 0.001 = 7$ and $\text{var}(n) = 7(1-0.001) + 4899.3 = 4906.3$. In other words, a complete audit of each regulation may lead to an expected seven regulations to be noncompliant with a huge variance.

If partial compliance may be defined as, say, less than k noncompliant regulations are deemed acceptable, compliance has a probability

$$R^k(t) = \sum_{i=1}^{k}\binom{N}{i}\frac{B(\alpha+i)B(N+k+\beta-i)}{B(\alpha,\beta)B(N+k+\alpha+\beta)}$$

In this sense, compliance and noncompliance are defined by what the regulator claims, which is a function of the consequences resulting from noncompliance audits. For example, suppose that a trader bets $100 000 on a stock based on an illegal tip received. If the bet sours, and say the trader loses 25% of their bet, would they be compliant? Probably yes. If they were to realize a profit of $1 million, would they be compliant? Of course they are, if in fact the trader is detected by a regulator. In such a case, both profits may be clawed back and penalties may be applied. The implication of this exercise is that compliance and noncompliance may be difficult to detect a priori unless there are important signals (such as insider trading, or persistent profitable financial bets and transactions) to point to financial outliers. In this sense, there are two possibilities: either for the regulator to be "persistent", auditing until a noncompliance is detected (as we shall see shortly), or to game the regulated to assess the probability of the regulated being noncompliant based on the consequences of their being audited and noncompliant. Such an approach is considered subsequently.

10.4.5 The Persistent Regulator

Suppose that a "persistent" regulator audits a bank until one (or more) noncompliant regulation is detected. The number of regulations audited until one regulation is found noncompliant is then a random variable $\tilde{n}_{\text{RE},j}(1)$ dependent on the bank's actions j to comply and provide an internal assessment of a probability $p_{2,\text{B}}^{j}$ of noncompliance. An estimate of this probability by the regulator is $p_{2,\text{R}}^{j}$ (either based on private information, or based on industry data or insider information). The probability distribution of the number of statistically selected audits $\tilde{n}_{\text{R},ij}(1)$ by the regulator is thus a geometric probability distribution $p_{2,\text{R}}^{j}\left(1-p_{2,\text{R}}^{j}\right)^{\tilde{n}_{\text{R},j}(1)-1}$ whose mean and variance are

$$E\left(\tilde{n}_{\mathrm{R},j}(1)\right) = \frac{1}{p^{j}_{2,\mathrm{R}}} \quad \text{and} \quad \mathrm{var}\left(\tilde{n}_{\mathrm{R},j}(1)\right) = \frac{1 - p^{j}_{2,\mathrm{R}}}{\left(p^{j}_{2,\mathrm{R}}\right)^{2}}$$

If a penalty $P_{\mathrm{B}}(1)$ is applied when the bank is at last detected to be noncompliant, then the regulator cost is a function of the number of regulation audits made to detect a noncompliance whose regulation cost is a random variable linear in the expected number of audits, $C_{\mathrm{R}}\left(\tilde{n}_{\mathrm{R},j}(1)\right) = c_{\mathrm{R}}\tilde{n}_{\mathrm{R},j}(1)$. In this case, let $\tilde{n}_{\mathrm{R},j}(1) = P_{\mathrm{B}}(1)/c_{\mathrm{R}}$ and $E\left(\tilde{n}_{\mathrm{R},j}(1)\right) = 1/p^{j}_{2,\mathrm{R}} = P_{\mathrm{B}}(1)/c_{\mathrm{R}}$ or $P_{\mathrm{B}}(1) = c_{\mathrm{R}}/p^{j}_{2,\mathrm{R}}$. Thus, the more compliant the bank (i.e., $p^{j}_{2,\mathrm{R}}$ small), the greater the penalty.

Say that the probability distribution of noncompliance is now $f_{\mathrm{R}}(\tilde{p}_{\mathrm{R}})$, then the number of controls until one noncompliance is detected has the mixture distribution

$$\tilde{n}_{\mathrm{R},j}(1) \sim \int \tilde{p}_{\mathrm{R}}(1-\tilde{p}_{\mathrm{R}})^{\tilde{n}_{\mathrm{R},j}(1)-1} f_{\mathrm{R}}(\tilde{p}_{\mathrm{R}})\,d\tilde{p}_{\mathrm{R}} \quad \text{with} \quad f_{\mathrm{R}}(\tilde{p}_{\mathrm{R}}) = \frac{\tilde{p}_{\mathrm{R}}{}^{a-1}(1-\tilde{p}_{\mathrm{R}})^{b-1}}{\mathrm{B}(a,b)}$$

In this case, we have

$$\tilde{n}_{\mathrm{R},j}(1) \sim \int_{0}^{1} \frac{\tilde{p}^{a}_{\mathrm{R}}(1-\tilde{p}_{\mathrm{R}})^{\tilde{n}_{\mathrm{R},j}(1)+b-2}}{\mathrm{B}(a,b)}\,d\tilde{p}_{\mathrm{R}} = \frac{\Gamma(a+b)}{\Gamma(a)\Gamma(b)} \frac{\Gamma(a+1)\Gamma\left(\tilde{n}_{\mathrm{R},j}(1)+b-1\right)}{\Gamma\left(a+1+\tilde{n}_{\mathrm{R},j}(1)+b-1\right)}$$

and

$$\tilde{n}_{\mathrm{R},j}(1) \sim a\frac{\Gamma(a+b)}{\Gamma(b)} \frac{\Gamma\left(\tilde{n}_{\mathrm{R},j}(1)+b-1\right)}{\Gamma\left(a+\tilde{n}_{\mathrm{R},j}(1)+b\right)}$$

As a result, the expected number of audits the regulator will pursue until a noncompliance is detected is

$$E\left(\tilde{n}_{\mathrm{R},j}(1)\right) \sim a\frac{\Gamma(a+b)}{\Gamma(b)} \sum_{i=1}^{\infty} i\frac{\Gamma(i+b-1)}{\Gamma(i+a+b)}$$

which is greater than $E\left(\tilde{n}_{\mathrm{R},j}(1)\right) = 1/p^{j}_{2,\mathrm{R}}$; therefore, the greater the regulator noncompliance uncertainty, the greater the penalty the persistent regulator will impose (to at least recover its costs).

10.4.6 The Beta Prime Model

The Beta Prime model is derived from the Beta probability distribution odds. In other words, let p have a Beta probability distribution of noncompliance $b(p|\alpha,\beta)$ and let its odds be, $y = p/(1-p)$. Then, a Beta prime distribution is given by:

$$f_{\mathrm{B}'}(y) = \frac{(y)^{\alpha-1}(1+y)^{-\alpha-\beta}}{\mathrm{B}(\alpha,\beta)}; \quad E(y) = \frac{\alpha}{\beta-1} \text{ if } \beta > 1, \quad \mathrm{var}(y) = \frac{\alpha(\alpha+\beta-1)}{(\beta-2)(\beta-1)^{2}} \text{ if } \beta > 2$$

For practical purposes, let the regression of the odds of noncompliance be a function of n factors defining a score S:

$$\ln y = \ln\left(\frac{p}{1-p}\right) = S = a_{0} + a_{1}x_{1} + a_{2}x_{2} + \cdots + a_{n}x_{n}$$

Given a random score S, we have $y = e^S$ and $E(y) = \alpha/(\beta-1) = E\left(e^{\tilde{S}}\right)$, as well as a variance

$$\text{var}(\tilde{y}) = \frac{\alpha(\alpha+\beta-1)}{(\beta-2)(\beta-1)^2}, \quad \text{var}\left(e^{\tilde{S}}\right) = E\left(e^{2\tilde{S}}\right) - \left[E\left(e^{\tilde{S}}\right)\right]^2 = E\left(e^{2\tilde{S}}\right) - \left(\frac{\alpha}{\beta-1}\right)^2$$

Therefore:

$$E\left(e^{\tilde{S}}\right) = \frac{\alpha}{\beta-1}; \quad E\left(e^{2\tilde{S}}\right) = \frac{\alpha(\alpha+\beta-1)}{(\beta-2)(\beta-1)^2} + \left(\frac{\alpha}{\beta-1}\right)^2$$

which provides two equations in two unknowns for an approximate estimate of the Beta prime probability distribution of the odds of noncompliance:

$$\alpha = \Phi_\alpha\left(E\left(e^{\tilde{S}}\right), E\left(e^{2\tilde{S}}\right)\right); \quad \beta = \Phi_\beta E\left(e^{\tilde{S}}\right), E\left(e^{2\tilde{S}}\right)$$

By the same token, this provides an estimate of the noncompliance probability, since both are defined in terms of the same parameters. Note that if the score is normally distributed, the distribution of y has a lognormal distribution whose parameters (mean and variance) can be approximated by the Beta prime distribution. However, when scores are not normally distributed, one may still use the Beta prime approximation. In other words, if $\alpha = 0.1$ and $\beta = 3$, based on an estimate of the Beta probability distribution, we have

$$\frac{0.1}{3-1} = 0.05 = E\left(e^{\tilde{S}}\right); \quad \frac{(0.1)(0.1+3-1)}{(3-2)(3-1)^2} + \left(\frac{0.1}{3-1}\right)^2 = 0.055 = E\left(e^{2\tilde{S}}\right)$$

Inversely, if the score has an expectation $0.05 = E\left(e^{\tilde{S}}\right)$ and $0.055 = E\left(e^{2\tilde{S}}\right)$, we obtain $\alpha = 0.1$ and $\beta = 3$, regardless of the probability distribution of the score. Generally, the kth moment is then

$$E\left(\tilde{y}^k\right) = \frac{B(\alpha+k,\beta-k)}{B(\alpha,\beta)} = \frac{\Gamma(\alpha+k)\Gamma(\beta-k)}{\Gamma(\alpha)\Gamma(\beta)}, \quad k < \beta$$

Therefore:

$$\begin{cases} k=1 \to E(y)^1 = \dfrac{\Gamma(\alpha+1)\Gamma(\beta-1)}{\Gamma(\alpha)\Gamma(\beta)} = \dfrac{\alpha}{\beta-1}, & \beta>1 \\[2mm] k=2 \to E(y)^2 = \dfrac{\Gamma(\alpha+2)\Gamma(\beta-2)}{\Gamma(\alpha)\Gamma(\beta)} = \dfrac{\alpha(\alpha+1)}{(\beta-1)(\beta-2)}, & \beta>2 \\[2mm] k=3 \to E(y)^3 = \dfrac{\Gamma(\alpha+3)\Gamma(\beta-3)}{\Gamma(\alpha)\Gamma(\beta)} = \dfrac{\alpha(\alpha+1)(\alpha+2)}{(\beta-1)(\beta-2)(\beta-3)}, & \beta>3 \end{cases}$$

Say that $\alpha = 0.5$ and $\beta = 6$, then

$$k=1 \to \frac{0.5}{5} = 0.1; \quad k=2 \to \frac{0.5(1.5)}{20} = 0.375; \quad k=3 \to \frac{0.5(1.5)(2.5)}{60} = 0.03125$$

10.4.7 The Logit and Beta Prime Compliance Models

In practice, numerous statistical and data analytic techniques, based on multiple performance and noncompliance risk factors, are used to estimate the probabilities of noncompliance. We consider the common statistical logit model. Let x_{ij} be the specific score of a regulated i on a specific regulation j. Such information is assembled through questionnaires that the regulated fills in or are defined by public records performance and various information. Let a_j be a set of weights to be applied to each regulation. Given these weights (estimated using a logit or other models), an aggregate score for a regulated i is then found to be $S_i = \sum_{j=1}^{p} a_j x_{ij}$. To determine these weights, the logit model assumes a logistic probability distribution to predict the probability of noncompliance as a function of the regulated score. Explicitly, it assumes a number of observable characteristics (input factors) presumed to predict the probability of noncompliance. Say that the probability is

$$PNC_i = F(S_i) = \frac{1}{1 + e^{-S_i}}$$

or the odds of noncompliance are:

$$\frac{PNC_i}{1 - PNC_i} = e^{S_i}$$

where S_i is the score that points to the natural logarithm of the odds of noncompliance. As a result, a linear predictive model based on data is then constructed, which we can write as

$$\ln\left(\frac{PNC_i}{1 - PNC_i}\right) = \tilde{S}_i = \alpha + \sum_{j=1}^{k} \beta_j X_{ij} + \varepsilon_i$$

where $\tilde{S}_i$ is a normally distributed random score whose expectation is $\hat{S}_i = \alpha + \sum_{j=1}^{k} \beta_j X_{ij}$. In this case, the noncompliance probability is a logit probability distribution with its cumulative distribution function

$$P\{NC_i | S_i\} = F(S_i) = \frac{1}{1 + e^{-S_i}} = \left(1 + e^{-\alpha + \sum_{j=1}^{k} \beta_j X_{ij} + \varepsilon_i}\right)^{-1}$$

The probability distribution for a score is

$$\frac{dF(\tilde{S}_i)}{dS_i} = f(\tilde{S}_i) = e^{-\tilde{S}_i}\left(1 + e^{-\tilde{S}_i}\right)^{-2} = e^{-\alpha - \sum_{j=1}^{k} \beta_j X_{ij} + \varepsilon_i}\left(1 + e^{-\alpha - \sum_{j=1}^{k} \beta_j X_{ij} + \varepsilon_i}\right)^{-2}$$

where ε_i is a random normal error and β_j are parameters to be estimated by linear regression using the regulator's data set regarding the regulated population. When the logit model is deemed statistically acceptable and if the parameter estimates are also meaningful, the PNC is deemed predictive as stated earlier. The statistical score is then used to reach a decision to audit or not, based on the predicted score relative to a standard score S^*. Explicitly, if the score is below the standard score, an audit is made; otherwise, it is not:

$$\begin{cases} \text{Do not audit} & S_i \geq S^* \\ \text{Audit for noncompliance} & S_i < S^* \end{cases}$$

Audit risk probabilities are then

$$\begin{cases} \text{type I risk} = P(\tilde{S}_i | S_i \leq S^*); & \text{the probability of a regulated is audited and found compliant} \\ \text{type II risk} = 1 - P(\tilde{S}_i | S_i \geq S^*); & \text{the probability of not auditing a noncompliant regulated} \end{cases}$$

or

$$\text{type I risk}: \ P(NC_i | S_i \leq S^*); \quad \text{type II risk}: \ 1 - P(NC_i | S_i > S^*)$$

Noncompliance is then defined by a conditional probability. Explicitly, by Bayes' rule:

$$P(NC, S) = P(NC|S)P(S) = P(S|NC)P(NC)$$

and

$$P(NC|S) = \frac{P(S|NC)}{P(S)} P(NC) = \frac{P(S|NC)P(NC)}{P(S|NC)P(NC) + P(S|C)P(C)}$$

In other words, given a prior probability of NC (expressing the general economic conditions for example), then based on prior data that indicates the conditional probabilities $P(S|NC)$ and $P(S|C)$, we can obtain a score-dependent estimate for the probability of noncompliance.

For the logit model, we have, as seen earlier, the score distribution $f(S_i) = e^{-S_i} / (1 + e^{-S_i})^2$; therefore, type I and II risks are calculated by

$$P_G(\tilde{S}_i | S_i \leq S^*) = \int_0^{S^*} \frac{e^{-S_i}}{(1 + e^{-S_i})^2} dS_i \quad \text{and} \quad 1 - P_{NG}(\tilde{S}_i | S_i \geq S^*) = 1 - \int_{S^*}^{S^*} \frac{e^{-X_i}}{(1 + e^{-X_i})^2} dX_i$$

Other models may extend this approach. For example, the probit model, unlike the logit model, assumes that the probability of noncompliance is given by a cumulative normal probability distribution; that is, it is defined by

$$PNC_i = F(S_i) = \int_{-\infty}^{S_i} \frac{1}{\sqrt{2\pi}} e^{-(1/2)x^2} dx$$

Other models can be constructed in this spirit (such as ordered logit, probit, and so on).

10.5 A Multivariate Bernoulli Compliance and Audits

10.5.1 Bernoulli Compliance

Compliance is essentially a qualitative statement such as Y or N, 1 or 0. Similarly, regulatory items are either compliant or noncompliant. In this case, in a vector of 10 regulations, $n = 10$, we may define the compliant state $(1, 1, 1, 0, 0, 1, 0, 0, 0, 1)$. Labeling each regulatory jurisdiction as probabilistic, we can state that these are defined by a multivariate and dependent Bernoulli distribution if compliance of these regulatory items tend to be statistically dependent. A single regulatory jurisdiction assumes, as already stated, two values, 1 or 0, which we denote by $\tilde{x}_i \in \{1,0\}$ with probability $p(\tilde{x}_i = 1) = p_i$. Let $(\tilde{x}_i, \tilde{y}_j)$, $i = 0, 1, j = 0, 1$, be dependent and therefore of four potential states $\langle\{1, 1\}\{1, 0\}\{0, 1\}\{0, 0\}\rangle$, each with a joint probability $\{p_{ij} = p(\tilde{x}, \tilde{y})\}$ denoting the joint random variables $(\tilde{x}, \tilde{y})$. For discussion purposes, we let these random variables denote the probabilities that regulation i is noncompliant with probability $\tilde{x}_i$ while regulatory jurisdiction j is audited with probability $\tilde{y}_j$. In this case the probability of noncompliance if the regulator selects one regulation only is $P\{1, 1\}$. If two regulations out of five regulatory jurisdictions are audited, there are then 10 possibilities. Letting $\{p_1, p_2, p_3, p_4, p_5\}$, their statistical probability of noncompliance is

$$
\begin{cases}
1,1,0,0,0 \rightarrow p_1(1-p_2) + (1-p_1)p_2 + p_1p_2 = 1 - (1-p_1)(1-p_2) \\
1,0,1,0,0 \rightarrow p_1(1-p_3) + (1-p_1)p_3 + p_1p_3 = 1 - (1-p_1)(1-p_3) \\
1,0,0,1,0 \rightarrow p_1(1-p_4) + (1-p_1)p_4 + p_1p_4 = 1 - (1-p_1)(1-p_4) \\
1,0,0,0,1 \rightarrow p_1(1-p_5) + (1-p_1)p_5 + p_1p_5 = 1 - (1-p_1)(1-p_5) \\
0,1,1,0,0 \rightarrow p_2(1-p_3) + (1-p_2)p_3 + p_2p_3 = 1 - (1-p_2)(1-p_3) \\
0,1,0,1,0 \rightarrow p_2(1-p_4) + (1-p_2)p_4 + p_2p_4 = 1 - (1-p_2)(1-p_4) \\
0,1,0,0,1 \rightarrow p_2(1-p_5) + (1-p_2)p_5 + p_2p_5 = 1 - (1-p_2)(1-p_5) \\
0,0,1,1,0 \rightarrow p_3(1-p_4) + (1-p_3)p_4 + p_3p_4 = 1 - (1-p_3)(1-p_4) \\
0,0,1,0,1 \rightarrow p_3(1-p_5) + (1-p_3)p_5 + p_3p_5 = 1 - (1-p_3)(1-p_5) \\
0,0,0,1,1 \rightarrow p_4(1-p_5) + (1-p_4)p_5 + p_4p_5 = 1 - (1-p_4)(1-p_5)
\end{cases}
$$

Therefore, a regulator will choose the two regulations that will have the greatest probabilities of detecting noncompliance.

A general expression for dependent bivariate Bernoulli random variables $(\tilde{x}, \tilde{y})$ is thus

$$
p(x,y) = \{p_{11}\}^{xy} \{p_{10}\}^{x(1-y)} \{p_{01}\}^{(1-x)y} \{p_{00}\}^{(1-x)(1-y)}
$$

where $(x,y) \in [1,0]$ and $p_{11} + p_{10} + p_{01} + p_{00} = 1$. For a K vector of multivariate Bernoulli probability distribution (note the change in notation) we have

$$
p(x_1, x_2, \ldots, x_K) = \{p_{11\ldots1}\}^{\prod_{j=1}^{K} x_j} \{p_{011\ldots1}\}^{(1-x_1)\prod_{j=1}^{K} x_j} \cdots \{p_{00\ldots0}\}^{\prod_{j=1}^{K}(1-x_j)}
$$

which leads to the following moments (mean, variance, and covariation):

$$
\begin{cases}
E(x_1) = p_{10} + p_{11}, & \mathrm{var}(x_1) = (p_{10} + p_{11})[1 - (p_{10} + p_{11})] \\
E(x_2) = p_{01} + p_{11}, & \mathrm{var}(x_2) = (p_{01} + p_{11})[1 - (p_{01} + p_{11})] \\
E(x_1 x_2) = p_{11}
\end{cases}
$$

Since the sum of probabilities for all events is equal to one, we can write $p_{11} = 1 - p_{00} - p_{10} - p_{01}$. Further, setting $1 - p_{00} - p_{01} = p_1$ and $1 - p_{00} - p_{10} = p_2$ we obtain

$$
\begin{cases}
E(x_1) = p_1 = 1 - p_{00} - p_{01}, & \mathrm{var}(x_1) = p_1(1-p_1) \\
E(x_2) = p_2 = 1 - p_{00} - p_{10}, & \mathrm{var}(x_2) = p_2(1-p_2)
\end{cases}
$$

as well as

$$E(x_1x_2) = p_{11} = E(x_1)E(x_2) + \rho\sqrt{\text{var}(x_1)\text{var}(x_2)}$$

where ρ is the correlation of the bivariate Bernoulli distribution with

$$E(x_1x_2) = p_{11} = p_1 - p_{10} = p_2 - p_{01} = p_1p_2 + \rho\sqrt{p_1p_2(1-p_1)(1-p_2)}$$

$$\text{cov}(x_1,x_2) = \rho - p_1p_2$$

Say that $p_1 = 0.2$ and $p_2 = 0.1$ and then $\rho = 0.3$, $p_{11} = 0.038$, $p_{10} = 0.162$, $p_{01} = 0.062$, $p_{00} = 0.738$, while for an independent process we have $E(x_1x_2) = p_{11} = p_1p_2$ and $E(x_1x_2) = p_1 - p_{10} = p_2 - p_{01} = p_1p_2$ and therefore $p_{10} = p_1(1-p_2)$ and $p_{01} = p_2(1-p_1)$.

10.5.2 Bernoulli and a Codependent Model

Let x_1 be a random audit and x_2 be a random noncompliance. Assume that both are statistically dependent defined by a bivariate Bernoulli distribution as indicated in the Table 10.1.

The probability of being noncompliant in this case is $p_{01} + p_{11}$ while the probability of an audit is $p_{10} + p_{11}$. It may be generalized to a sampling inspection of say n inspections (or inspecting n articles in a regulation book). The probability distribution of detecting, say, r outcomes has then a bivariate binomial distribution whose probability generating function is

$$G^*(z_1,z_2) = (p_{11} + p_{01}z_1 + p_{10}z_2 + p_{00}z_1z_2)^n$$

with $E(x_1) = n(p_{01} + p_{00})$ and $E(x_2) = n(p_{00} + p_{10})$ and $E(x_1x_2) = n(n-1)[p_{00} + (p_{01} + p_{00})(p_{10} + p_{00})]$. But, since $E(x_1x_2) = E(x_1)E(x_2) + \rho\sigma_1\sigma_2$, we have

$$\rho = \frac{E(x_1x_2) - E(x_1)E(x_2)}{\sigma_1\sigma_2}$$

where $\sigma_1\sigma_2$ can be calculated by using the second derivatives of the probability-generating function.

Similar distributions can be formulated in different ways. For example, let $(\tilde{x}_1, \tilde{x}_2, \ldots, \tilde{x}_n)$ be n bivariate random variables, representing n regulations with them being compliant defined by the probabilities defined as follows:

$$f(\tilde{x}_i = 1|p_{1,i}) = p_{1,i}$$

$$f(\tilde{x}_i = 1, \tilde{x}_j = 1|p_{2,ij}) = p_{2,ij}, \quad i,j = 1, \ldots, n; \ i \neq j$$

$$\vdots$$

$$f(\tilde{x}_i = 1, \tilde{x}_j = 1, \ldots, \tilde{x}_n = 1|p_{k,i,j\ldots n}) = p_{k,i,j\ldots n}$$

Table 10.1 Compliance and inspection.

	Compliant	Not compliant
No inspection	p_{00}	p_{01}
Inspection	p_{10}	p_{11}

Since these are binary variables, we have

$$E(\tilde{x}_i|p_{1i}) = p_{1i}, \quad E\left(\tilde{x}_i\tilde{x}_j|p_{2,ij}\right) = p_{2,ij}; \quad \text{cov}\left(\tilde{x}_i,\tilde{x}_j|p_{1i},p_{1j}p_{2,ij}\right) = p_{2,ij} - p_{1i}p_{1j};$$

$$i \neq j \quad \text{and} \quad \rho_{ij}\left(\tilde{x}_i,\tilde{x}_j\right) = \frac{p_{2,ij} - p_{1i}p_{1j}}{\sqrt{p_{1i}(1-p_{1i})p_{1j}\left(1-p_{1j}\right)}}$$

Thus, if a regulator has three regulations to audit, they may calculate the appropriate parameters recursively. The number of parameters required to represent such dependence, between two, three, four, and more random variables (regulations), will require an increasing number of parameters which renders such an approach unrealistic. For this reason, other approaches can be devised to represent and capture the dependence essential characteristics and at the same time maintain a tractable model.

10.6 Regulation and Compliance Games

In this section we shall use some examples to highlight the effect of strategic behaviors on regulation audits and compliance. We shall also point out that the greater the effort to detect noncompliance, the far greater the penalty the regulated will assume (even for a mostly compliant regulated). These penalties arise from the regulator viewpoint, a priori committed to detect a noncompliance and therefore justifies the penalty by the institutional effort expended. In a statistical environment of compliance, the time needed to detect noncompliance may further take a far greater amount of time and therefore the detection of noncompliance is far more significant, leading to a greater penalty. For example, if a fund controlled persistently over years fails to lead to the detection of a noncompliant behavior, then, once detected, penalties in the millions are extracted from that fund. This is to be compared with a regulatory control that is quickly settled by relatively small penalties to avoid any further search that can lead to other noncompliant measures. In this sense, in a complex regulated environment, a common policy is to accept immediately being noncompliant, whether it is based on fact or based on a move to initiate persistent controls, and thus avoid at least the extraordinary costs the regulated assume in reputation and legal and other costs that are not incurred by a regulator. These situations highlight the strategic and confrontational nature of compliance and regulation evoked in this chapter. The usefulness of a game is not necessarily practical, but it can provide a better understanding of the complexity and the conflictual nature that regulators and financial institutions are confronted by. For audit and regulatory games, we refer, for example, to Avenhaus (1994), Avenhaus *et al.* (1995, 1996), Kogan and Tapiero (2007), and C.S. Tapiero (1995, 1996, 2005a–c). The following problem is used as a simple example.

For simplicity, consider only two regulations to highlight the effects of regulations dependence. In a complex regulation system, such dependence is necessarily present. For a zero-tolerance regulation of two $(= N_R)$ regulation items, we have a noncompliance probability $\tilde{P}_0^2 = 1 - (1-\tilde{p}_1)(1-\tilde{p}_2)$, and therefore its expected value is necessarily a function of their correlation. Assume that correlated noncompliance probabilities $(\tilde{p}_1, \tilde{p}_2)$ defined by a bivariate Bernoulli model with potential probability outcomes $(p_{00}, p_{01}, p_{10}, p_{11})$, where "0" and "1" define compliance and noncompliance respectively. If these probabilities are independent, then $p_{00} = 1 - \left(1-\hat{p}_0^1\right)\left(1-\hat{p}_0^2\right)$, where $\left(\hat{p}_0^1, \hat{p}_0^2\right)$ are the marginal noncompliance probabilities of 1 and 2 to be noncompliant. If these probabilities are dependent, then $1 - p_{00} = (p_{01} + p_{10} + p_{11})$ denotes the probability of noncompliance (i.e., at least one regulation is noncompliant). For the regulated, set $\{y_1^k \equiv \tilde{p}_1^k;\ y_2^k \equiv \tilde{p}_2^k\} \equiv \{1, 0;\ 1, 0\}$ and the joint distribution $f(y_1^k, y_2^k)$, which we model by

$$f(y_1^k, y_2^k | \alpha_1, \alpha_2, \rho) = \frac{(\alpha_1)^{y_1^k}(1 - \alpha_1)^{1 - y_1^k}(\alpha_2)^{y_2^k}(1 - \alpha_2)^{1 - y_2^k}\rho^{y_1^k y_2^k}}{1 - \alpha_1 \alpha_2 (1 - \rho)}$$

In this case, the probabilities are obtained as shown in Table 10.2.

The marginal distributions of (y_1^k, y_2^k) are Bernoulli probability distributions with parameters p_1 and p_2 with

$$1 - p_1 = \frac{(1 - \alpha_1)}{1 - \alpha_1 \alpha_2 (1 - \rho)} \quad \text{and} \quad 1 - p_2 = \frac{(1 - \alpha_2)}{1 - \alpha_1 \alpha_2 (1 - \rho)}$$

since

$$1 - p_1 = p_{00} + p_{01} = \frac{(1 - \alpha_1)(1 - \alpha_2)}{1 - \alpha_1 \alpha_2 (1 - \rho)} + \frac{(1 - \alpha_1)\alpha_2}{1 - \alpha_1 \alpha_2 (1 - \rho)} = \frac{1 - \alpha_1}{1 - \alpha_1 \alpha_2 (1 - \rho)}$$

and similarly for $1 - p_2$. The probability of noncompliance if both regulations are audited is then

$$1 - \frac{(1 - \alpha_1)(1 - \alpha_2)}{1 - \alpha_1 \alpha_2 (1 - \rho)}$$

(and one or both regulations are found to be noncompliant). The marginal probabilities of noncompliance are then $y_1^k = p_{10} + p_{11}$, $y_2^k = p_{01} + p_{11}$. Say $\alpha_1 = 0.1$, $\alpha_2 = 0.2$, and $\rho = 0.3$ are the parameters of the bivariate Bernoulli probability distribution, then $p_{01} = 0.18255$, $p_{11} = 0.00608$, $p_{00} = 0.73022$, and $p_{10} = 0.08113$; therefore, the probability of noncompliance is $1 - p_{00} = 0.2697$. The marginal probabilities of noncompliance are also $p_1 = 0.08113$ and $p_2 = 0.18863$. If these regulations were independent, then $p_{00} = 0.7346$ and $p_{00} = 1 - 0.7346 = 0.2654$, then $(0.2697 - 0.2654)/0.2654$, which is a growth rate of 1.6% in noncompliance due to their dependence. In terms of our probabilities, the marginal probabilities are

$$p_1 = \frac{\alpha_1(1 - \alpha_2) + \alpha_1 \alpha_2 \rho}{1 - \alpha_1 \alpha_2 (1 - \rho)} \quad \text{and} \quad p_2 = \frac{(1 - \alpha_1)\alpha_2 + \alpha_1 \alpha_2 \rho}{1 - \alpha_1 \alpha_2 (1 - \rho)}$$

Table 10.2 Probabilities for the regulation dependence case.

	$y_2^k = 0$, C	$y_2^k = 1$, NC
$y_1^k = 0$ C	$p_{00} = \dfrac{(1 - \alpha_1)(1 - \alpha_2)}{1 - \alpha_1 \alpha_2 (1 - \rho)}$	$p_{01} = \dfrac{(1 - \alpha_1)\alpha_2}{1 - \alpha_1 \alpha_2 (1 - \rho)}$
$y_1^k = 1$ NC	$p_{10} = \dfrac{\alpha_1(1 - \alpha_2)}{1 - \alpha_1 \alpha_2 (1 - \rho)}$	$p_{11} = \dfrac{\alpha_1 \alpha_2 \rho}{1 - \alpha_1 \alpha_2 (1 - \rho)}$

which are necessarily an increase in the noncompliance probability. As a result, for $N_R = 2$ (for a full audit) we have a noncompliance probability $\tilde{P}_u^{N_R} = 1 - (1 - \tilde{p}_1)(1 - \tilde{p}_2)$, while for the audit of one regulation only, selected with a probability 0.5, we have $\tilde{P}_u^{N_R} = \frac{1}{2}(0.08113) + \frac{1}{2}(0.18863) = 0.13488$, which is the conditional probability of a noncompliance when the audit of a regulation is random.

Next, assume that the probability that the kth regulated actually attends to its compliance with probability u^k and let the probability that an audit probability of a noncompliant regulation is made and noncompliance is not detected. Let the probability of detecting the first regulation be θ_1, then the probability of a control and not detecting it is $u_1^k(1 - \theta_1)p_1$, while the probability that an audit is made and a regulation is found to be noncompliant is $(1 - u_1^k)p_1$ (and similarly for regulation 2). As a result, their sum in the first regulation is $p_1(1 - u_1^k\theta_1)$, denoting the probability of noncompliance of regulation 1 less the probability of an audit and noncompliance detected. The type II errors probabilities for a control of regulations 1 and 2 are therefore, $p_1(1 - u_1^k\theta_1)$, $i = 1, 2$, with p_i replaced:

$$\beta_1 = (1 - u_1^k\theta_1)\left[\frac{\alpha_1(1 - \alpha_2) + \alpha_1\alpha_2\rho}{1 - \alpha_1\alpha_2(1 - \rho)}\right] \text{ and } \beta_2 = (1 - u_2^k\theta_2)\left[\frac{\alpha_2(1 - \alpha_1) + \alpha_1\alpha_2\rho}{1 - \alpha_1\alpha_2(1 - \rho)}\right]$$

Therefore, the probability that both regulations are noncompliant and not detected is $\beta_1\beta_2$. Four situations arise in this case, which we summarize in Table 10.3.

If the probabilities of regulations audits are q_1^k and q_2^k, the probability of an undetected noncompliance is $1 - (1 - q_1^k\beta_1)(1 - q_2^k\beta_2)$. Of course, this is the risk the financial and regulated agent will run if it is subject to the control of the regulator. For example, if the regulated audits the first regulation only, then the noncompliance risk is $1 - (1 - \beta_1)$. Generally, if there were n dependent regulations, then the risk of noncompliance is $1 - \prod_{k=1}^{n}(1 - q_k^k\beta_k)$, where the type II risks are calculated based on a multivariate Bernoulli-dependent noncompliant model (see C.S. Tapiero (2013b)).

Table 10.3 Type II errors.

	$u_2^k = 1$	$u_2^k = 0$
$u_1^k = 1$	$\beta_1 = (1 - \theta_1)\left[\dfrac{\alpha_1(1 - \alpha_2) + \alpha_1\alpha_2\rho}{1 - \alpha_1\alpha_2(1 - \rho)}\right]$	$\beta_1 = (1 - \theta_1)\left[\dfrac{\alpha_1(1 - \alpha_2) + \alpha_1\alpha_2\rho}{1 - \alpha_1\alpha_2(1 - \rho)}\right]$
	$\beta_2 = (1 - \theta_2)\left[\dfrac{\alpha_2(1 - \alpha_1) + \alpha_1\alpha_2\rho}{1 - \alpha_1\alpha_2(1 - \rho)}\right]$	$\beta_2 = \dfrac{\alpha_2(1 - \alpha_1) + \alpha_1\alpha_2\rho}{1 - \alpha_1\alpha_2(1 - \rho)}$
$u_1^k = 0$	$\beta_1 = \dfrac{\alpha_1(1 - \alpha_2) + \alpha_1\alpha_2\rho}{1 - \alpha_1\alpha_2(1 - \rho)}$	$\beta_1 = \dfrac{\alpha_1(1 - \alpha_2) + \alpha_1\alpha_2\rho}{1 - \alpha_1\alpha_2(1 - \rho)}$
	$\beta_2 = (1 - \theta_2)\dfrac{\alpha_2(1 - \alpha_1) + \alpha_1\alpha_2\rho}{1 - \alpha_1\alpha_2(1 - \rho)}$	$\beta_2 = \dfrac{\alpha_2(1 - \alpha_1) + \alpha_1\alpha_2\rho}{1 - \alpha_1\alpha_2(1 - \rho)}$

10.7 Satisficing Games and Regulation–Compliance

Game theory is fundamentally based on a Nash equilibrium. Such an approach leads to conflictual games that might not be the appropriate models that define compliance and regulation. In fact, we believe that regulation does not (or rather should not) seek to "get the better" of financial institutions. Rather, a rational economic banking (Bhattacharya *et al.*, 1998), economic stability (Minsky, 1992, 2008; Nier *et al.*, 2007). By the same token, financial institutions have a stake in the maintenance of an efficient regulation as it maintains a competitive fairness. Thus, rather than defining regulation and compliance as Nash conflict games, regulation may seek "satisficing" solutions that may be found by satisficing games (Stirling and Goodrich, 1999; Stirling, 2003; C.S. Tapiero, 2005c).

The problems that both a financial firm (FF) and a regulator are faced with are twofold: (1) the FF's efforts (and therefore costs) to prevent noncompliance; (2) the strategies a regulator may pursue and its costs (see also Tapiero (1996)). In order to focus our attention, assume that an FF has a noncompliance probability p which it may reduce by investments in preventive controls at a cost c_F. For example, let $C(p)$ be the cost of noncompliance with $\partial C/\partial p < 0$, $\partial^2 C/\partial p^2 < 0$, $C(0) = \infty$. In this sense, an FF strategy is defined by selecting the probabilities (p, x) of noncompliance and of exercising a preventive effort whose cost is c_F. By the same token, the regulator has the choice to audit (with probability y) or not, which may result or not in detecting a noncompliance. If a noncompliance is detected, then a penalty cost might be applied to the FF. Since there are "no winners in noncompliance," both the FF and the "financial system as a whole" end up penalized by noncompliance. These situations result in a random payoff game, given in Table 10.4.

Note that, for the FF, the basic payoff from its activity, as long as it is not detected, is $\pi_P - C(p)$, while the payoff if it applies preventive controls is $\pi_P - [C(p) + c_F]$. When the FF does not apply preventive measures and it is noncompliant and detected by the regulator, then the FF payoff is random, with $(1-\alpha)\widetilde{\Phi}$ —an additional penalty cost sustained, where $\widetilde{\Phi}$ is the noncompliance costs sustained by "the financial system" with $(1-\alpha)$ the FF share. Its complementary share $\alpha\widetilde{\Phi}$ is assumed by the "financial system." Next, let π_S be the financial system's payoff that arises from the activity of the FF, while c_S is its cost of regulation. A summary of the costs of the FF and by the regulator is given in Table 10.4.

For a regulator, the decision is to audit or not, while for the FF the decision is to choose a preventive strategy embedded in the cost function $C(p)$ or to resort to a preventive

Table 10.4 The (FF, regulator) payoff matrix.

	Audit by regulator, y	No audit by regulator, $1-y$
Control by FF, x	$\pi_P - [C(p) + c_F]; \pi_S - c_S$	$\pi_P - [C(p) + c_F]; \pi_S$
No control by FF, $1-x$	$\begin{cases} \pi_P - C(p) - (1-\alpha)\widetilde{\Phi} & p \\ \pi_P - C(p) & 1-p \\ \pi_S - c_S - \alpha\widetilde{\Phi} & p \\ \pi_S - c_S & 1-p \end{cases}$	$\begin{array}{c} \pi_P - C(p) \\ \begin{cases} \pi_S & 1-p \\ \pi_S - \widetilde{\Phi} & p \end{cases} \end{array}$

control. These result in a random payoff of a two-person non-zero sum game—see also Reyniers and Tapiero (1995a,b) and C.S. Tapiero (1995, 1996) for related studies. Randomness occurs from two sources: the mutual controls set by the FF and the regulator who acts as a proxy for "the financial system;" and the randomness of noncompliance (p) and the randomness of the costs due to noncompliance $\left(\tilde{\Phi}\right)$. To simplify our analysis we consider first an intuitive solution under a "risk neutrality assumption." In this case, all random payoffs in the bimatrix game (Table 10.5) are treated by their expected values.

Proposition 10.1 *For a risk-neutral FF and a risk-neutral regulator, the propensity to introduce preventive controls by the firm and the regulator to control the firm are given by the following:*

1) *If $c_S \geq (1-\alpha)p\hat{\Phi}$ then $y^* = 0$ and in all cases $y^* \neq 1$, $0 < p < 1$.*
2) *$0 < x^* < 1$ in all conditions.*
3) *If $c_S \leq (1-\alpha)p\hat{\Phi}$, then for a risk-neutral firm and regulator:*

$$x^* = 1 - \frac{c_S}{(1-\alpha)p\hat{\Phi}} \quad and \quad y^* = \frac{c_F}{(1-\alpha)p\hat{\Phi}}$$

4) *The Nash equilibrium values for both the FF and the regulator are given by*

$$V_F = \pi_P - C(p) - c_F \quad and \quad V_S = \pi_S - \frac{c_S}{1-\alpha}.$$

The implications of these results are noteworthy. Of course, we see that the effects of α, the financial system's share in "mitigating the effects of noncompliance," decreases the propensity for preventive controls by the FF and increases the propensity of the regulator to control the FF. By the same token, when the FF improves its noncompliance (p is smaller), then it uses less preventive controls while the regulator will use more audits (to compensate the reduction in preventive efforts applied by the FF)! Other aspects are treated in detail in Tapiero (1995, 1996).

The definition and the solution of games provide a wide range of interpretations and potential approaches that deal with regulation and compliance games that seek solutions that might be used to reduce the costs and the risks of regulation and compliance. There are, of course, many facets to game theoretic problems which could be considered and have not been considered. For example, risk aversion, the effects of risk sharing, applying cooperative efforts (such as through tax incentives and their like in other games; Katzman, 1988; Laffont, 1995), as well as applications of a satisficing principle (Stirling, 2003;

Table 10.5 The (polluter, regulator) risk-neutral payoff matrix.

	Audit by regulator	No audit by regulator
Control by firm	$\pi_P - [C(p) + c_F]$; $\pi_S - c_S$	$\pi_P - [C(p) + c_F]$; π_S
No control by firm	$\pi_P - C(p) - (1-\alpha)p\tilde{\Phi}$; $\pi_S - c_S - \alpha p\tilde{\Phi}$	$\pi_P - C(p)$; $\pi_S - p\tilde{\Phi}$

$\hat{\Phi}$ denotes the expected cost of a polluting event. The solution of this game is treated in C.S. Tapiero (1995, 1996), and therefore we shall only summarize the essential facets of its solution given by Proposition 10.1.

C.S. Tapiero, 2005c). The basic presumption of the "satisficing" solution to regulation–compliance games is that it is very difficult to fully enforce a full compliance on an FF when regulation is so complex that it, in fact, contributes to a transformation of the financial system which might not be efficient. As a result, some risk controls are needed to ensure that an FF is controlled so that the appropriate efforts carried out by the FFs contribute to their compliance.

10.8 Conclusion

Regulations are complex and dependent in a number of ways. First, they may be dependent statistically, and second due to the interconnectedness of regulations systems and the networking of financial institutions. These issues, although of fundamental importance, are rarely attended to.

There are numerous books and papers on statistical and quality controls as well as on experimental design that are relevant to compliance. Some references consulted include Kennett and Zacks (2004) and C.S. Tapiero (1996).

This chapter particularly addressed inspection games or strategic controls. These problems have been studied by Maschler (1996), Reyniers and Tapiero (1995a,b), Ruckle (1992), Von Stengel (1991), Avenhaus (1994), Avenhaus *et al.* (1995, 1996), Baston and Bostock (1991), Bird and Kortanek (1974), and others. Some applications include inspection games for industrial products, contracts compliance, and quality controls; for example, Reyniers and Tapiero (1995a,b), C.S. Tapiero (1995, 1996, 2005a–c), and Ruckle (1992). Finally, there is an intensive set of studies applying control in regulation.

Appendix 10.A: Games, Risk and Uncertainty

Games uncertainty results essentially from two sources:

- Uncertainty regarding the actions that will be taken by the "other" (or "others") party. When a party's potential set of actions regarding the other is completely defined, we shall assume that their "preferences are complete," while when they are not we shall assume that their "preferences are incomplete." Such a distinction differentiates between risk and uncertainty in the sense of Frank Knight (1921), which is due to incomplete statistical information and to both moral hazard and adverse selection risks when information and power asymmetry induce a state of uncertainty.
- Risks related to adverse conditional payoffs of a game (prevalent in random payoff games). When conditional consequences are known partially or not known to the counterparty, we will call such games incomplete in the sense of Harsanyi (1967, 1968a,b) (also called Bayesian games). Other games based on various manifestations of information will also be defined.

Therefore, games risks and uncertainties differ from the uncertainty and randomness we encounter in statistical models which assume that (randomness) uncertainty and risks are not motivated. For example, suppose that an import firm has negotiated the delivery from a foreign country of goods of a certain (well-defined and contracted) quality. Once the contract has been drafted with the exporter and implemented, what are the conditional consequences if the exporting firm does not meet the quality contracted? How can the importing firm control the terms of the contract in the first place? Similarly, how would a creditor confront a potential debtor's default due to external events (namely, independent of the debtor intents) or purposeful default (therefore, a "strategic default")? These intents assume many forms at both microeconomic and macroeconomic scales. For example, a debtor nation might follow purposely an inflationary policy to devalue its currency and thereby reduce gradually its outstanding debt. While default of the debt is not explicit, it is implicit in the erosion of the terms of the debt that a debtor may choose to alleviate their future debt burden. In general, firms act and counteract with broadly varying means, motivations, information, and asymmetries of all sorts. These situations can lead to conflicts and risks that are "endogenous," which are also strategic risks. These are risks that result from the internal actions and counteractions of the parties involved in the game, each pursuing a personal agenda.

These problems recur in global economics, finance and trade in many ways. Sovereign states may, for example, sign an agreement and then, for "political reasons," rescind it explicitly or implicitly by countering the intent of such agreements. Similarly, importers in some countries are protected legally if they declare bankruptcy proceedings. They may contract the import of certain goods by a down payment and then, once the goods are received and sold, declare bankruptcy. To better understand and study such and other strategic problems, concepts of games and their theories can be useful. Some of these are considered with applications to trade, FX rates, pricing international assets and investments, and other problems of global finance.

Appendix 10.B: Concepts of Games and Risk

Game theory was first proposed and defined by a French mathematician Emil Borel in 1921. The famed mathematician John von Neumann provided an analysis of games in 1928. In 1944, von Neumann, together with Oskar Morgenstern, published the first fundamental book on game theory, *The Theory of Games and Economic Behavior*. This book was published about the same time when Dantzig developed a simplex algorithm in linear programming that provided an extraordinary impetus to the computational solution of large optimization problems. A few years later, the relationship between certain types of games (explicitly, zero-sum games, where the gain to one party is its exact loss to the other) and their solutions by linear programming was pointed out. Subsequently, applications of game theory to study strategic alternatives and decisions for military problems, economic competition, and so many others have provided both an extensive and appreciable foundation to game theory and its uses.

Mathematically, game models can be categorized in many ways. Some examples include the following.

- *Discrete or continuous strategic games.* Each party selects a strategy from a discrete set or a continuous set of alternatives.
- *Two parties' games.* Games are defined between two specific parties with well-defined preferences known completely to each of the parties.
- *Zero-sum games.* Games with conditional payoffs for one party being conditional losses for the other. Their sum is therefore equal to zero or to a constant (constant-sum games).

- *Non-zero-sum games.* Games with conditional payoffs for the parties to the game with their sum not summing to zero. These basic games lead to a broad number of generic and specific solutions, such as the Nash conjecture (to be seen later), collaboration solutions, and so on.
- *Stackelberg games or leader--led games.* Games with one of the parties able to observe the strategy of the other based on such an observation select a strategy. In finance, some of these games are also called the "principal-agent" game with the principal a leader and the agent led. In these games, the "leader" announces their move first.
- *Information asymmetry games.* Games with some players having information that the others do not possess.
- *Random payoff games.* Games with conditional uncertain payoffs to at least one of the two parties. These games are therefore both strategic and risk games.
- *Coalition games.* Games with parties negotiating a strategy to collaborate and distribute the spoils of collaboration according to agreed-on rules or contracts.
- *Repeated games.* These are sequential games, repeated with learning and information acquired as the game evolves over time. These also include some Bayesian games, consisting of prior estimates of players' strategic selections by the parties, updated by the game being repeated with outcomes observed when a game is played.
- *Constrained games.* These are games with parties subject to individual or common constraints. For example, risk constraints, regulation constraints (as with value-at-risk regulation), trade constraints, and exchange constraints.
- *Intertemporal games or differential games.* Games repeated continuously in time. These games consist typically of underlying processes (discrete- or continuous-time differential equations and stochastic differential equations) with each party pursuing their own intertemporal preference defined over a given time span—finite or infinite. These games are notoriously difficult to solve.
- *Bayesian incomplete games.* Unlike Nash games, which assume that all parties have complete information, Bayesian games assume that parties have incomplete information. Explicitly, one party may be uncertain about the other party's payoffs or the utilities assigned to each of the games' payoffs. Incomplete game problems may use learning mechanisms such as Bayesian learning (based on prior estimates of the potential actions a party may take and their payoffs and probabilistic posterior-revision once experience is accumulated). A variety of situations, such as incomplete information regarding the alternatives available a party has, lead to games that are in fact reduced to approximate partial information games.
- *Mean field games.* These are games based on an individual agent in an environment where the outcomes are defined independently by an infinite number of other players. These games are difficult to solve but are the subject of current and extensive research and applications. They provide in certain cases a solution to games with a continuum of players or an infinite number of players with information available to each by the aggregate mean response of the whole.

Real examples in economics and finance abound. For example, they are used to assess strategic decisions and their risks in international problems, international pricing, contracts in outsourcing for codevelopment, in coproduction, international trade and FX, revenues and risks sharing. Game models can provide better guidelines to design and manage strategic situations and their consequential risks.

Games in such situations can be subject to many risks, which we summarize as follows:

- Ex-ante risks arising from partial information, a lack of knowledge, and/or of an asymmetry between the parties that can differ culturally and economically.
- Ex-ante strategic risks arising from parties' preferences and their power that can lead to conflicts between the parties to the game. These risks are often called in finance counterparty risks and abound in credit risk.
- Ex-ante risks arising from environmental randomness that parties may be subject to (and therefore leading to games where the payoffs or losses are defined in terms of random outcomes).
- Ex-post risks, resulting from negotiated agreements that are not maintained by the parties.
- Incomplete state preferences risks or stealth strategic risks. Such situations arise when one of the parties knows their alternatives but only part or none of the alternatives of the "other party." These are games with a Knightian uncertainty.

Partial information games are particularly challenging and induce strategic risks and uncertainty which are often denoted by one-sided moral hazard (e.g., with a single party, the exporter with an information edge over the second party, an importer) and two-sided moral hazard (where both parties have an information edge that affects the parties' conditional outcomes). Incomplete states, stealth, and partial information game, although encountered in current practice, involve many technical problems that are yet to be deciphered.

Formally, the solution of a game depends on the assumptions we make regarding the parties to the game, including:

- their information (whether shared or common, partial or not);
- their power and lead–led relationships (if any);
- the randomness of the game conditional consequences;
- the rationality that each party has.

Treating information in games is far from simple and neither easily formulated nor easily solved. Typically, in a game theoretic framework, the value of information is measured by the improvement of the (Nash equilibrium) solution players may reach with more (or less) information. In some cases, however, more information may have adverse effects, with some parties gaining and others losing.

Global and international firms, integrated fully or loosely through partnerships, an association of stake holders, consisting of independent and dependent agents, forming strategic alliances and reciprocity agreements, and operating across national borders, have redefined themselves as corporate (and often international or A-National) entities with common interest on the one hand and private agendas on the other hand. These entities have been organized to take advantage and profit from global economy. They require, therefore, a better appreciation and application of game models that can capture and reproduce their complexity. Outstanding current issues in economics and finance, such as a market's contagion and systemic risks, would profit from strategic gaming approaches. General classes of games applied to a broad set of problems are also defined by specific names. These include, among many others, the following:

- *Cournot games* (1838). These are non-coordinating (non-zero-sum) games applied to trade models, when both parties have full information of their stakes and reach their decisions simultaneously and independently. These lead to a simultaneous "game play" with each party's strategy a function of the other. Cournot games are associated with quantity competition games. Originally, Cournot did consider both price and quantity games, however. These games will be considered here. Cournot games are based on the Nash conjecture, assuming that it defines a stable equilibrium resulting from an unspecified learning process. This is in contradiction to incomplete games (see Bayesian games earlier) where a Nash solution results from an iterative process. By contrast, the Cournot equilibrium is defined uniquely, while incomplete games can result in games with multiple equilibria (i.e., multiple solutions and therefore incomplete in a financial sense).

- *Bertrand games.* These games are similar to Cournot's but with parties competing instead on price. In these games, firms are price setters rather than quantity setters (with price-sensitive consumers determining the quantity). Both Cournot and Bertrand games have profusely been used in economics and trade.
- *The prisoner dilemma.* Imagine two suspected parties (criminals) that are arrested, and proof is sought for the conviction of one and/or both for their criminal acts. One may squeal on the other or may decide to cooperate. Four situations arise then, each situation with separate consequences that define the game. The problem is to predict whether the prisoners will cooperate or not and how can such cooperation be built and be stable. Such situations arise in many problems in a global and economic environment.
- *Battle of the sexes.* This is a game between two parties, say a loving husband and a loving wife, one wanting to go to see a movie (the wife), the other wanting to go to a football game (the husband). There are again four sets of consequences for each of the parties that define the game. The problem is how to reconcile what they want.
- *The hawk–dove game.* Say that two countries are in conflict, each with two postures it can assume. One is that of a hawk consisting of escalating the conflict (say, between these countries) until the opponent retreats, while the other, a dove strategy, consists of displaying hostility but retreating prior to being injured in case the other party chooses to be a hawk. Again, there are four conditional outcomes and a "solution" (or "solutions") defined by the parties' conditional outcomes. The problem is predicting what each of the parties will do.
- *Inspection (or statistical control) game.* Unlike statistical sampling, this is based on the latent and inner conflicts between the parties to the game. In inspection (controls) games, "sampling alternatives" are then reached by the solution of the game. For example, inspections are selected to determine how best to control ex-ante agreements. What if an international contract of non-proliferation is agreed between the two parties? The agreement may call for both mutual (and potentially random) inspections to ensure that the contract is maintained. Inspection games will then define rules for an inspector to verify that another party adheres to "the game-contract" legal rules. The legal behavior may be defined by an arms control treaty, for example, with the inspected potentially violating these rules. Typically, an inspector's resources are limited so that verification can only be statistical. This situation defines a game, usually with two players, inspector and inspected—see Avenhaus *et al.* (1995) and earlier papers by Reyniers and Tapiero (1995a,b).

These and other games are tools that one may use to better comprehend and manage strategic alternatives in a global environment. Some of these games are formulated and solved simply to highlight their differences and specific usefulness.

References

Ai, C. and Sappington, D. (2002) The impact of state incentive regulation on the U.S. telecommunications industry. *Journal of Regulatory Economics*, **22**(2): 133–159.

Alexander, I., Mayer, C., and Weeds, H. (1996) Regulatory structure and risk: an international comparison. World Bank Policy Research Working Paper No. 1698.

Armstrong, M. and Sappington, D. (2005) Recent developments in the theory of regulation. In Handbook of Industrial Organization, vol. III, M. Armstrong and R. Porter (eds). North-Holland: Amsterdam.

Ashby, W., 1952, Design for a Brain, Chapman and Hall, England

Aubert, C. and Reynaud, A. (2005) The impact of regulation on cost efficiency: an empirical analysis of Wisconsin water utilities. *Journal of Productivity Analysis*, **23**: 383–409.

Aumann, R. (1976) Agreeing to disagree. *Annals of Statistics*, **4**: 1236–1239.

Aumann, R. (1988) *Lectures on Game Theory (Underground Classics in Economics)*. Westview Press: Boulder, CO.

Aumann, R. and Hart, S. (eds) (2002) *Handbook of Game Theory with Economic Applications*. North-Holland: New York.

Avenhaus, R. (1994) Decision theoretic analysis of pollutant emission monitoring procedures. *Annals of Operations Research*, **54**: 23–28.

Avenhaus, R., Stengel, B.V., and Zamir, S. (2002) Inspection games. In *Handbook of Game Theory with Economic Applications*, vol. 3, R.J. Aumann and S. Hart (eds.). North-Holland: New York.

Avenhaus, R., Canty, M.D., Kilgour, D.M., et al. (1996) Inspection games in arms control. *European Journal of Operational Research*, **90**(3): 383–394.

Banks, D., Petralia, F., and Wang, S. (2011) Adversarial risk analysis: Borel games. *Applied Stochastic Models*, **27**(2): 72–86.

Barth, J.R., Caprio, G., and Levine, R. (2001) Banking systems around the globe: do regulations and ownership affect performance and stability? In *Prudential Supervision: What Works and What Doesn't*, F.S. Mishkin (ed.). University of Chicago Press: Chicago, IL.

Barth, J.R., Caprio, G., and Levine, R. (2004) Bank regulation and supervision: what works best? *Journal of Financial Intermediation*, **13**: 205–248.

Barth, J.R., Caprio, G., and Levine, R. (2008) *Rethinking Bank Regulation: Till Angels Govern*. Cambridge University Press: New York.

Basel Committee on Banking Supervision (2009) *Guidelines for Computing Capital for Incremental Risk in the Trading Book*. http://www.bis.org/publ/bcbs159.pdf (accessed May 31, 2017).

Baston, V.J. and Bostock, F.A. (1991) A generalized inspection game. *Research Logistics*, **38**: 171–182.

Bassan, B. (2003) Pricing stocks and options with Bayesian games. Dipartimento di Matematica, Università "La Sapienza," Piazzale Aldo Moro 5, I-00185 Rome, November 20.

Bassan, B. and Natoli, G. (2003) Strategic option pricing. Preprint, Dipartimento di Matematica, Università "La Sapienza," Piazzale Aldo Moro 5, I-00185 Rome, Italy, November 20.

Bassan B., Gossner, O., Scarsini, M., and Zamir, S. (2003) Positive value of information in games. *Journal of Game Theory*, **32**: 17–31.

Beck, T., Demirguc-Kunt, A., and Levine, R. (2006) Bank supervision and corruption in lending. *Journal of Monetary Economics*, **53**: 2131–2163.

Bhattacharya, S., Boot, A., and Thakor, A. (1998) The economics of bank regulation. *Journal of Money, Credit, and Banking*, **30**: 745–770.

Bird, C.G. and Kortanek, K.O. (1974) Game theoretic approaches to some air pollution regulation problems. *Socio-Economic Planning Sciences*, **8**: 141–147.

Bisias, D., Flood, M., Lo, A.W., and Valavanis, S. (2012) A survey of systemic risk analytics. Office of Financial Research, Working Paper #0001. https://www.financialresearch.gov/working-papers/files/OFRwp0001_BisiasFloodLoValavanis_ASurveyOfSystemicRiskAnalytics.pdf (access June 1, 2017).

Brandenburger, A. and Dekel, E. (1987) Rationalizability and correlated equilibria. *Econometrica*, **55**: 139–1402.

Camerer, C. (2003) *Behavioral Game Theory, Experiments in Strategic Interaction*. Princeton University Press: Princeton, NJ.

Carney, J. (2016) Protectionist walls are popping up…around banks. *The Wall Street Journal*, December 27, p. B1.

Eavis, P. (2016) New doubts about 'too big to fail' banks rattle foundation of regulations. *The New York Times*, March 3.

Foerster, J.-H. and Onaran, Y. (2016) Deutsche Bank to Settle U.S. Mortgage Probe for $7.2 Billion. *Bloomberg*, December 23. https://www.bloomberg.com/news/articles/2016-12-23/deutsche-bank-to-settle-u-s-mortgage-probe-for-7-2-billion (accessed July 15, 2017).

Gonzalez, F. (2005) Bank regulation and risk-taking incentives: an international comparison of bank risk. *Journal of Banking & Finance*, **29**: 1153–1184.

Harsanyi, J.C. (1967) Games with incomplete information played by "Bayesian" players, I–III. Part I. The basic model. *Management Science*, **14**(3): 159–182.

Harsanyi, J.C. (1968a) Games with incomplete information played by "Bayesian" players. Part II. Bayesian equilibrium points. *Management Science*, **14**(5): 320–334.

Harsanyi, J.C. (1968b) Games with incomplete information played by "Bayesian" players, I–III. Part III. he basic probability distribution of the game. *Management Science*, **14**(7): 486–502.

Harsanyi, J.C. and Selten, R. (1987) *A General Theory of Equilibrium Selection in Games*. MIT Press: Cambridge, MA.

Jackson, P. and Walter, S. (2013) The future of financial regulation. In *Risk Management in Financial Institutions*, S. Shahin and G. Feiger (eds). Euromoney Books: London; pp. 255–285.

Katzman, M.T. (1988) Pollution liability insurance and catastrophic environmental risks. *Journal of Risk and Insurance*, **55**: 75–100.

Kennett, R. and Zacks, S. (2004) *Modern Industrial Statistics: The Design and Control of Quality and Reliability*. Thosom Publishing.

Keppo, J., Kofman, L., and Meng, X. (2010) Unintended consequences of the market risk requirement in banking regulation. *Journal of Economic Dynamics & Control*, **34**: 2192–2214.

Kim, D. and Santomero, A. (1994) Risk in banking and capital regulation. *Journal of Finance*, **43**: 1219–1233.

Knight, F.H. (1921) *Risk, Uncertainty, and Profit*. Houghton Mifflin: Boston, MA.

Koehn, M. and Santomero, A. (1980) Regulation of bank capital and portfolio risk. *Journal of Finance*, **35**: 1235–1244.

Kogan, K. and Tapiero, C.S. (2007) *Supply Chain Games: Operations Management and Risk Valuation*. Springer Verlag.

Laffont, J.J. (1995) Regulation, moral hazard and insurance of environmental risks. *Journal of Public Economics*, **58**: 319–336.

Langlois, R.N. and Cosgel, M.M. (1993) Frank Knight on risk, uncertainty and the firm: a new interpretation. *Economic Inquiry*, **31**(3): 456–465.

Macey, R.J. (2013) Theories of regulatory risk: the surprise theory, the arbitrage theory and the regulatory mistake theory. In *Risk Management in Financial Institutions*, S. Shahin and G. Feiger (eds). Euromoney Books: London; pp. 165–188.

Maschler, M. (1966) A price leadership method for solving the inspector's non-constant sum game. *Naval Research Logistics Quarterly*, **13**: 11–33.

May, R.M. and Arinaminpathy, N. (2010) Systemic risk: the dynamics of model banking systems. *Journal of the Royal Society Interface*, **7**: 823–838.

Minsky, H. (1992) The financial instability hypothesis. Working Paper No. 74, Levy Economics Institute of Bard College. http://www.levy.org/pubs/wp74.pdf (accessed June 1, 2017).

Minsky, H.P. (2008) *Stabilizing an Unstable Economy*, McGraw-Hill: New York.

Nash, J.F. (1950) Equilibrium points in *n*-person games. *Proceedings of the National Academy of Sciences of the United States of America*, **36**: 48–49.

Nash, J.F. (1951) Non-cooperative games. *Annals of Mathematics*, **54**: 286–295.

Nau, R.F. and McCardle, K.F. (1990) Coherent behaviour in non-cooperative games. *Journal of Economic Theory*, **50**: 424–444.

Nier, E., Yang, J., Yorulmazer, T., and Alentorn, A. (2007) Network models and financial stability. *Journal of Economic Dynamics and Control*, **31**: 2033–2060.

Nocera, J. (2012) Keep it simple. *The New York Times*, January 17. http://www.nytimes.com/2012/01/17/opinion/bankings-got-a-new-critic.html (accessed June 1, 2017).

Owen, B.M. and Braeutoigam, R.R. (1978) *The Regulation Game: Strategic Use of the Administrative Process*. Ballinger: Cambridge, MA.

Posner, R.A. (2013) *Reflections on Judging*. Harvard University Press.

Reyniers, D.J. and Tapiero, C.S. (1995a) The supply and the control of quality in supplier–producer contracts. *Management Science*, **41**: 1581–1589.

Reyniers, D.J. and Tapiero, C.S. (1995b) Contract design and the control of quality in a conflictual environment. *European Journal of Operations Research*, **82**(2): 373–382.

Roubini, N. (2008) Ten fundamental issues in reforming financial regulation and supervision in a world of financial innovation and globalization. White paper. *RGE Monitor*, March 31. http://web-docs.stern.nyu.edu/salomon/docs/crisis/Nouriel-RegulationSupervisionMarch08.pdf (accessed May 31, 2017).

Ruckle, W.H. (1992) The upper risk of an inspection agreement. *Operations Research*, **40**: 877–884.

Russell, C.S. (1990) Game models for structuring monitoring and enforcement systems. *Natural Resource Modeling*, **4**: 143–176.

Schaefer, S. (2016) Goldman Sachs says $5.1 billion mortgage settlement will knock $1.5 billion off Q4 Earnings. *Forbes*, January 14. https://www.forbes.com/sites/steveschaefer/2016/01/14/goldman-sachs-says-mortgage-bond-settlement-will-knock-1-5b-off-q4-earnings/#4eab8d7a24db (accessed July 15, 2017).

Schneider, F. (2012) The shadow economy and work in the shadow: what do we (not) know? IZA DP No. 6423. http://ftp.iza.org/dp6423.pdf (accessed June 1, 2017).

Schneider, F. (2015) Size and development of the shadow economy of 31 European and 5 other OECD countries from 2003 to 2015: different developments. http://www.econ.jku.at/members/Schneider/files/publications/2015/ShadEcEurope31.pdf (accessed June 1, 2017).

Shahin, S. and Feiger, G. (eds) (2013) *Risk Management in Financial Institutions*. Euromoney Books: London.

Stirling, W.C. (2003) *Satisficing Games and Decision Making: With applications to Engineering and Computer Science*. Cambridge University Press: Cambridge.

Stirling, W.C. and Goodrich, M.A. (1999) Satisficing games. *Information Sciences*, **114**(1–4): 255–280.

Tapiero, C.S. (1994) Complexity and industrial management. *OR Insight*, **7**(1): 12–19. doi: 10.1057/ori.1994.19.

Tapiero, C.S. (1995) Acceptance sampling in a producer–supplier conflicting environment; risk neutral case. *Applied Stochastic Models and Data Analysis*, **11**: 3–12.

Tapiero, C.S. (1996) *The Management of Quality and Its Control*. Chapman and Hall: London.

Tapiero, C.S. (2005a) Environmental quality control: a queueing game. *Stochastic Environmental Research and Risk Assessment*, **19**: 59–70.

Tapiero, C.S. (2005b) Environmental quality control and environmental games. *Environmental Modeling and Assessment*, **9**: 201–206.

Tapiero, C.S. (2005c) Environmental quality and satisficing games. *Journal of Science and Engineering B*, **2**(1–2): 7–30.

Tapiero, C.S. (2013a) Reengineering risk and the future of finance. In *Risk Management in Financial Institutions*, S. Shahin and G. Feiger (eds). Euromoney Books: London; pp. 233–254.

Tapiero, C.S. (2013b) *Engineering Risk and Finance*. Springer: New York.

Tapiero, C.S. (2014) Financial regulation, non-compliance risks and control: a statistical approach. *Risk and Decision Analysis*, **5**(2–3): 113–127.

Tapiero, O.J. (2013a) The relationship between risk and incomplete states uncertainty: a Tsallis entropy perspective. *Journal of Algorithmic Finance*, **2**(2): 141–150.

Tapiero, O.J. (2013b) Financial decisions and quantum calculus. *Risk and Decision Analysis*, **4**(4): 291–301.

Tapiero, O.J. (2013c) The economics of uncertainty. In *Engineering Risks and Finance*, C.S. Tapiero. Springer: New York; chapter 10.

The Economist (1999) The shadow economy: black hole. August 26. http://www.economist.com/node/324323 (accessed June 1, 2017).

The Economist (2012a) The Dodd-Frank act: Too big not to fail. February 18. http://www.economist.com/node/21547784 (accessed June 1, 2017).

The Economist (2012b) United States' economy: over-regulated America. February 18. http://www.economist.com/node/21547789 (accessed June 1, 2017).

The Economist (2013) World economy: the gated globe. October 12. http://www.economist.com/news/special-report/21587384-forward-march-globalisation-has-paused-financial-crisis-giving-way (accessed June 1, 2017).

The Economist (2014) International banking: poor correspondents. June 14. http://www.economist.com/news/finance-and-economics/21604183-big-banks-are-cutting-customers-and-retreating-markets-fear (accessed June 1, 2017).

Von Stengel, B. (1991) Recursive inspection games. Technical Report S-9106, University of the Federal Armed Forces, Munich.

Index

Note: Page numbers in *italic* denote figures, those in **bold** denote tables.

Globalization, Gating, and Risk Finance, First Edition. Unurjargal Nyambuu and Charles S. Tapiero.
© 2018 John Wiley & Sons Ltd. Published 2018 by John Wiley & Sons Ltd.